Reading and Learning to Read

FOURTH EDITION

Jo Anne L. Vacca
Kent State University

Richard T. Vacca
Kent State University

Mary K. Gove
East Cleveland Schools

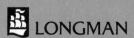
LONGMAN

An Imprint of Addison Wesley Longman, Inc.

New York • Reading, Massachusetts • Menlo Park, California • Harlow, England
Don Mills, Ontario • Sydney • Mexico City • Madrid • Amsterdam

To Laurie Kidwell and Lianne Lantz, teachers at the Paul Jones
Child Development Center, Kent State University, who lovingly
orchestrated the wedding ceremony of the guinea pigs,
Cookie and Armanzo, on a sunny April day.

And for Simon and his friends Amelia, Zachary, Connor,
and the rest of the class who made the preparations and witnessed
this memorable event. What a tale they have to tell!

Editor in Chief: Priscilla McGeehon
Acquisitions Editor: Virginia L. Blanford
Director of Development: Lisa Pinto
Developmental Editor: Nancy Crochiere
Marketing Manager: Renée Ortbals
Supplements Editor: Joy Hilgendorf
Project Manager: Ellen MacElree
Design Manager and Text Designer: Wendy Fredericks
Cover Illustration: P. C. Vey
Art Studio: ElectraGraphics, Inc.
Photo Researcher: PhotoSearch, Inc.
Electronic Production Specialist: Sarah Johnson
Electronic Page Makeup: Heather Peres
Printer and Binder: Quebecor Fairfield
Cover Printer: The Lehigh Press, Inc.

For permission to use copyrighted material, grateful acknowledgment is made to the copyright
holders on p. C-1, which are hereby made part of this copyright page.

Copyright © 2000 by Addison-Wesley Educational Publishers Inc.

Please visit our website at www.awlonline.com

ISBN 0-321-02060-X

2345678910—ARF—02010099

Brief Contents

Contents

CHAPTER 3   EARLY LITERACY: FROM BIRTH TO SCHOOL   67

CHAPTER 4   INVITING BEGINNERS INTO THE LITERACY CLUB   103

CHAPTER 5 WORD IDENTIFICATION   147

CHAPTER 6 READING FLUENCY   195

CHAPTER 7   READING COMPREHENSION   229

CHAPTER 8   VOCABULARY KNOWLEDGE AND CONCEPT DEVELOPMENT   273

CHAPTER 9 READING-WRITING CONNECTIONS   311

CHAPTER 10 BRINGING CHILDREN AND LITERATURE TOGETHER   357

CHAPTER 11   BASAL READERS AND INSTRUCTIONAL MATERIALS   397

CHAPTER 12   MAKING THE TRANSITION TO CONTENT AREA TEXTS   437

CHAPTER 13   MEETING THE LITERACY NEEDS OF DIVERSE LEARNERS   483

CHAPTER 14   ASSESSING READING PERFORMANCE   519

CHAPTER 15   MANAGING AND ORGANIZING AN EFFECTIVE CLASSROOM   563

Preface

The headline on the front page of a Los Angeles newspaper proclaimed the end of an "educational fad" as a state reading task force approved a new instructional framework for teaching reading in California schools. The article described the "failure" of the *whole language movement* and championed the return of *phonics* in the teaching of reading. What was troublesome for us, as authors of a comprehensive textbook on the teaching of reading, was the simplistic pitting of an important philosophy of literacy learning (whole language) against an important instructional tool in learning to read and spell (phonics). The sidebar to the article, however, drove home for us the controversy and confusion that exists over instructional practices related to the teaching of reading and writing today.

The sidebar, which accompanied the major news story, showed the writing of a first grader in response to having heard the story *Jack and the Beanstalk* read aloud by the teacher. In big bold letters, the headline read: "DOOMED KIDS?" Here's what the child wrote:

> If I wd hf mg ics I wd save the
> bses and one I sav the bes then
> I wd g thm way the end

The child's writing illustrates the use of *invented spelling* and, when translated into conventional spelling, it reads: "If I would have magic beans, I would save the beans. And when I save the beans, then I will give them away. The end." What troubled us about the depiction of the child's writing was the insinuation that young children—beginning readers and writers—who use invented spelling in their writing may somehow be "doomed" as literacy learners. *Doomed,* after all, is a pretty strong word.

This edition of *Reading and Learning to Read* begins at a time when there is much controversy and confusion over how to teach children to read. The news story in the Los Angeles paper is one of countless articles that have appeared recently in newspapers throughout the country questioning literacy practices in today's schools. Although there have been heated debates over the teaching of reading at various times throughout the twentieth century, the stakes have never been higher, or the level of national concern greater, for children to learn to read well—and for teachers to teach reading well. The public call for accountability for improved reading performance weighs heavily on the shoulders of children and teachers in the wake of legislative mandates and curriculum reform; national, state, and district "report cards" and "high-stakes assessments" of reading proficiency.

It is within the context of concern and controversy over the teaching of reading that we approached this revision of *Reading and Learning to Read.* How to teach reading well to all children is the subject of this book. Effective teachers use their *knowledge and beliefs about reading* to adapt instruction to individual differences among children in their class-rooms. Student diversity in today's classrooms is greater than at any time in our nation's history. Yet it is tempting to embrace a "one size fits all" approach to instruction as if there is a single "correct" way to teach reading to everyone, regardless of the diversity that exists in today's classroom. In this book, we reject the notion of a single "best" way to teach reading and examine how to develop a balanced, comprehensive reading program based on *best practices* rooted in current knowledge and research on how children learn to read.

CORE BELIEFS AT THE CENTER OF THIS EDITION

A set of core beliefs underlie this edition of *Reading and Learning to Read.* These beliefs are grounded in research and current thinking about how children become literate. As authors, we use our core beliefs about literacy learning to frame important questions related to the teaching of reading and to interpret best practices in a comprehensive reading program. Some of our core beliefs about reading and learning to read include the following:

◆ Children use language to seek and construct meaning from what they read, hear, and view.

◆ Reading, writing, speaking, listening, and viewing are interrelated and mutually supporting as children learn and use them.

◆ Learning to read involves learning how to decode words quickly and accurately.

◆ Children learn to read as they read to learn, enjoy, communicate, and solve problems.

◆ Children need to be exposed to a broad spectrum of reading materials and literature, including electronic texts.

◆ Children develop skills and strategies through explicit instruction and purposeful, meaningful use.

◆ Children deserve assessment techniques and processes that mirror the authentic ways they demonstrate their continually developing literacy.

◆ Children benefit from classroom communities in which materials, curriculum, instruction, practice, and assessment celebrate their diverse contributions.

◆ Teachers, parents, and administrators should make decisions based on how children learn and how they can best be taught.

Balanced literacy programs represent a goal. They require that teachers develop or identify their own core beliefs because it's important to build a program on an informed philosophical stance. Teachers then are in a good position to *think about what must be done to get literacy instruction ready for children,* rather than trying to get children ready for reading. In achieving balance, teachers base decisions on how children learn and how they can benefit from best practices, reflecting the interactive nature of the reading process. Moreover, we contend that teachers who actively search for balance are in a better position to achieve it when they engage in a process of defining and refining their beliefs about reading and learning to read.

In this fourth edition of *Reading and Learning to Read*, we invite you to engage in this process as you read the chapters, participate in discussions and activities, and seek answers to improve your own teaching. Defining and refining one's beliefs is not an easy process. But it is possible. How? By talking about *what* we do and *why* we do it; by observing one another and asking why; by self-examination and reflection. We hope that the new content and format features in this edition will serve as effective tools to help readers as they inquire into their beliefs and practice.

FEATURES OF THE FOURTH EDITION

The content in all 15 chapters is intended to offer prospective and veteran teachers a contemporary view of comprehensive instruction in literacy from birth into middle childhood and beyond. What it means to *integrate reading and writing instruction through a balanced approach* is our emphasis throughout, beginning in Chapter 2. Other substantial areas are featured, including:

◆ The latest information about phonemic awareness and strategies for teaching phonics have been incorporated into Chapter 3.

◆ Coverage of word identification has been expanded in Chapter 5.

◆ Explicit strategy instruction for reading comprehension is emphasized in Chapter 7.

◆ Ideas for integrating technology into instruction and examples of how teachers and students use electronic materials in connection with reading, writing, assessment, and communication are given throughout the book. Chapters 9, 11, 14, and 15, in particular, contain information and authentic samples.

◆ Students with special needs are integrated throughout the book, beginning with a Viewpoint feature in Chapter 1 about a hearing-impaired child's journey into reading, written by his mother, who is also a school principal.

◆ Authentic assessment and portfolio assessment, discussed mainly in Chapter 14, are expanded on with current information and related to other topics where appropriate.

The format of this edition features three types of boxes, offering explicit, practical examples with direct application to instruction:

◆ **Viewpoint:** Views of teachers, parents, administrators, students, and experts in literacy on critically important topics such as assessment, inclusion, phonemic awareness, phonics, diverse learners, and classroom communities

◆ **Class Works:** Descriptions of strategies at work in classroom environments and other interactive, natural situations, followed by questions to guide reflective inquiry

◆ **Best Practice:** Strategies and instructional guidelines recommended as effective and enhancing to the practice of successful literacy teaching and learning

Other features in the fourth edition intended to assist readers are found in the chapter opener, which starts with a chapter overview—a graphic organizer illustrating the major concepts in the chapter. This is followed by a list of what students will learn about in that chapter. Next, a vignette tells a story about the chapter's topic. Viewpoint, Class Works, and Best Practice boxes appear, in different combinations, in every chapter. At the conclusion of each chapter, Teacher-Action Researcher suggestions for further inquiry engage students in thoughtful activities for both the field and the college classroom, capitalizing on concepts just learned in the chapter. Key Terms, as a final reinforcement, are connected to major chapter concepts and the end-of-book Glossary.

Acknowledgments

Our professional colleagues who reviewed this edition deserve and have our thanks for their efforts to provide constructive feedback: Jerry Aldridge, University of Alabama at Birmingham; Beatrice Berlin, Loyala University; Joseph Douglas Cawley, Metropolitan State College of Denver; Marie Ice, California State University, Bakersfield; Donna Jamar, Emporia State University; Linda Labbo, University of Georgia; Debra Bayles Martin, San Diego State University; Linda Pohlabel, Ball State University; L. Bill Searcy, Southern Illinois University at Edwardsville; Laura Staal, University of New Mexico; and Brenda Toler, Ohio State University.

We appreciate and applaud the talents of Linda Burkey of Mount Union College and Christine McKeon of Walsh University for their work on the revision of our *Instructor's Manual* and the accompanying Web site. Our editor, Ginny Blanford, deserves more praise than we have room for on this page. We gratefully acknowledge many others who are associated with Longman, especially Nancy Crochiere, Ellen MacElree, Wendy Fredericks, Renée Ortbals, and Bruce Emmer.

J. L. V.
R. T. V.
M. K. G.

CHAPTER

1

Knowledge and Beliefs About Reading

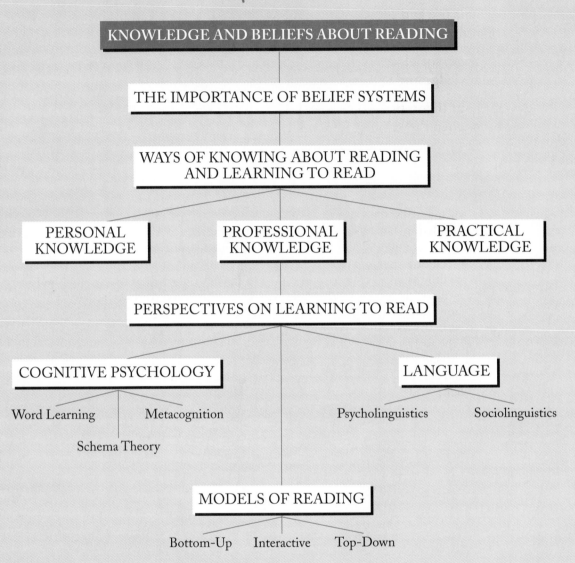

Chapter Overview

KNOWLEDGE AND BELIEFS ABOUT READING

THE IMPORTANCE OF BELIEF SYSTEMS

WAYS OF KNOWING ABOUT READING
AND LEARNING TO READ

PERSONAL
KNOWLEDGE

PROFESSIONAL
KNOWLEDGE

PRACTICAL
KNOWLEDGE

PERSPECTIVES ON LEARNING TO READ

COGNITIVE PSYCHOLOGY

LANGUAGE

Word Learning   Metacognition

Psycholinguistics   Sociolinguistics

Schema Theory

MODELS OF READING

Bottom-Up   Interactive   Top-Down

Between the Lines

In this chapter, you will discover:

◆ **How beliefs about literacy learning influence instructional decisions
and practices**

- How teachers use and construct personal, professional, and practical knowledge about literacy learning

- How language, social, and psychological perspectives on reading inform knowledge and beliefs about literacy learning

- How different theoretical models of the reading process describe what humans do when they engage in reading

On an unusually warm and humid day in May, the furnace at Lincoln Elementary School is blasting hot air into one of the first-grade classrooms. Two building custodians are trying to turn off the heat while the teacher and the students are trying to work despite the physical discomfort. The windows are wide open; a fan moves the hot air around the room, to little avail.

Lincoln Elementary, built in the 1940s, is an inner-city school. Although the physical plant shows its age, temporary inconveniences, such as the heating system's going haywire, don't get in the way of teaching and learning. For example, in the midst of all the commotion in the first-grade classroom, one of the students is at her desk, busy with paper and pencil, as she writes a note to the teacher. She folds it in half, writes "Mrs. H" on the front, and delivers it posthaste. The teacher, Mrs. Henderson, opens the note and much to her delight, reads:

Plese turn of the fan Them guys smell like my brother when he mos the grass.

Toni P.

The note to Mrs. Henderson has a great deal to say about "literacy in the making." As lighthearted as it may seem on the surface, it reveals much about Toni's literacy development. Just ask yourself, for example, "Does Toni know what writing and reading are for? Does she get her message across effectively? Does she have a sense of the teacher as a reader?" And as a language user, "Is Toni empowered? Is she willing to take risks?" The answers to questions such as these are as revealing about Toni's literate development as the grammatical and spelling errors that she made.

Although the school year is rapidly coming to a close, Mrs. Henderson recalls Toni's first day in her class. She hardly spoke a word. Yet today, Toni has blossomed into a confident and competent reader and writer. Some of her literacy strengths are mirrored in the note that she has written to Mrs. H. Not only does Toni express a strong, clear, concise message, but her writing also exhibits good sentence structure, word usage, and for the most part, mechanics (spelling, punctuation, and grammar). In a small but significant way, the note reflects the progress that she has made since the beginning of the school year.

Although she misspelled three words, Toni's written approximations of *please, off,* and *mows* are phonetically regular and close to the conventional spellings of the words. Though she neglects to use a period at the end of the first sentence, Mrs. Henderson attributes the omission to "fast writing" rather than Toni's lack of understanding of a punctuation mark at the end of a sentence. Developmentally, Toni writes the way she talks. In time, she'll understand why it is grammatically inappropriate to use *them* when she means *those.*

Throughout the year, Mrs. Henderson's literacy program has centered around the development of confident and competent readers and writers. She wants her students to be *motivated, thoughtful,* and *skillful* as they engage in literacy learning. Toni is motivated and thoughtful, and she is in the process of becoming skillful as a reader and writer. Mrs. Henderson makes a mental note to work with Toni on learning the conventional spellings of *please, off,* and *mows.* She plans to teach these words *explicitly* because of their irregular letter-sound patterns. But not immediately.

Instead, Mrs. Henderson reads Toni's note and acts on the plea—quickly, we might add—by turning off the fan. And at the same time, she can't help but appreciate Toni's use of language to communicate. Mrs. Henderson recognizes that a powerful and authentic **literacy event** has just taken place between a writer and a reader. She decides, on the spot, to extend the transaction that has just occurred between the two of them.

So she writes a note to Toni thanking her. She tells Toni that the way the day has begun reminds her of the story that she had read to the class awhile ago about Alexander, who had a *terrible, horrible, no-good, very bad day!* And because of Toni's note, she will read the story again to the class "so we can all feel better about this morning!" Mrs. Henderson's decision to continue and extend the communication reflects not only what she knows about reading and learning to read but also what she believes about teaching, learning, and the process of becoming literate.

How teachers come to know and develop beliefs about reading and learning to read is the subject of this chapter. Examine the chapter overview. It depicts the connections among several key concepts related to the role of of teacher knowledge and beliefs in reading instruction. A **belief system** represents a teacher's informed philosophy of reading and learning to read. What teachers believe about reading and learning to read is closely related to what they know about literacy learning and the teaching of literacy. As you study this chapter, pay close attention to how teachers come to know about literacy learning through (1) personal experiences—past and present—as readers and writers; (2) practical experiences and knowledge of their craft as they work with and learn from children; and (3) professional study that allows them to develop and extend their knowledge base about teaching and learning literacy.

Also in this chapter, we emphasize how different perspectives related to reading and learning inform teachers' knowledge and beliefs about literacy learning. Language, social, and psychological perspectives are not mutually exclusive domains of knowledge. Often effective literacy practice, sometimes referred to as **best practice,** requires teachers to use multiple perspectives as they plan and enact literacy instruction in their classrooms. As suggested in the graphic organizer, the final section of this chapter describes various theoretical models of the reading process. Understanding reading and learning to read within the context of theoretical models will enable you to connect knowledge and beliefs about reading to issues and approaches related to instructional practice in Chapter 2.

THE IMPORTANCE OF BELIEF SYSTEMS

Knowledge and beliefs about reading and learning to read are wedded in ways that influence almost every aspect of a teacher's instructional decisions and practices. To illustrate, consider what Mrs. Henderson does after she writes her reply to Toni's note.

Connecting the events of the morning to *Alexander and the Terrible, Horrible, No Good, Very Bad Day* (Viorst, 1972) is an opportune, authentic way to demonstrate one of the *language functions* that reading serves. As we discuss later in the chapter, reading can be put to use in different ways for different purposes, one of which is to entertain—or, in the classroom situation that the first graders find themselves, to provide some pleasure and relief from the heat in the room.

In addition, sharing the book with the class results in a "commercial" for another book, Patricia Reilly Giff's *Today Was a Terrible Day* (1980), which is part of the classroom library collection. This is a story about a boy named Ronald who has a terrible day in school until he discovers that he can read (without any help) a personal note written to him by the teacher. Toni's teacher previews the story with the class and makes a connection between the notes that she and Toni have exchanged and the note that the teacher in the story writes to Ronald. She then builds anticipation for the story by inviting the students to think about the "terrible days" experienced by Alexander and Ronald, what contributes to making a day terrible, and what people can do to turn a bad day into a good one.

Throughout the remainder of the day, as you might anticipate, children asked if they could leaf through or read *Today Was a Terrible Day* between class activities. Some of them even wrote about terrible days in their journals, which are an integral part of the literacy curriculum in this first-grade classroom.

All of the reading and writing activities that evolved from the unanticipated events of the morning provided children with a demonstration of the *intertextuality* of stories. Stories are products of the imagination, but the problems and themes that they portray reflect the human experience. *Intertextuality* is a fancy word used by literary theorists to describe the connections that exist within and between texts. Think about the personal connections made by Toni and her classmates. They were able to build on the morning's heating crisis to make connections between the two stories shared by the teacher, as well as the texts that some of them created by writing in their journals. The children in Toni's class are exploring what it means to be *meaning-seekers* and *meaning-makers*. Their use of texts to construct meaning is the nexus by which they link the stories and explore a theme that will recur throughout their lives.

Not a bad day's work on a hot, muggy day in May. The work of teachers sometimes takes unexpected twists and turns—"teachable moments," if you will, that usually beget reasons for reading and writing. Yet taking advantage of a teachable moment, as Toni's teacher did, requires a philosophy of reading and learning to read. Some educators call a teacher's philosophical stance a *worldview;* others call it a *belief system.*

For one reason or another, some teachers would probably have reacted differently to Toni's note. Perhaps a teacher would have praised Toni for her effort in writing the note but rather than extend the literacy event, concentrate on the misspellings or punctuation error. Another teacher might have been too busy or preoccupied with the heating crisis or other matters to respond to the note in a manner that connects literacy learning to life in the classroom. Other teachers might simply have been oblivious to the teachable moment because they did not understand or appreciate the literacy event that occurred. Our point, therefore, is that a teacher's knowledge and beliefs about the nature and purposes of reading and the ways in which it should be taught contribute significantly to whatever decisions a teacher makes in a given situation.

Different Beliefs, Different Instructional Decisions

Just about every teacher we've ever talked to agrees on the main goal of reading instruction: to teach children to become independent readers and learners. Differences among teachers, however, often reflect varying beliefs and instructional perspectives on how to help children achieve independence. Because they view the reading process through different belief systems, teachers have different instructional concerns and emphases. The decisions they make will vary.

In addition, effective teachers of reading use their knowledge and beliefs about reading to adapt instruction to individual differences among children in their classrooms. The students they work with may have different academic, language, cultural, or physical needs. Student diversity in today's classrooms, as we explain more fully in Chapter 13, is greater today than at any time in this century. There is an increasing number of students whose first language is not English and whose culture does not reflect the beliefs, values, and standards of the mainstream culture in American society. Moreover, the movement toward inclusive classrooms, where students with "special needs" are mainstreamed into regular classrooms, demands teachers who are knowledgeable about the nature and purposes of reading acquisition.

The Viewpoint in Box 1.1, written by a parent, is a poignant reminder of the importance of teachers who know *how* to respond to students' literacy needs and *why.*

The main goal of reading instruction is teaching children to become independent readers and learners.

No two teachers, even if they work with children at the same grade level and in classrooms next door to each other, teach reading in exactly the same way. Even though they may share the same instructional goals, adhere to literacy guidelines established within the school district or state department of education "standards," teachers often make decisions and engage in practices based on what they know and believe to be worthwhile. Observe how Arch and Linda, two first-grade teachers, introduce beginners to reading and learning to read.

Arch invites his first graders to explore and experience the uses of oral and written language in a variety of instructional situations. He chooses all kinds of authentic and functional reading material, "anything that's real and important to the kids," for reading and learning to read: signs, boxtops, labels, poems, nursery rhymes, children's books, interactive stories, and games on the computer. His students also create their own texts, and these become the basis for reading. They write about what they read in journals, make books from original stories that they share with one another, and dictate stories that Arch captures on chart paper. In addition, Arch uses "big books" and storybooks to build concepts and skills related to reading. Often he begins a big-book lesson by reading the story aloud and discussing it with the class. Over the course of several days, he rereads the story in unison with the children once, twice, or even more times and then invites individual students to read parts of the story on their own.

Arch pays some attention to sound-letter relationships in the context of the writing and reading activities that children engage in. He encourages students to invent spellings during journal writing and other writing activities by assisting them "to spell the words the

BOX 1.1   VIEWPOINT

Adam's Journey
Karen A. Whitmer

I don't know if we can teach your son to read if he cannot hear the difference between sounds.

Your son will have to learn to read in a special class, because he learns differently.

Why do you read aloud to your son if he cannot hear you?

Adam can skip library time to go to speech. He's probably not interested in books anyway.

These are the types of comments my hearing-impaired son and I have heard when he entered school. At times we have been upset and discouraged by the way some people have written him off as a reader and a learner. Today, however, we are able to laugh at such narrow ways of thinking because my son, Adam, is learning. Adam *is* reading—and he is loving it! Adam's journey into reading clearly illustrates what is, for me, an important principle underlying reading and learning to read: *When reading is meaningful, children learn to read.*

When my son was 4 years old, we had an established ritual each evening, which we would go through before his bedtime. Adam would take his bath, and while he was doing that, we would take time to name every object around him: soap, water, boat, shampoo, towel. We would also use the objects to show action: boat floats, water splashes, soap sinks. We would use the dressing ritual to show sequence: first, we put on underwear; next, we put on our bottoms; last, we put on our top. We would end the evening with a story, which I would read aloud. Adam would try to read along with me, and sometimes he could, if he had the text memorized. I noticed that his language was improving and that his articulation errors were fewer and fewer, but he wasn't transferring this knowledge to the decoding of printed words. Silently, I worried. Being a teacher, I knew what was to come for him.

This frustration remained my own until Adam entered school. Once he saw everyone else learning to read, he began to feel that same frustration. One night he left me a note by his bed (something he had never done before). On that note was a picture of a boy with tears rushing down his face. Next to the boy's head was the word "Adam." Without even thinking, I found a pencil and drew a picture of me with tears and wrote "Mom" next to it.

The next morning, Adam and I cuddled in his bed and talked about the reason for our tears. We were both sad that Adam was having trouble with reading. I assured Adam that I would talk to his teacher and that I would help him myself.

We began labeling everything in his room with index cards. This was the same thing we had been doing verbally, but now we were putting those utterances into print. Each evening, we would quiz each other on several of the cards. We also kept writing to each other in that notebook by his bed. Pictures and one-word labels eventually turned into phrases and sentences. I am sure these actions helped Adam on the road to becoming a reader. We capitalized on his strengths (memory and writing) as we fine-tuned his weakness (hearing sounds in words).

BOX 1.1 CONTINUED

However, the thing that sparked Adam's reading was his desire to learn. I truly believe Adam had a need to read. He wanted to be successful in school. He wanted to be included, to be a part of the community of readers in his classroom. He had to find a way to read that made sense to him, his own way.

Adam's way was through writing. It still is. We are still writing to each other on a daily basis. We no longer have his room full of index cards, however. Instead, Adam attempts to label unfamiliar objects or subjects that he needs for his writing. Adam also writes to his teacher, a pen pal, and his favorite professional baseball player. He writes to find out information. He reads now because those people are writing back with the information he asked for. If they write words he cannot decode, we work together to figure them out. Then Adam writes those words in a notebook and illustrates them, if appropriate. He uses that notebook for future reference and for future writings.

Adam still has trouble hearing the difference between sounds, but he can tell you all kinds of words that contain those sounds. He can also tell you what your mouth looks like when you produce those sounds, and he can make them himself. This "sounding-out" process is a slow and frustrating one for Adam. He prefers to read through a visual modality. He relies heavily on remembering what he writes. It is very common to see Adam running up to his room saying, "I've got to write that down!"

It takes a special teacher to allow Adam to "do it his own way," but we have been fortunate to find several teachers like that. Adam is not in a special class, and he is reading on grade level. He is in control of his learning. His desire to learn drives his journey into reading and learning to read. Recently, Adam drew another picture of himself. The picture shows a happy boy on a soccer field scoring a winning goal for his team. The caption under the picture reads, "Adam's the winner!" What more can I possibly say?

Note: In addition to being a mom, Karen Whitmer is an elementary school principal.

way they sound." In doing so, he responds individually to children's invented spellings. For words that he thinks a child should know how to spell correctly, he provides explicit intervention. For others, he accepts the child's invention if it approximates the conventional spelling. In addition, during big-book readings, Arch will periodically stop to point out and discuss initial letters and sounds, letter combinations, or endings. When students read aloud, Arch places little importance on word-perfect reading. He says, "I tell my kids not to let one or two words prevent them from reading; they might be able to understand what the story is about and to enjoy it without identifying all of the words."

Linda also teaches reading to 6-year-olds. But her approach is different from Arch's. She believes quite strongly that beginning readers must start with letter-sound correspondences, translating print into speech. Other than occasional "experience charts" in the first weeks of the school year, Linda doesn't attempt to introduce writing until most of her children make the monumental "click" between the black squiggly marks on a page and the sounds they represent.

Of the "click," Linda says, "You can't miss it." When she sees children making the connection between print and speech, Linda begins to aim for mastery.

Word study centers around story selections from the basal reading program that her school adopted several years ago. The basal program provides Linda with "great literature, big books, everything that you need to teach reading." When she began teaching 15 years ago, Linda taught letter-sound relationships by relying heavily on workbooks and worksheets from the basal program. Her students spent a lot of time on isolated drill and rote memorization of phonics rules. "I didn't know better then. Using workbook exercises was accepted practice by the teachers in my building, and I thought I was doing the right thing."

Today, however, Linda bases much of what she does on research related to how children learn words. Each day she blocks out 15 to 20 minutes for word study. She still goes about the teaching of letter-sound relationships in a direct and systematic manner but relies more on *explicit instruction*. That is, Linda makes it a practice to *model* skills and strategies that children need to decipher unknown words, *explain* why it is important for students to learn the skill or strategy under study, and *guide* students in their acquisition of the skill or strategy. She makes sure, for example, at the beginning of the school year that her students have rudimentary skills related to hearing sounds in words, recognizing letters and sounds, and blending sounds into words. Linda uses story selections from the basal reading anthology and big books to identify words for study and to provide practice and application in the use of the skill or strategy. Rather than dispense worksheets that require students to circle letters or draw lines to pictures, Linda says, "I do a lot more teaching about phonics skills and strategies so that it makes sense to students as they learn to decode words."

The perspectives from which Linda and Arch teach reading reflect different beliefs about learning to read that result in different instructional emphases and practices. Arch uses authentic, real-world literature such as children's books and functional materials like signs and boxtops. Linda relies on materials from a basal reading program that includes literature anthologies and a wide range of ancillary materials. Linda begins instruction with an emphasis on phonics skills and strategies. Arch begins with immersion in reading and writing. Comprehension is as important to Linda as it is to Arch, but the two differ in belief. Linda's understanding of reading suggests that when children decode words accurately and quickly, they are in a better position to comprehend what they read than children who are not accurate and automatic decoders. Arch's view is that children who engage in authentic literacy experiences will search for meaning in everything they read and write.

The Reading Wars: A Clash Between Two Belief Systems

What Linda does to teach reading reflects beliefs that embody a **phonics** or skills perspective. What Arch does underlies a belief system that reflects a **whole language** perspective. Much of the recent debate, confusion, and controversy over the teaching of reading has centered around these two opposing perspectives, both of which will be examined in various parts of this book. Although teaching reading doesn't conform to a "one size fits all" instructional mentality, people outside of education often do not understand why there isn't a single "correct" way to teach reading to everyone, regardless of the diversity that exists in today's classroom. Public dissatisfaction with and confusion over student performance on state and national assessments of reading have rekindled the heated debate on how to teach reading. The main controversy has focused on beginning instruction and the role of phonics and whole language in the teaching of reading.

The debate has sparked the "reading wars," so called by pundits in the media because the clash between phonics and whole language has taken on the kind of religious fervor witnessed in a holy war. The advocates of each approach have waged an emotional and intellectual battle over issues and practices related to beginning instruction. But is it really necessary to take sides? The Viewpoint in Box 1.2 was written by one of the authors of this book during his year as president of the International Reading Association (IRA).

Why isn't there more consensus on how to teach children to read? Although it is perfectly natural to want to know the "right way" to do something, a case can be made for both phonics and whole language in a comprehensive reading program, because both are grounded in knowledge and beliefs that can be supported by a body of research as well as common sense about the teaching of reading. From a professional perspective, the danger of buying into the "right way" to teach reading is this: some teachers can become dependent on others' telling them how to help children develop as readers rather than using on their own professional expertise and judgment. If teachers are to be empowered as professionals, they must apply their knowledge and beliefs about reading and learning to read to decide what is best practice for readers.

In the pressured world of teaching, it is sometimes easy to lose sight of what we know and believe about children, reading, and how children learn to read. The common thread that runs through the literacy practices of Mrs. Henderson, Arch, Linda, and countless other reading professionals is that they view reading and learning to read through belief systems that define and shape their roles as classroom teachers. Through what set of beliefs do you view reading and learning to read? How do you believe reading and writing should be taught in an effective literacy program? Throughout your teaching career, from the time you begin studying to become a teacher and all the while you practice your craft, you will be continually developing answers to these questions as you build and refine your knowledge and beliefs about what counts as literacy learning in your classroom.

Are some belief systems better than others? The answer to the question lies not with the authors of this or any comprehensive textbook on reading telling you the "right way" to think about teaching and learning to read but in the process of coming to know about literacy learning. The more you know about what readers and writers do and the roles that reading and writing play in the lives of children, the more empowered you are to respond to a question of such personal and professional importance.

Belief systems related to literacy learning are not a collection of naive assumptions and presuppositions but rather a set of beliefs that are grounded in research and current thinking about reading and writing. As suggested in the International Reading Association's *Standards for Reading Professionals* (1998), the beliefs of teachers "are a filter on the world and evolve as the world and our understanding of literacy change" (p. 12). In the Preface to this book, we outlined the core beliefs that underlie the writing of this book.

BOX 1.2   VIEWPOINT

The Reading Wars
Richard T. Vacca

The "reading wars" are here. They are being waged along several battle fronts: in the media, in legislatures, in school districts, and among colleagues. Newspaper coverage, in particular, has characterized the wars as a bloody conflagration between the proponents of phonics and whole language. I don't get it. I'm a proponent of phonics. I'm a proponent of whole language. Am I missing something here?

Phonics is a tool needed by all readers and writers of alphabetically written languages such as English. While I am not a proponent of isolated drill, overreliance on worksheets, or rote memorization of phonic rules, I support the teaching of phonics that children actually need and use to identify words quickly and accurately. These strategies need to be taught explicitly in well-planned lessons. Every effective classroom teacher that I have ever known has never questioned whether phonics should or should not be taught, but rather asked how, how much, to whom, and when it is most appropriate to teach phonics.

Learning to read has been the subject of controversy throughout much of the twentieth century. But today, the debates are no longer primarily confined to the groves of academe. Reading now rates prime-time coverage. In the September 1993 issue of the U.S. Department of Education's *News Bulletin,* Secretary of Education Richard Riley elevated the importance of reading: "America will go from great to second rate if our children cannot read well enough." The jobs of tomorrow demand complex skills and high-level performance. "The basics aren't good enough anymore."

Kudos to Secretary Riley for his leadership on behalf of literacy and for recognizing that lives are in the balance if children don't read well enough. But lest we forget, or diminish its importance, learning to read well is about more than jobs. Reading is a liberating force in our lives. It sets us free: to wonder, to challenge, to respond, to think and feel more deeply, and to make better decisions. The quality of our lives is diminished if we have not learned how to read well and to read often. Why, then, aren't the reading wars focused on our children's ability to read critically or to use reading to solve problems in a highly complex world?

Perhaps the reading wars are not as much about phonics pitted against whole language as they are about the role of phonics in reading and writing. Phonics is an important part of literacy instruction and needs to be taught well in classrooms where children read and write each day. Although phonics is a tool needed by readers and writers, the teaching of phonics, necessary as it is, isn't sufficient to develop thoughtful, comprehending readers who value reading and its many uses.

As Secretary of Education Riley recognizes, the basics aren't enough. It's time to recognize that the debate on phonics versus whole language diverts attention away from real issues that will make a difference in the reading and writing lives of our children.

Source: Adapted with permission from the International Reading Association and Richard T. Vacca. "The President's Notebook," *Reading Today,* October–November 1996, p. 4

Suffice it to say that what we, as authors of this book, believed about some aspects of reading and learning to read has changed considerably since entering the teaching field three decades ago, primarily because the *knowledge base* has changed. Nevertheless, there are some beliefs about children, teachers, teaching and learning, and how children learn to read and use reading to learn that have remained constant since we entered the teaching profession. If we were to characterize our worldview of reading and learning to read today, we would affirm that our beliefs are rooted in an *interactive* view of the reading process and a *balanced* view of reading instruction—concepts that will be developed in this chapter and the next.

How Teachers Come to Know About Reading and Learning to Read

Teachers come to know in different ways. For example, in a lifetime of interaction with the world about us, we acquire knowledge about reading and learning to read by *building it from the inside* as we interact with people, processes, ideas, and things. Jean Piaget's theory of **constructivism** provides a compelling explanatory framework for understanding the acquisition of knowledge. Piaget, one of the preeminent child psychologists of the twentieth century, theorized that children do not internalize knowledge directly from the outside but construct it from inside their heads, in interaction with the environment (Kamii, 1991). When constructivist thinking is applied to the acquisition of knowledge about teaching and learning, it holds that teachers engage in a process of seeking and making meaning from personal, practical, and professional experiences.

Constructing Personal Knowledge

Personal knowledge of reading and learning to read grows out of a teacher's history as a reader and a writer. Consider, for example, the influences in your life that have shaped the literate person that you are. From birth, you have interacted with *people* (parents, teachers, siblings, friends, significant others) and *things* (all kinds of literacy artifacts and texts, including books, signs, letters, labels, pencil and paper, word processors) to construct knowledge about the *processes* of reading and writing. By engaging in reading and writing, you come to know in a very personal way what readers and writers do and the contributions that reading and writing make to a life. You belong to what Frank Smith (1988) calls the "literacy club" by virtue of the fact that you read and write.

The development of an *autobiographical narrative* is a powerful tool that helps you link your personal history as a reader to instructional beliefs and practices. Not all teachers like to read, even though they know how. Some may read well and be well read. But others may have struggled as readers and bear the emotional scars to prove it. How do these realities affect what teachers do in classroom situations?

An autobiographical narrative helps you inquire into the past so as better to understand what you do in the present and what you would like to do in future classroom situations. Teachers who engage in narrative inquiry explore mental pictures of memories, incidents, or situations in their lives. The inquiry allows you to reflect, make connections, and project. As Connelly and Clandinin (1988) put it, "Where we have been and where we are going interact to make meaning of the situations in which we find ourselves" (p. 6).

To develop a reading autobiography, consider the questions in Figure 1.1. You may wish to share your narratives with others. What beliefs, values, and attitudes are an integral part of your stories? How do your personal histories of reading and learning to read influence where you are in your thinking about reading and where you would like to be?

Constructing Practical Knowledge

Teachers also construct practical knowledge, which is closely related to personal knowledge in that it grows out of experience both in and out of the classroom. The more that you work with and observe children in literacy situations in classroom and community contexts and reflect on their behavior *and* your own, the more you develop theories about what is the best practice for the readers and writers with whom you work. Practical knowledge is characterized by the beliefs, values, and attitudes that you construct about readers and writers, texts, reading and writing processes, learning to read and write, and the role of the teacher in the development of children's literate behavior.

In teacher education programs, field experiences and student teaching are vehicles for acquiring practical knowledge. In addition, interactions with and observations of practicing teachers influence the way you might think about reading and learning to read in classroom situations. Often preservice teachers find incongruities between what is taught in education courses and what they observe in the field. These incongruities create conceptual conflict, which is healthy because it helps reflective students of literacy think more deeply about their own understandings, beliefs, and practices.

◆ FIGURE 1.1

Developing a Reading Autobiographical Narrative

Re ect on how you learned to read, the reading habits you have formed, home and school in uences on your reading development, and the kinds of reading you do. Prepare an autobiographical sketch that captures these personal memories. How did you learn to read? What home reading experiences do you recall? What kinds of instructional activities and practices were you involved in as an elementary school child? Which ones do you recall fondly? Which, if any, do you recall with regret? In retrospect, what belief systems and views of reading and learning to read did your elementary school teachers seem to hold? Were you effectively taught how to handle the variety of reading tasks you face in the real world?

The construction of practical knowledge extends beyond classroom situations and includes interactions within the cultural context of school and community. For example, a teacher's beliefs about reading and learning to read may be affected by peer pressure, the beliefs of colleagues and administrators, school board policies, curriculum guidelines, the publishing and testing industry, public opinion, and standards for teaching reading.

Constructing Professional Knowledge and Expertise

As an integral part of their professional development, teachers interact with the world of ideas. Professional education organizations, such as the International Reading Association, refer to what teachers ought to know and be able to do to teach reading well as *standards* or the *knowledge base.*

Professional knowledge is knowledge acquired from an ongoing study of the practice of teaching. What teacher education programs do best is help preservice and inservice teachers build a knowledge base that is grounded in current theory, research, and practice. Throughout their professional development, the books and journals teachers read, the courses and workshops they take, and the conferences they attend contribute to the vision they have of reading and learning to read.

The instructional differences among teachers reflect the knowledge they put to use in classroom situations. While few would argue that nothing is as practical as a good theory, we embrace the notion that "there's nothing so theoretical as a good practice." Teachers construct theories of reading and learning to read, based on their ways of knowing, which influence the way they teach, including the way they plan, use and select texts, interact with learners, and assess literate activity. In turn, the decisions teachers make about instruction influence students' reading performance and their perceptions of and attitudes toward reading, as illustrated in Figure 1.2.

Coming to know what readers do is no easy matter. Part of the challenge that teachers encounter comes from the complex, elusive nature of the reading process. Who can ever really know a process that takes place in the head? The best we can do is investigate reading and learning to read by inquiring into literacy teaching and learning. Personal, practical, and professional experiences are the stepping-stones to knowing about reading and learning to read.

A reading professional, whether novice or veteran, continually needs to study the knowledge base from *multidisciplinary* perspectives. Because reading and learning to read are complex human activities, no one field of study provides us with all the answers. Understanding reading from multiple perspectives allows us to affirm, change, or let go of what we believe and value in light of new knowledge and research. Multidisciplinary perspectives on reading and learning to read enrich and broaden the knowledge base so that teachers are in the very best position to use their professional expertise and judgment to make instructional decisions.

A single discipline cannot provide a teacher with the insights and understandings needed to guide and support literacy learning in the modern world. The fields of education, linguistics, cognitive psychology, technology, sociology, and anthropology, to name a

◆ FIGURE 1.2   Relationships Among Teacher Knowledge, Decisions, and Actions and Students' Literate Activity and Attitudes Toward Reading and Writing

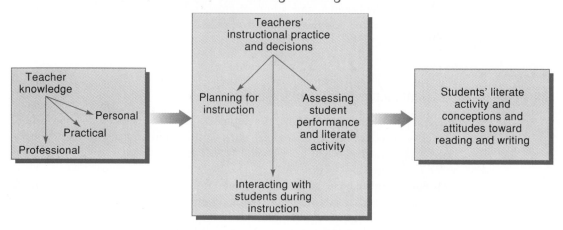

few, contribute in important ways to knowledge and beliefs about reading and learning to read. From a *cognitive* perspective, for example, an elementary teacher needs to understand, among other things, how children learn words in an alphabetic system of writing such as English; from a *language* perspective, how children's knowledge of written language emerges and develops naturally in early childhood to form the basis for literacy learning; and from a *sociocultural* perspective, how children's home language and community values influence language use and literacy learning.

Research on reading in the past three decades has centered primarily around the roles of cognition and language in reading acquisition. Cognitive studies have provided insights into how people comprehend and learn as they process written symbols. Cognitive scientists and researchers are interested in how reading works inside people's heads—how readers learn to *decode* words accurately and automatically in an alphabetic writing system, how readers use prior knowledge *(schemata)* to understand what they are reading, and how readers use and develop *strategies* to *regulate* and *monitor* comprehension as they learn from written language.

Language and literacy learning are inseparable. Learning to read needs to be understood in terms of learning to use written language effectively. One of the most important ways people learn is through the use of language, spoken, written, or signed. Goodman (1986) puts it this way: "Language enables us to share our experiences, learn from each other, [and] plan together, and greatly enhances our intellect by linking our minds with others of our kind" (p. 11). Children are inherently social. If children perceive little use of written language, they will have a difficult time learning to read and write. However, if written language is meaningful, the social and cultural situations in which it is used allow children to discern what reading and writing are all about.

Cognitive Insights into Reading and Learning to Read

A university colleague of ours, a cognitive psychologist by training, says he's been re-searching and studying the reading process for more than two decades because he's inter-ested in "how the mind works." How the mind works is another way of saying that he's in-terested in understanding *cognitive* and *metacognitive processes* in reading. His inquiries into the reading process embrace a psychological perspective. One of the important con-tributions from cognitive psychology focuses on beginning readers' discovery of the **alpha-betic principle** in languages such as English. Learning to read English involves learning how an alphabetic writing system works.

The Alphabetic Principle and Learning to Read

The alphabetic principle suggests that there is a correspondence between letters *(graphemes)*, which are the basic units of writing, and sounds *(phonemes)*. Pearson (1996) likens the discovery of the alphabetic principle to learning a great secret: When children "have learned the great secret—that English writing represents sounds—two entire worlds open to them: first, that well-spring of inner oral language; and second, through that lan-guage, a seemingly unending world of books" (p. 270). A teacher needs to understand how beginning readers come to master the alphabetic system and use their knowledge of Eng-lish writing to identify words.

However, before considering how beginners learn to identify words accurately and quickly, participate in the two demonstrations that follow. These demonstrations make clear what *skilled* readers know about the alphabetic system and how they use their knowl-edge for accurate and automatic word identification.

Suppose the following lines were flashed on a screen in half-second intervals, and you were asked to write down what you could remember after each line was flashed.

Line 1	─○─ □ ⊗ ⊓ ⊔ ╪ ⎍ ⊔
Line 2	xmrbacdy
Line 3	boragle
Line 4	institution
Line 5	flour wiggle come stove investigate girl door yell
Line 6	the beautiful girl ran down the steep hill

When we have conducted this demonstration with preservice teachers in reading methods classes, here's what usually happens.

Most class members are unable to recall accurately the squiggly black marks on line 1. However, they are able to remember some, but not all, of the letters in line 2. Both the nonword *boragle* in line 3, which follows conventional English spelling patterns, and the word *institution* in line 4 are usually recalled. After line 5 is flashed, students are unable to recall all the words in the string, but the whole string of words in line 6, which makes a sentence, is usually recalled.

What can we learn from this demonstration? Human beings can make about four fixations per second with their eyes (Smith, 1985). When looking at the flashed items, skilled readers use about 50 milliseconds of visual intake and then use 200 milliseconds to process the intake. During the intake, they can probably attend to only about five to seven items—the range of items most human beings can hold in short-term memory. When looking at each of the six lines for a half-second, the limitations of short-term memory (being able to recall five to seven items) operate. What changes line by line is the nature of the items. Skilled readers are able to recognize some of the items quickly and accurately because they are able to perceive them as letter patterns or units of written language. These patterns are recognized by skilled readers as familiar *spelling patterns* or *sight words*.

In line 1, skilled college-level readers are unable to group the marks, which we'll call "squiggles," into meaningful patterns. The reason is simple: they have no prior knowledge of the squiggles. These squiggles have not been learned as an *orthography*. Skilled readers have internalized the shapes of aphabetic letters, their names, and the sounds they symbolize. But they aren't the least bit familiar with the shapes of the individual squiggles in line 1 or whether the squiggles function as written symbols that represent sounds.

In line 2, the black squiggly marks are recognized as individual letters in English writing. However, within the time constraints of a half-second interval, college readers cannot group all of the letters into meaningful letter patterns. As a result, they have difficulty holding all the letters in short-term memory.

In lines 3, 4, and 5, skilled readers can group the letters into familiar spelling patterns. *Boragle* and *institution* are easily recalled by most college students when flashed on a screen. Even though *boragle* is a nonsense word, the letter patterns are consistent and predictable. *Institution* is recalled as a known sight word.

Most of the college students in our classes cannot in a half-second recall all of the words in line 5 because these words cannot be strung together into a meaningful utterance. However, the students stand a greater chance of recalling line 6 precisely because the string of words makes a meaningful sentence that they are able to decode, based on their immediate sight recognition of known words.

Now read these two lists, both containing nonwords:

LIST 1	LIST 2
scrass	tblc
sook	gfpv
tolly	oeaiu
amittature	rtbm
lanfication	gdhtaiueo

Which list is easier to read? Use what you learned from the first demonstration to respond to the question.

List 1, of course, is fairly easy for skilled readers to read, but list 2 is nearly impossible. The reason why list 1 is easier to read than list 2, as you might have surmised, involves your skill at identifying letters patterns. Written English contains predictable letter patterns that skilled readers are able to associate with sounds very rapidly and accurately (Juel, 1988; Venezky & Massaro, 1979). Skilled readers know that *scr* is likely to occur in English writing but that *tblc* is not likely to occur. When skilled readers encounter multisyllable words (or even nonwords that contain common orthographic patterns), they depend on their ability to group these patterns into syllables. This is done by using their knowledge of likely and unlikely letter sequences. We know that the letters *lan* would go together to pronounce "lan," that *fi, ca,* and *tion* should be treated as a cluster of letters that we chunk together or treat as a group. Cognitive studies show that skillful readers chunk words into syllables automatically, *in the course of perceiving letters.* Skilled readers are able to do this because of their knowledge of likely spelling patterns, or **orthographic knowledge.** This knowledge is so thoroughly learned that skilled readers do not have to put any energy into identifying words (Adams, 1990).

From an instructional perspective, then, it is important to know how to help beginning readers develop into skilled readers who can identify words quickly and accurately as they read. When young children begin reading, their eyes encounter three units of written language: letters, words, and sentences. While Holdaway (1979) notes the importance of the alphabetic principle in learning to read, he also points out that the visual display of print on the page makes the learning of words critical:

> We think of the alphabet principle as a wonderful invention. **BUTWEOVERLOOKANINVENTIONALMOSTASBRILLIANTAND CERTAINLYMORESIMPLE**—namely the visual display. . . . Indeed, written language is perceived as words, not as a series of individual letters. (p. 83)

Because of the use of spaces—a print convention that evolved with Gutenberg's invention of the printing press in the fifteenth century—the visual display of written language creates a system of distinct, perceptual units called *words.* According to Ehri (1995), during the course of learning to read, the eyes come to favor written words over letters and sentences: "The advantage of words over sentences is that words can be assimilated in one glance. The advantage of words over letters is that written words correspond more reliably to spoken words than letters correspond to sounds" (p. 171). Because words are the primary units of written language, helping beginners develop word-reading skill is one of the important instructional responsibilities of teachers in learning to read. Although beginners have developed some knowledge of written language prior to first grade, explicit instruction becomes essential as children progress through various phases of word-reading development and develop strategies to read words quickly and accurately. We will examine instructional issues and practices related to word-reading development and strategies for word study in Chapters 3 through 6.

How children think and reason with print is an important concern in this book. A cognitive view of reading suggests that the reader's ability to construct meaning is at the core of the process. The constructive processes characteristic of reading comprehension have been of intense interest to cognitive psychologists and reading researchers for more than a decade. In particular, they have studied the role that schemata play in comprehending texts.

Schema Theory and Reading Comprehension

Schemata reflect the prior knowledge, experiences, conceptual understandings, attitudes, values, skills, and procedures a reader brings to a reading situation. Children use what they know already to give meaning to new events and experiences. Cognitive psychologists use the term *schema* to describe how humans organize and construct meaning in their heads. Schemata have been called "the building blocks of cognition" (Rumelhart, 1982) and "a cognitive map to the world" (Neisser, 1976) because they represent elaborate networks of concepts, skills, and procedures that we use to make sense of new stimuli, events, and situations.

For example, do you possess the schemata needed to interpret the passage in Figure 1.3?

Upon first reading, Bransford and Johnson's passage may seem difficult to understand unless you were able to activate an appropriate schema. How many of you recognized that the passage had to do with washing clothes? Once a schema for washing clothes is activated, the words and phrases in the passage take on new meaning. Now try rereading the passage. Upon rereading, you will probably react by saying, "Aha! Now that I know the passage is about washing clothes, it makes sense!" Ambiguous words such as *procedure* and word streams such as "A mistake can be expensive" are now interpreted within the frame-

◆ FIGURE 1.3

What Is the Passage About?

The procedure is quite simple. First you arrange things into different groups. Of course, one pile may be suf cient depending on how much there is to do. If you have to go somewhere else due to lack of facilities that is the next step; otherwise you are pretty well set. It is important not to overdo things. That is, it is better to do few things at once than too many. In the short run this may not seem important but complications can easily arise. A mistake can be expensive as well. At rst the whole procedure will seem complicated. Soon, however, it will become just another facet of life. It is dif cult to foresee any end to the necessity for this task in the immediate future, but then one can never tell. After the procedure is completed one arranges the materials into different groups again. They can be put into their appropriate places. Eventually they will be used once more, and the whole cycle will then have to be repeated. However, this is part of life. (Bransford & Johnson, 1973, p. 400)

Source: From "Considerations of Some Problems of Comprehension," by J. D. Bransford and M. K. Johnson, in *Visual Information Processing,* edited by W. C. Chase (New York: Academic Press, 1973). Used by permission.

work of what you know about washing clothes. The more you know about washing clothes, the more comprehensible the passage becomes. When readers activate appropriate schemata, *expectations* are raised for the meaning of the text. Your expectations for the passage help you anticipate meaning and relate information from the passage to things you already know.

The more we hear, see, read, or experience new information, the more we refine and expand existing schemata within our language system.

Schemata, as you can see, influence reading comprehension and learning. For comprehension to happen, readers must activate or build a schema that fits with information from a text. When a good fit occurs, a schema functions in at least three ways to facilitate comprehension. First, a schema provides a framework that allows readers to *organize* text information efficiently and effectively. The ability to integrate and organize new information into old facilitates retention. Second, a schema allows readers to *make inferences* about what happens or is likely to happen in a text. Inferences, for example, help children predict upcoming information or fill in gaps in the material. And third, a schema helps readers *elaborate* on the material. Elaboration is a powerful aspect of reasoning with print. When children elaborate on what they have read, they engage in cognitive activity that involves speculation, judgment, and evaluation.

Metacognition and Learning

Metacognition, defined generally by Ann Brown (1985), refers to knowledge about and regulation of some form of cognitive activity. In the case of reading, metacognition refers to (1) *self-knowledge*—the knowledge students have about themselves as readers and learners; (2) *task knowledge*—the knowledge of reading tasks and the strategies that are appropriate given a task at hand; and (3) *self-monitoring*—the ability of students to monitor reading by keeping track of how well they are comprehending.

Consider the following scenario, one that is quite common when working with reading beginners: A first grader, reading orally, comes to a word in the text that he doesn't recognize. Stymied, he looks to the teacher for help. The teacher has at least four options to consider in deciding how to respond to the reader: (1) tell him the word, (2) ask him to "sound it out," (3) ask him to take an "educated guess," or (4) tell him to say "blank" and keep on reading.

What would you do? A rationale, based on what you know and believe about teaching reading, can be developed for each of the options or, for that matter, a combination. For example, "First, I'd ask him to sound out the word, and if that didn't work, I'd tell him the word." Or, "First, I'd ask him to take a good guess based on what word might make sense, and if that didn't work, I'd ask him to say 'blank' and keep on reading."

Options 2 through 4 represent strategies to solve a particular problem that occurs during reading—identifying an unfamiliar word. Sounding out an unfamiliar word is one strategy frequently taught to beginners. When using a sounding-out strategy, a reader essentially tries to associate sounds with letters or letter combinations. An emphasis on sounding out in and of itself is a limited strategy because it doesn't teach or make children aware of the importance of monitoring what is read for comprehension. A teacher builds a child's metacognition when sounding out is taught in conjunction with making sense. For example, a teacher follows up a suggestion to sound out an unfamiliar word by asking, "Does the word make sense? Does what you read sound like language?"

Option 3, taking an educated guess, asks the reader to identify a word that makes sense in the context of the sentence in which the word is located or the text itself. The **implicit** message to the reader is that reading is supposed to make sense. If a child provides a word other than the unfamiliar word but preserves the meaning of the text, the teacher would be instructionally and theoretically consistent by praising the child and encouraging him to continue reading.

The fourth option, say "blank" and keep on reading, is also a metacognitive strategy for word identification because it shows the reader that reading is not as much a word-perfect process as it is a meaning-making process. No one word should stop a reader cold. If the reader is monitoring the text for meaning, he may be able to return to the word and identify it or decide that the word wasn't that important to begin with.

The teacher can make the implicit messages about reading strategies **explicit.** Throughout this book, we will use terms associated with explicit instruction: *modeling, demonstrating, explaining, rationale-building, thinking aloud, reflecting.* From an instructional point of view, these terms reflect practices that allow the teacher to help students develop *metacognitive awareness* and *strategic knowledge.* For example, Arch, the first-grade teacher discussed earlier in this chapter, chooses to engage the reader, after she has taken a good guess at the unfamiliar word and completes reading, in a brief discussion of the importance of identifying words that "make sense" and "sound like language" in the context of what's being read. Such metacognitive discussions have the potential to build self-knowledge and task knowledge and also to strengthen the reader's self-monitoring abilities.

Self-Knowledge.   Do children know what reading is for? Do they know what the reader's role is? Do they know their options? Are they aware of their strengths as readers and learners? Do they recognize that some texts are harder than others and that all texts should not be read alike? Questions such as these reflect the self-knowledge component of metacognition. When readers are aware of *self* in relation to *texts* and *tasks,* they are in a better position to use reading strategies effectively (Armbruster, Echols, & Brown, 1982).

Task Knowledge.   Experienced readers are strategic readers. They use their task knowledge to meet the demands inherent in difficult texts. For example, they know how to analyze a reading task, reflect on what they know or don't know about the text to be read, establish purposes and plans for reading, and evaluate their progress in light of purposes for reading. Experienced readers are often aware of whether they have understood what they have read. And if they haven't, they know what to do when comprehension fails.

Self-Monitoring.   Reading becomes second nature to most of us as we develop experience and maturity with the process. Experienced readers operate on "automatic pilot" as they read, until they run into a problem that disrupts the flow. For example, read the following passage:

Teachers sometimes engage readers in brief discussions on metacognitive strategies.

The boys' arrows were nearly gone, so they sat down on the grass and stopped hunting. Over at the edge of the woods they saw Henry making a bow to a little girl who was coming down the road. She had tears in her dress and also tears in her eyes. She gave Henry a note, which he brought over to the group of young hunters. Read to the boys it caused great excitement. After a minute but rapid examination of their weapons, they ran down the valley. Does were standing at the edge of the lake, making an excellent target. (author unknown)

Now reflect on the experience. At what point during reading did a "built-in sensor" in your head begin to signal to you that something was wrong? At what point in the passage did you become aware that some of the words you were misreading were homonyms and that you were choosing the inappropriate pronunciations of one or more of the homonyms? What did you do to rectify your misreadings? Why do you suppose the "sensor" signaled disruptions in your reading?

As experienced readers, we expect reading to make sense. And as we interact with a text, the metacognitive "sensor" in each of us monitors whether what we're reading is making sense.

What reader hasn't chosen an inappropriate pronunciation, come across a concept too difficult to grasp, or become lost in an author's line of reasoning? What experienced reader hasn't sensed that a text is too difficult to understand the first time around? The difference, of course, between the experienced and inexperienced reader is that the former knows when something's wrong and often employs correction strategies to "get back on track." This is what monitoring comprehension is all about.

Metacognitive ability is related to both age and reading experience (Stewart & Tei, 1983). Older students are more strategic in their reading than younger students, and good readers demonstrate more ability to use metacognition to deal with problems that arise during reading than readers with limited proficiency. Nevertheless, the instructional implications of metacognition are evident throughout this book. Becoming literate is a process of becoming aware not only of oneself as a reader but also of strategies that help solve problems that arise during reading. A classroom environment that nurtures metacognitive functioning is crucial to children's literacy development.

READING FROM A LANGUAGE PERSPECTIVE

Cognition and language are crucial components in human development. Although the acquisition of language is a complex process, many children understand and use all of the basic language patterns by the time they are 6 years old. A child's apparent facility with language is best understood by recognizing the active relationship between cognition and language.

Jean Piaget (1973) spent most of his life observing children and their interactions with their environment. His theory of cognitive development helps explain that language acquisition is influenced by more general cognitive attainments. As children explore their environment, they interpret and give meaning to the events that they experience. The child's need to interact with immediate surroundings and to manipulate objects is critical to language development. From a Piagetian view, language reflects thought and does not necessarily shape it.

Lev Vygotsky (1962, 1978), the acclaimed Russian psychologist, also viewed children as active participants in their own learning. However, at some point in their early development, children begin to acquire language competence; as they do so, language stimulates cognitive development. Gradually they begin to regulate their own problem-solving activities through the mediation of egocentric speech. In other words, children carry on external dialogues with themselves. Eventually external dialogue gives way to inner speech.

According to both Piaget and Vygotsky, children must be actively involved to grow and learn. Merely reacting to the environment isn't enough. An important milestone in a child's development, for example, is the ability to analyze means-ends relationships. When this occurs, children begin to acquire the ability to use language to achieve goals.

The linguistic sophistication of young children cannot be underestimated or taken for granted. Yet the outdated notion that children develop speech by imitation still persists among people who have little appreciation or knowledge of oral language development. The key to learning oral language lies in the opportunities children have to explore and experiment with language toward purposeful ends. As infants grow into toddlers, they learn to use language as an instrument for their intentions: "I want" becomes a favorite phrase. No wonder M. A. K. Halliday (1975) described learning oral language as a "saga in learning to mean."

When teachers embrace reading as a language process, they understand the importance of learning oral language but are also acutely aware that written language develops in humans along parallel lines. Children learn to use written language in much the same manner that they learn to use oral language—naturally and purposefully. As Goodman (1986) put it, "Why do people create and learn written language? They need it! How do they learn it? The same way they learn oral language, by using it in authentic literary events that meet their needs" (p. 24).

Ultimately, there's only one way to become proficient as a writer and reader, and that's by writing and reading. When opportunities abound for children to engage in real literacy events (writing and reading), they grow as users of written language.

When language is splintered into its parts, and the parts are isolated from one another for instructional purposes, learning to read becomes more difficult than it needs to be. The whole language concept, originated by Kenneth and Yetta Goodman, reflects the way some teachers think about language and literacy. They plan teaching activities that support students in their use of all aspects of language in learning to read. Keeping language "whole" drives home the point that splintering written language into bits and pieces, to be taught and learned separately from one another, makes learning to read harder, not easier. According to Kenneth Goodman (1986):

> Many school traditions seem to have actually hindered language development. In our zeal to make it easy, we've made it hard. How? Primarily by breaking whole (natural) language up into bite-size, but abstract little pieces. It seemed so logical to think that little children could best learn simple little things. We took apart the language and turned it into words, syllables, and isolated sounds. Unfortunately, we also postponed its natural purpose—the communication of meaning—and turned it into a set of abstractions, unrelated to the needs and experiences of the children we sought to help. (p. 7)

Support for whole language teaching comes from two areas of language inquiry: **psycholinguistics** and **sociolinguistics**.

Psycholinguistics and Reading

A psycholinguistic view of reading combines a psychological understanding of the reading process with an understanding of how language works. Psycholinguistic inquiries into the reading process suggest that readers act on and interact with written language in an effort to make sense of a text. Reading is not a passive activity; it is an active thinking process that takes place "behind the eyes." Nor is reading an exact process. All readers make mistakes—"miscues," Kenneth Goodman (1973) calls them. Why? Miscues are bound to occur because readers are continually *anticipating* meaning and *sampling* a text for information cues based on their expectations. In fact, readers search for and coordinate *information cues* from three distinct systems in written language: the **graphophonemic,** the **syntactic,** and the **semantic.**

Graphophonemic System.   The print itself provides readers with a major source of information: the graphic symbols or marks on the page represent speech sounds. The more experience readers have with written language, the more they learn about regular and irregular sound-letter relationships. Experienced readers acquire enough knowledge of sounds associated with letter symbols that they do not have to use all the available graphic information in a word in order to decode or recognize it.

Syntactic System.   Readers possess knowledge about how language works. *Syntactic information* is provided by the grammatical relationships within sentence patterns. In other words, readers use their knowledge of the meaningful arrangement of words in sentences to construct meaning from text material.

The order of words provides important information cues during reading. For example, although children may be able to read the words *"ran race the quickly children the,"* they would make little sense out of what they read. The meaning is not clear until the words are arranged like so: *"The children quickly ran the race."* In addition, readers use syntactic information to anticipate a word or phrase that "must come next" in a sentence because of its grammatical relationship to other words in the sentence. For example, most children reading the sentence *"I saw a red _____."* would probably fill in the blank with a noun because they intuitively know how language works.

Semantic System.   The semantic system of language stores the schemata that readers bring to a text in terms of background knowledge, experiences, conceptual understandings, attitudes, beliefs, and values.

Sociolinguistics and Reading

In the child's first several years, skill in spoken language develops naturally and easily. Children discover what language does for them. They learn that language is a tool that they can use and understand in interactions with others in their environment. They also learn that language is intentional; it has many purposes. Among the most obvious is communication. The more children use language to communicate, the more they learn the many special functions it serves.

Halliday (1975) viewed language as a reflection of what makes us uniquely human. His monumental work explored how language functions in our day-to-day interactions and serves the personal, social, and academic facets of our lives. Frank Smith (1977) expanded Halliday's functions of language by describing ten of its uses. He proposed that "the uses to which language is put lie at the heart of language comprehension and learning" (p. 640). The implications of this proposition for learning to read will become apparent throughout this book.

These are the ten uses of language Smith (1977, p. 640) described:

1. *Instrumental:* "I want." (Language as a means of getting things, satisfying material needs)

2. *Regulatory:* "Do as I tell you." (Controlling the behavior, feelings, or attitudes of others)

3. *Interactional:* "Me and you." (Getting along with others, establishing relative status) Also, "Me against you." (Establishing separateness)

4. *Personal:* "Here I come." (Expressing individuality, awareness of self, pride)

5. *Heuristic:* "Tell me why." (Seeking and testing knowledge)

6. *Imaginative:* "Let's pretend." (Creating new worlds, making up stories, poems)

7. *Representational:* "I've got something to tell you." (Communicating information, descriptions, expressing propositions)

8. *Divertive:* "Enjoy this." (Puns, jokes, riddles)

9. *Authoritative/contractual:* "How it must be." (Statutes, laws, regulations, agreements, contracts)

10. *Perpetuating:* "How it was." (Records, histories, diaries, notes, scores)

Children recognize the meaningfulness of written language once they become aware of its uses. As Halliday (1975) noted, if children have difficulty learning to read, it is probably because beginning instruction often has had little to do with what they have learned about the uses of oral language.

The work of Harste, Woodward, and Burke (1984), which explores the literacy development of preschool children, reveals that even 2-year-olds use language strategies, often in concert, to make sense of written language. Four strategies in particular characterize the literacy expectations of beginners:

1. *Text intent.* Children expect written language to be meaningful. Their encounters with text support the expectation that they will be able to re-create and construct an author's message.

2. *Negotiability.* Because children expect print to make sense, they use whatever knowledge and resources they possess to negotiate meaning—to create a meaningful message. Negotiation suggests that reading is a give-and-take process between reader and author.

3. *Risk-taking.* Children experiment with how written language works. They take risks. They make hypotheses and then test them out. Risk-taking situations permit children to grow as language users.

4. *Fine-tuning.* An encounter with a written language becomes a resource for subsequent literacy events and situations. The more children interact with authors and texts, the better they get at constructing meaning.

Because reading is uniquely human, learning to read requires sharing, interaction, and collaboration. Parent-child, teacher-child, and child-child relations and participation patterns are essential in learning to read. To what extent do children entering school have experience operating and communicating in a group as large as that found in the typical classroom? Children must learn the ropes. In many cases, kindergarten may be the first place where children must follow and respect the rules that govern how to operate and cooperate in groups. Not only must they know how and when to work independently and how and when to share and participate, but they must also learn the rules that govern communicative behavior.

Communicative competence, as defined by Hymes (1974), develops differently in different children because they have not all had the same set of experiences or opportunities to engage in communication in the home or in the community. Some preschoolers have acquired more competence than others as to when to and when not to speak and as to what to talk about, with whom, where, and in what manner. The sociolinguistic demands on a 5- or 6-year-old are staggering.

Since a large part of learning to read will depend on the social and cultural context of the classroom, opportunities must abound for discussions and conversations between teacher and child and among children. Within this context, children must demonstrate (1) an eagerness to be independent; (2) an unquenchable zest to explore the new and unknown; (3) the courage to take risks, try things out, experience success as well as some defeat; and (4) the enjoyment of being with others and learning from them.

MODELS OF READING

Models of the reading process often depict the act of reading as a communication event between a sender (the writer) and a receiver of information (the reader). Generally speaking, language information flows from the writer to the reader in the sense that the writer has a message to send and transmits it through print to the reader, who then must interpret its meaning. Reading models have been developed to describe the way readers use language information to construct meaning from print. *How* a reader translates print to meaning is the key issue in the building of models of the reading process. This issue has led to the development of three classes of models: *bottom-up, top-down,* and *interactive.*

Bottom-Up Models of Reading.   **Bottom-up models** assume that the process of translating print to meaning begins with the print. The process is initiated by **decoding** graphic symbols into sounds. The reader first identifies features of letters; links these features together to recognize letters; combines letters to recognize spelling patterns; links spelling patterns to recognize words; and then proceeds to sentence-, paragraph-, and text-level processing.

Top-Down Models of Reading.   **Top-down models** assume that the process of translating print to meaning begins with the reader's prior knowledge. The process is initiated by making predictions or "educated guesses" about the meaning of some unit of print. Readers decode graphic symbols into sounds to "check out" hypotheses about meaning.

Interactive Models of Reading.   **Interactive models** assume that the process of translating print to meaning involves making use of both prior knowledge and print. The process is initiated by making predictions about meaning and/or decoding graphic symbols. The reader formulates hypotheses based on the interaction of information from semantic, syntactic, and graphophonemic sources of information.

The terms *top-down, bottom-up,* and *interactive* are used extensively in the fields of communication and information processing. When these terms are used to describe reading, they also explain how language systems operate in reading.

Models of reading attempt to describe how readers use semantic, syntactic, and graphophonemic information in translating print to meaning. It is precisely in these descriptions that bottom-up, top-down, and interactive models of reading differ. Figures 1.4 and 1.5 show the flow of information in each reading model. Note that these illustrations are general depictions of information processing during reading and do not refer specifically to models such as those in Singer and Ruddell's *Theoretical Models and Processes of Reading* (1985).

◆ Figure 1.4   Bottom-Up and Top-Down Models

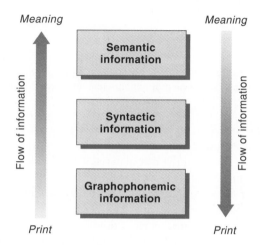

TOP-DOWN PROCESSING:
The act of reading is triggered by the reader's prior knowledge and experience in order to construct meaning.

Meaning   *Meaning*

Flow of information   Flow of information

Semantic information

Syntactic information

Graphophonemic information

Print   *Print*

BOTTOM-UP PROCESSING:
The act of reading is triggered by graphophonemic information such as letters, syllables, and words in order to construct meaning from print.

Bottom-Up Models

As illustrated in Figure 1.5, the process of deriving meaning from print in bottom-up models is triggered by graphic information embedded in print. This is why bottom-up models are described as being "data-driven." Data in this case are the letters and words on the page. A prototype model for bottom-up processing was constructed by Gough (1985), who attempted to show what happens in "one second of reading." In Gough's model, reading involves a series of steps that occur within milliseconds in the mind of the reader. The reader takes one "linguistic step" after another, beginning with the recognition of key features in letters and continuing letter by letter, word by word, and sentence by sentence until reaching the top—the meaning of the text being read.

The reading model by Samuels (1994) is also essentially bottom-up. However, the Samuels model incorporates the idea of *automaticity.* The concept of automaticity suggests that humans can attend to only one thing at a time but may be able to process many things at once so long as no more than one requires attention. Automaticity is similar to putting an airplane on automatic pilot and freeing the pilot to direct his or her attention to other things.

◆ Figure 1.5   Information Processing in Interactive Models of Reading

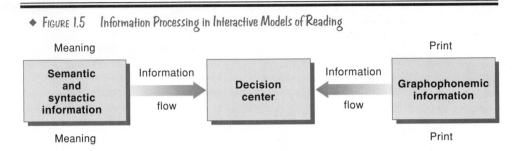

INTERACTIVE PROCESSING: The act of reading is triggered by the reader's prior knowledge and experience as well as graphophonemic information in order to construct meaning.

In reading, *decoding* and *comprehending* vie for the reader's attention. Readers must learn to process graphophonemic information so rapidly that they are free to direct attention to comprehending the text material for meaning.

The young reader is similar to the novice automobile driver. When learning to drive a car, the beginner finds the mechanics of operating the automobile so demanding that he or she must focus exclusively on driving. However, with practice, the skilled driver pays little conscious attention to the mechanics of driving and is able to converse with a passenger or listen to the radio. Likewise, the beginning reader must practice decoding print to speech so rapidly that decoding becomes automatic. As beginners become more fluent in decoding, they can devote their attention to comprehending the writer's message.

Top-Down Models

Top-down models emphasize that information processing during reading is triggered by the reader's prior knowledge and experience in relation to the writer's message. Obviously, there are no pure top-down models because readers must begin by focusing on print. As opposed to being data-driven, top-down models are said to be conceptually driven. That is to say, ideas or concepts in the mind of a reader trigger information processing during reading. As Frank Smith (1985) put it, "The more you already know, the less you need to find out" (p. 15). In other words, the more readers know in advance about the topic to be read, the less they need to use graphic information on the page.

To get a better idea of how reading is conceptually driven, read the following story:

FLAN AND GLOCK

Flan was a flim.
Glock was a plopper.
It was unusual for a flim and a plopper to be crods, but
Flan and Glock were crods. They medged together.
Flan was keaded to moak at a mox. Glock wanted to kead
there too. But the lear said he could not kead there.
Glock anged that the lear said he could not kead there
because he was a plopper.

Although you've never heard of Flan and Glock and don't know what a flim or a plopper is, it is not difficult to interpret from this short story that Glock was discriminated against. How did you figure this out? Your knowledge of capitalization may have led you to hypothesize that Flan and Glock are proper names. Knowledge of grammar, whether intuitive or overt, undoubtedly helped you realize that *flim, plopper, crods,* and *mox* are nouns and that *medged* and *keaded* are verbs. Finally, your knowledge of the world led you to predict that since the lear said, "Glock could not kead there because he was a plopper," Glock is probably a victim of discrimination.

Note that these interpretations of the story are "educated guesses." However, both prior knowledge and graphophonemic information were required to make these guesses. From our perspective, reading is rarely totally top-down or bottom-up. A third class of models helps explain the interactive nature of the reading process.

Interactive Models

Neither prior knowledge nor graphophonemic information is used exclusively by readers. Interactive models suggest that the process of reading is initiated by formulating hypotheses about meaning *and* by decoding letters and words. According to Kamil and Pearson (1979), readers assume either an active or a passive role, depending on the strength of their hypotheses about the meaning of the reading material. If readers bring a great deal of knowledge to the material, chances are that their hypotheses will be strong and that they will process the material actively, making minimal use of graphophonemic information. Passive reading, by contrast, often results when readers have little experience with or knowledge of the topic to be read. They rely much more on the print itself for information cues.

Effective readers know how to interact with print in an effort to understand a writer's message. Effective readers adapt to the material based on their purposes for reading. Purpose dictates the strategies that readers use to translate print to meaning. Two of the most appropriate questions that readers can ask about a selection are "What do I need to know?" and "How well do I already know it?" These two questions help readers establish purposes for reading and formulate hypotheses during reading. The questions also help decide how to *coordinate* prior knowledge and graphophonemic information.

Note that the models of reading just described don't take into consideration the social nature of reading and learning to read. In this sense, they're incomplete. However, models are useful in some respects: they help you reflect on your beliefs, assumptions, and practices related to reading instruction—the topic of Chapter 2.

SUMMARY

We organized this chapter around knowledge and beliefs about reading to suggest that teachers view what they do in the classroom through belief systems that focus and clarify their instructional decisions and practices. Belief systems bring into focus what teachers know, believe, and value not only about their roles as classroom teachers of reading but also about reading, readers, curriculum, and instruction. Teachers develop belief systems about reading and learning to read through personal, practical, and professional study and experience.

Because we believe that all teachers are theorists in that they have reasons for their instructional decisions, we examined the reading process from cognitive, linguistic, and social perspectives and described three models that involve the processing of language information.

The next step in thinking about reading and learning to read is to study how belief systems influence instructional practices and strategies. Chapter 2 explores the concept of balance in the teaching of reading as we examine two major instructional perspectives: phonic skills and whole language.

TEACHER-ACTION RESEARCHER

Teachers who engage in reflection and inquiry find themselves asking questions and observing closely what goes on in their classrooms. Action research is a way for teachers who want to reflect and inquire to better understand within the context of their own teaching more about themselves as teachers and their students as learners. At the end of each chapter, several ideas for action research are presented. Some are intended to be done in the field; others are for the classroom.

1. Observe a teacher in an elementary school. Record what you see and hear during reading instruction time. Based on the interactions recorded between teacher and students, what did you learn about the teacher's knowledge and beliefs about literacy?

2. Using the idea of the reading autobiography, prepare an autobiographical narrative following the directions in Figure 1.1. Share your autobiographical sketch with other members of the class or with colleagues in your school, or with a family member or roommate. What differences in reading development and attitude are evident? What similarities exist?

3. Suppose you are going to be on a panel discussion at a local community center. The topic is, "The Right Way to Teach Reading"; you'll have time for a five-minute statement. What would you say?

KEY TERMS

alphabetic principle
belief system
best practice
bottom-up model
constructivism
decoding
explicit
graphophonemic cues
implicit

interactive model
literacy event
metacognition
orthographic
    knowledge
phonics
professional
    knowledge
psycholinguistics

schemata
semantic cues
sociolinguistics
syntactic cues
top-down model
whole language

CHAPTER

2
Balanced Instruction

Chapter Overview

BALANCED INSTRUCTION

BELIEF SYSTEMS AND THE SEARCH FOR BALANCE

Beliefs About Reading
Interview

Theoretical Orientation to Reading
Profile

CURRICULUM PERSPECTIVES

Skills-Based Curriculum

Whole Language Curriculum

INSTRUCTIONAL APPROACHES

| Phonics | Basal Reading | Language Experience | Integrated Language Arts | Literature-Based | Technology-Based |

ACHIEVING A BALANCED LITERACY PROGRAM

Scaffolding Literacy
Experiences

Explicit Instruction

Meaningful Use of
Skills and Strategies

Between the Lines

In this chapter, you will discover:

♦ The relationship between balanced instruction and beliefs about reading

♦ How beliefs are connected to different theoretical models of reading.

♦ Differences between a skills-based and whole language curriculum

♦ Instructional approaches in the teaching of reading

♦ What it means to achieve a balanced reading program

Gay's gift wasn't what she had expected. Her mother's Christmas present in years past had always been unusual, but this year the woman had outdone herself. Wrapped in shiny foil, much to Gay's surprise, was a worn-out, overstuffed, red-covered notebook. There it was—Gay's old red notebook, which she hadn't seen for more than 20 years—reunited once again with its owner.

Between the covers of the red notebook were those wonderful, creative, misspelled stories that Gay had written as a child. She was about 8 years old when she penned her first story, "Hankie and the Hawk." Story after story filled hundreds of pages now yellowed with time. And then the idea struck her. Gay could hardly wait to get back to the students that she taught and share her childhood stories with them.

Since then, Gay introduces "the old red notebook" to her students on the opening day of each school year. In her own words, "the book" has become the centerpiece of a strategy she uses to introduce her third-grade class to reading and writing: "Here I am, starting the morning of the first day of the school year by reading stories to my class that sound like something the children would have written. The book is falling apart, the pages are yellow, and the crazy teacher is grinning like a fool! Soon, however, an 'ah ha' or two can be heard as I read the author's name with each story: 'Hankie and the Hawk' by Miss Gay Wilson, April 3, 1957; 'How the Pig Got a Curly Tail' by Miss Gay Wilson, December 10, 1959; 'Sue's Birthday' by Miss Gay Wilson, February 21, 1958.

"The dates and the name Wilson carry little meaning, but a few of my students recognize the name Gay as mine and soon catch on to what's happening. 'These are stories *you* wrote when you was a little girl,' blurts a precocious listener. The looks on the children's faces are worth their weight in gold. Sheer delight!

"They beg for more, and I promise more another day. There are enough stories to read every day for most of the school year. So I make a promise to them that I will not break: 'Every day this year you'll get to read, and every day this year you'll get to write.' I want them to feel the specialness of this promise. Then we discuss the author in each of them.

"What do we do next? Write, of course. Do any of the children say, 'I don't know what to write about?' Not at all. Of course, not all of them do write; some, on the first day, draw. But all the children approach writing with confidence. What do they do next? Read, of course. Since I read to them what I had written as a child, they now read to one another."

First days are important. Why did Gay make the decision to use her childhood writings on the first day of school as an instructional tool? "It was a natural decision to make," says Gay, "because I believe strongly in my role as a model. What better way to model what it means to be an author and a reader than to use my own childhood stories." So the old red notebook became part of a strategy—a plan of action—designed to build community, set expectations, and contribute to a classroom environment that supports a *balanced literacy program.*

In this chapter, you will learn about the importance of balanced instruction in a contemporary reading program. There are many variables to be taken into consideration as teachers strive for balance in their classrooms. Balanced instruction evolves from teachers' knowledge and beliefs about reading and learning to read. Gay's story opens this chapter because it illustrates how a teacher's beliefs about learning to read and write influence what she does in the classroom.

How does Gay's "old red notebook" strategy build a learning environment that contributes to a balanced literacy program? The question is more than rhetorical. We raise it to guide your search for what it means to achieve balance in a classroom literacy program. As a third-grade teacher, Gay's goal is to immerse students in authentic literacy experiences. But as you will see later in the chapter, she also attempts to balance these experiences with explicit teaching in the skills and strategies that her students need to use to be successful readers and writers. Teachers like Gay recognize that skills and strategies are learned best through meaningful use.

This chapter helps you make another connection between theory and practice as you explore issues related to achieving balance in the teaching of reading. As you study the chapter overview, note the relationships among beliefs, curricular perspectives, approaches to instruction, and balanced literacy programs.*

BELIEF SYSTEMS AND THE SEARCH FOR BALANCE

The search for balance in classroom literacy programs is critical to today's teacher but must be approached with caution. As Dorothy Strickland (1996), former president of both the International Reading Association and the National Council of Teachers of English, reminds us:

> Achieving balance in our literacy programs is not meant to imply that there is one specific Balanced Approach. Nor should it suggest a sampling method in which a little of this and a little of that are mixed together to form a grouping of disparate approaches. . . . Finally, balance does not mean having two very distinct, parallel approaches coexisting in a single classroom in the name of "playing it safe"—for example, literature-based instruction on Mondays and Wednesday and skills worksheets the remainder of the week. (p. 32)

In her cautionary words, Strickland uses expressions such as "mixing together," "approaches," "skills worksheets," and "literature-based instruction." As you unravel what it means to achieve a balanced literacy program, these terms will take on greater meaning.

Balanced literacy programs require an informed philosophical stance. A teacher's philosophical stance, or belief system, is crucial to achieving balance in the teaching of reading because instruction involves the kinds of decisions that teachers make based on how children learn to read and how they can best be taught.

As noted in Chapter 1, what teachers do to teach reading usually reflects what they know and believe about reading and learning to read. One way to examine your beliefs about reading and learning to read is to connect them to theoretical models of the reading process. Does your philosophical stance reflect a bottom-up view of reading? Top-down? Or interactive? Throughout this book, we contend that teachers who search for balance are in a better position to achieve it in the teaching of reading when their instructional decisions and practices reflect the *interactive* nature of the reading process. Interactive mod-

---

*This vignette is based on "The Gift," by G. Fawcett, 1990, *The Reading Teacher, 43,* p. 504. Used by permission.

◆ FIGURE 2.1   Beliefs About Reading Visualized as a Continuum

els, as we examined in Chapter 1, underscore the important contributions that both the reader *and* the text make in the reading process.

Alan Watts, a contemporary philosopher dealing with existential questions such as "Who am I?" and "Where am I going?" once said, "Trying to define yourself is like trying to bite your own teeth." We invite you to engage in a process of defining and refining your beliefs about reading and learning to read. The task is not easy, but unlike trying to bite your own teeth, it *is* in the realm of the possible.

One important way to define who we are as teachers of reading is by talking about *what* we do and *why* we do it or by observing one another in a teaching situation and asking *why* we did what we did. Another way is through self-examination and reflection. The tools that follow will help you inquire into your beliefs about reading in relation to instructional practices.

Beliefs About Reading Interview

Your beliefs about how students learn to read in all likelihood lie on a continuum between concepts that reflect bottom-up, interactive, and top-down models of reading. By participating in the Beliefs About Reading Interview (see the Viewpoint in Box 2.1), you will get a *general indication* of where your beliefs about learning to read lie on the continuum illustrated in Figure 2.1.

Your responses in the interview will often mirror **units of language** emphasized for instructional purposes. For example, the smallest units of written language are letters; the largest unit is the text selection itself. In Figure 2.2, concentric boxes help illustrate units of written language. The largest box represents the text as a whole. It may be a story, a poem, or an article on the Civil War. This unit of language is made up of *paragraphs*, which are made up of *sentences*, which are made up of *words*, which are made up of *letters*.

Teachers who possess a bottom-up belief system believe that students must decode letters and words before they are able to construct meaning from sentences, paragraphs, and larger text selections. Consequently, they view reading acquisition as mastering and integrating a series of word identification skills. Letter-sound relationships and word identification are emphasized instructionally. Because recognizing each word is believed to be an essential prerequisite to being able to comprehend the passage, accuracy in recognizing words is seen as important. If you hold a bottom-up set of beliefs, you may consider the practice of correcting oral reading errors as important in helping children learn to read. Or you may believe that helping students read a passage over and over or read orally into a tape recorder are important instructional activities because they

◆ Figure 2.2   Units of Written Language

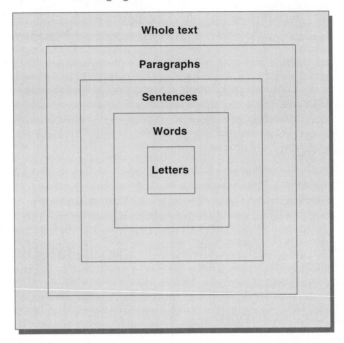

develop accurate word recognition. Teachers who hold bottom-up belief systems often emphasize the teaching of skills in a sequential and systematic manner.

Teachers who have a top-down belief system consider reading for meaning an essential component of all reading instructional situations. They feel that the majority of reading or language arts instructional time should involve students in meaningful activities in which they read, write, speak, and listen. These teachers may also emphasize the importance of students' choosing their own reading material and enjoying the material they read. Sentences, paragraphs, and text selections are the units of language emphasized instructionally. Since recognizing each word is not considered an essential prerequisite to comprehending the passage, word errors during oral reading may not be corrected. Instead, the teacher may advocate noninterference during oral reading or encourage a student to use the context or meaning of the passage to identify unrecognized words.

Teachers who hold an interactive view of reading and learning to read fall between bottom-up and top-down belief systems on the beliefs continuum. Such teachers recognize that a reader processes both letter-sound cues and meaning cues during reading. Reading as a meaning-making activity is utmost in their thoughts about reading and learning to read, but they also believe that readers must be able to identify words quickly and accurately if they are going to make sense of what they read. Moreover, teachers with interactive belief systems integrate reading, writing, speaking, and listening activities, and in the process of doing so, they *scaffold* children's literacy experiences. Scaffolding,

BOX 2.1　VIEWPOINT

What Do You Believe About Reading and Learning to Read?

Use this opportunity to express your views and beliefs about reading.

If you are a preservice teacher studying reading for the first time, you may find it difficult to answer some of the questions in Form A. However, we encourage you to respond to all of the questions based on whatever sources of knowledge and beliefs you currently hold about the reading process and how it should be taught. Knowledge sources may include your own school experiences, observations in the field, experiences as a reader, and previous study. Toward the end of the semester, you may wish to respond to the interview questions again. This will provide a good measure of the growth you have made in thinking about reading and learning to read. Team up with a partner, if possible, and take turns interviewing each other. Study the directions and respond to Form A or Form B of the Beliefs About Reading Interview.

Use Appendix A to analyze and interpret your beliefs about reading and learning to read. Appendix A will provide you with a general framework for determining whether you view reading and learning to read from a bottom-up, interactive, or top-down perspective.

BELIEFS ABOUT READING INTERVIEW

Directions: Select *Form A* of the interview if you are preparing to become a teacher. Select *Form B* of the interview if you are presently a teacher. Respond to each question, thinking in terms of *your own* classroom, either the one in which you plan to teach or the one in which you now teach. As you respond to each question, explain *what* you (would) do and *why* you (would) do it.

Form A: Preservice Teachers

1. You have just signed a contract for your first teaching position in an elementary school. Which goals for reading instruction do you feel most confident in making progress in during the school year?

2. Suppose that a student is reading orally in your class and makes a reading error. What is the first thing you will probably do? Why?

3. Another student in your class is reading orally and doesn't know a word. What are you going to do? Why?

4. You have read about and probably tried out different kinds of strategies and activities for teaching students to read. Which ones do you feel will be the *most* important in your classroom? Why?

5. What kinds of activities do you feel your students should be involved in for the *majority* of their reading instructional time? Why?

6. Here are the typical steps in a directed reading activity as suggested in basal reader manuals: (1) introduction of vocabulary, (2) motivation or setting purposes, (3) reading, (4) questions and discussion after silent reading, and (5) skills practice for reinforcement.

(Continued)

BOX 2.1 CONTINUED

Rank these steps in order from *most* important to *least* important (not necessarily in the order you will follow them).

7. Is it important to introduce new vocabulary words *before* students read a selection? Why or why not?

8. Suppose your new students will be tested to give you information to help you decide how to instruct them in reading. What would this diagnostic test include, and what kind of information would you hope that it gives you about your students?

9. During silent reading, what do you hope your students will do when they come to an unknown word?

10. Look at the oral reading mistakes, which are underlined below, on these transcripts of three readers. Which of the three readers would you judge as the best or most effective reader (Harste & Burke, 1977)?

READER A   I live near this <u>canal</u> [channel]. Men haul things up and down the <u>canal</u> [channel] in big boats.

READER B   I live near this <u>canal</u> [1. ca / 2. candle]. Men haul things up and down the <u>canal</u> [candle] in big boats.

READER C   I live near this <u>canal</u> [1. ca / 2. candle]. Men haul things up and down the <u>canal</u> [cannel] in big boats.

Form B: Inservice Teachers

1. Of all the goals for reading instruction that you have in mind as a teacher, which do you think you have made good progress toward accomplishing this year? Cite one or more, and for each, explain why.

2. What do you usually do when a student is reading orally and makes an oral reading error? Why?

3. What do you usually do when a student is reading orally and doesn't know a word? Why?

4. You probably use different kinds of strategies and activities in teaching reading. Which ones do you feel are the *most* important for your students? Why?

5. What kinds of activities do you feel students should be involved in for the *majority* of their reading instructional time? Why?

6. Here are the typical steps in a directed reading activity as suggested in basal reader manuals: (1) introduction of vocabulary, (2) motivation or setting purposes, (3) reading, (4) questions and discussion after silent reading, and (5) skills practice for reinforcement. Rank these steps in order from *most* important to *least* important (not necessarily in the order you follow them).

7. Is it important to introduce new vocabulary words *before* your students read a selection? Why or why not?

BOX 2.1 CONTINUED

8. Assuming that your students were tested to provide you with information that helped you decide how to instruct them in reading, what did diagnostic testing include, and what kind of information did it give you about your individual students?

9. During silent reading, what do you hope your students do when they come to an unknown word?

10. Look at the oral reading mistakes that are underlined on the transcripts of three readers in item 10 of Form A. Which of these three readers do you deem the best or most effective reader?

as you will learn in more detail later in the chapter, suggests that teachers provide instructional support and guidance in the development of skills and strategies. Because they recognize the importance of teaching skills and strategies, interactive teachers blend *explicit* instruction with children's immersion in various reading and writing activities. Teachers who possess interactive belief systems are likely to achieve balance in the teaching of reading because they strike an equilibrium between children's immersion in reading and writing experiences and their development as skillful and strategic readers and writers.

Table 2.1 summarizes the beliefs defining bottom-up, top-down, and interactive belief systems.

Theoretical Orientation to Reading Profile

The **Theoretical Orientation to Reading Profile (TORP),** designed by Diane De Ford (1985), is a survey instrument that uses a Likert scale to determine teacher beliefs about practices in reading instruction. De Ford identifies three belief systems or theoretical orientations associated with instructional practices in beginning reading: *phonics, skills,* and *whole language.* Phonics and skills orientations are equivalent to bottom-up beliefs about reading. A whole language orientation is associated with top-down beliefs.

Appendix B contains the TORP survey and guidelines for determining your theoretical orientation toward reading. We invite you to complete the TORP survey because it will help you extend your thinking about instructional practices associated with learning to read. A teacher who holds a phonics or skills orientation, for example, is likely to enact a curriculum that is quite different from a teacher who maintains a whole language orientation. Understanding the differences between a skills-based curriculum and a whole language curriculum is essential in a teacher's search for balance in the teaching of reading.

TABLE 2.1

Defining Bottom-Up, Top-Down, and Interactive Beliefs About Reading

	Bottom-Up Beliefs About Reading	Top-Down Beliefs About Reading	Interactive Beliefs About Reading
Relationship of word recognition to comprehension	Believe students must recognize each word in a selection to be able to comprehend the selection.	Believe students can comprehend a selection even when they are not able to identify each word.	Believe students can comprehend by identifying words quickly and accurately.
Use of information cues	Believe students should use word and letter-sound cues exclusively to identify unrecognized words.	Believe students should use meaning and grammatical cues in addition to letter-sound cues to identify unrecognized words.	Believe students process letter-sound and meaning cues simultaneously to identify unrecognized words.
View of reading	Believe reading requires mastering and integrating a series of word identification skills.	Believe students learn to read through meaningful activities in which they read, write, speak, and listen.	Believe students learn to read by developing skills and strategies in meaningful contexts.
Units of language emphasized instructionally	Emphasize letters, letter-sound relationships, and words.	Emphasize sentences, paragraphs, and text selections.	Emphasize letters, letter-sound relationships, words, sentences, paragraphs, and text selections.
Where importance is placed instructionally	View accuracy in identifying words as important.	View reading for meaning as important.	View accurate word identification as contributing to meaningful reading.
Assessment	Think students need to be assessed on discrete skills.	Think students need to be assessed on the kind of knowledge constructed through reading.	Think students need to be assessed on the basis of their performance in meaningful contexts.

Curriculum Perspectives

The term *curriculum* has various shades of meaning in education. One of the long-held conceptions of curriculum practice is that it centers on the selection and organization of objectives, content, and instructional activities and on the evaluation of learning (Tyler, 1949). The objectives of a curriculum become the "standards" that teachers use to make decisions about instruction and assessment. One way to think about curriculum, albeit a static conception, is that it represents *courses of study* that are based on national, state, and local school district policies. A curriculum course of study provides a blueprint for instruction that teachers are expected to follow.

A more dynamic conception of curriculum, however, is that it reflects what teachers and students *do* as they engage in classroom activity. As Henderson and Hawthorne (1995) put it, "Perhaps the most visible aspect of curriculum is a teacher's educational activities—what actually occurs in the classroom" (p. 16). If curriculum represents what teachers and students actually do in the classroom, a teacher's beliefs about literacy learning invariably contribute to curriculum decisions. These decisions involve, among other things, (1) the instructional objectives the teacher emphasizes for the classroom literacy program; (2) the materials the teacher selects and uses for instruction; (3) the learning environment the teacher perceives as most conducive to children's development as readers and writers; (4) the practices, approaches, and instructional strategies the teacher uses to teach reading and writing; and (5) the kinds of assessment the teacher perceives are best to evaluate literacy learning.

Curriculum-related questions every teacher has struggled with (or is struggling with) concern the teaching of literacy skills and strategies: What should children know and be able to do as readers and writers? Which skills and strategies are important? How do I teach skills and strategies? Answers to these questions will differ, depending on the curriculum perspective underlying the literacy program.

Two curriculum perspectives, each supported by differing assumptions and principles about learning to read and write, have resulted in dramatically different objectives, materials, practices, and decisions related to literacy instruction. For much of the twentieth century, the dominant practices related to learning to read have been tied to a **skills-based curriculum**. Only in the past two decades has a skills-based perspective been seriously challenged by educators. The challenge has come from a **whole language curriculum** perspective. Although whole language has transformed the way many of today's teachers think about and enact a literacy curriculum in their classrooms, some educators and policymakers are questioning the effectiveness of a whole language curriculum to develop skillful and competent readers and writers. Some are calling for a return to skills-based curricula. Others are calling for balanced instruction in which teachers draw on the best practices of both a skills-based and whole language curriculum.

Skills-Based Curriculum

In a skills-based literacy curriculum, learning to read and write presumes the acquisition of a finite but rather large number of skills that are considered essential in the development of reading and writing competence. Skills-based programs break down the reading process into smaller components called *skills*. The skills are sequenced from simple to complex and from smaller to larger.

A child's progression from simple to complex skills can be compared to walking a railroad track. Visualize children walking on a railroad track. To reach their destination, the children must step on one railroad tie at a time. If you have ever walked a railroad track, you have experienced how challenging it is to maintain a steady pace, without stumbling, when you walk a tie at a time. In reading programs that emphasize the teaching of skills, each skill is like a railroad tie. Children master one skill before progressing to the next skill as if they were walking a railroad track one tie at a time. If a child happens to stumble on one of the ties (a component skill) on the "skills track," the teacher is expected to provide *direct instruction* through additional practice and reinforcement until the child masters the component skill that he or she stumbled on.

Direct Instruction Model.   Inherent in a skills-based curriculum is the notion of direct teaching to the weaknesses or deficits that children exhibit in their skills development. It is the teacher's job to "identify the essential skills, find out what skills students lack, and teach those skills directly" (Carnine, Silbert, & Kameenui, 1990, p. 3). Grounded in a behaviorist theory of learning, direct instruction leads to mastery of skills when teachers provide students with immediate feedback, reinforcement, and extensive practice.

Reading Mastery (formerly called *Distar*) embodies a direct instruction model. The program developers of *Reading Mastery* based the skills design on a behavioral analysis of decoding (Kameenui, Simmons, Clark, & Dickson, 1997). The skills sequence in the program progresses from students learning letter sounds to blending the sounds into words to reading words in context. The skills lessons are fast-paced and carefully structured based on the task analysis of decoding skills.

The goal of direct instruction is to overlearn skills so that they become habitual and automatic in their use by readers. Because habit formation plays an important role in a child's skills development, the skills are taught in highly structured, repetitive lessons that require teachers to adhere strictly to the lesson format. In *Reading Mastery*, the steps in the lessons are scripted word for word in the teacher's program book. Children work in small groups, configured by ability level. As the teacher works with a group of students, she follows the script of what she is to say as she engages students in fast-paced, high involvement repetitive routines.

Skills Management.   In addition to provisions for direct instruction, another important feature of a skills-based curriculum is a "skills management" system. Typically, skills management programs have been designed to track students' progress in the development of essential reading skills identified by the program developers. As a result, skills management programs usually include a sequentially ordered set of skills written as behavioral objectives, sets of mastery tests, directions for determining what level of achievement constitutes mastery, and program materials that may include workbooks, additional practice and reinforcement exercises, games, and other activities for skills development. The mastery tests are administered periodically by the teacher to test the students' performance on the set of behavioral objectives or skills identified as essential for learning to read. Usually students are considered to have achieved a level of skills mastery if they can answer 80 percent or more of the test questions correctly.

The Teacher's Role in a Skills-Based Curriculum.

Teachers who work from a skills-based curriculum engage in the techniques or technical aspects of teaching reading—matters related to the scope and sequence of skills, planning lessons, and managing activities, for example. Technicians are usually good at what they do, but what they do is often limited to specific methods or prescriptive programs of instruction. Teachers who are technicians often reduce the complexity of teaching and learning to a set of instructional routines that may include a variety of drill-and-practice techniques, a heavy reliance on seatwork, and question-and-answer recitations. Nanci Atwell (1993) reflects on her beginnings as a "teacher-technician":

> When I became a teacher, the work was not real. I was the classic teacher-technician, and my work was classroom management. I managed the kids, the programs, and the paperwork. I viewed academics as the experts who were going to manage me, and I looked to them to be the "someone elses" who would tell me what to do with my students in my classroom. When the methods didn't work or didn't work with everyone, I blamed the experts. Or worse—I blamed the kids. Then I looked around for new gurus and recipes. (pp. vii–viii)

Atwell struggled with her role as a technician and gradually altered the way she taught children. Instead of viewing herself as a skills developer or program manager, she began to observe and reflect on her students' literate behavior "so I could teach them what they need to know."

What do readers need to know? Do they need to be able to master a set of component skills to become effective readers? Or can children become skillful readers without having to learn separate skills in a linear, skills-based curriculum? Answers to these question depend on whether you believe reading to be a skill or a set of skills.

Reading: Skill or Skills?

Is reading a single skill or is it a set of subskills? John Downing (1982), a noted reading researcher, wondered. He reasoned that if reading could be classified as either a skill or as a set of skills, then all that is known in psychology about the nature of a skill and a set of skills could be applied to reading. As Downing surveyed the psychological literature, he found a comprehensive definition of a skill provided by McDonald (1965): "From a psychological point of view, playing football or chess or using a typewriter or the English language correctly demands complex sets of responses—some of them cognitive, some attitudinal, and some manipulative." McDonald stresses that it is not merely a matter of motor behavior. The player must also understand the game, enjoy playing it, and have appropriate attitudes about playing the game. "The total performance . . . is a complex set of processes—cognitive, attitudinal, and manipulative. This complex integration of processes is what we usually mean when we refer to 'skill'" (p. 387).

Downing points out that psychologists have technical terms for parts of a skill—*subskills* or *subroutines*. Maybe that is what reading skills are. What do psychologists mean by subskills or subroutines of a skill?

Does the skill of reading have subskills or prerequisite skills that students need to be able to perform in order to read? Downing (1982) makes a very strong statement about the "reading skills" described in many reading method texts: "These bits of alleged behavior . . . mostly have no basis in objective data from studies of actual reading behavior. In other words, these so-called 'reading skills' are largely mythical" (p. 535).

Taking a more moderate stance than Downing, Samuels (1976) believes that it may be possible to determine a true hierarchy of subskills in reading. However, he admits, "despite the fact that . . . commercial reading series, with their scope and sequence charts, order the reading tasks as if we did know the nature of the learning hierarchy in reading, the sad truth is that the task is so complex that a validated reading hierarchy does not exist" (p. 174).

Yet just about all published reading programs identify sequences of skills to be taught. When these skills sequences are compared, there is rarely agreement as to the sequence of skills. Some first-grade and kindergarten programs begin with the alphabet, proceed through consonant letter-sound associations, and then begin introducing vowel letter-sound associations. Others begin with rhyming elements and graphic shapes and then present some words and letter-sound associations. Likewise, no agreement is to be found when comparing lists of skills from different publishers of upper-grade reading programs.

The view of learning to read by mastering word recognition and comprehension subskills is based on a bottom-up model of reading. Conversely, a whole language curriculum reflects top-down and interactive beliefs that students learn to read through meaningful experiences. These experiences include students' reading, writing, speaking, and listening about things important to them.

Whole Language Curriculum

In practice, teachers often associate whole language with what they do in their classrooms. They believe that a whole language curriculum creates child-responsive environments for learning that are supported by literature-based instruction and curriculum integration. Not only are the language arts integrated, but so is curriculum across content areas. Language is for learning. Teachers develop curriculum *with* students (Watson, 1989). Together, teacher and students enact and negotiate a whole language curriculum day by day throughout the school year.

Whole language teachers believe in weaving into their teaching the use of authentic texts for children to read, discuss, listen to, or write about. One of the main goals of a whole language curriculum is to support children in the skillful use of language. They develop skills and strategies, but they do so in the context of meaningful learning. The development of skills and strategies is not assumed to occur in linear progression as in a skills-based curriculum. Instead, children grow as readers and writers, both vertically and horizontally. Some children will experience periods of accelerated learning followed by plateaus in their development. Some may need more time than others to "roam in the known" before they make noticeable progress in their use of language. Teachers provide the type of supportive environment that enables learners to develop confidence and competence with language and its many uses.

Some Principles Underlying Whole Language Practices.   Although classroom descriptions of whole language practices may vary from teacher to teacher, some basic principles guide every teacher's actions. For example, teachers believe that language serves personal, social, and academic purposes in children's lives. Language therefore cannot be severed from a child's quest to make sense; language and meaning-making are intertwined. In addition, whole language teachers recognize that oral and written language are parallel; one is not secondary to the other. Language, whether oral or written, involves a complex system of symbols, rules, and constructs that govern the content and form of language in the context of its use. For the whole language teacher, keeping language "whole" means not breaking it into bits and pieces or isolating the subsystems of language for instructional emphasis.

Through language use, children learn to reflect on their own experience, to express themselves symbolically, to make meaning and create knowledge, and to share their meanings with others. Gordon Wells (1986) depicts children as "meaning-makers" who, in the process of learning language, use language to describe, explain, and inquire about the world around them and to share their knowledge with others. Wells's 15-year study of language users described patterns of oral and written language development and explains children's individual differences in learning language and literacy. He concluded from his longitudinal study that parents and teachers best serve children's language and literacy development as collaborators in learning. If parents and teachers are to help children achieve full potential as meaning-makers, the role of parents and teachers is to guide, encourage, and facilitate.

Respect for the child as a learner is paramount to a successful classroom environment. Whole language teachers believe that children are natural learners who learn how to read and write best under natural conditions. Because learning to read and write involves trial and error, whole language teachers hold firm to their convictions that children must learn to take risks in classroom contexts. Child development experts often characterize young children from birth through age 5 as "examiners," "experimenters," "explorers," "exhibitors," and "experts" (Owens, 1988). Teachers extend these images of children into their classrooms.

Classrooms are "communities" in a whole language curriculum. Teacher and students come together as a community of learners to engage in reading, writing, and other collaborative acts of meaning-making. Language learners help one another. They talk to each other about what they are writing and what they are reading. They engage in partnerships around projects and thematic studies. They share their understandings of how to solve problems encountered while reading and writing.

Conditions for Learning in Whole Language Classrooms.   Certain conditions for learning permeate classroom learning communities. These conditions have been described by various whole language theorists and educators (see Goodman, 1986; Cambourne, 1984; Smith, 1989). For example, *immersion* and *authenticity* are two necessary conditions for a whole language curriculum. Children must be immersed in written language. As learners, they need to engage in explorations of a wide range of texts, including those they produce by

In the whole language curriculum, classrooms are communities of learners, with children coming together to engage in reading, writing, and other collaborative activities.

writing and those they use for reading. They need to be surrounded with all kinds of literature. When they are immersed in literature, children are given numerous occasions to explore real texts to satisfy real needs. In a whole language curriculum, authentic texts may include children's actual writings as well as books representing different literary genres. Books may be big or little in size, wordless, predictable, informational, imaginary, biographical, historical, or realistic. Books may be anthologies of poetry or collections of short tales. In addition, genuine texts may also serve the functional, everyday needs of children and may include "environmental print" (street signs, posters, boxtops, labels), reference materials, textbooks, newspapers, and magazines.

In addition, *demonstration* and *engagement* are essential conditions for whole language learning. Teachers and students alike demonstrate the role literacy plays in their lives. Demonstrations show how reading and writing can be used to satisfy the user's purposes and functional needs. As Frank Smith (1989) observed, a teacher who is bored by what she or he is teaching demonstrates to children that what is being taught is boring. Likewise, a reading skills workbook containing meaningless exercises demonstrates to children that reading can be meaningless. In a whole language curriculum, children encounter numerous, demonstrations of reading and writing in use. Sometimes demonstrations are strategic—for example, the teacher models a learning strategy that shows students how to solve a problem encountered during reading or writing.

Engagement suggests the learner's commitment, mental involvement, and willingness to participate in a demonstration. In a whole language curriculum, there is a strong expectation that children who are engaged in learning will succeed. Teachers create environments that reinforce the expectation that children will be successful and then provide the means for them to succeed.

Ownership, time, and *response* are also conducive to learning in a whole language curriculum. Children take ownership for their own learning, but teachers play an important role in helping children assume responsibility for their learning. For example, teachers may plan and gather resources for a thematic unit, but they include their students in setting goals and making decisions about texts, activities, and patterns of participation. Learning is invitational. Harste, Short, and Burke (1988) define "invitations" to learn within the framework of choice and hypothesis testing: "Choice is central in curriculum because students test different hypotheses according to their different needs, interests, and experiences. Children should be invited rather than forced to engage in specific literacy activities" (p. 15). Invitations to participate in literacy events allow children to retain ownership of the processes in which they are engaged during a learning activity.

Time to read and write also is essential. Children need time to engage in literacy events. In whole language classrooms, opportunities for reading, writing, speaking, and listening occur throughout the day and are not compartmentalized into periods or time blocks.

If children are to realize their potential as language users, they need not only time to read and write but also response. Whole language teachers recognize this and build systems for response into their classroom procedures. In whole language classrooms, it is not uncommon to see children "conferencing" with one another or with the teacher as they share what they are reading or writing. It is also not uncommon to observe them talking about books or using journals to write their personal responses to what they are reading.

Another condition involves *approximation.* Cambourne (1984) suggests that children approximate written language as they learn to read and write. They experiment with written language as they put literacy to use in purposeful situations. With trial comes error. Conditions that favor *trial-and-error* learning help children become risk-takers. Nonconventional spellings, the child's "inventions," are interpreted as signs of growth as children develop toward conventional spelling competence. Oral reading errors (miscues) may represent a child's attempt to construct meaning during reading and should not automatically be interpreted as mistakes that must be remedied. Errors are welcomed, not frowned on, in a whole language curriculum. Knowing *when* and *why* to correct is an important part of whole language teaching.

The Teacher's Role in a Whole Language Curriculum.

Teachers who work from a whole language curriculum perspective do not necessarily view their primary roles as technicians or classroom managers, as might be the case in a skills-based curriculum. Instead, in schools throughout the country, so-called whole language teachers are apt to think of themselves as learners who engage in problem solving and classroom inquiry. Such is the case of Marné Isakson, who describes how a parent-teacher conference aroused her curiosity and prompted her to raise questions about the conditions underlying learning in her classroom:

> "My son has read more in the last six weeks than he has in the last six years. I don't know what you are doing in that classroom of yours, but, whatever it is, it's working." This

comment, made by a father at a parent-teacher conference, . . . started me thinking. . . .
Why? What was occurring [in my classroom] that supported [my students] as readers?
(Isakson & Boody, 1993, p. 26)

Isakson's curiosity led to other questions. She recognized that she could have listed the techniques, materials, strategy lessons, activities, and other student activities that she had initiated in her class, but these planned activities would tell her little "about what was really going on, especially from the perspective of individual students" (p. 27). Her inquiry into why students "turned on" to reading in her classroom included the use of field notes, interviews, and analyses of students' writings in response to what they were reading.

What effect did the inquiry have on Isakson's teaching? Here is what she says:

I think I have grown more as a teacher since I started looking closely at what was happening in my classroom than ever before in my professional life. I started looking at people instead of at lesson plans. I became involved in the classroom—reading with the students, writing with them, puzzling over difficult questions with them—instead of just directing activities. I started to take risks with my learning. (p. 33)

The axiom "To teach is to learn" takes on new meaning for teachers who reject tightly structured skills-based methods to read, write, and learn along with their students. Often teachers who engage in whole language practice use words like *coaching* to describe what they do in the classroom. *Coaching* is a concept that more likely evokes images of playing fields and athletic contests than classrooms and learning events. Applied to school contexts, however, *coaching* evokes images of child-centered practices. Consider what it means to coach another person's work. Coaches know that the burden of responsibility to do well always rests with the people with whom they work. Coaches try to get the most out of the natural talent of their players and performers. The teacher who coaches prepares, models, guides, supports, and stretches students to the limits of their potential as readers and writers.

Coaches will tell you that the key to successful coaching lies in the attitude they bring to their work. Kirby, Latta, and Vinz (1988) describe an interview with Quincy Jones, the Grammy Award–winning musician and record producer. Jones captured "the secret to coaching anyone's work" when he was asked how he was able to draw out the best work from the world-class singers, songwriters, and musicians with whom he has worked. His response: "You have to love what they do, and you have to try to understand what they do and not be promiscuous with what they do." Rather than focus indiscriminately on what they can't do, a great coach leads students to what they can become.

Skills-based and whole language perspectives are at opposite ends of an instructional continuum. Various approaches to the teaching of reading can be explained within the context of this continuum.

INSTRUCTIONAL APPROACHES

Approaches to reading represent general instructional plans for achieving goals and objectives in a literacy curriculum. Instructional approaches respond to curriculum-related questions concerning content, methods, and materials in the teaching of reading. Skills-

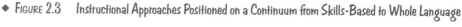

◆ FIGURE 2.3   *Instructional Approaches Positioned on a Continuum from Skills-Based to Whole Language*

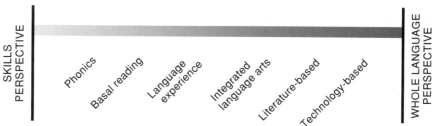

based curricula, for example, have spawned approaches to the teaching of reading that emphasize content, methods, and materials that are quite different from approaches associated with whole language curricula. In balanced literacy programs, teachers are likely to draw on their knowledge of different approaches to make decisions about instruction. Often, however, these decisions are consistent with teachers' beliefs about reading.

Several major approaches have dominated classroom literacy practice at various times in the twentieth century. These include traditional and contemporary approaches to phonics instruction, the basal reading approach, the language-experience approach, integrated language arts, literature-based instruction, and technology-based instruction. Figure 2.3 depicts these instructional approaches on a continuum from skills-based to whole language curriculum perspectives.

Approaches to Phonics Instruction

Approaches to phonics instruction have been classified as either traditional or contemporary (Stahl, Duffy-Hester, & Stahl, 1998). Traditional approaches reflect the type of instruction that the parents and grandparents of today's school-age children remember—often with mixed feelings. On one hand, students from previous generations recall the drudgery and boredom associated with repetitive "skill and drill" routines, an endless stream of worksheets, and rote memorization of phonics rules. On the other hand, they recall with some pride that they learned to read because phonics taught them how to "sound out" words. As Stahl and colleagues put it, traditional approaches to phonics instruction "are approaches that were in vogue during the 1960s and 1970s but seem to be returning as teachers grapple with how to teach phonics" (p. 344). Contemporary approaches to phonics instruction, however, are approaches that emerged in the 1990s.

Traditional Approaches.   Traditional phonics instruction includes *analytic, linguistic,* and *synthetic* approaches. These approaches are favored by teachers who devote large chunks of time to early, intensive, and systematic instruction designed to help children master the alphabetic principle. The instructional emphasis is on the teaching of isolated letter-sound correspondences separate from meaningful reading activities. Goff (1998), a leading advocate of early, intensive, and systematic phonics instruction, argues for a separation between phonics instruction and comprehension instruction. Simply stated, traditionalists believe in isolated instruction in the alphabetic code. The more phonics information that children acquire and apply to decode words in print, the better. As Goff puts it, "By minimizing the task of comprehension of word meanings, children can devote most of their mental energy to developing accurate and rapid (automatic) word recognition skills" (p. 140).

The key words associated with traditional phonics instruction are *early, intensive,* and *systematic.* The word *early* suggests that children's initial exposure to formal reading instruction should emphasize the alphabetic principle. "Phonics first" proponents believe that teachers who emphasize comprehension in beginning reading situations are putting the cart before the horse. Implicit in "phonics first" instruction is a bottom-up belief that children must learn letter-sound correspondences early in their school experience in order to build a foundation for reading meaningful texts.

Intensive and *systematic* are tandem concepts that are often mentioned in the same breath by proponents of traditional phonics approaches. The word *intensive* suggests a thorough and comprehensive treatment of letter-sound correspondences. Phonics instruction lacks intensity if letter-sound correspondences are taught *only as needed* when a child is in the process of constructing meaning from text. Traditional phonics instruction isn't intensive enough, for example, if letter-sound correspondences are taught within the context of listening to or reading stories. From a traditional phonics perspective, the chances are greater that there will be gaps in children's phonic knowledge if instruction is embedded within meaningful contexts. *Systematic* implies that phonics instruction should be organized around the ordered, logical arrangement of decoding skills taught in well-structured lessons. Of course, there are variations in systematic teaching procedures within lessons, depending on the approach to phonics instruction.

Analytic Phonics Instruction.   **Analytic phonics** is defined in the *Literacy Dictionary* as "a whole-to-part approach to word study in which the student is first taught a number of sight words and then relevant phonic generalizations, which are subsequently applied to other words" (Harris & Hodges, 1995, p. 9). Once students have learned a corpus of sight words containing specific letter-sound correspondences, they are taught to discover alphabetic relationships. Suppose, for example, that first-grade students recognize the word *bat* at sight. The teacher might begin an analytic lesson involving the consonant sound /b/ by writing the word *bat* on the board and directing students' attention to the /b/ sound: "The letter *b* at the beginning of the word *bat* makes a /b/ sound." She then writes other words within the students' sight vocabulary on the board—*bag, rib, Betty, baseball, able*—and asks them what the words have in common. Once students have discussed the consonant letter-sound relationship, the teacher would then assign a workbook page reinforcing the alphabetic relationship.

The analytic approach is highly visible in the word identification instructional strand of many of the basal reading programs of the 1970s and 1980s. Analytic lessons in basal reading programs rely heavily on the use of workbooks and practice exercises. A major criticism of the analytic approach is that teachers invest too little time on the initial teaching of alphabetic relationships and students spend too much time on paper-and-pencil exercises. Oral instruction from the teacher simply serves as an introduction to worksheets rather than to help students clarify relationships and make discoveries (Durkin, 1988; Stahl et al., 1998).

Linguistic Instruction. The *Literacy Dictionary* defines **linguistic instruction** as "a beginning reading approach based on highly regular sound-symbol patterns, temporarily substituted for the term 'phonic' early in the 1960s" (Harris & Hodges, 1995, p. 139). In the 1960s, linguists voiced their concerns over instructional practices associated with conventional phonics programs. Leonard Bloomfield and Clarence Barnhart, for example, wrote *Let's Read: A Linguistic Approach* (1961) as an alternative to "sounding out" practices. Bloomfield and Barnhart emphasize learning to decode words through regular letter patterns—for example, *dish, fish, wish, swish.* Charles Fries, another linguist, endorsed the linguistic approach in the *Merrill Linguistic Readers* in 1966. Other linguistic programs published at about the same time included the *SRA Basic Reading Series* (1964) and *Programmed Reading* (1963).

These programs include stories written so that there is a gradual introduction and numerous repetition of specific letter-sound relationships. The readers were full of sentences such as "The fat cat sat on the mat" and "The car was parked at the market." Patterns that were considered simpler, such as the "cat, sat, mat" pattern, were introduced before more difficult ones, such as the "car, park, market" pattern.

Linguistic approaches instructional materials resulted in "easily lampooned texts such as 'Dan is a man / Nat is a cat / Nat is fat. / Nat sat on a mat'" (Stahl et al., 1998, p. 344). The reading materials made little sense and were difficult to read aloud because they were loaded with similar words.

Synthetic Phonics Instruction. **Synthetic phonics** is defined in the *Literacy Dictionary* as "a part-to-whole phonics approach to reading instruction in which the student learns the sounds represented by letters and letter combinations, blends these sounds together to pronounce words, and finally identifies which phonic generalizations apply" (Harris & Hodges, 1995, p. 250).

Whereas in the analytic phonics approach students break down words into letter-sound units, in synthetic phonics students build words up letter by letter. In using the synthetic phonics method, teachers show beginning readers that *c* goes with a /k/ sound, *a* goes with an /a/ sound, and *t* goes with a /t/ sound. When these phonemes, or minimal sound units, are blended together, the child would read "*c-a-t—cat.*" This is where the expression "sound it out" comes from.

Contemporary Approaches to Phonics Instruction. These approaches do not emphasize an overreliance on worksheets, skill-and-drill activities, or rote memorization. Instead, contemporary approaches are rooted in constructivist principles of learning where students engage in word study based on strategies to learn spelling patterns, make words, and draw analogies between known and unknown word parts. Throughout this book, we draw on the most effective aspects of traditional phonics instruction but primarily advocate the use of contemporary approaches to phonics instruction in balanced literacy programs.

The Basal Reading Approach

Basal reading programs, the dominant approach to classroom reading instruction, are examined at length in Chapter 11. Teachers who traditionally use the reading lesson or story with a small group of students during a specified time in a regular location are most likely to use the **basal reading approach.** They constitute the majority in terms of numbers of classroom teachers around the country using a particular approach.

Most of today's basal programs are advertised as literature-based. They now feature anthologies and journals while providing a scope and sequence of skills and strategies to be taught at various levels and grades. Depending on your beliefs, basal instruction could be considered bottom-up approach, presenting skills to be taught in a sequence, or an interactive program, featuring unedited children's literature selections, strategy instruction, and writing opportunities.

In addition to having scope and sequence charts, the basal reading approach outlines a standard lesson framework with slight variations in differing programs. The *directed reading activity* (DRA) is the common label for the lesson framework in basal series. The DRA has four major instructional components: (1) motivation and background building, (2) guided reading, (3) skill development and practice, and (4) follow-up enrichment. These components are discussed in Chapter 11 and are important because they are based on interactive assumptions that students learn to read by reading, writing, and talking about meaningful topics. As a major approach to reading instruction, basal reading is easily observable in elementary classrooms in small reading groups. It spans a large segment of the skills–whole language continuum due to its relationship to both bottom-up and interactive theories of reading. Basal reading, frequently described as *eclectic,* runs the gamut from word recognition skills to extended and meaningful reading, discussing, and writing.

The Language-Experience Approach

Teachers often use language-experience activities in combination with other approaches to reading instruction. However, the **language-experience approach** (LEA) is especially prevalent in kindergarten and first-grade classrooms. We will examine LEA later in chapters related to emergent literacy and beginning instruction.

LEA is often associated with *story dictation,* recording the language of children on chart paper or newsprint and using what they say as the basis for reading instruction. There is more to LEA, however, than just recording the ideas of students after they have taken a trip to the school nurse or the zoo. LEA includes planned and continuous activities such as individual- and group-dictated stories, the building of word banks of known words, creative writing activities, oral reading of prose and poetry by teacher and students, directed reading-thinking lessons, the investigation of interests using multiple materials, and keeping records of student progress.

Stauffer (1970) and Allen (1976) have been strong proponents of LEA. Allen summed up the theory behind the language experiences from the young reader's point of view: What I think about, I can talk about; what I can say, I can write or someone can write for me; what I can write, I can read; and I can read what other people write for me to read.

Teachers who subscribe to LEA have common viewpoints about children and their language. For example, they would probably agree that children's oral and written expression is based on their sensitivity to classroom and home environments. Further, they would support children working with their *own* language.

Thus the language-experience approach is based on the idea that language should be used to communicate thoughts, ideas, meaning. It is very much an interactive approach to teaching reading. As such, it is placed more toward the whole language side of the continuum. How to use dictated stories and word banks, the directed reading thinking procedure with comprehension strategies, and ways to extend children's writing and reading into more writing and reading are all examples of related instruction.

Integrated Language Arts

An **integrated language arts approach** to instruction extends the concept of language experience throughout the grades by immersing students in reading, writing, talking, listening, and viewing activities. Integrated language arts instruction is mostly associated with a whole language curriculum perspective. Just as teachers believe that systems of language should not be separated and taught as isolated skills, so too do they believe that reading, writing, speaking, listening, and viewing should be taught in concert, not in separate lessons. In a whole language curriculum, the language arts support one another and are connected through the use of informative and imaginative literature.

Teachers preserve the powerful bonds that exist among the various language arts by helping children make connections. The IRA/NCTE *Standards for English Language Arts* (1996) underscore the importance of preparing students at all grade levels for the literacy demands of today and tomorrow. Literacy expectations have accelerated in this century and are likely to increase dramatically in coming decades. When the process of developing national standards began, IRA and NCTE recognized that being literate means being active, critical, and creative users not only of printed and spoken language but also of visual language. The IRA/NCTE *Standards* underscore the importance of integrating the language arts so that students will learn how to use language to think clearly, strategically, critically, and creatively.

Language is for learning. One of the more visible aspects of an integrated approach is the use of language as a tool for disciplinary learning. Teachers integrate language learning across the curriculum by organizing instruction around themes, inquiry-based project learning, and literature study. Various chapters throughout this book highlight the connections among the language arts, content area learning, and literature study.

Literature-Based Instruction

Literature-based instruction approaches accommodate individual student differences in reading abilities and at the same time focus on meaning, interest, and enjoyment. Veatch and Acinapuro (1966) designed a program for individualizing reading and articulated the how-to's of this approach. In literature-based instruction, teachers encourage their students to select their own trade books (another name for popular books).

In classrooms using literature in this way, children delight in the exploits of Curious George, Madeline, Encyclopedia Brown, and Pippi Longstocking. The rationale is that an important part of classroom life should be *reading:* reading literature that makes children wonder, weep, laugh, shiver, and gasp.

Pieces of literature are used as springboards for writing. Children can write differing endings for stories or incidents in their own lives that reflect conflicts similar to ones about which they have read. Students also look at story structures such as the repetitive structure in "The Three Little Pigs" and devise stories using the same kind of structure. Further, the conflicts between characters in literature can be used to help students gain insights into their own life situations. Students are encouraged to write about these also.

Self-selection of trade books or literature books is part of personalizing reading through the individualized approach. Teachers hold conferences with individual students about the books they are reading. Other forms of organization are also used. For example, a group of students reads and responds to the same piece of literature. Or students read different books with similar themes and then share and compare insights gained. Reading instruction delivered in this way emanates from assumptions about the reading process that are interactive and top-down. Literature-based approaches depend on teachers who know children's literature and classroom organization. These topics are discussed in Chapters 10, 11, and 15.

Technology-Based Instruction

Technology-based instruction approaches in today's schools can make a dramatic difference in children's literacy development. Computers run on literacy. Reinking (1995) argues that computers are changing the way we communicate and disseminate information,

In literature-based reading programs, students are encouraged to personally select their own trade books to read.

how we approach reading and writing, and how we think about people becoming literate. Learning to read with computers will become as commonplace in twenty-first-century classrooms as basal reading programs in the twentieth century.

In the early 1980s, when computers began to play an increasingly important role in classrooms, computer-related technologies were primitive compared to the powerful technologies that are available today. A little more than a decade ago, the computer's potential for classroom learning revolved mainly around word processing and as a teaching machine for computer-assisted instruction (CAI). CAI makes use of instructional software programs to help students learn. CAI programs in the 1980s included the use of drills, tutorials, games, and simulations. Some computer programs, mainly simulations such as *Oregon Trail* (MECC), were engaging and interactive. But many weren't. Drill and tutorial software, for example, often provided students with dull, uninviting "electronic worksheets" to practice skills and reinforce concepts.

Today, technology-based instruction is changing the face of literacy learning and instruction. The development of the CD-ROM (compact disk, read-only memory), for example, makes learning to read with computers highly engaging and interactive. CD-ROM technology makes possible multimedia environments for learning. Multimedia programs link text, sound, graphics, photographs, video, and other nonprint media in ways not possible in the 1980s.

Computers allow students to access and retrieve information, construct their own texts, and interact with others. The Internet, a technology for communication and information retrieval, is having a tremendous impact on classroom learning (Mike, 1996). Online learning opportunities on the Internet allow students to communicate with others throughout the world and to access significant and relevant text documents. In addition, computers as word processors allow children to create texts that can serve as the basis for learning to read. As they become more sophisticated in the use of word processing programs, children become skillful in their ability to organize, revise, and edit what they write.

Throughout various chapters of this book, we examine how to integrate technology-based instruction into balanced literacy programs. Achieving balance, however, isn't easy. What does it mean to achieve balance in literacy programs? Let's take a closer look.

ACHIEVING A BALANCED LITERACY PROGRAM

Balance is one of those elusive concepts that means different things to different people. The word *balance* suggests a state of equilibrium or harmony in the arrangement of various aspects or elements in a design. Yet what may be a state of equilibrium or a harmonious arrangement for one person may not be for another. Consider the concept of balance as it applies to various aspects of life in contemporary society.

◆ Many of us seek to achieve the "right" balance between work and leisurely activity. Yet striking a balance between work and leisure will vary from individual to individual. Some people find time each day to exercise or to pursue personal interests and hobbies. Others knock themselves out throughout the workweek and relax on weekends.

◆ Family physicians, nutritionists, and health and fitness experts espouse the importance of a balanced diet. Yet finding the "right" balance of foods to eat is a personal matter. The food pyramid provides a framework for making decisions about various foods, but achieving balance is a matter of individual choice in response to issues such as why, what, when, where, and how much to eat on a daily basis.

◆ Many people search for the "right" balance between worldly and spiritual matters. Some achieve balance in their lives through daily meditation and service to others. Or they read "self-help" books to improve their spiritual outlook. Others may affiliate with religious and spiritual groups that share similar values and beliefs. Still others may do all of these things.

Certainly, there are no simple answers or prescriptions on finding the "right" balance in our everyday lives, let alone in literacy programs that support the development of human processes as complex as reading and writing.

Consequently, balanced literacy instruction, according to Pressley (1996), is very difficult to do:

> First, teachers must know a great deal about children's literature and be committed to learning much more. They must also understand decoding, comprehension, and composition processes well enough that they can explain these processes and model them for students. More than that, however, they must be able to re-explain and re-model the processes in light of particular student difficulties and misconceptions. (p. 278)

Balanced instruction is all the more complicated because it has become a political as well as an educational issue. In the search for balanced literacy programs, educators, legislators, and policymakers invariably differ on what is the "right" balance in literacy instruction as much as next-door neighbors might differ on what it means to achieve a balanced lifestyle. At least three interpretations of what it means to engage in balanced teaching have emerged in the past several years.

Balanced Instruction as an Extension of the Back-to-Basics Movement

Some educators, legislators, and policymakers have called for balanced literacy programs as a means of ensuring that children receive systematic instruction in the "basic skills" associated with reading and writing. Balanced instruction, as viewed from this perspective, is an extension of the **back-to-basics movement.** The back-to-basics movement, which champions the return to direct and intensive instruction in the teaching of skills such as phonics and spelling, is a response to a whole language philosophy of literacy learning. Whole language is a progressive, child-centered movement that took root in the 1960s and blossomed in the 1980s. Proponents of a return to basic instruction contend that as teachers widely embraced a whole language philosophy, there has been a decline in reading achievement as measured by student performance on large-scale assessments such as statewide proficiency tests, national assessment surveys, and districtwide standardized tests.

As a result, balanced instruction has been linked politically and educationally to *accountability* in the wake of declining reading scores. As Johns and Ellish-Piper (1997) note:

> Rightly or wrongly, test scores appear to have contributed to the call for balance. In California, for example, declining reading scores on the National Assessment of Educational Progress and state reports were considered by a Reading Task Force representing teachers, parents, principals, business people, superintendents, community members, professors, and school board members. One of the recommendations of the task force focused on a balanced reading program that would combine skill development with literature and language-rich activities. (p. xiii)

Implicit in the recommendation of the California Reading Task Force is that whole language does not result in literacy practices that develop skillful readers. Whether such an implication is warranted or not has been the subject of much debate and controversy (see the discussion of the "reading wars" in Chapter 1).

Balanced Instruction as a Return to Eclectic Methods of Teaching Reading

The recommendation of the California Reading Task Force to combine skill development with literature and language-rich activities calls for a mix of different instructional approaches in a balanced literacy program. The combination of instructional methods and approaches, often called **eclectic instruction,** has some support from one of the most influential and ambitious undertakings in reading research during the twentieth century: the United States Cooperative First-Grade Studies (Bond & Dykstra, 1967). The First-Grade Studies compiled data from 27 individual research projects examining the effects of instructional approaches on beginning reading and spelling achievement. These instructional approaches included phonics, linguistic readers, basal programs, initial teaching alphabet, literature-based reading, language experience, and various grouping schemes and combinations of instruction. The First-Grade Studies found that *no instructional approach was superior to the others* for students at either high or low levels of readiness. Instead, the findings suggest "that although no single method proved best, combinations of methods were associated with the highest achievement" (Shanahan & Neuman, 1997).

The First-Grade Studies, more than anything else, underscored the importance of the "teacher variable" in children's reading achievement. Teachers make a difference. The more informed and knowledgeable they are, the more teachers are able to deal with the complexities of literacy learning as they respond to the how, when, and why of instruction.

How, when, and why a teacher combines instructional approaches and strategies involve questions of balance. Some teachers may find it difficult to "mix" one method of teaching with another, if the two methods are diametrically opposite from a theoretical and curricular perspective. Take the case of Katie, who began her teaching career at the age of 23 in an urban first-grade classroom. What follows is a brief description of her first year of teaching as she struggled to reconcile holistic teaching with skills-based teaching.

Katie attended a private college located in a suburb of the city. The college offered a small teacher education program. Katie's reading and reading-related courses included elementary reading, children's literature, and language arts. The reading and language arts courses were taught by the same instructor. Katie participated in numerous hours of field experience throughout the junior and senior years of the program. She especially enjoyed her reading courses because the instructor "challenged us to think about reading as language, not just skills to be taught in itsy-bitsy pieces." During many of her visits "in the field," the instruction that Katie observed wasn't congruent with what she was learning in her reading classes. The incongruity was the subject of much inquiry and debate: Should future teachers maintain the status quo, or should they be innovators who bring new ideas into the teaching profession, especially about the teaching of literacy?

Katie's school is situated in the inner city. About 70 percent of the children are from minority backgrounds. The principal is considered a "strong instructional leader." She believes that an "effective school must maintain high expectations for student achievement, an orderly climate, and a rigorous assessment program to monitor children's educational progress." As a result, the principal is a proponent of a "teach, test, teach" model for instruction. She indicates to Katie that it is OK to try out new teaching strategies, "as long as you are teaching the skills the children need." How well children scored on achievement tests is one of the main indicators of a teacher's success.

Katie feels the pressure of "having to teach skills in isolation." This approach, she admits, is not "what I believe in," but she feels obligated to follow the curriculum "like all of the other teachers."

Prior to the opening of school, Katie had spent two weeks planning what she was going to do. One of her first tasks was to fix up the room so that it would "invite kids to learn." The room has a reading corner and a "writer's nook." Both areas are stocked with children's books, paper, pencils, markers, scissors, and posters. The reading corner has a throw rug, a book rack, and an old couch that Katie got from her parents. The writer's nook has a round table and an electric typewriter.

The reality of teaching reading skills is omnipresent, despite Katie's attempts to provide meaningful experiences for her first graders. Periodically, she is required to test children to determine mastery of the skills. The principal also requires weekly lesson plans to be in her office in advance on Friday afternoons. Katie's plans are returned on Monday morning, before the start of school, with comments and notations.

In practice, Katie tries to teach a dual reading curriculum. She teaches the skills using workbooks in the morning, and she "smuggles in the good stuff" whenever she can find the time. Needless to say, Katie goes home each day exhausted and frustrated. She complains that she spends more time giving tests than she spends on instruction. The reading corner and the writer's nook are underused. "At least," Katie says, "I still read the class a story every day."

Although she tries to combine skills teaching with more holistic activities, Katie's instruction is out of balance. Her philosophical stance is in direct conflict with the principal's beliefs about learning to read. The external pressure to conform to the principal's expectations for skills instruction forces Katie to put her knowledge and beliefs about learning to read on hold. Although she attempts to mesh literature and language-rich activities with skills instruction, it simply doesn't work for her because she is caught between two disparate instructional methodologies. Her efforts to be "eclectic" simply create a disjointed mishmash of instructional activity. Balanced instruction does *not* mean sampling methods from different curricular perspectives or simply doing "a little bit of this" and "a little bit of that."

Balanced Instruction as an Integration of Instructional Approaches and Strategies

Eclectic instruction is not self-defeating when it is grounded in teachers' understanding of theoretical and research-based principles from the knowledge base on reading and learning to read. *Principled eclectic instruction* allows teachers to exercise flexibility in the use of approaches and strategies that are associated with different curricular perspectives. Effective teachers achieve balanced literacy programs by integrating reading and writing instruction throughout the school day. Weaving approaches and strategies into a seamless pattern of instruction is one of the hallmarks of a balanced literacy program.

A recent research project supports the notion that highly effective teachers are an informative source of knowledge about exemplary literacy practices (Pressley et al., 1996a; Pressley et al., 1996b). The project, conducted by a team of researchers from the National Reading Research Center, investigated the nature of outstanding literacy instruction in primary classrooms. In a series of studies, the research team conducted surveys, interviews, and extensive observations of primary teachers who were considered by their supervisors to be outstanding teachers of literacy. As a result of the project, the researchers determined that highly effective first-grade teachers strike a balance between children's immersion in literacy experiences and explicit instruction. The characteristics of highly effective literacy teachers includes the thorough integration of reading and writing activities and the extensive use of **instructional scaffolding** to support the development of children's literacy skills and strategies.

One of the important ways that teachers achieve balance is to scaffold instruction so that students become aware of and competent in the use of skills and strategies that they need to be successful. Used in construction, scaffolds serve as supports, lifting up workers so that they can reach areas they could not otherwise reach. The scaffold metaphor suggests helping students do what they cannot do on their own at first. Instructional scaffolding allows teachers to support literacy learning by showing students how to use skills and strategies that will lead to independent learning.

Instructional scaffolding means giving students a better chance to be successful with reading and writing. Teachers provide literacy scaffolds through the use of well-timed questions, explanations, demonstrations, practice, and application. These scaffolds provide instructional support for children in two ways: (1) the application of skills and strategies *at the point of actual use* during reading and (2) explicit instruction in the development of skills and strategies through minilessons.

Minilessons allow the teacher to provide **explicit strategy instruction** for students who need instructional guidance in the development and use of skills and strategies. The minilesson can be a short, unanticipated interchange between the teacher and students lasting a minute or two. Or it can be a planned lesson that may take five to ten minutes to complete. Minilesson, regardless of duration, allow teachers to share insights and knowledge that students might otherwise never encounter. These explicit lessons create a framework that will unify skill and strategy development by making provisions for children to become aware of, use, and develop control over skills and strategies that can make a difference in their literate lives.

Explicit instruction helps students by providing an alternative to what we have called direct instruction in a skills-based curriculum. A direct instruction model, as we noted earlier, is rooted in behavioral principles of learning. Students are taught what to do, given immediate feedback, and afforded extensive practice until discrete skills become habitual and automatic in their use. Students seldom grasp the rationale or payoff underlying the particular skills that are taught.

When teachers make instruction explicit, however, students construct knowledge about the use of skills and strategies. Explicit instruction involves strategic learning, not habit formation. Minilessons follow a pattern that usually includes (1) creating awareness of the strategy, (2) modeling the strategy, (3) providing practice in the use of the strategy, and (4) applying the strategy in authentic reading situations. Awareness of a strategy often involves a give-and-take exchange of ideas between teacher and students. These exchanges may include explanations and strategy tips and are built around questions such as "Why is the strategy useful?" "What is the payoff for students?" "How does this improve learning?" and "What are the rules, guidelines, or procedures for being successful with the skill or strategy?" Students should come away from these discussions recognizing the rationale and process behind the use of the skill or strategy under consideration.

Once students understand the what and how of the skill or strategy, the teacher might want to extend a minilesson by modeling its use and providing students with practice. Modeling may include walking students through the steps and raising questions about the procedures. Initiating a "think-aloud" procedure allows the teacher to share with the students the thinking processes that she or he uses in applying the skill or strategy. Practicing the strategy in a trial run using a short selection is a logical extension of modeling. Minilessons that include strategy awareness, modeling, and practice are designed to build procedural knowledge of skills and strategies. Once students have developed understandings about strategy use, regular and authentic class reading experiences should encourage application.

Notice how Gay, whose literacy vignette began the chapter, uses modeling to explain the importance of visual imagery when students are reading. She is working with a group of third graders during a guided reading lesson. She uses a think-aloud to model how she tries to visualize what she reads when she is reading.

> GAY: When I am reading, I try to form pictures in my head. Sometimes I even close my eyes and try to see what I am reading. To do this, I always try to use what I know or have experienced in my own life. When I came to the word *cliff* in the story, I tried to picture in my mind what the cliff looked liked.

As the discussion continues, Gay, through her questions, invites the group to participate in a dialogue with her related to the visual imagery of the cliff in the story.

GAY: In the story we read about a cliff. Who formed a mental picture of the cliff?

JOE: I did. *(Gay encourages Joe to describe his image, and Joe responds by relating an incident in his life.)* One day we were driving along and my mom yelled at her boyfriend to look out. He was about to drive right over a cliff!

GAY: So when you saw the word *cliff* in the story, did a picture enter your mind?

JOE: Yeah!

GAY: What did it look like?

JOE: It was like this hill and then it dropped off real fast. *(Joe uses hand motions to explain what he means.)*

GAY: *(provides an explanation)* Joe has a picture in his mind. He reads well because he does what all good readers do. When they read something it reminds them of something that has happened to them or that they've seen on TV or read about or heard someone else talk about. Good readers form pictures in their mind, and that helps them understand the story. Did anyone else get a mental picture when you read about the cliff?

SCOTT: One time me and my friend were riding our bikes and he skidded and went right over a cliff.

GAY: So the picture you saw was different from Joe's, but both of your pictures helped you understand the story.

Several other children contribute their picture of what a cliff looks like, based on their prior knowledge and experience. Gay then redirects the process discussion by asking another question.

GAY: How was the cliff in the story different from or the same as the ones all of you pictured in your head?

MEAGAN: They were all steep. A cliff is a cliff no matter what you did with it.

GAY: *(thinks aloud and then asks the students to visualize other images from the story)* It always helps me to make pictures in my mind while I am reading. Like I said earlier, I even close my eyes so I can see things that I am reading about. Now I would like all of us to close our eyes. I will also. Now let's try to picture some other things we saw in the story besides the cliff.

In addition to think-alouds, Gay will engage students in "process discussions" to scaffold students' use of strategies. In the following process discussion, she centers the minilesson around self-help strategies for monitoring reading when readers come across a word that is difficult.

GAY: Before we begin reading our story today, I'm curious about something. How important are words when you're reading?

NATALIE: Words help you make sense.

GAY: That's right! But how do we know when the words in the story make sense?

NATALIE: They just do. When the words make sense I understand what I'm reading.

DUSTY: You put what you know with what the author tells you and then you just "get it."

GAY: Yes. When you read for meaning, you're "getting it"; what you're reading is making sense. What are some of the things that good readers like you do when they come to hard words that they don't recognize?

CHRIS: We fix our mistakes.

GAY: Sure you do; that's because you know that reading has to make sense. If it doesn't, then you have to fix it. What else?

TIA: I make pictures in my head when I'm reading.

NATALIE: We take risks.

GAY: And what do you mean by that, Natalie?

NATALIE: I'm not afraid to try hard books.

GAY: What other kinds of risks do you take?

JESSICA: We aren't afraid to try hard words. I try [to identify a word] before I ask for help.

ANNA: If I don't know a word, I try to figure it out.

GAY: And how do you do that, Anna?

ANNA: Lots of ways. I try to sound it out or figure it out by using the clues in the story; or I just skip it if I can't still figure it out. Sometimes I just ask someone if it's really bothering me.

GAY: Anna, all of those ways are called "strategies." The important thing is that reading has to make sense. We'll learn even more strategies you can use as the year goes along.

The hallmark of balanced instruction is the integration of reading and writing experiences with scaffolded instruction in the use of skills and strategies. Skills and strategies are best learned through meaningful use. When students are engaged in meaningful and authentic reading and writing activities, there are numerous opportunities to scaffold their literacy experiences, as you will discover in the chapters that lie ahead.

SUMMARY

An underlying assumption in this book is that when teachers are in touch with their beliefs about reading and learning to read, they are in a better position to balance literacy instruction in the classrooms. When you analyze your beliefs, connecting what you practice with what you know and believe, you are better able to understand what you do and why. The reading autobiography suggested in Chapter 1 lends itself to a narrative inquiry that helps teachers discover some of the events and experiences that contribute to the development of beliefs and attitudes related to reading and learning to read. In this chapter, the Beliefs About Reading Interview and the TORP survey were suggested as tools that also permit teachers to inquire into their beliefs.

We explored two predominant curricula, one founded on a skills-based perspective and the other on a whole language perspective. Is reading a skill or a set of separate skills? What principles underlie a whole language curriculum? These questions allowed us to make distinctions between two very different curricular views associated with the teaching of reading. We showed how different instructional approaches to reading lie on a continuum between skills-based and whole language perspectives. These approaches include phonics instruction, basal reading programs, language experience, integrated language arts, technology-based instruction, and literature-based programs.

Teachers enact curricula in varied and complex ways, based on their perspectives of the reading curriculum, the particular context in which they teach, and the desire to achieve a balanced literacy program.

TEACHER-ACTION RESEARCHER

1. Is there someone you now work with, a teacher who stands out in the school in which you are interning, or a fellow classmate, whom you believe achieves a balanced literacy program? Describe the teacher and his or her literacy program. Organize your description of this teacher with the following: (a) background information including some personal history, (b) beliefs about reading, (c) the school context, and (d) how he or she balances literacy instruction.

2. Interview and observe a teacher who uses a whole language curriculum or is in the process of making a transition from a skills-based curriculum to a whole language curriculum. How does the teacher encourage children who don't want to read? Describe how the teacher keeps track of what each child is reading and the child's reading progress. How does the teacher encourage children to respond to what they read?

3. Interview a skills-based teacher. How does the teacher differ in practice from the teacher described in item 2?

4. Interview a fellow student using the Beliefs About Reading Interview (Box 2.1). Analyze the person's implicit theories of reading as suggested in this chapter. If there is time, ask her or him to interview another classmate and form a small group to compare the various responses.

KEY TERMS

analytic phonics

back-to-basics movement

basal reading approach

eclectic instruction

explicit strategy instruction

instructional scaffolding

integrated language arts approach

language-experience approach

linguistic instruction

literature-based instruction

skills-based curriculum

synthetic phonics

technology-based instruction

Theoretical Orientation to Reading Profile (TORP)

units of language

whole language curriculum

CHAPTER

3

Early Literacy:
From Birth to School

Chapter Overview

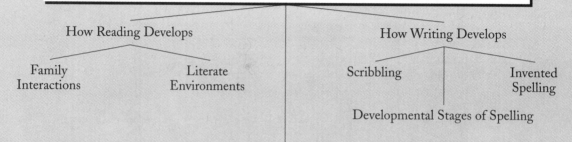

EARLY LITERACY: FROM BIRTH TO SCHOOL

CHILDREN'S DEVELOPMENT IN EARLY READING AND WRITING

How Reading Develops

Family Interactions

Literate Environments

How Writing Develops

Scribbling

Developmental Stages of Spelling

Invented Spelling

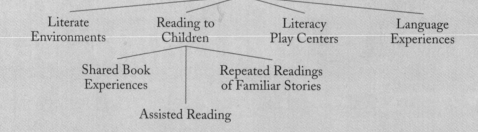

DEVELOPMENTALLY APPROPRIATE PRACTICES FOR BEGINNERS

Literate Environments

Reading to Children

Literacy Play Centers

Language Experiences

Shared Book Experiences

Repeated Readings of Familiar Stories

Assisted Reading

Between the Lines

In this chapter, you will discover:

♦ The continuum of children's literacy development as they progress through various phases of learning to read and write

♦ How reading and writing develop in home environments that support literacy learning

♦ The importance of developmentally appropriate practices

♦ How to create literate environments

♦ Developmentally appropriate literacy practices emphasizing play, language experiences, and reading to children

Beginnings are important. Literacy beginnings, as crucial as they are to children's development as readers and writers, often take diverse paths. For example, when Leslie Anne was born, her grandmother, a reading specialist by trade, gave her granddaughter the book *Goodnight Moon.* And she gave Leslie Anne's dad (her son) some motherly, if not professional, advice, telling him that it was time to begin reading aloud to his daughter. According to the grandmother, Margaret Moorehead (1990), her son "looked at me like I was crazy. 'Mom, Leslie Anne is only 2 days old. This is silly. She wouldn't understand'" (p. 332). Moorehead countered her son's incredulity, saying that Leslie Ann was already being talked to, even though she didn't understand everything that was being said. Then why not read to her?

On that auspicious occasion Leslie Anne began her journey to literacy. Her parents developed the habit of reading to her daily. At 6 months, Leslie Anne was sitting on her grandmother's lap, helping to hold a book, when she began "reading" in a voice distinctively different from her usual cooing and babbling. According to Moorehead (1990), Leslie Anne read aloud, "'A baa baa, a baa baa,' and turned the page. Six months old, and already she knew that you hold a book up, that there are just a few sounds on each page, that those sounds are different from ordinary talking, and that you turn a page and say something else" (p. 332). The love of books quite naturally blossomed for Leslie Anne in a family environment that supported and nurtured literacy learning. Going to the library and listening to stories became as routine a family activity as grocery shopping.

Leslie Anne, as you have probably surmised, is in the process of becoming literate in a family context that values reading and communicates strong feelings and attitudes about literacy to her. The family's own interest in reading, manifested by a willingness to spend time talking and reading with Leslie Anne, provides the supportive, natural learning environment that she needs in order to grow as a reader.

Irma, by way of contrast, is a child who lives in a housing project in East Los Angeles with her mother and four younger siblings. Her mother can't read. Neither she nor her brothers and sisters have ever heard a nursery rhyme or story. Irma is trapped in a cycle of illiteracy that is passed from one generation to another: "Irma had never had a chance even to hold books before entering school" (Rosow, 1992, p. 525).

Now during the first week of the first grade, Irma checked out two library books. But what was she expected to do with the books? Where were the models of literate activity in her life? For one reason or another, the books disappeared once she brought them home. The school sent a note to the home, pinned to Irma's shirt, requesting the return of the books, lest Irma's family pay a fine and she lose her library privileges: "But the note to the nonreading mom, who herself had never had library privileges, failed to recover the books or collect the fines, so Irma spent her first year in school without books. She had no one to read to her, and she had no hope of reading to herself" (Rosow, 1992, p. 525). As bleak as the prospects for Irma's **literacy development** may seem, Irma's story could be different. To realize the promise of literacy in Irma's life, appropriate school experiences could very well bring the intergenerational cycle of illiteracy to an end.

The stories of Irma and Leslie Anne—two young children from culturally diverse family backgrounds—underscore the importance of understanding the needs of all children and the conditions underlying their literate development. If we are going to make a difference in children's literacy development, we must be aware of the learning environment of the home, respect the diverse cultural milieus from which children learn to use language, and develop strategies to build on family strengths. Irma and Leslie Anne will not bring the same kinds of knowledge, values, attitudes, and strategies for literacy learning to school. Yet their school experiences will play a pivotal role in realizing their full potential as literacy learners.

This chapter is about literacy beginnings. It is forged on the dynamic and powerful connections between children's oral language and written language development. As you study the chapter overview, keep in mind several main ideas about learning to read and write in early childhood. First, there is a continuum of children's development in early reading and writing. Young children develop as early readers and writers from birth as they progress from awareness and exploration in their preschool years to independent and productive reading and writing by the end of the third grade. Second, early readers and writers develop literacy skills through developmentally appropriate practice as they participate in purposeful and meaningful activities. And third, speaking, listening, viewing, writing, and reading are interrelated, mutually supportive activities. Language experiences provide the foundation for learning to read and write.

In this chapter, we tackle important issues related to the early literacy learning of children before they enter school and the implications of such learning for beginning instruction. What do teachers of young children need to know about young children's knowledge of and experiences with literacy? How can teachers make the child's first encounter with formal reading and writing instruction smooth and developmentally sound?

Children's Development in Early Reading and Writing

More than three decades of research show that children begin their journey as readers and writers early in life. From birth through preschool, young children begin to acquire basic understandings about reading and writing and its functions through home experiences with print. Children continue their literacy development as they enter school through a variety of learning experiences that allow them to experiment with language and develop early reading and writing skills in kindergarten and first grade. Learning to read and write, based on developmentally appropriate practice, takes on a more formal nature throughout the primary grades as teachers balance systematic instruction in the alphabetic code with many opportunities for fluency development and meaningful reading and writing (Snow, Burns, & Griffin, 1998). From the time children enter third grade, literacy instruction emphasizes the development and use of strategies to become independent and productive readers and writers.

The much heralded position statement on young children's development in early reading and writing, jointly adopted by the International Reading Association (IRA) and the National Association for the Education of Young Children (NAEYC) in 1998, proposes a continuum of children's development in early reading and writing to account for literacy learning from birth through the primary grades. Figure 3.1 illustrates the phases of children's development on the **reading-writing continuum** as suggested in the joint position statement by IRA and NAEYC. As you study the figure, keep in mind

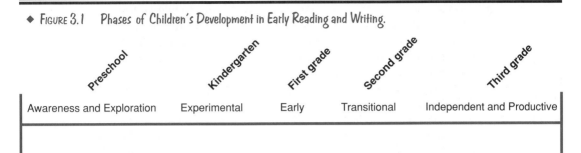

◆ FIGURE 3.1   Phases of Children's Development in Early Reading and Writing.

Source: Adapted from *Learning to Read and Write: Developmentally Appropriate Practices for Young Children,* A Joint Position Statement of the International Reading Association and the National Association for the Education of Young Children, adopted 1998.

that children at any grade level will function at a variety of phases along the reading-writing continuum.

Phases of Literacy Development

As indicated in Figure 3.1, the continuum of children's literacy development encompasses a sequence of distinct phases.

1. *Awareness and Exploration Phase.* The **awareness and exploration** phase begins at birth and progresses through a child's preschool years. Children explore their environment and build the foundations for learning to read and write. The awareness and exploration phase of literacy development marks the time when children become curious about print and print-related activities. For example, they enjoy listening to and talking about stories and understand that print carries a message. In addition, young children demonstrate *logographic knowledge* by identifying labels, signs, cereal boxes, and other types of environmental print. They also begin to *pretend-read* during their preschool years and engage in paper-and-pencil activities that include various forms of scribbling and written expression. Another literacy accomplishment in this phase occurs when young children begin to identify some letters and letter-sound relationships and write letters or approximations of letters to represent written language.

2. *Experimental Reading and Writing Phase.* Early awareness and exploration lead children to experiment with oral and written language. Children enter the **experimental** phase of the reading-writing continuum right around the time they enter kindergarten. This phase reflects their understanding of basic concepts of print, such as left-to-right, top-to-bottom orientation. Young children enjoy being read to and begin to engage in sustained reading and writing activities. They also continue to recognize letters and letter-sound relationships, become familiar with rhyming, and begin to write letters of the alphabet and high-frequency words.

3. *Early Reading and Writing Phase.* The **early phase** of children's development usually occurs in first grade when instruction becomes more formal. Children begin to read simple stories and can write about topics about which they have much prior knowledge and strong feelings. They can read and retell familiar stories and begin to develop strategies, such as predicting, for comprehension. They are beginning to develop accurate word identification skills through their increasing knowledge of letter-sound patterns. In addition, children's ability to read with fluency becomes more evident, as does their ability to recognize an increasing number of words on sight. Moreover, their writing shows awareness of punctuation and capitalization knowledge as they continue to engage in writing about topics that are personally meaningful to them.

4. *Transitional Reading and Writing Phase.* By second grade, students begin to make the transition from early reading and writing to more complex literacy tasks. They are reading with greater fluency and using cognitive and metacognitive strategies more efficiently when comprehending and composing. During the **transitional** phase, children demonstrate an ever-increasing facility with reading and writing in all facets of activity, including use of word identification strategies, sight word recognition, reading fluency, sustained silent reading, conventional spelling, and proofread what they have written.

5. *Independent and Productive Phase.* As children progress from the transitional phase, they engage in a lifelong process of becoming **independent and productive** readers and writers. The third grade marks the beginning of their journey into independent and productive learning as they use reading and writing in increasingly more sophisticated ways to suit a variety of purposes and audiences. From this point on in their development as readers and writers, children extend and refine their literacy skills and strategies.

Appendix C provides a list of reading and writing accomplishments that successful literacy learners are likely to achieve from kindergarten through third grade. The accomplishments were compiled by the Committee on the Prevention of Reading Difficulties in Young Children as part of an analysis and synthesis of research on children's early reading acquisition commissioned by the National Research Council (Snow et al., 1998). The list of reading and writing accomplishments is not designed to be exhaustive or comprehensive but highlights children's typical achievements related to reading and writing revealed through several decades of research.

The set of reading and writing accomplishments in Appendix C provides, at best, a summary sketch of young children's literacy development and should not be interpreted rigidly. Teachers must take into account enormous individual differences in children's literacy development as they enter school. According to the IRA/NAEYC joint statement on children's early literacy development:

> Experienced teachers throughout the U.S. report that the children they teach today are more diverse in their backgrounds, experiences, and abilities than were those they taught in the past. Kindergarten classes now include children who have been in group settings for 3 or 4 years as well as children who are participating for the first time in an organized

early childhood program. Classes include both children with identified disabilities and children with exceptional abilities, children who are already independent readers and children who are just beginning to acquire some basic literacy knowledge and skills. Children in the group may speak different languages at varying levels of proficiency. Because of these individual and experiential variations, it is common to find within a kindergarten classroom a 5-year range in children's literacy-related skills and functioning (Riley, 1996). What this means is that some kindergartners may have the skills characteristic of the typical 3-year-old, while others might be functioning at the level of the typical 8-year-old. (pp. 4–5)

What children's literacy development makes clear is that the foundations for reading and writing begin at home and that schools build on these foundations to develop skillful and strategic readers and writers. In this chapter and the next, we will examine closely the beginnings of reading and writing in the awareness and exploration, experimental, and early phases of literacy development. The remaining chapters of this book explore the roles that teachers and texts play in children's literacy development as they progress from early and transitional reading and writing to independent and productive reading and writing.

With this in mind, let's take a closer look at how reading and writing develop in the context of family interactions and home experiences. **Family literacy** is a relatively new concept that describes how family members and caregivers influence the oral and written language development of young children and provide the context in which they learn to read and write (Neuman, Caperelli, & Kee, 1998; Benjamin & Lord, 1996; Taylor & Dorsey-Gaines, 1989; Taylor, 1983).

How Reading Develops

Most children enter school with expectations that they're "gonna learn how to read." It doesn't matter to Michael, a 5-year-old, that he can already read many signs—for example, "Stop" and "Zoo"—that have a great deal of meaning to him. It also doesn't matter that Michael "knows" most of the alphabet by name and often "reads along" by reciting favorite passages from bedtime stories that his mother and father read to him. Nor does it matter that Michael's mother still chuckles over his behavior at around age 2 when he first recognized a McDonald's billboard from the backseat of the family car. Michael "oohed" and "aahed" and chanted, "Stop! Stop! Hungry, Mommy."

Michael doesn't grasp the significance of these events because he is on the threshold of starting school. Nor does his mother recognize the importance of these abilities. Despite Michael's observable reading and readinglike behaviors at home, there remains a trace of uncertainty on his mother's part. Although the groundwork has been laid for Michael to continue to grow as a reader, his mother expresses some concern as to whether he will achieve success in learning to read. She is sure that he will but adds, "We'll wait and see."

Does Michael's mother need to assume a "wait and see" attitude? A child such as hers grows up immersed in a print-oriented world. Children see written language all around them—in books. supermarkets, department stores, fast-food restaurants, and on television, signs, and a variety of printed materials from the TV listings to labels on household products. Print is everywhere. When aren't children confronted with written language in some form in their immediate environment? The child may also see parents, brothers, sisters, and others using written language to some degree—whether to read recipes, follow directions, do homework, solve problems, acquire information, or enjoy a story. The plethora of print that confronts young children on a daily basis plays a subtle but important role in their desire to understand written language and use it for personal and social means.

Today's preschooler acquires much more intuitive and conscious knowledge about print and its uses than most adults would imagine. As early as 1958, James Hymes observed that reading "sells itself" to the young child because written language is "in the limelight" constantly. Everyday living "beats the drums" for reading with a bombardment of print that no formal program of instruction could ever match.

Although this may be the case, informal "teachable moments" await children in a print-rich world. Parents (and teachers) should make a *conscious* effort, whenever appropriate, to create awareness of print in meaningful and functional ways. By way of illustration, 4-year-old Sandy's parents seize whatever opportunity is available to demonstrate the purposeful nature of print. Whenever they go to a restaurant, for example, they encourage Sandy to "read" the menu and to select the foods she prefers. Although Sandy may not be able to read most of the words on the menu, she pretend-reads. Her parents support her use of print by showing her the menu, by engaging in dialogue with her over possible food choices, and by pointing to the printed words as they read the menu with her.

This example, simple and straightforward as it may appear, illustrates the subtle but powerful role that parents play in literacy learning. The parent's role (and the teacher's) is to lead, model, and facilitate literacy learning by being supportive, by socializing children in the uses of written language, by engaging them in conversation about written language, and by encouraging and accepting children's constructions of meaning through written language.

The Importance of Family Interactions.   Michael and Sandy already know a lot about written language and have had some valuable early literacy experiences. They are learning to read informally through family interactions. More than likely, they will continue their growth as literacy learners and should experience success in school. As teachers, we have much to gain from the study of family literacy. The Class Works featured in Box 3.1 illustrates this point. Read it and reflect on the family interactions that occur between a mother and her children as they are grocery shopping.

Some children learn to read naturally. They develop the ability to read through a process that can best be described as trial-and-error learning. These early readers make discoveries about written language in a *low-risk* family environment that is relatively free from anxiety and criticism.

In school, however, the stakes are usually high and the risks involved in learning to read are greater than at home. The margin for error isn't what it was at home, especially if the emphasis in school is on learning through memorization, analysis, and recitation. As a result, children are often introduced to reading instruction with emphasis on the smallest possible print units, for example, letters. For children who have little background experience with print, confusion mounts quickly in what often becomes a high-risk learning situation. In such contexts, little, if any, time is spent on functional, meaningful literacy activity. Children are denied the opportunities to experience and learn from their participation in the uses of written language.

Kid-Watching at the Supermarket

One of our students, Meg, plans on teaching in the primary grades. As part of a field experience, she decided to "shadow" unobtrusively a mother and her two children as they shopped in a local supermarket. Here are Meg's observations as recorded in her field notes.

> The mother pushed the shopping cart with the younger of the two children sitting in the child seat. I learned that the two children were named Brian and Kate when overhearing the mother talking in line. Brian was around 14 months old and Kate about 3 or 4 years old. Kate sat on the bottom shelf of the cart. When the mother stopped in the produce area, she said to the children, "Look at the bananas. Don't they look good?" Brian looked at the bananas and said, "Bananas." The mother continued in an easy, slow voice to comment on the color of the bananas and what she planned to use them for. At this time, I decided to observe Kate more closely.
>
> As her mother went up the dairy aisle, Kate walked between the cart and her mother. As Kate walked around the store, she asked questions like "What's this?" pointing to specific items on the shelves. Her mother would always answer and explain about the item if more questions were asked. At one point, a can was thrown out of the cart by Brian while the mother was looking over the cereals. She walked over to the cart, picked up the thrown can, and asked Kate what had happened. Kate pointed to Brian saying, "He throwed it." The mother then asked Kate to find the cereal that she was looking for. (I couldn't hear what kind.) Kate roamed the aisle looking for the cereal and eventually found it. Throughout shopping, Kate was quite active and inquisitive. She would look at items in the store and always wanted to know more about them. For some products she would finger the letters on the box or can and ask, "What does this say, Mommy?"

Reflective Inquiry

- What does this case tell you about the uses of language?

- In what ways does the older child demonstrate knowledge of written language?

- How does the mother's interaction with the children support and encourage language learning?

"The amount of written language confronting a child can come as a surprise to an adult who normally pays only passing attention to it. But adult readers have learned to ignore this plethora of print, while to an inquiring, learning child it must be a stimulating situation" (Smith, 1976, p. 298). Perhaps this is why most adults form the expectation that learning to read is solely a function of formal instruction in school. Does a similar expectation exist for a child's growth and development in spoken language? Of course not. Most parents play an important role in the oral language development of their children. Yet few, until recently, had begun to believe that learning to read begins through interaction with parents and other significant members of a family. The foundations of literacy are built on children's social and linguistic interaction with their world and the persons in it. Home is where literacy learning begins.

Studies of early readers indicate that learning to read is strongly associated with positive home environments (Neuman & Roskos, 1993; Strickland & Morrow, 1990; Teale, 1978). Early readers have access to a variety of easy reading materials in the home, and they can also use the local library. Moreover, early readers are attracted to reading *anything* that interests them in their immediate everyday print environment, from labels on cans and cereal boxes to TV listings to cookbooks, telephone directories, and bus timetables.

Although books, billboards, and package labels are all potential sources for reading in a young child's home environment, children must learn how print functions in their lives. In this respect, reading aloud to children is one of the most important contributing factors in the learning environment of early readers. Early readers' homes are frequently characterized by one or more parents and older siblings who read regularly.

As a result, children learn about reading by observing the significant people in their lives modeling reading behaviors naturally—for real purposes—in a variety of ways. They might see, for example, a parent reading a recipe while cooking or baking, studying a map on the family's vacation, singing from a hymnal at church, or reading the assembly instructions for a new bike. Some children will rivet their attention on the television screen as words flash before them during a commercial. Others quickly become aware that newspapers and magazines impart information about events occurring locally and in the world. Others realize that books may be read to learn and to entertain. Indeed, reading is part of their environment. Children need to become aware of the many purposes for reading and become involved in different kinds of reading activity frequently.

The quality of interaction that the child has with family members—whether they are parents, older siblings, grandparents, aunts, or uncles—plays heavily in reading development. Often, however, assistance in learning to read is not consciously given. Instead, significant others, such as parents, read to children repeatedly (by reading certain stories over and over) and *answer questions that children ask about reading*. There is no better way to help the child make the connection that print is meaningful than to respond to the question, "What does this say?" as the child points to a printed page.

The Importance of Literate Environments.   As you might surmise, a **literate environment** for young children is one that fosters interest in and curiosity about written language and supports children's efforts to become readers and writers. Learning, not instruction, is the dominant force in a child's literacy development. Early readers thrive in environments where parents and other significant persons hold a high regard for reading. Reading to children is a highly valued and recurring event. The environment is punctuated by a genuine willingness to respond to children's questions about print. Within a literate environment, there is also a preoccupation with scribbling, drawing, and writing—so much so that Durkin (1966) characterizes children who learn to read naturally as "paper-and-pencil kids."

Reading outloud to children is one of the most important contributing factors in the learning environment of early readers.

Early readers spend significant amounts of time expressing themselves through scribble writing, drawing, copying words, and inventing spellings for words. Writing is an important though often underestimated factor in learning to read. Materials that encourage and facilitate writing should be readily accessible to young children. Crayons, markers, pencils, pens, paper, postcards, stationery, and chalkboards invite self-expression and should be kept in reach of children. Parent-child activities, such as the following, extend children's interest in and knowledge about written language by providing opportunities to observe, as well as participate in, meaningful, functional writing activities.

◆ Parents should encourage their children to help write the family shopping list.

◆ Parents and children may communicate with one another through written messages, such as writing notes. A bulletin board or a chalkboard provides a designated location for writing and receiving notes.

◆ Parents should create occasions to write, such as writing a Christmas list or a letter to Santa. In the same vein, they should encourage children to correspond with a responsive pen pal, perhaps a "best friend" or a relative living in another area who's about the same age. Writing invitations for a birthday party or a sleep-over or writing the instructions to give to the person who will temporarily care for a pet provide meaningful writing occasions.

How Writing Develops

Some young children are prolific with pencil and paper. Others are just as handy with crayon, ink marker, or paintbrush. Sometimes a convenient wall or refrigerator door substitutes nicely for paper. The common denominator for "paper-and-pencil kids" is a strong desire and a need for self-expression and communication.

The noted Russian psychologist Lev Vygotsky (1962) suggests that an infant's gestures are the first visible signs of writing: "Gestures are writing in air, and written signs frequently are simply gestures that have been fixed." As Calkins (1986) explains: "The urge to write begins when a baby, lying in her crib, moves her arms and we draw close to the crib, our faces lighting into smiles. 'She's waving at us,' we say. Because we attach meaning to what could be called meaningless gestures, the gestures assume meaning. Babies learn the power of their gestures by our response to them" (p. 35). As infants learn about the power of signs and symbols, there is, in Vygotsky's words, "a fundamental assist to cognitive growth."

Klein (1985) distinguishes between the terms *writing* and *written expression*. Written expression comes earlier than writing. Scribbles and drawings are examples of written expressions *if* they have symbolic meaning to the child. The difference, then, is in the child's ability to produce units of written language—that is, letters, words, and sentences. For Klein, a working definition of writing should include written expression: Writing is the "ability to employ pen or pencil and paper to express ideas symbolically so that the representations on the paper reflect meaning and content capable of being communicated to another by the producer" (pp. 3–4). How youngsters move from various representations of written expression to units of written language is a natural and important evolution.

Young children learn writing through exploration. As Clay (1988) observes, most 5-year-olds "have definite ideas about the forms and uses of writing gained from their preschool experience: exploring with a pencil, pretending to write, inventing messages, copying an important word like one's name, and writing labels, messages, or special words in favorite story books" (p. 20). The key to early writing development is found not in a child's motor development or intelligence but in the *opportunities* the child has to explore print. According to Clay, new discoveries about writing emerge at every encounter a child has with paper and pencil: Young children write "all over the paper in peculiar ways, turning letters around and upside down and letting the print drift over into drawing and coloring from time to time. We should be relaxed about this exploration of spaces and how print can be fitted into them" (p. 20). What can be learned from observing how young writers progress in their development?

The Importance of Scribbling.   **Scribbling** is one of the primary forms of written expression. In many respects, scribbling is the fountainhead for writing and occurs from the moment a child grasps and manipulates a writing tool. Children take their scribbles seriously, if Linda Lamme's (1984) quotation from a scribbler is any indication: "Dat's not a scrwibble. It says, 'What's for dinner, Mom?'" (p. 37). Lamme has described the progression of scribbling in children's writing development in her excellent handbook for parents.

Early Scribbling.   Early or uncontrolled scribbling is characterized by children making random marks on paper. Evidence of early scribbling can be gathered for most youngsters before their first birthday. Very young children who scribble soon learn that whatever it

◆ Figure 3.2   Taylor's Scribbling. She Points to a "Face" in the Upper Right-hand Corner.

is that is in their hands, it can make marks. Early scribblings, according to Lamme, compare with babbling in oral language development. In Figure 3.2, Taylor, at 21 months, is constantly preoccupied with her scribbles and often talks spontaneously as she expresses herself with paper and pencil. She tells her mother as she scribbles that she likes to make lots of "tapes" and points to a "face" in the upper right-hand corner of the scribble in Figure 3.2.

Since early scribbles are not usually representational (i.e., they do not convey meaning), parents and teachers should suppress the urge to ask a child, "What is this?" Instead, encourage a child to make markings on paper without pressure to finish a piece of work or tell what it's about, unless the child is eager to talk about it.

Controlled Scribbling.   Movement away from early scrawls becomes evident in children's scribbles as they begin to make systematic, repeated marks such as circles, vertical lines, dots, and squares.

Controlled scribbling occurs in children's written work between the ages of 3 and 6. The marks are often characterized as *scribble writing* in the sense that the scribbles are linear in form and shape and bear a strong resemblance to the handwriting of the child's culture, as Harste, Woodward, and Burke (1984) demonstrated. When they asked three 4-year-olds from different countries to "write everything you can write," the children produced print that reflected their native languages—English, Arabic, and Hebrew (see

◆ FIGURE 3.3   Dawn, Najeeba, and Dalia's Writing Samples Show They Have More Knowledge About Print Than Adults Would Expect.

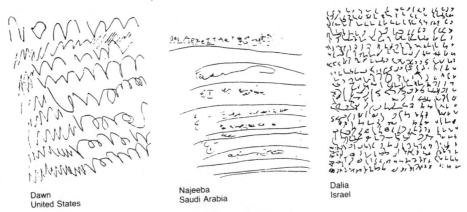

Dawn
United States

Najeeba
Saudi Arabia

Dalia
Israel

Source: Writing Samples from Three Four-Year-Olds. From "Children's Language and World: Initial Encounters with Print" by Jerome Harste, C. L. Burke, and V. A. Woodward from *Reader Meets Author/Bridging the Gap: A Psycholinguistic and Sociolinguistic Perspective.* J. A. Langer and M. T. Smith-Burke, eds. Reprinted by permission of Jerome C. Horste and the International Reading Association.

Figure 3.3). These writing samples show that young children have more knowledge about print than some adults might realize.

According to Harste and his collaborators, Dawn's controlled scribbles look undeniably like English. When Najeeba finished her writing, she said, "Here, but you can't read it because it is in Arabic." Najeeba went on to point out that in Arabic one uses "a lot more dots" than in English. Dalia is an Israeli child whose whole writing bears the look of Hebrew. Kindergarten and first-grade children build on their knowledge of written language by participating in planned and spontaneous writing activity. In doing so they acquire knowledge about reading *by* writing.

In the remainder of this chapter and in Chapters 4 and 5, we show how beginners can explore the natural relationship between writing and reading through language experiences and independent writing.

Scribble writing stands in contrast to *scribble drawing*, which is more pictographic in expression. Children use drawing as a means of written expression. According to Klein (1985), "Drawing is possibly the most important single activity that assists both writing development and handwriting. It is critical to the child's evolving sense of symbol, and it directly assists muscle and eye-hand coordination development" (p. 40). Children between the ages of 4 and 6 use drawings or pictographs as a form of written expression in their work.

Name Scribbling.   Name scribbling is an extension of scribble writing. Scribbles become representational to the child writer: The scribbles mean something. At this point, parents or teachers should begin to model writing and write with children. This is where the language experience activities described in Chapter 2 play an important role in the writer's development. Make cards, lists, or signs with child writers; label things. Have children dictate stories as you write them as well as encourage independent writing.

When children differentiate between drawing and scribbling as means of written expression, they begin to make great strides in their knowledge of print. Name scribbling underscores this differentiation and results in the formation of valuable concepts about written language—namely, that markings or symbols represent units of language such as letters and words, which in turn represent things and objects that can be communicated by messages.

Four-year-old Matthew engaged in name scribbling in Figure 3.4. His writing represents a thank-you note. What do you notice in Matthew's writing?

◆ FIGURE 3.4   Matthew's Thank-you Note.

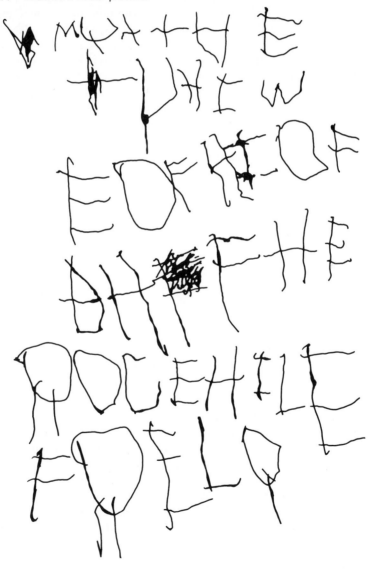

When Matthew's mother asked him to read the thank-you message aloud, he approximated a speech-to-print match. That is, he matched his spoken words to the letters and marks on each line of print. Here's what he read:

> This is Matthew Padak
> speaking, Rich Vacca
> and Jo Anne Vacca. Thank you
> for coming to our house.

What does Matthew's written expression tell us about his development? Matthew is acutely aware of the message-sending function of writing. He has developed a "message concept." Through his many encounters with print in his environment, Matthew has also developed alphabet-letter awareness. He knows, too, some of the conventions of writing peculiar to the English language. Writing, for example, moves from left to right, then back to the left at the end of a line, and from top to bottom on a page. Also, Matthew has developed an awareness of audience—in this case, the Vaccas. His thank-you message is direct and to the point. In case you're wondering what the two solid markings are that appear at the beginning of the first two lines, Matthew's explanation is both sensible and pragmatic: "That's where they [the Vaccas] can put the nails through." In other words, when the Vaccas display Matthew's thank-you note on their bulletin board, they'll know where to place the thumbtacks!

Matthew's note is also revealing by what it doesn't reflect. At age 4, Matthew's writing doesn't indicate word awareness (i.e., that words are composed of letters and are separated from one another by "boundaries" or white spaces). Matthew might be called a one-letter speller. A letter or several letters on each line of text may represent a word, a phrase, or an entire sentence.

As Matthew continues to grow as a writer, his writing will become increasingly more sophisticated. He will develop a concept of word and a knowledge of letter-sound correspondence. We are confident that Matthew will soon be writing words and sentences with the aid of invented spellings. Spelling invention will give way to convention as he gains greater knowledge and control of letter-sound relationships. Other writing conventions, such as punctuation and capitalization, will also evolve with continued writing experiences in an environment that encourages growth and supports Matthew's literacy development. How parents and teachers view the conventions of writing, particularly invented spellings, in beginning situations is crucial to writing development.

The Importance of Invented Spelling.   **Invented spelling** is a name given to children's written words before they have learned the rules of spelling. Most children don't begin school having mastered letter-sound correspondence. Yet children come to school with varying degrees of knowledge about the structure of written language because of their early explorations with reading and writing. Through their use of invented spellings, children expect their writing to make sense and have meaning.

Take the case of Paul Bissex, an early reader and writer, whose mother documented his literacy development by keeping a detailed diary of his progress (Bissex, 1980). At age 4, Paul clearly recognized the connection between writing and reading. For example, when he read his writing, complete with invented spellings, he explained: "Once you know how to spell something, you know how to read it" (p. 1). As Bissex observes, Paul developed multiple strategies because of his use of invented spellings: "Paul seemed to be asking himself not only 'What does this word *sound* like?' and 'What does this word *look* like?' but 'What does it mean?'" (p. 102).

Invented spellings signal to parents and teachers that children are beginning to analyze speech sounds in print. By first grade, for example, most children know something about letters. They may know the names and shapes of some letters. Others may be making associations between sounds and letters. The more that children explore letter-sound associations in their writing, the more progress they make toward conventional spelling. Bobo, a second grader, is a case in point.

Bobo was an "average" second grader in Sharon Piper's class. A regular classroom event in Mrs. Piper's room is journal writing. Early in the school year, Bobo's journal entries indicated that he was using several systematic strategies in his writing. His entries on October 27 and 28, for example, indicated that he was employing both a letter-name strategy (*cam* for *came*) and a transitional strategy showing awareness of lax vowels and the *e* marker (*scerry* for *scary; gucy* for *guy*).

Mrs. Piper decided to follow Bobo's development as a speller by examining words that recurred through different entries over time. Here's what she discovered.

	TODAY		SNOW
Nov. 3	to daey	Nov. 20	sarrow
Nov. 20	taooday	Dec. 9	sniwing
Dec. 3	teay	Jan. 18	snowing
Jan. 5	today		

	YESTERDAY		TOMORROW
Nov. 19	ewastdoaday	Nov. 7	tamarro
Dec. 11	yesdday	Apr. 28	tomorrowe
Feb. 5	yesterday	Apr. 29	tomrrow

	OPENING MY PRESENTS		VACATION
Dec. 14	opting my poisis	Dec. 7	waicing
Dec. 18	opning my pisins	Dec. 16	facishin

	COMING		OUTSIDE
Dec. 17	ciming	Nov. 5	altt
Feb. 4	caming	Nov. 20	aitsadd
Feb. 11	comming	Dec. 9	awtside
Apr. 16	comeing	Jan. 21	owtshd
		Feb. 24	outsid
		May 3	outside

All of the examples show progress toward a correct form. The important point, however, is that Bobo's progress reveals how children *invent* and *reinvent* spellings as they experiment with written language. Chomsky (1970) points out that the child doesn't *memorize* spellings but invents them each time to approximate the correct spelling. Invention, then, reflects that spelling is a process that is refined over time and that children have little trouble making the transition to conventional spelling when they have many opportunities to write freely.

Advantages of Invented Spelling. The gradual sophistication in children's invented spellings should be celebrated by teachers and parents as a display of intelligence and emerging competence with written language. When "correct spelling" isn't an obstacle in the path of young writers, they are free to get their ideas down on paper. Invented spellings help children place ideas before notions of correctness. Every primary teacher knows the interruptions that can occur in class when youngsters constantly ask for the correct spelling of practically every word they don't know. What we sometimes fail to recognize, however, is that children probably seek correct spellings because they perceive that the teacher values accuracy in their writing. When children are bound by notions of correctness, writing becomes a laborious undertaking rather than a meaning-making act. A supportive learning environment, however, encourages children to try to spell words as best they can during writing and to experiment with written language without the restrictions imposed by demands for accuracy and correction.

Sowers (1982) lists the advantages of not placing a premium on accuracy:

1. Children build independence because they don't have to ask for every word they don't know.

2. By emphasizing ideas rather than correctness, children become fluent in their writing. They can elaborate and play on paper without interruptions.

3. Children move efficiently through the stages of spelling development when they have opportunities to apply strategies about sound-symbol correspondences at their own pace and level of sophistication.

4. Children develop control and responsibility for their writing by taking risks and trying out the "rules" that they are forming about spelling. As Sowers noted, "The worst outcome of an unsuccessful invention is that communication stops temporarily." But if the invention succeeds, so does the child: "Real rewards await the child who writes fearlessly about a FROSHUS DOBRMAN PENSR instead of a BAD DOG" (p. 48).

The whole idea behind encouraging spelling invention is to build on the emerging competence of the beginner. As children put their ideas ahead of concerns for correct spelling, they will develop confidence in their ability to write; they will recognize the value of taking risks.

Developmental Stages of Spelling.   During the past three decades, spelling researchers have explored the developmental relationship between spelling ability and reading and writing (Read, 1971; Clay, 1979b; Henderson & Beers, 1980; Bear & Templeton, 1998). From their work it is clear that young children apply systematic strategies to relate speech sounds to print. These strategies are applied through definable **developmental stages of spelling**. These stages are broadly defined as follows.

1. *Prephonemic Spelling*. Once children know some letters, they begin to experiment with the relationship between the letters and their sounds. One early concept that develops is that there is a one-to-one correspondence between the initial consonant or final consonant and the word. The word *back* is spelled with a *B* or *sink* with a *K*. This concept is gradually expanded to include the consonant boundaries of words. For example, *ML = mail* and *DR = dear*. Matthew, whose thank-you note is illustrated in Figure 3.4, is an early prephonemic speller.

2. *Phonemic Spelling*. At this stage, vowels begin to appear in children's invented spellings. Children of 6 or 7 learn to sound their way through a word, making letter-sound matches as they go. There is still a tendency to use a one-to-one match, although it is now much more refined than in the previous stage. For example, *MAL = mail; ESTR = Easter; COT = coat; SRPRIS = surprise*. Note that long vowels are represented with the corresponding letter name. Often, logical substitutions are made for short vowels, such as *SEK = stick* or *JRAS = dress*.

3. *Transitional Spelling*. As a result of extended opportunities to read and write in and out of school, children begin to abandon the notion that there has to be a one-to-one match between a spoken sound and a graphic symbol. They now actively search for chunks or patterns of letters that represent spoken sounds. They begin to develop greater spelling awareness by observing the consonant-vowel-consonant (CVC) pattern, *GET = get;* the CVVC pattern, *DAER = dear* and *CEAP = keep;* and the CVCe patterns, *TAKE = take; LIKE = like; CAER = care*.

4. *Conventional Spelling*. By the third grade, children have developed many accurate notions of how to spell words that conform to the standard rules of the language. They use correct spellings more and more often in their attempts to communicate.

Knowing how reading and writing develop allows teacher to plan instruction that is developmentally appropriate. The IRA/NAEYC joint position statement on learning to read and write contends that developmentally appropriate practices should be challenging but achievable with sufficient teacher support. Since ideal conditions for literacy development may not exist for all children, what do some of the insights from learning to read and write suggest for developmentally appropriate practices in kindergarten and first grade?

DEVELOPMENTALLY APPROPRIATE PRACTICES

The idea of **developmentally appropriate practice** suggests that the curriculum match or be geared to children's developing abilities (Schickedanz, 1998; Bredekamp, 1987). From a literacy development perspective, a child's first contact with a language arts curriculum in school should match his or her level of emergent literacy.

David Elkind (1989) argues that developmentally appropriate practice takes into account one's beliefs and conceptions of the learner or the learning process, of knowledge, and of the goals of education. From a developmental perspective, the child, as a learner, is viewed as having *developing* abilities. All children, perhaps with the exception of those who are mentally, emotionally, or linguistically impaired, are capable of attaining these abilities. However, not all children will attain these abilities at the same age. In terms of literacy learning, not all children entering school will have developed abilities to read and write at the same level of proficiency or rate of growth. Thus the differences in children should weigh heavily in planning initial literacy experiences.

Elkind also contends that a teacher's conception of the learning process and of knowledge affects developmentally appropriate practices. From a developmental viewpoint, learning always involves *creative* activity. Nowhere is this proposition more evident than in literacy learning. As we have already observed, young children must "try out" literacy on their own terms by exploring and experimenting with written language. Not only is the learning process creative, but the learner is always involved in the *construction* of knowledge. Within a literate environment, young children act on objects (e.g., paper, pencil, books) and events (e.g., a bedtime story) to make sense of written language.

Teachers' conceptions of the aims and goals of education are interlaced with their conceptions of the learner, the learning process, and knowledge. Elkind (1989) put it this way: "If the learner is seen as a growing individual with developing abilities, if learning is regarded as a creative activity, and if knowledge is seen as a construction, then the aim of education must surely be to facilitate this development, this creative activity, and this construction of knowledge" (p. 115).

Effective teachers of literacy know how to plan developmentally appropriate experiences and how to rally instruction around children's diversity. Individual differences, however, need not suggest a unique program of instruction for each child. Individualizing a literacy program is as much a state of mind as it is a fixed or prescriptive approach to instruction. How teachers go about individualizing says more of their beliefs about reading and learning to read than it does about any specific method.

Individualized instruction is sometimes narrowly translated to mean "learning small things in small steps," where each child completes an individualized program "except for some differences in pacing" (Moffett, 1975). A teacher's responsibility, first and foremost, is to establish a classroom environment in which individual learning takes place during literacy instruction. Holdaway (1979) argues that it is impossible to determine the right level, content, pace, and style of learning for each child, each day. But teachers can set the conditions for developmentally appropriate learning by creating literate environments and giving enough instructional support to each child to learn to read and write successfully.

Creating Literate Environments

Insights from the early literacy experiences of preschool children have yet to be reflected in beginning reading in schools. Instruction for beginners should not be a carbon copy of practices that are appropriate for older children or that emphasize drill, repetition, and memorization. Instead, the beginner needs supportive, meaningful situations in learning to read. In this respect, there is much to be learned from the behavior of parents of preschool readers.

A teacher of beginners should consider focusing literacy instruction around the natural methods of parents whose children learned to read before school entry. A literate classroom environment for reading places less attention on instructional methods and more emphasis on individual attention and a warm, accepting relationship between child and teacher. A literacy learning environment in school establishes ideal conditions for learning to read in much the same way that the home environment of the child establishes ideal conditions for learning to speak.

In a classroom environment that promotes literacy development. children feel free to take risks because errors are expected and accepted. Risk taking is an important factor in literacy learning. Beginners should feel free to ask questions with the expectation that interested adults will listen and respond constructively. As Routman (1988) noted, respect for each child is a critical factor: "If [children] feel respected, they will feel secure and be able to take risks. So it is with us as adults too. Respect is necessary for optimal learning" (p. 32).

Holdaway (1982) describes some of the characteristics of a natural, or home-centered, language-learning environment that operates efficiently in a preschooler's mastery of oral language.

1. Young children are allowed to develop in their own way and at their own rate using language functionally to meet their needs.

2. Parents are positive and rewarding in their reception of most responses that children attempt. In learning oral language, children have a built-in support system provided by their parents that does not stress criticism or correction but allows for trial and approximations.

3. Parents demonstrate tremendous faith and patience.

4. Parents do not create competitive situations in which children learn language. Parents may compare a child's performance with what he or she did yesterday or a week ago, but rarely do they make close comparisons of their child's performance with another child.

5. Children learn in meaningful situations that support the language being learned.

6. Children have models to emulate. Because the language-learning process is innately rewarding, they spend much of their time voluntarily practicing.

It is evident from the studies cited earlier in this chapter that many of the conditions necessary for language learning were operating in the lives of early readers. Teachers of reading beginners must approximate these ideal conditions in their classrooms. Consider, then, establishing some of the hallmarks of a home-centered environment for learning to read.

Not only is a literate classroom environment home-centered, but it is also playful. A play-centered environment allows young children in day care or kindergarten classrooms to develop a "feel" for literacy as they experiment with written language.

Designing Literacy Play Centers

Literacy play centers in preschool and kindergarten provide an environment where children may play with print on their own terms. Play provides a natural context for beginners to experiment with literacy. Play centers promote literacy by giving children opportunities to observe one another using literacy for real reasons (Neuman & Roskos, 1997; Morrow, 1990; Schickedanz, 1986).

Roskos (1986, 1988) closely observed eight children, aged 4 and 5, for six months during free-play situations to analyze the kinds of reading and writing activities they engaged in naturally during play. She was amazed to discover the quantity and quality of early literate activity in pretend-play situations.

In free-play situations, the children Roskos observed were involved in literacy in two fundamental ways. First, during **pretend play,** they commonly engaged in "story making." The stories that were spontaneously created during play frequently included a setting, characters, a goal or central concern, specific events that constituted a plot, and a resolution. Some of the stories that children created included taking trips to Sea World and domestic problems like "the naughty daughters."

Second, literacy socialization—what children know about reading and writing from living in a literate society—was also observed during spontaneous free-play activities. The young children in Roskos's study were highly aware of the reading and writing activities that occur naturally on a daily basis, and they exhibited their knowledge of literacy when they used it during pretend play.

As a result of her study, Roskos makes three recommendations for teachers in day-care, preschool, and kindergarten settings:

1. Create and frequently use play centers that facilitate sustained pretend play and prompt experimentation with reading and writing. In addition to the traditional housekeeping and block areas, teachers should consider developing play centers like the office, the travel agency, the store, the bank, or the play school that stimulate young children to explore the routines, functions, and features of literacy.

2. Ask young children to share their pretend-play stories, which can then be recorded on chart paper and used for extended language experience activities. From play accounts like these, teaching points about story sense, print forms, directionality, and sight vocabulary can easily be inserted.

3. Begin to observe more closely the literacy at work in the pretend play of youngsters. These observations tell us much about the young child's literacy stance and may guide us in our instructional efforts to connect what is known about written language to the un-

known. Scribbled recipes from the housekeeping area, stories created at the sand table, and book handling in the play school are literacy signals that should not be ignored.

In the Best Practice featured in Box 3.2, examine several factors to be considered when designing literacy play centers.

Teachers often assume the role of participant in a play episode, but their main responsibility is to facilitate literacy development, which may involve appropriately intervening to create opportunities to include children in literacy-related activities during play. This may entail suggesting the need for making a list, recording an appointment, requesting a telephone number, checking food labels, or reading a bedtime story.

Notice how a kindergarten teacher, Ms. Green, participates in and facilitates two timely literacy routines.

Four children are busily working in the housekeeping area when the teacher walks by.

Ms. Green:	Mmmm! It smells wonderful in here. What are you cooking?
Lonnie:	I'm making applesauce.
Tim:	Well, I'm making some pizza.
Ms. Green:	Applesauce and pizza will make a terrific lunch!
Karen:	Yeah! Let's have pizza and applesauce for lunch. Pizza is my favorite.
Ms. Green:	Even the baby can eat applesauce. He can't chew pizza yet because he doesn't have teeth, but he can eat applesauce.
Karen:	Oh, no! The baby is crying again. That baby is crying too much!
Ms. Green:	I will help you take care of the baby while you fix lunch. Let's see. I think that he would like to hear a story. *(She selects a small board book from the bookshelf in the housekeeping center and sits down to read to the "baby.")* Yes, the baby should enjoy this book. This is a story that my children liked to hear when they were babies. *(She holds the doll and reads the book. Several children come over to watch as she reads to the baby.)*
Emily:	OK, lunch is ready. Do you want some lunch, Ms. Green?
Ms. Green:	I would love to have lunch with you. I like pizza and applesauce.

Everyone pretends to eat.

Tim:	Well, how do you like my pizza, Ms. Green?
Lonnie:	How's my applesauce?
Ms. Green:	Everything is delicious. Will you both share your recipes for pizza and applesauce with me?
Tim and Lonnie:	Sure!

The teacher then provides paper for Tim, Lonnie, and the other children to write their recipes. The children's writings used a combination of scribbles, letters, and invented spellings.

BOX 3.2 BEST PRACTICE

Literacy Play Centers

Consider the following when designing literacy play centers.

◆ *Setting.* Literacy play centers are usually designed around places and contexts that are familiar to young children—for example, a doctor's or dentist's office, the post office, or a bank. The setting should be general enough so that children create their own stories and themes as they engage in play talk and action.

◆ *Location of Centers in the Classroom.* Literacy play centers are located in a designated area of the classroom, labeled accordingly at children's eye level. Neuman and Roskos (1997) illustrate several classroom play settings that they have studied in their research.

Three Literacy-Related Play Settings

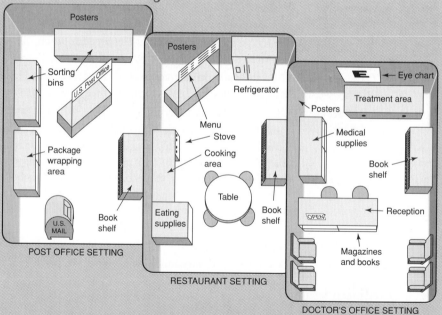

Source: From Susan B. Neuman and Kathleen Roskos, Literacy knowledge in practice: Contexts of participation for young writers and readers, *Reading Research Quarterly, 32,* 1, p. 16.

◆ *Props in a Play Center.* Furnish a play center with real props found in the environment. The props may be used for dramatic effect *(dramatic props)* or for literacy-related activity *(literacy props).* For example, dramatic props in a doctor's office play setting may include a doctor's kit (with stethoscope, light, etc.), a nurse's hat, a blanket for the examining table,

Box 3.2 continued

and dolls as patients. Literacy props may include patient charts, prescription pads, sign-in sheets, magazines in the waiting room, bill forms, and checkbooks. The appropriateness of props in a play center depends on their authenticity, use, and safety. Any literacy-related item found in the "real world" may become part of a center. Neuman and Roskos (1990) list the types of props that may be used in several different literacy play settings.

TYPES OF PROPS FOUND IN LITERACY PLAY CENTERS

Kitchen Center

Books to read to dolls or stuffed animals
Telephone books
A telephone (preferably a real one)
Emergency number decals on or near telephone
Cookbooks
Blank recipe cards
Small plaques or decorative magnets
Personal stationery
Food coupons
Grocery store ads/fliers
Play money containers
Empty grocery containers
Small message board or chalk-boards
Calendars of various types
Notepads of assorted sizes
Pens, pencils, markers
Large plastic clips

Office Center

Calendars of various types
Appointment book
Message pads
Signs (e.g., open/closed)
Books, pamphlets, markers
Magazines
File folders
Racks for filing papers
In/out trays
Index cards
Business cards
Assorted forms
Play money and checklike pieces of paper
Ledger sheets
Typewriter or computer keyboard
Clipboards
Post-it notes and address labels
Note cards
Large and small plastic clips
Pens, pencils, markers
Trays for holding items

Post Office Center

Envelopes of various sizes
Assorted forms
Stationery
Pens, pencils, markers
Stickers, stars, stamps, stamp pads
Post office mail-box
Tote bag for mail
Computer address labels
Large and small plastic cups
Calendars of various types
Small drawer trays
Posters and signs about mailing procedures

Library Center

Library book return cards
Stamps for marking books
A wide variety of children's books
Bookmarks
Pens, pencils, markers

Paper of assorted sizes
A sign-in/sign-out sheet
Stickers
ABC index cards
A telephone
Telephone books
Calendars of various types
Posters for children's books
File folders

Teachers may also wish to extend and elaborate on a play episode by inviting children to think about and discuss what they did during play. Pictures, three-dimensional materials, and written work (involving children's scribbles or invented spellings) may provide a basis for children to recall what they did and what they liked about the play episode.

In a post office center, a kindergarten teacher, Mrs. Chones, provided additional experiences and activities designed to extend children's prior knowledge of the responsibilities of postal workers and the process of transporting mail. She began by guiding a discussion to determine what the children already knew about the post office, what they needed or wanted to know, and any misconceptions they may have had. The children's responses were recorded on chart paper and were posted on the wall near the post office center. As a follow-up to the discussion, the teacher showed the children an interesting, current, age-appropriate video about the post office. A brief discussion followed to determine if the video provided answers to any of the questions or clarified any misconceptions.

In addition, the children were taken on a field trip to the local post office. The remaining unanswered questions from the wall charts were transferred to smaller strips of paper for the children to carry with them to the post office. The children drew pictures to accompany their questions and to serve as visual aids to help them remember what questions they wanted to ask. A postal worker served as a tour guide and patiently answered the children's questions, impromptu and planned. When the children returned to their classroom, they helped the teacher revise the wall charts based on the knowledge gained from the field trip.

As a result, the play episodes that occur in the post office center are likely to be more involved and sophisticated, because the teacher provided relevant experiences designed to extend the children's knowledge and to stimulate their interest. At times, the teacher guided the children's play in the post office center by acting as a participant. For example, she mailed a package, she bought stamps and requested a receipt, and she asked for help in locating an address for a letter that she was sending.

A home-centered, play-centered environment extends children's literacy learning in developmentally appropriate, creative ways. A language-centered environment provides language experiences that are crucial to a beginner's growth as a literacy learner.

Exploring Print Through Language Experiences

Young children need to have the time and space to explore language in order to clarify its uses and gain facility in its production and reception. Children who experience language and its intricacies take giant steps on the road to becoming literate.

It is no coincidence that many preschool readers are also early writers. They have a strong desire to express themselves in symbolic terms through drawing, scribbling, copying, and ultimately, producing their own written language. Exploring written language with paper and pencil helps children form expectations that print is meaningful.

Talking, Creating, Singing, and Dancing.   The main feature of a language experience approach is that it embraces the natural language of children and uses their background experiences as the basis for learning to read.

Language experience activities in beginning reading instruction permit young children to share and discuss experiences; listen to and tell stories; dictate words, sentences, and stories; and write independently. The teacher can revolve language experiences around speaking, listening, visual expression, singing, movement, and rhythmic activities.

Use conversation to encourage individual or group language experience stories or independent writing. A language experience story is a story that is told by the child and written down by the teacher for instructional purposes.

1. Talk about everyday sights and occurrences.

2. Provide problem-solving tasks (e.g., making a milkshake) or highly motivating situations (e.g., making peanut butter and jelly sandwiches) to elicit oral language.

3. Tell stories through pictures. Wordless picture books are particularly useful for stimulating language development through storytelling and creative writing.

4. Discuss enjoyable occasions (e.g., birthdays, holidays, special events such as the World Series, the class picnic).

5. Use visual experiences to stimulate conversation (e.g., television, book illustrations, artwork). Visual expression through art activity, in particular, provides exciting opportunities for language experiences.

Use art as a vehicle for personal expression. Artistic expression represents a powerful force in children's lives. Through various forms of aesthetic and manipulative activity, children learn that there are many ways to express what they are thinking or feeling. What children draw, paint, or sculpt today can be the basis for what they talk or write about tomorrow and then what they eventually read.

Every classroom for young children should provide enough space to work on and display art projects. Art materials should include crayons, colored chalk, clay, paints, felt-tip pens, scissors, paste and glue, paper, newsprint (unprinted newspaper), and an assortment of junk (e.g., straws, wire, boxes, soap bars, toothpicks, Styrofoam, pipe cleaners, and anything else that might lend itself to manipulative activity).

Singing, dancing, and other rhythmic activities are valuable means of expression in their own right. Such activities can also be linked easily and naturally to reading and writing instruction. For example, you can do any or all of the following:

1. Encourage readalongs as children sing familiar and favorite songs. Create large cue cards that contain the lyrics to the songs. As children sing, the teacher directs their attention to the lyrics, moving a hand across the card, left to right, top to bottom, pointing under each word, and synchronizing the movement with the music.

2. Create new lyrics for familiar songs that have a highly repetitive pattern. In one kindergarten class, the children changed "Old MacDonald Had a Farm" to "Old MacDonald Had an Amusement Park." Imagine the new lyrics that were contributed by the children!

3. Create dances that tell a story. Songs such as "The Eensy Weensy Spider" can be used to encourage movement and interpretation through dance.

4. Improvise movement stories inspired by poems and familiar stories. Chenfield (1978) suggests that as you read with the students, include movement as a way to further express and interpret the reading material. Children make fine choreographers, creating spontaneous movement sequences for "The Gingerbread Man," "Peter Cottontail," and other action stories.

Role Playing and Drama.   Young children delight in pretending. Role playing and dramatic activities in a beginning reading program not only stimulate the imagination but also provide many opportunities to use language inventively and spontaneously.

Role playing affords children the chance to approach ordinary or unusual events and situations from different perspectives and points of view. Children begin to recognize that there are different levels and uses of language appropriate for different situations. Role playing can be easily adapted to stimulate writing and to enhance reading comprehension throughout the elementary grades.

The objective of drama in the classroom is self-expression. Children "play along" in structured and unstructured situations. **Dramatic play** activities require very little planning and involve unstructured, spontaneous expression such as pretending to be a leaf falling from a tree or an astronaut going to Mars. *Creative drama* is more structured in that children often have definite parts to play as they act out a favorite story or event. Props, costumes, and scenery may be called for. A third kind of dramatic activity, *pantomime,* involves wordless communication in which children use their bodies to translate reality and convey meaning.

The teacher should have a dress-up area for dramatic activities. Because drama is so unlike traditional classroom activities, the teacher's approach, much like a parent's, is one of continuous encouragement and facilitation. Consider some of these language experiences.

1. Use children's literature for drama. Folktales such as *Little Red Riding Hood* or *Henny Penny* provide simple plot structures and clearly defined characters. Action-filled poems can be valuable for pantomime and movement activities.

2. Engage children in problem situations as a start for spontaneous dramatic activity. Rose (1982) suggested the following problems:

   ◆ You have been called at school to go home immediately.

   ◆ You are waiting in line at McDonald's or Burger King and are very hungry. On two occasions, people get ahead of you. What do you do the third time it happens?

   ◆ You have just broken your mother's pearl necklace, and the pearls are scattered on the floor. You are picking them up when your mother enters the room.

   ◆ You run into the police station to report that your bicycle has been stolen. The police seem to doubt your story.

In addition to language experiences, one of the most important developmentally appropriate practices for beginners, as well as children throughout the grades, is to read aloud from storybooks. The IRA/NAEYC joint position statement on early reading and

Improvisation and creativity expand and enhance classroom self-expression

writing underscores the importance of reading to children: "The single most important activity for building understandings and skills for reading success appears to be reading aloud to children (Bus, Van Ijzendoorn, & Pellegrini, 1995; Wells, 1985)."

Reading to Children

There is no better way to create a love for books than by reading to children. Reading to children sparks their imagination and gives them a sense of wonder. According to Cramer (1975), reading to children will help them appreciate the gift of literature, develop and enrich their own language, and build implicit concepts about reading and writing.

Reading to children helps them learn to read in subtle but important ways. It is through reading that children develop a schema or a sense for stories. In Chapter 7, we discuss the role of *story structure* in learning to read and how children can use their schema for stories to comprehend material. A story schema is developed early in the lives of children who have been read to frequently. Moreover, reading to children provides models for writing as they develop a sense of plot, characterization, mood, and theme.

Cramer (1975, pp. 461–462) provides valuable guidelines for reading to children:

1. Plan each day's reading selection in advance. Normally one should have certain days reserved for the reading of a continuing story. It is also useful to reserve at least one

day a week for special selections—poetry, surprise readings, or readings designed to mesh with other daily or weekly classroom activities.

2. Select reading material best suited for the children being read to. Keep in mind age and interest levels. Many teachers choose to consult various sources in selecting appropriate books.

3. Interpret the mood, tone, and action of the passage being read. Don't be afraid to be dramatic. Inhibition, shyness, or fear of making a fool of oneself often prevents teachers from entering into the drama of a story.

4. Differentiate the reading-to-children time for the directed reading-and-listening-activity time. It is neither necessary nor desirable to make the reading-listening time into a structured lesson. The primary objective is enjoyment.

5. When reading a narrative that will be continued the next day, stop at a point that is likely to invite anticipation for the next episode. Judicious use of this device can have a positive effect on attendance and sustained high interest level in the selection being read.

Reading activities may be planned to focus on children's authors and illustrators. Children may learn about the authors and illustrators by reading or listening to their stories, by corresponding with them, by creating stories in their style, or by comparing and contrasting the stories.

Jim Trelease's *New Read-Aloud Handbook* (1989) is a valuable resource for parents and teachers who want to make reading to children a regular routine. Trelease not only provides the dos and don'ts of reading aloud but also includes annotated references of read-aloud books that can be used to make reading come alive for children.

Reading to children is an important way of sharing books. The act of sharing books with children provides valuable stimulation for relating speech to print. Almost all of the early readers in various studies came from book-oriented homes. Reading to and with children captures their fascination with print. They progress from sheer delight in the human experience of story sharing to recognition that the pictures in books "tell a story" to the awareness that the black squiggly marks (not the pictures on a page) have a direct association with spoken language.

Books may be shared in a variety of contexts. Young children will hear good children's literature during a library story hour or on television programs such as *Reading Rainbow*. Excellent literature is also available to children through book and cassette combinations that are sold in bookstores or may be borrowed from a public library.

Sharing Books.   The bedtime story, and the intimacy that surrounds it, is one of the most important ways that parents can share the joy of reading with their children. The **shared book experience** is a teaching strategy that incorporates the intimate effects of sharing books with children (Butler, 1988; Holdaway, 1979). The idea behind the shared book experience is to use a "big book" (usually a book with a 15- by 24-inch format) to share a story with a group of children or the whole class. In Chapter 4, we provide an extensive discussion on the use of big books in primary classrooms.

The big book allows all the children in the class or in a small group to participate actively in the reading of the story. Because the print and illustrations are large enough for all the children to see, the teacher captures their attention immediately and focuses instruction around key goals. For example, the teacher should read the story aloud often enough so that children learn it by heart. The story then becomes the basis for discussion and language-related activities (i.e., story dramatization) as well as teaching children about directionality and other print-related concepts.

The shared book experience involves the teacher and a class of beginners partaking in the reading and rereading of favorite stories, songs, poems, and rhymes. Andrea Butler (1988) likens the shared book experience to a ritual that should occur daily in the class-room lives of teachers and children. She recommended the use of shared book experience as a way of creating opportunities for children to learn what a book is, what an "expert" reader does with a book as it is read, and what makes a story a story. In the Best Practice featured in Box 3.3, study the various steps in a shared book experience lesson.

Repeating the Reading of Favorite Stories.   Repetition of favorite stories and eventually "memory reading" play a crucial role in the child's understanding that print is supposed to sound like language. The phenomenon of memory reading involves recalling and rehearsing favorite segments of stories by heart. Young children learn to use a variety of strategies to achieve some sense of independence over their favorite stories. As part of sharing books and reading aloud, the teacher should be ready and willing to read and reread favorite books and to invite children to participate as much as possible. The language patterns of the books should be predictable, melodic, and rhythmic. We will have more to say on predictable materials and book choices for young children in Chapter 6.

Two additional suggestions should be considered. First, create a listening library for the classroom by recording stories on audiotapes for children to listen to as they follow the story in the book. Second, children will enjoy repeating and retelling favorite stories by using a flannel board or puppets or through creative play and dramatics.

Some adults are quick to point out that children who memorize stories are just pretending to read, just "going through the motions." Pretending, however, shouldn't be discouraged. In fact, imitation establishes good models. The readinglike behaviors associated with an imitative stage in reading provide children with important early book experiences.

BOX 3.3   **BEST PRACTICE**

The Shared Book Experience

Consider the following steps when sharing books with early readers and writers.

STEP 1: INTRODUCE, TALK ABOUT, AND REREAD A NEW STORY

◆ Show children the cover of the book and invite discussion of the illustration. Ask, "What does the illustration on the cover remind you of?" "What do you think this story will be about?"

(Continued)

BOX 3.3 CONTINUED

◆ Tell children the title of the story. Invite further predictions as to the story's content.

◆ Read the story dramatically. Once children have experienced the joy of hearing the story, invite conversation: "What did you enjoy about the story?" "Were the characters like you?" It is better not to overdo the discussion with lots of questions. Accept the children's personal reactions and responses, and support their efforts to express their enjoyment of the story and to talk about the meaning that it had for them.

◆ Encourage children to retell the story in their own words. Allow them to use picture clues and assist them as needed.

◆ Reread the story, inviting children to participate in some way by focusing on repetitive elements, or chants, and having them join in with you. Keep the emphasis on meaning and enjoyment.

STEP 2: REREAD FAMILIAR STORIES

◆ Once the children have become familiar with several stories, ask them to choose a favorite to be reread.

◆ Strive for increased participation by the children by creating *readalong* situations.

◆ Create *book experiences* to build children's book knowledge. For example, as you read, point to the words in the text, and demonstrate skills such as page turning and directionality (e.g., left to right, top to bottom).

◆ Teach children about *book conventions* (e.g., front and back cover, title and author page, pictures to support the story).

◆ Make children aware of *written language conventions* (e.g., words, pages, spaces between words, the use of capital letters in proper names or at the beginning of a sentence, punctuation marks, quotation marks to indicate dialogue between characters). We will examine the development of written language and book conventions in more depth in Chapter 4.

STEP 3: DEVELOP READING SKILLS AND STRATEGIES

◆ As children progress in the sharing and rereading of favorite stories, teach them literacy skills and strategies (e.g., recognizing letter-sound relationships in words, using context to identify words, building a sight-word vocabulary, developing oral reading fluency, comprehending meaning). These strategies and others will be examined in subsequent chapters.

STEP 4: ENCOURAGE INDEPENDENT READING

◆ Develop a classroom library of books that have been shared and reread many times.

◆ Encourage students to read favorite books on their own and with others.

Just consider some of the print concepts they learn: Books have pages, the pages can be turned, books have a right and wrong way up, the pictures help tell a story, and books are a source of enjoyment and pleasure.

Providing Assistance as Needed.   Parents of early readers answer questions when their children ask for assistance. The parent usually follows the child's lead, not vice versa. Children choose their own activities and materials, and when questions arise, a parent or other adult is there to help.

One of our preservice students who is studying to be an elementary school teacher observed her two children, Ben and Matt, interacting with each other just before bedtime. The brothers share the same bedroom and often read bedtime stories together. Ben is 8 and Matt is 5.

BEN: Matt, pick out a story. *(Matt proceeds to do so while Ben plays with the dog.)*

MATT: Ben, can I read the big words?

BEN: *(points to the book)* Are these the big words?

MATT: Yeah, those words.

BEN: Why don't I read the black words and you read the red ones? OK?

MATT: *(points to book)* You mean these?

BEN: Yeah.

MATT: But I don't know all the words.

BEN: Well, I'll just help ya—OK?

MATT: OK, I'll try. *(Matt sighs and the story begins.)* Will you help me with that? *(Matt points to a word on the page.)*

BEN: *Scissors.*

MATT: *Scissors.*

BEN: Yeah, good. That's right. *(The story continues until Matt reads the word* fish *for* goldfish.*)*

BEN: No. What kind of fish?

MATT: Goldfish?

BEN: Yeah, good. *(Ben points to a picture of the goldfish. After a while, Ben gets tired of giving Matt hints about the words.)*

BEN: Can I read the rest?

MATT: Yeah, but I want to read the last page.

BEN: OK. *(Ben reads the book until the last page.)* Are you goin' to read this?

MATT: Yeah. *(Matt attempts the last page and does fairly well with Ben's occasional assistance.)*

BEN: Good. Matt! You're learnin' to read real well.

Assisted Reading

Consider these stages when using assisted reading with beginners.

STAGE 1: READ TO CHILDREN AND HAVE THEM "ECHO" THE READING

In this initial stage of assisted reading, the teacher reads to children, and they repeat the phrases or sentences after the person doing the reading. This practice is sometimes called *echo reading*. Not only does echo reading encourage young children to memorize text, but it also assists them to make the connection between print and speech and to develop a concept of *word*.

STAGE 2: HAVE CHILDREN ANTICIPATE WORDS DURING READING

Children enter this stage when they recognize that some of the words occur repeatedly in stories they are reading. At this point, leave out some of the words that you think children know. The children supply the missing words as they read.

STAGE 3: HAVE CHILDREN DO MOST OF THE READING

Children enter this stage when they do most of the reading of familiar stories that have been read to them on a repeated basis. The teacher fills in the words children may not know or may have trouble recognizing. The goal is to maintain as smooth a flow of reading as possible.

Matt has acquired knowledge of written language and has developed concepts of reading by being immersed in stories from a very early age. He is learning how to read by reading with help from Ben and his parents and on his own. Matt seeks assistance when he needs it and doesn't recognize such help as corrective or critical.

Hoskisson (1975) recommends a strategy that he devised called **assisted reading** that combines all of the features of home-centered learning: reading with children, sharing books, repeating favorite stories, memorizing text, and providing assistance as needed. Parents or teachers can easily adapt the three stages associated with the strategy (see the Best Practice featured in Box 3.4).

We have scratched the surface in presenting some of the implications of early reading for beginning instruction. We will continue the discussion in the next chapter.

SUMMARY

In this chapter, we dealt with the developmental aspects of literacy learning in relation to children's early reading and writing. We inquired into the nature of beginning reading instruction by looking at preschoolers' knowledge of and experiences with print. Children progress through various phases in literacy development in early reading and writing from birth through the primary grades.

Early in life, some children use what they have learned and experienced daily to build positive associations with books. Through such natural activities as the bedtime story and other types of storybook interaction, children develop a "set for literacy." Preschoolers are immersed in a world of meaningful print; they exhibit early reading behaviors well before they enter a classroom. What kinds of experiences, then, are needed to get the kindergarten child off to a good start?

Beginning readers benefit from developmentally appropriate practices that are home-centered, play-centered, and language-centered. *Home-centered* refers to supportive situations in which a warm, accepting, and patient relationship develops between teacher and child. Reading to children, sharing books, and assisting with reading are among the activities that can be easily transferred from the parent to the teacher. *Play-centered* refers to activities that allow children to explore literacy in spontaneous play contexts. Literacy play centers are powerful contexts for helping children experiment with literacy. *Language-centered* refers to experiences in which children explore spontaneous activities. Speaking, visual expression, singing, movement and rhythmic activities, role playing, and drama are all instructional devices for teachers who want to approximate ideal conditions for learning to read in their classrooms.

TEACHER-ACTION RESEARCHER

1. Locate a kindergarten or preschool classroom that has a play-centered environment in which children can develop a "feel" for literacy as they experiment with written language. Collect data describing how children experiment with literacy in a natural context. How do play centers promote literacy? As children engage in pretend play, what do they do that will assist in their literacy development? Tape-record or take notes of conferences that occur, interview children, collect anecdotes of interactions among the children, and compile all the information into a study of one or more children's literacy learning.

2. Refer to the Class Works in Box 3.1. Observe a preschool child or several children learning about reading and writing in a natural setting. Unobtrusively record what you see and hear as the child interacts with written language. What do your notes tell you about the child's use of language? In what ways does the child demonstrate knowledge of written language? If an adult is observed interacting with the child, how does the adult's behavior support and encourage language learning? (If possible, observe in a multicultural preschool setting.)

3. Reflect on the literate environment that you experienced personally as a child or that a child you know well experienced. Use the following questions to guide your retrospective inquiry:

   a. Were stories read or told?

   b. How much time was spent listening to stories?

    c. Describe an instructional situation and the child's responses.

    d. Was child given encouragement and support, perhaps a hug or an accepting word, in the learning situation?

    e. How much time was spent doing worksheets?

    f. Was time spent scribbling, drawing, or writing? Describe the nature of the child's participation.

What can be drawn from your personal reflection?

4. Analyze the invented spellings of first, second, third, and fourth graders from writing samples that you have collected or from those provided by your instructor. What are the developmental stages of spelling of the children whose writing you have analyzed? What does the analysis of spelling tell you about each child's knowledge of words and of letter-sound relationships? How would you design instruction to help each of the children continue to grow and develop as spellers?

KEY TERMS

assisted reading

awareness and
    exploration

developmentally
    appropriate
    practice

developmental
    stages of spelling

dramatic play

early phase of reading
    and writing

experimental phase
    of reading and
    writing

family literacy

independent and
    productive
    reading and
    writing

invented spelling

language experience
    activities

literacy development

literate environment

literacy play center

pretend play

reading–writing
    continuum

scribbling

shared book
    experience

transitional phase
    of reading and
    writing

Chapter Overview

INVITING BEGINNERS INTO THE LITERACY CLUB

EMERGENT LITERACY PROGRAMS

LITERACY LEARNING THROUGH STORYBOOKS

Big Books

Interactive Reading and Writing

LEARNING ABOUT LETTERS AND SOUNDS

Phonemic Awareness

Letter Recognition

LEARNING ABOUT FEATURES OF WRITTEN LANGUAGE

Linguistic Awareness

Concepts About Print

Observing Children's Emerging Literacy Accomplishments

LEARNING ABOUT THE RELATIONSHIP BETWEEN SPEECH AND PRINT

Uses of Written Language

Language-Experience Stories

Between the Lines

In this chapter, you will discover:

♦ What it means to be a member of the literacy club

♦ The rationale for an emergent reading program

♦ The importance of storybooks in the lives of early readers and writers

♦ How to develop and assess linguistic knowledge, concepts of print, and literacy-related knowledge and skills

♦ How to develop phonemic awareness and alphabet knowledge

The first day of school is always full of anticipation and excitement for children and teachers alike. Thoughts of children from previous years flash through Sandra's mind a half-hour before she meets a new group of first graders. The room's ready. She's ready. And she's sure that the children will be ready to continue their development as literacy learners.

This is Sandra's fourth year as a teacher. She's just as eager to get started as she was on her very first day and as full of expectation as her children. She's confident about her ability to work with 6- and 7-year-olds. She knows that she must anchor the teaching of reading and writing in knowledge of what children bring to her classroom, how they learn, and how language works.

Sandra understands that children come to school expecting to learn to read. She begins the first day of the first grade by introducing the children to a poem from a selection of read-aloud rhymes for young children (Prelutsky, 1986). The poem is about a child growing up and making discoveries about himself. Sandra has printed and illustrated the poem on a large piece of poster board. She reads it to the children several times, pointing to each word.

When Sandra feels that the children are sufficiently familiar with the poem, she invites individuals to read the poem and to tell the class something about themselves. As each child responds, she creates an "About Me" story by recording on chart paper exactly what each child has said, and then reading the poem aloud.

Joey said, "My best TV show is 'Rugrats.'"
Sally said, "I like to eat pizza."
Jeff said, "I have a new baby brother. His name is Tyler."
Jenny said, "My cat wakes me up every morning."

Sandra then makes copies of the poem and the "About Me" story to send home with the first graders at the end of the school day to share with their families.

Through the social interactions that occur in the classroom, Sandra invites all of her students into the **literacy club** on the first day of school. In this club, nobody pays dues, and nobody's excluded from joining. Sandra recognizes that when young children identify themselves as part of a community of readers and writers and are accepted as such, they will build on the literacy knowledge they bring to school. Confidence with print breeds competence.

The literacy club consists of the group of readers and writers with whom a child interacts (Smith, 1985). If children are to understand reading and writing and what these literacy processes are for, they must become members of the literacy club. The only requirement for membership is a mutual acknowledgment of acceptance into a group of people who use reading and writing in meaningful and purposeful ways. In other words, children must perceive of themselves as readers and writers and in turn be perceived by others as readers and writers. The chapter overview suggests the importance of membership in the literacy club. Emergent literacy programs provide children with invitations to join the literacy club by building on and extending their knowledge and awareness of language and literacy.

Emergent Literacy Programs for Beginners

Emergent literacy, as we began to develop it in Chapter 3, is a concept that supports learning to read in a positive home environment where children are in the process of becoming literate from birth. Literacy development begins from the time children hear their first nursery rhymes and stories. The acquisition of reading should be as natural as oral language development, given ideal learning conditions. What happens in the classroom influences children's emerging literacy skills and concepts of reading, as well as their motivation to read. Children need good role models, invitations to learn, and support in their development toward skilled reading and writing, much of which they can get from effective teachers. Beginning instruction, then, should serve to extend literacy development in early childhood.

Three questions underlie instruction and assessment in an emergent literacy program: (1) What does a child already know about print? (2) What reading behaviors and interests does a child already exhibit? and (3) What does a child need to learn? Answers to these questions will demonstrate that beginning instruction for 5- and 6-year-olds is not a period of time in which children progress from nonreading to reading behavior. When planning beginning instructional experiences for 5- and 6-year-olds, a basic principle of emergent literacy should guide your actions: Rather than thinking about getting children ready for reading, consider what must be done to get literacy instruction ready for children.

The notion of **reading readiness** evolved from the belief that readiness is largely the result of maturation to the present-day conception that children benefit from instructional experiences before engaging in reading. Although early proponents of reading readiness contended that children must reach a certain level of physical, mental, and emotional maturity to profit from teaching, there has been a dramatic shift from a maturational perspective to an instructional emphasis.

From the 1930s, readiness has implied that there is a best time to benefit from reading instruction. The idea of a best time often translated into one-dimensional indicators of reading readiness such as a child's mental maturity as reflected by a score on an intelligence test. The importance of mental age, for example, was supported by the views of Morphett and Washburne (1931). For many years, a 6.5 mental age became the benchmark for deciding matters of reading instruction. Even today, there are remnants of the best-time-for-teaching-reading theory; we still award children performance scores on a reading readiness test. But reliance on a single readiness test score, or for that matter mental age, tends to minimize the differences that children bring to reading instruction and negates a developmental view of learning to read.

Reading readiness programs are based on a logical analysis of reading skills grounded in a bottom-up view of the reading process. As a result, most programs generally include activities to develop prerequisite skills such as auditory memory and discrimination and visual memory and discrimination. In addition, children are expected to master the smallest units of written language (recognizing letters and sounds) before progressing to larger units (letter patterns, words, simple sentences). To facilitate mastery, readiness programs are organized around a "scope and sequence," a hierarchy of skills through which children progress. Monitoring a child's skills acquisition through periodic assessment is a major feature of today's readiness programs.

A predominant view of reading readiness has been to treat it as a period of transition extending over several weeks or months. According to Clay (1979b), a transitional view of readiness upholds the notion that children gradually change from nonreaders to beginning readers. At best, such a view pays lip service to a developmental concept of reading. It leads to the unwarranted assumption that children bring little, if anything, to school in the way of knowledge about and experience with print. Most children are bound to have some knowledge of print and book experiences before entering school, as limited as they may seem in some cases.

Teale and Sulzby (1986) contend that reading readiness, as institutionalized by schools, curricula, and publishers of tests and instructional programs, is no longer an appropriate way to conceptualize instruction for beginners. In its place, they suggest emergent literacy as a developmentally appropriate view on which to build literacy curricula, instructional practice, and assessment for beginners.

Table 4.1 compares readiness and emergent literacy along several dimensions.

If beginners are going to make a smooth transition from emergent to fluent literacy, they must feel from the outset that they belong to a classroom community of readers and writers. The challenge of working with beginners lies in scaffolding learning and weaving together experiences that build on children's knowledge of language and their previous interactions with texts. Working with beginners requires knowing about the book experiences they have had, their desire to read, and their awareness of concepts related to print. Because young children come to school with diverse family literacy backgrounds, their acquaintance with texts will vary dramatically. Some will have little or no prior knowledge or

TABLE 4.1

Comparison of Emergent Literacy and Reading Readiness

	Emergent Literacy	Reading Readiness
Theoretical perspective	Children are in the process of becoming literate from birth and are capable of learning what it means to be a user of written language before entering school.	Children must master a set of basic skills before they can learn to read. Learning to read is an outcome of school-based instruction.
Acquisition of literacy skills and strategies	Children learn to use written language and develop as readers and writers through active engagement with their world. Literacy develops in real-life settings in purposeful ways.	Children learn to read by mastering skills arranged and sequenced in a hierarchy according to their level of difficulty.
Relationship of reading to writing	Children progress as readers and writers. Reading and writing (as well as speaking and listening) are interrelated and develop concurrently.	Children learn to read first. The skills of reading must be developed before introducing written composition.
Functional-formal learning	Children learn informally through interactions with and modeling from literate significant others and explorations with written language.	Children learn through formal teaching and monitoring (i.e., periodic assessment) of skills.
Individual development	Children learn to be literate in different ways and at different rates of development.	Children progress as readers by moving through a scope and sequence of skills.

experience with books and little interest in learning to read. Others will have rich experiences and considerable desire to extend what they already know about print. Many will fall somewhere between the two extremes. Invitations into the literacy club build on the instructional implications of literacy learning in early childhood. Bethany's story in the Class Works featured in Box 4.1 illustrates this point. Storybooks and their many uses beckon young children to membership.

BOX 4.1   CLASS WORKS

Bethany's Membership in the Literacy Club: In, Out, and In Again!

Bethany's encounters with reading instruction in kindergarten capture the *disempowerment* that occurs when a young child feels excluded from participation in a literate community (Searcy, 1988). Before entering school, Bethany was an active member of the literacy club. She engaged in much of the literate activity of early readers and writers described in Chapter 3. For example, at 13 months she pointed to a logo in the corner of a place mat at a local fast-food restaurant and read, "Pepsi." By age 2, she was enjoying books and joining in on the reading by supplying words for predictable text. Throughout her early literacy development, Bethany had learned that she did not have to be perfect to belong to the literacy club and that taking risks was part of what it meant to be a user of written language. But when she entered kindergarten, Bethany soon found that she was "into school and out of the literacy club."

Kindergarten was not what Bethany had expected. Although her teacher was warm, caring, and enthusiastic, the *reading readiness program* was contrary to everything she had learned about literacy and what it meant to be a user of written language. For most of the year, Bethany's "reading" consisted of doing worksheets designed to teach letter names and to associate sounds with letters. For example, early in the school year, one worksheet task consisted of drawing lines from "Mr. B with Beautiful Buttons" to pictures whose labels started with the sound of the letter *b*. Whenever she erred on tasks such as these, her mistakes were corrected in red pencil by the teacher. Eventually, the red marks convinced Bethany that she could not read. It wasn't until April of her kindergarten year that Bethany began to regain her confidence and restore her self-concept as a reader. Her class had finally progressed through the readiness worksheets to exercises that involved reading simple sentences, but the key to her return to the literacy club occurred outside of school at the public library. The children's librarian had encouraged Bethany to read a book by reassuring her that she "could do it." Literacy was beginning to make sense again.

Reflective Inquiry

◆ What is the significance of Bethany's story?

◆ How do the actions of teachers help or hinder children's literacy development?

LEARNING LITERACY THROUGH STORYBOOKS

Storybooks unlock the mysteries of reading, rivet children's attention to print, and provide models of writing that build on and extend the young child's concepts of texts and how they work. In Chapter 3 we explored the value of reading storybooks aloud, repeated

◆ Figure 4.1   Storybook Literacy Experiences for Beginners

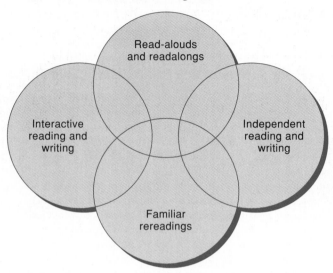

readings of familiar stories, and shared reading experiences around the use of **big books**—enlarged versions of children's storybooks. As Figure 4.1 illustrates, a literature-rich curriculum for young children will offer numerous opportunities to interact with storybooks. Literacy lessons immerse children in **storybook experiences.** These experiences aren't mutually exclusive, but as the illustration in Figure 4.1 suggests, they are interlocking and connected. All are designed to further children's explorations with texts and to develop concepts related to print as well as strategies to construct meaning.

Immersing beginners in storybook literacy experiences, which include read-alouds and readalongs, **interactive reading** and **writing,** rereadings of favorite texts, and independent reading and writing, helps accomplish a variety of instructional goals:

- ◆ To motivate beginners to want to read and write

- ◆ To interest beginners in listening to, reading, and writing stories with emphasis on predicting, sharing, and extending personal meanings

- ◆ To help beginners understand what reading and writing are all about

- ◆ To encourage beginners to respond to stories by drawing, writing, and dramatizing their explorations of texts

- ◆ To invite beginners to construct meaning through the use of picture cues and storybook illustrations

- ◆ To help beginners gain familiarity with "book language" and the meaning of terms that figure in literacy instruction

◆ To teach beginners about directionality, the left-to-right, top-to-bottom orientation of written language

◆ To teach beginners the meaning of *word* and the function of space in establishing boundaries between words

◆ To teach beginners alphabetic principles of written language

◆ To teach beginners to predict words that "must come next" in a sentence

◆ To teach beginners to recognize words that they are interested in learning or that occur frequently in meaningful contexts

These goals are not sequential in the sense that one must be accomplished before another is attempted. In classrooms where storybook experiences are an integral part of the school day, several or more may be accomplished over time in combination or simultaneously. The translation of these goals into classroom activities and experiences lies in having a developmental perspective of beginning reading. Big books, a recent phenomenon in American classrooms, provide a developmentally appropriate context for interactive reading and writing experiences.

Big Books in American Classrooms

Big books are one of the easiest and most effective ways to get beginners involved in the exploration of texts. The use of big books as an instructional resource began in the late 1960s in New Zealand, when teachers began to make their own big books from heavy brown butcher paper. Teacher-made big books retold nursery rhymes, poems, and popular stories such as "The Gingerbread Man." The critical feature common to these big books was that the stories and poems provided beginners with strong rhythms and predictable patterns of language.

The predictability of the plot and language of big books makes them easy to understand and remember. For example, after two or three readings, most 5- and 6-year-olds easily memorize Mem Fox's *Hattie and the Fox* (1987) or Bill Martin Jr.'s *Brown Bear, Brown Bear, What Do You See?* (1983). Big books such as these, with their simple, repetitive refrains, colorful animal illustrations, and cumulative plot endings, allow children to make predictions and participate immediately in shared reading experiences.

New Zealand researchers, spearheaded by the pioneering work of Don Holdaway, observed and documented the influence of big book teaching on children's literacy development and their social interactions in the classroom (Holdaway, 1979). Children were learning to read naturally in the company of other children and the teacher. In the 1970s, authors such as Joy Cowley and June Melser began publishing the first big books in New Zealand for use in classrooms. Cowley's amazingly popular *Mrs. Wishy-Washy* (1987) is used today in classrooms for beginners throughout the world. According to Cowley (1991), the popularity of her big books is in the inherent appeal they have for children: "It is important to me . . . that the big books I write relate directly to the child's world and not to an adult view of what the world is or should be" (p. 19). (See her Viewpoint featured in Box 4.2.) Today's big books not only capture the child's view of the world but also range in content from traditional tales to books of poems to informational books in different content areas.

The popularity of big books in New Zealand coincided with whole language movements throughout English-speaking countries. Big books soon began to appear in classrooms throughout the United States and became associated with whole language teaching. In addition to the pleasure and enjoyment that children get when they participate in shared readings and rereadings of big books, big book formats are versatile in helping to achieve all of the instructional goals for beginners. The chart in Figure 4.2 suggests some of the activities that teachers and children engage in when they use big books.

Interactive Reading and Writing

When the teacher and children engage in interactive reading and writing experiences, they demonstrate that literacy learning is social and collaborative. In interactive reading, they collaborate to construct meaning and enjoy a story. In the process, children develop strategies and concepts related to print. In interactive writing, the teacher and students create a text together. The texts that are created—lists, letters, labels, story retellings, alternative texts of stories that have been shared, and language experience stories—demonstrate some of the important uses of written language and show children what reading is all about.

Interactive reading and writing, as you might surmise, are reciprocal processes. What children read together is the basis for what they will write together; and in turn, what they write together is the basis for what they will read together. And what they read and write together often is the springboard for independent reading and writing.

Interactive Reading. Interactive reading, as the name suggests, encourages children to interact verbally with the story being read, the teacher, and other children. Interactive reading has many of the same features of the shared book experience described in Chapter 3. The difference between the two practices lies in the instructional tone and emphasis of interactive reading. Whereas the primary goal of the shared reading experience is to create an intimate context for reading much like that surrounding the bedtime story, interactive reading events engage students not only in the enjoyment of a story but also in the development of skills and strategies. During the shared book experience, the teacher begins with a straight-through reading of a big book as children listen to the story. Through a series of repeated readings, the literacy event becomes more instructional as the teacher interacts with children to explore reading processes and construct meaning. During interactive reading, by contrast, the teacher poses questions throughout the read-aloud using either a big book or regular-size picture book.

When working with beginners in preschool, kindergarten, and first grade, shared book experiences make good sense. However, as children begin to make the transition into more skillful and strategic reading, primary grade teachers devote considerable time to interactive read-alouds. Figure 4.2 provides an excellent sequence of instructional proce-

BOX 4.2   VIEWPOINT

Joy Cowley on Big Books

Big book reading is a big plus for all children. It puts children in a no-risk situation where they can read with a group at their own skill level. Children who lack confidence in reading will especially benefit from big book reading. Their reading is reinforced by their peers, and they can enjoy the pleasure of stories within a group until they are ready to attempt the stories on their own.

Enthusiasm is the key emotion associated with big book reading. A confident, enthusiastic teacher will readily communicate those feelings to his or her students. Usually I introduce a big book by reading the story a couple of times to the class and inviting discussion. Then the students and I can read the book together. Big books invite student participation, not just in reading but in using a pointer for following along, turning pages, and so on. Children may extend the large group experience by reading to each other in smaller groups, reading individually, dramatizing the text, making recordings complete with sound effects, and writing their own books using a similar theme or pattern.

Mrs. Wishy-washy

by Joy Cowley

Whatever the follow-up or innovation, it is important to remember that reading and writing are activities we do to share ourselves with others. Big books are especially good tools for sharing. It's for that reason, I think, that teachers around the world are having such success in using big books to bring literature to the lives of children.

Source: From "Joy of Big Books," by Joy Cowley, *Instructor,* October 1991, p. 19. Copyright © 1991 by Scholastic, Inc. Reprinted by permission of Scholastic, Inc.

◆ FIGURE 4.2

Big Book Activities Before, During, and After Reading

What the Teacher Does	What the Child Does	Objective
BEFORE READING		
(1) Stimulates discussion about relevant content and concepts in text.	(1) Talks and listens to others talk about relevant content and concepts.	(1) To focus listening and speaking on vocabulary and ideas about to be met in print. To activate background knowledge related to text.
(2) Reads aloud title and author; uses words *title* and *author* and briefly explains what they mean.	(2) Notes what the words on the book cover represent.	(2) To build vocabulary and concepts: title, author, authorship.
(3) Asks children what they think story might be about, based on title, cover. Or, thinks aloud about what s/he thinks this story might be about.	(3) Uses clues from title and cover together with background knowledge to formulate predictions about the story. Or, observes teacher model the above.	(3) To use clues from text and background knowledge to make inferences and formulate predictions.
(4) Shows pleasure and interest in anticipation of the reading.	(4) Observes as teacher models personal interest and eagerness toward the reading.	(4) To build positive attitudes toward books and reading.
DURING READING (TEACHER READS ALOUD)		
(5) Gives lively reading. Displays interest and delight in language and story line.	(5) Observes teacher evoke meaningful language from print.	(5) To understand that print carries meaning.
(6) Tracks print with hand or pointer.	(6) Follows movement of hand or pointer.	(6) To match speech to print. Directionality: left to right.
(7) Thinks aloud about her/his understanding of certain aspects of the story (self-query, making predictions, drawing conclusions, etc.).	(7) Observes as teacher monitors her/his own understandings.	(7) To develop an understanding of the reading process as thinking with text.
(8) Hesitates at predictable parts in the text. Allows children to fill in possible words or phrases.	(8) Fills in likely words for a given slot.	(8) To use semantic and syntactic clues to determine what makes sense.
(9) At appropriate parts in a story, queries children about what might happen next.	(9) Makes predictions about what might happen next in the story.	(9) To use story line to predict possible events and outcomes.

◆ Figure 4.2   Continued

What the Teacher Does	What the Child Does	Objective
AFTER READING		
(10) Guides discussion about key ideas in the text. Helps children relate key concepts.	(10) Participates in discussion of important ideas in the text.	(10) To reflect on the reading: to apply and personalize key ideas in text.
(11) Asks children to recall important or favorite parts. Finds corresponding part of the text (perhaps with help of children) and rereads.	(11) Recalls and describes specific events; parts of text.	(11) To use print to support and confirm discussion.
(12) Guides group rereading of all or specific parts of text for errorless repetition and reinforcement.	(12) Joins in the reading in parts s/he feels confident about.	(12) To develop fluency and confidence through group reading.
(13) Uses cloze activities (flaps to cover words) to involve children in meaningful (contextually plausible) offerings. Discusses response with children.	(13) Fills in possible words for a given slot.	(13) To use semantic and syntactic clues to determine what words fit in a slot and why.
AFTER READING, FOR REPEATED READINGS ONLY		
(14) Focuses children's attention on distinctive features and patterns in the text: repeated words, repeated word beginnings (letters, consonant clusters), punctuation marks, etc. Uses letter names and correct terminology to discuss these features. Extends discussion to developmentally appropriate level.	(14) Notes distinctive features and patterns pointed out by teacher and attempts to find others on her/his own.	(14) To analyze a known text for distinctive features and patterns. To develop an understanding of the elements of decoding within a meaningful context.
(15) Makes books and charts available for independent reading.	(15) Selects books and charts for independent reading and reads them at own pace.	(15) To increase confidence and understanding of the reading process by practicing it independently.

dures to engage children in interactive reading. In addition, Barrentine (1996) provides the following suggestions for planning an interactive read-aloud:

◆ Select high-interest picture books with rich language, well-developed plots and characters, and multiple layers of meaning. Great stories will engage students in numerous opportunities for learning.

◆ Read the book several times to yourself before reading aloud to children. Think about the story's structure (e.g., the setting, the sequence of events leading to plot conflict and resolution), characters, images, illustrations, point of view, themes, and the author's use of language.

◆ Identify instructional goals for the interactive reading, including the reading strategies that might be developed.

◆ Decide on points in the story where you might pause to ask children to make predictions. Also anticipate where you may need to build children's background knowledge so that they will understand concepts with which they may not be familiar. For example, Barrentine describes how a teacher invited her students to make predictions before the reading of *Blueberries for Sal* by Robert McCloskey (1963). The teacher, Mrs. Herbert, displayed the illustrated endpaper of the book and asked the children to make predictions about the setting of the story and the characters.

TEACHER:	Let's preview the pictures here. Who do you think this might be? *(She displays the endpaper and points to Sal's mother, who is in the kitchen pouring blueberries into a canning jar.)*
STUDENT 1:	They're gonna make berry pie!
STUDENT 2:	The mama.
TEACHER:	And who might this be?
STUDENT 3:	The— the— Sal!
TEACHER:	Very good. Do you think they live in the city or the country?
STUDENTS:	*(overlapping comments)* Country. City. They might be both.
TEACHER:	Country? What makes you think they live in the country?
STUDENT:	'Cause there's a lot of trees.
TEACHER:	A lot of trees. OK. Do you see any big, tall buildings and skyscrapers like we've talked about in our social studies book?
STUDENTS:	No.
STUDENT:	They live in the country.
STUDENT:	They live in the forest.
TEACHER:	Here's the title page, *Blueberries for Sal*. This is by Robert McCloskey. He's written some other stories that we have read. Raise your hand if you've heard *Make Way for Ducklings*.

◆ Plan how and when you will ask questions during the interactive reading, but be prepared to relinquish your plans in order to be responsive to children's needs.

Take your lead from children responses, and tailor questions to the dialogue that develops through the interaction.

◆ Plan follow-up activities that help children extend the shared meaning constructed during the interactive reading.

Interactive Writing.   During interactive writing, there are many opportunities for explicit instruction in which teachers demonstrate early writing strategies (Clay, 1985). Following steps associated with the language experience approach, the teacher becomes a scribe for a text dictated by the children. The focus, first and foremost, is always on the composing of the text. The teacher, as well as the children who volunteer, will often read, then reread, the text for emphasis and make additions and changes to clarify meaning. Within this meaningful, collaborative context, opportunities abound to demonstrate early writing strategies such as word-by-word matching, left-to-right directionality, use of space to create boundaries between words, and other print conventions. As children gain experience with the conventions of print, the teacher uses shared writing activities to focus on spelling patterns and word analysis.

Let's take a look at how interactive reading and writing are played out in Stephanie Hawking's first-grade class (Hawking, 1989). Stephanie and the children have been sharing Jack Kent's story *The Fat Cat* (1982). After the third rereading, she and the children decide to write an alternative text to the story, which they titled "The Fat Cat at Big Boy." The inspiration for the alternative story is the Big Boy restaurant, which is located near the school.

The children wondered what would happen if the Fat Cat ever prowled for food at the Big Boy. So their first interactive writing experience involved brainstorming a list of what the Fat Cat would eat at Big Boy. One student, Miranda, suggested that the Fat Cat could eat men. Stephanie invited her to write the word *men* on a list, saying, "You know how to write *ten*. Can you use ten to help you write *men*?" (Hawking, 1989, p. 7). Miranda first practiced on the blackboard and then wrote *men* on a chart titled "Big Boy." The class worked on the chart for several days, and when it was finished, the children taped it to the wall to use as a resource.

Stephanie and the children then began writing the alternative text together. Talk, as you might predict, was crucial to the success of the story. As Stephanie explains, "The talk surrounding shared writing is a rich source of information. . . . As the children discuss what to write and how it should be written, the teacher finds out more about their developing concepts of story and their understanding of the writing process" (Hawking, 1989, p. 7). The class began by talking about how to begin the story. Everyone agreed that it should begin with the words "once upon a time" because it was going to be a "fake" story. Stephanie used this "teachable moment" to underscore the connection the children made between their story and the fairy tale genre. She told them that another name for a particular kind of fake story is a folktale.

As the text began to develop, Stephanie wrote on the chart as children dictated, but she also invited the children to add to the story by volunteering to write parts. Stephanie observed what the children who volunteered knew about the mechanics and conventions of writing and listened to their comments and suggestions as other children added to the text. When she served as a scribe for the children, she was able to focus their attention on the use of quotation marks for portions of the text that contained dialogue. As the class finished each page of the chart, the children would tape it to the wall so that they could refer to it whenever necessary to check on continuity of story line. At other times, they would search for the spelling of a word they knew had already been written on a previous page.

The interactive writing of "The Fat Cat at Big Boy" was eventually made into a class big book. The children illustrated the story with drawings, decided on the sequencing of pages, and assembled the entire big book text, rereading each page several times. Stephanie served as proofreader for the final copy—the public copy—of the big book by changing children's invented spellings to conventional forms. The big book's construction followed guidelines similar to the Best Practice guidelines in Box 4.3.

The children in Stephanie's class were so proud of the big book they had created that they decided to dedicate it "To All the Cats in the Neighborhood."

Alternative texts such as "The Fat Cat at Big Boy" are popular forms of interactive writing in Stephanie's class. Some of the children were so excited about the project that they wanted to write Fat Cat stories on their own. And they did. What began as interactive reading of a popular storybook for young children turned into independent reading and writing.

Learning About the Relationships Between Speech and Print

Children must be able to figure out what spoken language and written language have in common. Without learning the relationship between speech and print, the beginner will never make sense of reading or achieve independence in it. Earlier we suggested that reading often to children, repeating favorite bedtime stories, and providing opportunities to draw, scribble, and interact with print in their immediate environment are some of the ways that children naturally learn to make sense out of reading and its uses. Nevertheless, many 5-year-olds enter school with only vague notions of the purpose and nature of reading. They are not yet aware that what is said can be written, that written language is made up of words and sentences, or that reading involves directionality, attending to the spacing between words, punctuation cues, and other conventions of print. There are several ways of going about this important instructional task.

Understanding the Uses of Written Language

From the beginning of their school experience, children must learn that the value of reading or writing lies in its uses as a tool for communicating, understanding, and enjoying. A 5-year-old or a 75-year-old should engage in reading and writing for real reasons and in real situations. Effective teachers make their own opportunities and should consider teaching about the uses of written language when any interesting or natural occasion arises in the classroom.

Publishing Big Books in the Classroom

Big book publishing is an excellent collaborative group writing activity. Because children love big books, they will enjoy their own published stories. The models and directions below will involve children in creating their own big books for classroom use.

MODELS

Use commercially published big books as models for the types that children will make. Consider these possibilities:

- Poem books

- Alternative books (based on stories read in class)

- Alphabet and number books

- Reaction books (the scariest thing I ever saw)

- Riddle and rhyme books

- Informational books (based on theme studies)

- Innovations on a text (imitative stories based on the predictable language patterns of books read in class)

DIRECTIONS FOR MAKING BIG BOOKS

Mural Style

- Fold even-size pages of butcher paper in a back-and-forth manner (each page should be 12 inches wide). Fold one page per child, plus one each for the cover and the title page. If you plan to display sculpturally (see "Display Options"), be sure to back each page with oaktag or cardboard.

- Children can draw and color directly onto their assigned pages or glue on illustrations and text. This kind of big book does not easily lend itself to lamination.

Construction Paper Style

- Have students draw and write directly onto 12-by-18-inch white construction paper.

- After each page is decorated, laminate or cover with contact paper.

- Put pages in sequence. Turn the first two pages face down, lay on a flat surface, and bind with masking or colored craft tape. Continue taping pages to the already bound ones, in right-to-left fashion. Be sure to fold the hinged pages back and forth as you finish each one to keep the book flexible.

BOX 4.3 CONTINUED

Variations

◆ Create a book that never stops by continuing the story line and illustrations right around the back of the last page, ending up on the reverse of the title page.

◆ Make an upside-down topsy-turvy book by turning the book over and using the reverse side in regular left-to-right fashion. This can be done with two separate stories or with two made-up versions of a favorite fairy tale.

◆ Use real objects as illustrations if they complement the story. Some you might try include photos, stickers, wrappers, and yarn. Staple, glue, or stitch in place before laminating. There will be a tiny bulge on any page you decorate this way.

◆ Use colorful sentence strips to fit the pages above or below the illustrations. Have the children write text onto the strips.

Display Options

◆ Hang with clothespins from an overhead wire.

◆ Use a clamp to hold the book's pages while you read aloud (if the clamp has holes, hang the book from a hook).

◆ Display sculpturally on the floor or around a table.

◆ Hang across a bulletin board.

Source: From "Do-It-Yourself Big Books," by Ethel Huttar, *Instructor,* October 1991, p. 21. Copyright © 1991 by Scholastic, Inc. Reprinted by permission of Scholastic, Inc.

ITEM: The teacher and children are gathered around the guinea pig cage discussing their new pet. The teacher is explaining the food guinea pigs eat and is showing the children the food they will be feeding the pet. One of the children remembers that the class goldfish died because too much food was put in the bowl. The teacher suggests that the class make a sign to put on the package telling the right amount of food and a chart to put near the cage to be checked on the day he is fed. She discusses the reasons these written records will help. (Taylor & Vawter, 1978, p. 942)

Situations such as the guinea pig scenario evolve naturally in the classroom. Nevertheless, seizing the opportunity to help children recognize the value of reading and writing requires a certain amount of awareness and commitment. For example, Taylor and Vawter (1978) illustrate how two teachers approach an everyday event differently. As children prepare for a field trip to a farm, one kindergarten teacher passes out name tags routinely and without explanation. Another teacher, however, poses a problem to be solved by the children: "If the farmer wants to ask one of us a question, how can we help him know our names?" Through give-and-take discussion, the children offer solutions that range from "tell him" to "I don't know" to "wear our names." As the discussion progresses, the teacher passes out the name tags and suggests that names are written so that someone can read them and that writing a name helps identify someone.

In Chapter 1 we outlined the **uses of oral language.** These language functions can and should be adapted to print at the beginning of instruction. Not only will children become aware of the purposes of written language, but many of the activities outlined here build word awareness. Therefore, beginners should be introduced to some of the more obvious uses of print.

In general, the classroom should reflect a living example of written language put to purposeful ends. The classroom environment should be filled with print to suit specific instructional goals. Print should be evident everywhere in the form of labels for classroom objects, simple messages, rules, directions, and locations where a specific activity takes place, such as a story-reading area or an art center. Specifically, consider these uses of written language.

Perpetuating Uses.   Show children how to bridge the gap between time and space through print, or *perpetuate*. To do this, *keep records and charts of a daily activity.* For example, Durkin (1980) recommends developing a weekly weather chart with the days of the week at the top and slots for inserting descriptive cards under each day. The children can then use words to describe the day's weather.

Monday	Tuesday	Wednesday	Thursday	Friday
awful	foggy	sunny	———	———
rainy	cloudy	clear	———	———
sticky	dark	dry	———	———

Post the names of room helpers for each week. Each morning, make a point of going to the chart and having the children identify who will help the teacher for the day.

Vote or poll children on various classroom events or activities and tally the results. For example, ask children to suggest names for the new pet rabbit. List the names, limiting the number to three or four possible choices, and tally the results for the children to see.

Thumper (6)

Whitey (3)

Long Ears (11)

Use children as messengers to deliver notes to other teachers or to parents. Explain the purpose of the note and why it was written. Or *display notes from the principal* congratulating children for work well done. Also post thank-you notes, letters, the school lunch menu for each day, and many other forms of communication.

Finally, *keep a classroom scrapbook,* beginning from the first day of school and including important events throughout the year. For example, use instant photographs or magazine pictures, and record the importance of each event.

Regulatory, Authoritative-Contractual Uses. Show children how print can be used to control and direct behavior and to establish rules and agreements. For example, *list classroom rules and use print to give directions such as lining up for the bus or going to the library. Establish official written contracts with children for various classroom activities* (e.g., clean-up after art activities, taking milk count for the week).

═══ OFFICIAL CONTRACT ═══

_____ *hereby agrees to* _____
      (name)   *(activity)*

for _____
        (date)

To use print to give directions, a teacher can *make recipe charts for cooking projects* that may include pictures and words explaining what to do. Pictures can depict *ingredients* such as flour, sugar, or eggs (cut from a magazine advertisement) or *processes* (e.g., a sketch of eggs being broken). In addition, children can *follow directions with clue cards that use pictures and simple words* or they can *play scavenger hunt using simple messages to direct the hunt.*

Instrumental Uses. Children should learn that print can be used to express personal needs. Teachers and children can *list materials needed to participate in various activities:*

ART	MUSIC	BUILDING
clay	bells	wood
scissors	shakers	glue
paint	piano	cardboard
brushes	record player	blocks

PLANTING	FIELD TRIP	SLEEPOVER
seeds	lunch	toothbrush
water	boots	PJ's
pots	warm clothes	pillow
tools	25¢	teddy bear

The teacher can *write gift lists or birthday wishes dictated by the children. Signs can be used to invite children to participate in various activities:*

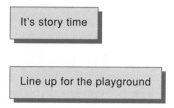

It's story time

Line up for the playground

Diversion Uses.   Demonstrate the value of print as a tool for enjoyment, or *diversion. Read aloud to children on a daily basis.* Also consider storytelling. (We will explain a variety of reading-aloud and storytelling procedures and activities in Chapters 6 and 10.) In particular, introduce children to humorous and nonsensical literature. Consider such classics as Dr. Seuss's *Cat in the Hat* (1957), Mayer's *Billygoofang* (1968), Pincus's *Tell Me a Mitzi* (1970), and Krauss's *Backward Day* (1950). Read to children those that you especially enjoy.

Tell puns, jokes, riddles, brain teasers, and the like. For example, ask children, "What's white and can be poured in a glass?" and record the responses. Or consider posting a riddle and joke on a section of the bulletin board, with the answer or punch line written on the inside flap.

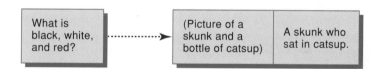

What is black, white, and red?   (Picture of a skunk and a bottle of catsup)   A skunk who sat in catsup.

Use simple language patterns to introduce children to rhythms of language. Later in the year, use patterned stories and poems to model language patterns in writing. These patterned stories are highly predictable, enjoyable, and repetitious enough that children are naturally attracted to them. Bill Martin's *Instant Readers* or Dr. Seuss's materials develop children's sensitivity to hearing language. The following lines by Dr. Seuss (1960) provide an example:

> One fish, two fish.
> Red fish, blue fish.
>
> This one has a little star.
> This one has a little car.

As the year progressed in one kindergarten class, children were creating their own writing by dictating familiar patterns to the teacher.

One bear, two bear.
White bear, brown bear.

This one has a big red nose.
This one has big fat toes.

Personal Uses. Children need to learn that written language can be used to express individuality, pride, and awareness of self—a *personal* use of language. *Develop a "this is me" book for each child.* The book might be bound and contain the child's drawings and descriptions of self and family. The first page might begin. "This is me," and include a self-portrait drawn by the child. Other pages may include "This is my family." "This is my pet." "My favorite game is _____." "My favorite book is _____." "I like _____." "I want to be _____." "My best friend is _____."

In a similar vein, have the students make "me" cards that tell the names of pets, favorite toys, books, colors, television programs, or movies. Names of places of interest, places recently visited, or exciting places to explore in the community can also be included.

As children develop letter and sound awareness, have them suggest self-descriptive words for each letter in their names: For example, John might choose *Jolly, open, happy, nice.* Ask children for "best" words and write them on the blackboard. Then read them to other members of the class. Write words that name special people, such as family members or friends. Then attach a photograph of the person to accompany the name.

Connecting Speech and Print Through Language Experience

There is no more appropriate way to help children understand what reading is all about than to show them how language is transcribed into print. A **language experience** story is just what it implies—an account that is told aloud by a child and printed by another person. In the beginning of instruction, there are numerous ways to involve children in producing experience stories. For example, many of the suggestions for teaching about the uses of written language can serve to stimulate the child's dictation or, for that matter, a group-dictated story. Not only does an experience story vividly show the relationship between speech and print, but it also introduces children to the thrill of personal authorship.

This doesn't mean that children should not engage in independent writing experiences. However, when language-experience stories are coupled with regular writing time, children make great strides in learning about written language. Some argue that language-experience activities are superfluous in light of the recent emphasis on writing process. (See Chapter 9 for an extended discussion.) We disagree. From a learning-to-read perspective, young people will benefit greatly from *both* language experience and writing.

The value of language experience lies in the physical ease by which text is produced *to achieve reading instructional goals.* When a child dictates, the physical burden of writing is removed. This often results in more of a child's ideas being put in print than would otherwise be possible in beginning situations. In Chapter 9, we advocate regular, ongoing writing activity from the first day that children enter school. Dictated language-experience stories should be phased out as children's independent writing fluency increases.

When children have opportunities to converse naturally and spontaneously, their language is likely to be colorful and expressive, to have an almost poetic quality. For example, the following language-experience story was based on a conversation among a group of 5-year-olds as they experienced the visit of a pet mouse. It was recorded verbatim by Mrs. Ruttan, their kindergarten teacher.

> This mouse is soft.
> Soft as a baby sister?
> Soft as a little tiny ball?
> She's so small somebody could step on her.
>
> I'm afraid to hold her.
> I'll touch her and pet her,
> But I'm afraid to hold her.
> Does her tail tickle?
> Does it really?
> Are you scared of a mouse?
> No. But they tickle, you know.
>
> Feels like a pillow in my hand.
> Feels like I could sleep on her.
> Feels like a feather.
>
> I just love mouses.
> I wish we had our very own mouse.
> I held her for just a minute.
> Her claws tickled me.
> She was soft though.
> I told you I liked mouses.

Study another language-experience story based on a conversation a group of children had about a new baby guinea pig in Mrs. Ruttan's class.

> We have a baby guinea pig.
> Her name is Nothing.
> She's not much of anything at all.
> She doesn't even weigh a pound.
>
> She wants to hide from us.
> Maybe she's scared.
> Why should she be scared?
> This is the first time she saw us.
> I think she's scared of us.
>
> Maybe she's just not used to us.
> Maybe she's just playing hide-and-go-seek.
> Maybe she's got to take lessons about knowing about people.

Much can be learned about what young children think and know and how they feel through language-experience-based instruction. An emergent literacy curriculum becomes more relevant, meaningful, and appropriate when it is based on children's own language, existing knowledge, and interests.

Steps to Follow in Producing Language-Experience Stories.   A child can dictate a complete story, or several children can collaborate on an account by contributing individual sentences. In either case, the first step is to provide a stimulus (e.g., a classroom guinea pig, pictures, concrete objects, an actual experience a child has had) that will lead to dictation. Whatever the stimulus, it should be unusual and interesting enough for children to want to talk about it and to remember it two or three days later when the dictation is reread.

As children dictate, it's important to keep their spoken language intact. Therefore, write down exactly what is said regardless of grammatical errors and incomplete sentences. By capturing language just as it is spoken, the teacher preserves its integrity and ensures the child's total familiarity with the print to be read.

Once the story is written down, the teacher should read it aloud several times, carefully but steadily moving left to right, top to bottom, and pointing to each word or line as it is read and then sweeping to the next line. After that, the account should be read in unison with the teacher continuing to model left-to-right, top-to-bottom orientation to print.

A dictated story need not be long. It can represent free-flowing language or controlled responses elicited by guiding questions. Suppose students are conversing about their summer activities. The teacher might say, "Let's tell each other what we did on our summer vacations." Jim begins, "I went fishing for the first time." As he says this, Mrs. Phillips, the kindergarten teacher, writes this verbatim on an "experience chart" (a large sheet of newsprint). The other children contribute to the story, with Mrs. Phillips writing out each contribution, beginning with the child's first name. The account was dictated as follows:

Jim said, "I went fishing for the first time."

Dory said, "We went to my grandma and grandpa's in Florida."

Tony said, "I didn't do nothing but swim."

Sheila said, "My family and me fished too."

Michele said, "I went to Sea World."

The Value of Language Experience.   Examine what can be accomplished when young children engage in the writing of language-experience stories (Durkin, 1980):

◆ It can motivate children to want to read.

◆ It personalizes instruction.

◆ It demonstrates the connection between spoken and written language.

- It demonstrates the left-to-right, top-to-bottom orientation of written English.

- It demonstrates that the end of the line does not always mean the end of a thought.

- It demonstrates the value of written language for preserving information, ideas, and feelings.

- It teaches the meaning of *word* and the function of space in establishing word boundaries.

- It teaches the function of capitalization and punctuation.

In Mrs. Phillips's case, the story was read three times as the children watched her move left to right, top to bottom. Next, they read the story aloud two more times as she continued to model left-to-right orientation. She then had each child read his or her contribution, directing the children to "read it the way you said it." As a child read, she moved her hand along the bottom of each line, coordinating with the child's voice and reading in unison with each child.

Mrs. Phillips wanted to build confidence among her readers as she unobtrusively provided them with valuable learning opportunities. In addition to a "reading experience," she also spent time engaging the children in building the concept of *word*. First, she read the entire story in a natural speaking voice, pointing to each word as it was being read. By suggesting to the children that they read their individualized contributions, she reinforced word understanding. Mrs. Phillips also asked the children questions such as "Which word appears the most?" and discussed how space separates one word from another. Finally, Mrs. Phillips asked the children to draw an illustration for the sentence or part that each contributed to the account. These illustrations were pasted around the chart as they were completed, and the chart was posted on a bulletin board for other class members to read.

LEARNING ABOUT FEATURES OF WRITTEN LANGUAGE

Children's understanding of the relationship between speech and print is a vital first step in learning to read. They become aware of what reading is all about by recognizing the functionality of reading—that the purpose of reading, in its broadest sense, is to communicate ideas. A second step, or stage, is to become aware of the technical features of reading (Downing, 1979). These technical features (printed letters, words, sentences, syllables, sounds, punctuation marks, etc.) make up children's "technical vocabulary" for reading, or, according to Reid (1966), the language available to children "to talk and think about the activity of reading itself" (p. 57). To understand the technical features of reading, children must develop **linguistic awareness.**

Linguistic Awareness

Children of 5 and 6 may not be aware that words are language units. Spoken language, after all, is a steady stream of sounds that flow one into the other. Words and other print conventions (e.g., punctuation marks) were created to better represent spoken language in print and thus facilitate the reading of written language. For the 5-year-old, the six-word written message *Did you visit the fire station?* sounds like one big word—*Didjavisitthe-firestation?* Even more difficult concepts for young children to learn are that spoken words are made up of smaller sounds (phonemes), that written words are made up of letters, and that in a written word, there is a close approximation between letters and sounds.

If children are to succeed in reading, they must acquire linguistic awareness and understand the language of reading instruction. They must learn the technical terms and labels that are needed to talk and think about reading and to carry out instructional tasks. What, for example, is the child's concept of "reading"? Of a "word"? Of a "sound"? Does the child confuse "writing" with "drawing" and "letter" with "number" when given a set of directions? Without an awareness of these terms, cognitive confusion in the classroom mounts quickly for the child (Downing, 1979). The teacher's job is to make explicit what each child knows implicitly about written language.

Some children show consistent interest in reading books on their own.

The technical features of written language are learned gradually by children and are best taught through real reading and readinglike activities and through discussions designed to build concepts and to untangle the confusion that children may have. Within the context of shared-book experiences, language-experience stories, and writing activities, children will develop linguistic sophistication with the technical features of print. These vehicles for instruction not only provide teachers with diagnostic information about children's print awareness but also form the basis for explicit instruction and discussion.

Agnew (1982) shows how to use language-experience stories to assess young children's emerging print awareness. The various procedures and tasks she proposed can easily be adapted to big book and language-experience stories.

PROCEDURES

1. Obtain a short story dictated by the child.

2. Print three or four nouns or verbs from the story on index cards.

3. Print two sentences from the story on separate pieces of paper.

4. Have available a supply of separate letters made from wood, felt, cardboard, or other materials.

5. Ask the child to complete any or all of the tasks outlined below. Record responses and impressions on the evaluation form.

6. Results should be viewed as tentative hypotheses about the child's print awareness. You'll want to validate results through classroom observation.

TASKS

1. Ask the child to point to any word on the chart story, then to "cup" his or her hands around or circle the word. (The child does not have to say the word but only show that he or she knows where the word begins and ends.) Ask the child to repeat the task with three or four other words.

2. Ask the child to match an individual word card with the same word in the story. (The child does not have to say the word; he or she simply needs to make a visual match.) If the word occurs more than once in the story, ask the child to locate the word in another place in the story. Repeat the task with several other word cards.

3. Ask the child to match a sentence with its counterpart from the story. (The child does not have to read the sentence.) Repeat the task with the other sentence.

4. Show the child an individual word card and provide him or her with the individual letters necessary to spell the word. Ask the child to build the word he or she sees on the card, using the separate letters. Ask the child for the names of the letters he or she is using. Probe the child about his or her understanding of the difference between letters and words. Repeat the exercise with two or three other word cards.

5. Ask the child to point to any letters he or she can name in the story. (Note whether the child points to letters rather than words.)

The Concepts About Print Test

As part of a research study to investigate young children's acquisition of concepts about print, Marie Clay (1979a) developed the Concepts About Print Test. She examined not only what knowledge of print children possessed but also how their understanding of print changed. The underlying question that guided the study asked, "To what degree do young children possess reading-related concepts and linguistic abilities considered to be essential in learning to read?"

The Concepts About Print Test is individually administered to a child within the context of an interview. The examiner asks the child if he or she will help in the reading of a story. For example, if the test were being used by a teacher to acquire diagnostic information, particularly for children experiencing difficulty in a beginning program, the teacher might tell the child, "I'm going to read you a story, but I want you to help me." A child's book, *Sand*, is then introduced to the child to begin the assessment interview. During the interview, which usually takes 15 to 25 minutes to complete, up to 24 questions may be asked to evaluate concepts about print such as directionality and the differences between word and letters.

In addition to *Sand*, Clay (1979c) developed a second child's book, *Stones*, also to be used to assess concepts of print. Full instructions for the administration of the Concepts About Print Test may be found in Clay's book *The Early Detection of Reading Difficulties* (1985). The types of reading-related and linguistic concepts tapped by Clay's assessment tool are examined in Figure 4.3.

Observing Children's Emerging Literacy Accomplishments

Teachers can use **observation** to assess children's emerging literacy accomplishments. A wealth of information can be garnered from daily classroom interactions. Many of the instructional activities suggested in this book will reveal important information to help you make instructional decisions. For example, as you interact with children, ask yourself these questions (McDonnell & Osburn, 1978):

1. *Do children attend to the visual aspects of print?* If I am reading a story, can the child tell me where to start and where to go next? Is the child able to point to words as I read them, thereby demonstrating knowledge of directional patterns of print? Does the child understand the concepts of words and letters? Can he or she circle a word and letter in the book? To eliminate the good guesser, this ability should be demonstrated several times.

2. *Do children use their intuitive knowledge of language?* Can the child look at a picture book and invent a story to go with the pictures? Does the invented story, when the teacher begins to write it down, indicate the child is using a more formalized language that approximates the language used in books (i.e., booktalk) rather than an informal conversational style? Does the child recognize that the print and the pictures are related? Can the child "read the words" of a memorized text such as a nursery rhyme,

◆ Figure 4.3

Reading-Related and Linguistic Concepts Assessed in the Concepts About Print Test
by Marie Clay

Print Concept	Child's Task
1. Front of book	Identifies the front of the book
2. Difference between a picture and a page of print	Identifies a page of text (and not the picture on the opposite page) as the place to begin reading
3. Left-to-right directionality	Identifies the direction of reading as a left-to-right process
4. Return sweep	Identifies the return sweep as the appropriate reading behavior at the end of a line
5. Word pointing	Points out words as a teacher reads a line of print slowly
6. Beginning and end	Identifies the first and last parts of a story, page, line, or word
7. Bottom of a picture	Identifies the bottom of a picture that is inverted (upside down) on a page
8. Inverted page of print	Identifies the appropriate place to begin, left-to-right direction, and return sweep
9. Line order	Identifies line sequence as the correct answer when asked, "What's wrong with this?" (The teacher reads a printed sentence in which the line sequence is jumbled.) *Example:* and began to swim. I jumped into the water
10. Left page begins a text	Identifies the left page as place to begin reading when two pages of text are side by side
11. Word order	Identifies word order as the correct answer when asked, "What's wrong with this?" (The teacher reads a printed sentence in which the word order is distorted.) *Example:* I looked and looked I but could not find the cat.
12. Letter order	Identifies that the letters in simple words are not sequenced properly when the teacher reads, as if correct, a text in which the letters of the words are out of order *Example:* The dgo chased teh cat thsi way and thta way. The cta ran pu a tree.

even though the spoken words are not completely accurate matches for the print? Is this recall stimulated or changed by the pictures?

3. *Are children beginning to show signs of integrating visual and language cues?* Are they beginning to read single sentences word by word, pointing to each word with a finger while reading? Can the child use all the cues available to a reader: the predictability of language, word order, a beginning sound, and an appropriateness to context while reading? Does he or she stop and correct, without prompting, when a visual-vocal mismatch occurs?

4. *Does the child expect meaning from print?* Does he or she demonstrate that a message is expected by relating a sensible story?

You can also adapt Clay's Concepts About Print assessment to observe young children's emerging literacy concepts. Gray-Schlegel and King (1998), for example, developed a set of questions based on Clay's work to improve preservice teachers' understanding of beginners' emerging print-related concepts. The Emergent Literacy Observation (see the Best Practice featured in Box 4.4) allows teachers to use storybooks as an assessment tool to interview and observe a child's concepts about print. The questions for the Emergent Literacy Observation can be adapted to any picture book for beginners. Use the questions to think about why a child responded to each question in the manner that he or she did. Many of the preservice teachers in Gray-Schlegel and King's classes believed that their views on young children and emergent literacy changed as a result of using the Emergent Literacy Observation.

LEARNING ABOUT LETTERS AND SOUNDS

Language-experience stories help children discover that the string of sounds in spoken language can be broken down into units of print made up of words and sentences. But children must also learn that a word can be separated into sounds and that the segmented or separated sounds can be represented by letters. Such learning involves the beginnings of *phonics*, a topic discussed in depth in Chapter 5. The smallest sound unit that is identifiable in spoken language is known as a *phone*. Although phones describe all the possible separate speech sounds in language, they are not necessarily represented by the letters of the alphabet. *Phonemes* are the minimal sound units that can be represented in written language. The *alphabetic principle* suggests that letters in the alphabet map to phonemes. Hence the term *phonics* is used to refer to the child's identification of words by their sounds. This process involves the association of speech sounds with letters. In the beginning of reading instruction, key questions that need to be asked are "Is the child able to hear sounds in a word?" and "Is the child able to recognize letters as representing units of sound?"

One of the first indications that children can analyze speech sounds and use knowledge about letters is when they invent their own spellings during writing. As discussed in Chapter 3, invented spellings are a sure sign that children are beginning to be conscious of sounds in words.

BOX 4.4   BEST PRACTICE

Emergent Literacy Observation Questions

Use the interview questions to observe a young child demonstrate knowledge of print. Consider tape-recording the interview. Reflect on the child's response to each question. What are the child's literacy accomplishments? What does the child need to learn?

EMERGENT LITERACY OBSERVATION QUESTIONS

1. Holding the book by its spine and letting it hang downward, hand it to the child and ask: *Show me the front of the book. Turn to the page where I should start reading.*

2. Once you've turned to the first page of the story, ask: *Where should I begin to read? Please show me with your finger. And then which way should I go? Show me what I should read when I come to the end of the line.* (Make sure you ask this question on a page with more than one line of print.)

3. Read the next few pages aloud and ask no questions. Note the child's attentiveness and interest.

4. Turn the page and ask (there must be an accompanying picture): *What do you think this page will be about?*

5. Read another page or two. Then ask: *Can you show me a word? Can you show me another word?*

6. Frame a line of print with your fingers and ask: *How many words are between my fingers?*

7. As you are reading another page, leave out a word in one of the sentences. Be sure to choose a sentence that provides lots of clues for the missing word. Ask: *What do you think is the missing word?* (You might want to do this a second time with a different sentence to make sure of the results.)

8. Finish reading the story. Note any spontaneous remarks the child might say at the end of or anywhere during the story.

9. After the story is read, ask: *What would be a good title (name) for this story?* (Important: Don't tell the child the book's title at the beginning of this exercise!)

10. Ask: *What would be a good title (name) for this story?* (Important: Don't tell the child the book's title at the beginning of this exercise!)

11. General observations: *Did the child appear eager to read with you? Was his/her interest sustained throughout the story? Did he/she make comments about the story as it was being read? Did he/she ask questions, comment on the illustrations, make predictions, etc.?*

Source: From "Introducing Concepts About Print to the Preservice Teacher: A Hands-On Experience," by M. A. Gray-Schlegel and Y. King, *California Reader*, Fall 1998, p. 18. Reprinted with permission of the authors.

TABLE 4.2

Spellings by Three Kindergartners

Word	Monica's Spelling	Tesscha's Spelling	James's Spelling
monster	monstr	mtr	aml
united	unintid	nnt	em3321
dressing	dresing	jrasm	8emaaps
bottom	bodm	bodm	19nhm
hiked	hikt	hot	sanh
human	humin	hmn	menena

Table 4.2 records invented spellings from several samples of writing from three kindergartners, Monica, Tesscha, and James. Their spellings reflect varying levels of sophistication in hearing sounds in words and in corresponding letters to those sounds. Gentry and Henderson (1980) contend that Monica demonstrates the most **phonemic awareness** and James the least. A perusal of Monica's list of words indicates that she has learned to distinguish sounds in sequence and can correspond letters directly to the surface sounds that she hears. Tesscha has also developed an awareness of sounds and letters, though not to the same extent as Monica. James is the least ready of the three to benefit from letter-sound instruction. For James (and other 5- and 6-year-old children at a similar level of development), analyzing sounds in words and attaching letters to those sounds is beyond present conceptual reach. Making initial reading tasks too abstract or removed from what James already knows about print will not help him progress in reading.

Children can easily become confused when taught to identify sounds in words or correspond letters to sounds if they have not yet developed a concept of what a word is. Likewise, the level of abstraction in recognizing a word is too difficult for children if they have yet to make any global connection that speech is related to print. This doesn't mean that program goals for learning about letters and sounds are not worthwhile. However, learning letter-sound relationships must be put into perspective and taught to beginners in meaningful contexts and as the need or opportunity arises.

Recognizing Letters

Letter recognition has been a well-established predictor of first-grade success in reading (Durrell, 1958). However, studies by Ohnmacht (1969) and Samuels (1972) show that teaching children to master the recognition of letters does not necessarily help them become better readers by the end of the first grade. Therefore, teachers of beginning reading should not assume that the relationship between letter naming and reading success is *causal.* The ability to recognize letters and to succeed in reading probably results from a more common underlying ability. Venezky (1978) contends that letter recognition scores on a reading readiness test can be interpreted as a sign of general intelligence or positive home experiences and a child's early exposure to print.

No doubt today's 5-year-old brings more letter knowledge to beginning reading instruction than the 5-year-old of a half-century ago. Television plays a big part in this phenomenon. Children's programs such as *Sesame Street* are largely responsible for increasing children's letter awareness.

Kindergarten and first-grade teachers should capitalize on children's knowledge of letters in a variety of ways. Plan instruction in letter recognition around daily classroom routines and activities. Also help children discriminate small but significant differences among letters, not necessarily in isolated activity, but in meaningful written language contexts. Traditionally, visual perception tasks have involved letter identification and discrimination. While these tasks are more justifiable than discrimination activities involving geometric shapes, the teacher should move quickly to letter recognition and discrimination within words and sentences. Consider the following instructional activities:

◆ *Discuss letters in the context of a language-experience story or key words that children recognize instantly because they are personal and meaningful.* (See Chapter 5 for a discussion of key word instruction.) For example, ask children to find at least one other child in the room whose first name begins with the same letter. If a child can't find a match, ask the class to brainstorm some names that begin with the same letter as the child's name. Write the names on the board for discussion and analysis.

◆ *Use alphabet books.* Every kindergarten and first-grade class should have a collection of alphabet books. Ask children to find the page that a certain letter is on. Compare and contrast the illustrations of the letter in the different books. The children can illustrate their own rendition of the letter, and over time the class can develop its own alphabet book.

◆ *Target a letter for discussion.* Have children search for the letter on labels of cans and other commercial products (e.g., Special K), in magazines, newspapers, and other sources of print. Children can make a letter collage by cutting the letters they find and arranging and pasting them onto a big letter poster that the teacher has made from construction paper.

◆ *Tie letter recognition to writing.* Begin with each child's name. Encourage children to write their names by tracing copies of the letters or writing independently. Ask children to count the number of letters in their names, to examine their names for repeating letters, and so on.

◆ *Create letters through art activities.* Art plays a very important part in the child's school experience, by giving children the opportunity to learn that there are many ways to express their thoughts, feelings, and points of view. Art also heightens children's awareness of their physical environment, involving them through the manipulation of different materials and the development of visual and sensory capacities. For this reason, one small but significant form of expression might be to create letters through drawing, finger painting, sculpting, and making collages such as the letter poster previously described.

Learning single alphabet letters contributes greatly to learning to read, although it is not sufficient by itself. Often some teachers may be tempted to have children memorize single alphabet letters through the use of *flash cards*. Schickedanz (1998), however, recommends avoiding flash cards to teach young children letter naming and recognition because the practice is devoid of a meaningful context. As she puts it:

> In meaningful activities, children are able to see and appreciate a connection between what they are learning and some application of it—some reason for its importance or usefulness. If children are exposed to letters and their names through the use of flashcards . . . the purpose of alphabet letters is not obvious. But if children are exposed to letters and letter names in looking at their own names, classroom signs, or titles of storybooks, the purpose of letters is obvious. (p. 23)

To illustrate her point, Schickedanz provides several best practice instructional scenarios for teaching alphabet letter naming and recognition. Study these Best Practice scenarios featured in Box 4.5.

Developing Phonemic Awareness

One of the concepts related to print that beginners must become aware of is that a word is made up of a series of sounds. Yopp (1992) explains that young children typically lack phonemic awareness, the understanding that speech is composed of a series of individual sounds: "Cat . . . is simply a cat, a furry animal that purrs. Young children are unaware that the spoken utterance *cat* is a word that is made up of a series of sounds, or phonemes, /k/, /a/, and /t/ . . ." (p. 696). The lack of phonemic awareness contributes to children's inability to identify unknown words. If beginners are to benefit from phonics instruction, they must first develop an ability to manipulate sounds in words.

Based on their research analysis, the authors of the International Reading Association's position statement, *Phonemic Awareness and the Teaching of Reading*, emphasize the importance of phonemic awareness in learning to read and spell (Cunningham, Cunningham, Hoffman, & Yopp, 1998). Research on early reading acquisition clearly demonstrates that phonemic awareness is a powerful predictor of young children's later reading development (Juel, 1988). So consistent are the research findings on the relationship between phonemic awareness and learning to read that Stanovich (1994) concludes that phonemic awareness tasks "are the best predictors of the ease of early reading acquisition—better than anything else that we know of, including IQ" (p. 284).

Why is phonemic awareness such an important ability in learning to read and spell? Because the orthographic system of the English language is based on the alphabetic

BOX 4.5 BEST PRACTICE

Instructional Scenarios for Teaching Alphabet Letters

1. Building a model of a trolley station in the block area, a child asks a teacher how to spell the words *Outbound Green Line*. The teacher dictates *O* and *U*, but vocalizes the *T* and *B* phonemes, leaving the letter selection to the child. Soon, the child asks the teacher to take over the writing, explaining, "It's too much." But the child remains involved, dictating *G, R, E*, and *N*, for *green* and *L, I*, and *N*, for *line*, as the teacher sounds out the words and writes the letters. As the teacher forms *G*, she says, "A line right here makes this letter *G*, not *C*."

2. When Samantha writes her name on the picture she has drawn, she asks if her *S* looks how "it is supposed to." The teacher explains that it is backward. The teacher writes a correctly oriented *S* on another piece of paper, as Samantha watches. Soon, Samantha writes her name again. But despite having studied the teacher's *S* before starting, she writes her *S* backward once more. She shakes her head no and asks the teacher to help. This time the teacher proceeds differently: "Put your marker right here" (pointing to a spot). "Now, move your marker that way" (pointing again). "Now change directions . . ." (moving Samantha's hand in the new direction). "Keep gooooing . . . Stop!" The teacher takes Samantha's hand to guide it in the other direction.

3. A child is playing with alphabet-matching material at a puzzle table. He matches loose letter tiles to letters printed on a background board and then does it again. As the child matches the letter tiles for the third time, a teacher stops by and comments, "That's the other *K*. There's the *T*. Mmm, yes, *N* goes right there."

4. All but six children have been dismissed from music time to go with a teacher to the bathroom and then to snack. To avoid a long wait in the bathroom area, a second teacher keeps a small group to play an alphabet-matching game. First the teacher draws a long vertical line on her paper. One child guesses that the teacher was thinking of *T*. Another guesses *L*. A third guesses *M*. The teacher confirms that she might be thinking of any of these letters. Next, the teacher draws a short horizontal line to the right of the vertical line, at the top. "I was right, *L*," one child exclaims. The teacher says that it will be necessary to rotate the paper (she rotates it 180 degrees), and then turns the paper over and traces the faint outline showing through from the other side. "*L* is a good guess, but not the letter in my mind."

    The child who suggested earlier that the teacher was thinking of *T* continues to maintain that this letter is in the teacher's mind. Another child thinks it could be *E* or *F*. For the next clue, the teacher starts in the middle of the long, vertical line, and draws a short line to the right. "*F!*" the children shout. The teacher confirms that this is the letter of which she has been thinking.

(Continued)

BOX 4.5 CONTINUED

5. The children sing the song "Willoughby Wallaby Woo" during music time, and then make up some verses using names of children in the class.

6. A child uses a teacher-made manipulative. Pictures of flowers children have seen on walks and in classroom bouquets donated by parents who have home gardens are mounted on the background board. Velcro-backed name tiles (such as tulips, daffodils, or lilies of the valley) are in a small dish. The child says the name of a flower to himself and then searches for the tile bearing this name. As the child searches the tiles, he can be heard saying *"t," "d,"* or *"l."*

Source: From "What Is Developmentally Appropriate Practice in Early Literacy?: Considering the Alphabet," by J. A. Schickedanz, in S. B. Neuman & K. A. Roskos (Eds.), *Children Achieving: Best Practices in Early Literacy* (pp. 20–37). Copyright © 1998. Reprinted with permission of the International Reading Association.

principle, children must have an understanding of how spoken language maps onto written language. Phonemic awareness helps a child grasp this understanding. Without phonemic awareness, a child might be able to learn letter-sound relationships by rote but will not understand how to use and coordinate letter-sound knowledge to read or spell new words. As a result, phonemic awareness plays a critical role in the development of skills required in the manipulation of phonemes—namely, phonics and spelling skills (Griffith & Olson, 1992).

Several kinds of tasks are involved in phonemic awareness. Children should be able to perform these tasks as a precursor to phonics and spelling instruction (Adams, 1990).

◆ *Rhyming.* Tasks that require children to rhyme words or to recognize rhymes are probably the easiest phonemic awareness tasks for them to perform.

◆ *Blending.* A more difficult task involving phonemic awareness requires children to blend a series of orally presented sounds to form a word; for example, given the separate sounds /c/, /a/, /t/, the child says *cat.*

◆ *Segmenting beginning and end sounds in words.* Children who have developed the capacity to hear sounds in words are able to perform phonemic awareness tasks that require them to isolate and identify the sound at the beginning or end of a word. A teacher might ask, "What sound do you hear at the beginning of the word *pig?*" or "What sound do you hear at the end of the word *hit?*"

◆ *Segmenting separate sounds in a word.* This is the most difficult of the phonemic awareness tasks. Children who can segment separate sounds in a word are considered to be phonemically aware.

When children develop phonemic awareness, they recognize that words can rhyme, can begin or end with the same sound or different sounds, and are composed of phonemes that can be separated or blended in different ways to form words. Most children, about 80 percent, develop phonemic awareness by the middle of the first grade. Because phonemic awareness appears to develop naturally in young children, some people might question whether it needs to be taught or emphasized in early reading. The IRA position statement, however, makes clear that "insofar as it is natural for parents to read to their children and engage them with print and language, then phonemic awareness may develop naturally in some children. But if we accept that these kinds of interactions are not the norm, then we have a great deal of work to do in encouraging parents to engage their young children with print" (Cunningham et al., 1998).

Not only do parents have an important role to play in children's phonemic awareness, but so do teachers. Kindergarten and early first grade are the most appropriate times to plan activities that will develop children's ability to manipulate sounds in words. How can phonemic awareness be taught? The Viewpoint featured in Box 4.6 is from IRA's position statement on phonemic awareness in response to that question.

Developing Phonemic Awareness in Children.

Instruction has it greatest impact on phonemic awareness when teachers *balance* a high level of interaction with print and explicit instruction in various tasks related to manipulating sounds in words. Consider the following practices in the development of a child's phonemic awareness.

Play with language through read-alouds. Use read-aloud books, nursery rhymes, riddles, songs, and poems that play with language and manipulate sounds in natural and spontaneous ways. Choose language-rich literature that is appropriate for young children and deals playfully with speech sounds through the use of rhyme, alliteration, assonance, and other forms of phoneme manipulation (Griffith & Olson, 1992). In doing so, draw children's attention to the sounds of spoken language and examine language use.

Playing with sounds through interactive reading experiences integrates phonemic awareness instruction within the context of enjoying stories, nursery rhymes, songs, poems, or riddles. You can create numerous opportunities for children to develop phonemic awareness through the questions you pose to draw children's attention to the sounds in words. For example, ask questions such as "Did you notice how those words rhymed?" "Which words start alike?" and "What sound do you hear at the beginning of all these words?" In addition, extend interactive read-alouds by creating alternative versions of the story or additional verses while maintaining the same language patterns. Appendix F contains an annotated list of read-aloud books to develop children's phonemic awareness.

Create games and gamelike activities to reinforce and extend children's awareness of sounds in words. As children develop a familiarity with the concept of rhyme, make or purchase games that use rhyming words. For example, make a bingo-style board on which children cover pictures that rhyme with those drawn from a bag or a box. Other phonemic awareness activities might include these:

◆ Clapping the number of syllables heard in a name or a word. To begin, say the name or word and then repeat it in unison with the children as they clap with you.

How Should Phonemic Awareness Be Taught?

The answer to this question has both theoretical and practical implications. Theorists interested in determining the causal contribution of phonemic awareness to learning to read have conducted experimental studies in which some students are explicitly taught phonemic awareness and some are not. Many of the early studies in this genre focused on treatments that emphasize oral language work only. The findings from these studies suggest phonemic awareness can be taught successfully.

More recently, there have been studies of phonemic awareness training that combine and contrast purely oral language approaches to the nurturing of phonemic awareness abilities, with approaches that include interaction with print during the training. These studies suggest that programs that encourage high levels of student engagement and interaction with print (for example, through read-alouds, shared reading, and invented spelling) yield as much growth in phonemic awareness abilities as programs that offer only a focus on oral language teaching. These studies also suggest that the greatest impact on phonemic awareness is achieved when there is both interaction with print and explicit attention to phonemic awareness abilities. In other words, interaction with print combined with explicit attention to sound structure in spoken words is the best vehicle toward growth.

Some research suggests that student engagement in writing activities that encourage invented spelling of words can promote the development of phonemic awareness. These findings also are consistent with continuing research into the sources of influence on phonemic awareness abilities before students enter school. It is clear that high levels of phonemic awareness among very young children are related to home experiences that are filled with interactions with print (such as being read to at home, playing letter games and language play, and having early writing experiences).

Source: From *Phonemic Awareness and the Teaching of Reading: A Position Statement from the Board of Directors of the International Reading Association,* prepared by J. Cunningham, P. M. Cunningham, J. V. Hoffman, and H. K. Yopp, adopted April 1998. Reprinted with permission from the International Reading Association.

◆ Play guessing games or use riddles to help children become sensitive to the sounds in words. For example, "What am I thinking of?" is a guessing game that helps children blend spoken sounds together to form a word (Yopp, 1995). Here's how it works: First, choose a category from which you will select words. Then, in a deliberate, segmented fashion, say each sound of the word and ask children, "What am I thinking of?" For example, given the category "sea animals," a teacher might say the following sounds: /c/, /r/, /a/, /b/.

◆ Play with tongue twisters to build awareness of the sounds in beginning letters. Have children say tongue twisters as quickly, and as slowly, as they can. Once children can recite tongue twisters from memory, write them on poster boards. Direct children's attention to the beginning sounds.

◆ Have children line up for lunchtime or recess by the beginning sound in their names. For example, say, "Anyone whose name begins with /b/, please line up" (Cunningham & Allington, 1999). This activity involves *sound matching*. Sound-matching activities can be adapted in numerous ways. For example, ask children to decide which of several words begins with a given sound or to generate a word beginning with a particular sound. Yopp (1992) recommends giving children a series of pictures of familiar animals or objects (e.g., snake, dog, cat, bird) and asking them to select the one that begins with the /s/ sound. Also, to the tune of "Jimmy Crack Corn and I Don't Care," have children generate words that begin with a particular sound by singing,

> Who has a /d/ word to share with us?
> Who has a /d/ word to share with us?
> Who has a /d/ word to share with us?
> It must start with the /d/ sound.

As the class sings together, call on individual children to volunteer words that begin with the /d/ sound. Then incorporate the words that have been contributed by the children into the song, e.g.: "*Dog* is a word that starts with /d/. *Dog* is a word that starts with /d/. *Dog* is a word that starts with /d/. *Dog* starts with the /d/ sound." Make sure throughout the activity that the children sing the phoneme sound, not the letter name.

◆ In addition to sound matching, Yopp (1992) presents several other useful phonemic awareness activities that involve *sound isolation, blending, segmentation, sound addition*, and *sound substitution*.

Engage children in numerous occasions to write. Provide children with many opportunities to experiment with language through writing. Daily writing experiences may be beneficial for children who lack phonemic awareness (Griffith & Klesius, 1990). The more children write, the better they become at hearing sounds in words as they attempt to invent spelling. As they become more adept at segmenting sounds in words, encourage children to approximate spelling based on the way words sound. Teacher-child interactions should provide enough instructional support as the child needs to approximate the spelling of a word.

Notice how Mrs. Nicholas scaffolds instruction for a first grader who asks for help as she attempts to spell *hospital* in the story that she is writing (Cramer, 1978, p. 132).

JENNY:	Mrs. Nicholas, how do you spell *hospital?*
MRS. NICHOLAS:	Spell it as best you can, Jenny.
JENNY:	I don't know how to spell it.
MRS. NICHOLAS:	I know you don't know how to spell it, honey. I just want you to write as much of the word as you can.

JENNY:	I don't know any of it.
MRS. NICHOLAS:	Yes, you do, Jenny. How do you think *hospital* starts? *(Mrs. Nicholas pronounced* hospital *distinctly with a slight emphasis on the first sound, but she deliberately avoided grossly distorting the pronunciation.)*
JENNY:	*(very tentatively)* h-s.
MRS. NICHOLAS:	Good! Write the *hs.* What do you hear next in *hospital? (Again Mrs. Nicholas pronounced* hospital *distinctly, this time with a slight emphasis on the second part.)*
JENNY:	*(still tentatively)* p-t.
MRS. NICHOLAS:	Yes! Write the *pt.* Now, what's the last sound you hear in *hospital? (While pronouncing* hospital *for the last time, Mrs. Nicholas emphasized the last part without exaggerating it unduly.)*
JENNY:	*(with some assurance):* l.
MRS. NICHOLAS:	Excellent, Jenny, *h-s-p-t-l* is a fine way to spell *hospital.* There is another way to spell *hospital,* but for now I want you to spell words you don't know just as we did this one.

Because Mrs. Nicholas was willing to accept invented spellings in a beginning situation, Jenny benefited. Not only did she have an opportunity to map spoken language onto written language, but Jenny also had the opportunity to test the rules that govern English spelling in an accepting environment.

Teach children to segment sounds in words through explicit instruction. Individual children who may be having trouble segmenting sounds in words may benefit most from explicit instruction. Clay (1985) recommends the use of Elkonin boxes (named after a Russian psychologist) as a phonemic segmentation strategy. The following procedures can be incorporated into individual or small group instruction once the children are identified as ready for training in phonemic segmentation. To benefit from such instruction, children must have developed strong concepts of print as "talk written down" as well as a concept of "word." Because the initial stages of training in segmenting a word into sounds is totally aural, children need not be aware of letters to profit from this type of instruction. Eventually, children learn to attach letters to sounds that are separated.

1. *Give the child a picture of a familiar object.* A rectangle is divided into squares according to the number of sounds in the name of the object. Remember that a square is required for every sound in a word, not necessarily every letter. For example, if the picture were of a boat, there would be three squares for three sounds:

b	oa	t

2. *Next say the word slowly and deliberately, allowing the child to hear the sounds that can be naturally segmented.* Research has shown that it is easier to hear syllables than individual phonemes in a word (Liberman, Shankweiler, Fisher, & Carter, 1974).

3. *Now ask the child to repeat the word, modeling the way you have said it.*

4. *Continue to model.* As you segment the word into sounds, show the child how to place counters in each square according to the sounds heard sequentially in the word. For example, with the word *boat,* as the teacher articulates each sound, a counter is placed in a square:

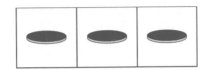

5. *Walk the child through the procedure by attempting it together several times.*

6. *Show another picture and then the word.* Ask the child to pronounce the word and separate the sounds by placing the counters in the squares. The teacher may have to continue modeling until the child catches on to the task.

7. *Phase out the picture stimulus and the use of counters and squares.* Eventually, the child is asked to analyze words aurally without teacher assistance.

In time, the teacher should combine phonemic segmentation with letter association. As the child pronounces a word, letters and letter patterns can be used instead of counters in the squares. The child can be asked, "What letters do you think go in each of the squares?" At first, the letters can be written in for the child. Clay (1985) suggests that the teacher accept any correct letter-sound relationship the child gives and write it in the correct position as the child watches. She also recommends that the teacher prompt the child with questions such as "What do you hear in the beginning?" "In the middle?" "At the end?" and "What else do you hear?"

Hearing sounds in words is no easy reading task for 5- and 6-year-olds. The research of Liberman and her associates (1977) points out that preschool and kindergarten children have a more difficult time with segmentation tasks than first graders do. As we suggested earlier, helping children sound out words may be premature if they are not yet phonemically aware. That is why it is important to assess children's ability to manipulate sounds in words.

Assessing Phonemic Awareness. Teachers can assess children's phonemic awareness through ongoing instruction as they engage in various activities. Observing children perform phonemic awareness tasks is an informal means of assessment that will help you plan and adapt instruction according to children's needs. Formal measures of phonemic awareness create a testlike environment but provide useful indicators of children's capacity to manipulate sounds in words. For example, the Yopp-Singer Test of Phoneme Segmentation in Figure 4.4 measures a child's ability to separately articulate the sounds of a spoken word in order. Validation studies of the Yopp-Singer Test show not only that it is a valid

◆ Figure 4.4

A Test for Assessing Phonemic Awareness in Young Children

Name: _____   Date: _____

Score (number correct) _____

Directions: Today we're going to play a word game. I'm going to say a word and I want you to break the word apart. You are going to tell me each sound in the word in order. For example, if I say "old," you should say "/ō/-/l/-/d/." (Administrator: Be sure to say the sounds, not the letters, in the word.) Let's try a few together.

Practice items: (Assist the child in segmenting these items as necessary.)

      ride,   go,   man

Test items: (Circle those items that the student correctly segments; incorrect responses may be recorded on the blank line following the item.)

1. dog	_____	12. lay	_____
2. keep	_____	13. race	_____
3. fine	_____	14. zoo	_____
4. no	_____	15. three	_____
5. she	_____	16. job	_____
6. wave	_____	17. in	_____
7. grew	_____	18. ice	_____
8. that	_____	19. at	_____
9. red	_____	20. top	_____
10. me	_____	21. by	_____
11. sat	_____	22. do	_____

Source: From "A Test for Assessing Phonemic Awareness in Young Children," by H. K. Yopp, *The Reading Teacher, 49,* 1, p. 22. Copyright © 1995. Reprinted with permission.

and reliable measure of phonemic awareness ability but also that it can be used to identify children who are likely to experience difficulty in reading and spelling (Yopp, 1995).

To administer the Yopp-Singer Test, orally present the set of target words one at a time and ask a child to respond by segmenting each target word into its separate sounds. For example, you say the word *red* and the child responds /r/, /e/, /d/; say the word *fish* and the child says /f/, /i/, /sh/. As the child progresses through the 22-item test, it is appropriate to provide feedback. If the child responds correctly, nod approval or say, "Good job; that's right." If a child gives an incorrect answer, provide the correct response and then continue down the list.

You can determine a child's score on the Yopp-Singer Test by counting the number of items correctly segmented into all constituent phonemes. Although no partial credit is given, a child's incorrect responses should be noted on the blank line following the item. These incorrect responses provide much insight into the child's developing awareness of sounds in words. As you score each test item, note that consonant and vowel *digraphs* are counted as a single phoneme (e.g., /sh/ in *she;* /th/ in *three;* /oo/ in *zoo;* /oi/ in *boy;* a more detailed explanation of digraphs and other phonics elements is given in Chapter 5).

Expect wide variation in young children's performance on the Yopp-Singer Test. Yopp (1995) reports that second-semester kindergarten students drawn from the public schools in a West Coast city in the United States obtained scores ranging from 0 to 22 correct responses on the test items. Guidelines for evaluating a child's performance include the following:

◆ Correct responses for *all* or *nearly all* of the items indicate that a child is phonemically aware.

◆ Correct responses for *some* of the items (about 12 correct responses, with a standard deviation of 7.66) indicates that a child displays emerging phonemic awareness.

◆ Correct responses for *few* items or *none at all* indicate that a child lacks phonemic awareness.

The Yopp-Singer Test allows teachers to identify children who are likely to experience difficulty learning to read and spell and give them instructional support using practices described earlier. In the next chapter, we will examine how children use their knowledge of sounds in words to engage in code instruction as they develop word identification skills and strategies.

SUMMARY

In this chapter, we explored the difference between reading readiness and emergent literacy as views on which to begin instruction. If reading is viewed developmentally, teachers will make use of children's preschool experiences with and knowledge of print to get beginners started in reading and writing. The principle behind instruction is to teach for literate behavior. In other words, beginning reading and writing should center around readinglike situations rather than on activities that are unrelated to having children interact with printed language.

Three strands of instruction characterize beginning reading. First, children should participate in storybook literacy experiences as well as learn what reading is all about. We showed how to use stories and incorporate language functions into instructional practices.

Through these activities, children learn that the string of sounds in spoken language can be broken down into units of print made up of words and sentences. Moreover, they should be getting instruction in which they learn that a word can be separated into sounds and that these separated sounds can be represented by letters. Finally, a third phase should center around the language of instruction. Children must learn the terms and labels that are needed to talk about reading and carry out reading tasks.

We emphasized informal assessment because it provides daily judgments of children's preparedness and progress in beginning reading situations. Assessment through teaching and observation yields valuable information about a child's abilities, as well as about the teaching methods that seem to be easiest and of greatest interest to individual children. Formal measures such as the Concepts About Print Test and the Yopp-Singer Test of Phoneme Segmentation, are also valuable tools for assessment in early reading.

TEACHER-ACTION RESEARCHER

1. Suppose you were planning to conduct an interview with a young child to determine the child's concepts about print. What questions would you develop to tap the child's knowledge about books and print? Develop a set of questions to use both before and during reading. Compare your questions with those of several of your classmates.

2. Roberto is an active kindergartner who loves to be "on the move," playing with games, building blocks and Lego blocks. He will sit to hear a good book, but when asked to follow along, he doesn't know where to begin. Sometimes he points to the top right side of the page and sometimes to the middle of the page. In collaboration with a fellow class member, design several classroom experiences with print from which Roberto may benefit.

3. Choose a popular children's story and make a big book. Then prepare a lesson that involves reading the big book aloud, discussion, and dramatization. Share your big book lesson with others in the class. If you have access to a classroom or a young child, teach this lesson.

4. An editorial in your local newspaper advocates a strong phonics program beginning in kindergarten. Write a letter to the editor in which you explain the importance of developing children's concepts about print and phonemic awareness before teaching phonics. Use language that parents in the community will understand.

KEY TERMS

big books	literacy club	storybook
emergent literacy	observation	experiences
interactive reading	phonemic awareness	uses of oral language
interactive writing	phonemic	
language experience	segmentation	
linguistic awareness	reading readiness	

CHAPTER

5

Word Identification

Chapter Overview

WORD IDENTIFICATION

Defining Word Identification

Phases of Development in
Word Identification

APPROACHES AND GUIDELINES FOR PHONICS

STRATEGIES FOR TEACHING PHONICS

Consonant-Based
Strategies

Analogy-Based
Strategies

Spelling-Based
Strategies

**USING MEANING AND LETTER-SOUND
INFORMATION TO IDENTIFY WORDS**

Strategies for
Using Context

Strategies for
Cross-Checking Meaning

RAPID RECOGNITION OF WORDS

High-Frequency Words

Key Words

Between the Lines

In this chapter, you will discover:

- ◆ **Phases of word-reading development**
- ◆ **Guidelines and strategies for teaching phonics**
- ◆ **Strategies for rapid recognition of words**
- ◆ **Strategies for analyzing words in context**
- ◆ **The importance of self-monitoring while reading**

Steve, 3½ years old, was staring at a gum wrapper with PAL written on it. He said, "This says 'gum.'" Was Steve reading? We like to think so. Literacy has begun to emerge for Steve. He has made the association between speech and print and knows intuitively that reading is supposed to make sense. At his present level of development, Steve makes use of information in his immediate surroundings to determine what print says. This is one way environmental context cues are used by emergent readers. As Steve continues to develop as a reader, he will learn to use word identification cues from the context in the flow of print and within words themselves.

Words inevitably enter into the discussion when children attempt to explain what they are doing during the class time they spend on learning to read. Some children report that they are studying or learning new words. Others explain what they do when they come to a word they don't know. For example, two first-grade children from different classrooms talk about what they do when they come to words that they do not recognize during reading. The first child, Suzanne, is learning to read in a classroom that places emphasis on identifying words by sounding out letters and blending them. The second child, William, is learning to read in a classroom that places emphasis on sounding out *and* using context to identify words during reading. Here are Suzanne's responses to her teacher's questions:

TEACHER: What would you do if you were reading by yourself and you came to a word you didn't know?

SUZANNE: Sound it out.

TEACHER: What would you do if you tried to sound it out and you still couldn't figure it out?

SUZANNE: I'd ask you to help me sound it out.

TEACHER: What if you are all alone?

SUZANNE: I'd call my brother. He could tell me the word.

TEACHER: What could you do by yourself to figure it out?

SUZANNE: I'd go next door. Someone there could help me sound the word out.

TEACHER: If no one were around to help you?

SUZANNE: I'd yell, "Anybody come and help me!"

TEACHER: But what if no one heard you yelling for help?

SUZANNE: I'd stop reading.

Suzanne has developed a *single strategy* for word identification. If sounding out an unfamiliar word fails, she would either seek help or just stop reading until help arrives!

In contrast, here is how William answers his teacher's questions:

TEACHER: What would you do if you were reading by yourself and you came to a word that you didn't know?

WILLIAM: I would sound it out.

TEACHER: What would you do if you tried to sound it out and you still couldn't figure it out?

WILLIAM: I'd skip over the word and then read the next sentence. Then I'd try to figure it out. I'd look at the letters to see if they are the same as the word I guessed. Then I'd go back to the beginning and see if it makes sense.

TEACHER: What would you do if you still couldn't figure the word out?

WILLIAM: I'd keep on reading.

The teacher in Suzanne's classroom is operating from a bottom-up perspective of learning to read. Her counterpart in William's classroom, however, is more interactive in her orientation toward reading. The instructional emphasis in Suzanne's classroom rests squarely on learning *letter-sound relationships*, because the teacher believes *phonics* provides the most efficient means for transferring learning from one reading situation to another. William's teacher believes that children should make use of phonemic knowledge but must also take advantage of meaning information while reading. The two teachers have different instructional emphases but the same instructional goal in mind: Both want their students to achieve independence in word identification while reading.

How teachers invest their time in helping readers identify words is an important instructional question and the subject of much debate. Although there are differences in practice, it is the philosophical differences that seem to predominate (Stahl, 1992; Stahl, Duffy-Hester, & Stahl, 1998). In some circles, stating how words should best be taught can unleash heated arguments, as different approaches can have good or bad connotations, depending on one's perspective.

As depicted in the chapter overview, we suggest strategies that will result in two broad instructional goals of word identification instruction. The first is that children should learn how to deal with unfamiliar words *rapidly* and *independently*. If children cannot quickly identify new words on their own, reading soon becomes tedious, if not overwhelming. Misty, a first grader, put it this way: "I'm in big trouble if I miss words when I'm reading." Furthermore, if word identification takes up most of the reader's energy and attention, comprehension and enjoyment will suffer (Samuels, 1994, 1996).

A second goal of instruction is that readers should develop *multiple strategies* for word identification. Readers must learn how to use phonics and meaning clues to help identify unfamiliar words while reading.

DEFINING WORD IDENTIFICATION

Several terms have been associated with identifying words: *word attack, word analysis, word recognition,* and *decoding.* These terms are often used interchangeably. Figure 5.1 illustrates the relationship of these terms to word identification.

Word identification means putting a name or label on words that are encountered in print. It is a comprehensive term that encompasses the use of phonemic and meaning cues to identify unfamiliar words.

◆ Figure 5.1   Terms Related to Word Identification

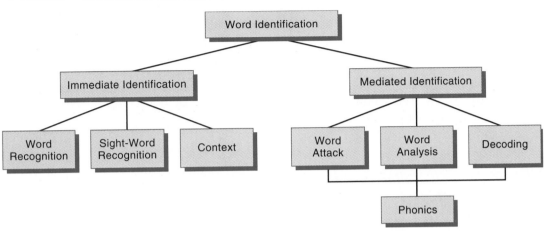

Word recognition suggests a process that involves *immediate identification.* Immediately recognized words are retrieved rapidly from *lexical memory.* Word recognition is sometimes referred to as *sight-word recognition* or *sight vocabulary.* These terms suggest a reader's ability to recognize words rapidly and automatically. In this chapter we use *immediate word recognition* to describe rapid recognition. Keep in mind, however, that the process of immediate word recognition is far more complicated than merely recognizing words on flash cards. When a word is retrieved rapidly from memory, the process is often triggered by the application of letter-sound knowledge. Learning to read words rapidly involves making associations between particular spellings, pronunciations, and meanings by applying knowledge of letter-sound relationships (Ehri, 1995). Skilled readers use the strategy of immediate word recognition on 99 percent of the printed words they encounter.

The terms *word attack, word analysis,* and *decoding* suggest the act of translating print to speech through analysis of letter-sound relationships. These terms have been used frequently with what is commonly referred to as *phonics.*

Phonics provides readers with a tool to "attack" the pronunciation of words that are not recognized immediately. A good way to think of phonics is that it "embraces a variety of instructional strategies for bringing attention to parts of words. The parts can be syllables, phonograms (such as *an*), other letter strings (such as *pie*), or single letters" (Beck & Juel, 1995, p. 22). Phonics, then, always involves *mediated word identification* because readers must devote conscious attention to "unlocking" the alphabetic code.

Few teachers of beginning readers would deny that phonics has an important role to play in children's development as readers and writers. Yet how best to teach children to read and write has the been the subject of debate and controversy throughout the twentieth century. No wonder Cunningham and Allington (1999) argue that phonics is not *the* solution to the development of skilled readers, but neither is just immersing beginners in reading and writing. Study the Viewpoint featured in Box 5.1. Cunningham and Allington explain why teachers should be wary of those who advocate phonics instruction as a solution, not a means, to developing independent readers.

Teachers are in the most strategic position to make decisions about the phonics that children actually use to read and write well. Rather than engage in debates about whether phonics should or should not be an integral part of literacy instruction, effective teachers ask *when, how, how much,* and *under what circumstances* word identification strategies should be taught. Understanding the phases of development that children progress through in their ability to identify words is important knowledge that teachers can use to make decisions about instruction.

PHASES OF DEVELOPMENT IN CHILDREN'S ABILITY TO IDENTIFY WORDS

It is through frequent experiences with books and print, as we suggested in Chapters 3 and 4, that children develop knowledge about reading and writing prior to school. They do so at different rates, in different ways, and in different settings. When young children engage in frequent book and print experiences, the development of word knowledge emerges during the preschool years without much, if any, formal instruction. Yet the capacity to read words cannot be left to chance or immersion in print. Teachers must build and expand on the word-reading knowledge that children bring to school.

Children progress through various developmental phases of word identification while learning to read (Ehri, 1991, 1994). In the course of their development, they first learn to identify some words purely through *visual cues,* such as distinctive graphic features *in* or *around* the words. As children continue to grow as readers, they use their developing knowledge of letter-sound relationships to identify words. The development of word learning can be divided into four phases, as illustrated in Figure 5.2: the *prealphabetic, partial alphabetic, full alphabetic,* and *consolidated alphabetic* phases (Gaskins, Ehri, Cress, O'Hara, & Donnelly, 1997).

The *prealphabetic phase,* which has also been called the *logographic* or *visual cue* phase, occurs before the development of alphabetic knowledge. Children are able to recognize some words at sight during this phase because of distinctive visual and contextual cues in or around the recognized words. The ability to read cereal box labels, restaurant logos, and other kinds of environmental print is one of the first literacy accomplishments of a preschool child. The octagonal shape of a stop sign, for example, may prompt preschoolers to shout "stop" as their parents slow down at the sign. In addition, young children learn to attend to visual cues in words. As shown in Figure 5.2, preschoolers and kindergarten children may read the word *yellow* because they remember the two "tall posts" in the middle of the word.

Children progress to the *partial alphabetic phase* when they begin to develop some knowledge about letters and detect letter-sound relationships. For example, at 4½ years old, Simon reads his name by remembering that the letter *s* looks like a snake and makes a

◆ FIGURE 5.2   Developmental Phases in Children's Ability to Read Words

Prealphabetic phase
(Remembering a distinctive, purely *visual* cue)
Example: tall posts

yellow

Partial alphabetic phase
(Remembering limited matches between salient letter sounds)
Example: matches between *K* and *N* only

KitteN
↓   ↓
k it n

Full alphabetic phase
(Remembering matches between *all* letters and sounds)
Example: 4 letter units matched to 4 sound units

C L O CK
↓ ↓ ↓ ↓
k l o k

Consolidated alphabetic phase
(Remembering matches between multiletter units and symbolic units)
Example: matching onset and rime units

CR ATE
↓   ↓
kr   at

Source: From "Procedures for Word Learning: Making Discoveries About Words," by I. W. Gaskins, L. C. Ehri, C. Cress, C. O'Hara, and K. Donnelly, *Reading Teacher, 50,* p. 317. Copyright © 1997. Reprinted with permission of the International Reading Association and the authors.

hissing /s/ sound; and the letter *i* sounds like its name. The partial alphabetic phase emerges during kindergarten and first grade for most children, when they acquire some knowledge of letters and sounds. They remember how to read specific words by detecting how a few letters correspond to sounds in the word's pronunciation. As indicated in the example in Figure 5.2, a child might recognize *kitten* by remembering the letter-sound relationships between the initial *k* and final *n* letters, but not the letter-sound matches in between. Early readers who function at the partial alphabetic phase are likely to misread some words sharing the same partial letter-sound cues—for example, misreading *kitchen* as *kitten*. This is especially the case when the word is read in isolation rather than in the context of a story.

The *full alphabetic phase* emerges in children's literacy development when readers identify words by matching all of the letters and sounds. They have developed enough knowledge about letter-sound relationships to unlock the pronunciations of unknown words. As shown in Figure 5.2, readers at this phase would be able to segment the word *clock* into four letter units that match the four sounds in the pronunciation. Sounding out letters and blending them into words may be laborious and slow at the beginning of the full alphabetic stage, but as children become more accomplished at decoding unknown words, they progress to more rapid word analysis. Some children enter first grade with the capacity to analyze words fully. Others do not and will benefit from explicit, carefully planned lessons that help them make discoveries about letter-sound relationships in words (Gaskins et al., 1997).

Why Phonics Is Not the Solution . . . But Neither Is Just Reading*

Patricia M. Cunningham and Richard L. Allington

Patricia M. Cunningham and Richard L. Allington are distinguished leaders in the field of reading and recognized for their research on contemporary phonics instruction and literacy policy analysis. Cunningham is a professor at Wake Forrest University, and Allington is a professor at the State University of New York at Albany. Here they explain how phonics fits into the teaching of word recognition.

At several points in American educational history, code-emphasis instruction (the phonics approach) has been touted as "the answer" to teaching all children to read. Both of us began our teaching in the 1960s, the last time phonics was offered as the answer. It wasn't the answer then and it isn't today. But once again there are claims being made for the effectiveness of phonics approaches and once again some folks are overstating and exaggerating evidence to support code-oriented materials and methods. There is a convergence of research evidence pointing to the critical role that good decoding skills play in good reading. However, there is no convergence in the research evidence indicating what types of phonics instruction, of what intensity, over what duration will produce the largest numbers of children who read well and willingly.

But this lack of evidence doesn't seem to matter to many proponents of a pro-phonics agenda. Product advertisements, legislative testimonies, and various other materials have recently contained a set of strikingly similar assertions about phonics teaching and learning—assertions that are simply distortions of the research available even though often couched in terms such as "scientifically rigorous research." Here are some assertions that have appeared repeatedly and that we consider "unscientific"—assertions that cannot be drawn from the available scientific evidence.

UNSCIENTIFIC ASSERTION #1. NO ONE TEACHES PHONICS

Two recent large-scale federally funded studies provide overwhelming evidence that virtually all primary grade teachers teach phonics, usually daily. Smaller, more intensive studies of exemplary teachers point to the same conclusion but also point to an interesting phenomenon— these exemplary teachers rarely report using commercial phonics curriculum material. Instead, they teach phonics knowledge and strategies to children rather than teaching the pages in a phonics workbook.

UNSCIENTIFIC ASSERTION #2. THERE IS A PHONEMIC AWARENESS CRISIS

Recently, a new wrinkle has been added to the phonics campaign—a crisis in phonemic awareness. Oversimplifying a bit, phonemic awareness is the ability to isolate individual sounds (phonemes) in spoken words. For instance, being able to count three sounds in "cat." The evidence indicates that phonics instruction offers little benefit for children who have not developed phonemic awareness. There is compelling evidence to support the conclusion that phonemic awareness is an important understanding in learning to read an alphabetic language like English. But the evidence also indicates that most (80–85 percent) children acquire phonemic awareness by the middle of first grade. The research also indicates that 2 of those 3 or 4 children in each classroom who don't develop phonemic awareness initially can develop it within a few weeks, if offered some targeted tutorial or small group intervention. The remaining children may require a more intensive intervention.

Box 5.1 CONTINUED

We have learned much about the importance of children developing phonemic awareness, but the research still offers no clear basis for advocating particular instructional materials or methods. Phonemic awareness is important and it can and should be developed, but it is not "the root of all reading problems" nor will the implementation of elaborate time-consuming commercially produced phonemic awareness programs solve all our reading problems!

UNSCIENTIFIC ASSERTION #3. EXPLICIT, SYSTEMATIC PHONICS IS THE ONLY WAY TO GO

There is suddenly much ado about the need to ensure that "explicit, systematic" phonics instruction is offered. Often "incidental, opportunistic" phonics instruction is contrasted negatively against the "scientific" assertions for "explicit, systematic" phonics. The problem is that the available studies of exemplary teachers portray powerful phonics instruction that is "direct and opportunistic" (and it seems systematic also). It seems obvious that well-planned instruction based on student needs would be more effective than a series of random instructional activities. But exactly what sort of "explicit, systematic" or "explicit, opportunistic" phonics instruction does the research endorse?

Simply said, there is no convergence of research on just what sort of phonics instruction should be offered. Often publishers of commercial materials seem to be suggesting that their material has been developed from some set of "scientific" principles, which suggests that there is research evidence found on just what order letters and sounds should be taught and whether the instruction should focus on synthetic or analytic approaches and so on. But there simply is no convergence of research on such points. There is no "scientifically" determined sequence of instruction and no conclusive evidence on what sorts of phonics lessons, or of what duration would most effectively develop the optimum level of decoding efficiency in children.

UNSCIENTIFIC ASSERTION #4. DECODABLE TEXTS ARE ESSENTIAL

Finally, the most recently touted unscientific assertion has to do with the role of, or need for, "decodable texts." Such texts are described as offering children "only words that they have been taught the phonics skills to sound out." The decodable texts displayed at the recent meeting of the International Reading Association reminded us of the 1960s "Nan can fan Dan" and "Nat the Rat" readers. The key point is that there isn't a single study that supports the exclusive use of decodable texts in beginning reading!

In fact, there is evidence that restricting beginning reading materials to any single text type will likely produce a limited set of reading strategies—though the strategies developed seem to vary by the type of text restrictions in place. There is research support for providing children with "manageable" texts—texts that they can read without too much difficulty. There is also evidence that some of the recently published reading series provide reading material that is quite difficult. But none of this suggests that a return to "Nat the Rat" is the solution.

AN UNSCIENTIFIC ASSERTION FROM THE LAST ERA—CHILDREN WILL ACQUIRE DECODING SKILLS FROM JUST READING

This is the unscientific assertion most responsible for the current phonics frenzy! Both the research and our experience indicate that children need to be taught effective decoding skills and strategies. Most children don't become skillful at pronouncing unknown words just by reading. Phonics instruction is an essential part of a reading program—but it is not the reading program!

Source: From *Classrooms That Work: They Can All Read and Write* (2nd ed.), by P. M. Cunningham and R. L. Allington (New York: Longman, 1999), pp. 3–5. Used by permission of Addison-Wesley Educational Publishers, Inc.

As children become more skilled at identifying words, they rely less on individual letter-sound relationships. Instead, they use their knowledge of familiar and predictable letter patterns to speed up the process of reading words. They do so by developing the ability to analyze chunks of letters within words. The recognition of predictable letter patterns begins to emerge in the first grade as children engage in reading and begin to recognize many words with similar spelling patterns. In the example in Figure 5.2, readers at the *consolidated alphabetic phase* would be able to segment the word *crate* into two larger letter or spelling patterns, *cr* and *ate,* and match them to larger sound units known as *onsets* (the initial consonants and consonant patterns that come at the beginning of syllables) and *rimes* (the vowel and consonants that follow them at the end of syllables). The recognition of letter patterns in the consolidated alphabetic phase allows children to analyze multisyllabic words rapidly.

IMPLICATIONS FOR WORD IDENTIFICATION

Learning to read cannot be limited to experiences with words alone. Children need to have ample experiences with books, frequent encounters with oral and printed language, and early opportunities to write. Adams (1990) put it this way: "Children do need explicit instruction in letters and sounds, but such instruction *must* take place in an environment where they are surrounded by print in the form of storybooks, notes, displays, charts, and so forth" (p. 48). Furthermore, engaging children in writing develops knowledge about phonics. This is true in situations where children do not feel required to use conventional spelling; they can sound out words as they think they are spelled. In this way, students extend their knowledge of letter-sound associations.

When teachers revolve instruction around interesting and informative texts with predictable language patterns, children become aware of and understand how print on a page relates to making meaning. Part of this learning includes recognizing the relationships between letters and sounds. This understanding is needed by all readers and writers of alphabetically written languages such as English. Some of the ways in which teachers and parents support and develop children's knowledge of phonics include reading stories, poems, and songs and discussing letter-sound relationships and letter patterns in words that rhyme; encouraging children to listen for and identify sounds in words; encouraging children to spell the sounds they hear in words as they write; and comparing and contrasting letter-sound patterns in children's names, high-interest words, and words drawn from the books children are reading and the stories they write.

Phonics instruction is most appropriate when it is related to children's developmental needs. Certainly, students may need more explicit instruction than indicated in the suggestions given here. "Some children," according to Stanovich (1994), "do not discover the alphabetic principle on their own and need systematic direct instruction" (p. 285). Phonics instruction, however, should minimize the use of isolated drills, worksheets, and rote memorization of phonics rules. Children do not acquire word identification abilities efficiently by being exposed to jargon-filled instruction. Cunningham and Allington (1999, p. 123) provide an example:

Consider some of the traditional phonics instruction given to children:

♦ The *e* on the end is silent and makes the vowel long.

Immediate identification of words is the result of experience with reading, seeing, discussing, using, and writing words.

♦ When a vowel is followed by *r,* it is controlled.

♦ When there are two consonants in the middle of a word that are not a digraph or a blend, divide between them.

This kind of rule-based, jargon-filled instruction is confusing to many children and does not represent what people actually do when they come to an unfamiliar word in their reading, or when they are trying to figure out how a word might be spelled. The traditional phonics rules are descriptions of how the letter-sound system works. *They are not what you use when you need to pronounce or spell an unfamiliar word* [emphasis added].

Instead, children are likely to look at all the letters in the word in a left-to-right sequence, search their memory for similar letter-sound patterns, produce a pronunciation that sounds like a word that they already know, and cross-check the pronunciation with meaning (Cunningham, 1995).

Instead of phonics being driven by rules and jargon, teachers need to model for students how to use phonics to identify unknown words through explicit strategy instruction *and* integrated instruction during reading. Word study should emphasize short, planned lessons in classrooms where children read and write every day.

Approaches and Guidelines for Teaching Phonics

Teachers sometimes find themselves spending an inordinate amount of time on instruction in phonics that is isolated from meaningful text. Some teachers lament that they are unable to find time for their students to practice the application of phonics to relevant reading material. As a result, children can easily form the wrong message about phonics: that *reading* consists of phonics or sounding out words.

In the past, many commercially published phonics programs have been based on *traditional approaches* to the teaching of phonics. These programs often have fallen "short of the ideal" (National Institute of Education, 1985, p. 43). Two of the major traditional approaches described in Chapter 2, *analytic phonics* and *synthetic phonics,* are often incorporated into the instructional design of commercially published phonics programs. The steps of the analytic approach, you may recall, proceed from the whole word to a study of its constituent parts. The sequence of instruction usually involves the following steps:

1. Observe a list of known words with a common letter-sound relationship, for example, the initial consonant *t.*

2. Begin questioning as to how the words look and sound the same and how they are different.

3. Elicit the common letter-sound relationship and discuss.

4. Have the learners phrase a generalization about the letter-sound relationship—for example, all the words start with the sound of the letter *t.* The sound of the letter *t* is /t/ as in *top.*

The synthetic approach takes a different route to developing phonics skills. It uses a building-block approach to understanding letter-sound relationships. The sequence of instruction goes something like this:

1. Teach the letter names.

2. Teach the sound or sounds each letter represents.

3. Drill on the letter-sound relationships until rapidly recognized. Discuss rules and form generalizations about relationships that usually apply to words (when vowels are short or long, for example).

4. Teach the blending together of separate sounds to make a word.

5. Provide the opportunity to apply blending to unknown words.

There are similarities between analytic and synthetic phonics. Both approaches address rules, discuss isolated letter-sound relationships, break words apart, and put them back together again. In so doing, the danger of fragmenting word identification from actual text situations is always present.

Teachers who engage children in the analysis of words must be well versed and knowledgeable in the content and language of phonics. In Figure 5.3, we highlight some of the basic terms associated with phonics instruction.

The alternative to traditional approaches to phonics is to engage children in word identification programs based on **contemporary phonics** approaches (Stahl et al., 1998). Contemporary approaches are strategy-based and grounded in the phonics that children actually use to decode words.

Contemporary word study approaches place emphasis on the use of spelling patterns to identify words (Bear, Invernizzi, Templeton, & Johnston, 1996). As children move through the developmental phases of word identification, they grow in their ability to read words automatically without having to think consciously about spelling patterns. To get to that point, a teacher needs to provide students with abundant opportunities to practice identifying words in a variety of contexts: in isolation, in stories and expository text, and in writing words (Stahl et al., 1998).

Here are some guidelines for contemporary phonics instruction that work both in classrooms where the basal reader is the core text and in classrooms where reading instruction centers around literature-based programs.

1. Phonics Instruction Needs to Build on a Foundation of Phonemic Awareness and Knowledge of the Way Language Works.

In Chapter 4, we emphasized that young children differ in their phonemic awareness of sounds in spoken words. Once children are able to segment sounds, they also need to be shown the blending process. As you may recall, blending means joining together the sound represented by letters and letter clusters in a word. Essentially, the reader links the sound sequence with the letter sequence.

Whenever possible, children should practice segmenting and blending unfamiliar words that are *encountered in meaningful print context*. Remember, phonics instruction is designed to help children approximate the pronunciation of unfamiliar words. When approximations occur within a print context, readers can rely on meaning cues as well as phonic information to assist in word identification.

In addition to differing in phonemic awareness, children also come to phonics instruction with varying degrees of generalizations about the way the written language works. Their generalizations constitute a particular level of linguistic awareness as described in Chapter 4. Informally, teachers may engage young children in experiences concerning the notions of word, letter, and alphabet through such activities as cutting language experience stories into strips and asking individual children to cut off the words and having children sort words and letters.

2. Phonics Instruction Needs to Be Integrated into a Total Reading Program.

At least half of the time devoted to the teaching of reading, and probably more, should be spent on the actual reading of stories, poems, plays, and trade books. Furthermore, no more than 25 percent of the time, and possibly less, should be spent on phonics instruction and practice (Stahl, 1992).

It is important to show children how to use phonics taught in actual reading of texts. Unfortunately, too many phonics programs are not related to the actual reading children are asked to do. Children seem to learn letter-pattern knowledge best if they observe a pattern appearing in many different words, rather than in repetitions of the same word.

A Primer on the Content and Language of Phonics

Consonants. *Consonants* are all the sounds represented by letters of the alphabet except *a, e, i, o, u*. Consonants conform fairly closely to *one-to-one correspondence*—for each letter there is one sound. This property of consonants makes them of great value to the reader when attempting to sound out an unknown word. There are some consonant anomalies:

The letter *y* is a consonant only at the beginning of a syllable, as in *yet.*.

The letter *w* is sometimes a vowel, as in *flew*.

Sometimes consonants have no sound, as in *know*.

The letters *c* and *g* each have two sounds, called hard and soft sounds:

Hard *c: cat, coaster, catatonic* (*c* sounds like /k/)
Soft *c: city, receive, cite* (*c* sounds like /s/)

Hard *g: give, gallop, garbage* (*g* sounds like /g/)
Soft *g: giraffe, ginger, gym* (*g* sounds like /j/)

Consonant Blends. *Consonant blends* are two or three consonants grouped together, but each consonant retains its original sound. There are several major groups of blends:

l blends: *bl cl fl gl pl sl*

r blends: *br cr dr fr gr pr tr*

s blends: *sc sk sm sn sp st sw*

three-letter blends: *scr spr str*

Consonant Digraphs. When two or more consonants are combined to produce a new sound, the letter cluster is called a *consonant digraph*. The most common consonant digraphs are these:

ch as in *chin*   *ph* as in *phone*

sh as in *shell*   *gh* as in *ghost*

th as in *think*   *-nk* as in *tank*

wh as in *whistle* *-ng* as in *tang*

Vowels. *Vowels* are all the sounds represented by the letters *a, e, i, o, u*. The letter *y* serves as a vowel when it is not the initial sound of a word. Sometimes *w* functions as a vowel, usually when it follows another vowel. There is *rarely a one-to-one correspondence* between a letter representing a vowel and the sound of the vowel. Vowel sounds are influenced heavily by their location in a word and by the letters accompanying them. Several major types of vowel phonemes are worth knowing about.

A *long vowel* sound is a speech sound similar to the letter name of the vowel. A *macron* (‾) is sometimes used to indicate that a vowel is long. *Short vowel* sounds are speech sounds also represented by vowel letters. Short sounds are denoted by a *breve* (˘). An example of the long and short sound of each vowel letter follows:

SHORT VOWEL SOUND	LONG VOWEL SOUND
/ă/ as in *Pat*	/ā/ as in *lake*
/ĕ/ as in *bed*	/ē/ as in *be*
/ĭ/ as in *pit*	/ī/ as in *ice*
/ŏ/ as in *hot*	/ō/ as in *go*
/ŭ/ as in *hug*	/ū/ as in *use*

Often when a vowel letter initiates a word, the short sound will be used, for example: *at, effort, interest, optimist,* and *uncle.*

Vowel Digraphs.   *Vowel digraphs* are two vowels that are adjacent to one another. The first vowel is usually long and the second is silent. Vowel digraphs include *oa, ee, ea, ai, ay* as in *boat, beet, beat, bait,* and *bay.* There are notable exceptions: *oo* as in *look, ew* as in *flew, ea* as in *read.*

Vowel Diphthongs.   *Vowel diphthongs* are sounds that consist of a blend of two separate vowel sounds. These are /oi/ as in *oil,* /oy/ as in *toy,* /au/ as in *taught,* /aw/ as in *saw,* /ou/ as in *out,* and /ow/ as in *how.* Generally children do not need to be taught these formally.

Consonant-Influenced Vowels.   The letter *a* has a special sound when followed by an *l* as in *Albert* or *tallow.* R-controlled vowels occur when any vowel letter is followed by an *r: star, her, fir, for,* and *purr.* The power of *r* over vowel sounds is perhaps the most beneficial to point out to children, although in the process of forming their own generalizations about short and long vowel sounds children have probably incorporated *r*-controlled notions (Heilman, Blair, & Rupley, 1986).

Phonograms.   *Phonograms* (also called *rimes*) are letter patterns that help to form word families or rhyming words. Letter clusters such as *ad, at, ack, ag, an, ap, ash, ed, et, ess, en, ine,* and *ike* can be used to develop families of words; for example, the *ad* family: *bad, dad, sad, fad,* and so on. Phonograms may be one of the most useful letter patterns to teach because they encourage children to map speech sounds onto larger chunks of letters.

Syllables.   A *syllable* is a vowel or a cluster of letters containing a vowel and pronounced as a unit. Phonograms, for example, are syllables. The composition of the syllable signals the most probable vowel sound. Examine the following patterns:

Long vowels	CV	*be*
	CV*e*	*like*
		rote
	CVVC	*paid*
		boat
Short vowels	VC or CVC	*it*
		hot
R-controlled	V*r*	*art*
	CV*r*	*car, her*
Digraph/diphthong Variations	VV	*saw, book*
		boil, out

◆ FIGURE 5.3 *Continued*

These patterns underlie the formation of syllables. The number of syllables in a word is equal to the number of vowel sounds. For example, the word *disagreement* has four vowel sounds and thus four syllables. The word *hat* has one vowel sound and thus one syllable.

There are three primary syllabication patterns that signal how to break down a word into syllabic units.

- *VCCV.* When there are two consonants between two vowels, the word is usually divided between the consonants: *hap-pen, mar-ket, es-cape*. However, we do not split consonant digraphs such as *sh* or *th* or *ng*, as in *sing-er, fa-ther*. There is a variation of this pattern— the VCC*le* pattern. A word with this pattern is still divided between the consonants: *sad-dle, bot-tle, rat-tle, pud-dle*.

- *VCV pattern 1.* When one consonant is between two vowels, the division is before the consonant: *re-view, o-pen, be-gin*. Again there is a slight variation with the VC*le* pattern, but still divide before the consonant: *peo-ple, ta-ble, cra-dle*.

- *VCV pattern 2.* If using VCV pattern 1 does not result in a familiar word, divide after the consonant, as in *sal-ad* or *pan-el*.

Trachtenburg (1990) proposes a means to integrate phonic skills with reading print. She recommends a "whole-part-whole" sequence:

1. *Whole:* Read, comprehend, and enjoy a whole, high-quality literature selection.

2. *Part:* Provide instruction in letter-sound relationships and patterns by drawing from or extending the preceding literature selection.

3. *Whole:* Apply the new phonics skill when reading (and enjoying) another whole, high-quality literature selection.

For example, the teacher would first read *Angus and the Cat* aloud and engage the children in a discussion of it. Next the children could read it chorally together. Then the teacher would provide instruction in *-an* and *-at* phonograms, which are high-utility phonograms. This instruction could include finding the words in the story, the children writing sentences using these words, cloze exercises, and sorting words having these elements and reading them to partners. Finally, children could read books such as *The Cat in the Hat* or *Who Took the Farmer's Hat?* which also contain many words with these letter patterns. This sequence may span five or six lessons for beginning readers. Trachtenburg (1990) also provides a list (see Appendix D) of trade books with a high percentage of common letter-sound relationships.

3. Phonics Instruction Needs to Focus on Reading Print Rather Than on Learning Rules.

As noted earlier, skilled readers do not refer to phonics rules but see words in terms of patterns of letters. Adams (1990) points out that they recognize new words by comparing them or spelling patterns in them to words they already know. For example, when Stahl (1992) asked skilled readers to pronounce *minatory*, most people said the first syllable was /min/ as in *minute* or *miniature*, comparing it to a pattern in a word they already know how to pronounce. Phonics instruction should help children do this. Teachers need to first draw their attention to the order of letters in words and then encourage them to examine common patterns in words, through sounding out words and showing similarities between words.

Vowel letter-sound associations are often taught with phonics rules. Adams (1990), however, points out the vowel letter-sound correspondences are more stable when one looks at rimes than when letters are looked at in isolation. She gives the example that *ea* taken alone is thought of as irregular. However, in the rime *-ead*, it is regular in such words as *bread, read,* and *dead.* Clymer (1963) noted that children generally find it easier to learn to read words by using rhyming phonograms, and research on the relative ease with which children learn differing kinds of phonograms has reinforced this insight (Adams, 1990).

4. Phonics Instruction Needs to Include the Teaching of Onsets and Rimes.

Instead of teaching phonics rules, teach children to use onsets and rimes. An **onset,** or the part of the syllable before the vowel, is a consonant or consonant blend or digraph; a **rime** is the part from the vowel onward. As we have noted earlier, consonant letter-sound associations are fairly consistent. In addition, phonograms or rimes have been found to be generalizable. One study found that of the 286 phonograms that appear in primary grade tests, 95 percent were pronounced the same in every word in which they were found (Durrell, 1963). In addition, these 272 stable phonograms are contained in 1437 of the words commonly found in the speaking vocabularies of primary aged children (Murphy, 1957). According to Wylie and Durrell (1970), nearly 500 primary grade words can be derived from only 37 consistent rimes.

As children grow in their ability to identify words, it is easier and quicker for them to identify words when rimes and other letter patterns are taught than when they attempt to sound out all of the individual letters and blend them. Many successful teachers use *analogy-based strategies* for phonics instruction (Fox, 1996; Gaskins et al., 1997). (These will be discussed in the next section.)

5. Phonics Instruction Needs to Include Spelling-Based Strategies.

When children are encouraged to write and to use invented spellings as discussed in Chapter 3, they use their knowledge of letter-sound relationships. Writing with invented spelling improves children's awareness of phonemes, an important precursor to learning to decode words. When word study reflects spelling-based strategies, it is a powerful way to teach phonics (Bear et al., 1996).

Strategies for Teaching Phonics

The five guidelines just given are broad statements of principle by which teachers can become actively involved in the teaching of phonics based on contemporary approaches to instruction. These principles are grounded in research discoveries related to the phonics children use to identify words. Contemporary phonics approaches support children's ability to identify words through explicit strategy-based instruction and integrated learning during reading and writing activities. Throughout this section, we draw heavily on the strategies and activities described in what we believe to be three of the best resources for contemporary phonics instruction: *Phonics They Use: Words in Reading and Writing* (Cunningham, 1995), *Strategies for Word Identification: Phonics From a New Perspective* (Fox, 1996), and *Words Their Way: Word Study for Phonics, Vocabulary, and Spelling Instruction* (Bear et al., 1996).

Consonant-Based Strategies

In Chapter 4, we emphasized the importance of letter recognition. Recognizing and naming letters is one of the important accomplishments of early readers because it sets the stage for beginners to become involved in more sophisticated manipulations of letters and sounds. Consonant letters represent all of the individual phonemes associated with letters of the alphabet except for the vowels *a*, *e*, *i*, *o*, and *u*. Because consonants generally have one sound for each letter, they lend themselves well to instructional strategies that allow children to make discoveries about words. Once children have developed a good grasp of consonant letter-sound relationships, they can engage in activities that will help them recognize consonant digraphs and blends. Consider the following consonant-based phonics instruction strategies and activities.

Letter Actions.   Physical actions can be used to help children learn the consonants (Cunningham, 1995). Children who are kinesthetic learners benefit particularly from this technique. Simply choose your favorite action for each of the letters. On a large card, print the letter on one side and write the action on the reverse. For young children, a simple drawing of the action can be used in place of the word. When choosing the actions, make sure that each one can only represent one letter. For example, you wouldn't want to choose giggle for *g* and laugh for *l*—this might confuse the children. Introduce new letters as they are mastered. A simple activity to do is to mix the letter cards up and show them for five to ten seconds at a time. After the letter is shown, the children can act out the letter until you put the card down. You can increase the speed with which new letters are revealed as time goes on. Another variation is to pass out the letter cards to the students. They can act out a letter for the others to identify. A third activity is to have one child pick a card from the pile, begin acting it out, and then invite their classmates to do the same. The leader then picks another card and changes activities. Here is a list of actions for each consonant:

B:	bend, bounce, bob
C:	catch, creep, crawl, clap
D:	dance, duck, dive
F:	fall, freeze, flap
G:	gallop, giggle, grunt
H:	hop, hide, hit, holler

J:	jump, juggle, jog
K:	kick, kiss
L:	laugh, lick, lunge
M:	march, mix, munch
N:	nap, nod
P:	punch, push, paint
R:	run, rest, rip
S:	salute, sit, sing, slap, skip
T:	tiptoe, talk, tickle, tap
V:	vacuum, vanish
W:	wiggle, walk, wave
Y:	yawn, yell
Z:	zip, zigzag

Favorite Foods. Cunningham (1995) incorporates children's association with favorite foods to suggest another strategy for developing knowledge about consonant letters and sounds. The strategy calls for you to select favorite or unique foods, one food per letter. Prepare the food and share it as a class. Pictures of each food can be posted with each letter in the classroom. Children will easily be able to recall a letter when they look for things they have eaten. Help children make the connection between the consonant letter that begins each food and the initial sound they hear when the say the name of the food.

B:	bread, bananas, bagel
C:	cake, cookies, carrots, candy, celery
D:	donuts, dill (pickle), dressing
F:	fish, fettuccine, fruit
G:	gum, gingerbread, grapes, grapefruit, graham crackers
H:	hamburgers, ham, hummus, hotdogs
J:	jelly beans, Jell-O, jelly, juice
K:	Kool-Aid, kisses (Hershey's), kidney beans, kabobs
L:	lettuce, lemonade, lasagna, lemon, lime
M:	macaroni, meatballs, milk, mushrooms
N:	noodles, nuts
P:	potatoes, pancakes, pizza, pumpkin pie
R:	radishes, raisins, rice
S:	soup, salad, spaghetti
T:	toast, tea, tomatoes, turkey
V:	vegetables, V-8 juice, vanilla, vinegar
W:	watermelon, walnuts, water, waffles
Y:	yogurt, yams
Z:	zucchini bread, zucchini

The class members can keep a cookbook with the recipes they prepared during the year. Copies of the recipe books can be sent home with the children to enjoy at home.

Consonant Substitution.   As students develop consonant letter-sound knowledge, there are numerous activities that you can use to assist them with learning to read words that rhyme or belong to the same *word family*. These activities involve consonant substitution. The Best Practice featured in Box 5.2 outlines a basic procedure for consonant substitution. Bear et al. (1996) provide teachers with many options and variations.

Flip Books.   One variation on the basic consonant substitution procedures is to create flip books. Flip books are made from sentence strips, which are ideal for creating small booklets for word study. One large sentence strip is used for writing the rime (on the right side of the strip). Strips that are half the size of the larger one are cut for the onsets. Consonants, consonant blends, and consonant digraphs are written on these smaller cards and then stapled or attached with spiral binding to the longer card. Students flip through the booklet, reading each word. *Man* is changed to *can* or *ran* with the flip of the page.

From *Words Their Way: Word Study for Phonics, Vocabulary, and Spelling Instruction,* by D. R. Bear, M. Invernizzi, S. Templeton, and F. Johnston (Columbus, OH: Merrill, 1996), p. 177. Used by permission.

Making Words.   Flip books make students aware of their word-making capability when they substitute different consonants at the beginning of a rime. To engage children in the process of making words, consider these steps (Cunningham, 1995):

1. Decide on the rime that you wish students to practice, and develop a rime card for each of the students. Example:

> all

BOX 5.2   **BEST PRACTICE**

Consonant Substitution

The consonant substitution strategy actively involves students in learning words that rhyme or belong to the same word family. The basic steps for consonant substitution are as follows:

1. Target a rime for instructional emphasis, for example, *at*.

2. Develop a set of word cards that include the *at* rime.

3. Ask students to identify the first word in the set, for example, *bat*. If the students do not know the word, tell them. Then have them read the word after you. Place the word in a pocket folder or on the bulletin board so that it is visible to the students.

4. Show students the next word, *cat*. Invite them to read the word, and if they don't know it, tell them. Place the word in the pocket folder next to the first word. Help students detect letter differences between the first two words and discuss how the pronunciation of each word changes when the consonant letter is substituted.

5. Repeat the activity with the remaining word cards, and provide assistance as needed as you engage in discussion.

2. Develop a set of consonant letter cards for each student that can be used to make words with the rime that has been targeted for practice. Example:

3. Direct students to use the letter cards to make the first word, *ball*.

4. Invite students to now change the word to make *call*.

5. Repeat the activity until all of the words have been made.

In addition to letter and rime cards, students could use letter tiles to make words. Decide on the rime you would like students to study. Select the letter tiles for the rime and a number of consonants on additional tiles. Have the students construct the words on their desks or a carpet square. Also use slate squares or mini-chalkboards for consonant substitution. Students write the rime and then change the initial consonant to make words.

Other variations are possible: Use magnetic letters on a filing cabinet, cookie sheet, or chalkboard to make words. Consider spreading shaving cream on a table or on each student's desk. Have the children write a word from the rime in the cream. With each new word, just wipe away the beginning letter and replace it with a different consonant. Fill a cookie sheet with sand or Jell-O mix. Students write the words in the medium, changing only the beginning of the word. To erase the entire word, simply tap the sides of the tray lightly. This activity works well as a learning center. Remember to have a list of the rimes on hand for the children to refer to.

Finally, create pocket holders for cards. Large tagboard can be folded to hold letter cards in a bottom pocket. The sides can be folded in to create a trifold effect. The teacher can call out a specific three-letter word to be formed. Students slip the letter cards into the appropriate pockets. When the words are formed, the teacher calls out "show me." Students turn their pocket folders around for the teacher to check. The following short-vowel rimes are ideal for this activity:

an	*ap*	*ar*	*ab*	*ad*	*ag*	*am*	*at*
ed	*en*	*et*					
id	*in*	*ig*	*im*	*ip*	*it*		
ob	*od*	*op*	*og*	*ot*	*ow*		
ub	*ug*	*um*	*un*	*ut*			

From *Words Their Way: Word Study for Phonics, Vocabulary, and Spelling Instruction,* by D. R. Bear, M. Invernizzi, S. Templeton, and F. Johnston (Upper Saddle River, NJ: Prentice-Hall, 1996), p. 182. Used by permission.

Cube Words. Consonant substitution activities can also be developed using letter cubes. Students roll the cubes, using four to six cubes, depending on their ability level. Words are formed with the letters that are rolled. Words are recorded on a sheet of paper that is divided into columns marked with the numbers 1 through 5. Words with one letter are recorded into the first column, words with two letters in the second, and so on. Students can work independently or in pairs. Students who work in pairs may take turns rolling the cubes, forming the words, and writing the words in the appropriate columns. A sand clock or egg timer may be used. When time is up, students review the words and count up the total number of letters used as the score (Bear et al., 1996).

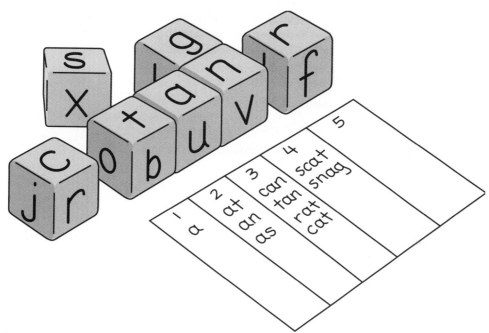

From *Words Their Way: Word Study for Phonics, Vocabulary, and Spelling Instruction,* by D. R. Bear, M. Invernizzi, S. Templeton, and F. Johnston (Upper Saddle River, NJ: Prentice-Hall, 1996), p. 188. Used by permission.

Once the children have a strong understanding of consonants, they are ready to begin work with consonant digraphs and blends. Many of the same activities done with consonants can be adapted for the digraphs and blends.

Digraph Actions and Food Associations.
For example, association with actions and foods can readily be done. Here is a list of words that correspond to various digraphs. The digraphs can be written on large cards, and the actions can be written or illustrated on the reverse side. When the cards are shown, the children do the corresponding action. Students may take turns or may act out the digraphs all together. Pictures of the foods can also be placed on large cards. Each food can be prepared and shared. The recipes can be added to the class cookbook.

	ACTIONS	FOODS
ch:	cheer, chirp, chop	cheese, chips, chocolate
sh:	shout, shake, shiver	sherbet, shortcake, shrimp
th:	think, throw, "thumbs up"	three-bean salad
wh:	whistle, whisper, whirl, whisk	white/wheat bread, whitefish

Digraph Tongue Twisters.   Cunningham (1995) recommends that you create consonant digraph tongue twisters for word learning. The tongue twisters can be written on large chart paper or on sentence strips for easy reference. Children enjoy hearing and reciting the silly sayings such as the examples given here. Be sure to explain the meanings of any difficult words. As part of the activity, have students illustrate the tongue twisters and write sentences to match. Also, have them underline the digraphs at the beginnings of the words on both the large chart paper and on their individual copies.

EXAMPLES OF TONGUE TWISTERS

Charles cheerfully chose cherry cheesecake.

Shy Shelly shall shake shells.

Theodore throws thistles through three thickets.

Analogy-Based Strategies

One of the ways that readers identify unknown words is to read them *by analogy* to known words (Goswami, 1988; Goswami & Bryant, 1990). The analogy strategy is used by all readers. It is based on the premise that words with similar onset and rime patterns also have similar pronunciations. For example, if a reader knew the word *cat*, she would be able to separate it into the *c* onset and *at* rime. Furthermore, the reader would also identify other *c* words such as *cap, call,* and *cut*, as well as other *at* words such as *sat, hat,* and *rat*.

Justin, a first grader, was reading the following poem which the teacher and students constructed during an interactive writing lesson.

In winter it's so nice,
To slip and slide on the ice,
Slip-sliding once,
Slip-sliding twice,
On ice that's white as rice.

His class had written it in their poetry notebooks and recited it each morning as a part of their morning poetry time. Justin was reading through his poems during quiet reading time and was slowly pointing to the words as he read. Each time he came to a word with the *ice* rime, he paused as if deep in thought. His teacher, who was close by, made these observations. "Justin was experiencing an 'aha' moment. He was piecing together what we had been talking about in class. He was making connections between the rhyming words and their letter patterns. It was almost as if I could see his mind separating the onsets and rimes and joining them back together. Justin would pause and say 'n-ice,' 'r-ice,' and 't-wice.' Later that day he came upon the word *mice* in a story he was reading. Immediately, he said, 'Look, this is another *ice* word.' He turned to the poem in his poetry notebook and carefully wrote the word *mice* at the bottom."

Each time that Justin pronounced the *ice* words, he left the rime intact. He automatically saw the letters *i-c-e* as a unit. He discovered that it was easier to pronounce the entire rime than to pronounce each sound separately. Since the pronunciations of onsets and rimes are consistent from word to word, it is wise to teach them in these forms.

A second-grade class was learning the *ock* rime pattern. The class studied words such as *block, sock* and *knock.* Throughout their word study, the students kept lists of additional words that contained the *ock* pattern, such as *padlock* and *peacock.* When they began to study the *oke* pattern in words such as *joke, smoke,* and *stroke,* they realized that the vowel *o* is pronounced differently in the two rimes. The different pronunciations were more easily remembered when they were learned as a part of a rime. Every onset is worthwhile to learn. The onsets of words give important clues about what an unknown word might be. Readers can often make predictions about words based on the onset alone.

Rimes are so numerous that teachers will need to select the most frequent patterns that their students will encounter. As we noted earlier in the chapter, 37 rimes make up over 500 of the most frequent words:

ack	*ain*	*ake*	*ale*	*all*	*ame*	*an*	*ank*
ap	*ash*	*at*	*ate*	*aw*	*ay*	*eat*	*ell*
est	*ice*	*ick*	*ide*	*ight*	*ill*	*in*	*ine*
ing	*ink*	*ip*	*ir*	*ock*	*oke*	*op*	*or*
ore	*uck*	*ug*	*ump*	*unk*			

The Random House Rhyming Dictionary (Stein, 1990) and *Webster's Compact Rhyming Dictionary* (1987) are excellent resources for words containing rime patterns.

All syllables have a rime. Whereas single-syllable words have only one rime and one onset, multisyllable words have any number of onset and rime combinations. Some words

Through phonics instruction, children learn to recognize words in text through letter patterns developed by using consistent sound-letter associations.

such as *at* and *it* have only a rime. To determine the onsets and rimes within a word, simply break the word apart into syllables. The number of syllables will be equal to the number of vowel sounds heard during the pronunciation of the word. For example, the word *finish* has one onset, *f*, and two rimes, *in* and *ish*. Examples of single and multisyllable words are shown in Figure 5.4.

The Analogy Strategy.   When students have difficulty identifying particular words, analogies can be made with familiar onsets and rimes. Emily, a third grader, was reading a passage from the story *Peter and the Wolf*. She had difficulty with the word *meadow* in the following sentence: "Around Peter's house was a garden and beyond the garden was a meadow." When the word *meadow* is analyzed closely, it can be divided as *m* (onset), *ead* (rime), *ow* (rime). Emily's teacher was quick to see that she was having difficulty with the word and provided her with assistance in this manner:

1. The teacher first covered up the *ow* rime at the end of the word.

2. The teacher asked Emily to think of other words that have the *ead* rime.

3. Emily supplied the words *lead* and *head*.

◆ FIGURE 5.4

Examples of Onsets and Rimes in Single-Syllable Words

onset	+ rime	= word
l	+ ive	= live
d	+ ark	= dark
	and	= and

Examples of Onsets and Rimes in Multisyllable Words

onset	+ rime	+ onset	+ rime	+ onset	+ rime	= word
gr	+ and	+ f	+ a	+ th	+ er	= grandfather
f	+ or		+ est			= forest
g	+ ar	+ d	+ en			= garden
b	+ e	+ y	+ ond			= beyond
m	+ ead	+	+ ow			= meadow

4. The teacher then asked her to think how *m-ead* would be pronounced.

5. Emily blended the onset and rime together to get /med/.

6. The teacher then had Emily predict what the word could be based on the beginning of the word and the context of the sentence.

7. Emily correctly stated the word *meadow* and then confirmed that it would make sense in the context of the story.

The Word-Building Strategy.   The word-building strategy is based on the knowledge that children frequently use pronounceable word parts as a decoding strategy (Gunning, 1995). For instance, if a child would encounter the word *train,* she may first say *rain* and then *train.* With simple C-V-C words like *cup,* children may say the beginning *c* sound and then the entire word, thus naturally dividing the word into the onset and rime. Word building capitalizes on students' natural tendency to use onsets and rimes when decoding words. Study the Best Practice steps for the word-building strategy in Box 5.3.

Rimes in Nursery Rhymes.   Nursery rhymes are ideal for onsets and rimes. Poems and rhymes can be printed on large chart paper and posted in the classroom. Particular attention can be paid to the rime and onset patterns. Students can circle or highlight the letter patterns with colorful markers. When the poems are hung in the classroom, the children will easily be able to see the onsets and rimes from a distance.

Word Building with Onset and Rime Tiles.   Fox (1996) recommends the use of onset and rime tiles to make words. Create word tiles with index cards or sentence strips. Print the onsets and rimes that occur most frequently in daily classroom reading. Individual students may use smaller tiles while the teacher uses oversized tiles with a pocket chart. Begin with three or four onsets and one rime. Have the students practice joining the tiles together to create words such as *top, mop, pop,* and *hop.* Discuss that the rime remains the same in each word; only the onset changes. Model the procedure with the large tiles and the pocket chart. When the students have mastered one rime, add another. Put the two rimes side by side in the pocket chart, and discuss what words can be made with the onsets. You may wish to have multiple tiles for each rime. Clues may be given for creating words. For instance, the teacher might say, "Place the *at* tile in the center of your work space. Look for the letter that begins the words *hill* and *heart.* Add that tile to *at.* What word have you made?" Repeat the procedure using clues for different onsets. Observe the students to make sure they are correctly identifying the onsets. This strategy can be adapted for older students. The rimes can be more difficult vowel patterns, and the onsets can be blends and digraphs.

Hink Pinks.   As students begin to explore rimes, they will soon discover creative combinations called "hink pinks" (Cunningham, 1995; Fox, 1996). *Sad dad, bee tree,* and *flat mat* are a few examples of hink pinks. As students encounter these colorful and often unconventional combinations, they can keep a record of them. Lists of hink pinks can be added to personal dictionaries or journals. Favorite examples can be illustrated for a class book or made into pictures for display in the classroom. One variation is to have students write the

Word-Building Strategy

The word-building strategy begins with the identification of the specific rime pattern to be studied. If the rime *ine* was the focus, it would be presented in the following manner.

STEP 1: BUILDING WORDS BY ADDING THE ONSET

Write *ine* on large chart paper on the overhead. Ask students to supply different consonants to create the words *mine, nine, line,* and *dine.* As each word is written, carefully enunciate the beginning consonant and the rime and then the whole word. For example, *mine* would be *m-, -ine, mine.* Repeat the procedure for each new word formed. Attention may then be paid to the *ine* rime. Discussion may clarify the relationship between the long *i* and silent *e.*

STEP 2: BUILDING WORDS BY ADDING THE RIME

To ensure that students have a clear understanding of the onset and rime, present the onset and have the students supply the rime. Write *m* and have the children tell what would be added to create the word *mine.* After adding the *ine,* say the word in parts, *m-, -ine,* and then as a whole. Point to each letter pattern as it is said.

STEP 3: SELECTING A MODEL WORD

Choose a common word that easily illustrates the specific letter pattern. The *ine* rime can be shown with a picture of the number 9. Illustrations can be added to the children's personal dictionaries or anyplace else that can be easily referenced.

STEP 4: GUIDED PRACTICE

Provide many opportunities for the students to practice using the letter pattern. Possibilities include sharing big books with the pattern, using magnetic letters on cookie sheets, writing words on mini-chalkboards, tumbling letter blocks to form words, or making flip books with the rime pattern.

STEP 5: APPLICATION

Provide opportunities for students to read stories, poems, chants, and rhymes with the specific letter pattern. It may be helpful to keep a list of appropriate titles or copies of poems and rhymes in a binder or folder marked with rimes and letter patterns.

rimes on sentence strips and then illustrate them on a separate piece of paper. The illustrations and sentence strips can be mixed up and then put back together again. Pictures can be displayed on the bulletin board. Small hooks or thumbtacks could be placed under each picture. The sentence strips could then be matched with the pictures. Definitions can be written for each hink pink. For example, "an unhappy father" would be a *sad dad,* and an "overweight feline" would be a *fat cat.* The rhyming words and their definitions could also be mixed and matched. Hink pinks will not only help students think about rimes and word definitions but also engage them in mind-stretching activities.

Spelling-Based Strategies

Spelling-based strategies for word identification were pioneered by Henderson (1990) and his research associates. These strategies are designed to engage children in word study (Bear et al., 1996). Through the use of *word bank, word wall,* and *word sorting* strategies, children examine words and word patterns.

Word Banks.
Word banks are simply boxes of word cards that individual students are studying. Word banks are a natural extension of the language-experience approach in which students learn to read words from dictated stories. Students make word cards from the words in their language-experience stories and study them. A quick way of helping children begin a word bank without using dictation is to have students read a selection that is fairly easy for them. The students underline words that they could not immediately recognize and words that they cannot figure out, as well as words that they consciously used context or mediated strategies to figure out. The students then write each of these words on word cards. Words for word banks can be gleaned from basal readers, trade books, signs, labels, and print with which the children are involved. Words in the word banks can then be used in word sorting activities, as we will describe shortly.

Word Walls.
Another way to study words and word patterns is through **word walls.** A word wall may be started when students notice words that rhyme but are not spelled with the same letter patterns. For example, in Susan Valenti's second-grade classroom, the class participated in a shared-book experience as the teacher read Shel Silverstein's "Enter This Deserted House." In this poem, the poet rhymes the words *do, too, blue,* and *few* as he creates for readers young and old the eerie feeling of entering a deserted house.

As Susan read the poem, the children noticed that *do, too, blue,* and *few* all rhymed but were not spelled with the same letter pattern. So Susan and her class started a word wall for this sound. The word wall was constructed on a sheet of shelf paper hung on the wall. Students were asked to find words for each of the spellings of the sound /oo/. The following are some of the words they found:

do	*too*	*blue*	*few*
tool	clue	dew	
fool	sue		

Word walls may be adapted for a variety of word study purposes at different grade levels. Kindergarten classrooms, for example, often begin word walls by listing the letters of the alphabet in large, bright letters. **High-frequency words,** words that occur repeatedly in text, are added to the wall underneath the letters of the alphabet. Tonya, a kindergarten teacher, uses poetry to highlight specific words for the wall. Each week Tonya introduces a poem, chant, or rhyme. She selects three focus words from the poem to add to the wall. When her students learned the nursery rhyme "Jack and Jill," they focused on the words *pail, water,* and *Jack.* The words were written on colored construction paper and cut out along letter boundaries. Illustrations were added as an aid in word identification. The words were stapled underneath the beginning letter, where they served as a reference for the children's reading and writing all year long.

Primary grade word walls may also include words that are high-frequency sight words, follow a specific rime or phonogram pattern, or are commonly used in the children's writing. One first-grade classroom has a word wall dedicated to the 37 rime patterns introduced earlier in the chapter. Each week the class studies a new vowel pattern within the context of poetry. Words that followed the specific rime pattern are added to the wall. As new words are identified, they too are listed under the rime.

Intermediate and middle-level teachers often target homophones, compound words, or commonly misspelled words for students to reference. Words that are a part of a theme or topic study may also be emphasized for word study on a classroom word wall. A sixth-grade class studying the Civil War included words like *slavery, Confederate, secede, union, soldier,* and *battlefield* on the word wall.

Word walls may be permanent or temporary. They may stay up for the entire school year or only for a particular unit of study. They can be written on sentence strips, word cards, poster board, or chart paper. Charts are ideal for classrooms with limited space. They may be displayed when needed and then stored away when not in use. The charts can be put back on display for review or comparisons with other word study charts.

Portable word walls can be made with file folders. Manila folders can be divided into categories according to alphabet, letter patterns, rimes, themes, and so on. Students can copy words onto the folder for personal reference at home or school. This technique may be especially helpful for intermediate grades where students are in different classrooms each day.

Word Sorting.   Classifying stimuli into classes according to their common properties is one of the most basic and powerful operations of human thinking and is responsible for much of a child's natural learning ability. This is why **word sorting activities** are so suitable for studying words. When sorting words, students look for similarities in words, including letter pattern similarities.

There are two kinds of word sorts: open and closed. In both, children are guided toward *discovering* similarities in words, rather than *being told* how they are alike.

For open word sorts, the following steps are suggested:

1. Each child in a small group has a word bank. Sorting activities can be done with children seated on the floor or at a table.

2. The children are asked to go through their word banks and group some words that go together in some way.

3. After grouping words, each child tells what words they have grouped. Then another student "reads their minds" by telling how the group of words is alike.

4. In open word sorts, there is no one correct answer. Students just have to be able to explain why they grouped words as they did. For example, Jill grouped *top, tickle, to,* and *terrible* because they all begin with the letter *t.* John sorted *tomato, potato, tomorrow,* and *butterfly* because they all have three syllables. Sue sorted *mother, father, sister,* and *brother* because they are all family members. Helen classified *pretty, ugly, green,* and *fat* together because they all describe something. Notice that students can sort words by attributes concerning letter-sound relationships, the meaning of the words, or their function in sentences.

In closed word sorts, the students search to group words according to a specific attribute the teacher has in mind. There is a correct way to sort the words in closed sorts. The students figure out what that correct way is.

The ability to generalize from the known to the unknown is a fundamental aspect of all word analysis. The closed word sort is an excellent way to get students to think about letter patterns in words. As students are learning the consonants and consonant blends, they can sort pictures of objects beginning with those consonants and consonant blends.

Students can also group words by letter patterns. *In having students sort words into groups of those with the same letter patterns, you are teaching the process of looking for letter patterns; you are not just teaching individual letter patterns.* Just as skilled readers have not learned to recognize 50,000 English words instantly by sight by studying 50,000 word cards, skilled readers have not learned English letter patterns by studying them in isolation. They have learned how English letters are patterned by reading and writing. So the purpose in having students sort words by letter patterns is to encourage children to look for graphic similarities in words. Students can be given word cards with letter patterns that are not similar.

> sad   pad   glad   ladder   radish   tadpole   advertise
> dip   rip   lip   zipper   tulip   hippopotamus   shipwreck

A harder task is to have students sort word cards with letter patterns that are somewhat similar.

> sad   glad   admit   admiration
> made   grade   lemonade

Students can also be asked to sort words with inflectional endings.

> plays   wishes   played   wished

Notice that these words could be sorted by the words with the same roots or by the words with plural versus past-tense endings.

Have-a-Go.   The Have-a-Go strategy originated in Australia and was made popular in the United States by Regie Routman (1991). The strategy simply involves the use of a Have-a-Go sheet to record words from children's daily writing that are particularly challenging to spell. Students choose misspelled words from their work and then "have a go" at the standard spelling.

Here's how the strategy works: The students write the words that they think they misspelled in the first column of the Have-a-Go sheet (see Figure 5.5). Then they attempt to improve on the spelling in the second and third columns as they meet with the teacher for additional instruction. Each of the students schedules time to meet in conference with the teacher to discuss these misspellings.

Alyson Meyer explains how she uses the Have-a-Go strategy in the Class Works featured in Box 5.4.

Using Meaning and Letter-Sound Information to Identify Words

As noted in Chapter 3, some preschool children develop an expectation that print should make sense. They have heard stories frequently read to them and are immersed in a language-rich environment. These young children rely heavily on pictures or other aspects of the immediate situation in deciding what printed words say.

Steve, the 3-year-old introduced at the beginning of this chapter, makes use of meaningful information from his immediate surroundings, his *environmental context*. But as he continues to develop as a reader, he will learn to use with greater sophistication various kinds of *meaning and letter-sound information from the text itself.*

◆ Figure 5.5

Have-a-Go Sheet

Word	Attempt 1	Attempt 2	Correct Spelling

Strategies for Using Context

Readers use meaning clues to identify words they have heard but may not have experienced visually in print. When readers can combine meaning clues with phonic information, they have developed a powerful tool for word identification. Cloze-type activities help show readers how to use the *context* of a sentence or passage.

Modified Cloze Passages.

Modified *cloze passages* can be constructed from materials that are at first relatively easy to read. The material used can be stories and poems from basal readers, language-experience stories, other student-written products, or subject matter texts. Gradually, the difficulty of the reading material can be increased. Note that cloze-type materials are available commercially from publishing companies. However, teachers often produce the most effective cloze passages because they are in the best position to gear the material to the needs of their students.

Cloze activities can contain as little as one deletion in a sentence or up to 20 deletions in a passage. There are different deletion systems: selective word deletion, systematic word deletion, and partial word deletion. The kind of deletion system used determines what aspects of the passage are focused on as students complete the cloze passages and discuss their responses.

Using *selective word deletion*, important nouns, verbs, adjectives, and adverbs can be left out. These words carry the meaning of the context of what the author is saying. When selected nouns, verbs, adjectives, and adverbs are deleted, the focus is on meaningful information from the passage. In addition, vocabulary characteristics of a subject are emphasized. For example, if the subject of a cloze passage is going to the zoo, such words as *yak* and *zebra* are discussed in terms of how their meaning contributed to the meaning of the passage.

In *systematic word deletion*, every *n*th word in a passage is deleted—for example, every fifth, tenth, or twentieth word. When such a cloze deletion system is used as a teaching device, many function words will be deleted; therefore, much of the discussion will consider examples such as "Bill went _____ the hill." Did Bill go up, down, or around the hill? The students must deduce appropriate words from the context of the rest of the passage.

In *partial word deletion*, every *n*th word or selected word is partially deleted. Three types of partial deletions can be used: (1) Initial consonants, initial consonant blends, digraphs, or initial vowels are given, and all other letters are deleted. (2) The letters mentioned in option 1 plus terminal consonants or terminal consonant digraphs are given, and all other letters are deleted. (3) Consonants are given and vowels are deleted.

Cloze passages in which only the initial letters are given help children understand that initial letters serve to reduce the number of meaningful substitutions available. The discussion of this type of cloze would include how useful the content plus some graphic information can be. The more graphic information given, the more certain the reader will be of what the word is. Study examples of the three types of cloze activities in Figure 5.7.

Cloze with Choices Given.

If students find it difficult to complete cloze activities, giving choices for the deleted words makes the task easier. Here are some differing procedures to use in devising the choices for the cloze blanks.

The Have-a-Go Strategy (The Incredible Inventor)

Alyson Meyer uses the Have-a-Go technique with her third graders. Although she calls it an "Incredible Inventor" sheet, the idea behind it is the same. She changed the name of Have-a-Go because children were not familiar with the Australian expression.

Alyson's students keep their "Incredible Inventor" sheet in their writing folder, where it can be readily accessed during personal writing time and writing conferences (see Figure 5.6). Students add words that they had trouble spelling to the first column of their Incredible Inventor sheet during the first draft of their writing.

After writing, the students meet in conference with Alyson. They bring their writing journals and Incredible Inventor sheets to the conference. One aspect of writing conference time is discussing the words on the Incredible Inventor sheets. Some children may have four or five words to discuss with her; others may have twice that many. Alyson will guide the students toward standard spellings of the words with comments such as "You're missing a letter here. What do you think it might be?" or "Think about how to spell the word _____. Part of this word is the same." She never just gives the students the correct answer but instead leads them to a better understanding of word and letter patterns. If a student is at a dead end,

◆ FIGURE 5.6   Incredible Inventors

Word	Attempt 1	Attempt 2	Correct Spelling
Squorrl	Squrorl i	Squrriol *squirrel*	Squirrel ☺
Champatison	Campatison *tion*	Campation *competition*	competition
Srink	Shrink ☺		Shrink
algaba	algabra *e*	algebra ☺	algebra
wagen	wagen	wagan *o*	wagon
Scopian	Scorpion ☺		Scorpian
mointian	mantion	mountain ☺	mountain

BOX 5.4 CONTINUED

she leads them by writing three possible spellings of a word and then gives them the chance to select the word that looks correct.

During one writing conference, a student had misspelled the word *skate*, writing *skait* instead. Alyson guided the conference by saying, "I see that you used a common word pattern for the long *a* sound, but that's not the right pattern for this word. Think of another spelling pattern for long *a*." The student then suggested both the *ay* and *a*-silent *e* patterns. The student experimented with both combinations in the "first attempt" and "second attempt" columns of the Incredible Inventor sheet and decided that the *a*-silent *e* pattern was the correct one for this particular word. The fourth column is reserved for the conventional spelling of the word.

After the writing conference, students then correct their own writing, using what they learned during conference time. Alyson knows that her students learn best when they are given the opportunity to experiment with letter and word patterns and when they are challenged to discover spelling conventions. The Have-a-Go strategy provides a framework to experiment with and explore words so that students can gain a deeper understanding of the English language and its conventions.

1. The incorrect item, or *foil*, can be a different part of speech as well as different graphically.

    The doctor was _____ that the patient got better so quickly.

    MONKEY/AMAZED

2. The foil can be graphically similar to the correct item but a different part of speech.

    The doctor was _____ that the patient got better so quickly.

    AMAZON/AMAZED

3. The foil and correct answer can be graphically similar and the same part of speech.

    The doctor was _____ that the patient got better so quickly.

    AMUSED/AMAZED

4. Three choices can also be given: the correct response, a word of the same part of speech that is graphically similar, and a word of a different part of speech that is and graphically similar.

    The doctor was _____ that the patient got better so quickly.

    AMAZED/AMUSED/AMAZON

A discussion of these particular cloze examples would include a discussion of why a doctor would be more likely to be *amazed* than *amused* by a patient's progress in getting well. Students would also note that "The doctor was *amazon* that the patient got better so quickly" makes no sense.

◆ FIGURE 5.7

Three Different Types of Cloze Activities

Selective Word Deletions

Slim and Shorty were _____ who lived on a big ranch a long way from town.

Slim and Shorty had five mules. One day Slim _____, "We're almost

out of _____. We have to go to _____. We'll take the

_____ to carry the food home."

Systematic Word Deletions

Slim and Shorty began to line _____ the mules. Slim got on the

_____ at the front of the line. _____ got on the mule at the

_____ of the line.

Partial Word Deletions

Then Shorty s_____, "How will we get all five m_____ to town?"

Slim said, "You w_____ the mules. That way we won't l_____

any."

Cryptography and Mutilated Messages.   Many children enjoy deciphering codes and writing messages in code. When something is written in code, something has been done to change the graphic display, so context is used to break the code.

Here are a few ways messages can be changed. You and your students can think of more ways. There are also trade books on cryptology that your students can enjoy.

Color names are inserted. (Look red under blue the green table.)

Bottom of letter is covered.

Words are scrambled. (Door the open.)

No spaces are left between words and a letter is inserted between words. (Illustrateathebpoemcondpageefifty-sixfofgyourhbook.)

Notice that each of these coded messages tells the reader to do something. This is a good way to use codes. Jane Jones, a second-grade teacher, devised some coded messages that led her students on a treasure hunt. Students read directions in coded messages telling them to look specific places, for example, "Look behind the red geraniums." Behind the geraniums was another coded message that told them to look in another place. These coded messages finally led them to a treasure.

Reader-Selected Miscue Strategy. How important is a single word? This is a question readers need to ask about words they find troublesome. To get this notion across, have students read a somewhat difficult selection. Ask them to put light marks by words that they do not recognize, but tell them *not to try to figure them out.* This is actually hard to do! After students have read the selection, ask them to summarize what the author was saying. Then go back and discuss the words the students have marked. Do they know what these words are now? Many of the words they will know in spite of the fact that they did not actually try to figure them out. What about the words they are still unable to recognize? Students need to decide, "Are these important to understanding the selection?" If students feel the word is important to understanding the selection, decide how meaning cues and letter-sound cues can be used to determine what the word is. The point of this lesson, though, is to realize that often a selection can be read and understood without recognizing every word. Students can categorize difficult words that they think are crucial to understanding the selection and those that are not and then discuss why they placed particular words in each category.

Lessons such as this one can be structured to convey the idea that some words contribute more to understanding a selection than others. Also, a teacher needs to encourage students informally to ask themselves about unrecognized words they meet as they read; for example, "How important is this word to understanding what the author is saying?"

Watson (1978) devised a teaching strategy that she called *reader-selected miscues* to help children become aware that they are in control of making sense out of print. Children should know that they have a range of options available to them when they encounter words they don't recognize or passages they don't understand during reading.

Study the Best Practice featured in Box 5.5 for basic procedures related to the reader-selected miscue strategy.

Using Context to Cross-Check and Self-Monitor Meaning

Cross-checking and *self-monitoring* strategies help readers combine letter-sound and meaning information to make sense while reading. **Cross-checking** simply involves rereading a sentence or two to "cross-check"—confirm, modify, or reject—probable pronunciations of unknown words encounter during reading. If the sentence makes sense, the meaning confirms the reader's cross-checking; if the sentence doesn't make sense, the reader tries again.

The cross-checking strategy takes little preparation and is very effective for teaching phonics in meaningful contexts. For example, notice how cross-checking brings together students' knowledge of digraph sounds and the use of context clues for decoding words. On large chart paper, sentence strips, or the overhead, write sentences similar to the ones given here. Cunningham (1995), a proponent of cross-checking, notes that children love to see their names used in the sentences, so make sure to include them.

Reader-Selected Miscue Strategy

The following procedures may be adapted to fit a variety of reading situations that may arise during the course of a school day:

◆ Children are assigned to read a selection (fiction or nonfiction) silently and without interruption.

◆ When a troublesome word is encountered or something is not making sense, the child inserts a bookmark or lightly marks the page to indicate the problem and then continues reading.

◆ When the reading is completed, the children review the words or concepts they have marked and select *three* that caused the greatest difficulty.

◆ In addition, the children are asked to explain *how* some of the problems or words that they encountered seemed to "solve themselves" as they continued to read.

◆ Finally, the students are to examine passages involving the troublesome words or ideas that they had marked and help each other in clarifying them.

What do readers learn from this procedure? For one thing, they learn that everyone makes mistakes; no one reads "word-perfectly." Readers also see that they are the ones to decide what is hard for them and what comes easily. They see that a portion of a text may be quite readable to some readers and less readable for others but that everyone runs into words or concepts that perplex them. Finally, they see from reader-selected miscues that with a keep-going strategy, many unknowns will be clarified by the text as they continue reading.

Emily likes to eat <u>chocolate chip</u> cookies.
Kate likes to have <u>wheat</u> bread for her sandwiches.
Zachary likes to eat <u>sherbet</u> on a hot day.
Matthew is good at <u>throwing</u> Frisbees.
Joseph <u>cheers</u> for his team to win.

Cover the underlined word in each sentence up with a Post-it note or index card. Have the students read the sentence and predict what words would make sense in the blank spot. Reveal just the initial digraph and have the children check their predictions, crossing out any that do not begin with the specific digraph. Record new words that make sense and begin with the digraph. Finally, uncover the word and see if any of the predictions match the original word.

The central importance of cross-checking, even at the earliest stages of development, is crucial in learning to read. When a teacher places a high premium on students' word-perfect oral reading performance, young developing readers are at risk of not developing strategies for **self-monitoring.** Such readers become dependent on the teacher or other able readers to help them when they encounter a hard word. One of your main goals is to train children to self-monitor their reading by encouraging cross-checking.

Another way to help children self-monitor is to discuss with them what to do when they come to unknown words. When children attempt to figure out unknown words in text, encourage them to use meaning and letter-sound information. Direct the process by fostering a search for information cues as described in the previous section. Help children monitor their searches by using a chart similar to the one in Figure 5.8. Explain the procedures listed on the chart and give children practice using them.

RAPID RECOGNITION OF WORDS

There is more to rapid word identification than flashing a sight-word card and requiring an instant response. Immediate identification of words is the result of *experience with* reading, seeing, discussing, using, and writing words.

◆ FIGURE 5.8   Monitoring an Unknown Word

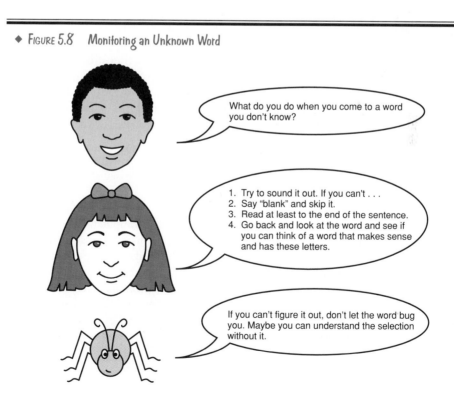

Several reasons are usually given for beginning word identification with whole words. One is that students learn to recognize words by their *configuration* (their length and general contour or shape). The configuration of a word, however, has been shown to be *a low-utility cue in word identification* (Marchbanks & Levin, 1965). A word's general contour loses its usefulness because there are many words that have similar configurations.

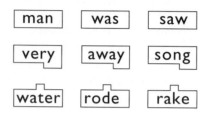

Configuration clues may be more useful for unusual-looking words. For example, we may speculate that words such as *elephant* and *McDonald's* are quickly identified by young children because of their distinctive shapes.

Yet we may also argue that words such as these are identified automatically by a child because they are charged with personal meaning.

Durkin's (1980) rationale for whole word instruction still makes the most sense. She suggested whole word methodology at the outset of reading instruction on the following grounds: Whole word learning allows children to sense "real reading" quickly. It can also be of greatest interest to most children, because they are apt to be familiar with the concept of a *word* rather than linguistic concepts associated with phonics, such as *letter* or *sound.*

High-Frequency Words

Numerous lists of high-frequency words have been compiled. Figure 5.9 contains Edward Fry's "instant words." According to Fry (1980), the first 100 instant words on his list make up half of all written material and the 300 words make up 65 percent of all written text.

High-frequency word lists contain a large number of words that are grammatically necessary—words such as articles, conjunctions, pronouns, verbs of being, and prepositions that bind together information-bearing words. These words are called *function words;* they do much to help a sentence function, but they do not get across the meaning of a passage by themselves. Nouns, action verbs, adjectives, and adverbs are *content words;* they supply the content or information of the topic.

Compare the following paragraphs to get a better idea of how these two types of words work together in running print.

The Instant Words

First Hundred

Words 1–25	Words 26–50	Words 51–75	Words 76–100
the	or	will	number
of	one	up	no
and	had	other	way
a	by	about	could
to	word	out	people
in	but	many	my
is	not	then	than
you	what	them	first
that	all	these	water
it	were	so	been
he	we	some	call
was	when	her	who
for	your	would	oil
on	can	make	now
are	said	like	find
as	there	him	long
with	use	into	down
his	an	time	day
they	each	has	did
I	which	look	get
at	she	two	come
be	do	more	made
this	how	write	may
have	their	go	part
from	if	see	over

Common suffixes: *-s, -ing, -ed*

Second Hundred

Words 101–125	Words 126–150	Words 151–175	Words 176–200
new	great	put	kind
sound	where	end	hand
take	help	does	picture
only	through	another	again
little	much	well	change
work	before	large	off
know	line	must	play
place	right	big	spell
year	too	even	air
live	mean	such	away
me	old	because	animal
back	any	turn	house

Source: From *Elementary Reading Instruction,* by Edward Fry (New York: McGraw-Hill, 1977). Reprinted with permission of McGraw-Hill Companies, Inc.

Second Hundred (cont.)

Words 101–125	Words 126–150	Words 151–175	Words 176–200
give	same	here	point
most	tell	why	page
very	boy	ask	letter
after	follow	went	mother
thing	came	men	answer
our	want	read	found
just	show	need	study
name	also	land	still
good	around	different	learn
sentence	form	home	should
man	three	us	America
think	small	move	world
say	set	try	high

Common suffixes: -s, -ing, -ed, -er, -ly, -est

Third Hundred

Words 201–225	Words 226–250	Words 251–275	Words 276–300
every	left	until	idea
near	don't	children	enough
add	few	side	eat
food	while	feet	face
between	along	car	watch
own	might	mile	far
below	close	night	Indian
country	something	walk	real
plant	seem	white	almost
last	next	sea	let
school	hard	began	above
father	open	grow	girl
keep	example	took	sometimes
tree	begin	river	mountain
never	life	four	cut
start	always	carry	young
city	those	state	talk
earth	both	once	soon
eye	paper	book	list
light	together	hear	song
thought	got	stop	leave
head	group	without	family
under	often	second	body
story	run	late	music
saw	important	miss	color

Common suffixes: -s, -ing, -ed, -er, -ly, -est

PARAGRAPH 1

Once upon a _____ there was a _____ _____ _____
_____. One _____ _____ _____ an _____ in the
_____ _____ _____, "An _____ _____ has a
_____ of _____. I'll _____ this _____ _____ me to
his _____ of _____."

PARAGRAPH 2

_____ _____ _____ time _____ _____
_____ mean man named Grumble. _____ day Grumble saw _____
elf _____ _____ woods. Grumble said, "_____ elf always
_____ _____ pot _____ gold. _____ make _____ elf
take _____ _____ _____ pot _____ gold."

When reading paragraph 1, can you tell what the paragraph is about? All of the content or information-bearing words were taken out. When reading paragraph 2, at the very least you know that the story is about a mean man named Grumble and an elf. By studying paragraph 2, you might even have figured out that Grumble wanted to take the elf's pot of gold.

How Should Function Words Be Taught?

Function words like *was, there, the, has,* and *of* should be taught as sight words early in children's reading instruction. The rationale for teaching rapid recognition of these words is this: Beginning readers who can quickly and accurately identify high-frequency words will more readily read across *any line of print,* because these words make up 65 percent or more of *all* written material. Readers who are able to identify these common words rapidly are much more able to use context to help identify words while they read.

Another reason children have been taught high-frequency function words as sight words is because a large number of them are not phonically regular. Words like *the, one,* and *of* do not conform to predictable letter-sound associations.

High-frequency function words are also troublesome to young readers because of the similarity of their graphic features. Some children frequently become confused, for example, over words beginning with *wh* and *th* (*that, what, then, when, where*). Instructional strategies are needed to help children deal with function words to the point of an immediate, automatic recognition.

Children are less likely to confuse such words as *was* and *saw* when meaning is being emphasized. When these two words are interchanged in a sentence, *the sentence does not make sense.* Jan, a first-grade teacher, knew the usefulness of introducing confusing sight words like *was* and *saw* using predictable language. The day after her class took a fall nature walk, she had her students dictate a caption story in which each caption described something they had seen on the walk.

I *saw* an oak tree.
I *saw* a squirrel.
I *saw* some poison ivy.

Jan and her students first read the story in unison, and then individual students read it aloud. The students then illustrated the sentence that they had contributed to the captioned story.

A week or so later, Jan read *Feelings from A to Z,* by Pat Visser. After discussing the feelings of the children and the situations that were described in the book, Jan asked her students to remember a feeling that they had experienced and to draw a picture of the situation that caused them to feel that way. The captions written under their illustrations used the pattern "I was _____ when _____."

> I *was* embarrassed when I sat down in green paint.
> I *was* scared when I went through a haunted house at Halloween.
> I *was* happy when my mother came home from the hospital.

The students then compared the two sets of caption stories they had dictated, framing the words *was* and *saw* in the highly predictable contexts. Once she felt confident that the students could read the stories, Jan gave them further practice in reading these confusing pairs by sending illustrated copies of the captioned stories home with them to read to their parents.

Words such as *was* and *saw, every* and *very,* and *what* and *that* are *graphically* similar. That is, these words *look alike.* Context activities such as the one Jan used sensitize students to minimal differences in words. A beginning reader learns that words that look alike must make sense and sound right in the context of what is being read.

Sometimes young readers habitually misidentify function words (or content words for that matter) that have minimal graphic differences. A first grader, for instance, may start a sentence that begins with *then* by reading the word *when.* This miscue may occur out of habit, probably for no other reason than a beginner often relies heavily on what is grammatically *familiar.* A young child is apt to begin more sentences orally with the word *when* than the word *then.* In cases such as this, the child's schema for how language works plus a graphic cue from the word itself contributes to the observed response.

We recommend that children listen to themselves read so that they can develop an ear for the kinds of misidentifications just described. The tape recorder is a valuable learning resource. As children listen to themselves read aloud, ask, "Does this (the misidentification) sound right?" "Does what you just heard make sense?"

Teaching Key Words

One of the quickest and most interesting ways to ease children into reading is through key word teaching. **Key words** are a fundamental aspect of language-experience instruction. Key words are charged with personal meaning and feeling, for they come out of the experience and background of the young child. The concept of key words emerged from the work of Sylvia Ashton-Warner (1959, 1963, 1972).

Teachers help students identify words quickly through key word instruction. Key words become the core of what might be traditionally called *sight-word development.* The emphasis in learning words is to tie instruction to meaningful activity through *seeing, discussing, using, defining,* and *writing* words.

Ashton-Warner (1972) suggested that each child keep a file or word bank of special personal words drawn both from personal experiences and experiences with literature. The word cards could be used in the following way. The personal word cards of a group of children are jumbled together. The children sort out their own word cards and read them to each other before placing them back into their files. Cards that are not recognized are left out and later discarded. Thus the words kept by each child retain personal meaning and use.

Group Activities with Key Words. There are many useful strategies for key word instructional activities in small groups (Veatch, Sawicki, Elliot, Flake, & Blakey, 1979). Consider the following:

- *Retrieving words from the floor.* Children's word cards (the word cards of a group or half the class are usually best) are placed on the floor face down. Each child is asked to find a word, hold it up, and read it to whoever is watching.

- *Classifying words.* Select a topic according to a classification (e.g., desserts, television characters, funny words, places, scary words). All of the children who have a dessert word, for example, would stand in one area of the room. The teacher might want to label the area with a sheet of paper that says "dessert." Children who have words of other classifications also stand in their designated areas. (See word sorting activities in this chapter.)

- *Relating words.* If one child has the word *cake* and another the word *knife*, a child might relate the words by saying, "A knife can cut a cake." The teacher should try to get the children to relate words by asking questions such as "What can my word do to the cake?" "How can my word be used with the cake?" "Is there something that my word can do with the cake?" The teacher can continue this by asking the children, "Does someone else have a word that can be used with the word *cake*?"

- *Exchanging words.* If a child does not know a word, the teacher can say, "That doesn't make any difference. Just put it in the exchange box." Children may go through the exchange box at any time, and if they find a word they want and *know*, they can take that word and add it to their stockpile. If they lose a word and cannot find one to replace it, they may get another one from the teacher.

- *Learning a partner's words.* Each child chooses a partner, and they teach each other their own words.

- *Coauthorship.* Two or more children get together and combine their words or ideas to make longer words or stories from their original words or ideas.

- *Using two words in a story.* In pairs, each child selects one word from a stockpile of favorite words. The children then use the two words to write a silly story, a funny story, a sad story, or a make-believe story.

- *Acting out words.* If the key word is conducive to acting out, a child could dramatize the word for the other children to guess. Examples of good words for acting out are *rabbit, owl, bird, clock,* and *leaf.*

- *Hiding words.* The teacher writes a word on a medium-sized piece of heavy paper (perhaps 4 by 5 inches). When the children are not in the classroom (e.g., at recess), the word cards are placed around the room in easy-to-spot places. In various ways, the children can find the words.

Individual Activities with Key Words.   The following make engaging individual activities for key word learning (Veatch et al., 1979):

◆ *Making booklets.* The teacher or the children make a booklet of words and pictures. The booklet should be designed so that when it is open, both picture and word can be seen at the same time.

◆ *Making alphabet books.* After children are confident that they know their words and can claim them for their own, they can record the words in the correct section of an alphabet book divided by initial letter.

◆ *Making sentences.* Children write their words on a piece of paper or on the board and then proceed to add other words, such as function words, to make sentences of varying length. The following are some examples of sentences written for key words: Get the *lion*. Casper, the *ghost*, can fly.

◆ *Illustrating.* Children draw a picture about the key word and then dictate to the teacher a caption for the picture.

◆ *Inventing words.* Children create combination words using two words from the word bank (e.g., *kangaroo* and *rooster* combine to form *kangarooster*). They can illustrate and/or write about the newly created word.

◆ *Exploring feelings.* Children choose words to describe their present feelings.

◆ *Exploring identity.* Children choose a self-descriptive word for each letter in their name.

◆ *Naming special people.* Children select words that describe family members, friends, teachers. A photograph of the person is attached to the name and put on a bulletin board titled, "Special People."

Personal words and other sight-word strategies help children learn to identify words without having to focus on individual letters and the sounds that are associated with them.

SUMMARY

The underlying premise of this chapter is that *how* teachers help children with word identification is extremely important. We looked at word identification abilities within the context of the developmental phases associated with children's ability to identify words. Rather than teach word identification with worksheets, rules, and jargon-filled instruction, this chapter presented a variety of strategies that children actually use to decode words. Instructional strategies were examined for teaching phonics, context, and rapid recognition of high-frequency words and key words.

When readers can combine meaning cues with phonic cues, they have developed a powerful tool for word identification. This is why readers must learn how to use contextual information to recognize words. Various kinds of contextual activities can be designed to help students coordinate semantic, syntactic, and phonemic information. These activities involve cloze-type passages in which target words are deleted from the text. These words can be deleted selectively or systematically, depending on the teacher's purposes. Readers must also become aware that a text selection can be read and understood without identifying every word. Context-centered activities such as the reader-selected miscue strategy can help students in this respect.

TEACHER-ACTION RESEARCHER

1. Arrange to visit a first- or second-grade classroom during a lesson involving phonics. Observe how the teacher helps children with word identification. What does the teacher's approach reveal about his or her beliefs about reading? To what extent are the observed approaches and activities integrating aspects of word identification into real reading? Arrange to observe in another classroom, preferably in another school, and ask the same kinds of questions.

2. Compare Fry's instant words in this chapter to other lists of basic sight words (for example, the Dolch list). What do the lists have in common? Which list do you prefer the most? Why?

3. Collect several samples of writing from a child in primary school. Analyze the writing to determine the child's letter-sound knowledge. Then interview the child's teacher to determine his or her perceptions of the child's strengths and gaps in phonics. Does your analysis match the teacher's perceptions? Why or why not?

4. Analyze the word identification strand of a basal reading program. How is decoding or word identification defined? What are the major components of the strand? How is phonics taught—for example, is phonics taught analytically or synthetically? What provisions are made to help children develop multiple strategies for identifying unknown words? How comprehensively is context taught and reinforced?

5. Now compare the word identification strand with a published supplementary phonics program. How are the two alike? Different? Describe the extent to which the supplementary program is compatible with the basal's word identification program.

6. What should be the role of parents in helping children identify words? Brainstorm ways in which parents can help children with word identification at home.

7. Prepare and teach a word identification lesson to a small group of second or third graders. Make provisions in the lesson to combine phonics with context usage and application so that the focus of the lesson is not on learning rules but on reading print. Describe the reactions and interactions of the children during the lesson. How would you change the lesson if you were to work with the same group of children tomorrow? How would you extend the lesson?

8. Prepare a list of words found in a picture book, and have a child read the list to you. Note which words are read correctly. Have the same child read the picture book itself while you note how the child reads the words. Did you discover any differences in the child's ability to read the words on the list as compared to the same words in the book? What did the reader seem to know about the relationship of print to sound? How do you explain your findings?

KEY TERMS

contemporary
  phonics
cross-checking
high-frequency
  words

key words
onset
phonograms
rime
self-monitoring

word banks
word sorting
  activities
word walls

CHAPTER
6
Reading Fluency

Chapter Overview

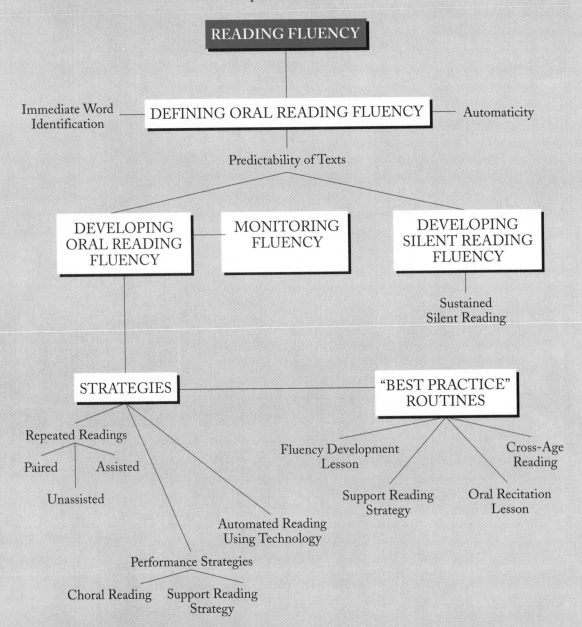

Between the Lines

In this chapter, you will discover:

♦ The importance of developing fluency in young readers

♦ What classroom routines, strategies, and reading materials help foster fluency development during oral reading

♦ Why a program of sustained silent reading (SSR) is so critical for independent reading

Jamie, a first grader, labored as she read out loud. Word by word, she started, then stopped, then started again. Haltingly slow. Disjointed. She read the story in a monotone, as if the words from the story were on a list rather than a conversational flow of sounds in oral language.

"Jamie, read the story with expression, like you're talking to us," Mrs. Leonardo said in a supportive voice. Teachers like Mrs. Leonardo often encourage the reading beginner to be expressive. Perhaps they have known intuitively what researchers are beginning to investigate and understand: Reading with expression is a sign of progress, a sign that a child is reading fluently and with comprehension.

In the delightful book *The Wednesday Surprise* by Eve Bunting (1989), Anna, a 7-year-old, teaches her grandmother to read by reading together with her on Wednesday evenings. Anna says, "I sit beside her on the couch and she takes the first picture book from the bag. We read the story together, out loud, and when we finish one book we start a second." When asked by her mother, "When did this wonderful thing happen?" Anna explains. "On Wednesday nights. . . . And she took the books home, and practiced."

Anna's a smart 7-year-old. The role of practice in learning to read is extremely important. As the authors of *Becoming a Nation of Readers* (1985) suggest: "No one would expect a novice pianist to sight read a new selection every day, but that is exactly what is expected of the beginning reader" (p. 52). A budding pianist practices a piece over and over to get a feel for the composition, to develop control over it, and to become competent and confident with it.

So it is with young readers. In this chapter, we underscore the value of having readers develop fluency in oral and silent reading situations. Examine the chapter overview. It depicts the connections among key concepts related to developing fluent reading, an important part of reading instruction that was formerly overlooked. We begin by defining reading fluency as *reading easily and well with a sense of confidence and knowledge of what to do when things go wrong*. By examining the concepts of immediate word identification and automaticity we see that fluent reading is key to comprehension. After considering how materials influence fluency development, we describe teaching strategies and routines to teach fluency, as well as ways to monitor oral reading fluency. Included are descriptions of "best practices" that help orchestrate the teaching and training of fluency with the teaching of comprehension.

Let's begin by focusing on immediate word recognition, which allows a skilled reader to concentrate on comprehension.

Defining Oral Reading Fluency

The term *fluent* is often associated with doing something easily and well. When applied to reading, **fluency,** in everyday terms, means reading easily and well. With this ability comes a sense of control and confidence, and often a knowledge of what to do when the reader gets bogged down or entangled in a text. Allington (1983) equates fluent oral reading with *prosody* or prosodic reading. Prosody is a linguistic concept that refers to such features in oral language as *intonation, pitch, stress, pauses,* and the *duration* placed on specific syllables. These features signal some of the meaning conveyed in oral language.

Have you ever sat in a class or served on a committee with a person who used few prosodic cues while speaking? Sometimes it's difficult to focus on what the person is trying to say or what the person means. In the same way, reading with expression, or using prosodic features while reading orally, has the potential of conveying more meaning than reading without expression. In addition, prosodic cues convey moods and feelings. Children generally know instantly when a parent is irritated with them. A mother's tone of voice (intonation) is usually enough to signal, "Mom is mad."

In learning to understand oral language, children rely on prosodic features. Similar conditions appear to be necessary in learning to understand written language. Schreiber (1980) found that students learned how to put words together in meaningful phrases, despite the fact that a written text provides few phrasing cues and uses few graphic signals for prosodic features in print. When Mrs. Leonardo asked Jamie to read with expression or as if she were talking to others, she was suggesting to Jamie that she rely on her intuitive knowledge or prosodic features in oral language, not only to help convey meaning to others but also to help her understand what she was reading.

Instruction in fluent oral reading produces readers who move from word-by-word reading to more efficient phrase reading (Chomsky, 1976; Samuels, 1979). Fluency instruction has also resulted in improved reading achievement, assessed through measures of comprehension (Dowhower, 1987).

Immediate Word Identification

The term **immediate word identification** is often used to describe rapid recognition. Keep in mind, however, that the process of immediate word identification is far more complicated than recognizing words on flash cards. When a word is retrieved rapidly from long-term memory, the process is often triggered by well-developed schemata that the reader has developed for a word. In immediate word identification, semantic or physical features in a word (e.g., a single letter or a letter cluster) trigger quick retrieval of that word.

Immediate word identification is the strategy used by skilled readers on 99 percent of the printed words they meet. It is also the method used by children when they identify their first words. Often one of the first words children learn to identify in print is their name. Jessica, a 4-year-old, can recognize her printed name but may not attend to each individual letter. She recognizes her name because some distinctive feature triggers rapid retrieval from long-term memory.

In Chapter 5, we looked at children acquiring phonic knowledge as one tool in identifying words. We also considered how to help children analyze syllabic or meaning-bearing units in unfamiliar words. Both phonic and structural analysis involve *mediated word identification*. Mediation implies that the reader needs more time to retrieve words from long-term memory. Readers use mediating strategies when they don't have in place a well-developed schema for a word: The schema is lacking in either semantic or physical features sufficient for rapid retrieval.

We think that experiencing problems in fluency is a major contributor when students lag behind in reading ability. Rasinski and Padak (1996) studied elementary school children from a large urban district who were referred for special tutoring in reading in the Title One program. The children read passages near their grade level and were measured on word recognition, comprehension, and reading fluency. Although the students' performance tended to be below grade level on all measures, only reading fluency was drastically below grade level. Their oral reading was slow and belabored.

How do skilled readers reach the point at which they read fluently and don't have to rely on mediated word identification strategies? Researchers are finding that *repetition is extremely important in learning to recognize words*. The amount of repetition needed for beginning readers to be able to recognize words immediately has not been appreciated. Traditionally, repetition of reading texts has not been systematically included in reading instruction.

As mature readers, we are able to identify immediately or sight-read thousands and thousands of words. How did we learn to identify these words? Did we use flash cards to learn each one? Did we first sound out each word letter by letter? Probably not.

In the past few years, the effects of developing oral reading fluency in meaningful texts have been studied with impressive results (Chomsky, 1976; Samuels, 1979; Allington, 1983; Dowhower, 1987; Koskinen & Blum, 1986).

Automaticity

Samuels (1988) argues that word recognition needs to be accurate and *automatic*. To explain the term **automaticity,** an analogy is often made to driving a car. Most of the time, a skilled driver will focus little attention or use little mental energy while driving. Skilled drivers frequently daydream or ponder happenings in their lives as they drive, yet they still manage to drive in the appropriate lane at an appropriate speed (most of the time!). They drive on automatic pilot. Nevertheless, when the need arises, a driver can swiftly focus attention on driving—for example, when a warning light goes on or when weather conditions suddenly change. In other words, most of us drive with automaticity, with little use of mental energy, but when necessary, we're able to refocus rapidly on what we're doing as drivers.

When readers are accurate but not automatic, they put considerable amounts of mental energy into identifying words as they read. When readers are both accurate and automatic, they recognize or identify words accurately, rapidly, easily, and with little mental energy. Like the skilled driver, the skilled reader can rapidly focus attention on a decoding problem but most of the time will put energy into comprehending the text.

Fluency strategies are also one way of getting rid of the "uh-ohs," which are a part of learning any new skill. When taking tennis lessons, the beginner often makes mental comments such as "Uh-oh, I need to hit in the middle of my racket" or "Oh, what a crummy backhand shot." Each hit is judged as either good or bad. Children are also prone to struggle with the "uh-ohs" when learning to read. This happens especially when they think about which words they can and cannot identify. As with the beginning tennis player, the reading beginner often gets anxious because the "uh-ohs" interfere with constructing meaning from the text. Developing automaticity is one way to give beginning readers a feel for reading without anxiety.

Predictability of Reading Materials

For children to develop into confident, fluent readers, they need to read lots of texts that are easy for them. For first and second graders, *predictable literature* can be read with ease. Rhodes (1981) has delineated several characteristics of predictable stories. Some criteria for predictable literatures are outlined in Figure 6.1.

Predictable books have a context or setting that is familiar or predictable to most children. The pictures are supportive of the text; that is, there is a good match between the

◆ Figure 6.1

Characteristics of Predictable Stories

1. Is the context (setting) one that is familiar or predictable to the reader?

2. Are the pictures supportive and predictable given the text?

3. Is the language natural? That is, does the author use common language patterns?

4. Is the story line predictable after the book has been started? Are the transitions clear?

5. Does the language "flow"?

6. Does the book reflect creativity, capture an interesting thought, or communicate something worthwhile, worthy of the title "literature"?

7. Is there repetition of specific language?

8. Are there cumulative episodes in the plot?

9. Is there rhyme?

text and the illustrations. The language is natural, meaning that common language patterns are used. The story line is predictable. There is a repetitive pattern of the mother rocking the child at night regardless of the trials during the day. There is also repetitive language in the refrains. Further contributing to the predictability of the book is the rhyme of language.

Other characteristics of predictable books delineated by Rhodes (1981) are rhyme and the use of cumulative patterns, as in *The Great Big Enormous Turnip:*

> The black dog pulled the granddaughter.
> The granddaughter pulled the old woman.
> The old woman pulled the old man.
> The old man pulled the turnip.
> And they pulled—and pulled again.
> But they could not pull it up.

Predictable texts are particularly helpful in developing fluency because children can rely on these characteristics of predictability. With predictable stories, less able readers can use intuitive knowledge of language and sense rather than rely on mediated techniques that draw on their mental energy. Using predictable texts, readers can develop fluency by reading them repeatedly with less and less assistance.

Developing Oral Reading Fluency

Children learn to become fluent in an environment that supports oral reading as communication. In mindless situations where children take turns reading in round-robin fashion, little constructive is accomplished. In round-robin reading, children often do not view their role as tellers of a story or as communicators of information. Instead, their role is to be word perfect. Accuracy, not automaticity or comprehension, permeates round-robin reading. While we are strong proponents of oral reading in classrooms, the emphasis during oral reading must be on communication and comprehension, not word-perfect renderings of a reading selection. Let's take a closer look at several classroom routines and strategies that can help foster fluency during oral reading.

Repeated Readings

Repeated readings, as defined in earlier chapters, mean simply having a child reading a short passage from a book, magazine, or newspaper more than once with differing amounts of support. Samuels (1979) proposes the method of repeated readings as a strategy to develop rapid, fluent oral reading. Here are several steps Samuels suggests when using the method of repeated readings:

1. Students choose short selections (50 to 200 words) from stories that are difficult enough that they are not able to read them fluently.

2. Students read the passage over several times silently until they are able to read it fluently.

3. The teacher can involve students in a discussion of how athletes develop athletic skills by spending considerable time practicing basic movements until they develop speed and smoothness. Repeated reading uses the same type of practice.

4. Samuels suggests that students tape-record their first oral rendition of the passage as well as their oral rendition after practice so that they can hear the difference in fluency.

Lauritzen (1982) proposes modifications to the repeated-reading method that make the method easier to use with groups of children. Mrs. Leonardo, a first-grade teacher, used the repeated-reading method in this way. She began by reading aloud to her students and discussing what happened in *Love You Forever,* a predictable text written by Robert Munsch and illustrated by Sheila McGraw. It begins:

A mother held her new baby and very slowly rocked him back and forth, back and forth.
And while she held him, she sang:

> I'll love you forever, I'll like you for always,
> As long as I'm living my baby you'll be . . . .

However, when the baby grew and pulled all the food out of the refrigerator and took his mother's watch and flushed it down the toilet, sometimes his mother would say, "This child is driving me crazy!"

But at night, while she rocked him, she sang:

> I'll love you forever, I'll like you for always,
> As long as I'm living my baby you'll be.

After this initial reading by the teacher, Mrs. Leonardo read it with the children in choral reading fashion. She and individual children next took turns reading parts of the passage, with the children reading the refrain with repetitive language: "I'll love you forever, I'll like you for always, / As long as I'm living my baby you'll be." Then Mrs. Leonardo asked the children how they thought the mother felt when she was rocking her son at night and how they could read the refrain to show that feeling. She also asked how the mother felt when she said, "This child is driving me crazy!" and how she showed this with her voice.

Finally, each child chose a passage in the book and read the passage silently and then several times orally to a partner. Some of the children also read along while listening to a tape-recorded version of the story. These activities were continued until each child was able to read the passage with accuracy and fluency.

Studies on repeated readings have fallen into two categories: *assisted* repeated readings, in which students read along with a live or taped model of the passage, and *unassisted* repeated readings, in which the child engages in independent practice (Dowhower, 1989).

In both assisted and unassisted repeated readings, students reread a meaningful passage until oral production is accurate and smooth and resembles spoken language. Notice that Mrs. Leonardo used both assisted and unassisted readings to develop reading fluency, beginning initially with assisted reading. First, she read the passage and the students listened and discussed the story. Then she gradually assisted students less as they continued to reread the story.

When teachers discuss the repeated-reading strategy, they frequently ask, "Don't students find repeated readings of the same story boring?" To the contrary, teachers who have used repeated readings find that young children actually delight in using the strategy. Children plead to have their favorite bedtime story read over and over. In the same vein, they get very involved in practicing a story with the goal of reading it accurately and fluently and are eager to share their story with parents and classmates.

Paired Repeated Readings

In paired repeated readings, students select their own passage from the material with which they are currently working. The passage should be about 50 words in length. Students, grouped in pairs, should each select different passages, which makes listening more interesting and discourages direct comparison of reading proficiency. The material should be predictable and at a level where mastery is possible.

When working together, the students read their own passage silently and then decide who will be the first reader. The first reader then reads his or her passage out loud to a partner three different times. Readers may ask their partner for help with a word. After each oral reading, the reader evaluates his or her reading. A self-evaluation sheet might ask the reader, "How well did you read today?" Responses to be checked might range from fantastic to good to fair to not so good. The partner listens and tells the reader how much improvement was made after each rendition of the reading; for example, if the reader knew more words and read with more expression during the final reading. A listening chart can be used to help a student evaluate a partner's reading (see Figure 6.2). The partners then switch roles.

◆ FIGURE 6.2   A Listening Chart

Reading 3

How did your partner's reading get better?

He or she read more smoothly   _____

He or she knew more words   _____

He or she read with more expression   _____

Tell your partner one thing that was better about his or her reading.

Peer Tutoring.   Another way to organize fluency practice is to use a **paired reading** strategy with peer tutoring. This is a particularly useful strategy in second and third grade, where differences between the most fluent and the least fluent readers become evident.

Topping (1989) notes that the collaborative work of children in pairs has enormous potential, but teachers must be able to organize and monitor this activity carefully. He advocated structured pair work between children of differing ability in which a more able child (tutor) helps a less able child (tutee) in a cooperative learning environment.

Teachers often recognize the value of extra reading practice in a paired reading situation for less able children but sometimes express concern about the worth of the activity for more able students. Research reviews on the effectiveness of peer tutoring with paired reading have shown that the more able reader accelerates in reading skill at least as much as the less able reader (Sharpley & Sharpley, 1981).

For growth in fluent reading to be maximized, the teacher needs to pair students carefully. One way to do this is to match the most able tutor with the most able tutee. This procedure seems to aid in matching pairs with an appropriate *relative competence* to each other, which maximizes the success of using this technique. As in any collaborative learning group, do not group best friends or worst enemies. You also need to consider how to handle absences.

Here's a general plan for paired reading with peer tutoring. The tutee chooses a book that has been read to the children or used in direct instruction. The book needs to be within the tutor's readability level (i.e., 95 to 98 percent accuracy level). The tutor and the tutee discuss the book initially and throughout the reading. They read together aloud at the tutee's pace. If the tutee happens to make a word error, the tutor says the word cor-

Paired reading is a useful strategy for developing reading fluency.

rectly. The pair continues reading together. When the tutee wants to read alone, he or she signals nonverbally—for instance, with a tap on the knee. The tutor praises the tutee for signaling, then is silent and the tutee reads alone. The tutor resumes reading when requested by the tutee. If the tutee makes an error or does not respond in five seconds, they use the correction procedure just described, and then the pair continues to read together. At the conclusion, the pair discusses the story based on questions developed by the tutor before the session.

This procedure allows tutees to be supported through the text with higher readability levels than they would attain by themselves. The text level also ensures stimulation and participation for the tutor, who promotes discussion and questioning on the content of the text.

Parents and Paired Reading.   The subject of reading is often perceived by parents as too complicated for them to teach to their children. All to often, attempts at "teaching" word attack skills end in frustration for both child and parents. Paired reading offers the possibility of making parental involvement in the reading growth of their children easy, effective, and enjoyable (Rasinski & Fredericks, 1991). Several years ago, teachers in the Akron, Ohio, public schools decided to emphasize at parent meetings that paired reading is easy to learn and do, works with all ages of children using texts from books to newspapers, takes only a few minutes a day, and is proven to improve reading fluency. After reading teachers were introduced to paired reading, Title 1 parents were asked to participate in paired reading with their children for five minutes each day. Many did and, at the end of the school year, a mother of a Title 1 child reported, "At first I thought this was silly and that it couldn't make much difference in Katie's reading. Then I saw the improvement myself. We both had fun together, and she was reading. I now believe in the program and really enjoy it" (p. 515).

Sylvia, a whole language teacher in a mixed class of kindergarten, first-, and second-grade inner-city students, has developed a home reading program that includes activities like paired reading (Vacca & Rasinski, 1992). The children may take home classroom books that have been coded (one dot for "easy"). Their parents are "expected to read to or with their children or listen to their children read" (p. 83). Parents reading daily with children can be most effective.

Automated Reading

Another practice that supports children as they increase oral reading fluency is **automated reading,** or listening while reading a text. An automated reading program employs simultaneous listening and reading (SLR), a procedure suggested by Carol Chomsky (1976). In the SLR procedure, a child reads along with a tape recorder or a record. The steps in SLR are as follows:

1. Students listen individually to tape-recorded stories, simultaneously following along with the written text. They read and listen repeatedly to the same story until they can read the story fluently.

2. Students choose the book or a portion of the book in which they want to work. When they are making their selections, the teacher explains that they will continue listening

In simultaneous listening and reading, children listen individually to recorded stories while following along with the written text.

to the same story until they are able to read it fluently by themselves. Students need to choose a book that is too hard to read right away but not out of range entirely.

3. Students are to listen to their books every day, using earphones and following along in the text as they listen. They need to listen to the whole story through at least once; then they can go back and repeat any part they choose to prepare more carefully. They can also record themselves as they read along with the tape or tape-record themselves as they read aloud independently.

4. Every three or four days the teacher listens to the students read orally as much as they have prepared. Students are encouraged to evaluate themselves on how fluently they read the selection they have prepared.

Sometimes it takes students a while to get accustomed to working with tape recorders, and at the beginning they can keep losing their place in the book. It takes practice to coordinate their eyes and ears in following along with the text. Once students become familiar with a story, keeping their place is not a problem.

Chomsky (1976) reported that when students first begin using this method, it may take as long as a month before they are able to read a fairly long story aloud fluently. As they become more proficient with SLR, the time can be reduced by as much as half.

When students are able to read the story fluently without the aid of the tape, they need to be given opportunities to read the story to their parents, the principal, or fellow students.

Students using this strategy could not present the story without having a book to follow, so they have not really memorized the book. However, a combination of memorization and reading enables students to have an experience of successful, effective, fluent reading.

These techniques are effective with students of all ages. The Viewpoint in Box 6.1 gives an inside look at how an adult learned to read at age 30.

Several schools in Madison, Wisconsin, use SLR in an automated reading program (Dowhower, 1989). Children are sent to the library to choose a book, accompanied by an audiotape, that is not too easy or too hard for them to read. The criteria for selecting tapes for the automated reading program include high interest, appropriate pacing, language patterns, clear page-turning cues, and lack of cultural biases. To monitor the difficulty level of books chosen, each child takes a test by reading a list of 20 words from the story. If the child knows more than 15 words, the book is probably too easy; if 8 or fewer words, the book may be too hard. Another way to monitor book difficulty level is for the child to read a short section orally, with a teacher, librarian, or aide keeping a running record of miscues made. Dowhower (1989) indicated that on the first reading, a child should read with 85 percent accuracy or better before starting to practice; otherwise, the text is too hard.

Once a book is selected, the child then reads along with the audiotape several times daily until the story can be read smoothly and expressively. When children are ready, they read the whole book (or several pages, if the book is very long) to an adult.

To provide further fluency practice, the SLR strategy can be used with CD-ROM disks. Some CD-ROMs read the book to the child, allow the child to slow down and speed up the reading speed, to click on text to have it reread, to click on a word to be given help, and to click on an illustration to learn additional information or activate animation. Some examples of this technology is *Discis Books* for Apple Macintosh Plus computers, with such notable stories as Beatrix Potter's *Tale of Peter Rabbit* (1953), Sean O'Huigin's *Scary Poems for Rotten Kids* (1988), and Robert Munch's *Paper Bag Princess* (1980). *Some Stories and More* is an IBM CD-ROM series of literature-based read-aloud programs for primary school children.

The SLR strategy as used in automated reading is a useful way for students to develop fluency through practice reading. It is important, however, that students be involved in experiences in which expressive oral reading is modeled and texts are discussed, in addition to having the opportunities for practice that SLR provides. With this word of caution, we turn next to two performance strategies that actively engage students in fluent and accurate oral reading.

Choral Reading

Telling students to read with expression is not enough for many developing readers. Rather, many children need to listen to mature readers read with expression and interpret and practice different ways of orally reading selections. **Choral reading** is an enjoyable way to engage children in listening and responding to the prosodic features in oral language in order to read with expression. In essence, through the use of choral reading techniques, students consider ways to get across the author's meaning using prosodic cues like pitch, loudness, stress, and pauses.

Craig's Story

Craig learned to read at the age of 30. With the help of friends, he began using the repeated reading and simultaneous listening and reading strategies to read texts that were meaningful to him. In a quite natural way, Craig joined the community of readers after being painfully aware of not being able to read for many years. Here's his story.

Because I did not learn to read, elementary school was quite rough. I felt out of place—like I was in a foreign country. For one thing, there was so much competing. The teachers gave out stars, A's, and sparkles for the best readers, but I didn't learn to read. We had those desks that one pulls up to open. Well, I would steal some stars and A's and put them in my desk because I couldn't win one. I was told I was "slow," so I came to believe I wasn't smart. I excelled in art and mechanical drawing. And in high school I learned to type. Also, most things I heard I could remember.

I would sweat when I was asked to read aloud. Someone would tell me a word and then the next paragraph I couldn't remember it. Consonants and vowels made no sense to me. I am just starting to understand about nouns and action words. Words like *though, through,* and *thought* all looked the same to me. Once in third grade I covered my paper with my hands and the teacher hit me severely. I couldn't stand up and read because people would laugh, so I wouldn't go to school. I remember not going to school, just walking around. I remember leaving by the fire escape.

I remember being with my friends on a cloudy day. We walked by a store. They could read the name of the store, but I couldn't.

In elementary school and junior high I would listen because the stories were so interesting to me. One story that brought tears to my eyes was *Flowers for Algernon.* It is about Charley, who had about a 70 IQ and was put into an experiment that made him smart. At the beginning of the story Charley was just like me—stupid, dumb, couldn't read. He talked like me. I wished and dreamed that a drug like that would work on me. A teacher read *Flowers for Algernon* over and over to me.

The Big Book, the book of Alcoholics Anonymous, says, "No man likes to think he is mentally and physically different from his fellow man." I definitely felt different! By high school I read about second-grade level and was resentful and rebellious. I couldn't be a nerd or a jock, so I was a rebellious person. I felt inferior—I had an ego complex. I couldn't get a job because I couldn't fill out an application. I created a street hustle. I was on the other side of the law for about ten years. I ran with a certain gang who experimented with alcohol and drugs. All through this scenario I feared what people thought of me; I had no way to fit in. I was an actor who watched what "normal" people did. For example, I would get a newspaper because other people did. No one knew I didn't know how to read.

As an adult, I moved to a place where people were less rebellious and were willing to help me. They found out I couldn't read. People began reading the Big Book to me, and I could interpret to them what they read. They perceived me as smart. Someone gave me a tape

BOX 6.1 CONTINUED

recorder and brought me books on tape. They read pamphlets into a tape recorder and I would listen to them. I would listen to the same pamphlet over and over. Even when I wasn't reading, I would play the tape recorder. I could repeat what many of the pamphlets said. The first book I read through was *Jonathan Livingston Seagull* by Richard Bach. I had to read it over and over because I got stuck on words. The next was *Illusions*, also by Richard Bach. Then I read *Joshua* by Joseph Girzone and *The Sermon on the Mount* by Emmit Fox. I read *Tao Te Poo*. Then I began reading all kinds of stuff. *The Prophet* by Kahlil Gibran, *Zen Beginner's Mind* by Suzuki Roshi. I got an audiotape of *Sidhartha* by Hermann Hesse. I listened to the same book over and over. I read these books fast. More recently I have read the commentary of the Tao Te Ching many times as well as the Tao Te Ching itself.

It is still difficult for me to take words apart, but I can remember words. Spelling is difficult. Sometimes I can see words in my mind. When I put it on paper, it usually doesn't come out right.

A teacher, a poet, and someone I called a "cowboy" helped me by putting books on tape. I could listen and follow and then read. They were friendly and made me feel comfortable. So I no longer feel like an outsider.

Choral reading is defined as the oral reading of poetry that makes use of various voice combinations and contrasts to create meaning or to highlight the tonal qualities of the passage. McCanley and McCanley (1992) extend this definition to include sound effects, exclamatory words, crowd noises, asides, and simple movements like exaggerated raising of the eyebrows. Further, primary children enjoy choral reading combined with puppetry. For example, with the cumulative story *An Invitation to the Butterfly Ball* by Jane Yolen (1976), children can use paper bag puppets representing ten different kinds of animals invited to a dance by a tiny elf. The story begins, "One little mouse in great distress looks all around for a floor-length dress," and adds two moles, three rabbits, and so on, up to ten porcupines (Walley, 1993).

In preparing for a choral reading of a text, the teacher models one way the selection can be read while the children listen. Then students identify how the teacher read the passage. Were parts read loudly or softly? What was the tempo? Did the teacher emphasize particular syllables? Was his or her voice pitched higher or lower in different parts of the passage? Students are then invited to try different ways of reading or interpreting a part, and they may want to respond to the mood or feeling that each interpretation imparts (Cooper & Gray, 1984).

Choral reading increases reading fluency (Bradley & Talgott, 1987; Chomsky, 1976; Dowhower, 1987; Samuels, 1979; Schreiber, 1980). In addition, it provides a legitimate, fun way for children to practice and reread a text that leads to a decreased number of oral reading miscues (Herman, 1985).

There are four major types of choral reading: refrain, line-a-child, dialogue, and unison. Each type works well with different kinds of selections (Miccinati, 1985).

Mrs. Leonardo used the *refrain* type of choral reading with *Love You Forever*; that is, she read the stanzas and the children chimed in on the refrain. The refrain is the easiest type of choral reading to model and learn.

Mrs. Leonardo used the *line-a-child* type of choral reading with "Five Little Chickens," an old jingle from *Sounds of Powwow* by Bill Martin and Peggy Brogan (1980):

> Said the first little chicken with a queer little squirm,
> I wish I could find a fat little worm.
> Said the second little chicken with a queer little squirm,
> I wish I could find a fat little bug. . . .

After the five little chickens have spoken:

> Said the old mother hen from the green garden-patch,
> If you want any breakfast, just come here and scratch!

She had the whole group read the lines that began with *said* and individual children read what the little chicken and the mother chicken said. The line-a-child format can be easily used on selections in which there are different characters who have lines to speak. When using this type of choral reading, children learn that listening for one's cue is essential or the choral reading breaks down.

Mrs. Leonardo's children giggled when she read to them "The Deaf Woman's Courtship."

> Old woman, old woman, will you do my washing?
> Speak a little louder, sir; I'm rather hard of hearing.
> Old woman, old woman, will you do my ironing?
> Speak a little louder, sir; I'm rather hard of hearing.
> Old woman, old woman, can I come a-courting?
> Speak a little louder, sir; I think I almost heard you.
> Old woman, old woman, marry me tomorrow.
> GOODNESS GRACIOUS MERCY SAKES! NOW I REALLY HEARD YOU!

Then the class discussed and practiced the *dialogue* type of choral reading with the boys reading the male part and the girls reading the old woman's responses. This selection was also useful to discuss with the children when to use soft and loud voices and when to pitch their voices high or low.

A fourth type of choral reading is the *unison* choral reading, which is often used by teachers who work on oral reading fluency. Yet from a choral reading perspective, this is the most difficult because the entire group speaks all the lines and responds to the prosodic cues simultaneously. Timing, parallel inflections, and consistent voice quality are of prime importance; otherwise, there is a singsong effect. This points to the need for the teacher to model how to read a selection with expression and to discuss how to use stress, pitch, intonation, and loudness when reading in unison. Otherwise, students may get the idea that oral reading should be done in a singsong fashion.

Readers' Theater

Another way to involve children in orally reading literature to other children is through **readers' theater.** McCaslin (1990) defines readers' theater as the oral presentation of drama. prose, or poetry by two or more readers. Readers' theater differs from orally reading a selection in that several readers take the parts of the characters in the story or play. Instead of memorizing or improvising their parts as in other types of theater productions, the players read them. Since the emphasis is on what the audience *hears* rather than sees, selection of the literature is very important. Readers' theater scripts generally contain a great deal of dialogue and are often adapted from literature. An example of a readers' theater script for Kraus's *Leo the Late Bloomer* (1971) is illustrated in Figure 6.3.

During a readers' theater program, the members of the audience use their imagination to visualize what is going on, because movement and action are limited. Although there is no one correct arrangement of the cast in presenting readers' theater, an effective procedure is to have the student readers stand in a line facing away from the audience and then turn toward the audience when they read their part.

In preparing for readers' theater, students read the selection silently, then choose parts and read the selection orally. Students need to practice reading expressively. Props and scenery may be used but should be kept simple. As with oral reading of literature, giving an introduction and setting the mood before the presentation are important.

After students have presented several readers' theaters using teacher-made or commercially prepared scripts, students can write their own scripts, either adapting literature they enjoy or using stories they have written. Here's how to guide students to develop their own scripts: Once children have read a story, they transform it into a script through social negotiation. The writing of a story into a script requires much rereading as well as knowledge and interpretation of the text. Once the script is written, the children formulate, practice, and refine their interpretations. Finally, the readers' theater is presented to an audience from handheld scripts (Shanklin & Rhodes, 1989).

Choral reading and readers' theater motivate children to read the same material repeatedly to increase fluency. Many children will rehearse a part enthusiastically to present it to an audience.

ROUTINES FOR FLUENCY DEVELOPMENT

Next we will examine four Best Practice routines: the **fluency development lesson** (Box 6.2), the **oral recitation lesson** (Box 6.3), the **support reading strategy** (Box 6.4), and **cross-age reading** (Box 6.5). Each emphasizes specific aspects of fluency training and integrates the teaching of fluency with teaching other important aspects of reading like comprehension and word recognition.

Routines such as the fluency development lesson, the support reading strategy, the oral recitation lesson, and cross-age reading are best practices that need to be included in the teaching of reading. Not only do they provide systematic fluency instruction and practice, but they also focus on comprehension.

Next the focus shifts to informal ways to assess and monitor fluency development. How does a teacher know if students are developing fluency? There are no formal tests to measure automaticity in reading.

◆ FIGURE 6.3

A Readers' Theater Script: LEO THE LATE BLOOMER

Characters (5)
Narrator 1 (N-1)
Narrator 2 (N-2)
Father
Mother
Leo

N-1: *(Each person should turn around and then back as they are introduced.)* This is the story of a tiger, Leo the Late Bloomer. I am the first narrator. Next to me is the second narrator. The characters are Father, Mother, and Leo.
N-2: Leo couldn't do anything right.
N-1: He couldn't read.
N-2: He couldn't write.
N-1: He couldn't draw.
N-2: He was a sloppy eater.
N-1: And he *never* said a word.
Father: What's the matter with Leo?
Mother: Nothing! Leo is just a late bloomer.
Father: Better late than never.
N-1: Every day Leo's father watched him for signs of blooming.
N-2: And every night Leo's father watched him for signs of blooming.
Father: Are you sure Leo's a bloomer?
Mother: Patience! A watched bloomer doesn't bloom.
N-1: So Leo's father watched television instead of Leo.
N-2: The snows came. Leo's father wasn't watching. But Leo still wasn't blooming.
N-1: The trees budded. Leo's father wasn't watching. But Leo still wasn't blooming.
All: Then one day, in his own good time, Leo bloomed!
N-1: He could read!
N-2: He could write!
Father: He could draw!
Mother: He ate neatly!
N-1: He also spoke. And it wasn't just a word.
N-2: It was a whole sentence. And that sentence was . . .
Leo: I made it!
All: The end.

Source: The script is adapted from *Leo the Late Bloomer,* by Robert Kraus (New York: Windmill Books, 1971).

The Fluency Development Lesson

The fluency development lesson (FDL) was devised for primary teachers to work with increasing fluency (Rasinski, Padak, Linek, & Sturtevant, 1994). The FDL takes about 10 to 15 minutes to complete. Each child has a copy of passages from 50 to 150 words.

STEPS IN THE FLUENCY DEVELOPMENT LESSON

1. The teacher reads the text to the class while students follow along silently with their own copies. This step can be repeated several times.

2. The teacher and students discuss the content of the text as well as the expression she used while reading to the class.

3. The class, along with the teacher, reads the text chorally several times. For variety, the students can read in antiphonal and echo styles.

4. The class practices reading the text in pairs. Each student takes turns reading the text to a partner three times. The partner follows along with the text, provides help when needed, and gives positive feedback.

5. Working with the entire class, volunteers perform the text. Individuals, pairs, and groups of four perform for the class. Arrangements are made for students to read to the principal, the secretary, the custodian, or other teachers and classes. Students are also instructed to read the text to their parents. In this way students are given much praise for their efforts.

Rasinski and colleagues (1994) worked with primary grade teachers in implementing FDL three to four times a week from October to June. The children in these classes experienced greater improvement in overall reading achievement, word recognition, and fluency than a comparable group of children who received a more traditional type of supplemental instruction using the same passages. The greatest gains were made by the children who were the poorest readers at the beginning of the year.

BOX 6.3   **BEST PRACTICE**

The Oral Recitation Lesson

The oral recitation lesson (ORL) also provides a useful structure for working on fluency in daily reading instruction (Hoffman, 1985). ORL has two components: *direct instruction* and *student practice*.

STEPS IN THE ORAL RECITATION LESSON

Direct Instruction Component

1. The teacher models fluency by reading a story to the class.

2. The teacher leads a discussion of the story, and students are asked to summarize what happened. (As a variation, the children can predict what will happen as the story unfolds. Hoffman emphasizes that predictable stories should be used in the ORL.)

3. The teacher and students talk about what expressive oral reading is like—that it is smooth, not exceedingly slow, and that it demonstrates an awareness of what punctuation marks signal.

4. Students read in chorus and individually, beginning with small text segments and gradually increasing the length of the segment. (We suggest that choral reading techniques be used. This can show students how prosodic cues facilitate meaning for listeners.)

5. Individual students select and orally read a portion of the text for their classmates. Other class members provide positive feedback to students on the aspects of expressive oral reading discussed.

Student Practice Component

Students practice reading orally the same text used in the direct instruction component. The goal is to achieve oral reading fluency. Hoffman suggests that second graders should reach the goal of reading 75 words per minute with 98 percent accuracy before moving to another story. This component takes from 10 to 15 minutes, with students doing soft or whisper reading. The teacher checks on individual mastery and maintains records of students' performance on individual stories.

Pairs of students:

1. Read a personally selected portion of the selection silently.

2. Read to partner three times.

3. Self-evaluate each repetition.

4. Evaluate improvement in smoothness, word accuracy, and expression.

The Support Reading Strategy

The support reading strategy was designed to integrate several aspects of fluency growth into traditional basal instruction over a three-day period. Morris and Nelson (1992) used this strategy in a second-grade classroom with low-achieving students who had made little progress in the preceding 11 months and thus were at the initial stages of reading development. Their reading achievement increased substantially after six months of the support reading strategy.

STEPS IN THE SUPPORT READING STRATEGY

1. The first day, the teacher reads a story to a small group of children in a fluent, expressive voice. Throughout the reading, the teacher stops and asks the children to clarify what is happening in the story and then to predict what will happen next. The teacher and children echo-read the story, with the students reading their own books. The teacher monitors each child's reading and provides assistance where needed.

2. The next day, the teacher pairs the readers, and the pairs reread the story; each reader reads alternating pages. Each pair is then assigned a short segment from the story to practice reading orally with fluency.

3. The third day, while the class is working individually or in small groups on writing or other tasks, individual children read the story to the teacher. The teacher monitors the reading by taking a running record, a procedure for monitoring word recognition strategies (see Chapter 14).

MONITORING ORAL READING FLUENCY

There are several ways to monitor a reader's levels of fluency. One way to include children in the monitoring of fluency and to build awareness of fluency is to have paired readers use a checklist like the one in Figure 6.2. However, the quickest and perhaps the most effective way to monitor a reader's fluency is simply to listen to the child read orally. By listening to phrasing, rate, and expression, teachers informally monitor which students are not

Cross-Age Reading

Labbo and Teale (1990) claimed that a significant problem with many struggling readers in the upper elementary grades is a lack of fluency. Cross-age reading provides these readers with a lesson cycle that includes modeling by the teacher, discussing the text, and allowing for opportunities to practice fluency.

Cross-age reading also provides upper-grade youngsters with a legitimate reason for practicing for an oral reading performance. In short, cross-age reading seems to be a powerful way to provide upper elementary students with purposeful activities to develop reading fluency, as well as to provide younger students with valuable literary experiences.

The cross-age reading program described by Labbo and Teale (1990) has four phases: preparation, prereading collaboration, reading to kindergartners, and postreading collaboration.

STEPS IN CROSS-AGE READING

1. In the *preparation* phase, the older students are helped by their teacher to prepare for a storybook-sharing session in three specific ways. First, the teacher helps select appropriate books. Students can be guided to select books they personally like, that have elements in the story that the kindergarten students can identify with, and that have illustrations that complement the story.

   Second, the teacher helps the students prepare by having them engage in repeated readings of the text. Students may be paired with partners who can give each other positive feedback concerning growth in fluency and expressiveness of oral reading. Students should also rehearse on their own to gain control over and confidence with a story.

   Third, as part of preparation, the teacher helps the students to decide how their books will be introduced, where to stop in their books to discuss the story, and what questions to ask to ensure the kindergartner's involvement in the story.

2. The purpose of the *prereading collaboration* phase is to ensure that the students are ready to share their books orally. In a 15- to 20-minute session a few days before the actual reading to the kindergartners, the older students set personal goals concerning their reading, report on and try out their ideas for involving the kindergartners, and receive and give feedback in a positive, supportive environment.

3. Once the readers are prepared, they are ready for *reading to kindergartners*. They go as a group with the teacher to the kindergarten classroom and read their prepared story to small groups of youngsters. This activity generally generates enthusiasm among both readers and kindergartners.

Box 6.5 continued

4. The *postreading collaboration* phase is an opportunity for the students to share and reflect on the quality of the storybook reading interactions. The reflective nature of these postreading discussions can also help students develop strategies to improve subsequent readings.

In an urban district in Texas, fourth graders regularly read to kindergartners and first graders in a cross-age reading program. But soon after the program began, the fourth-grade teachers realized they were not able to provide sufficient support to help their students read fluently and lead the younger children through a directed listening-thinking activity. Some children needed more encouragement to practice the book enough to become fluent themselves—particularly since teachers expected the fourth graders to be able to ask the younger children for predictions about a reading as well as answers to simple comprehension questions. To help solve the problem, fourth-grade teachers enlisted the aid of high school students. Soon the fourth graders were paired with high school buddies. Once a week each pair met to practice fluency and to prepare ways to engage the kindergartners and first graders in making predictions at different junctures in the story.

Cross-age reading has expanded to involve having the older children write stories for the younger children to read and then to write stories with the younger children (Leland & Fitzpatrick, 1994). Cross-age reading and writing programs often also have both the older and younger students read the stories to their parents or some other caring adult (Fox & Wright, 1997; Leland & Fitzpatrick, 1994).

fluent readers. Particularly for students who read word by word, teachers may also use a simply fluency rating scale, as shown in Figure 6.4. Because the text difficulty level often affects fluency, note the selection on which the student's fluency is rated. As you work with children using these fluency-building strategies, periodically rate their oral reading.

The rate at which one reads is related to fluency. Poor fluency is characterized by slow, word-by-word reading. Thus calculating a reading rate offers an approach to monitoring fluency for teachers who desire a more quantitative approach. Rasinski and Padak (1996) suggest the fluency-monitoring procedure in Figure 6.5.

There is another simple, informal procedure a teacher can use to check students' ability to read fluently. First, the student reads orally from a passage that he or she has not previewed or practiced. After reading, the student retells everything that he or she remembers about the passage. The teacher can follow up with questions that probe comprehension, if the child does not provide enough information.

This informal test gives the teacher two indications of automaticity. First, does the child read with few hesitancies and with expression? Lack of expression is an indicator of a disfluent reader. The second indicator is the quality of the child's retelling of the story or the ability to answer questions about it. If the child can read orally and comprehend the text at the same time, as these task conditions demand, the decoding had to be automatic (Samuels, 1988).

◆ FIGURE 6.4

Rating Fluency

As a child reads, listen and decide which of the descriptions below best describes his or her general fluency during reading. Chart fluency each time a child reads. In the process, you may want to take notes about what seems to influence the child's reading performance.

Rating

• POOR: Reads primarily word by word

• FAIR: Reads primarily in phrases with little intonation, ignores some punctuation

• GOOD: Reads fluently with expression

Adapted from *Classrooms That Work: They Can All Read and Write,* 2nd ed., by P. M. Cunningham and R. L. Allington (New York: Addison Wesley Longman, 1999), p. 49. Reprinted by permission of Addison-Wesley Educational Publishers.

◆ FIGURE 6.5

Monitoring Fluency by Calculating Reading Rates

Ask the reader to read the text in a normal manner as you time the reading. The text should be at or slightly below the level the student can read and understand with little difficulty. Keep track of when the reader has read for one minute. Then count the number of words read. This is the reader's rate per minute. You need several 60-second samples before you can calculate an average rating. Compare the reader's oral reading rate against the following second-semester grade-level estimates.

• Grade 1: 80 words per minute

• Grade 2: 90 words per minute

• Grade 3: 110 words per minute

• Grade 4: 140 words per minute

• Grade 5: 160 words per minute

• Grade 6: 180 words per minute

Readers who read at a rate that is consistently and substantially below the appropriate grade-level reading rate need assistance in developing reading fluency.

Adapted from *Holisitic Reading Strategies: Teaching Children Who Find Reading Difficult,* by T. Rasinski and K. N. Padak (Columbus, Ohio: Merrill, 1996), p. 70.

In addition to developing oral reading fluency, students also need time in class to develop fluency in silent reading, where comprehension is the sole reason for reading. Next we shall concern ourselves with the silent reading program.

Developing Silent Reading Fluency

At the beginning of this chapter, we defined fluent reading as reading easily and well with a sense of confidence and knowledge of what to do when things go wrong. Fluent readers are seasoned readers, just as some individuals are considered to be seasoned runners. A seasoned runner has knowledge of what it is like to run for long periods of time. Although seasoned runners have developed patterns of running, they choose when, where, and how far to run. They have gained much knowledge about themselves, how to assess how they feel so they do not run too far (or that they run far enough), and what they can do to protect themselves from a running injury. Self-knowledge contributes to self-confidence as a runner. In short, seasoned runners have *metacognition* for running—they know about the task of running, about themselves as runners, and how to monitor themselves during running.

Fluent readers are seasoned readers in that they are able to sustain reading for longer periods of time. They know that productive silent reading means accomplishing as much silent reading as possible during a period of time. They know that to do this they must keep their mind on the ideas being expressed, responding to high-potency words and sentences and giving less attention to ideas of lesser importance. Although there are distinct patterns in their reading, they choose daily what they are going to read, for what purposes, and how long they need to read to suit those purposes. They know that on some days and with some reading materials, they probably won't be able to concentrate as well as on other days or with other materials.

Similar to seasoned runners, fluent readers develop a metacognition for reading. They know about the task of reading, about themselves as readers, and how to self-monitor their reading. Fluent readers perceive of themselves as able readers. They engage in a reading task with confidence that they will succeed.

Fluent readers grow in leaps and bounds from silent reading experiences. A *sustained silent reading* program, where children read materials they choose themselves, is extremely important to the development of reading fluency.

Sustained Silent Reading

As explained by Hunt (1970), **sustained silent reading (SSR)** is a structured activity in which students are given fixed time periods for reading self-selected materials silently. Here are the essential steps.

1. Each student must select his or her own book.
2. Each student must read silently without interruption for a fixed period of time.
3. The teacher reads along with the students and permits no interruptions.
4. Students are not required to answer content-related questions or give reports or their reactions to what they have read during SSR.

A major reason why a structured reading activity like SSR is so important is that despite teacher encouragement, many students do not choose to read on their own. SSR provides for all students the kind of reading experience in school that avid readers get on their own—the chance to read whatever they want to read without being required to answer questions or read orally. In other words, reading for the sake of reading should not be reserved for only the good readers.

The overall goals of SSR are (1) to produce students who choose reading *over other activities* and (2) to encourage students to read voluntarily material *selected by themselves* for information or pleasure. We believe that if students are to learn to enjoy reading and choose it as an activity, they need to participate in structured silent reading during regular class time. Through SSR experiences they begin to see that they can read for extended periods of time and that it is an enjoyable activity.

Even the most reluctant reader will read when a structured period of silent reading is provided. Levine (1984) found that special education high school students who read six to eight years below grade level became engrossed in reading during SSR. In fact, children who say they do not like to read and who disrupt classes will read during SSR.

Learning to read independently is a major benefit. Without SSR, some students may never obtain independence and self-direction in reading and in choosing what they would like to read. Students will read if they are given time to read, if they are permitted to choose their own reading selections, and if what they read does not have to be discussed, labeled, or repeated back to the teacher.

McCracken and McCracken (1978), who have contributed much to the concept of SSR, identified seven positive messages about reading that children learn by participating in SSR.

1. *Reading books is important.* Children develop a sense of what the teacher values by noting what the teacher chooses to have them do. Children who spend most of their time completing ditto sheets will perceive of this work as important. Children who read only basal-reader-length stories will perceive of reading stories five to ten pages in length as important. If teachers want their students to choose to read fully developed pieces of literature, they must provide time for children to reach such materials.

2. *Reading is something anyone can do.* Since no one watches them, poor readers can make mistakes without worrying. Able readers are "relieved they do not have to prove that they are bright every time they read something" (McCracken, 1971, p. 582). When one is allowed to choose one's own material and read at one's own rate, reading is something *everyone* can do.

3. *Reading is communicating with an author.* Reading is often perceived by students as communicating with a teacher if it is done only in situations where short snatches of material are read with reactions then elicited by the teacher. One of the most exciting reactions to SSR we have observed in students is their individual responses to an author's message.

4. *Children are capable of sustained thought.* Many teachers are concerned that students "have short attention spans" and that they "don't stick to a task for very long." Stu-

dents, however, have relatively little trouble sustaining their reading for long periods of SSR. They actually look forward to the extended peacefulness.

5. *Books are meant to be read in large sections.* If basal reading is the main way students participate in reading, they often get the notion that reading involves reading three- to ten-page segments, not whole selections of literature. In SSR, students get to read larger chunks of material.

6. *Teachers believe that pupils are comprehending.* It is neither possible nor desirable for teachers to know what each student has learned and felt about every story or book read. Students take something away from every reading experience. One way teachers can show students they trust them to learn from reading is not to question them about what they read during SSR.

7. *The teacher trusts the children to decide when something is well written.* When SSR programs are functioning, students are not asked to report on what they have read. What often happens is that students will want to spontaneously share what they have read and feel is worth sharing.

Classrooms without voluntary, sustained reading often foster the idea that reading is something one does when forced and only for short periods of time. Each of these positive messages about reading is an important notion to get across if we want students to choose reading over other activities.

Putting SSR into Action

When beginning SSR with your class, talk over with students the reasons for having it and the rules: (1) Everyone reads. (2) Everyone is quiet. (3) Everyone stays seated (Hilbert, 1993). If they are near the end of a book, they need to have a new choice at hand. Many teachers do not require that students sit at their desks during SSR, but students must decide where to sit before SSR begins. A "Do Not Disturb" sign outside the classroom door is often helpful.

Initially, begin with short periods of SSR, perhaps 5 to 10 minutes for first and second graders and 10 to 20 minutes for third through sixth graders. Gradually extend the time to 30 to 45 minutes for the upper-elementary grades. Hilbert (1993) suggests beginning the timing when the last child has actually begun to read.

During SSR, children read books of their own choosing. At first many reluctant readers choose comics, joke books, and other short books with pictures. Often, as the year goes on, children begin selecting more challenging pieces of literature as well as nonfiction selections (Hilbert, 1993). This is particularly true when SSR is combined with other strategies, such as literature circles (see Chapter 10). It often takes a month of daily SSR for the more reluctant or restless reader to get into reading for a sustained period of time.

SSR for Beginning Readers and Less Able Readers

The standard procedures for SSR imply that students must already have some degree of reading proficiency before they can participate fully. Nevertheless, it's very important to establish and nurture the habit of sustained attention to a self-selected book in children's earliest classroom reading experiences. Hong (1981) has described some procedures for adapting SSR for younger readers in what she called *booktime*. Booktime was used with a group of first graders who had been placed in the lowest reading group in their class. Characterized by their teacher and the reading specialist as having exceptionally short attention spans, the children appeared uninterested in reading and lacked a basic sight vocabulary and word identification skills. Here are the procedures for booktime, which Hong says "evolved gradually as the children made clear what they need and want in their reading environment."

1. Booktime is held at the same time each day so that children come to expect this period as a permanent part of their routine. Repetition of instructions quickly becomes unnecessary. Younger and slower readers will probably have to begin with one to five minutes. With these readers, an eventual 10- to 15-minute session should be sufficient each day.

2. The reading group for booktime consists of five to seven students, rather than a whole class. This contributes to a certain intimacy and allows some sharing without getting too noisy and hectic.

3. Introduction and accessibility of books are critical factors. Booktime assumes that the teacher regularly reads aloud to the children. After books are read to the group, they should be placed in the classroom library. The library will gradually accumulate a set of books, each of which will have been introduced to the group in an earlier reading-aloud session. This avoids the problem of a child's trying to select a book from a collection of unknown ones. New titles will constantly be added to the library, and less popular or overly familiar ones can be removed.

4. Children select just one book. They may go through several books in one period, but they must peruse only one at a time. And no one may "save" books by tucking them under one's arm or sitting on them while reading another book.

5. Because children may go through more than one book in a given session, booktime is best conducted with children sitting on the floor near the book collection, rather than each child taking a book back to his or her seat. There should be little or no people traffic through the reading area. If possible, larger, noisier activities are restricted to the opposite side of the room.

6. The teacher reads with the children as in standard SSR but may also respond to children's questions about print, such as, "What's this word?" or "Does this say *wait*?" This gives children feedback on their hypotheses about print. They feel encouraged

when they learn they've successfully decoded a new word, and they know when they have to revise their conclusions. However, teachers will want to avoid becoming word machines, spewing out every unknown word. Children should be encouraged to read as best they can and to try to figure out words on their own.

As in SSR, teachers don't interrogate children either during or after the reading; teachers only respond. With such a limited teacher role, other individuals can help with booktime.

7. Children may read in pairs and talk to each other quietly. The sharing of a book avoids the fuss that comes when two children want the same book. The quiet talk also has educational benefits. It can be helpful in reviewing a story (i.e., for comprehension and sense of story), exchanging reactions and feelings (i.e., a response to literature), and figuring out some of the text (i.e., word identification skills).

8. Children are guided toward treating books with respect, with no throwing or rough handling of books tolerated. This reinforces the perception that books are something special.

Hong (1981) reports that the success of booktime depends on the quality of the books that are presented. A major criterion is that the plot be clear, well paced, and predictably sequential. The language should be whole, using complete, natural sentences that create a flow and rhythm. Predictable, patterned books are excellent choices for booktime.

As the children described by Hong (1981) participated in booktime, they became more accustomed to it. They began by focusing their attention on specific books, then developed favorites to which they often returned. The children progressed from a merely general interest and a focus on illustrations toward paying more specific attention to the features of print. After several weeks of booktime, it was not unusual to see the children spend an entire session on the first few pages of a single book, attempting to read the text using a combination of context clues and decoding.

Parents and SSR

Often parents want to help students with their academic progress. However, helping students with workbook pages or with oral reading can become frustrating for both the child and the parents. Encouraging parents to have short, sustained silent reading times with their children is one way for parents to do something specific that assists their children's school progress but limits the activities to low-pressure, pleasurable interactions. Spiegel (1981) suggests the following schedule for sending a series of newsletters to parents to acquaint them with the recreational reading program of which SSR is a major part.

Newsletter 1 (day 1): Explain what a recreational reading program is and how it will work in your class, and include a schedule of what information will be contained in subsequent newsletters.

Newsletter 2 (day 3): Present a rationale for having a recreational reading program, with emphasis on how it fits into the basic curriculum. Include a short statement of support from the principal and reading teacher.

Newsletter 3 (day 5): Make suggestions about how parents can help support the program through their efforts at home.

Newsletter 4 (day 7): Make a list of the ways parents can volunteer their time in the classroom to support the program.

To prepare parents for what to expect, some teachers begin the school year with a letter sent home. Vacca and Rasinski (1992) write about Gay, a third-grade teacher who sends a letter to parents highlighting her philosophy toward literacy. She explains in the communique that "children learn to read and write by reading and writing" (pp. 159–160). Informal chats, formal conferences, and telephone calls to parents in the evenings are other ways to keep parents informed about how their children are doing and why they are spending time on such activities as SSR.

There is one other person whose support parents and teachers can enlist to promote independent sustained reading: the principal. Explain to the principal the importance of a recreational reading program and the need for a large supply of books. The principal can also be invited to participate in classroom SSR and thus be an important model. This is a good way to convey the idea that reading is important to everyone.

Teaching Sustained Silent Reading

Productive reading can be strengthened by helping readers realize that success means learning to sustain themselves with print for longer periods of time. Children can keep track of the amount of silent reading accomplished during the reading period through charts (see Figure 6.6) or graphs (see Figure 6.7). Such demonstrations of growth are particularly important for lower-achieving or at-risk readers.

◆ FIGURE 6.6   A Chart for Sustained Silent Reading

| Name _____ |
| Title of Book _____ |

Monday	Tuesday	Wednesday	Thursday	Friday
_____	_____	_____	_____	_____
pages	pages	pages	pages	pages

Date _____

◆ FIGURE 6.7   Graph for Charting Progress in Sustained Silent Reading

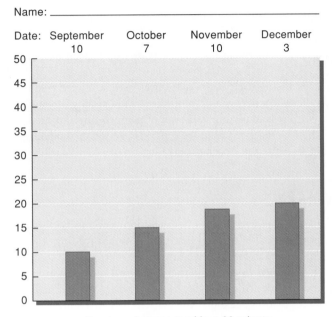

Name: _____

Date: September   October   November   December
            10   7   10   3

Number of pages read in a 20-minute
sustained silent reading program

After a silent reading session, the teacher can build the climate for productive silent reading and self-evaluation by discussing—individually, in small groups, or with the whole class—students' responses to the following questions (Hunt, 1970):

1. How did you read today? Did you get a lot done?

2. Did you read better today than yesterday?

3. Were you able to concentrate today on your silent reading?

4. Did the ideas in the book hold your attention? Did you have the feeling of moving right along with them?

5. Did you have the feeling of wanting to go ahead faster to find out what happened? Were you constantly moving ahead to get to the next good part?

6. Was it hard for you to keep your mind on what you were reading?

7. Were you bothered by others or by outside noises?

8. Could you keep the ideas in your book straight in your mind?

9. Did you get mixed up in any place? Did you have to go back and straighten yourself out?

10. Were there words you did not know? How did you figure them out?

11. What did you do when you got to the good parts? Did you read faster or slower?

12. Were you always counting to see how many pages you had left to go? Were you wondering how long it would take you to finish?

13. Were you kind of hoping that the book would go on and on—that it would not really end?

By discussing their own experiences with sustained silent reading and using questions such as these, teachers can develop the understanding in young readers' minds that reading means getting as many big ideas out of print through sustained silent reading as they possibly can. The teacher's main role in SSR is one of modeling the importance of reading, showing students the "teacher as reader."

SUMMARY

This chapter explored how to help children develop both oral and silent reading fluency. An important goal of reading instruction, fluent reading with expression and comprehension, requires practice and rereading.

We examined how automaticity in word recognition leads to the growth of competence and confidence in the developing reader. We defined and discussed repeated readings, choral reading, readers' theater, the use of technology, and routines and strategies that can be used to foster and develop fluency. Ways to involve parents and older students were suggested through paired reading and cross-age tutoring.

To provide all students with the kind of experience in school that avid readers get on their own—reading without having to respond immediately to questions—we believe in building a program of sustained silent reading. Sustained silent reading (SSR) is crucial in developing independent readers. We presented numerous practical suggestions for implementing SSR and showed how it can be part of a comprehensive plan to incorporate independent reading time into daily classroom routines.

TEACHER-ACTION RESEARCHER

1. Either interview several elementary teachers or conduct a short survey in an elementary school about the different ways that teachers provide practice in oral reading for the purpose of developing reading fluency. Compile a list of the ideas in this chapter, including the oral recitation lesson (ORL), paired repeated readings, choral reading, cross-age reading, and automated reading. Based on what the teachers report, which of the ideas on your list seem to be the most popular ways of developing oral reading fluency in students? Furthermore, how does a teacher monitor for oral reading fluency? What are some of the indicators that a child is a disfluent reader? If the opportunity presents itself, observe one or two of the classrooms and describe what actual practices are used.

2. Develop a plan to use sustained silent reading (SSR) regularly in a primary, intermediate, or middle school class. Use the following questions, and add several of your own. Then compare plans with your classmates.

   a. How often would you conduct SSR? At what time of day?

   b. In what ways will your students benefit from SSR?

   c. How would you set up your classroom for SSR?

   d. Describe some changes you might expect to see after a few weeks.

   e. How will your school principal and others participate in SSR? What effect do you think this will have?

KEY TERMS

automaticity
automated reading
choral reading
cross-age reading
fluency
fluency development
   lesson (FDL)

immediate word
   identification
oral recitation
   lesson (ORL)
paired reading
predictable texts
readers' theater

repeated readings
support reading
   strategy
sustained silent
   reading (SSR)

CHAPTER

7

Reading Comprehension

Chapter Overview

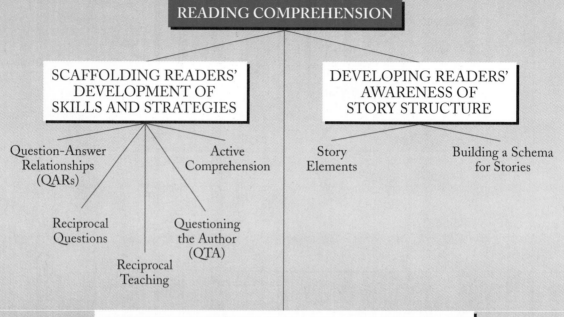

READING COMPREHENSION

SCAFFOLDING READERS' DEVELOPMENT OF SKILLS AND STRATEGIES

DEVELOPING READERS' AWARENESS OF STORY STRUCTURE

Question-Answer Relationships (QARs)

Active Comprehension

Story Elements

Building a Schema for Stories

Reciprocal Questions

Questioning the Author (QTA)

Reciprocal Teaching

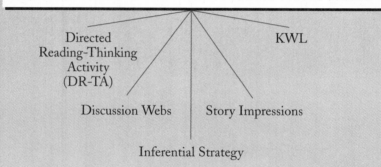

GUIDING READERS' INTERACTIONS WITH TEXTS

Directed Reading-Thinking Activity (DR-TA)

KWL

Discussion Webs

Story Impressions

Inferential Strategy

Between the Lines

In this chapter, you will discover:

♦ **Explicit instructional strategies to model and guide the development of comprehension skills and strategies**

♦ **The importance of story structure as an aid to comprehension**

♦ **Instructional strategies to scaffold readers' awareness of story structure**

♦ **Instructional strategies to guide readers' interactions with texts**

*T*hird graders have just finished sustained silent reading and are sharing their stories with one another. Hannah is eager to start and jumps at the opportunity to tell her classmates, "I read this story about a girl who's spoiled and she's going to have a baby sister." The teacher models a listener's response for her students by asking Hannah, "Does the author tell you she's spoiled? Does the author come right out and say, 'That girl's spoiled'?"

Hannah doesn't waste a second in replying, "Well, no. But I just knew."

"How did you know? Were there some clues?"

"Well," Hannah answers, "she was always yelling at everyone, and she had to have her own way all the time."

In response, the teacher moves from modeling to an explanation to reinforce one of the concepts she and her students have been working on during the year—an awareness of *sources of information* in text. "That's really good, Hannah! Authors give us information in different ways, don't they?" She then waits for Hannah's reply.

"Sure," Hannah says. And she proceeds to recite the names she has learned for the sources one can turn to in seeking answers after a reading. "Right There, Think and Search, Author and You, and On Your Own."

Addressing Hannah's classmates, the teacher asks, "Which one of those do you think Hannah used to figure out that the girl in her story was spoiled?"

"Think and Search," several of the children respond in unison.

The exchange between the teacher and her students takes about 30 seconds. The children then return to sharing the content of their stories. Thirty seconds doesn't seem like much time to make a difference in the way children interpret text, but informal, opportunistic occasions to *make explicit* a strategy for constructing meaning contribute to children's comprehension development. Exemplary literacy teachers take advantage of these spontaneous, often unplanned opportunities throughout the day to *embed* the teaching of skills and strategies within the context of meaningful reading, writing, and discussion activities. But that's not all they do.

Exemplary teachers also engage children in explicit strategy instruction through the use of well-planned lessons or *minilessons*. Minilessons allow teachers to take the mystery out of comprehension and learning by sharing insights and knowledge that students might otherwise never encounter. Explicit strategy lessons create a framework that provides the instructional support that students need to become aware of, use, and develop control over comprehension skills and strategies. Striking a balance between strategy instruction and readers' actual interactions with texts is the key to comprehension development.

As the chapter overview suggests, you will explore three dimensions of reading comprehension instruction: (1) how to scaffold students' development and use of comprehension strategies through explicit instructional techniques; (2) how to develop students' awareness of *story structure*, the underlying organization of stories, to facilitate comprehension of narrative texts; and (3) how to guide students' interactions with texts as they read. In Chapter 12, we will continue to examine comprehension strategies within the context of content area learning.

As you study the various instructional ideas in this chapter, think about reading comprehension as a dialogue between the author of the text and the reader. Authors use written language to communicate their ideas or tell a good story to someone else—an audience of readers. Readers use *cognitive and metacognitive strategies* to engage their minds in the dialogue so that they can understand, respond to, question, and even challenge the author's ideas. Students are in a strategic position to comprehend whenever they use their prior knowledge to construct meaning. Prior knowledge is the sum total of the student's world. It represents the experiences, conceptual understandings, attitudes, values, skills, and strategies that students put into play to comprehend what they are reading. How can you create strategy lessons that scaffold explanations, demonstrations, and practice in the use of strategies that students need to construct meaning and "take on" the author? How can you demonstrate to students the importance of prediction making, raising questions, questioning the author, and other strategies that connect their world to the world of the text—a world of ideas?

Scaffolding the Development and Use of Comprehension Strategies

When students know how to ask questions before, during, and after reading, they have learned an important strategy for comprehending and constructing meaning. Learning how to ask questions in relation to reading is no easy task for students. Strategy instruction can provide explicit demonstrations related to the importance of raising questions before reading and questioning the author while reading. The instructional strategies that follow promote students' active search for meaning and response to reading.

Active Comprehension

Whenever children are engaged in a process of generating questions throughout reading, they are involved in **active comprehension.** According to Singer (1978), teachers encourage active comprehension when they *ask questions that elicit questions in return.* A first-grade teacher, for example, might focus attention on a picture or an illustration from a story or a book. Instead of asking, "What is the picture about?" the teacher poses a question that gets questions in response: "What would you like to know about the picture?" In return, students might generate questions that focus on the details, main idea, or inference from the illustration.

Ms. Mayer, a fourth-grade teacher, read the opening paragraph of *The Best Christmas Pageant Ever* to her class.

> The Herdmans were absolutely the worst kids in the history of the world. They lied and stole and smoked cigars (even the girls) and talked dirty and hit little kids and cussed their teachers and took the name of the Lord in vain and set fire to Fred Shoemaker's old broken-down toolhouse.
>
> The toolhouse burned right down to the ground, and I think that surprised the Herdmans. They set fire to things all the time, but that was the first time they managed to burn down a whole building.

> I guess it was an accident. I don't suppose they woke up that morning and said to one another, "Let's go burn down Fred Shoemaker's toolhouse" . . . but maybe they did. After all, it was a Saturday, and not much was going on.

She then asked, "What more would you like to know about the Herdmans?" As her fourth graders responded, Ms. Mayer wrote their questions on the board.

> Why were the Herdmans so bad?
>
> Did they enjoy setting fire to the toolhouse?
>
> Did they feel guilty after the toolhouse burned down?

Not only do these questions stimulate interest and arouse curiosity, but they also draw students into the story. In the process, students' reading comprehension will be more goal-directed. That is, they will read to satisfy purposes that *they*, not the teacher, have established.

Nolte and Singer (1985) explain that teachers can show students how to generate their own questions for a story by adhering to a "phase-in, phase-out" strategy. "Phase-in, phase-out" simply means that you gradually shift the burden of responsibility for question asking from your shoulders to those of your students. A good deal of this strategy involves modeling question-asking behavior and making students aware of the value of questions before, during, and after reading. The following plan will ensure a smooth transition from teacher-directed questions to student-generated questions. Although the steps in the plan were recommended for 9- and 10-year-old students, they can easily be adapted for younger or older readers.

1. Discuss the importance of asking questions as you direct students' comprehension of a story.

2. Model the types of questions that can be asked about central story content, including setting, main character, problem or goal, and obstacles encountered while attempting to resolve the problem or achieve the goal.

3. As you work through a story, ask questions that require questions in response: for example, "What would you like to know about the setting of the story? The main character?" "What would you like to know about what happened next?" Spend several class periods guiding question generation in this manner.

4. Divide the class into small groups of four to six children. One student in each group is designated to serve in the role of teacher by eliciting questions from the other members. Circulate around the room to facilitate the group process. Spend several class periods in small group question generation. Allow several minutes toward the end of each class period for debriefing with students; for example, "How did the questioning go?" "Were there any problems?" "Why does question asking make a story easier to read?"

5. Have students work in pairs, asking each other questions as they read.

6. Have students work on their own to generate questions. Discuss the questions they raise as a whole group.

In following these steps, Nolte and Singer found that training students to ask questions resulted in superior comprehension on the part of 9- and 10-year-olds as compared to children the same age who did not receive such training.

Reciprocal Questioning (ReQuest)

Reciprocal questioning, also known as **ReQuest,** can easily be used to help students think as they read in any situation that requires reading. ReQuest encourages students to ask their own questions about the material being read (Manzo, 1969; Vacca and Vacca, 1999). Should you use ReQuest, consider the following steps.

1. Introduce ReQuest to students.

2. Both the students and the teacher silently read a common segment of the reading selection. Manzo recommended one sentence at a time for poor comprehenders. This may also be appropriate for beginning readers. Consider varying the length of reading for older students. For example, both teacher and students begin by reading a paragraph.

3. The teacher closes the book and is questioned about the passage by the students.

4. Exchange roles. The teacher now asks students questions about the material.

5. Upon completion of the student-teacher exchange, the next segment of text is read. Steps 3 and 4 are repeated.

6. At a suitable point in the text, when students have processed enough information to make predictions about the remainder of the assignment, the exchange of questions stops. The teacher then asks broad questions such as "What do you think the rest of the assignment is about?" "Why do you think so?"

7. Students are then assigned the remaining portion of the selection to read silently.

8. The teacher facilitates follow-up discussion of the material.

The ReQuest procedure also works well in groups when you alternate the role of student questioner after each question. By doing so, you will probably involve more students in the activity. Also, once students understand the steps and are aware of how to play ReQuest, you may also try forming ReQuest teams. A ReQuest team made up of three or four students challenges another ReQuest team.

Whenever students are asked to generate questions, some will not know how to do so. Others will ask only literal questions, because they don't know how to ask any others; they don't know how to ask questions that will stimulate inferential or evaluative levels of thinking. One way to deal with these situations is to provide a model that students will learn from. Your role as a questioner should not be underestimated. Over time you will notice the difference in the ability of students to pose questions and in the quality of questions asked.

Notice how in a third-grade class, the teacher used her children's penchant for asking detailed questions to an advantage. ReQuest was being played from a social studies textbook, and the text under consideration consisted of two pages, one explaining map symbols and the other a map of the city of Burlington to practice reading the symbols or key. The children sensed that it would be difficult for the teacher to recall every detail relating to the map of Burlington. So they zeroed in, hoping to stump the teacher with precise questions. Notice how the teacher (T) uses the occasion to make students (S) aware of how to interact with the text.

S: Where is the lake in Burlington?

T: Oh-oh. I'm not sure I studied the map well enough. Let me think. *(closes eyes)* I'm making a picture in my head of that map. I can almost picture that lake. I think it's in the northeast corner of Burlington.

S: You're right.

T: I'm glad I made that mental picture as I was reading.

S: Where are the railroad tracks in Burlington?

T: I'm not sure. My mental picture is pretty good, but I don't have every single detail.

S: Close to City Hall.

S: Where is the hospital?

T: *(closes eyes)* Near the center of town.

Questioning continued in this manner with the teacher knowing some of the answers and the students informing her of others. At the conclusion of the lesson, the teacher summarized this way: "Who would have ever thought you'd get so many questions from two short pages of social studies? I'm glad you asked all those. I sure learned a lot about reading maps! When we do ReQuest, I do two things that might help you, too. First, if there's a chart, picture, or map, I try to take a photograph of it in my head. Then if you ask me questions about it, I can bring it up in my memory. Also, as I'm reading, I ask myself questions that I think you might ask me. Then I'm ready for them! This is a good thing to do anytime you're reading. Stop, ask yourself questions, and answer them. That helps you understand and remember what you have read."

Question-Answer Relationships (QARs)

When asking questions, special attention should be given to the most likely source of information the reader needs to answer the question. Certain questions can be thought of as *textually explicit* because they promote recall or recognition of *information actually stated in the text*. Other questions are *textually implicit* because they provoke thinking. Readers must search for text relationships and think about the information presented. If students are to integrate ideas within a text, textually implicit questions are likely to be the most useful. Finally, some questions usually place the reader's knowledge of the world at the center of the questioning activity. Such questions are *schema-based*. Students must rely on their own resources as well as the text to solve problems, discover new insights, or evaluate the significance of what was read.

Question-answer relationships (QARs), as proposed by Raphael (1986), help learners know what information sources are available for seeking answers to different types of text questions. Through this strategy, readers become more sensitive to the different mental operations and text demands required by different questions. As a result, teachers and students become cognizant of the three-way relationships that exist among the question, the text to which it refers, and the background knowledge and information at the reader's disposal. QARs enhance children's ability to answer comprehension questions by teaching them how to find information they need to answer questions. Explicit instruction will make students sensitive to two information sources where answers can be found.

The first information source is the *text*. Some answers to questions can be found *right there* in the text. Other answers found in the text, however, demand a *think-and-search* strategy in which students *search* the text for information and *think* about the relationships that exist among the bits of information found.

The second information source is the *reader*. Some questions signal to the reader "I am on my own." Other questions may signal "It's up to the author and me." In either case, the text may help, but answers must come from inside the reader's head. The use of *Right There, Think and Search, Author and You,* and *On My Own* are mnemonics to help readers recognize question-answer relationships. A chart such as the one in Figure 7.1 can be used to make readers aware of QARs. The Best Practice steps featured in Box 7.1 will assist students in their understanding and use of QARs.

Questioning the Author (QtA)

Questioning the author (QtA) is an instructional strategy that models for students the importance of asking questions while reading. Beck, McKeown, Hamilton, and Kucan (1997) devised the QtA strategy to demonstrate the kinds of questions students need to ask in order to think more deeply and construct meaning about segments of text as they read. The strategy is based on the notion that successful readers act on the author's message. If what they are reading doesn't make sense to them, successful readers raise questions about what the author says and means. QtA shows students how to read text closely as if the author were there to be challenged and questioned.

QtA places value on the quality and depth of students' responses to the author's intent. While reading, it is important that students keep their minds active as they engage in a dialogue with an author. A successful reader monitors whether the author is making sense by asking questions such as "What is the author trying to say here?" "What does the author mean?" "So what? What is the significance of the author's message?" "Does this make sense with what the author told us before?" "Does the author explain this clearly?" These questions, according to Beck et al. (1997), are posed by the teacher to help students

◆ Figure 7.1   Introducing Question-answer Relationships

Where Are Answers to Questions Found?

Think and Search

The answer is in the text, but the words used in the question and those used for the answer are not in the same sentence. You need to think about different parts of the text and how ideas can be put together before you can answer the question.

Author and You

The answer is not in the text. You need to think about what you know, what the author says, and how they fit together.

or

In the Text:

Right There

The answer is in the text. The words used in the question and the words used for the answer can usually be found in the same sentence.

In My Head:

On My Own

The text got you thinking, but the answer is inside your head. The author can't help you much. So think about the question, and use what you know already to answer it.

Steps in the Development of Students' Understanding of QARs

The QAR instructional strategy enhances students' ability to answer comprehension questions. Raphael (1982, 1986) recommends the following steps for developing students' understanding of QARs.

DAY 1

◆ Introduce the concept of QARs by showing students the chart in Figure 7.1 or an overhead transparency containing a description of the basic question-answer relationships. The chart should be positioned in a prominent place in the classroom so that students may refer to it whenever the need arises.

◆ Begin QAR instruction by assigning students three short passages (no more than two to five sentences in length). Follow each reading with one question from each of the QAR categories on the chart.

◆ Then discuss the differences between a Right There question and answer, a Think and Search question and answer, an Author and You question and answer, and an On Your Own question and answer. Explanations should be clear and complete.

◆ Reinforce the discussion by assigning several more short passages and asking a question for each. Students will soon begin to catch on to the differences among the QAR categories.

DAY 2

◆ Continue practicing with short passages, using one question for each QAR category per passage. First, give students a passage to read with questions *and* answers *and* identified QARs. Why do the questions and answers represent one QAR and not another?

◆ Second, give students a passage with questions and answers; this time they have to identify the QAR for each.

"take on" the author and to understand that text material needs to be challenged. Through QtA, students learn that authors are fallible and may not always express ideas in the easiest way for readers to understand. QtA builds metacognitive knowledge by making students aware of an important principle related to reading comprehension: *Not comprehending what the author is trying to say is not always the fault of the reader.* As a result, students come to view their roles as readers as "grappling with text" as they seek to make sense of the author's intent.

BOX 7.1 CONTINUED

♦ Finally, give students passages, decide together which strategy to use, and have them write their responses.

DAY 3

♦ Conduct a brief review. Then assign a longer passage (75 to 200 words) with up to five questions (at least one each from the QAR categories).

♦ First have students work in groups to decide the QAR category for each question and the answers for each.

♦ Next, assign a second passage, comparable in length, with five questions for students to work on individually. Discuss responses either in small groups or with the whole class.

DAY 4

♦ Apply the QAR strategy to actual reading situations. For each question asked, students decide on the appropriate QAR strategy and write out their answers—for example:

What is Jack's problem?

_____ Right There

_____ Think and Search

_____ Author and You

_____ On My Own

Answer:

(Discussion follows.)

♦ Once students are sensitive to different information sources for different types of questions and know how to use these sources to respond to questions, variations can be made in the QAR strategy. For example, during a discussion, consider prefacing a question by saying, "This question is *right there* in the text" or "you'll have to *think and search* the text to answer" or "You're *on your own* with this one." Make sure that you pause several seconds or more for "think time."

Planning QtA lessons for narrative or informational texts is a three-stage process. Planning requires the teacher to (1) identify major understandings and potential problems with a text prior to it use in class, (2) segment the text into logical stopping points for discussion, and (3) develop questions or *queries* that model and demonstrate how to "question the author." Let's take a closer look at each stage in the planning process.

Identify major understandings and potential problems. Read the text closely, and note the author's intent, the major ideas and themes, and any areas or potential obstacles in the material that could affect children's comprehension. Reflect on your own comprehension as you read the text. Take note of any passages that you reread or pause to think about, knowing that these sections will most likely be problematic for students.

Segment the text. Determine where to stop the reading to initiate and develop discussion. The text segments may not always fall at a page or paragraph break. Sometimes you may want to stop reading after one sentence to ask a query.

Develop queries. Plan questions that will help students respond to what the author says and means. Queries prompt students' responses to the text and encourage them to dig deeper and make sense of what they are reading. There are two types of queries to develop: *initiating queries* and *follow-up queries.* Pose initiating queries at the beginning of the reading. Develop these queries to draw students' attention to the author's intent with questions such as "What is the author trying to say here?" and "What is the author talking about?" By discussing these questions, students begin to build an understanding of the main ideas and key concepts instead of simply retrieving information.

Use follow-up queries to focus the direction of the discussion and assist students as they integrate and connect ideas. These questions help students to figure out why certain ideas were included by the author. Beck et al. (1997) provide some examples of follow-up queries: "What does the author mean here?" "Does this make sense with what the author told us before?" "Why do you think the author tells us this now?" "Does the author explain this clearly?"

When using QtA to comprehend stories, pose narrative queries. Through the use of narrative queries, students become familiar with an author's writing style as they strive to understand character, plot, and underlying story meaning. The following queries help students think about story characters: "How do things look for this character now?" "Given what the author has already told us about this character, what do you think the author is up to?" Understanding the story plot can be accomplished with queries such as these: "How has the author let you know that something has changed?" "How has the author settled this for us?"

The thoughtful use of queries is vital for classroom discussion. As students actively explore and clarify meaning, guide the discussion as you progress from one text segment to the next. Beck et al. (1997) recommend the use of a variety of "discussion moves" to guide the discussion:

Marking: Drawing attention to certain ideas by either paraphrasing what a student said or by acknowledging its importance with statements such as "Good idea" or "That's an important observation"

Turning back: Making students responsible for figuring out ideas and turning back to the text for clarification

Revoicing: Assisting students as they express their ideas; filtering the most important information and helping students who are struggling to express their ideas by rephrasing their statements

Modeling: Thinking aloud about an issue that is particularly difficult to understand and students are unable to reach without assistance

Annotating: Providing information that is not in the text so that students can understand the concepts more fully

Recapping: Summarizing the main ideas as a signal to move on in the lesson (this can be done by either the teacher or the students)

To get a better sense of how to orchestrate a QtA lesson, study the Class Works featured in Box 7.2. It illustrates how a third-grade teacher plans a QtA lesson for a discussion related to the characteristics and habitats of bats.

BOX 7.2 CLASS WORKS

Planning a QtA Lesson on Characteristics and Habitats of Bats

Ann Marie Greene, a third-grade teacher, uses QtA regularly in her classroom. She has noticed a positive difference in her students' comprehension of text material and increased participation during discussion. She notes, "My students now realize that the author may not be expressing ideas in the clearest way. They see themselves as detectives, whose job it is to determine the author's intent and put together the related concepts." Before beginning the lesson, she reminds them of the fallibility of the author and their responsibility as readers: to figure out what the author is trying to say.

The class has been studying the characteristics and habitats of bats from the book *Zipping, Zapping, Zooming Bats* (Earle, 1995). Notice how Ann Marie segments the following passage according to the ideas about which she wants students to question the author. During the lesson, the students sit in a circle on the carpet, read each text segment together, and then stop to respond to the queries. The queries that Ann Marie posed to the students after each text segment are given in italics.

Sometimes when people explore caves, they kill bats by accident.
("What do you think the author means by this?" "Give some examples of ways that you think people kill bats accidentally.")

If you went into a cave where bats were hibernating, you would wake them up.
("What does the author mean when she uses the word hibernating?" "Does she explain the concept clearly?")

Then they would fly to another part of the cave. Each time that happens, the bats use up about a month's supply of fat. If they use up too much stored food, they will starve before spring, when they can hunt again.
("Does the author explain this clearly?")

If you go into a cave in June or July, be sure to look for baby bats. If you do see pups, never touch or bother them. Leave quickly and quietly.

Bats are mammals. They are the only flying animals that nurse. This means that the mothers' bodies make milk to feed their babies. Bat pups hang together in large groups called nurseries. Each mother returns to feed her pup at least twice a night.

(Continued)

BOX 7.2 CONTINUED

The pups need their mothers' milk to survive. If you disturb a nursery cave, the frightened mothers may leave, and the pups will starve.
("How does this connect to what the author has told us so far?" "Does the author explain this clearly?")

Besides disturbing their caves, people harm bats by destroying their homes. People close off their attics and tear down old barns. They seal off empty mines and cut down forests, where bats like to live.
    Several kinds of bats are now in danger of dying out.
(Why do you think that the author tells us this now?")

In some places there aren't enough bats left to keep down the number of insect pests. Farmers lose crops, and mosquitoes feast on us. People could use poisons to kill bugs, but poisons can be dangerous to humans, other animals, and plants.
("What is the author trying to say?")

Reflective Inquiry

◆ How are Ann Marie's queries different from the types of questions students are typically asked about passage content?

◆ How does Ann Marie's lesson contribute to students' awareness and understanding of their roles as questioners during comprehension?

Source: Text segments from *Zipping, Zapping, Zooming Bats,* by A. Earle (New York: HarperCollins, 1995), pp. 23–26. Copyright © 1995 by Ann Earle. Used by permission of HarperCollins Publishers.

Reciprocal Teaching

Reciprocal teaching, as devised by Palincsar and Brown (1984), depends on the teacher's ability to model how an expert reader uses four comprehension activities to understand a text selection: (1) raising questions about a text segment, (2) predicting what the segment is about, (3) summarizing the important points, and (4) clarifying difficult vocabulary and concepts.

In reciprocal teaching, the teacher begins the lesson by modeling each of the four comprehension activities while leading a discussion of the text. During this phase of the lesson, the quality of the dialogue between teacher and students depends on how explicit the teacher is in demonstrating each of the comprehension activities.

After observing the teacher, students are invited to share or add to what the teacher has stated and then to teach the remaining sections of the text selection. For example, a student assumes the role of the teacher and proceeds to model one or more of the comprehension activities on the next segment of text. If the student runs into trouble with any of the activities, the teacher recenters the lesson to provide support by adjusting the demands of the task. Gradually, the teacher withdraws support and the student continues teaching the lesson.

Planning is the key to reciprocal teaching. Herrmann (1988) suggested that teachers plan a lesson in two phases. In the first phase, you should become familiar with the text selection. This entails the following:

Identify which text segments will be used to demonstrate the four comprehension activities.

Identify salient questions in the selection and generate additional questions about the material.

Generate possible predictions about each text segment.

Underline summarizing sentences and generate possible summaries for each text segment.

Circle difficult vocabulary or concepts.

In reciprocal teaching, a student assumes the role of the teacher and models one or more comprehension activities from a text.

The second phase of planning requires two additional decisions on the part of the teacher. First, you will need to decide to what extent students already use the comprehension activities. Which activities do they use effectively? What will they need to help them comprehend? Second, decide on the level of support that various students require to lead each of the activities.

In the Best Practice featured in Box 7.3, Herrmann (1988) provides an excellent model of a reciprocal teaching lesson.

Reciprocal teaching helps students think more strategically about reading. Our experience with the procedure suggests that it is a complicated strategy; teachers will need to work with it several times before they feel accomplished with its implementation. Nevertheless, if used often enough, students will begin to approach learning from text knowing what to do and how to do it.

Strategy instruction lets children in on the secrets of reading comprehension. What they discover through explicit instructional techniques like reciprocal teaching and QtA is that meaning doesn't lie hidden in text like buried treasure, waiting for readers to dig it out. On the contrary, readers must actively engage in reading to construct meaning. Reading comprehension is triggered by the knowledge that readers bring to print. Not only must children use prior knowledge to comprehend, but they must also bring into play knowledge about the text itself. As readers mature, they become more sophisticated in recognizing how texts are organized in stories and informational writing. To engage in reading as a meaning-making process, readers must be aware of and search for structure in everything they read. In the next section, we pay attention to the underlying elements that make up the structure of well-told stories. In Chapter 12, we will focus on text structures commonly found in content area texts.

Developing Readers' Awareness of Story Structure

Stories are basic to any school's reading curriculum. Because stories are central to children's reading development, much time and effort have been spent attempting to understand how stories are comprehended. A child's knowledge of stories begins to develop at an early age. In Chapters 3 and 4, we explained how children hear and tell simple stories and then read and view them in both home and school experiences. Children learn implicitly that well-told stories are predictable. There is an underlying structure that all simple stories appear to have in common. As children develop a **story schema,** they begin to sense what comes next.

A simple story actually isn't as simple as it might appear on the surface. The underlying structure of a story can be quite complex. Attempts have been made to identify the basic elements that make up a well-developed story (Mandler & Johnson, 1977; Thorndyke, 1977; Stein & Glenn, 1979). These efforts have led to the development of several variations of **story grammar.** Just as sentence grammar provides a way of describing how a sentence is put together, story grammar helps specify the basic parts of a story and how they tie together to form a well-constructed story. What do most well-developed stories have in common? Although individual story grammars may differ somewhat, most people would agree that a story's structure centers around *setting* and *plot*.

Model of a Reciprocal Teaching Lesson

1. Read the text title and have the students tell what they expect or would like to learn from the selection. Summarize the group's predictions and, if appropriate, add a few of your own. Note how the lesson begins in the following lesson excerpt.

    T: What's the title of our new passage?

    S: "The Miracle of Butterflies."

    T: Right. What's the miracle of butterflies? In your own words, what would you predict this is going to be about?

    S: How butterflies fly?

    T: Oh, that's a good prediction!

    S: What they do.

    S: What season they come out, like summer.

    T: Okay. Those are some excellent predictions. Let's begin.

2. Read a small portion of the text aloud, paragraph by paragraph.

3. Ask a question about the content. Invite the group to answer the question. Invite individuals to share additional questions generated while they read the selection.

    T: My question is: What have the people of Butterfly City, U.S.A., done to protect the butterflies?

    S: They made a law making it illegal.

    T: To do what?

    S: To kill butterflies.

    T: Exactly. Does anyone else have a question?

4. Summarize what has been read by identifying the gist of the segment and explain how you arrived at this summary. Invite the group to comment on the summary. Note how the teacher summarized in the following lesson excerpt.

    T: My summary is that this is about the migration of monarch butterflies. I thought of that summary because the authors introduced the story with a good topic sentence. That was a good clue. Do you have anything that should be added to my summary?

    (Continued)

BOX 7.3 CONTINUED

5. Lead a discussion to clarify any words or ideas that are unclear or confusing.

T: Let me ask you something here. Is there an unclear meaning in this paragraph?

S: Yes. Where it says "scrawls in wavy light."

T: Now, does the sun ever write a message in the sky?

S: No.

T: No. What is the author doing here?

S: Making up the whole thing in his mind.

T: All right. It doesn't really happen but the author is using this expression to say that the sun sends us a message and that it can be used as an energy source. But certainly you will never look at the sky and see a message written by the sun.

Source: From "Two Approaches for Helping Poor Readers Become More Strategic," by B. A. Herrmann, *The Reading Teacher, 42* (1988), p. 27. Reprinted by permission of the International Reading Association.

Elements in a Story

The setting of a story introduces the main character (sometimes called the *protagonist*) and situates the characters in a time and place. The plot of a story is made up of one or more *episodes*. A simple story has a single episode. More complex stories may have two or several episodes, as well as different settings. Each episode is made up of a chain of events. Although the labeling of these events differs from story to story, the following elements are generally included:

A beginning or initiating event—either an idea or an action that sets further events into motion

Internal response (followed by a goal or problem)—the character's inner reaction to the initiating event, in which the character sets a goal or attempts to solve a problem

Attempts—the character's efforts to achieve the goal or alleviate the problem; several attempts may be evident in an episode

One or more outcomes—the success or failure of the character's attempts

Resolution—the long-range consequence that evolves from the character's success or failure to achieve the goal or resolve the problem

A reaction—an idea, emotion, or a further event that expresses a character's feelings about success or failure to reach a goal or resolve a problem or that relates the events in the story to some broader set of concerns

The events in the story form a causal chain. Each event leads to the next one as the main character moves toward reaching a goal or resolving a problem.

Keeping the elements of story grammar in mind, read the story "People of the Third Planet" in Figure 7.2 and then analyze its structure. To help you map the story's structure, use the chart in Figure 7.3. In the spaces provided on the chart, write what you believe to be the major story parts, including the setting and chain of events.

After you have completed the chart, compare your mapping of the story elements with those of other members of your class. Although there will undoubtedly be some differences in the way the story elements are interpreted, there will probably be a fair amount of similarity among ideas of in what constitutes the elements of story grammar in "People of the Third Planet."

Knowing the underlying elements of a story benefits both teacher and students. You can use story organization to plan instruction more effectively and to anticipate the problems students might have in following a specific story's action, especially if it lacks one or more story elements. Students can build and use the story schema to make better sense of what they read. The closer the match between the reader's story schema and the organization of a particular story, the greater the comprehension is likely to be. This is why a *story map* is an important planning tool in the hands of teachers.

Mapping a Story for Instructional Purposes

An analysis of a story's organizational elements strengthens instructional decisions. Beck, McKeown, McCaslin, and Burket (1979) recommend creating a **story map** as a way of identifying major structural elements, both explicit and implicit, underlying a story to be taught in class. A chart such as the one in Figure 7.3 helps you map the relationships that exist among the major events in a story. Once these relationships are established, they form the basis for developing a line of questions that will help students grasp the story parts under discussion. According to Beck and her associates, students should thoroughly understand the general framework of the story before broader, evaluative questions can be considered.

The following generic questions are easily applied to specific stories. As you examine these questions, consider how you would adapt them to "People of the Third Planet."

SETTING:

Where did the story take place? When did the story take place? Who is the main character? What is _____ like? What is _____'s problem? What did _____ need? Why is _____ in trouble?

INTERNAL RESPONSE AND GOAL/PROBLEM:

What does _____ decide to do? What does _____ have to attempt to do?

People of the Third Planet
by Dale Crail

The silver flying saucer came down silently and landed in a parking lot in a small town on earth. It was one o'clock in the morning, and the streets were dark.

Slowly a section of the saucer slid open. Two creatures from another world stepped out. For a moment they thought no one was near. Then they noticed a line of figures standing before them.

One creature whispered to the other, "Over there I see some people of the Third Planet. But they do not come forward to greet us. Perhaps this is not the time to tell the people of the Third Planet about our world."

The other creature shook his head. "No, our orders are clear. Now is the time. We must approach these earth people and arrange a meeting with their leader."

He stepped forward and began to speak. "People of the Third Planet—or Earth, as you call it. We greet you in peace. We are messengers from a world that is millions of years older than your own. We wish to establish a peaceful link between our two worlds and exchange ideas with you. We would like to speak to someone of importance on your planet. Please direct us to such a person." No one in the line of figures moved. They did not even seem interested in the space creature's words.

After several seconds the creature stepped back and whispered to his friend, "These earth people act as if they do not understand what I am saying. How can that be? We monitored their radio signals and listened to them speak. I am sure we are using their language correctly."

"Stay calm," said the other creature. "I will speak to them."

He raised his voice and said, "Earth friends! Perhaps you are frightened by our sudden appearance. Or perhaps you do not fully understand our message. I assure you that it is of the greatest importance. It is necessary that we speak to the leader of the Third Planet. Please tell us where we may find this person."

The figures remained absolutely still.

"We will not harm any of you," the space creature went on. "We only wish to talk with your leader. But—if you do not cooperate—we will be forced to take one of you with us for questioning."

No one figure moved or said a word.

The creature from the saucer began to get angry. He clenched his fists and whispered to his friend, "Apparently these Earth people will not tell us anything. Let us take one aboard. We will force the Earth person to speak."

He shouted at the figures standing before him, "You have left us no choice! We will have to use force."

He was amazed that even these words had no effect. The figures did not turn and run. They did not move at all.

In a fury he raced up to the first figure in line and said, "You are my prisoner. March forward to the saucer!"

Nothing happened.

Then he hit the figure hard, but still the figure did not move.

"It is no use," he said. "I cannot force this Earth person to walk. It is as if the Earth person has roots that go deep into the ground."

"Use your ray gun!" his friend yelled. "Cut the Earth person away from the Earth that these people love so much."

◆ FIGURE 7.2   Continued

> There was a single flash of fire from the space creature's gun. The Earth person fell noisily to the ground.
>
> Even then none of the other figures moved.
>
> This was more than the space creatures could believe.
>
> "People of the Third Planet!" the first creature said. "We greeted you in peace, and you did not answer us. We captured one of your people, and you did not stop us. You are strange people with no feelings for anyone. Farewell, people of the Third Planet. Farewell."
>
> The two creatures put the captured figure into their saucer and then climbed in themselves. With a sudden flash of light the flying saucer took off from Earth.
>
> A police car was coming down the street just as the saucer flashed up into the sky.
>
> "What was that?" one of the police officers asked.
>
> "Looked like an explosion in the parking lot," his partner said. "Better see what happened."
>
> The car raced toward the lot and screeched to a stop. The driver jumped out and flashed his light and found the officer down on one knee, pointing to a metal base that was still hot to the touch.
>
> "Something sliced off this thing," the police officer said. "Did a neat job of cutting too. But what for? They could only get away with a few pennies. Why would anyone want to steal a parking meter?"

Source: Adapted from *People of the Third Planet* by Dale Crail. Copyright © 1968 by Scholastic, Inc. Reprinted by permission of Scholastic, Inc.

ATTEMPTS AND OUTCOMES:

What did _____ do about _____? What happened to _____? What will _____ do now? How did it turn out?

RESOLUTION:

How did _____ solve the problem? How did _____ achieve the goal? What would you do to solve _____'s problem?

REACTION:

How did _____ feel about the problem? Why did _____ do _____? How did _____ feel at the end?

When students have responded to questions related to the story line, engage them in discussion centered around other important aspects of the story, such as its theme, character development, and the reader's personal response to the story.

THEME:

What is the moral of the story? What did you learn from the story? What is the major point of the story? What does this story say about _____? Why do you think the author wanted to write this story?

◆ FIGURE 7.3

Mapping Story Structure

CHAIN OF EVENTS

Time and place:	Character(s):

CHAIN OF EVENTS

The beginning event that initiates the action	
Internal response and goal/problem	
Attempt(s) and outcome(s)	
Resolution	
Reaction	

CHARACTERS:

Why do you think _____ did that? What do you like about
_____? Dislike? Does _____ remind you of anyone
else that you know?

PERSONAL RESPONSE:

Is there anything you would have changed in the story? How did the story make you feel?
Happy? Sad? Angry? Bewildered? Was there anything about the story that didn't make sense?

Not only is story mapping useful for planning questions, but it also provides you with information about "break points" during reading. A break point occurs whenever students are asked to stop an in-class reading to discuss story content. When and where to stop reading, as we will explain later in this chapter, is one of the most important decisions you can make when guiding reading.

Building a Schema for Stories

We don't advocate teaching story elements for the sake of teaching story elements. Such practice can turn out to be counterproductive. However, making children aware of the predictability of a well-developed story is appropriate, especially if the children don't appear to use a story schema during reading. You can put story structure to good use in the classroom when there is access to reading materials that are written around recognizable story structures. Moreover, avoid using narrative selections that masquerade as stories. These so-called stories go nowhere; they're incomplete and severely lacking in one or more story parts.

How did the story make you feel? Is there anything you would have changed? Did any of the characters remind you of someone you know?

The following activities and suggestions will help students build a sense of story and reinforce their awareness of story structure.

Read, Tell, and Perform Stories in Class.

There is no better substitute for building experience with stories or extending students' knowledge of how stories are put together than to read, tell, and perform stories in class on a regular basis. These types of experiences with stories are as paramount in the upper grades as they are in the beginning grades. In Chapter 10, we will emphasize the nuts and bolts of storytelling. In earlier chapters, we have explained the importance of reading stories aloud, writing stories, and performing stories through dramatic play. Language experiences such as these are integral to the development of concepts related to literacy.

Don't Teach the Language of Story Grammar as an End in Itself.

Although children need to be aware of the language of instruction, avoid teaching jargon for the sake of learning technical terms. Children develop a story schema gradually and implicitly, mainly through direct experience and interaction with stories. However, when teaching story parts explicitly to children, use language that is simple and familiar. For example, instead of asking a child to identify the "initiating event" in the story, you may want to phrase the question in more familiar language such as, "What happened in the beginning of the story to get things started?"

Build on children's concepts of *problem* and *trouble*. You might ask "What does trouble mean? Have you ever been in trouble with a parent or a friend? What kind of trouble happens in stories you have read? How did (the main character) get into trouble? How did (the main character) get out of trouble?"

The concept of trouble is closely related to the central problem in a story. Most fiction in the elementary and middle grades revolves around a problem. Because a problem gives coherence to a story, it is probably one of the most important story parts for readers to recognize. For this reason, build on students' sense of problems in their own lives. Categorize the types of problems that they have experienced (e.g., problems related to needing, wanting, feeling). Then relate these problems to stories children have read and will read.

Show Relationships Among Story Parts.

Flowcharts reflect best practices for mapping relationships that exist among events in the story. Flowcharts give children a visual image of how stories are organized. Gordon and Braun (1983) suggest giving students copies of a diagram without the story information. As information is discussed relating to the story parts depicted on the flowchart, students can write what is being said on their own copies.

Pearson (1982) claims that children as young as 8 years old are successful, with much teacher modeling, at representing a story on a flowchart. Flowcharting can take many different forms, including the one illustrated in Figure 7.4. Study the generic flowchart and how a second-grade teacher adapted that format to develop a story map based on students' suggestions during discussion.

The value of flowcharting lies in the discussions that take place before, during, and after the activity. Discussions should revolve around the relationships of one event to another. The goal behind a discussion is to make students consciously aware that events in a story form a causal chain. With much teacher-led discussion, modeling, and guided practice, many students beginning in the second or third grade will grasp how to map story parts and make flowcharts on their own. Once this is the case, have stu-

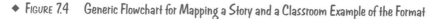

♦ Figure 7.4   Generic Flowchart for Mapping a Story and a Classroom Example of the Format

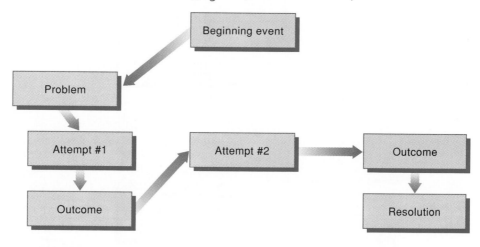

dents share their products with one another. Rather than emphasize accuracy during sharing sessions, ask for reasons and rationales. Encourage speculation and risk taking. Also, allow students the opportunity to revise or alter their individual efforts based on the discussion.

Reinforce Story Knowledge Through Instructional Activities.

Children's understanding of story structure can be extended through varied instructional tasks. Whaley (1981) suggests two activities: **macrocloze stories** and **scrambled stories**. A third activity involves the use of **story frames.**

Macrocloze Stories. A macrocloze story is based on the same principle that operates for a cloze passage. A teacher constructs cloze material by deleting single words from a passage. Children are then given copies of the cloze passage and are required to supply the missing words. When constructing a macrocloze story, instead of omitting single words, delete one or more parts from the story—for example, a sentence, several sentences, or an entire paragraph. Reproduce copies of the story with rules indicating where the text deletions have been made. Students should then read the story and discuss the missing information orally or in writing.

Scrambled Stories. A second instructional task involves scrambled stories. As the name implies, a story is separated into its parts and jumbled. Students must then read the scrambled story and reorder it. Try your hand at reordering the story events in Figure 7.5 from Aesop's fable "The Crow and the Pitcher." Decide which story event comes first, second, third, and so on. Compare your reordering with others in your class.

◆ Figure 7.4   Continued

Problem

The bear ate too much. People got mad at the bear because he ate everything edible that he could get his paws on.

Beginning Event

When Johnny found a small baby black bear in the woods behind a stump.

First Attempt

Johnny tried to get rid of the bear by taking him back to the woods.

Outcome

The bear came back to his farm and started eating again.

Second Attempt

He tried to get rid of the bear again by taking him to an island.

Outcome

But the bear came back again and he wasn't even very wet.

Third Attempt

Johnny and his father discussed what had to be done. They had to shoot the bear.

Outcome

Johnny was about to shoot the bear in the woods when the bear smelled something and started to run. The bear ran into a bear trap.

Response

Johnny was happy because he got rid of the bear without killing him and he could still visit the bear.

Resolution

The zoo people said they had set the trap to catch a bear for the zoo. They said Johnny could visit the bear any time he wanted and that the bear would have enough food.

Story Frames. Story frames present a third way of heightening an awareness of stories. Fowler (1982) showed that story frames may be particularly appropriate in the primary grades or in situations where students are at risk in their development as readers. A story frame provides the student with a skeletal paragraph: a sequence of spaces tied together with transition words and connectors that signal a line of thought. Fowler identified five story frames, each with a different emphasis: *plot summary, setting, character analysis, character comparison,* and the story's *problem.*

◆ FIGURE 7.5   Scrambled Story from Aesop's Fable, "The Crow and the Pitcher"

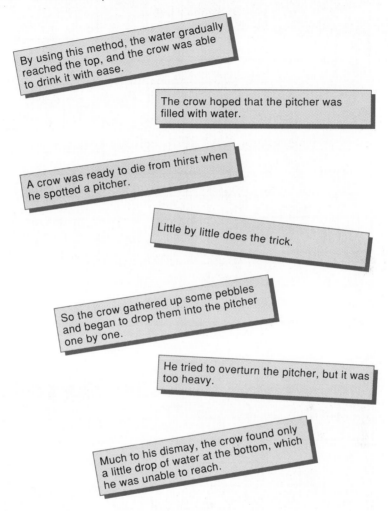

In Figure 7.6, examine how two third graders completed a frame for the story "Owl at Home." The frame centers on the story's problem. The children bring differing abilities to the task, yet both capture the central focus of the story.

Examples of story frame formats are illustrated in Appendix E.

As students become familiar with using story frames, you may want to involve them simply in writing summary paragraphs that focus on different elements of the story. Building a schema for stories is an important aspect of comprehension instruction. No less important is how readers interact with texts. As students become sensitive to story structure, you will find it easier to guide reader-text interactions.

◆ FIGURE 7.6   Comparison of Story Frames for "Owl at Home"

Tanner's Frame

In this story the problem starts when ___ Owl thought the moon ___
___ was following home. ___

___

After that, ___ He started walking and he said that ___
___ the moon was still following him. ___

Next, ___ He was almost home and he still thougt ___
___ the moon was still following him. ___

___ Then,
___ he went inside his house and he got ___
___ his p.J's on. ___

The problem is finally solved when ___ Owl looks out the ___
___ window and says night to the moon and ___
___ went to bed. ___ The story ends ___ with owl ___
___ sleeping. ___

Renee's Frame

In this story the problem starts when ___ everything was dark ___

___

___

After that, ___ a tip of the moon appeared over ___
___ the seashore. ___

Next, ___ Owl watched the moon go ___
___ higher, higher. ___

___ Then,
___ They became good friends. ___

___

The problem is finally solved when ___ Owl went to bed ___

___

___ The story ends ___ good ___

___

GUIDING INTERACTIONS BETWEEN READER AND TEXT

On the road to reading maturity, young readers need to become aware of and skilled at recognizing when shifts in thinking occur during reading. The shift may involve an author's transition to a new topic, changes in setting, twists in the plot, and so on. Or the author may put demands on the reader's ability to make inferences. For whatever reason, many youngsters run into trouble while reading because they don't know *how* or *when* to adjust their thinking as a particular reading selection demands.

Suppose you were teaching a class in which most of the students had appropriate background knowledge for the reading selection. Discussion before reading activates schemata, and students approach the selection with anticipation of what lies ahead in the material. But somewhere during reading, you sense that the readers are having trouble understanding the story. Some look confused as they read; a couple raise their hands to ask for clarification. Others just plow ahead; whether they are comprehending is anyone's guess.

Readers sometimes get lost in a welter of details or bogged down in the conceptual complexity of the selection. The prereading activity that was initiated at the beginning of the lesson, though necessary, wasn't sufficient to maintain readers' interactions with the text. As a result, they're able to process only bits and pieces of information but fail to grasp the author's intent and message. How can you help?

Assigning questions *after* reading may clarify some of the confusion but does little to show readers how to interact with the author's ideas *during* reading. This is why guiding reader-text interactions is an important part of comprehension instruction. In this section, we explain several instructional strategies that teachers have found useful for this purpose.

Directed Reading-Thinking Activity

The *directed reading-thinking activity (DR-TA)* builds critical awareness of the reader's role and responsibility in interacting with the text. The DR-TA strategy involves readers in the process of predicting, verifying, judging, and extending thinking about the text material. Throughout this process, the teacher agitates thinking by posing open-ended questions. The learning environment for DR-TA lessons must be supportive and encouraging so as not to stifle or inhibit students' participation. For example, never refute the predictions that children offer. To do so is comparable to pulling the rug out from under them.

"Think time" is important in a DR-TA lesson. We suggest that you pause several seconds or more for responses after posing an open-ended question. If there is silence during this time, it may be an indication that children are thinking. So wait and see what happens.

To prepare a DR-TA for a story, analyze its structure first. Map the story as we suggested earlier. Once you have identified the important story parts, decide on logical stopping points within the story. In Figure 7.7, we indicate a general plan that may be adapted for specific stories.

Linda Fleckner, a sixth-grade teacher, used the DR-TA to guide reader-text interactions for the short story "People of the Third Planet." Earlier you were invited to map the elements of this story. Study the dialogue that occurred between Ms. Fleckner and two students at the beginning of the lesson.

◆ Figure 7.7   Potential Stopping Points and Open-ended Questions in a DR-TA

Title

**What do you think
this story is going
to be about?**

Why do you think so?

Setting, introduction of characters,
and beginning event

**What do you think
is going to happen next?**

Why do you think so?

Character's response and
goal or problem

**What do you think
is going to happen next?**

Why do you think so?

Attempts made to alleviate
problem and achieve goal

**What do you think
is going to happen next?**

Why do you think so?

Outcomes or attempts
and resolution of problem

Character's reaction to events

Ms. F.:   *(writes title on the board before assigning the story)* What do you
think this story's about?

Student: It's about outer space.

Ms. F.:   Why do you say that?

Student: Because it's about a planet.

Ms. F.:	*(writes the prediction on the board)* Let's have some more predictions.
STUDENT:	This is about space, I think. But something happens on Earth.
Ms. F.:	Why do you think it's about Earth?
STUDENT:	Earth is the third planet from the sun, right?
Ms. F.:	*(writes the prediction on the board)*

Note that Ms. Fleckner used two open-ended questions and resisted posing additional questions to clarify students' predictions. In doing so, she set a tone of acceptance and didn't turn the question-response exchange into an interrogation session. In addition, she wrote the predictions on the board. Later, she returned to the predictions and asked students to verify their accuracy, reject them outright, or modify them in light of information gained from reading.

After five or six predictions about the title were written on the board, Ms. Fleckner assigned the first segment of text. Students read through the story's initiating event, the first eight lines from the story. Study the exchange that followed with the student who predicted that the Third Planet was Earth.

Ms. F.:	*(points to the board)* Well, how did some of your predictions turn out?
STUDENT:	I was right. It's about Earth.
Ms. F.:	You certainly were! So what do you think is going to happen now that the space ship has landed on Earth?
STUDENT:	War will break out. Someone's going to report the space ship. The creatures are going to come out and capture the people.
Ms. F.:	Why do you say that?
STUDENT:	Because that's what happens in the movies.
Ms. F.:	That's a possibility! *(turns her attention to the class and asks for other predictions)*

Initial predictions are often off the mark. This is to be expected since students' predictions are fueled by background knowledge and experience.

The DR-TA begins with very open-ended or divergent responses and moves toward more accurate predictions and text-based inferences as students acquire information from the reading. See the Best Practice featured in Box 7.4 for general procedures in using the DR-TA strategy. Compare the DR-TA to the *inferential strategy,* which also makes substantial use of students' ability to use background knowledge and make predictions.

Inferential Strategy

The **inferential strategy** was designed for elementary children, especially those in the primary grades (Hansen, 1981). Unlike the DR-TA, the inferential strategy does not require

Steps in the Directed Reading-Thinking Activity (DR-TA)

Two features that distinguish the DR-TA from some of the other instructional strategies for guiding reader-text interactions are (1) that the students read the same material at the same time and (2) that the teacher makes frequent use of three questions to prompt inquiry and discussion: "What do you think?" "Why do you think so?" and "Can you prove it?"

STEPS IN THE DR-TA PLAN

◆ Choose an interesting narrative or informational text. If you choose a story, for example, initiate the DR-TA by having students focus on the title and illustrations and ask them to predict what the selection will be about. Ask, "What do you think this story will be about?" "Why do you think so?"

◆ Write students' predictions on chart paper or the chalkboard so that there is a visible record to which students can refer during discussion. Then invite students to read silently to a logical stopping point. Ask, "Now that you have had a chance to read the beginning of the story, what do you think it is about?" "Would anyone like to change predictions or make new ones?" After students have made or refined predictions, ask, "How do you know? Read the lines that prove it." Redirect questions as needed.

◆ When there are no more ideas, invite students to read the next segment of text silently. Ask similar questions and other related ones.

◆ Have students continue reading the text, stopping at logical points, and engaging in the same cycle of questions until the story is finished.

stopping points throughout the reading selection. Instead, it relies on several questions *before* reading and discussion afterward.

Consider the following steps in the inferential strategy:

1. Analyze the content selection for important ideas central to the material. Before assigning the class to read the material, select three ideas that are important or might be difficult to understand.

2. Plan prereading questions. Develop *two* questions for *each idea* identified in the content analysis. One question is posed to tap background knowledge relative to the idea; the other is intended to elicit prediction—for example:

Background: How do you react when you feel uncomfortable in a social situation?

Prediction: In the selection you are about to read, Tim feels unsure of himself on his first blind date. How do you think Tim will react when he meets his date?

Ask students to write predictions before discussion takes place.

3. Discuss responses to background and prediction questions *before* reading. Discuss both students' previous experience with the topic and their predictions for the selection.

4. Upon finishing the prereading discussion, assign a selection to read.

5. After reading, relate predictions to what actually happened in the selection. Evaluate the three or four ideas that motivated background and prediction questions.

For example, in Mrs. Conti's second-grade class, the children read "The Lion and the Mouse" from their basal reader. It contained the following story line:

Setting: A happy little mouse is running and jumping in the grass in the morning.

Beginning event: The mouse gets lost in the grass and is picked up by a lion who says he wants to eat him.

Internal response: The mouse is frightened; he wants to be set free.

Attempt: The mouse promises to help the lion if the lion will set him free.

Outcome: The lion laughs in disbelief but decides to let the mouse go free.

Resolution: The lion gets caught in a net and the mouse chews him free.

Reaction: The lion is grateful—a little mouse helped him after all.

Mrs. Conti chose three ideas around which to ask background questions and prediction questions: (1) A kindness is never wasted, (2) everybody needs someone, and (3) you can use your head to get out of trouble.

Study the background and prediction questions that Mrs. Conti asked for the third idea.

Background question: All of us have probably been in trouble at some time, maybe with a friend, a brother or sister, or a parent. Sometimes we have to use our heads to get out of trouble. What are some of the things that you have done to get out of trouble?

Prediction question: In this story, a mouse got caught by a lion who wants to eat him. What do you think he'll do to get out of trouble?

During the prereading activity, the children shared their answers to the questions. They had much to contribute. They then read the story in its entirety. After reading, the predictions that were made were compared with inferences derived from the story.

KWL (What Do You <u>Know</u>? What Do You <u>Want</u> to Find Out? What Did You <u>Learn</u>?)

KWL, as described by Ogle (1986), is a three-step teaching plan designed to guide and to motivate children as they read to acquire information from expository texts. The strategy helps students think about what they know or believe they know about a topic, what they need to find out by reading the text, and what they learned by reading and what they still need and want to learn about the topic from other information sources. The KWL model is outlined on a chart that children use as they proceed through the steps of the strategy (see Figure 7.8).

The first two steps in the model are prereading activities. The beginning step (K—What do you *know?*) involves brainstorming with a group of students to help them focus on their current knowledge of a topic. The teacher's questions should lead children to think about and to respond *specifically* to the topic being discussed. The

◆ FIGURE 7.8

KWL Chart

K What do you <u>know</u>?	W What do you <u>want</u> to find out?	L What did you <u>learn</u>?

CATEGORIES OF INFORMATION YOU EXPECT TO USE

A.   E.

B.   F.

C.   G.

D.   H.

purpose of this process is to activate children's prior knowledge to help them understand what they will read in the text. The children's responses will be recorded on the board or on an overhead projector. The teacher, however, will not merely accept children's ideas or statements. As the discussion progresses, the teacher will encourage children to extend their thinking by asking questions that require them to consider the source as well as the substance of their information. Children will be asked to reflect on where they learned their information and on how they might prove that what they said is accurate.

Organizing children's statements into general categories of information that they may come across as they read and discussing the kinds of information that they are likely to find in the article will provide additional structure, guidelines, and direction for children as they read. The teacher will demonstrate how key categories are determined and will invite children to offer additional categories. Students who are not ready for or accustomed to this level of thinking may need additional support and practice.

The next step (W—What do you *want* to find out?) evolves naturally from assessing the results of the brainstorming and categorizing activities. As children identify areas of controversy and/or key categories that contain little or no information, a purpose for reading is developed. Although this step is done mainly as a group activity, each student will write the questions that he or she is most interested in learning about on the worksheet. Students' personal interests will guide and motivate their reading. The length and the complexity of the material will determine whether children can effectively read and derive information by reading the entire text or if the piece should be read in steps that provide opportunities for children to think, at logical intervals, about what they are reading.

During the final step of the KWL process (L—What did you *learn?*), the students will record their findings on their worksheets. They have the option of writing down information either as they read or immediately after they finish reading. With teacher guidance and assistance, the students will assess whether their questions and concerns were satisfactorily answered by reading the text. When students need or want additional information about a topic, they should be guided to other sources of information.

In Figure 7.9 examine the KWL chart that was developed by a third-grade class. Also study the interactions that occurred between the teacher (T) and students (S) as they developed the chart.

> *T:* Fold your paper into three columns. In the first column write a *K.* That stands for things you know. The next column will be titled *W.* That stands for what you want to know. The last column should be labeled *L.* That is for what you learned when the story is all finished. Now what is the title of the story?
>
> *S:* "Eastern Chipmunks."
>
> *T:* What kinds of things do you already know about chipmunks that you could put in the first column? *(The children's responses are listed in the first column of the worksheet. They were not certain, however, whether or not chipmunks were nocturnal. They decided to move that question to the next column—What you want to find out.)*

◆ FIGURE 7.9

Completed KWL Chart

K What do you <u>know</u>?	**W** What do you <u>want</u> to find out?	**L** What did you <u>learn</u>?
1. They run fast. 2. They eat nuts. 3. They dig holes. 4. They climb trees. 5. They are afraid of people. 6. Some are brown.	1. Do they come out in the daytime or at night? 2. How old are they when they live on their own? 3. How long do they live? 4. What colors are they? 5. How fast can they dig? 6. How fast can they run? 7. How deep can they dig?	1. I learned that they live under rocks. 2. Their holes are 20 to 30 feet long. 3. Cats eat them. 4. Baby chipmunks grow up in one month. 5. *Chipmunk* is an Indian word. 6. They have two pouches for storing food. 7. They work, play, and rest at different times during the day and night. 8. They have eyes on the side of their heads. 9. They have sharp claws and teeth. 10. They are good at hiding. 11. They nibble on leaves.

CATEGORIES OF INFORMATION YOU EXPECT TO USE

A. Where chipmunks live (homes)

B. How they look (appearance)

C. How they act (behaviors)

D. What they eat

T: Now take a look at what you have here. We are going to put what you believe you know about chipmunks into groups. We'll make concept groups like we do when we do concept circles. Does anyone have a group or concept?

S: Where they live.

T: Which things would go into that group?

S: They live in the ground.

S: They live in forests.

T: What other groups do you see?

S: Things like run fast.

T: What else could go with that?

S: Climb trees.

T: These seem to be things that they do. Could we call this group behaviors?

S: Yes.

S: Food.

T: Good. Find all the statements on your page that refer to their food and read them to yourself.

S: I know another one. How they look.

T: Which ones would go there?

S: They are brown with striped tails.

S: They are small.

The same type of questions were asked to help the children think about what more they wanted or needed to know about chipmunks.

As the students completed the prereading phase of the KWL strategy, they were assigned the text to read. After reading, the discussion that followed went something like this.

T: Now write in the last column on your chart the things that you learned when you read the story. Was there anything that we wanted to know that was not in the story?

S: How deep their tunnels are.

T: How could we find out?

S: I have an encyclopedia at home. I could bring it in tomorrow.

T: Great! Bring in the encyclopedia volume with chipmunks in it and we'll look it up. We might find some other things that we didn't know about chipmunks also.

Discussion Webs

Discussion webs require students to explore both sides of an issue during discussion before drawing conclusions. When classroom discussions occur, they can quickly become dominated by the teacher or a few vocal students. In an effort to move the discussion forward, the teacher may ask too many questions too quickly. Usually children are more reticent to participate or become involved when discussions are monopolized by teacher talk or the talk of one or two students.

Donna Alvermann (1991) recommends the use of discussion webs as an alternative to discussions that are teacher-dominated. The discussion web strategy makes use of cooperative learning principles that follow a "think-pair-share" discussion cycle (McTighe & Lyman, 1988). According to Alvermann, "Students *think* individually about the ideas they want to contribute to the discussion and then discuss these ideas with a partner. Next, the partners *pair* up with a different set of partners to work toward consensus. . . . Finally, the two sets of partners, working as a group of four, decide which ideas a spokesperson from the group will *share* with the entire class in the whole-group discussion that follows" (p. 93).

The discussion web strategy uses a graphic aid to guide children's thinking about the ideas they want to contribute to the discussion. The graphic aid is illustrated in Figure 7.10. In the center of the web is a question. The question reflects more than one point of view. Students explore the pros and cons of the question in the No and Yes columns of the web—in pairs and then in groups of four. The main goal of the four-member group is to draw a conclusion based on the discussion of the web.

Alvermann (1991) suggests the following steps in the use of discussion webs for classroom discussions:

1. Prepare students for reading by activating prior knowledge, raising questions, and making predictions about the text.

2. Read the selection and then introduce the discussion web by having students work in pairs to generate pro and con responses to the question. The partners work on the same discussion web and take turns jotting down their reasons in the No and Yes columns. Students can use key words and phrases to express their ideas and need not fill in all of the lines. They should try to have an equal number of pro and con reasons represented on the web.

3. Combine partners into groups of four to compare responses, work toward consensus, and reach conclusions as a group. Explain to students that it is OK to disagree with another member of the group, but they should try to keep an open mind as they listen to others during the discussion. Dissenting views can be aired during the whole class discussion.

4. Give each group three minutes to decide which of all the reasons given best support the group's conclusion. Each group selects a spokesperson to report to the whole class.

5. Have students follow up the whole class discussion by individually writing their responses to the discussion web question. Display students' responses to the question in a prominent place in the room so that they can be read by others.

When students use discussion webs, there is usually a high degree of participation; they are eager to hear how other groups reach consensus and draw conclusions. In Gloria Rieckert's class, sixth graders use discussion webs to think about several dilemmas that Billy, the main character, faces in the book *Where the Red Fern Grows*, by Wilson Rawls. The discussion web shown in Figure 7.10 asks the question, "Should Billy have cut down the big, old sycamore tree in order to get the coon?" Reyna, Pam, Jessica, and Kim reach a yes consensus on the question, but Reyna still has her doubts and Jessica clearly voices a dissenting view. Each member follows up the discussion by writing his or her response to the question.

Discussion Web

Reyna
Pam
Jessica
Kim

Should Billy have cut down the big, old sycamore tree in order to get the coon?

Yes

Because he shouldn't disapoint his dogs

Because his dogs worked for it

Because he said he would cut a tree down when a coon was up there

He wanted to keep his word

Because he felt he had to

No

Because it would take a long time to grow

Because when it fell it could have hurt something

Part of nature

Because animals lived there

Because it was his favorite tree

Conclusion

Yes, because he wanted to keep his word.

> Reyna: I felt that Billy shouldn't have cut the sycamore tree down because he could have really hurt himself. Plus the tree was part of nature, and that coon didn't deserve to die. The tree is a living thing. But I sort of changed my mind about Billy cutting the tree down after listening to Pam and Kim. Keeping your word is important.
>
> Pam: I think Billy should of cut down the big tree cause a promise is worth more than a tree and he was proud.
>
> Kim: I think he should of cut down the tree because he promised that coon to his dogs. It was also his first coon. If he wouldn't of cut down that tree he would never of gotten his coon skin hat. If he didn't cut down that tree he wouldn't have been a hunter.
>
> Jessica: I don't think he should have cut down the tree because it takes a long time to grow back. It hurt the environment and Billy didn't even think about that. I don't think he should have done it because it is a bad thing to do.

It is evident from these responses that discussion plays a role in guiding students' interpretation of what they are reading. Readers have an opportunity through discussion webs to view and refine their own interpretations of a text in light of the points of view shared by others.

Story Impressions

Story impressions is the name of a strategy that helps children anticipate what stories *could* be about. As a prereading activity, this strategy uses clue words associated with the setting, characters, and events in the story (the story impressions) to help readers write their own versions of the story prior to reading. McGinley and Denner (1987), originators of the strategy, describe it this way: "Story impressions get readers to predict the events of the story that will be read, by providing them with fragments of the actual content. After reading the set of clues, the students are asked to render them comprehensible by using them to compose a story of their own in advance of reading the actual tale" (p. 249).

Fragments from the story, in the form of clue words, enable readers to form an overall impression of how the characters and events interact in the story. The clue words are selected directly from the story and are sequenced with arrows or lines to form a descriptive chain. The chain of clue words triggers children's impressions of what the story may be about. Children then write a "story guess" that predicts the events in the story.

As McGinley and Denner (1987) explain, "The object, of course, is not for the student to guess the details or the exact relations among the events and characters of the story, but to simply compare his or her own story guess to the author's actual account" (p. 250). They suggest the following steps to introduce story impressions to the class for the first time:

1. Introduce the strategy by saying to the students, "Today we're going to make up what we think this story *could* be about."

◆ FIGURE 7.11   Story impressions for Chapter 9 of *Where the Red Fern Grows*

Story Chain	Story Guess
boy	Billy uses his ax to chop down the big sycamore tree. He doesn't chop it down, and he goes to his grandpa for help. His grandpa teaches him a trick. He shouldn't give up, and chop all day, and then, if it is not down, put a scarecrow by it. Then, go home and eat dinner. Billy did that, and he got some sleep. He had a lot of blisters in his hands. He went next day, and he tried to chop down the tree, but he didn't chop it down, and he had a lot of discouragement. He said a prayer that night, and at night, a gust of wind blew down the tree.

Story Chain:

boy
↓
ax
↓
big sycamore tree
↓
Grandpa
↓
trick
↓
scarecrow
↓
dinner
↓
sleep
↓
blisters
↓
discouragement
↓
prayer
↓
gust of wind
↓
success
↓
coon
↓
apology

2. Use large newsprint, a transparency, or a chalkboard to show students the story impressions (see Figure 7.11 for an example), saying, "Here are some clues about the story we're going to read." Explain that the students will use the clues to write their own version of the story and that after reading, they will compare what they wrote with the actual story.

3. Read the clues together, and explain how the arrows link one clue to another in a logical order. Then brainstorm story ideas that connect all of the clues in the order in which they are presented, saying, "What do we think this story could be about?"

4. Demonstrate how to write a story guess by using the ideas generated to write a class-composed story that links all of the clues. Use newsprint, the chalkboard, or a transparency for this purpose. Read the story prediction aloud with the students.

5. Invite the students to read the actual story silently, or initiate a shared reading experience. Afterward, discuss how the class-composed version is like and different from the author's story.

6. For subsequent stories, use story impressions to have students write individual story predictions or have them work in cooperative teams to write a group-composed story guess.

Story impressions work well in primary and intermediate classrooms. Younger readers may need more than one introductory lesson to model the strategy. With older readers, story impressions can easily be adapted for longer literary texts, which may involve several chapters or more. In Gloria Riechert's sixth-grade class, for example, readers use story impressions to predict events from the novel *Where the Red Fern Grows*. Figure 7.11 shows the story impressions for Chapter 9 of the book and compares the story guesses of two students. A class discussion of the strategy revealed that students felt that the clue words made it easier to make predictions about the story. According to some of the students, story impressions helped them key in on important events and aroused their curiosity about the chapter.

SUMMARY

In this chapter, we examined three dimensions of reading comprehension instruction from an active, meaning-making stance. The first instructional dimension involves explicit instruction in the development and use of strategies for comprehending text. We explored various instructional techniques devised to build knowledge and awareness of the student's role in reading comprehension and the questioning skills needed to construct meaning: active comprehension, reciprocal questioning (ReQuest), question-answer relationships (QARs), questioning the author (QtA), and reciprocal teaching. These strategies model and guide students' development of comprehension strategies.

The second dimension of comprehension instruction that we examined covered techniques for building and reinforcing children's awareness of a story's underlying structure.

The elements that comprise a well-told story were discussed, as were activities for building and reinforcing children's sense of stories. There is, however, no better way to build experience with stories than to have children read, tell, listen to, and perform them on a regular basis.

The third dimension of comprehension instruction focused on instructional strategies to model and guide reader-text interactions. Directed reading-thinking activities (DR-TA), the inferential strategy, KWL, discussion webs, and story impressions are useful instructional frameworks for guiding readers' responses to text and developing metacognitive and cognitive thinking strategies as readers engage in a dialogue with authors. All of these strategies involve prediction making, activating prior knowledge, engaging children actively in constructing meaning, and making inferences during reading.

TEACHER-ACTION RESEARCHER

1. Working with several class members or colleagues, plan to teach a reading selection. First, decide on the selection to use. Then use the questioning the author (QtA) strategy to plan the lesson. Finally, teach the lesson to other members of the class and evaluate the strategy.

2. Discuss with a group of children a story they have just read, and tape-record the conversation. Analyze the discussion to see if you followed these guidelines to keep students on task: (a) Ask a preliminary question to identify a problem or issue, (b) insert a question or two as needed to clarify or redirect the discussion, and (c) pose a final question or two to tie together loose ends or establish a premise for further discussion. Also check to see if you used declarative or reflective statements, state-of-mind queries, or deliberate silence as alternatives to questions.

3. Choose a story from a basal reader and construct a story map, using a chart similar to the one suggested in the chapter. Then examine the story map to determine where to create "break points" in planning a DR-TA. Try out the DR-TA with an appropriate group of elementary school students (or your classmates) and report on the lesson.

4. Construct a story map from another narrative selection, then design a lesson to reinforce or extend students' schemata for stories. The lesson might include the macrocloze or scrambled story activities suggested in the chapter. Finally, field-test the lesson with a group of students at the appropriate grade level.

5. Choosing different grade levels, observe three elementary school classrooms during reading instruction time. Take notes on what the teacher does to facilitate comprehension. Also watch what students are doing when they are not working directly with the teacher: Are they completing worksheets, reading selections longer than one or two sentences or a paragraph in length, or writing about what they have read? Are they involved in other instructional activities? Categorize what you see in terms of types of activities and instruction according to ideas presented in this and previous chapters.

KEY TERMS

active comprehension

directed reading-
   thinking activity
   (DR-TA)

discussion Webs

inferential strategy

KWL

macrocloze stories

question-answer
   relationships
   (QARs)

questioning the
   author (QtA)

reciprocal teaching

ReQuest

scrambled stories

story frames

story grammar

story impressions

story map

story schema

CHAPTER

8

Vocabulary Knowledge
and Concept Development

Chapter Overview

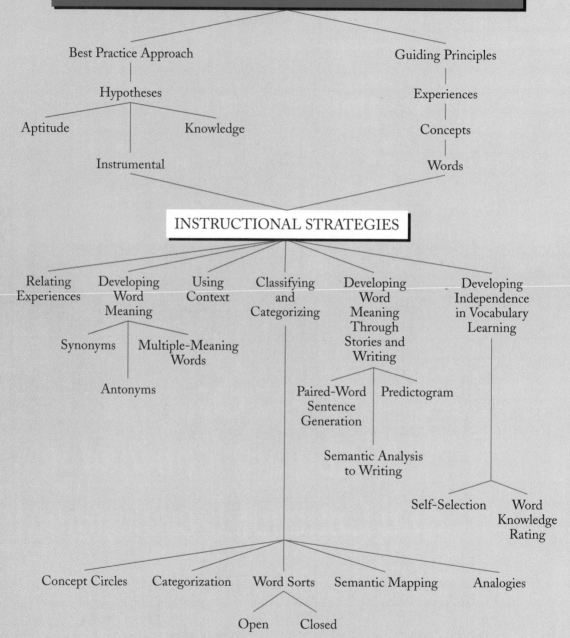

VOCABULARY KNOWLEDGE AND CONCEPT DEVELOPMENT

Best Practice Approach

Guiding Principles

Hypotheses

Experiences

Aptitude   Knowledge

Concepts

Instrumental

Words

INSTRUCTIONAL STRATEGIES

Relating Experiences

Developing Word Meaning

Using Context

Classifying and Categorizing

Developing Word Meaning Through Stories and Writing

Developing Independence in Vocabulary Learning

Synonyms   Multiple-Meaning Words

Antonyms

Paired-Word Sentence Generation   Predictogram

Semantic Analysis to Writing

Self-Selection   Word Knowledge Rating

Concept Circles   Categorization   Word Sorts   Semantic Mapping   Analogies

Open   Closed

Between the Lines

In this chapter, you will discover:

♦ The relationship among children's experiences, concepts, and words

♦ Principles that guide the teaching of vocabulary in elementary classrooms

♦ Instructional strategies for teaching vocabulary using a variety of activities

♦ Why vocabulary functions differently in literature and in content material

Simon is like many young children who, at age 5, are curious about language and undaunted in the use (and misuse) of words. Simon, in his zest to learn, plays with language, often experimenting and using words spontaneously to express himself or to describe new experiences and understandings. As his language expands, so does Simon's world. Ever since developing the concept of *word*, he doesn't hesitate to ask, "What's that word mean?" when he hears an unfamiliar word used in conversation or in the media. No one in his family even blinked when Simon asked, "What's *'peachment* mean?"

Because of its historic nature, media coverage of Bill Clinton's impeachment trial dominated radio and television news in early 1999, so much so that the word *impeachment* could not escape Simon's attention. Not only did he hear the word used repeatedly on television news programs, but he also observed the people closest to him, his parents and grandparents, engaged in spirited discussions on the pros and cons of the impeachment process. So the question, "What's *'peachment* mean?" took no one by surprise. Yet the question posed a dilemma. How do you begin to explain to a 5-year-old what it means to impeach the president of the United States? Simon's grandmother, whom he calls "Bama," gave it her best shot. She explained that the president of the United States is the leader of the country, just as Simon's mom and dad are the leaders of his family. Then Bama went on to explain, "The word *impeachment* means that attempts are being made to remove him from his office. You'll understand the word better when you get older and study about it in school. Am I making any sense, Simon?"

"I think so, Bama," Simon said in an unsure voice, abruptly shifting gears to playing with his Lego blocks. Several days later, however, Simon tested his newfound knowledge as his dad surfed the Internet on the computer in his home office. Gary has promised to play with Simon and says he'll be only a few more minutes on the computer. Simon waits until he can wait no more. "Daddy," he says, "I'm *impeaching* you now from your office! You promised we would go out and play."

It's like day and night, the difference between classrooms where children like Simon are allowed to experiment and play with words and classrooms in which the learning of words is focused on lists. Teachers in the former take advantage of children's natural spontaneity and creativity, knowing that part of the joy of teaching is the unpredictability of what children will say or do. They create classroom environments in which opportunities to experiment with words abound. Every time a student makes a decision as to which word is best in a piece of writing, vocabulary learning takes place. Mark Twain said that the difference between the right word and the almost right word is the difference between lightning and the lightning bug. Children experiment with words whenever they hear unfamiliar words read aloud in literature or whenever they encounter new words while reading. They develop an ear for language and an eye for the images created by language.

Nevertheless, teachers face real problems in developing vocabulary knowledge and concepts in their classrooms every day. For as "children's vocabulary grows, their ability to comprehend what they read grows as well" (Rupley, Logan, & Nichols, 1999, p. 336). Children are likely to have trouble understanding what they read if they are not readily familiar with most words they meet in print.

Too often we assume that children will develop an understanding of words from such staple activities as discussing, defining, and writing the words in sentences. We do little else instructionally. Yet students must not only be able to define words but also experience unfamiliar words in frequent, meaningful, and varied contexts. A major premise of this chapter is that *definitional knowledge* is necessary, but students must also develop *contextual* and *conceptual knowledge* of words to comprehend fully what they read.

Defining and using words in sentences are insufficient to ensure vocabulary learning. Students need to be involved in *constructing* meaning rather than memorizing definitions. In addition, they need to experiment with the relationship between the meanings of terms (Beck, Perfetti, & McKeown, 1982). The more that children encounter vocabulary in as many language contexts as possible, the more they will come to know and use words.

Have you ever heard a student who encounters a difficult word say with confidence, "I know what that word means!"? We share a concern that there are not enough children developing the I-know-that-word attitude. As depicted in the chapter overview, this chapter will emphasize ways to increase children's sensitivity to new words and their enjoyment in word learning. What instructional opportunities can be provided to influence the depth and breadth of children's vocabulary knowledge? What are the instructional implications of vocabulary for reading comprehension? How do students develop the interest and motivation to *want* to learn new words? How can students grow in independence in vocabulary learning? To answer these questions, we must first recognize that vocabulary development is not accidental. It must be orchestrated carefully not only during reading time but throughout the entire day.

The Relationship Between Vocabulary and Comprehension

The relationship between knowledge of word meanings and comprehension has been well documented by researchers and acknowledged by children. Many students admit that

Children experiment with words whenever they encounter new words while reading.

sometimes they don't understand what they're reading because "the words are too hard." The seminal work of F. B. Davis (1944) and other researchers such as Thurstone (1946) and Spearitt (1972) have consistently identified vocabulary knowledge as an important factor in reading comprehension.

Various explanations are used to account for the strong relationship between vocabulary and comprehension. Anderson and Freebody (1981) proposed three hypotheses: the **aptitude hypothesis,** the **knowledge hypothesis,** and the **instrumental hypothesis.** These three hypotheses are capsulized in Figure 8.1.

All three hypotheses have merit in explaining the relationship between word knowledge and comprehension. The implications of the aptitude and knowledge hypotheses signal the importance of reading aloud to children and immersing them in written language. Wide reading experiences develop a facility with written language. Further, the instrumental hypothesis is important to us as teachers: Teach word meanings well enough, and students will find reading material easier to comprehend. Unfortunately, vocabulary instruction research has provided contradictory evidence on this effect. Nagy (1988) summarizes some of the research this way:

> Imagine an experiment with two groups of students who are about to read a selection from a textbook. One group is given typical instruction on the meaning of some difficult words

◆ FIGURE 8.1

Three Hypotheses for the Strong Relationship Between Vocabulary and Comprehension

Aptitude Hypothesis

Both vocabulary and comprehension reflect general intellectual ability. A large vocabulary as measured by test performance is a solid indicator of verbal and mental ability. The relationship is explained this way: The more intellectually able the student, the more she or he will know the meanings of words and therefore comprehend better while reading. It is best to guard against the pessimistic attitude that only the most intelligent child profits from instruction in vocabulary. A child's environment and experiences, including those in the classroom, are crucial in learning concepts and words.

Knowledge Hypothesis

The knowledge hypothesis suggests that vocabulary and comprehension reflect general knowledge rather than intellectual ability. In other words, students with large vocabularies related to a given topic also have more knowledge about the topic, which in turn produces better comprehension. Closely tied to the schema view of reading, the knowledge hypothesis proposes that vocabulary words must be taught within a larger framework of concept development.

Instrumental Hypothesis

The instrumental hypothesis establishes a causal chain between vocabulary knowledge and comprehension. The instrumental hypothesis can be defended thus: If comprehension depends in part on the knowledge of word meanings, vocabulary instruction ought to influence comprehension.

from the selection; the other group receives no instruction. Both groups are given passages to read and are tested for comprehension. Do the students who received the vocabulary instruction do any better on the comprehension test? Very often they do not. (p. 1)

According to several studies, many widely used methods generally fail to increase comprehension (Mezynski, 1983; Pearson & Gallagher, 1983; Stahl & Fairbanks, 1986). Why might this be the case? One explanation may involve the very nature of practices associated with vocabulary instruction. This instruction usually involves some combination of looking up definitions, writing them down or memorizing them, and inferring the meaning of a new word from the context. These activities do not create enough *in-depth* knowledge to increase comprehension of difficult concepts. Good definitions and illustrations of how words are used in natural-sounding contexts seem to be minimal requirements for good instruction in vocabulary. Other studies indicate that comprehension is facilitated when vocabulary is taught *in depth* before reading begins (Beck et al., 1982; Stahl, 1983; Beck, McKeown, & Omanson, 1987).

We've noticed that many teachers spend instructional time introducing vocabulary words *before* students read but do not spend much time on vocabulary *after* students have read. For example, few teachers encourage children to use significant vocabulary words *after* reading texts in such activities as retelling and written, oral, artistic, and dramatic responses to what has been read. Researchers are also looking into the connection between intensive vocabulary instruction and writing. They are finding that students write better after intensive, in-depth work on vocabulary related to the writing topic (Duin & Graves, 1987; Beyersdorfer & Schauer, 1989).

Though wide reading provides students with rich and meaningful contexts for word learning, vocabulary instruction is also important. Poorer readers are at a double disadvantage in increasing their vocabulary if they are unmotivated or unable to do the amount of contextual reading required to extend their vocabularies. And, they are less likely to use context to access word meanings.

Moreover, the instrumental and knowledge hypotheses have many instructional implications, which we address throughout this chapter. Words need to be taught directly and well enough to enhance comprehension. Students must have quick access to word meanings when they are reading. Quick access can be achieved through a variety of strategies that make use of children's definitional, contextual, and conceptual knowledge of words.

Before examining instructional strategies, the relationship among children's experiences, concepts, and words needs to be explored. What are concepts? What does it mean to know words?

EXPERIENCES, CONCEPTS, AND WORDS

One way to define **vocabulary** is to suggest that it represents the breadth and depth of all the words we know—the words we use, recognize, and respond to in meaningful acts of communication. *Breadth* involves the size and scope of our vocabulary; *depth* concerns the level of understanding that we have of words.

Vocabulary has usually been classified as having four components: *listening, speaking, reading,* and *writing.* These components are often said to develop in breadth and depth in the sequence listed. Children of 5 and 6, for example, come to school already able to recognize and respond to thousands of spoken words. Children's first vocabulary without much question is listening vocabulary. However, as a child progresses through the school years, he or she eventually learns to identify and use as many written as spoken words. By adulthood, a person's reading vocabulary often outmatches any of the other vocabulary components.

As children progress through their school years, they learn to identify and use as many written as spoken words.

For this reason, it is more or less assumed that listening and speaking vocabularies are learned in the home, whereas reading and writing vocabularies fall within the domain of school. Although this assumption may generally hold, it creates an unnecessary dichotomy between inside and outside school influences. It is much safer to assume that both home and school are profoundly influential in the development of all components of vocabulary.

Words as Labels for Concepts

Although words are labels for **concepts,** a single concept represents much more than the meaning of a single word. It might take thousands of words to explain a concept. However, answers to the question "What does it mean to know a word?" depend on how well we understand the relationship among words, concepts, and experiences. Understanding this relationship provides a sound rationale for teaching vocabulary within the larger framework of concept development.

Concepts are learned through our acting on and interaction with the environment. Edgar Dale (1965) reminded us how children learn concepts best: through direct, purposeful experiences. Dale's "Cone of Experience" in Figure 8.2 depicts the levels of ab-

♦ FIGURE 8.2   Dale's Cone of Experience

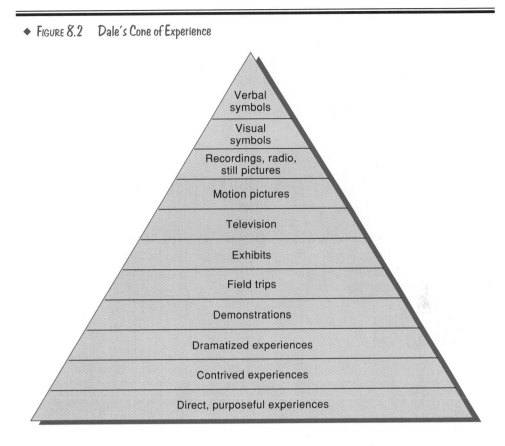

straction from the most concrete, nonverbal experiences beginning at the base of the cone to the most abstract and removed experiences at the tip of the cone—verbal symbols. For a child who has never ridden on a roller coaster, the most intense and meaningful learning would occur during a trip to an amusement park! The relationship of experiences to concepts and words sets the stage for an important principle of vocabulary instruction: To learn new or unfamiliar words, it is necessary to have experiences from which concepts can be derived.

Words and Concepts: A Closer Look

One way of thinking about a concept is that it is a mental image of something. By something, we mean anything that can be grouped together by common features or similar criteria—objects, symbols, ideas, processes, or events. In this respect, concepts are similar to schemata.

Concepts are synonymous with the formation of categories. We would be overwhelmed by the complexity of our environment if we were to respond to each object or event that we encountered as unique. So we invent categories (or form concepts) to reduce the complexity of our environment and the necessity for constant learning. Every canine need not have a different name to be known as a dog. Although dogs vary greatly, the common characteristics that they share cause them to be referred to by the same general term. Thus to facilitate communication, we invent words to name concepts.

Scan a page from any dictionary and you will discover that most words are the names of concepts. The only place that these words stand alone is on a dictionary page. In your head, concepts are organized into a network of complex relationships. Suppose you were to fix your eyes on the word *baboon* as you scanned the entries in the dictionary. What picture comes to mind? Your image of *baboon* probably differs from that of another person. Your background knowledge of *baboon*, or the larger class to which it belongs known as *primates*, will very likely be different from someone else's. So will your experiences with and interests in baboons, especially if you are fond of frequenting the zoo or reading books about primate behavior. The point is that we organize background knowledge and experiences into conceptual hierarchies according to class, example, and attribute relations. Let's take a closer look at these relationships.

Class, Example, and Attribute Relationships

We stated that the concept *baboon* is part of a more inclusive class called *primates*, which in turn is a member of a larger class known as *mammals*, which in turn is a member of an even larger class of animals known as *vertebrates*. These *class relationships* are depicted in Figure 8.3.

Class relationships in any conceptual network are organized in a hierarchy according to the **superordinate** and **subordinate** nature of the concepts. For example, in Figure 8.3, the superordinate concept is *animals*. There are two classes of animals, known as *vertebrates* and *invertebrates*, which are in a subordinate position in the hierarchy. However, *vertebrates* is superordinate in relation to *amphibians, mammals, birds*, and *fish*, which, of course, are types or subclasses of vertebrates. To complete the hierarchy, the concept *primates* is subordinate to *mammals* but superordinate to *baboons*.

By now you have probably recognized that for every concept there are examples of that concept. In other words, an *example* is a member of any concept under consideration. A *nonexample* is any instance that is not a member of the concept under consideration. Class example relationships are reciprocal. *Vertebrates* and *invertebrates* are examples of *animals. Mammals, birds, fish*, and *amphibians* are examples of *vertebrates*. A *primate* is an example of a *mammal*, and so on.

To extend this discussion, suppose we were to make *primates* our target concept. In addition to baboons, what are other examples of primates? No doubt, *apes, monkeys*, and *humans* come quickly to mind. These examples can be shown in relation to each other.

Note that the examples of primates given in Figure 8.4 are not exhaustive of all possible primates that we could have listed. Nevertheless, we might ask, "What do baboons, apes, monkeys, and *Homo sapiens* have in common?" Answers to this question would force

◆ Figure 8.3   Example of a Concept Hierarchy

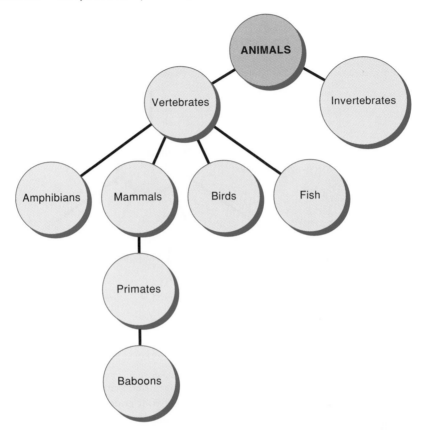

us to focus on relevant *attributes,* the traits, features, properties, or characteristics that are common to every example of a particular concept. In other words, the relevant attributes of primates refer to the characteristics that determine whether baboons, mónkeys, apes, and *Homo sapiens* belong to the particular class of mammals called *primates.*

All primates, from baboons to human beings, have certain physical and social characteristics, but not every primate shares each of these features. Nearly every example of a primate can grasp objects with its hands and/or feet. A primate has nails rather than claws. Vision is a primate's most important sense. Most species of primates live in groups, but some live alone. A social group is often considerable in size and highly organized. Primates have the capacity to communicate with one another by means of signals based on scent, touch, vision, and sound. And, of course, primate infants depend to a large extent on their mothers.

This discussion began when we asked you to form a mental image of *baboon.* The clarity with which you were able to picture a baboon in your mind depended, as you may have surmised, on how familiar you were with the characteristics of primates in general

◆ FIGURE 8.4   Class Example Relationships for the Target Concept PRIMATES

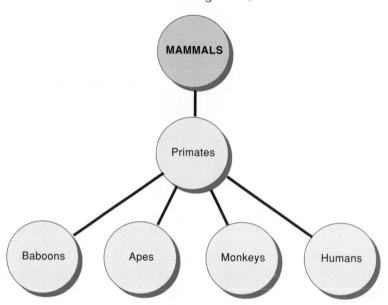

and baboons specifically. Baboons, apes, monkeys, and *Homo sapiens* share common characteristics, but they also differ.

In what ways are baboons similar to other primates? How are baboons different? These are important questions in clarifying your concept of *baboon* and sorting out the relationships that exist among the various examples. Concept learning involves a search for attributes that can be used to distinguish examples from one another and to differentiate examples from nonexamples.

To promote students' conceptual understanding of key vocabulary, Simpson (1987) culls an instructionally useful answer to the question "What does it mean to know a word?"

Suppose that a concept to be developed in a third-grade social studies unit was *wigwam*. Students would need to be able to generate that wigwam was a shelter or home for Native Americans and that it was not as sturdy as the house they live in. They could relate the wigwam to a tent they may have used on a camping trip or a scout outing, while noting that wigwams were made of lightweight wooden poles covered by layers of bark or reed mats. But suppose the concept in a science unit was a more abstract one like *energy*. In this case, students would need to be able to generate that they needed energy to play and work but that they did not need much energy to sleep or to watch television. As the concept *energy* was explored further, students would realize that our bodies need food to produce energy, just as cars and airplanes need fuel to keep running. Students could even come up with the notion that nuclear reactors split atoms to produce electrical energy, which lights their houses and runs their television sets and video games.

Through such understandings, children gain depth in their word learning. Next, before we examine teaching strategies, let's look at some guidelines for establishing vocabulary programs throughout the elementary grades.

Principles to Guide Vocabulary Instruction

In this section, we consider six principles to guide the teaching of vocabulary in elementary classrooms. They evolve from common sense, authoritative opinion, and research and theory on the relationship between vocabulary knowledge and reading comprehension.

Principle I: Select Words That Children Will Encounter While Reading Literature and Content Material

Readers can tolerate not knowing some words while reading; they can still comprehend the text selection. So vocabulary instruction that introduces a smattering of new words prior to a reading selection will boost comprehension significantly. However, when vocabulary learning is centered around acquiring a large percentage of words appearing in actual selections that will be read in class, comprehension is likely to be enhanced (Stahl, 1983; Beck & McKeown, 1983). Which words are the best choices for vocabulary instruction? Which aren't?

Words shouldn't be chosen for instructional emphasis just because they are big or obscure. Teaching archaic or difficult words just because they are unusual is not a legitimate reason for instruction. A reader learns to use monitoring strategies to overcome such obstacles. Nor should difficult words be chosen if they do not relate to the central meaning of the passage or important concepts in it. Maps or organizers of the reading material can be used to help identify the words for study. This is true for literature as well as for content area vocabulary instruction. For example, for the book *The Paperbag Princess,* by Robert N. Munsch (1980), one teacher chose the vocabulary from a map she constructed (see Figure 8.5).

Consider the following additional ways to choose words for instructional emphasis.

Key Words.   Key words come directly from basal, literature, or content text selections. These words convey major ideas and concepts related to the passage content and are essential for understanding to take place. Key words need to be taught, *and taught well,* because they present definite obstacles to comprehension that cannot be overlooked by the reader.

Useful Words.   Useful words are relevant. Children encounter useful words repeatedly in a variety of contexts. In some cases, a child may be familiar with useful words, having learned them in earlier stories or units or in previous years. However, it cannot be assumed that these words are old friends; they may be mere acquaintances.

Interesting Words.   Interesting words tickle the imagination and create enthusiasm, excitement, and interest in the study of words. Words that have unique origins, tell intriguing

◆ FIGURE 8.5

Map for THE PAPERBAG PRINCESS

Characters:

1. Elizabeth: a princess with expensive clothes
2. Ronald: a prince
3. dragon: dragon smashed castle, burned Elizabeth's clothes, and carried off Ronald

Problem:

Elizabeth wanted Ronald back.

Resolution:

Elizabeth outwitted dragon by telling him he was the "fiercest" dragon and got Ronald back. Ronald told her to "come back when dressed like a real princess." Elizabeth told Ronald he looked like a prince but he was a bum.

Big Ideas:

* Sometimes using your brains wins out over physical strength.
* At times what you do is more important than what you wear.

---

stories, or have intense personal meaning for students make good candidates for instruction. Children can get hooked on words through the study of interesting words.

Vocabulary-Building Words.   Classroom instruction should include words that lend themselves readily to vocabulary-building skills. **Vocabulary-building skills** allow children to seek clues to word meanings on their own. Words should be selected for instruction that will show students how to inquire into the meaning of unknown words—through structural analysis (i.e., drawing attention to word parts) or context analysis (Vacca & Vacca, 1999).

Principle 2: Teach Words in Relation to Other Words

Vocabulary words are often crucially tied to basic concepts. Children, as we have contended earlier, develop definitional knowledge when they are able to relate new words to known words. When words are taught in relation to other words, students are actively drawn into the learning process. They must use background knowledge and experiences to detect similarities and differences. When words are taught within the context of concept development, children develop a greater sensitivity to shades of meaning in communication. Rather than learning words randomly, children should deal with words that are related semantically and belong to categories.

Henry (1974) outlined four basic cognitive operations associated with learning concepts and words. The first involves the act of *joining*, or "bringing together." Comparing, classifying, and generalizing are possible through the act of joining. Asking children to explain how words are related or having them sort through word cards to put words into groups involves the act of joining.

The act of *excluding* is another conceptual operation worth considering when teaching words in relation to other words. Children must discriminate, negate, or reject items because they do not belong in a conceptual category. When a child must decide which word does not belong in a set of words, the process involves exclusion. In this case, the child would search through his or her background knowledge to distinguish examples from nonexamples or relevant attributes from irrelevant attributes.

So when a child is asked to decide which word does not belong in the list *flower, music, perfume, skunk,* on what set of criteria is a decision made? One immediate response may have been that music doesn't belong since it has little to do with the concept of smell.

A third conceptual activity or operation involves the act of *selecting*. Children learn to make choices and to explain why they made their choices based on what they have experienced, know, or understand. Synonyms, antonyms, and multiple-meaning words lend themselves well to the act of selecting. For example, select the *best* word from the choices given in the following sentence:

Tyrone's quiet behavior was mistaken for _____
SHYNESS/MODESTY/TERROR

Any of the choices might be acceptable. Yet the value of the activity is in providing a rationale for your choice by judging the worth of several potentially correct answers.

A fourth aspect of thinking conceptually involves the act of *implying*. Is a child able to make decisions based on if-then, cause-and-effect relationships among concepts and words? Dupuis and Snyder (1983) contend that the most common form of vocabulary exercise using implication is the analogy. They believe that the act of completing an analogy is such a complex activity that it actually requires the use of joining, excluding, and selecting processes.

Principle 3: Teach Students to Relate Words to Their Background Knowledge

Judith Thelen (1986) likened children's schemata of differing subjects to having file folders inside the brain. Let's suppose a math text reads, "A negative number is on the left of a number line." If Joe has a well-developed file folder for some schema for *number line,* this explanation of a negative number will be useful to Joe. But suppose Helen has heard of *number line* but has an underdeveloped file folder for the concept. In that case, the sentence defining negative numbers will have little meaning for Helen.

Pearson (1984) admonished educators by saying that we have asked the wrong question in teaching vocabulary. Instead of asking, "How can I get this word into the students' heads?" we should be asking, "What is it that students already know about that they can use as an anchor point, as a way of accessing this new concept?" If we ask the latter question, we will always be directing our vocabulary instructions to the file-folder issue—where does this word fit? Following Pearson's line of thinking, Joe and Helen's teacher could help each of them think, "How can I use what I know about a number line to learn what a negative number is?" In Helen's case, the teacher needs to show her a number line and have her work with it to develop her notions of the concept.

Principle 4: Teach Words in Prereading Activities to Activate Knowledge and Use Them in Postreading Discussion, Response, and Retelling

Through **prereading activities,** vocabulary words can be focused on *before* students read to help activate background knowledge in activities involving predicting. For example, Ms. Vizquel, a second-grade teacher, used vocabulary words she had chosen from *The Paperbag Princess* in a technique called Connect Two (Blachowicz, 1986). Her students predicted ways in which the terms would be connected in the story (see Figure 8.6). Then, since the words she chose reflected the story line, her students used them quite naturally when responding *after* reading. Here is a retelling given by Omar, a second grader:

Elizabeth was a princess who wore *expensive* clothes and was going to marry a prince named Ronald. A dragon *smashed* her castle and took Ronald. Elizabeth told the dragon,

◆ FIGURE 8.6   *Example of the Connect Two Strategy for* THE PAPERBAG PRINCESS

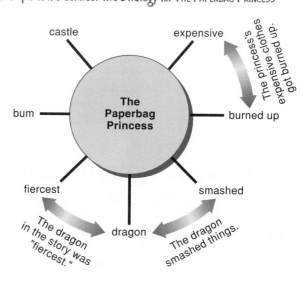

"Aren't you the *fiercest* dragon in the world?" and "Can't you burn up ten forests?" and stuff like that. The dragon did this stuff and got so tired he went to sleep so Elizabeth got Ronald. Then Ronald told her, "Come back when you look like a real princess." Elizabeth told him he looked like a prince but he was a *bum*.

In this way, Omar was able to integrate the words *expensive, smash, fiercest,* and *bum* as he retold the story.

Principle 5: Teach Words Systematically and in Depth

Teaching a word in depth means going beyond having students parrot back a definition. It means more than having students do something with a definition like finding an antonym, fitting the word into a sentence blank, and classifying the word with other words. All these are excellent activities and do need to be a part of a systematic vocabulary program. However, researchers are finding that for students to process vocabulary *in depth*, they must *generate a novel product using the term:* They could restate the definition in their own words, compare the definition to their own experiences with the concept, or make up a sentence that clearly demonstrates the word's meaning. These novel products can be written. But in fact, class discussion leads students to process words deeply by drawing connections between new and known information (Stahl, 1986).

By teaching systematically, we mean following a vocabulary program similar to the ones proposed by Beck, McKeown, and Omanson (1987) and Duin and Graves (1987). In these programs, 10 to 12 conceptually related words were taught and reinforced over a seven- to ten-day period. Networks of meanings of these words were established, as well as links to students' experiences. The activities included timed word matchings to facilitate students' automatic retrieval of new meanings. Finally, in the Duin and Graves study, students were engaged in group writing activities on a topic, using the vocabulary words in their writing.

Principle 6: Awaken Interest in and Enthusiasm for Words

Too often in elementary classrooms, vocabulary learning is one of the dullest activities of the school day. Children tend to associate vocabulary instruction with dictionary drill: looking up words, writing out definitions, and putting words in sentences. Though these activities have some merit, they quickly become routine. Children need to know *why, when,* and *how* to use dictionaries.

Nothing can replace the excitement about words that a good teacher can generate. The teacher's attitude toward vocabulary instruction can be contagious. What you do to illustrate the power of words is vital in improving children's vocabulary. Ask yourself whether you get excited by learning new words. Share words of interest to you with your students, and tell stories about the origin and derivation of words.

Help students play with words, as Cindy's third-grade teacher did. In one activity, her teacher, through discussion and demonstration, developed for the children the concept of facial expression, or "mugging." With a Polaroid camera, she took "mug shots" of her students and placed them prominently on the bulletin board. The children learned to "mug" for the camera by acting out "mug" words (e.g., happy mugs, sad mugs, angry mugs). The very last mug the children learned was the smug smile of satisfaction, or the "smug mug." Cindy's teacher explained that when a child knew something that no other person knew or took great pride in an accomplishment, he or she was to flash the "smug mug."

BEST PRACTICE: STRATEGIES FOR VOCABULARY AND CONCEPT DEVELOPMENT

Vocabulary instruction should not be neglected in the elementary classroom. Teachers in most grades worry that they "don't have the time to spend on vocabulary instruction." Direct vocabulary instruction need not take more than 20 minutes a day. Moreover, opportunities for incidental instruction and reinforcement arise in content area instruction throughout the school day.

Best practice in vocabulary instruction begins with the teacher's commitment to teach words well. So start slowly, and gradually build an instructional program over several years. We have already recommended that words be selected for emphasis that come from the actual materials that children read during the year, basal and literature selections as well as content area text selections. For best practice, the program should evolve from the instructional implications of the knowledge, instrumental, and aptitude hypotheses discussed earlier. Therefore, consider a three-component approach to classroom vocabulary instruction as illustrated in the Best Practice featured in Box 8.1.

Relating Experiences to Vocabulary Learning

Dale's Cone of Experience (Figure 8.2) is a good place to begin when planning and selecting vocabulary strategies that are experienced-based. The more direct, firsthand experiences students have, the better.

But different levels of vicarious experience can also establish bases for vocabulary learning. Vicarious experiences, though secondhand, are valuable in their own right. Dale's Cone of Experience indicates possibilities for planning experiences that are vicarious: demonstrations, simulations, dramatization, visual and audio media, reading to children, and reading on one's own.

Next we will consider how wide reading is useful for growth in vocabulary learning and how to help students use context to extend this growth.

Using Context for Vocabulary Growth

Teachers and experts know that in addition to defining new terms, children also need some examples of the concept; that is, children need to hear the new words used in differing contexts. Hearing a dictionary definition is not enough to learn a new word.

A Three-Component Approach to Classroom Vocabulary Instruction

Instructional strategies are not unique to any one component illustrated. In fact, strategies for teaching vocabulary should cut across components. Therefore, select strategies based on planning decisions that include provisions for a variety of activities, the types of information you wish to convey about words, and ways to link concepts to the children's experiences.

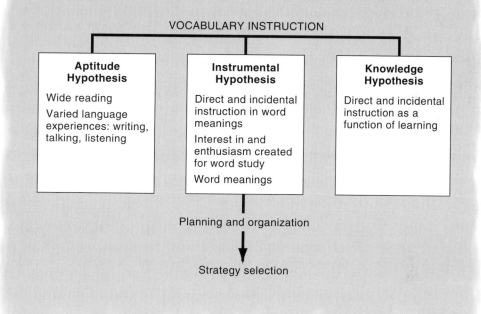

VOCABULARY INSTRUCTION

Aptitude Hypothesis	Instrumental Hypothesis	Knowledge Hypothesis
Wide reading Varied language experiences: writing, talking, listening	Direct and incidental instruction in word meanings Interest in and enthusiasm created for word study Word meanings	Direct and incidental instruction as a function of learning

Planning and organization

Strategy selection

Defining a word and using the word in a sentence or a context is a common and useful practice. In studying sound, a third-grade class learned that the definition of *vibrate* was "to move rapidly back and forth." They also discussed different contexts for *vibrate*—how a violin string vibrates and how blowing into a bottle or a flute makes the air vibrate. Even though we know that using context while reading is an important avenue for vocabulary growth, we agree with Nagy (1988) that when teaching *new* meanings, context alone is not effective. We know that the context provided in most texts tells us something about the word's meaning, but seldom does any single context give complete information (Deighton, 1970; Shatz & Baldwin, 1986). Nevertheless, we suggest that *the instructional goal should be to teach students to use context to gain information about the meanings of new terms.* For example, Judy led a group of first graders in reading a small book titled *Skylab* (Ribgy, 1993). First, when she asked the children what they thought a Skylab was, Jan said, "A lab in the sky, of course." Judy wrote this on the board. As Jan and the first graders read the book together, they made a list of what a skylab is:

> It is a space station.
> A rocket takes a skylab into space.
> A skylab goes around the earth.
> Astronauts stay on a skylab.
> A skylab has big solar collectors. Solar collectors change sunlight into electricity.

Helping students learn to use context to gain information about words new to them is particularly important for less fluent readers of any age. In addition, children need to know that they must accept partial word knowledge, some degree of uncertainty, and occasionally misleading contexts as they meet new words in their independent reading (Beck, McKeown, & McCaslin, 1983).

We will examine ways to help children grow in independence by using differing contexts to extend their vocabulary knowledge. But first, we look at more direct instructional strategies to develop word meanings.

Developing Word Meanings

Definitional knowledge, or the ability to relate new words to known words, can be built through synonyms, antonyms, and multiple-meaning words.

Synonyms are words that are similar in meaning to other words. **Antonyms** are words that are opposite in meaning to other words. Synonyms and antonyms are useful ways of having children define and understand word meanings. Antonyms, in particular, can demonstrate whether children really comprehend the meanings of new words. Moreover, words that have multiple meanings tend to confuse students, especially when they are reading and encounter the uncommon meaning of a word used in a passage.

Synonyms.
Synonym instruction has value when a child has knowledge of a concept but is unfamiliar with its label—the new word to be learned. In such cases, the focus of instruction is to help the student associate new words with more familiar ones. This particular strategy is a good example of the cognitive principle of bridging the gap between the new and the known.

For example, a fifth-grade teacher provided a synonym match for words that children were studying in a unit on ecology. Here are several of the matching items:

COLUMN A: NEW WORDS	COLUMN B: WORDS THAT YOU ALREADY KNOW
cultivate	change
erode	surroundings

environment   wearing away
modify   work

The children were directed to match the words from column B with the words from column A. A discussion followed with students giving reasons for their matchups. The discussion led to further clarification of each new term and the realization, as one child put it, that "some words just look hard but really aren't."

In another synonym-related activity, students were given overworked or unimaginative words in sentences or paragraphs, and asked to supply alternative words that would make each sentence or the paragraph more descriptive and interesting. Words such as *nice, great,* and *neat* are good candidates for this type of activity.

> Our trip to the zoo was *neat.* The entire family had a *swell* time. Dad thought that seeing the monkeys on Monkey Island was *fun.* So did I. But Mom *said,* "The monkeys were OK, but I liked the reptiles even more. The snakes were *terrific."* We all had a *great* time at the zoo.

This activity, and adaptations of it, can be used as a springboard for children to analyze a piece of their own writing, looking for overworked words and substituting more interesting and precise words.

Many word processing programs now have a built-in thesaurus. Children can be shown how to use the thesaurus to help find "just the right word" for what they want to say. Teachers can also use the thesaurus to develop exercises in which students must decide which synonyms would fit best in specific contexts, like the following:

> Which synonym would you most likely find in a funeral announcement or an obituary?
>
>   dead   departed   extinct

Exercises such as this one are a part of vocabulary instruction that promotes deep and fluent word knowledge.

Antonyms.   In addition to matching activities (in which students associate the target words with words that are opposite in meaning) and selecting activities (in which students select the best choice for an antonym from several listed), consider strategies that challenge children to work with antonyms in various print contexts.

For example, ask children to change the meanings of advertisements: "Change the ad! *Don't* sell the merchandise!" Children can ruin a good advertisement by changing the underlined words to words that mean the opposite. The following are examples of the antonym advertisment activity.

> Today through Tuesday!
> Save now on this <u>top-quality</u> bedding.
> The <u>bigger</u> the size, the <u>more</u> you save.

<u>GREAT</u> truckload sale!

Just take your purchase to the checkout, and the cashiers will <u>deduct</u> 30% from the ticketed price

Similar activities can be developed for a target word in a sentence or several new vocabulary words in a paragraph. You may devise an activity in which children work with sentence pairs. In the first sentence, the target word is underlined. In the second sentence, a child must fill in the blank space with an antonym for the target word.

1. The ship sank to the <u>bottom</u> of the ocean.

   The climbers reached the _____ of the mountain.

2. The <u>joyful</u> family reunion never had a dull moment.

   The funeral was the most _____ occasion I had ever experienced.

Sentence pairs will generate variations of antonyms. Therefore, children should be asked to defend their choices. In the first pair of sentences, *top, peak,* and *highest point* are acceptable antonyms for *bottom. Sad, solemn,* and *depressing* are all possible antonyms for *joyful.*

Multiple-Meaning Words.   Words with multiple meanings give children opportunities to see how words operate in context.

The *hall* was so long that it seemed endless.

The concert took place in a large *hall.*

The Football *Hall* of Fame is located in Canton, Ohio.

In content area textbooks, children frequently run across common words that have different meanings (e.g., *mean, table, force, bank, spring*). These can lead to confusion and miscomprehension. A strategy for dealing with multiple-meaning words involves prediction and verification (Vacca & Vacca, 1999).

1. Select multiple-meaning words from a text assignment. List them on the board.

2. Have students predict the meanings of these words and write them on a sheet of paper next to each term.

3. Assign the reading selection, noting the numbers of the pages where students can find each word in the text reading.

4. Ask students to verify their original predicted meanings. If they wish to change any of their predictions, they can revise the meanings based on how each word was used in the selection.

Classifying and Categorizing Words

When children manipulate words in relation to other words, they are engaging in critical thinking. Vocabulary strategies and activities should give students the experience of *thinking about, thinking through,* and *thinking with* vocabulary. Working with relationships among words provides this opportunity.

Through the aid of **categorization** and classification strategies, students recognize that they can group words that label ideas, events, or objects. Such strategies involve the processes of joining, excluding, selecting, and implying. Children will learn to study words critically and form generalizations about the shared or common features of concepts. Word sorts, categorization, semantic mapping, analogies, paired-word sentence generation, and collaborative learning exercises are all activities that help children conceptualize as well as learn and reinforce word meanings.

Word Sorts.   The process of sorting words is integrally involved in concept formation. Word sorting is an unbelievably simple yet valuable activity to initiate. Individually or in small groups, children sort through vocabulary terms that are written on cards or listed on an exercise sheet. The object of word sorting is to group words into different categories by looking for shared features among their meanings. The strategies can be used effectively at any grade level.

As discussed in Chapter 5, there are two types of word sorts: the *open sort* and the *closed sort.* In the *closed sort,* students know in advance what the main categories are. In other words, they must seect and classify words according to the features they have in common with a category. The closed sort reinforces and extends the ability to classify words. The *open sort* stimulates inductive thinking. No category or grouping is known in advance of sorting, and students must search for meanings and discover relationships among words.

Fifth-grade students participating in a unit on the newspaper discovered the many functions of a newspaper: to inform and interpret, influence, serve, and entertain. A closed-sort task that children participated in involved the completion of the following worksheet in small groups.

> *Directions:* In your groups, place the topics below under the proper headings. You may use a topic more than once. Base your decisions on class discussions and what is found in today's newspaper.

the largest picture on page A-1	the Market at a Glance column (business)
Weather Watch	the Transitions column (sports)
News Watch	the Bridge column
the first full-page ad	the classified index
the first Focal Point story	display advertising
legal notices	death notices
the first letter to the editor	the headline on page A-1
Dear Abby	the crossword puzzle
the astrology column	

Informs or Interprets	Influences	Serves	Entertains

Ms. Prince introduced a science unit on fish in this way. She had her third graders work in groups to brainstorm and list everything they could think of relating to the word *fish*. Their list included

good to eat	fun to catch	slippery
pretty	water	bugs
fins	tail	shiny

While the students were still in groups, she then asked them to come up with one or more categories or groups that two of the words could go into. The students came up with the following categories:

Fins and tail are *parts of a fish's body*.

Pretty, slippery, and shiny describe *how fish look*.

Good to eat and fun to catch tell about *things people like to do with fish*.

After the children had read the chapter on fish, Ms. Prince asked them to find words from the chapter that could go in the category or group that describes *how fish look*. The students very quickly added *scales* and *gills* to this category. In this way, Ms. Prince involved students in an open sort before reading and a closed sort (using a category identified by the children) after reading the text.

An excellent use of open sorting is to coordinate it with word banks. Word banks, closely associated with the language-experience approach, are collections of cards bearing words that a student does not recognize immediately. (Word banks were discussed in Chapter 5.)

Categorization.   Vocabulary activities involving categorization help students form relationships among words in much the same manner as open and closed sorts. The difference, however, lies in the amount of assistance a child is given. For example, a teacher may give students two to six words per grouping and ask them to do something with the sets of words. Different formats may be used to "do something" with the word sets. Consider giving the children sets of words and asking them to circle the word in each set that includes the meaning of the others. This exercise requires them to perceive common attributes or examples in relation to a more inclusive concept and to distinguish superordinate from subordinate terms. Children are involved in the cognitive process of joining.

Directions: Circle the word in each group that includes the meaning of the others in the group.

generals	ocean	spicy
troops	lake	sour
armies	water	taste
warriors	bay	salty

Other categorization exercises may direct students to cross out the word that does not belong in each set. This format forces students to manipulate words that convey the meanings of common items. In these activities, children learn to exclude words that are not conceptually related to other words.

Directions: Cross out the word in each group that doesn't belong.

meat	earth	judgment
butter	ground	treasure
oatmeal	stable	cash
fish oil	soil	price

The younger children are, the more manipulative and directed the categorization activity might be. Word cards may be used instead of worksheets. Working with sets of cards, a teacher may place one set at a time on a worktable and call on a child to remove the card that doesn't belong. The other children around the table must then attempt to explain the child's choice. Manipulative activities that require cutting, pasting, or drawing also work well.

Concept Circles.

Concept Circles.   A versatile activity appropriate for students at a wide range of grade levels, **concept circles** provide still another format and opportunity to study words critically and to relate words conceptually to one another. A concept circle simply involves putting words or phrases in the sections of a circle and then directing students to describe or name the concept relationship among the sections. In the example in Figure 8.7, Cheryl Goldstein asked her third graders, after they had read a story about scientists digging up dinosaur bones, to determine the main idea of the concept circle.

◆ FIGURE 8.7   Example of a Concept Circle

What is the main idea of this concept circle?

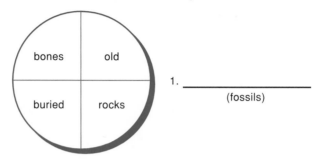

1. _____
                (fossils)

Alternatively, you might invite students to shade in the section of a concept circle containing a word or phrase that *does not relate* to the other words or phrases in the circle's sections and then identify the concept that they have in common. See Figure 8.8 for an example of a concept circle Brenda Kozma's fourth graders were asked to do in groups of three during their health lesson on food groups.

Other modifications include leaving one or more sections of the circle empty, inviting students to fill in the empty sections with a word or two relating in some way to the terms in the other sections. Students must then justify their choices by identifying the larger concept depicted by the circle.

Although these activities are similar to categorization exercises, students may respond more positively to the visual aspect of the sections in a circle than to category sorting because the circles seem less like tests.

Semantic Mapping.   **Semantic mapping,** or webbing, is a strategy that shows readers and writers how to organize important information. Semantic mapping can also revolve

◆ FIGURE 8.8   Variation on the Concept Circle

Directions: Shade in the section that does not relate to the other sections. What is the concept?

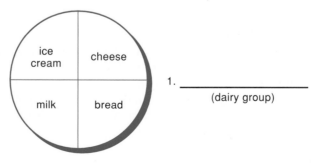

1. _____
                (dairy group)

around vocabulary learning by providing a visual display of how words are related to other words. Earlier in this chapter, semantic mapping was used to make distinctions among class, example, and attribute relations. Similarly, students can use semantic mapping to cluster words belonging to categories and to distinguish relationships. According to Smith and Johnson (1980), the procedures for semantic mapping can be varied to suit different purposes.

The first step in the semantic mapping of vocabulary is for the teacher to select a word central to a story or from any other source of classroom interest or activity and then write this word on the board. From this point, the procedures can vary, depending on the objective of the lesson. For example, the teacher can ask the students to think of as many words as they can that are in some way related to the word and jot them down. As students share the words they have written with the class, the words are grouped into categories on the

◆ Figure 8.9   A Semantic Map of the Five Senses

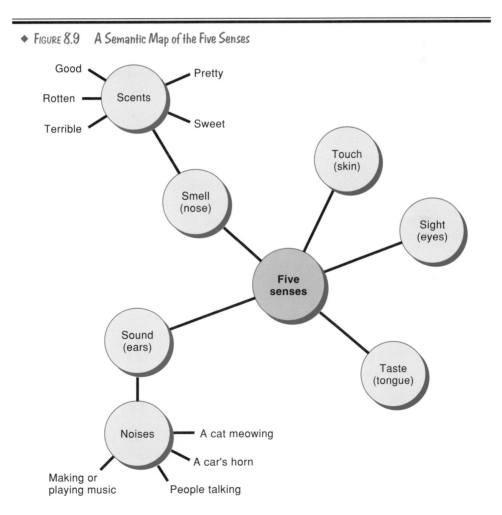

board around the central concept. The students can suggest names for the categories and discuss the category labels, relating their experiences to the words on the board.

Semantic maps can be elaborately developed or kept relatively simple, depending on the sophistication of the class and grade level. In Figure 8.9, a group of beginning readers developed a concept of the five senses through a mapping strategy.

The teacher began the map by writing the target concept, *five senses,* in the middle of the board. She then presented the class with a familiar situation: "How often have you known that your sister was making a snack even before you got to the kitchen to see or taste it?" The children responded by saying they could smell food cooking or hear a sibling preparing the snack. The teacher praised the student responses and continued, "You were using your senses of smell and sound to know that a snack was being fixed." She then wrote *smell* and *sound* on the board and connected the words to the central concept.

The children's attention was then directed to the bulletin board display of five children, each employing one of the senses. Through a series of questions, the class gradually developed the remainder of the semantic map. For example, when the concept of smell was being developed, the teacher noted, "We call a smell 'scent,'" and connected *scent* to *smell* on the map. She then asked, "How do you think flowers smell?" "What words can you tell me to determine different types of smells?" As the students volunteered words, the teacher placed them on the map. When the teacher asked, "When you think of sound, what's the first thing that comes to your mind?" the children quickly said "noises." The teacher connected *noises* to *sounds.* Further discussion focused on types of noises, both pleasant and unpleasant.

Analogies.   An **analogy** is a comparison of two similar relationships. On one side of the analogy, the words are related in some way; on the other side, the words are related in the same way. Analogies probably should be taught to students beginning in the intermediate grades. If they are not familiar with the format of an analogy, they may have trouble reading it successfully. Therefore, give several short demonstrations in which you model the process involved in completing an analogy.

1. Begin by asking students to explain the relationship that exists between two words. For example, write on the board a simple class example relationship:

   apple   fruit

2. Ask students, "What is the relationship between the two words?" Explanations may vary greatly, but arrive at the notion that an apple is a type of fruit.

3. Explain that an analogy is a comparison of two similar sets of relationships. Write on the board:

   Apple is to fruit as carrot is to _____

4. Suggest to students, "If an apple is a type of fruit, then a carrot must be a type of _____." Discuss the children's predictions, and provide additional examples.

5. Note than an analogy has its own symbols:

   apple:fruit::carrot: _____

6. Point out that the symbol : means *is to* and :: means *as*. Walk students through an oral reading of several analogies, saying, "An analogy reads like this." (The class reads the analogy in unison following the teacher's lead.)

7. Provide simple analogies at first, and gradually increase the complexity of the relationships.

8. Develop analogies from vocabulary used in stories, content area texts, or topics of interest in the classroom.

Ignoffo (1980) explained the value of analogies this way: "Analogies are practical because they carry an implied context with them. To work the analogy, the learner is forced to attempt various . . . procedures that involve articulation, problem solving, and thinking" (p. 520).

In Figure 8.10, we illustrate some of the types of word relationships from which many analogies can be developed.

Paired-Word Sentence Generation.   Students often need many exposures to new and conceptually difficult words in order to begin using these words in their speaking and writing vocabularies (Duin & Graves, 1987). After students have classified and categorized words through word sorts or other strategies, **paired-word sentence generation** can spur them into using these words in their speaking and writing.

Simpson (1987) described paired-word sentence generation as a task that could be used to *test* students' understanding of difficult concepts. We have taken her notion of paired-word sentence generation and developed it into a teaching strategy. In using this strategy, the teacher gives the students two related words. The goal of the strategy is to generate *one* sentence that correctly demonstrates an understanding of the words *and* their relationship to each other. However, there are several steps to help elementary students reach this goal. We will describe these steps by illustrating how Mr. Fratello used the strategy with his fifth-grade class as they worked with the concepts *reptile* and *cold-blooded*. First, Mr. Fratello had each student write sentences with the terms *reptile* and *cold-blooded* in them. The class came up with sentences like these:

> Reptiles are cold-blooded.
> Snakes, lizards, and turtles are reptiles.
> Cold-blooded means that when the air is warm, their bodies are warm, and when the air is cold, their bodies are cold.

Mr. Fratello then led the class in a sentence-combining activity to write a sentence that would give the reader information about what *reptiles* are and what *cold-blooded* means, as well as how the two concepts are related to each other. The class came up with sentences like these:

> Reptiles, like snakes, lizards, and turtles, are cold-blooded because they are cold when the air is cold and warm when the air is warm.

> Snakes, lizards, and turtles are reptiles that are cold-blooded, which means they are warm when the air is warm and cold when the air is cold.

◆ FIGURE 8.10

Using Word Relationships to Form Analogies

DIRECTIONS: Study each type of relationship, and for each example given, complete the analogy. Then compare your responses with a classmate or colleague.

1. Purpose relationship

   Teeth:chew::pen: _____
   Chair:sit::knife: _____

2. Part-to-whole relationship

   Antler:deer::tusk: _____
   Cat:feline::dog: _____

3. Synonym relationship

   Small:tiny::create: _____
   Copy:imitate::large: _____

4. Antonym relationship

   Black:white::day: _____
   High:low::morning: _____

5. Place relationship

   Book:bookcase::car: _____
   Flowers:vase::clothes: _____

6. Attribute relationship

   Rare:whale::common: _____
   Detective:clue::scientist: _____

7. Cause-and-effect relationship

   Furnace:heat::freezer: _____
   Seed:tree::egg: _____

Mr. Fratello asked his fifth graders to generate paired-word sentences throughout the school year. They first worked as a whole class and later worked in groups of four made up of both high and low achievers. Finally, they worked alone, devising their own sentences.

Developing Word Meanings Through Stories and Writing

Vocabulary functions differently in literature and in content material. First of all, when reading literature, knowing the meaning of a *new* word may not be necessary for under-standing the gist of the story. In contrast, content area vocabulary often represents major concepts that are essential for comprehension and learning. For example, children who cannot give a definition of *stamen* after reading about the parts of a flower have not grasped important content. But children can understand a story about a band even if they glean from context only that a *tambourine* is a musical instrument but don't know what ex-actly it is like. Second, vocabulary in literature often involves simply learning a new label for a concept already possessed, like learning that *desolate* means "very sad." In content ar-eas, often the purpose of the text is to teach the concepts as in the example of the second-grade science material labeling the parts of the flower, whereas this is not generally true in stories. Finally, in content texts, vocabulary terms often have a high degree of semantic re-latedness—as the terms *nectar, pollen, anther, stamen, stigma,* and *style* do. This is less likely to be true of vocabulary terms selected from literature (Armbruster & Nagy, 1992).

Yet, as mapping the story *The Paperbag Princess* illustrates, story grammar can be used to develop word meanings. The following two strategies, semantic analysis to writing and predictogram, draw on insights from story grammar.

Semantic Analysis to Writing. Since authors develop a theme through a series of related in-cidents, Beyersdorfer and Schauer (1989) reasoned that stories provide a situational con-text that could be used for rich development of word meanings. When using this strategy, the teacher narrows the selection of words to those semantically related to the theme. Stu-dents then develop definitions based on personal schemata for the theme.

In using *semantic analysis to writing:*

1. The teacher identifies the theme and composes a question involving critical thinking related to the theme.

2. The teacher selects words used by the author or consults a thesaurus to find about five words, both synonyms and antonyms, relating to the theme (words that are too closely synonymous are discarded).

3. The teacher constructs a **think sheet** (see Figure 8.11) for discussion purposes as well as for writing.

Brad, a sixth-grade teacher who was piloting a literature-based reading program, de-cided to involve his students in semantic analysis to writing with the thought-provoking book *A Wrinkle in Time,* by Madeleine L'Engle. In this story, Meg Murry, along with her precocious brother Charles Wallace and their friend Calvin O'Keefe, hope to rescue her

◆ FIGURE 8.11

Think Sheet for Extended Definition of Self-Reliance

QUESTIONS YOU WILL RESPOND TO IN AN ESSAY:

Was Meg in *A Wrinkle in Time* self-reliant? If so, how? What did she do that showed self-reliance? If not, what did she do that was not self-reliant? Further, did she change during the story?

What is self-reliance? _____

_____

DIRECTIONS:

1. As a class, we will define the terms. Write down definitions as we do this.

2. To this list add two words (numbers 6 and 7) suggested during brainstorming. Consult your dictionary and record a definition.

3. Decide which of the seven words contribute an essential characteristic to your definition of *self-reliance*.

4. Find evidence from the story that proves that Meg did or did not demonstrate the characteristics. Give the page number and a phrase description of the event.

5. Using the order of importance, rank the essential characteristics.

6. Write an essay. Define *self-reliance* and support the definition with evidence from *A Wrinkle in Time*.

TERM—DEFINITION	ESSENTIAL—YES/NO	ILLUSTRATION—STORY, PAGE NUMBER
1. Self-confidence		
2. Certainty		
3. Trust in oneself		
4. Independence		
5. Conviction		
6. *Courage*		
7. *Determination*		

father from a mysterious fate. The children travel through time to the planet Camazotz with the assistance of Mrs. Whatsit, Mrs. Who, and Mrs. Which. There they confront IT, the planet's intimidating force for conformity. Meg and friends find her father, but Charles Wallace gets swallowed up in IT. Meg's father cannot rescue Charles Wallace because he has been away from him so long that the familiar ties are too weak: Meg has to go back to IT and rescue Charles Wallace.

Although many themes can be derived from this book, Brad chose to use *self-reliance* in semantic analysis to writing because Meg, the main character, changed in terms of self-reliance through the many incidents in the book. Brad found that the dictionary definition of *self-reliance* was "sure of oneself and one's ability; needing, wishing for, and getting no help from others."

Brad then devised the questions "Was Meg in *A Wrinkle in Time* self-reliant?" "If so, how?" "What did she do that showed self-reliance?" "If not, what did she do that was not self-reliant?"

To make the think sheet, Brad used a thesaurus and chose the following words and phrases:

self-confidence	independence
certainty	conviction
trust in oneself	

Because he knew that the book would prove quite difficult for some of the readers in the class, Brad read the book orally to the class over a two-week period. He knew that some of these same readers would write interesting essays on self-reliance. Each day as he read the chapters, students wrote in a response journal (response journals will be described in Chapter 9), and the class had lively discussions comparing their responses.

Students were now prepared for Brad to involve them in the semantic analysis to writing strategy. As a result of class brainstorming and discussion, the terms *courage* and *determination* were added to the think sheet. Small group work then began in earnest to find incidents that showed that Meg was or was not self-reliant.

Next the class had an animated debate about whether Meg was or was not self-reliant, citing evidence for both positions. Many felt that Meg was not self-reliant and supported this with the incident when Meg finds her father and becomes disillusioned when her father is not able to get her brother, Charles Wallace, away from IT. Students who felt Meg became self-reliant cited the fact that Meg finally mustered the courage to attempt to save Charles Wallace from IT. Thus two different initial statements and story frames were formulated to help students begin writing their first drafts, after they had worked in pairs to rank the importance of their supporting evidence.

I think Meg in *A Wrinkle in Time* _____
self-reliant. I think this because _____ . Further, _____ .
In addition, _____
    In conclusion, _____
_____ .

Brad took home many stimulating essays to read after his students had eagerly read them to each other. Many students later chose their self-reliant essay from all those accumulated in their writing folder to revise and edit.

Predictogram.   Story elements—including the setting, the incidents in the plot, characterization, the character's problem or goal, how the problem or goal is resolved, and the theme or larger issue to which the problem or goal relates—can be used to develop students' meaning vocabulary with the *predictogram* strategy.

In planning for predictogram, teachers choose words from a story that they feel will be challenging to the students. The words and their meanings are discussed in class, and children relate their personal associations with the words. Finally, students work in groups to predict how they think the author might use each term in the story. Would the author use it to tell about the setting? The characters? The problem or goal or trouble the characters have? Would the author use the word to tell about how the problem or trouble was solved? Students then read to discover how the author did use the terms.

Mrs. Nowak, a third-grade teacher in the same school as Brad, was also beginning to use a literature-based program with the basal reading program she had used for five years. She was planning for a group of students to read *Crow Boy*, by Taro Yashima. The words she thought would be challenging included *forlorn, interesting, trudging, admired, announced, imagine, graduation, attendance, charcoal,* and *rejected*. To get students thinking about the problems in the story, she asked them to free-write about their thoughts on the idea that "sometimes kids tease a classmate who is shy or different." The students shared their free-writes. Then Mrs. Nowak told them what was happening at the beginning of the story. She led them in a discussion concerning how the meanings of the terms related to personal experiences and predicting which of the words the author would use for each story element.

Figure 8.12 shows how the group completed the predictogram for *Crow Boy*. The students then read the story, looking to see how the author actually used the challenging vocabulary terms. Next we suggest ways to help children gain control over their own vocabulary learning.

Developing Independence in Vocabulary Learning

There is no question that wide reading and thus learning the meaning of words from context is an important way for people to extend their vocabularies. Fielding, Wilson, and Anderson (1986) found that the amount of free reading was the best predictor of vocabulary growth between grades 2 and 5. Nagy (1988) theorized that after third grade, for children who do read a reasonable amount, reading may be the single largest source of vocabulary growth. Students are also exposed to terms as they listen to teachers, parents, and television.

Next we will look at the strategies of self-selection and word knowledge rating. These two strategies aid students in monitoring their own growth in vocabulary knowledge as they use context in reading and listening. The *self-selection* strategy helps children become sensitized to the many words that they read and hear in school and at home that they can

♦ Figure 8.12

Predictogram for Crow Boy by Taro Yashima

DIRECTIONS: Discuss with members of your group how you think Taro Yashima would use the vocabulary words below. Would he use them to describe the characters? Or the problem or goal of the character? Or the solution to the problem? Place each word in the appropriate square. Be prepared to tell why you think so.

Vocabulary words: forlorn   imagine
                    interesting   graduation
                    trudging   attendance
                    admired   charcoal
                    announced   rejected

Setting where the story took place	*charcoal* *interesting*
Characters the people in the story	*forlorn* *imagine* *trudging*
Problem or goal main character	*rejected*
Solution to problem or attainment *of goal*	*graduation* *attendance* *announced* *admired*

---

add to their meaning vocabulary. *Word knowledge rating* helps children develop an awareness of the extent to which they know the words they come across as they read and interact with others.

Self-Selection Strategy.   Words for the self-selection strategy can be drawn from basal readers, literature, content area instruction, or incidental learning experiences. As the name implies, children select the words to be studied. In describing how to use this strategy, Haggard (1986) explained that the first step is to ask students to bring to class one word they believe the class should learn; the teacher also chooses a word. These words are then written on the board and students give the definitions they gleaned from the context in which they found the word. Class members add any information they can to each definition. The students and teacher consult pertinent references like dictionaries, glossaries, and textbooks to add to definitions that are incomplete or unclear.

At this point, students can explain why they think a word is important to learn. Through this discussion, students narrow the list, agreeing to exclude terms that many already know or are not useful enough. The agreed-on terms and their definitions are recorded in vocabulary journals that are kept throughout the year. Students may also enter into their own vocabulary journal personal words that they chose but that were not chosen by the group. The class list of words is then used in activities like word sorts, analogies, synonym matching, or any of the other activities that have been described. The class-agreed words also become part of end-of-unit tests. By using this strategy, students become aware of many striking words that they see and hear in their daily lives.

Word Knowledge Rating.   Word knowledge rating is a way to get children to analyze how well they know vocabulary words. Words chosen by the teacher or by the students in the self-selection strategy are written on a worksheet or on the board. We suggest students rate words using Dale's (1965) continuum to explain the degrees of word cognition.

> I've never seen the word.
> I've heard of it, but I don't know what it means.
> I recognize it in context. It has something to do with _____.
> I know the word in one or several of its meanings.

After students have rated themselves on their knowledge of the words, lead them in a discussion using questions such as "Which are the hardest words?" "Which do you think most of us don't know?" "Which are the easiest?" "Which do you think most of us know?" (Blachowicz, 1986). The exchange could also involve consideration of the question "Which terms are synonyms for concepts we already know, and which are somewhat or totally new concepts to us?"

Through such discussions, students will begin to make judgments concerning the depth of their knowledge of vocabulary terms that they have encountered, as well as the amount of effort needed to add the term to their meaning vocabulary.

SUMMARY

Vocabulary instruction is one facet of reading instruction about which there is minimal controversy. Educators agree that it is possible to extend students' knowledge of word meanings, and it is important to do so because of the relationship between this knowledge and reading comprehension. This chapter explored that relationship, then delved into the instructional opportunities teachers can provide to expand children's vocabulary knowledge and to develop their interest and motivation to *want* to learn words and to monitor their own vocabulary learning.

Six guidelines for establishing vocabulary programs throughout the elementary grades were presented. For best practice, a three-component approach to classroom instruction was suggested, with numerous strategies for vocabulary and concept development that capitalize on children's natural spontaneity, using direct instruction and cooperative learning groups as well as reinforcement activities. These strategies can be adapted for teaching vocabulary through basal readers, literature, or content area instruction, providing a natural framework for concept development at all ages.

TEACHER-ACTION RESEARCHER

1. Choose any grade level, and plan a vocabulary lesson, teaching it to a small group of your classmates or children. The lesson should emphasize one of the following strategies discussed in the chapter: (a) relating experiences to vocabulary learning; (b) developing word meanings using synonyms, antonyms, or multimeaning words; and (c) classifying and categorizing words. In what ways did the strategy selected work well with the students?

2. Observe a classroom teacher during reading and language arts instruction for several consecutive days. Record the time spent on vocabulary instruction. Look for vocabulary instruction that reflects the aptitude and knowledge hypotheses as well as the instrumental hypothesis. How much time is devoted to vocabulary learning in each category? What kinds of activities have been incorporated into the instruction? What conclusions do you draw from your observations? What implications can you make for further instruction?

3. Develop a semantic map around a key concept. Overview the map with one or two of your fellow students, explaining the context for which it is intended. How much do they think that children will already know about the concept? What areas are most likely to require further development?

KEY TERMS

analogy
antonyms
aptitude hypothesis
categorization
class relationships
concept circles
concepts
definitional
    knowledge

instrumental
    hypothesis
knowledge
    hypothesis
paired-word sentence
    generation
prereading activities
semantic mapping
subordinate

superordinate
synonyms
think sheet
vocabulary
vocabulary-building
    skills

CHAPTER

9
Reading-Writing Connections

Chapter Overview

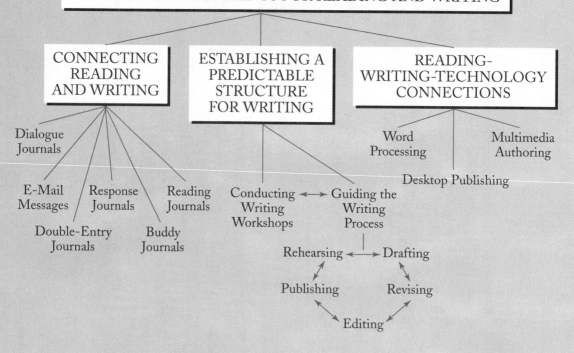

READING-WRITING CONNECTIONS

RELATIONSHIPS BETWEEN READING AND WRITING

CREATING ENVIRONMENTS FOR READING AND WRITING

CONNECTING READING AND WRITING

ESTABLISHING A PREDICTABLE STRUCTURE FOR WRITING

READING-WRITING-TECHNOLOGY CONNECTIONS

Dialogue Journals

E-Mail Messages

Response Journals

Reading Journals

Double-Entry Journals

Buddy Journals

Conducting Writing Workshops ←→ Guiding the Writing Process

Rehearsing ←→ Drafting

Publishing — Revising

Editing

Word Processing

Multimedia Authoring

Desktop Publishing

Between the Lines

In this chapter, you will discover:

♦ Relationships between reading and writing

♦ Conditions contributing to a classroom environment that supports reading-writing connections

♦ How to use journals to integrate reading and writing

◆ **How to create a predictable classroom structure for writing**

◆ **How to organize writing workshops and guide the writing process**

◆ **How to enhance reading-writing connections through technology**

In Kay Dunlop's first-grade class, the children listen to Kay read Jean Marzollo's *Happy Birthday, Martin Luther King* (1993), a wonderfully written and illustrated book highlighting the important events of King's life. It has become routine for the students in the class, as part of their development as a community of learners, to connect talking *and writing* to what they have read or have heard read to them. *Happy Birthday, Martin Luther King* provides an occasion to connect reading and writing as they think about and reflect on King's life.

So Kay asks, "What if Martin Luther King Jr. were alive today? What would he be disappointed about?" Some of you may wonder whether first graders have the wherewithal to think about and respond to such an analytic and speculative question. Yet in Figure 9.1, James, one of Kay's students, grapples with the question and speculates that King would be angry if he were alive today. James doesn't let the conventions of punctuation and spelling get in his way as he writes his response to the question in his reading journal. Nor does he shy away from the use of "big" words like *angry, violence, freedom,* and *separate* to express his feelings and thoughts. He knows that his teacher, in this learning situation, is more concerned with what's on his mind than with the surface features of his writing. This is not to say that Kay doesn't want James and his classmates to excel in all aspects of writing, including its mechanics, but she recognizes that important functions of writing are to make sense of experience and to think analytically.

Asking a "What if . . . ?" question prompts James's thinking about the story of Martin Luther King's life. He uses this occasion to connect reading and writing to express his dismay at the violence that is all too real in his world. James reasons that King would not want teenagers to bring guns to school and kill people. James also uses his understanding of the life and times of King to interact personally with the concept of integration as he asserts that King "dos not wut [want] poeple seprt [separate]." James even uses a refrain from one of King's speeches, "Let freedom ring," to support his assertion that King would be angry if he were alive today. James constructs meaning as he connects reading and writing to gain perspective on his world.

As the chapter overview suggests, in this chapter we show how writing helps children understand *and* be understood. Writing is thinking with paper and pencil, and therein lies one of its important links to reading. Our emphasis throughout the chapter is on the strong bonds that exist between learning to write and learning to read. These connections are powerful enough to suggest that children probably learn as much about reading by writing as they learn about writing by reading.

◆ FIGURE 9.1   James's Response to the Question, "If Martin Luther King, Jr. were alive today, what would he be disappointed about?"

if Martin L. king wher a liv he wood be age. dcos tenagrs are doing vials and. they bring guns to. scoohl and they kill poepel.

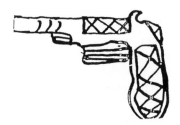

But he wats Feetm! to. Reiing he dos not wut poeple Sept he wats. Feetm!

RELATIONSHIPS BETWEEN READING AND WRITING

Common sense tells us that writing is intended to be read. When children are writing, they can't help but be involved in reading. Before writing, they may be collecting and connecting information from books, and during and after writing, they are revising, proofreading, and sharing their work with others. Children should be invited to write about what they are reading and to read about what they are writing. Therein lies the real value of *reading-writing connections.*

Writing and reading have been described as two sides of the same process (Squire, 1984). Yet in many elementary schools, writing and reading are strangers to one another, isolated and taught as separate curriculum entities. In the past, teachers have followed a much-traveled road to literacy instruction. Reading and writing have been taught separately and sequentially. The premise underlying this instructional path is that reading ability develops first and writing ability follows. Nevertheless, supported by new knowledge about literacy development, today's teachers recognize that when young children are engaged in writing, they are using and manipulating written language. In doing so, children develop valuable concepts about print and how messages are created.

There is compelling evidence to suggest that writing and reading abilities develop concurrently and should be nurtured together. Carol Chomsky (1970, 1979) was one of the first language researchers to advocate that children write first and read later. She contends that writing is a beneficial introduction to reading because children acquire letter and word knowledge through invented spellings. Marie Clay (1991) also supports the powerful bonds between writing and reading. She views reading and writing as complementary processes. Literacy development demands that children engage in reading and writing concurrently.

Reading and writing are related, and both are acts of making meaning for communicating.

The connections between reading and writing have been examined formally through research studies and theoretical explorations (Shanahan, 1990; Tierney & Shanahan, 1991). How are reading and writing related? The following are some of the conclusions that can be drawn about the relationships between reading and writing.

◆ Reading and writing processes are correlated; that is, good readers are generally good writers, and vice versa.

◆ Students who write well tend to read more books than those who are less capable writers.

◆ Wide reading may be as effective in improving writing as actual practice in writing.

◆ Good readers and writers are likely to engage in reading and writing independently because they have healthy concepts of themselves as readers and writers.

These conclusions suggest that reading and writing are related. The two processes share many of the same characteristics: Both are language- and experience-based, both require active involvement from language learners, and both must be viewed as acts of making meaning for communication. This is why children's writing should be shared with an audience composed of readers, in *and* out of the classroom.

As much as reading and writing are similar, Shanahan (1988) warns that research suggests that the two processes may be different as well. Some good readers, for example, aren't good writers, and some good writers may indeed be poor readers. Nevertheless, if writing is to have an impact on reading, and vice versa, then instruction in writing and reading must be integrated throughout the instructional program.

Integrating writing and reading is no easy task. An occasional foray into creative writing will not appreciably affect children's writing or reading development. Where does a teacher begin? How do you get started? How do you guide children's writing day in and day out throughout the school year?

CREATING ENVIRONMENTS FOR READING AND WRITING

Since the mid-1970s, Donald Graves (1983, 1994) and Jane Hansen (1987) have conducted research on the writing and reading development of elementary school children. Extensive field work in primary and intermediate classrooms has yielded valuable insights into the influence of the learning environment on children's writing and reading. Graves and Hansen have shown that *informal* learning environments increase the volume of writing and reading elementary children do. Not only do they write and read more, but they also take greater control over and responsibility for their writing and reading. Children need much less external motivation to write and read from their teachers when they have time to read and write and have the chance to select their own writing topics or reading material.

In school, children develop fluency and power in their reading and writing when they have *time* and *choice* on their side. We explore the importance of student choice and the uses of instructional time in a literature-based reading program in greater depth in Chapter 10.

Children must have numerous occasions to write about things that are important to them. This is why a teacher's positive attitude toward invented spellings contributes greatly to children's writing development. Concerns for the form and mechanics of writing matter but must be viewed from a developmental perspective. The first order of business for encouraging an environment that supports writers should be on the exploration of topics that matter to young writers.

Examine, for example, the following suggestions for encouraging classroom writing, and note the italics, which underscore connections between writing and reading.

1. Use children's experiences, and encourage them to write about things that are relevant to their interests and needs. Children must choose topics that they care about. Yet a fear that teachers often harbor is that students will have nothing to say or write about if left to select their own topics. Rarely is this the case. Children want to write. But before they begin, they should have good reason to believe that they have something to say. How can you help? Guide students to choose topics that they have strong feelings about; *provide opportunities for reading literature, surfing the Internet,* and brainstorming ideas before writing; show students how to plan and explore topics by using lists, jotting notes, and clustering ideas.

2. Develop sensitivity to good writing by reading poetry and literature to children. Young writers need to listen to written language. In Chapter 10, we explain ways to *bring children and literature together. Although literature is a mirror that reflects good writing to children, the writings of other children also serve as a powerful model.* Sharing good literature and children's writing helps young writers feel that they are capable of producing similar work.

3. Invent ways to value what children have written. Children need praise and feedback, the two mainstays of a built-in support system for classroom writing. *Sharing writing in progress* is an important way to ensure response, or feedback, in the classroom. *Displaying and publishing writing* is another.

   Children's writing reflects the functions of written language. Children, like adults, don't engage in writing for the sake of writing. Because their efforts are purposeful, their writing must result in products. Later in this chapter, we explain ways to *value children's products through publication.* Certainly one of the best ways to value writing and reading is through bookmaking. *Nowhere do children build a sense of authorship better than by writing and illustrating their own books.*

4. Guide the writing personally. As children are writing, you should circulate around the room to help and encourage. Conferencing then becomes the primary means to respond and to give feedback in the writer's environment. Teacher-student and peer conferences help create a collaborative, noncompetitive environment in which to write, *try out work in progress,* and *share what has been written with others.*

5. Write stories and poetry of your own and share them with your students. *Sharing your writing with students* or discussing problems that you are having as a writer signals to children that writing is as much a problem-solving activity for you as it is for them. There is no better way to model writing than to let students in on the processes you use as a writer. Children need to know that writing is as exciting for you as it is for them.

6. Tie writing in with the entire curriculum. Content area activities may provide the experiences and topics that can give direction and meaning to writing. *Writing to learn will help children discover and synthesize relationships among the concepts they are studying in social studies, science, mathematics, art, music, and health. The connection between reading and writing are especially meaningful when children explore concepts through written language.*

7. Start a writing center in your classroom. A writing center is a place where young writers can go to find ideas, contemplate, or *read other children's writing.* The center should be well equipped with lined paper of various sizes and colors; lined paper with a space for a picture; drawing paper of all sizes; stationery and envelopes; tag board; index cards; a picture file; pencils, colored pencils, crayons, and markers; paper clips; white glue and paste; paper punches; *book display stands; informational texts such as magazines, dictionaries, and encyclopedias; a classroom library for students' writing;* and *an address file of book authors, sports figures, celebrities, and magazines that print students' work.* A writing center isn't a substitute for having a classroom program where children work every day at developing the craft of writing. Instead, the center is a visible support that enhances the writing environment in your classroom.

When a teacher encourages children to write, they engage in reading activities in varied and unexpected ways. An environment that connects writing and reading provides students with numerous occasions to write and read for personal and academic reasons, some of which are suggested in Figure 9.2.

Connecting Reading and Writing

When journals are part of the writing environment, children use them to write about things that are important to them and that they have strong feelings about. Journals can be used to help children examine their personal lives and to explore literary and informational texts. A journal brings children in touch with themselves as they record their thoughts and feelings, and it is a gold mine for generating ideas. All forms of written expression are welcomed in journals—doodles, comments, poems, letters, and, for the purpose of the next section, written conversations between child and teacher and child and child.

Using Journals (and E-Mail Correspondence) for Written Conversation

If journals are to be used to generate ideas, time must be set aside by the teacher to read and respond to children's entries on a regular basis. Because child and teacher enter into a personal relationship through the vehicle of journal writing, there are, as we have seen, many occasions for a dialogue in writing.

◆ FIGURE 9.2

Occasions for Writing and Reading

- Pen pal arrangements with other classes within the building

- Pen pal and "key pal" (Internet correspondence through e-mail) arrangements with a class from another school in the same district or in classrooms around the world

- Writing stories for publication on the Internet

- Writing for a school or class newspaper

- Writing for a class, school, or electronic magazine on the Internet

- "Author of the Week" bulletin board that features a different student writer each week

- Entering writing contests in the local community or on the Internet

- Opportunities for students to read pieces of writing over the school's public address system

- Opportunities for students to read selected pieces of writing to a younger class

- Outings where students can read selected pieces of writing to children in a day-care center

- Displays of student writing in the classroom, on a classroom home page, and in the corridors of the school

- Videotapes of students reading their writing

- Multimedia authoring presentations of students' projects

- Play festivals featuring student-authored scripts

- Student-made publicity for school events

- Student-written speeches for school assemblies and programs

- A "young author festival" to highlight student-authored books

- Student-prepared speeches in the voices of characters from stories or from social studies

- Daily journals and diaries

- Biographical sketches based on interviews or research

- Songwriting

- Reviews of movies or television programs

- Cartoon scripts

Dialogue Journals. According to Gambrell (1985), the **dialogue journal** emphasizes meaning while providing natural, functional experiences both in writing and reading. Child and teacher use dialogue journals to converse in writing. A teacher's response to children's entries may include comments, questions, and invitations to children to express themselves. The Best Practice featured in Box 9.1 offers guidelines for using dialogue journals in the classroom.

Guidelines for Using Dialogue Journals

One of the most important ways to encourage reading is through an ongoing, sustained written conversation with students. Dialogue journals serve to scaffold reading-writing interactions through informal conversations. Guidelines for the use of dialogue journals include the following:

1. Use bound composition books. (Staple appropriate writing paper inside a construction paper cover. The paper should be large enough for several journal entries so children can see the developing dialogue.)

2. To motivate students, tell them journals are like letters. They will write to you and you will write back. Encourage writing about any topic of interest or concern to them.

3. For best results, write daily. Set aside a special time for writing and reading. For children in grades one and two, 10 minutes might be appropriate, whereas older children may need 20 minutes.

4. Focus on communication. Do not correct entries; instead, model correct forms in your response.

5. Respond in a way that encourages written expression such as, "Tell me more about . . . ," "I'd like to know more about . . . ," "Describe . . . ."

6. Dialogue journals are private. Convey to students that they belong to the two of you, but they may share their journals if they wish. Sharing should always be voluntary.

From "Dialogue Journals: Reading-Writing Interactions," by L. B. Gambrell, *The Reading Teacher, 38* (1985), pp. 512–515. Reprinted by permission of the International Reading Association.

In Figure 9.3, study how second-grade teacher Sharon Piper responded to Tammy Lynn's September 20 journal entry. Mrs. Piper's dialogue with Tammy Lynn encourages a response and a continuation of the conversation through subsequent journal writing.

Buddy Journals.   A **buddy journal** is a variant of the dialogue journal. However, instead of a teacher engaging in written conversation with a student, a buddy journal encourages a dialogue between children using a journal format (Bromley, 1989). Before beginning buddy journals, children should be familiar with the use of journals as a tool for writing and also be comfortable with the process of dialoguing with a teacher through the use of dialogue journals. To get buddy journals off and running, have the students form pairs. Each child may choose a buddy, or buddies may be selected randomly by drawing names

◆ FIGURE 9.3   Tammy Lynn and Mrs. Piper's Dialogue Entries

mRs. piper We have
Bunkbeds and my Sister
fell of and harT her head and
arm it was bresed bad but she
still vehT to school and my
mom Told me if i wanted to
Sleep on the Top becuse
every cuple munts my mom
puts up plair beds and
we take torns and it Was
kristys torn but She fell
off

Dear Tammy Lynn,
I am sorry to hear about Kristy's fall from
the bunkbed. I hope her bruise went away
and that she is feeling better. When will
you be sleeping on the top bunk? What
will you do to not fall out of the top bed?

from a hat. To maintain a high level of interest and novelty, children may change buddies periodically.

Buddies may converse about anything that matters to them—from sharing books they have been reading to sharing insights and problems. As Bromley (1989) advises, teachers who use buddy journals for natural writing occasions should promote student interaction, cooperation, and collaboration: "Buddy journals enhance socialization since they allow students a forum for learning about each other" (p. 128).

For example, in Megan's elementary school, the fifth-grade students participate in a family living class where they explore a variety of social, emotional, and psychological issues that, in Megan's words, "teaches us growing up." A textbook and supplementary materials, including imaginative and informational trade books, pamphlets, magazines, and newspaper articles, provide numerous reading opportunities for the students. An integral part of the class is to examine adolescent behavior and its effect on the family.

"Teenagers," Megan hears her teacher say in class discussion, "worry about a lot of things," "What things?" Megan wonders to herself, but the question is left unexplored as the discussion shifts to another subject.

When she gets home from school that day, the question of what teenagers worry about is still on Megan's mind: "I didn't have much to do and I was kinda bored, so I began to draw about what teenagers think." In her notebook, she sketches the drawing shown in Figure 9.4a, and titles it, "What Most Adolescents Think."

◆ Figure 9.4a   "What Most Adolescents Think," by Megan Woodrum

The next day, Megan brings her drawing to class and shows it to the teacher. Delighted, the teacher invites Megan to share the drawing with other class members. Later that morning, as the students write in their buddy journals, a classmate asks Megan about her drawing and why she thinks teenagers worry about such things as being normal, looking good, and fitting in. Megan responds to her writing partner with the journal entry in Figure 9.4b.

The buddy journal allows Megan to explore and clarify ideas encountered in class and in her own life experiences through informal written conversation with a classmate. It provides Megan with another tool, in addition to cartooning, for self-expression and meaning-making.

Electronic Mail (E-Mail) Conversations.   On the Internet, students (and teachers) can send and receive messages anywhere on the planet through the use of *electronic mail (e-mail)*. E-mail communication engages students in written conversations with others in the same learning community, at a neighboring school, or anywhere in the world. E-mail messages are sent electronically from one computer to another through the use of special software. When students use e-mail, reading-writing connections are both personal and social (through **key pal correspondence**—the electronic equivalent of pen pals) and educational (through **Internet projects**—a collaborative approach to learning on the Internet).

Key pal correspondence creates opportunities for children to communicate with other children from around the world, learn about different cultures, ask questions, and develop

◆ FIGURE 9.4b   *Megan's Response to Her Buddy's Question, "Why do teenagers worry?"*

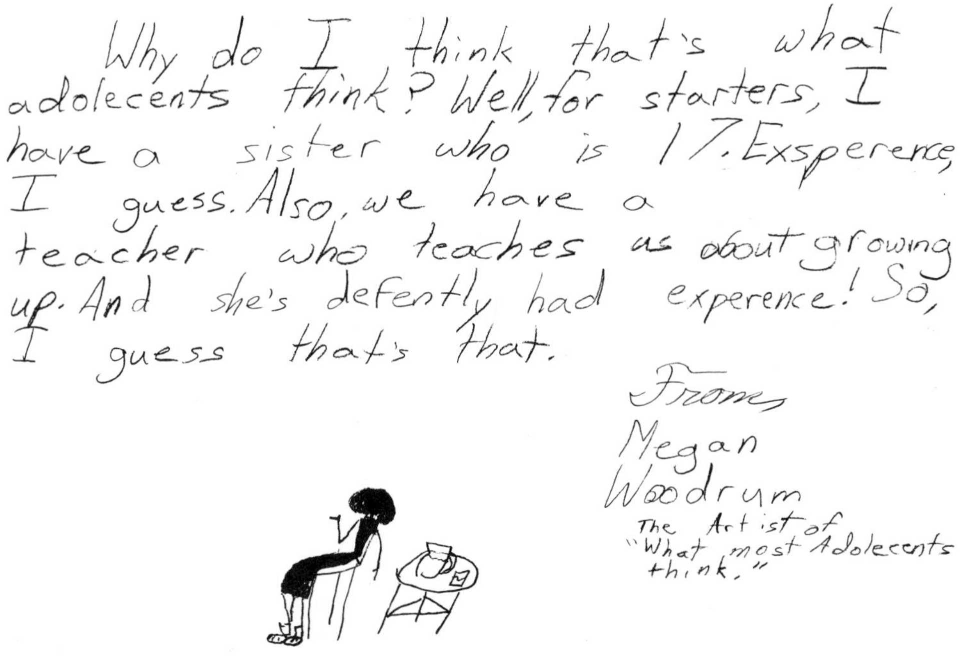

Why do I think that's what adolecents think? Well, for starters, I have a sister who is 17. Exsperence, I guess. Also, we have a teacher who teaches us about growing up. And she's defently had experence! So, I guess that's that.

From,
Megan
Woodrum
The Artist of "What most Adolecents think."

literacy skills. E-mail reduces the time between messages to a matter of seconds, making it possible for children to send messages anywhere in the world and receive responses quickly. Figure 9.5 illustrates the first two pages from Rigby Heinemann's Global Keypals site for students 5 to 10 years of age. Updated every week, this site allows teachers and students to make contacts and enter their own messages in the following age groups: 5–10, 11–13, and 14–18.

Internet projects also promote global conversations and learning connections between students. According to Leu and Leu (1999), Internet projects are designed within the framework of a thematic or topical unit. To proceed with an Internet project, a teacher plans an upcoming unit and writes a description of the project. The project description is then posted in advance on a site, such as Rigby Heinemann's Global Keypals, in order to locate classrooms that may be willing to become collaborating partners in the project. Planning and posting the project two or three months in advance will help identify classroom partners and provide enough time to work out the details of the collaboration. Teachers from the collaborating classrooms communicate electronically to make arrangements and plan project-related activities for students to engage in.

Leu and Leu (1999) recommend several sites as "jumping-off points" for Internet projects but indicate that there are numerous sites for teachers to explore on the Internet:

◆ *Intercultural E-Mail Connections* (http://www.stolaf.edu/network/iecc/index.html). Located at St Olaf's College, this site is recommended by Leu and Leu as one of the best sources for linking with key pals and classroom partners from different countries.

◆ *Pitsco's Launch to Keypals* (http://www.pitsco.com/keypals). This key pal site contains a master list of mailing lists that link teachers to teachers, students to students, and classes to classes.

◆ *eMail Classroom Exchange* (http://www.epals.com/). This site links partner classrooms by school, name, location, language, or grade level.

In one Internet project in northeastern Ohio, preservice teachers engaged in e-mail conversations with fourth graders (Vacca & Vacca, 1999). The collaborative project revolved around conversations about trade books that the preservice teachers and their fourth-grade partners were reading. The collaborative project was a joint venture between university instructors and classroom teachers. Throughout the semester, the e-mail partners dialogued about the books, engaged in authentic talk. In addition, the preservice teachers incorporated instructional strategies into electronic conversations. For example, in one correspondence just prior to reading the book *A Taste of Blackberries* (Smith, 1973), a preservice teacher invites his partner to make predictions about the book:

> Just to let you know before you start reading, the book is very sad and it involves people dying. I would like you to brainstorm a little bit about the name of the book and give me some guesses of what you think the story may be about. Then we will take your guesses, and after we read the book, we can find out how close you were with some of your guesses. I am really looking forward to hearing from you.

Not only did the e-mail collaboration serve to make reading-writing connections during the literature discussions, but also the e-mail partners got to know one another socially as

Rigby Heinemann Keypals
for students aged 5 - 10 years

Hey kids! Have you visited our links to great <u>Kidplaces</u> on the web?

Be aware! Read the <u>netiquette guide to keypals.</u>

Clicking on the <u>heading</u> for any of the following entries will allow you to send email to that person. You can put your own message here by using the <u>'Add your own Message'</u> section below (we update approximately weekly).

Please note that we do not publish surveys as such, but you may briefly outline the topic of your survey and request that interested people email you directly for the actual survey questions.

Email <u>**Click here to add your own message to this list**</u>
(send an email, not an attachment, please, and
don't forget to include your name and age)

Or answer some of these people by clicking on their <u>heading</u>:

 <u>Jessica, 10 y/o</u>

My name is Jessica Mathews. I am 10. I am from Missouri.
I like cats, and playing with friends.
Jessica
25 January 1999

◆ Figure 9.5   *Continued*

Jake (7 years old)

Hi , my name is Jake, and I will be eight in September. I
live in Australia, and am looking for penpals anywhere. I like
playing with my friends, I really like sports like soccer,
cricket, rugby, and base ball. My dad and me have just set
up my trainset, and I like that too. I will reply to any boys
or girls that write to me, Bye.
Jake
25 January 1999

Ali, 10 y/o

HI my name is Ali i am a female I am 10 years old I like
sports especially soccer. I dont care if I get a boy or a girl
key pal.
Ali
25 January 1999

Naina - aged 7

I go to school in England and am looking to write to a pal in
India who can tell me all about themselves and their school.
Naina
25 January 1999

Source: From Rigby Heinemann Keypals.

they shared information and asked questions about college life, hobbies, interests, and family life.

Using Journals to Explore Texts

Journals create a nonthreatening context for children to explore their reactions and responses to literary and informational texts. Readers who use journals regularly are involved actively in the process of comprehending as they record their feelings, thoughts, and reactions to various types of literature. Journals create a permanent record of what readers are feeling and learning as they interact with texts. As a result, they have also been called *logs* because they permit readers to keep a visible record of their responses to texts. Such responses often reflect thinking beyond a literal comprehension of the text and engage students in inferential and evaluative thinking.

Several types of journals may be used to explore texts: **double-entry journals, reading journals,** and **response journals.** What do these different types of journals have in common? Each integrates reading and writing through personal response, allowing readers to feel and think more deeply about the texts they are reading.

Double-Entry Journals.
A double-entry journal provides students with an opportunity to identify text passages that are interesting or meaningful to them and to explore—in writing—why. As the name of the journal implies, students fold sheets of paper in half lengthwise, creating two columns for journal entries. In the left-hand column, readers select quotes from the text—perhaps a word, a phrase, a sentence or two—that they find interesting or evocative. They then copy the text verbatim and identify the page from which each text quote is taken. In instances where the quoted passage is several sentences or a paragraph long, the student may choose to summarize rather than copy the passage verbatim.

Across from each quote, in the right-hand column, readers enter their personal responses and reactions to the text quotes. As Yopp and Yopp (1993) explain, students' responses to a text will vary widely: "Some passages may be selected because they are funny or use interesting language. Others may be selected because they touch the student's heart or remind the student of experiences in his or her own life" (p. 54).

Children as early as first grade have used double-entry journals with success, once they have developed some confidence and fluency reading simple stories (Barone, 1996). Teachers, however, must model and demonstrate how to respond to text using the two-column format. The Best Practice featured in Box 9.2 provides guidelines for scaffolding the use of double-entry journals with beginners.

Older children will not need as many demonstrations before they develop the knack of using double-entry journals, yet the payoffs will be readily evident in class discussions. One of the big benefits of a double-entry journal is that it encourages interactions between reader and text. Another benefit is that it makes children sensitive to the text and the effect the author's language has on them as readers. A third payoff is that students explore texts for personally relevant ideas.

For example, sometimes teachers use a double-entry journal format to help students respond personally to what they are reading. This format allows student to record dual entries that are conceptually related according to prompts given by the teacher. Often a

Guidelines for Using Double-Entry Journals with Beginners

Use double-entry journals in the context of interactive reading and writing experiences. With reading beginners, teachers sometimes follow these steps:

1. Help children interact with a text through a shared reading experience.

2. After sharing a story several times, have young readers gather around an experience chart.

3. Divide the chart paper into two columns; label the left column "What I Liked the Best" and the right column "Why I Liked It."

4. Illustrate how to use the double-entry format for response by sharing with the class a text quote or two that you like. You might say, "One of my favorite parts of the story is on page 5." Then you turn to page 5 and read it to the class. Next, copy the text quote in the left-hand column. Tell why you like the text quote—how it makes you feel or what it reminds you of. Write your personal reaction in the right-hand column.

5. Then invite children to volunteer some of their favorite words, lines, or parts from the text. Encourage them to share their reactions. Serve as a scribe by writing their quotes and reactions on the chart paper.

6. Vary the demonstrations with subsequent interactive writing experiences; for example, ask children to volunteer to write on the chart paper.

7. Introduce the class to double-entry journals. Begin by showing them how to make their own journals using 8½-by-11-inch lined paper. Encourage children to use the double-entry journal as a follow-up to a shared reading. Share the journal entries as a group. Phase children into the use of double-entry journals for texts read independently.

teacher will ask students to provide a description or explanation in one column and students' reaction or response in the other column. Younger children can use the entire left page of a notebook as one column and the right page as another column. Examine in Figure 9.6 a third grader's journal entry as she describes and reacts to the clothes worn by Pilgrim girls in response to her teacher's read-aloud of *A Thanksgiving Story* (Dalgliech, 1954).

Reading Journals. Another type of journal has been called a *reading journal.* In contrast to double-entry journals, reading journals provide students with more structure and less

◆ FIGURE 9.6   Example of a Third Grader's Double-entry Journal Response

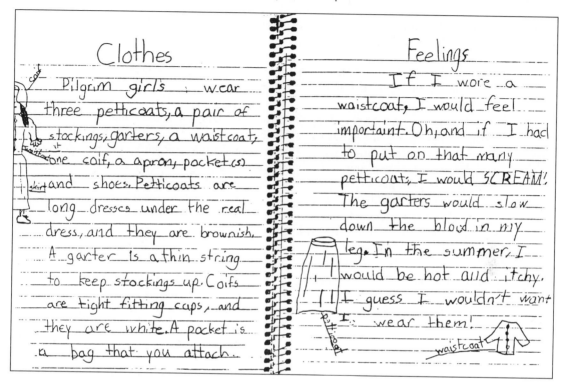

choice in deciding what they will write about. The teacher often provides a prompt—a question, for example—to guide students' writing after a period of sustained reading. Reading journals are usually used with a common or *core* text that everyone in a class is reading or listening to.

Prompts may include generic-type "process" questions such as the following: What did you like? What, if anything, didn't you like? What did you think or wonder about as you were reading? What will happen next? What did you think about the story's beginning? Its ending? What did you think about the author's style? Did anything confuse you? At times, reading journals use prompts that are more content-specific, asking readers to focus on their understanding of an important concept or some relevant aspect of plot, setting, character, or theme.

As second graders finished a class study of Donald Hall's *Ox-Cart Man* (1979), a story set in the distant past about a farmer and his family, the teacher, Laura Scott, prompted the students to write in their reading journals: "Would you like to be one of the ox-cart man's children?"

The students were eager to answer the question. One responded to the prompt in the affirmative:

I wolwd like to be the ox cart mans son bcose he wolwd by me a knife. also becose he grow food.

Another child responded from an alternate perspective:

I wod not like to be in his family becuse I wod have to wlak to the markit And I wod not like it if I wod have to eat the food I Do not like. And I wod have to live on a farm and I'am not talking abut the farming today but abut long go.

Many of today's basal reading programs are cognizant of the importance of reading-writing connections and often include a journal as part of the overall program. In fact, some basal programs have replaced the traditional workbook with a journal. Workbooks are designed, first and foremost, for readers to practice and apply skills. While journals represent a significant step forward in the evolution of basal programs, some basal reading journals remain workbooks in disguise. Teachers need to pay close attention to the prompts and activities contained in basalized journal formats. Do the prompts engage students in personal responses and explorations of meaning, or are they designed to reinforce specific skills?

Response Journals.   The main difference between a reading journal and a response journal is the amount of prompting that teachers use to elicit students' reactions to a text. Response journals invite readers to respond to literary texts freely, without being prompted. Hancock (1993a) suggests an extended set of guidelines (see the Best Practice in Box 9.3) for students who use response journals. These guidelines are perhaps best suited for intermediate and middle-grade students but can easily be adapted to the primary level.

Sixth-grade teacher Gloria Reichert introduces students to response journals with a letter at the beginning of the school year. In one section of the letter, she explains response journals this way:

I'm sure you are wondering about what a response journal is. It is a place where you will be able to write about books and stories that you will be reading throughout the year in our class. The response journal will be a great way to help us explore what we are feeling and thinking about what we are reading.

What will you be writing in your response journals? You can write anything you want about the book or story you are reading. You can express your thoughts, your feelings, or your reactions. How do you feel about the book? What does the book make you think about? What do you like or dislike about it? Who are the characters? Do you like them? Can you relate to their problems? What does the story mean to you?

Gloria then shows the class some different types of responses that she has collected from past students who read Wilson Rawls's *Where the Red Fern Grows*. One entry that she shows mixes literary commentary with personal involvement in the story:

I thought chap. 5 was very good. I'm glad Billy got the dogs. I thought it was really, really mean that all the people were laughing at him because he was carrying the pups in the gunny sack. I mean, come on. He had nothing to carry them in, and they needed air to

Guidelines for Response Journals

◆ *Feel free to write* your innermost feelings, opinions, thoughts, likes, and dislikes. This is your journal. Feel the freedom to express yourself and your personal responses to reading through it.

◆ *Take the time to write* down anything that you are thinking while you read. The journal is a way of recording those fleeting thoughts that pass through your mind as you interact with the book. Keep your journal close by and stop to write often, whenever a thought strikes you.

◆ *Don't worry* about the accuracy of spelling and mechanics in the journal. The content and expression of your personal thoughts should be your primary concern. The journal will not be evaluated for a grade. Relax and share.

◆ *Record the page number* on which you were reading when you wrote your response. Although it may seem unimportant, you might want to look back to verify your thoughts.

◆ *Use one side only* of your spiral notebook paper, please. Expect to read occasional, interested comments from your teacher. These comments will not be intended to judge or criticize your reactions, but will create an opportunity for us to "converse" about your thoughts.

◆ *Relate the book* to your own experiences and share similar moments from your life or from books you have read in the past.

◆ *Ask questions* while reading to help you make sense of the characters and the unraveling plot. Don't hesitate to wonder why, indicate surprise, or admit confusion. These responses often lead to an emerging understanding of the book.

◆ *Make predictions* about what you think will happen as the plot unfolds. Validate, invalidate, or change those predictions as you proceed in the text. Don't worry about being wrong.

◆ *Talk to the characters* as you begin to know them. Give them advice to help them. Put yourself in their place and share how you would act in a similar situation. Approve or disapprove of their values, actions, or behavior. Try to figure out what makes them react the way they do.

◆ *Praise or criticize* the book, the author, or the literary style. Your personal tastes in literature are important and need to be shared.

◆ *There is no limit* to the types of responses you may write. Your honesty in capturing your thoughts throughout the book is your most valuable contribution to the journal. These guidelines are meant to trigger, not limit, the kinds of things you write. Be yourself and share your personal responses to literature through your journal.

From "Exploring and Extending Personal Response Through Literature Journals," by M.R. Hancock, *The Reading Teacher, 46,* 6 (1993), p. 472. Reprinted by permission of the International Reading Association.

breathe. I can't believe a fight would actually start because it got so bad. The part where the mountain lion came, and the two pups saved Billy by howling was amazing. I thought the chapter had good action.

Another entry critiques a chapter from the perspective of someone who has had dogs as pets:

I didn't like chapter two. How can a kid get so sick from just not having a dog. Dogs are not always perfect anyways. They wake so early in the morning by barking there head off and sometimes they run around the house making a ruckus.

In Chapter 10, we will more closely examine some of the different types of responses that children write. Recognize, however, that by showing different examples of entries to her class, Gloria is making students aware that they should try to avoid just telling what the text is about.

When using response journals, some students, especially beginners, will be inclined to write about the plot of a story. Vacca and Newton (1995) illustrate how Eli, a third grader, responds in his journal to two of Cynthia Rylant's books for young readers.

ELI'S RESPONSE TO *GREEN TIME*:

I liked it. In the beginning, Henry and Mudge went on a picnic. There was a bee on Henry's pear. When Henry picked it up he got stung. He was yelling Ow! Ow! After awhile the pain went away and Henry was fine.

ELI'S RESPONSE TO *SMALL PIG*:

I didn't like it. It was about a pig that liked to sit in the mud and sink. One day the farmer's wife was cleaning the house. Then she cleaned the farm and sucked up the mud in the vacuum. So he went to the city and sat in wet concrete and it dried. The farmer had to get him out.

In both entries, Eli's expression of like or dislike is followed by a plot summary. For young readers, such responses are typical, as Vacca and Newton (1995) explain, particularly in cases where classroom time is spent on story structure or elements of a story that comprise its plot. Retellings, however, often give way to personal responses when teachers provide regular opportunities for students to use response journals and when they encourage children, as Gloria Reichert does in her class, to respond beyond retelling.

Response journals can be used flexibly to incorporate the features of dialogue and buddy journals. Several options are possible. The students engage in a dialogue with the teacher or with one another. In Reichert's sixth-grade class, she will often respond to students' entries directly or invite them to correspond with one another by writing **literary letters**, a response technique popularized by Nanci Atwell (1998).

When a literary letter becomes the discourse form for a response, it is written in the journal and delivered to the teacher or a classmate. The rule of thumb for returning a literary letter is this: If someone in the class receives a letter, he or she should write a response, in the form of a letter, in the sender's journal within 24 hours. Students in Reichert's class can write as many literary letters as they wish, but they are expected to write at least two letters per week, one to her and one to another student. She uses the opportunity to respond to students' letters as a means of validating their thinking and helping them explore their reactions.

Here's an example of an exchange of letters by Nick and Brian, two of Reichert's students, in response to *Where the Red Fern Grows:*

> Dear Brian,
>> I think Billy is veary strange. I would take his older sister's idea about him being crazy. It was cool how his dogs chased that coon all over God's creation. Personally I don't think the coon's up in that big old tree. Do you?

> Dear Nick,
>> I think he is crazy too. But I think Ann would be smart enough to catch that coon. I do think that coon is up that tree.

Journals, regardless of format, reflect writing in which children use language loosely, as if engaged in talk. Such writing does not place a premium on perfection or mechanics—spelling, punctuation, or grammar, for example. Indeed, teachers encourage children to write freely in journals, placing their reactions and responses ahead of concerns for correctness.

Journal writing is a vehicle for developing writing fluency among students. Students who write regularly in journals find that the more they write, the easier it becomes to express their feelings and thoughts about what they are reading. Not only does the volume of writing increase over time, but the facility to explore and clarify ideas is also sharpened.

ESTABLISHING A PREDICTABLE STRUCTURE FOR WRITING

No two writing classrooms are the same; nor should they be. Instructional routines and procedures vary from classroom to classroom. However, effective classrooms often have certain characteristics in common.

One classroom characteristic is that children have freedom of movement. Allowing them to choose where they want to write contributes to the writing environment. Many will choose to write at their desks or a nearby writer's table. Some may opt for the writing center or a private area of the room designated the "Writer's Nook" or "Writer's Hideaway." Arrange the room so that movement and easy access to classmates are possible. Access to classmates, in particular, will become an important part of trying out work in progress, reading drafts, and holding peer conferences.

A second characteristic involves continuity from day to day. It's crucial to establish a regular writing time that children will come to expect and anticipate. Set aside 30 to 60 minutes every day, if possible, for writing. This is not to suggest that children shouldn't be encouraged to write at other times of the day. However, it does suggest a set time for writing that will provide students with a sense of continuity and regularity. When there's a special time for writing every day, children learn to anticipate writing *when they are not writing* (during lunchtime, on the playground, or at home). Writing becomes habitual (Atwell, 1998).

In addition to journals, an integral part of the routine of classroom writing involves the use of folders or writing portfolios. In process-centered classrooms, there is often a box of writing folders that contain the collected pieces the children have written. The pieces are chosen by the children or the teacher. They may be selections that represent the children's best work or ones that demonstrate growth in writing. The folders are often stored in a brightly decorated cardboard box or in a filing cabinet within easy reach of the children.

Some teachers recommend using two writing folders: a *daily folder* that contains a child's immediate work in progress and a *portfolio* for completed pieces of writing. The portfolio has at least two important purposes. First, it documents students' writing development during the school year. Children (as well as parents or the principal) can study their progress and the changes that have occurred in their writing. They enjoy reading and reviewing the topics they've written about and the types of writing they've completed. Teachers find that folders are valuable for helping students understand the writing process. Second, when students accumulate their writings, they can see the investment that they have made. The folder, then, helps build a sense of pride, accomplishment, and ownership. It is a visible record of a child's growth as a writer (Graves, 1994).

A process-centered classroom should be guided by rules and procedures that set clear expectations for behavior and interaction and give children a sense of structure and stability. Rules or guidelines will emphasize different things in different classrooms. Yet you may want to consider some of the following (Graves, 1983, 1994):

◆ When engaged in drafting, writers shouldn't be disturbed. There will be plenty of time to talk about their writing and to share work in progress.

◆ Talk is an important part of writing, but there are limits set on the number of persons who share with one another at any one time.

◆ The class writes and shares every day.

Organizing the Writing Workshop

Many teachers think about writing time each day as a workshop. The classroom is the student writer's studio. Begin each day's **writing workshop** by providing students with the structure they need to understand, develop, or use specific writing strategies or by giving them direction in planning their writing or in revising their drafts. The **minilesson,** as the name implies, is a brief, direct instructional exchange (usually no longer than ten minutes) between the teacher and the writing group (which may include the whole class). The exchange isn't a substitute for individual guidance; instead, it is meant to get students started on a writing project or to address their specific problems or needs. For example, a minilesson can stimulate topic selection, brainstorm ideas and rehearse for writing, illustrate interesting versus dull writing, model literary style by reading passages from literature, illustrate good sentence and paragraph structure, teach or model strategies for revision, and teach a mechanical skill.

Calkins (1994) provides several in-depth examples of different types of minilessons that she has seen used by elementary teachers.

Following the minilesson is the actual time that the students spend "in process," whether they're collecting information, drafting, revising, or editing their work. For part of this time, you may find yourself working on your own writing. In addition, your role is primarily to facilitate the workshop by responding to the needs of writers as specific situations demand.

Two plans that teachers have followed in facilitating the writing workshop are outlined here.

PLAN 1

I. Minilesson (3–10 minutes)

II. Writing workshop
  A. Circulate to help individuals (10 minutes)
  B. Work with children in a group conference (15 minutes)
  C. Hold scheduled individual conferences (15 minutes)

III. Group share session (10 minutes)

PLAN 2

I. Minilesson (3–10 minutes)

II. Writing workshop
  A. Write with class (5–10 minutes)
  B. Circulate to help individuals (10–20 minutes)
  C. Hold scheduled individual conferences (10–15 minutes)

III. Group share session (10 minutes)

The main purpose of a **group share session** is to have writers reflect on the day's work. "Process discussions" focus on concerns implicit in the following questions:

How did your writing go today? Did you get a lot done?

Did you write better today than yesterday?

Was it hard for you to keep your mind on what you were writing?

What do you think you'll work on tomorrow?

What problems did you have today?

Calkins (1983, 1994) provided these guidelines to facilitate reading and discussion of children's drafts.

Raising concerns: A writer begins by explaining where he or she is in the writing process, and what help he or she needs. For example, a child might say, "I'm on my third draft and I want to know if it's clear and makes sense" or "I have two beginnings and I can't decide which is best."

Reading aloud: Usually, the writer then reads the writing (or the pertinent section) out loud.

Mirroring the content and focusing praise: The writer then calls on listeners. A classmate begins by retelling what he has heard: "I learned that . . ." or "Your story began . . ." Sometimes a listener may begin by responding with praise or showing appreciation for the writing.

Making suggestions: Questions or suggestions are then offered about the concern raised by the writer. Sometimes other things will come up as well.

Besides reflecting on the day's writing, reserve the share session for celebrating finished work. Ask volunteers to share their writing with an audience. The author's chair is an integral part of the sharing experience. The celebration that children take part in reflects their payoff for the hard work that writers go through to craft a piece of writing to their satisfaction. In the Class Works featured in Box 9.4, notice how Liz Crider, a second-grade teacher, makes the writing workshop an integral part of the school day.

Guiding Writing (and Observing Reading)

When teachers guide the writing process, they will have many opportunities to observe children in real, functional reading situations. Hornsby, Sukarna, and Parry (1988), in fact, show the kinds of reading opportunities that children have when they are involved in the writing process. Table 9.1 depicts these opportunities.

In a process-centered classroom, children quickly become aware that writing evolves through steps and stages. The *stages in the writing process* have been defined by different authorities in different ways. In this book, the stages are referred to as *rehearsing, drafting, revising and editing,* and *publishing.* These stages aren't neat or orderly; that is why they have been described as *recursive.*

Rehearsing.   Rehearsing is everything that writers do before the physical act of putting ideas on paper for a first draft. "Getting it out" is a useful mnemonic because it helps us re-

A Typical Day in a Writing Workshop

Liz Crider is a second-grade teacher who makes writing workshops an integral part of the school day. Here's how she describes a typical day for her students in a writing workshop.

I teach writing through demonstrations that show my students "what good writers do." To begin my writing program at the beginning of the school year, I invite a published writer to come into the class to let the children know that adult writers have some of the same problems in writing that children do. On one such occasion, one of my students was so inspired by a visiting professional writer that he made a statement that I will always remember. He said, "I'm writing a book too, but it's still in my head. I haven't even started writing it yet." This is a profound statement for a second grader to make, and the other students in the class responded by telling how writing also begins in their heads.

Not only do my students write in their response journals, but they also engage in the writing workshop. Before the workshop begins, I may conduct a focused minilesson to teach whatever skills the students might show a need for at the time. I frequently use the writing of other second graders and my own writing as a means of teaching these lessons.

The children write about 30 minutes a day. While they are writing, I conduct one-on-one conferences with as many students as I can during that half-hour period. I usually can see no more than two or three during that block of time. While I am conferencing with a student, partners conduct peer conferences. I model throughout the year so that the children will know what a good conference looks and sounds like. They work at being gentle, yet honest with their responses.

At the close of the workshop, two or three children read their writing. The piece that they read might be completed or in progress. They sit in the special "author's chair." They tell the group what their needs are: (1) if they would like the group to just listen, (2) if they would like suggestions, or (3) if they would like comments. This is used as a whole class conference. I constantly model, even during this activity. I record the students' comments on a large Post-it and give it to the author to attach to the story just shared. I frequently remind the children that authors own their writing. They may choose to accept or ignore our input.

All topics are generated by the children themselves. They write on whatever topic they desire. The children frequently choose to involve themselves in research during writing workshop. They write a report of their findings, complete with a simple bibliography. They then stand as the expert on whatever subject they investigated.

During the workshop, students' desks are arranged in groups of four for collaboration. Children freely share ideas and information. They support one another. The writing center is an important area in my room. There they gather to revise, edit,

(Continued)

Box 9.4 CONTINUED

peer conference, and share ideas about their writing. Though there is movement and noise in my classroom, children are engaged and active learning is taking place.

Reflective Inquiry

♦ What is your reaction to the writing workshop practices used by Liz Crider in her classroom?

♦ What does Liz mean when she says, "I teach writing through demonstrations that show my students 'what good writers do'?"

♦ Is it unrealistic to expect second graders to generate their own topics for writing?

member that rehearsal means activating background knowledge and experiences, getting ideas out in the open, and making plans for approaching the task of writing.

The rehearsing stage has also been called *prewriting*, a somewhat misleading term because "getting it out" often involves writing of some kind (e.g., making lists, outlining, jotting notes, writing in a journal). Regardless of terminology, rehearsing is a time to generate ideas, stimulate thinking, make plans, and create a desire to write. In other words, rehearsing is what writers do to get "energized," to explore what to say and how to say it: "What will I include?" "What is a good way to start?" "What is my audience?" "What form should my writing take?"

The teacher's job is to make students aware that the writing process must *slow down* at the beginning. By slowing down the process, the students can then discover that they have something worthwhile to say and that they want to say it.

There are many ways to rehearse for writing: talking, reading to gather information, brainstorming and outlining ideas, role playing, doodling, drawing, cartooning, jotting down ideas, taking notes, interviewing, and even forming mental images through visualization and meditation.

Drafting. "Getting it down" is an apt way to describe drafting. Once writers have rehearsed, explored, discovered, planned, and talked (and done whatever else it takes to get ideas out in the open), they are ready to draft a text with a purpose and an audience in mind. A child is reading when drafting. The writing workshop provides the in-class time for first-draft writing. As children draft, the teacher regulates and monitors the process. For example, while students are writing, teachers should not be grading papers or attending to other unrelated chores. They should either be writing themselves or keeping writers on task.

Drafting is a good time to confer individually with students who may need help using what they know to tackle the writing task. The teacher can serve as a sounding board, ask

TABLE 9.1

Opportunities to Read During Writing

Stage in the Writing Process	Reading Opportunities
Before writing (rehearsing)	Poetry reading
	Oral reading of stories in draft and published form
	Short story reading
	Play reading
	"Read-along" taped stories
During writing (drafting and revising)	Children's oral reading of their drafts to themselves and in conferences
	Silent reading during composition of drafts (to check meaning, to remind oneself of where the writing has been and where it should go, to regain momentum, to provide a breathing space, or even to avoid writing)
	Researching books for material for stories
	Functional reading and the development of reference, library, and study skills
	Reading aloud to check sense, to hear the sound of the language
After writing (publishing)	Oral reading for audience response
	Silent reading of own and other children's published stories
	Borrowing books from class and school libraries
	Choosing to read again a favorite book or story
	Reading and performance of plays written by children

Adapted from *Read On: A Conference Approach to Reading*, by D. Hornsby, D. Sukarna, and J. Parry (Portsmouth, N.H.: Heinemann, 1988), p. 117.

probing questions if students appear to be stuck, and create opportunities for a child to read what he or she is writing. A teacher may want to ask the following questions:

How is it going?

What have you written so far?

Tell me the part that is giving you a problem. How are you thinking about handling it?

I am not clear on _____ . How can you make that part clearer?

Are you leaving anything out that may be important?

What do you intend to do next?

How does the draft sound when you read it out loud?

What is the most important thing that you're trying to get across?

Once completed, a first draft is just that—a writer's first crack at discovering what he or she wants to say and how he or she wants to say it.

Revising.   Each interaction that occurs when a writer seeks a *response*, either from the teacher or from another writer in the class, constitutes a *conference*. Children have many opportunities to read their work critically during conferences. Simply stated, a conference may be held when a writer needs feedback for work in progress. The conference may last five seconds or five minutes, depending on the writer's needs. However, once a student decides to rework a first draft, conferencing becomes a prominent aspect of *revising* and *editing*.

Conferencing.   When writers work on a second or third draft, they have made a commitment to rewrite. Rewriting helps students take another look. This is why good writing often reflects good rewriting and rereading of a piece.

To conduct a teacher-child conference, a teacher must learn to define his or her role as listener. Graves (1983) noted that when conducting a conference, the child leads and the teacher intelligently reacts.

To elicit clarification of a piece of writing, a teacher might focus the conference with a specific question or two appropriate to the writer's needs.

The following general steps will help in conducting a conference.

1. The writer *reads* the draft out loud.

2. The teacher *listens* carefully for the meaning of the draft.

3. The teacher then *mirrors the content* ("Your draft is about . . ."), *focuses praise* ("The part I liked best about your draft is . . ."), *elicits clarification* ("Which parts are giving you the most trouble?"), *makes suggestions* ("I think you should work on . . ."), and *seeks the writer's commitment* ("Now that we have talked, what will you do with the draft?").

To illustrate how effective a conference can be in helping children revise their work, Wolf (1985) described her work with Jessica, a second grader. Jessica's first draft, displayed in Figure 9.7, is a fluent but rambling piece on a topic that evolved from a social studies lesson on the problem of pollution in big cities.

In this draft, Jessica's content is remarkable; her voice is strong. In conference with the teacher, Jessica realized that her ideas "jumped around." Jessica brings a "writer-as-reader" perspective to her draft and would need to help the reader keep the ideas straight. Here is the strategy that she and the teacher worked out: Jessica used a green marker to underline all the ideas about factories and how they pollute the air and a red marker to underline all the things about how pollution made people and animals sick. Jessica mentioned to the teacher that she also wanted to include her mother's problems with pollution. As a result, she underlined all of those ideas with a yellow marker. She then wrote a second draft, putting all the ideas underlined in green together, all the ideas underlined in red together, and all the ideas underlined in yellow together. The conference was a perfect opportunity to discuss paragraphing and the idea of indentation. Jessica's second draft is displayed in Figure 9.8.

Teachers who have regular conferences with students quickly realize two things: (1) It's an overwhelming, if not impossible, task to conference with every student who needs feedback during a day's writing, and (2) the class must assume responsibility for providing response to fellow writers.

Peer conferencing provides an audience of readers for a writer to try out work in progress. A child may arrange during the writer's workshop to hold a conference with another child, if it doesn't interfere with the other child's writing. In addition, time might be set aside for peer conference teams to meet.

A peer conference team consists of two, three, or four members. A team responds to a writer's draft from questions that the teacher has prepared and modeled through class discussion, demonstration, and individual student conferences:

What did you like best about this paper? What worked well?

Was there anything about this piece of writing that was unclear to you?

What feeling did this piece of writing convey to you?

Where in the paper would you like to see more detail? Where could the writer show you something instead of telling you about it? In other words, where could the writer use more description?

Editing.   During revision, students will be messy in their writing, and they should be encouraged to be messy. They should be shown how to use carets to make insertions and be allowed to make cross-outs or to cut and paste sections of text, if necessary. The use of arrows will help students show changes in the position of words, phrases, or sentences within the text.

Once the content and organization of a draft are set, children can work individually or together to edit and proofread their texts for spelling, punctuation, capitalization, word choice, and syntax. Accuracy counts. "Polishing" or "cleaning up" a revised draft shouldn't be neglected, but students must recognize that *concern for proofreading and editing comes toward the end of the writing process.*

◆ Figure 9.7   Jessica's First Draft on Pollution

Pollushein! By Jessica
I hate pollushun! It
comes from fackters. They pollut
the air. Pollushun can make you
sick! I sujest you stay away
from pollushun! Every day fater
ys pollut the ain even more.
When I go to teleto
I go in a car. We see
Lots of fackters polluting
The air. We see all sorst
of fackterys. facktery chimnis
are what pallut the
air If thay wod tink
about other pepill.

◆ FIGURE 9.7   Continued

Maybe if thay wod spend ther
money on geting their chimneys
clean the peopill won't
have to wach the air.
for the dascusting things in
it. Like my mom
she works down town
All so cars and
turuks polluth the air
When my mom parcks
her car she walks
To her offices. Whill
she is walking to her
ofies she smels the discust
ing smells in the air
When facktters dump ther junck

◆ FIGURE 9.7　Continued

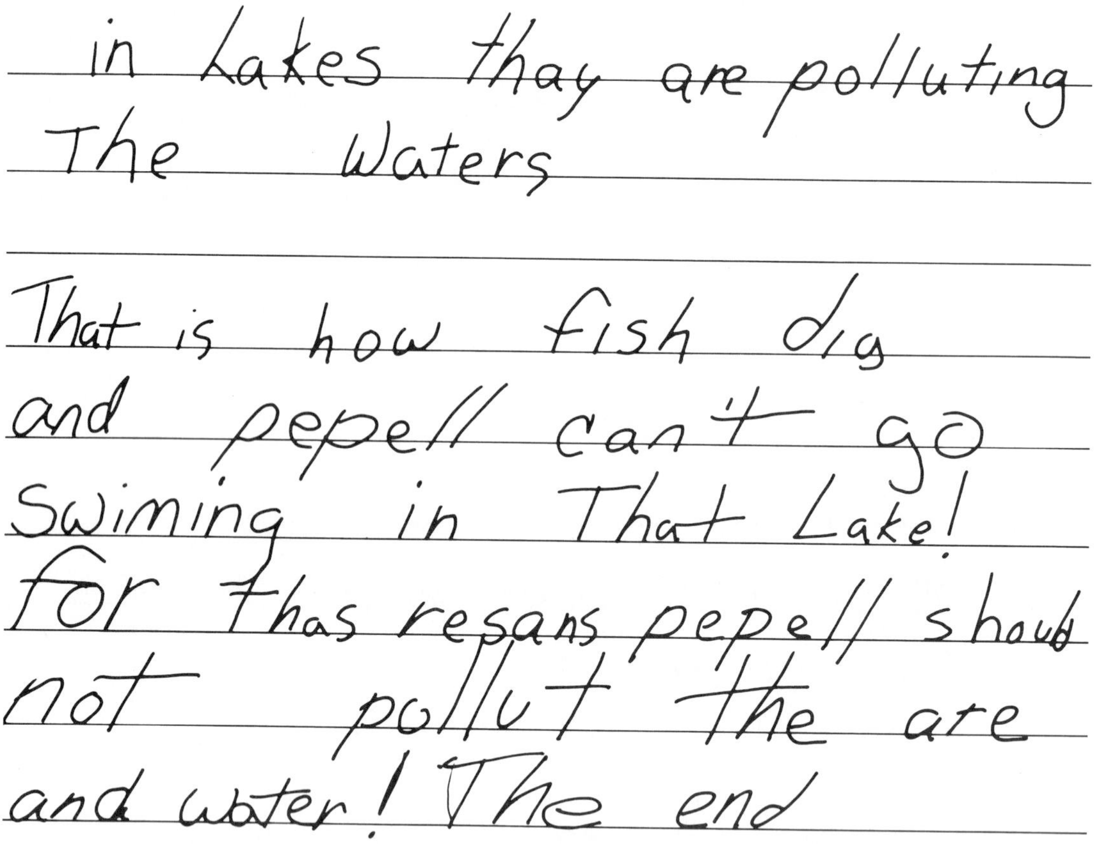

in Lakes thay are polluting
The Waters

That is how fish dia
and pepell can't go
Swiming in That Lake!
for thas resans pepell shoud
not pollut the are
and water! The end

　　　Children should edit for skills that are appropriate to their ability and stage of development as writers. An editing conference should provide a *focused evaluation* in which one or two skill areas are addressed. If children have edited their writing to the best of their ability, the teacher may then edit the remainder of the piece for spelling and other conventions.

Publishing.　If writing is indeed a public act, it is meant to be shared with others. Writing is for reading, and children learn quickly to write for many different audiences. When young writers have a sense of their audience, the task of writing becomes a real effort at communication.

　　　The pride and sense of accomplishment that come with *authorship* contribute powerfully to a writer's development. Publishing provides a strong incentive for children to keep writing and rewriting. But more than anything else, publishing in the classroom is fun. Consider the following vehicles for reading, displaying, sharing, and publishing student work.

◆ FIGURE 9.8   Jessica's Second Draft on Pollution

By Jessica   Second Draft

Pollushn By   Jesseca

I Hate pollushn! It came from fackters thay pullut the air Every day faterys pullut the air even more We see lots of fackters pulluting the air. We see all sorst of fackterys facktery chimns are what pullut the air. When fackterys dump ther junk into lakes thay are polluting the water That is how fich dys and pepell can't go swiming in that Lake

Pollushn can make you sick! I sujest you stay away from pollushn! When I go to Taketo I go in a car I see lots of fack. faktery chimnys are what pollut the air. Maybe if they whad spend ther manny on chimnys clean pepell whed not have to whach out for the air for the disgusting things in it. when fackterys

dump ther junk in the Lakes they are polluting the water that is how fish dys pepell can't go swiming in that lake!

If thay wod thingk about other pepell. maybe if thay wod spend ther many on getting ther chimnys cleand then pepell wod not have to wach the air for the discusting thing in it. Like my mom she werks down town allso cars & tracks pollut the air. when my mom parks her car she wocks to her offes. She smells the disgusting tings in the air!

We recommend the frequent use of read-aloud sessions as a way of sharing and celebrating writing. In this way, all children will at one time or another have an opportunity to read their work to the group. The group share session described earlier creates the opportunity for a child to present his or her work. Establish a tone of acceptance during oral readings of finished work. Having a child read a completed piece of writing from the "author's chair" is one way to celebrate authorship because it dignifies the hard work and effort that has been put into the writing.

Young people take great pride in writing and illustrating their own books. Producing a book often provides the impetus for writing and justifies all the hard work that goes into the final product. Writing a book creates a meaningful context and motivates youngsters to revise and edit stories, focusing on content, organization, sentence structure, interesting words, and correct spelling. Young writers are especially inspired to write books when they are exposed to children's literature on a regular basis—a topic we explain thoroughly in Chapter 10. They are also eager to make books when they can choose the type of book they want to write. Some possibilities for bookmaking are given in Figure 9.9.

Class-produced newspapers, magazines, anthologies, and books are excellent ways to publish student writing. The students should be involved in all phases of the publication's production. We suggest that children not only participate as writers but also work in groups to assume responsibility for editing, proofreading, design, and production. Production of a class publication need not be elaborate or expensive. Photocopied or computer-generated publications have the same effect on student writers as more elaborate presentations when they see their work in print. Finally, be sure to display student writing. Establish an author's day or a reading fair in which students circulate around the room reading or listening to as many pieces as they can.

Letters, community publications, commercial magazines, and national and state contests are all vehicles for real-world publishing outside of the classroom and school. Letters, in particular, are valuable because there are so many audience possibilities.

In addition to letters, the local newspaper, PTA bulletin, or school district newsletter sometimes provide outlets for class-related writing activity. Commercial magazines and national, state, local, or school writing contests also offer opportunities for publication. Commercial magazines and writing contests, of course, are highly competitive. However, the real value of writing for commercial publication lies in the authenticity of the task and the real-world audience that it provides. The International Reading Association publishes an excellent resource, *Magazines for Kids and Teens* (Stoll, 1997), which lists popular magazines for children and adolescents that publish student writing.

Finally, children are publishing their writing on the Internet. There are a growing number of central sites on the Internet that support school-age writers and provide a great location for children to read other children's stories. One of the most popular sites is KidPub (http://en-garde.com/kidpub/intro.html). A parent developed the KidPub site so that his daughter would have a place to publish her writing. KidPub accepts all children's work. Figure 9.10 shows the KidPub home page and the array of opportunities to make reading-writing connections for your students.

Ideas for Making Books

Type of Book	Sample	Construction
Shape books Stories about animals, objects, machines, people, etc.; poems; nursery rhymes; innovations	Poems ♡♡♡ · TALL TALES · Bubbles	Make pages in the shape of your book. Bind together with staples or masking tape or lace with yarn.
Ring books Group stories; word fun; poems; collection of poems	BOOKS	Punch holes in pages and use notebook rings or shower curtain rings to bind together.
Stapled books Individual stories; group contributions; alphabet books; word books; poems	The Silly Kid!	Pages and cover are stapled together, then bound with masking tape for added durability.
Fold-out books Poems; patterns; sequences; stories		Pages are folded accordion-style and then stapled or glued to covers.
Bound cloth books Poems; collections of poems; stories that have been edited and prepared for printing		(See extended directions on the next page.)

Extended Directions for Bound Cloth Books

Supplies: 1 piece of lightweight fabric (approximately ¹/₂ yard), several needles, white paper, dry-mount tissue, cardboard, masking tape, an iron, and an ironing area.

1. Each child should have 6 or 7 sheets of paper. This will give a finished book with 10 to 12 pages, but will not be too difficult to sew. Fold each sheet of paper in half (one by one). (Fig. 1)

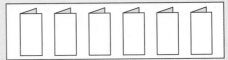

Figure 1

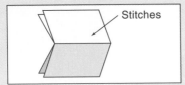

Figure 2

2. Bring the sheets together and sew along the fold. *Hint:* Start on the outside of the fold so that the knot will not be seen when binding is finished. (Fig. 2)

3. Cut out the fabric to measure 12" x 15". Prepare some templates from cardboard for students to use as guides. (Fig. 3)
4. Spread out the materials as pictured. (Fig. 3)

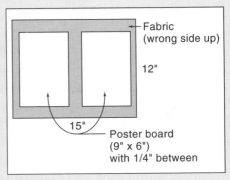

Figure 3

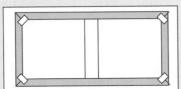

Figure 4

5. Fold the edges of the fabric over the two boards, and tape in place at the corners. (Fig. 4)

6. Now make a sandwich using the cover, then a piece of dry-mount tissue (8¹/₂" x 11"), then the sewn pages, and iron in place as pictured. Iron only on the endpapers since the pages can be scorched. (Fig. 5)

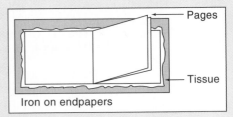

Figure 5

Welcome to

KidPub

You are visitor number 952944!

*More than **26,000** stories written by kids from all over the planet!*

- **Newest Stories**
- **Older stories (but goodies!)**
- **Search all KidPub stories** (New! Search by category!)
- **KidPub Schools:** Where classes publish their writing
- **Gary and Liz: Return to Gateway Mansion** Add the next paragraph to our never-ending story!
- **Questions and Answers:** Common questions about KidPub
- **The Story Form:** Use this handy form to submit a story...just fill in the blanks!
- **How to Publish *Your* Story:** A more detailed description of how to send stories to KidPub
- **Statistics:** How many stories are read each day? Where do our readers live?
- **KidPub Publisher's Picks** The Publisher's favorite stories and poems
- **KidPub KeyPals** Hook up with one of 21,000 Internet PenPals, or sign up yourself!
- **KidMud** is back.

You can contact us at KidPub@KidPub.Org

In addition to KidPub, Leu and Leu (1999) recommend that teachers explore the following locations, set a bookmark for each location, and invite children to take advantage of what each location offers them in the way of publishing their own work and reading the work of other children.

◆ *Cyberkids* (http://www.cyberkids.com/). A magazine for children ages 7 to 11. Young writers submit their stories as part of a contest. Readers then vote for the winners of the contest as part of a preliminary screening of the stories submitted.

◆ *The Book Nook* (http://I-site.on.ca/booknook.html). A location where children can publish reviews of books that they have read. Guidelines for developing book reviews are provided.

◆ *Parents and Children On-Line*
(http://www.indiana.edu/~eric_rec/fl/pcto/menu.html). This site publishes children's writing for its magazine, which is designed to support family reading at home.

The possibilities for reading-writing-technology connections are not limited to publication on the Internet. Teachers who use technology to support and enhance students' reading and writing development recognize the important role that computers can play in the literacy lives of children.

READING-WRITING-TECHNOLOGY CONNECTIONS

Advances in technology are quickly changing how human beings communicate and disseminate information. Technology, integrated into the curriculum for meaningful learning, can be a powerful tool in students' literacy development. E-mail conversations, as noted earlier, hone reading and writing skills by putting students in communication with other students and content experts throughout the world in a matter of seconds. Moreover, the digital forces of the computer have paved the way for an information age that affects the literacy learning of today's generation of students like no other generation before it. Students have instant access to **electronic texts** on the Internet or CD-ROM software. Electronic texts, which are constructed and displayed on a computer screen, are becoming an integral part of students' literacy lives in *and* out of classrooms. These texts are not fixed entities, set in print. They are fluid, interactive, and engaging.

Supporting students' writing of electronic texts is one of the important reading-writing-technology connections that can be made in the classroom. Using computers to construct electronic texts helps students examine ideas, organize and report information and inquiry findings, and communicate with others. Word processing, desktop publishing, and authoring software programs, for example, allow students to use and develop literacy skills to publish writing in creative ways and prepare multimedia reports and presentations relevant to curriculum objectives. The technology available today makes it possible for students to connect what they are reading and writing about to sound, graphics, illustrations, photographs, video, and other nonprint media in multimedia environments not possible in classrooms a mere decade ago.

Word Processing

Word processing offers much to classroom writing environments. The computer screen lends a pubic quality to writing that can encourage sharing and communication. It can encourage children to perceive text as flexible and malleable, and it can increase teacher involvement in writing and, paradoxically, student independence as writers.

The public nature of the computer screen has some pitfalls, which can be avoided. For some children and some writing tasks, the screen can become too public or too interactive. Rearranging the setting can ameliorate this problem. Do not get carried away by overediting children's writing. Resist viewing any printout or display as a final draft. Finally, think about your students' ability to type. If they have insufficient typing skills, they

Word processors can encourage children to see text as flexible and malleable.

may initially write less, be less spontaneous, or be loath to delete things they have written.

Here are some additional suggestions for teaching word processing:

◆ *Become familiar with the program yourself first.* Use it for your own writing. While learning, you may wish to make a poster and/or a duplicated sheet of major editing commands for your students.

◆ *Start simple.* Teach only a few basic commands; then add more to students' repertoires as necessary.

◆ *Consider introducing word processing in a whole class language-experience-story setting.* As each command is clicked or key is pressed, discuss what it does, why it is needed, and how to do it.

◆ *Work intensely with a small group to develop your first "experts."* Post children's names with the instructions for using the program so that others can ask them for help.

◆ *Continue presenting short, direct lessons to the class followed by work on the computer in pairs.*

◆ *If few computers are available, rotate groups using the word processor for compositions.* Or have students write their first draft in pencil. When they are done, they can sign up for a 20- to 30-minute session at the computer. Working in pairs, one student types in his or her own composition as the other student reads it, suggesting changes along the way. (If possible, try to work for just a minute with students during this time; it is exciting to be a coach during the writing rather than a critic afterward.) The children then switch places. One teacher who had only one computer every third week had a parent volunteer type in students' work after school during the two weeks in which the class did not have access to the computer. In the third week, students would read and revise their programs. Although these methods are compromises to an extent, students can still benefit from using the computer, especially in reviewing and revising, the final, crucial step in writing.

◆ *Model and follow the writing process as described in this chapter.*

Because students find themselves writing more, and more easily, on word processors, their work may be less organized and need more revision than paper-and-pencil writing does. Fortunately, this free, continuous writing followed by reflection and revision is one of the best ways to compose. The computer can also make revision much easier.

Compositions can be reviewed either as paper printouts or on the computer screen. "Reviewing" should mean that both the teacher and other students read and react to a child's writing. The real advantage for students is the ease of making corrections. Rather than messy erasures, confusing lines and arrows, and unwelcome rewriting, editing on the computer is like a game. Press a key—poof!—a paragraph disappears. Move to an earlier spot in the composition and press another key—the paragraph reappears in its new location. Or press a few keys and in less than a second every "din't" becomes "didn't."

Word processing allows students to create a text and change it in any way desired. Word processing software programs have the potential to make students more active writers as they engage in rehearsing, drafting, revising, and editing. For children who have trouble with fine motor control and find writing with paper and pencil difficult, computers can make writing easier by taking away some of the physical demands of putting ideas on paper. Freed from the physical tasks associated with writing, students can expend more cognitive energy on the communication itself.

Used correctly, word processors can help children write. Words are not carved in stone; they are painted in light, permitting effortless manipulation. The more students intelligently manipulate text—the more they read their work and revise—the better writers they will become.

Desktop Publishing and Multimedia Authoring

Desktop publishing and **multimedia authoring** software programs give students an authentic reason for reading and writing: publishing. These programs enhance the writing process and help students create stories and reports for classroom publication as part of writing workshops or thematic units of study. Software for desktop publishing typically permits students to integrate text and graphics, use different text styles, and arrange text in columns. Today many word processing programs include basic publishing features that make student authorship appealing. Multimedia authoring programs heighten even further the pride of authorship as students build stories and reports using text, colorful illustrations, sound, and animation. Programs such as HyperStudio, The Multimedia Workshop, Authorware Star, Toolbook, HyperCard, and SuperCard, along with Make-a-Book and My Own Stories for younger children, extend the writing process through the interaction of various media.

HyperStudio is one of the most popular multimedia authoring programs in the elementary grades. Older students can use HyperStudio software independently after some initial teacher guidance; young children may require more extended instructional support in the use of the program. HyperStudio is similar to other authoring systems in that it provides students with the ability to create information cards (containing text and graphics), use clip art, play sound (prerecorded or supplied by the student), and display writing in a variety of creative ways, including the development of card stacks and timelines.

When using multimedia authoring programs, it is best to begin with simple projects and presentations and gradually introduce students to more complicated uses of the software. Jane Fuller, a fifth-grade teacher, introduces students to HyperStudio by showing them how to make one card. She integrates the lesson into a review of American historical figures that students study as part of a unit on the Revolutionary War. First, Jane invites the class to design a "business card" for historical figures of the 1770s. She assigns the students to research the individuals they have chosen to determine their particular contributions or importance to American history. Once students have completed the research, they must then create a sentence or two, similar to what is found on business cards, "advertising" the historical person's talents and contributions. For example, George Washington's card might say, "A Tough Man for Tough Times" or "Leadership in Times of Danger and Discouragement." In addition to the "catchy" descriptions, students incorporate into the card's design basic data related to the lives of the historical figures and information concerning their accomplishments, using HyperStudio to position the information and select background choices, font, bold type, italics, and so on. Finally, the students print their cards, share, and display them.

The activity allows Jane's students to develop some understanding of the mechanics of making a card with HyperStudio software while reviewing the historical accomplishments of well-known Americans of a particular time period. Once the students become more familiar with a multimedia authoring system like HyperStudio, Jane initiates more complicated authoring projects for them. For example, as part of a unit on science, students prepare four- or five-card reports on animals they have selected for in-depth study. As part of the multimedia presentation, the students enhance their written texts with scanned photos and/or student illustrations as well as sound and video recordings.

SUMMARY

Learning to write is as natural to children as learning to read. Recent research has resulted in compelling evidence that suggests that reading and writing develop concurrently. Rather than teaching reading and writing as separate curricular entities, they should be taught in tandem.

One of the keys to writing and reading connections in classrooms rests with the environment that teachers create. Natural environments for learning provide encouragement and a built-in support system, and there is tremendous, patient faith that children will develop as writers. Time for writing, response to writing, and ownership of one's own writing are the hallmarks of a natural learning environment.

Writing leads to reading. Getting started with writing instruction is challenging. Teachers must establish a routine for writing. For example, there should be time to write every day, freedom of movement in the classroom, and occasions to write.

Reading is a natural springboard into children's writing. Making the connection between children's literature and writing and informational texts in content areas and writing is important because writing is a way of comprehending. Through journals, children can respond personally to text to explore, clarify, and extend meaning. Writing, we believe, can help children grow in every facet of reading. Journals and writing folders should be the focal point of the classroom writing program.

Process-centered classrooms allow for great flexibility, not anarchy, and have a predictable structure. Guidelines need to be established to set clear expectations for behavior and interactions in the classroom. In process-centered classrooms, students are encouraged to choose topics that matter to them and to rehearse for writing through talking, reading, brainstorming, and other prewriting strategies. Talking and journal writing, in particular, will help children discover and select topics for writing.

Drafting, revising, and editing are commonplace occurrences in process-centered classrooms. Throughout the stages of writing, children need a response from the teacher and other children. Conferences are the vehicles by which teacher and writers respond to one another in order to try out work and to get ideas on how to improve their drafts. Revising requires that the writer resee or rethink a piece. Only once the content of writing is set does editing become a major writer responsibility. Editing means preparing the writing for an audience and involves polishing the writing by attending to such matters as spelling, punctuation, and usage.

Publishing provides the payoff for the hard work that goes into the writing process. Encouraging students to value writing is crucial. Some suggestions include providing an author's chair; sponsoring class publications, bookmaking, oral presentations, and contests; and advising students about submission to magazines that publish student work, including locations on the Internet.

TEACHER-ACTION RESEARCHER

1. Think back to when you were a child and try to recall the first time you engaged in writing something. Start with your earliest memory and trace your journey as a writer up to and including the present time. Think about

teachers	settings
assignments	grades
advice	topics
feelings	habits
senses	idiosyncrasies

   Let these questions guide you:

   a. What are some words that come to mind when you think of "writing" in relation to your school experiences?

   b. Who were the teachers that mattered? That didn't matter?

   c. Do you like to write?

   d. Do you, or would you, like to teach writing?

   e. What are your most effective characteristics as a writer? Your least effective?

   f. Have you ever written anything you were proud of? What is it?

   g. When, where, and how do you usually write?

   h. What is your most effective characteristic as a teacher of writing? Your least effective?

   i. What are some good and bad experiences you're had as a writer?

   Add comments to make a portrait of yourself as a writer. Focus on what your personal journey shows you about the way writers develop—or don't develop. What does your experience show you about novice writers who are learning how to write? In what ways will your experiences influence the way you teach writing? What advice would you give to teachers of writing?

2. Observe an elementary school teacher during writing instruction time, taking notes on what the teacher says and does. What provisions does the teacher make for writing in-

struction? Is the teacher's approach to writing process- or product-centered? Analyze the lesson and your notes to answer the questions.

3. Design a process-centered writing lesson. Use what you have learned about the writing process and effective strategies to aid that process. Be sure to touch on these issues:

   a. What prewriting activities will you use to be reasonably sure that students will have something to say when they begin to write?

   b. How will you provide for in-process response to the writing?

   c. How will you provide for growth in mechanics and editing? Which skills will you try to develop?

   d. How will you arrange for the writing to reach an audience?

   e. How will you handle management problems such as finding time for the writing, keeping kids on task, arranging the classroom environment, and evaluating the work?

   You may design a lesson to be completed in several days or one that will take a week or two. Discuss the content of your lessons with other members of the class.

4. Locate a classroom in which process writing, including conferences, is used. Observe the interactions that occur when writers seek a response to their writing, from the teacher or other writers in the class. Do the children seem to have sufficient opportunities to read their work critically during conferences? How long do the conferences tend to last? In a week or two, collect the same type of data based on observations in another classroom either at the same or another grade level. Or revisit the same classroom each week for the same amount of time during the course of a month. Do you notice any changes in the conduct of the conferences or the interactions among the children?

5. Conduct a writing-process conference with an elementary grade student who has just completed a draft (use some of the suggestions in this chapter for conducting the conference). Describe what happened during the conference. What did you learn from the experience? (Tape-record, if permissible.)

6. Brainstorm ways to connect reading and writing during instruction. Share your ideas with others in the class.

7. Collect several journal entries of children at different grade levels. What do children write about? What kinds of responses do they make to literary texts? How would you plan instruction to help each child continue to grow and develop as a journal writer?

KEY TERMS

buddy journal
desktop publishing
dialogue journal
double-entry journal
electronic texts
group share session
Internet projects

key pal
  correspondence
literary letters
minilesson
multimedia
  authoring
reading journal

response journal
stages in the writing
  process
word processing
writing workshop

CHAPTER

10

Bringing Children
and Literature Together

Chapter Overview

BRINGING CHILDREN AND LITERATURE TOGETHER

SUPPORTING A COMMUNITY OF READERS

SURROUNDING CHILDREN WITH LITERATURE

ORGANIZING THE CLASSROOM AS CHILDREN RESPOND TO LITERATURE

Selecting Classroom Collections of Books with Multicultural Perspectives

Helping Children Select Books

Core Books and Literature Units

Free Response to Literature

Listening to Literature and Storytelling

Teacher-Led Book Talks

Teachers as Readers and Writers

Literature Circles, Student-Led Book Talks

Technology and Books

Between the Lines

In this chapter, you will discover:

♦ That literacy is personal and that readers benefit from a supportive environment

♦ What it means to bring children and books together in a literature-based program

♦ How to choose literature and involve children through activities

♦ Ways to organize classes around books and literature circles

♦ Major strategies for encouraging readers to respond to literature

Imagine the expression on Laura Pils's face when she received a brightly colored, handmade Valentine's Day card in the shape of a heart from Michael, a friend of one of Laura's first-grade students. In purple letters, the card said, "Happy Valentine's Day. I love you, Miss Piss" (Pils, 1993).

"It's so fitting," Laura thought of Michael's card. "It is these first attempts at literacy that are so wonderful. . . . All the parts are not in place yet, but the soul is there, speaking loud and clear while trying to find its own voice" (Pils, 1993, p. 653). Laura's first-grade class in Middleton, Wisconsin, personifies the type of literate community where all of the students, including those who fall behind the others in their literacy development and are not particularly eager to learn, feel that they are valued members of the class and that they have something to offer the rest of the children. Michael is a case in point. So is Dan.

Michael is Dan's friend. Although Laura never had Michael as a student, she came to know him through Dan. Dan was one of the needier students in Laura's class who had been struggling from the beginning of the school year with reading and writing. His language skills were limited; he had difficulty expressing himself other than through crying, acting out, and sometimes getting into verbal and physical fights with his classmates.

Dan's story is not unlike that of students in other schools and in other classrooms whose path to literacy, for one reason or another, is rough and uncertain. Yet within the literacy community that is Laura's classroom, there is an air of confidence that all of the children will find their way to literate activity. "But how to reach them?" That is the challenge that she faces. Twenty-five years of teaching experience with literacy beginners helps Laura realize that she must first establish a level of trust in the classroom and then find a "hook" that will connect literacy to the lives of the children. For many teachers, like Laura, literature is the hook.

Her attempts to reach Dan were eventually realized when Laura learned that his grandparents, with whom Dan spent summers near the ocean, were visiting from Connecticut. She arranged in advance for the grandparents to make a surprise visit to the classroom as "mystery readers." Throughout the year, mystery readers are invited into the classroom, unannounced to the children, to share in a surprise reading of a child's favorite book. Open invitations are extended to parents, grandparents, and older brothers and sisters to visit and read to the class. On the day that his grandparents visited the classroom, Dan "stood proudly next to his grandma and grandpa and introduced them. As they read, they stopped often and had Dan assist in the telling of the story. We took their picture with Dan and tacked it to the Mystery Reader board" (Pils, 1993, p. 652). On that eventful day, Dan took a giant step forward in his journey toward literacy; he felt, perhaps for the first time, that he had something of himself to give to the other students. Throughout the remainder of the year, he made steady progress and contributed to the community through the stories he wrote and shared with others.

Dan is now in the third grade and is still making an impact on the community of readers and writers in Miss Pils's first-grade class. He helps select books for her class: "Knowing that I like pigs, he checked out every pig book in the library. He came into the room beaming when he found a pig story that had just arrived; he was teaching me about a new book" (Pils, 1993, p. 653). And Michael, who once declared his love for Miss Pils, also helps select books for her class. Dan and Michael were even invited to participate in reading to the class books that they had liked "when they were little." As Laura Pils explains, "We took their pictures and put them on the Mystery Reader board. We wrote them thank-you notes. Their teacher said they were so proud. I was proud too" (p. 653).

The story of Dan and Michael illustrates convincingly that at its best, literacy is a personal and self-engaging activity. Children who view themselves as contributing members of a classroom of readers and writers develop a sense of self-worth and commitment. Bringing children and books together in a literate community fosters the ability not only to think better but also to feel and to imagine.

Reading literature requires children to respond to books affectively as well as cognitively. Children respond emotionally to the literary text as a whole. These feelings, by and large, are unique and tied to each reader's life experiences. Emphasizing personal involvement in literature develops in children an imagination, a sense of wonder, and an active participation in the literary experience. To our mind, bringing children and literature together is one of the highest acts of humanity in the classroom.

How teachers capture children's interest in books and bring them into a supportive community of readers is the subject of this chapter. Examine the chapter overview, depicting connections among several key concepts related to bringing books and children together. It is important to surround children with books, including those with a multicultural perspective, to immerse children in hearing literature and to help them find books they want to read.

We also emphasize in this chapter the importance of children's responding personally to literature as a way to extend critical thinking and make connections to other readers. We look at how to organize the classroom so that children can authentically respond to books. Children's freedom to choose what they read is considered in relation to different ways of organizing for instruction. Finally, we look at how teachers themselves can be involved in personal reading and writing.

Supporting a Community of Readers

There are long-term benefits implicit in bringing children and books together on a regular basis. First, reading expands children's experiential backgrounds. Children who have never milked a cow and been awakened by a rooster or never lived in a tenement apartment and played in the alley of a big city can expand their world through reading. Second, literature provides children with good models of writing. These models are valuable in children's own writing development and teach the unique characteristics of written language. Third, children learn to read by reading, a theme we have repeated throughout this book. When they are encouraged to read books regularly, children are more likely to develop patience with print and thus they gain valuable practice in reading. Fourth, when the prime purpose for reading is pleasure, children want to understand what they are reading and are likely to select books with familiar topics, themes, or characters. Natural reading situations are created that will promote students' use of reading strategies. And fifth, wide reading provides opportunities for children to develop vocabulary knowledge. Readers learn the meaning of words by meeting them again and again in a variety of contexts.

Literature-based reading programs have the potential for success with all types of students, but particularly with readers like Dan and Michael, who can easily "slip through the cracks" without a supportive environment for literacy development. Simply defined, a **literature-based reading program** may be viewed in the context of instructional practices and student activities using literature, books, novels, short stories, magazines, plays, and poems that have not been rewritten for instructional purposes. Furthermore, children's literature often *supplants,* rather than *supplements,* a basal reading program.

Studies have been conducted in classrooms where literature-based programs were beginning to be used with populations that had traditionally been unsuccessful in literacy learning in school. A landmark study, conducted by Cohen (1968) and later replicated by Cullinan, Jaggar, and Strickland (1974) with New York City second graders from low-socioeconomic neighborhoods, compared the growth of two groups of children in reading. One group was taught from a basal reader program, while the other participated in a literature-based program. The literature group showed significant increases over the basal reader group in word knowledge, comprehension, and quality of vocabulary. Also, children who speak limited English have made great gains in reading when immersed in real literature (Larrick, 1987; Roser, Hoffman, & Farest, 1990). The reading ability of emotionally handicapped children also increased significantly through a literature-based reading program (D'Alessandro, 1990).

Reading achievement studies of literature-based reading programs also report significant shifts in the children's attitudes toward reading. Tunnell, Calder, Justen, and Waldrop (1988), for example, found that with mainstreamed learning-disabled children in a literature-based program, "negative attitudes toward books and reading virtually disappeared as self-concept in relation to literacy rose" (p. 40). Literature-based programs seem to affect children's conceptions of reading, also. Rasinski and De Ford (1986) asked children from classrooms using different types of reading programs questions like "What is reading?" and "What happens when you read?" The responses from children in the different classrooms were dramatically different. Children in the literature-based classroom considered reading a more meaning-related activity than the children from a basal reading classroom and the children from a mastery learning classroom did.

No wonder reports such as *Becoming a Nation of Readers* (Anderson, Hiebert, Scott, & Wilkinson, 1985) call for reading programs that provide children with many varied opportunities to read high-quality literature.

The real value of literature-based reading programs is that they create a **community of readers.** Hepler and Hickman (1982) proposed the idea of a community of readers to characterize how children, in alliance with their friends and teacher, work together in classrooms in which school reading becomes like adult reading, where adults are motivated to read. In these classrooms, children informally and spontaneously talk over their experiences with books and recommend books to each other. In Hepler's (1982) yearlong study of a fifth- and a sixth-grade classroom, she found it common for children who discovered something of particular appeal to read that passage aloud to a friend, offer the book to a friend for approval, or simply nudge the nearest person and point out "the good part."

Hansen (1987) has expanded this idea into "a community of readers and writers." She explained that students should help each other learn, not out of a sense of duty, but because they know each other as people. Children sharing their thoughts on what they have read helps make this happen. In book-sharing talks, sometimes children have similar thoughts about a book, but often they have unique contributions to make to the discussions. The teachers who have worked with Hansen have come to realize that each child has something to share, that everyone knows something that others will find interesting. This attitude encourages students to have confidence in themselves and to take risks by eliminating the fear of not knowing the right answer. Hansen suggests, "When words, whether our own written words or our verbal responses to someone else's, give us a place in the group, print acquires a new dimension for us. Learning is usually social; we learn very little entirely on our own. Without a community, people have less desire to write or read" (p. 64).

Classrooms where children support each other as readers and writers do not arise spontaneously. Rather, "they are carefully structured environments that reflect a teacher's commitment to literature as a natural medium for children's reading and language learning as well as a source of fun and satisfaction" (Hickman, 1983, p. 1). In these classrooms, children's responses to literature are livelier and more positive than in the average classroom, and their choices of books seem to be made with more care.

Hooking children on books helps them realize their literacy potential. The Best Practice illustrated in Box 10.1 outlines some of the hooks we explore in this chapter, all of which support a community of readers in the elementary classroom.

SURROUNDING CHILDREN WITH LITERATURE

One thing that sets literature-based classrooms apart is that the teachers are enthusiastic about children's literature. Teachers who make a point of talking about their own favorite books or stories or are themselves engrossed in a new book often find their students wanting to read those same books for themselves. These teachers also show personal interest in books in other ways. Some teachers share autographed copies of books from their own collections or display book-related items such as ceramic or stuffed toy characters or posters designed by a picture-book artist.

Jill, a first-grade teacher, showed a stuffed rabbit with a blue jacket as she read Beatrix Potter's *Peter Rabbit*. Another teacher told the story of "Little Red Riding Hood" using a doll on which one end was Red Riding Hood and the upside-down end was a wolf wearing grandmother-type spectacles. No matter how the teacher's enthusiasm is expressed, it creates a setting where children know that attention to the world of books is authentic and desirable.

Selecting a Classroom Collection of Books

A major classroom characteristic that brings children and books together is many carefully selected books. These books come from different sources—the teacher's personal collection, the school library, the public library, and paperback book clubs. While the core col-

Hooking Students on Books

1. IMMERSE STUDENTS IN LITERATURE

◆ Create a classroom climate in which literature is an integral component.

◆ Use many genres of children's books with multicultural perspectives, including folktales, poetry, realistic fiction, historical fiction, and informational books.

◆ Select and organize a classroom collection of books.

◆ Read and tell stories. Show films and filmstrips of literature selections.

2. USE INSTRUCTIONAL TIME TO SHOW THE VALUE OF READING

◆ Find classroom time for students to read books of their choice.

◆ Model reading behavior and become a reader of children's books.

◆ Encourage students to respond to the aesthetic dimensions of literature.

3. HELP STUDENTS FIND AND SHARE BOOKS THEY WANT TO READ

◆ Help students find books of interest at the appropriate level.

◆ Tell or read the beginning of interesting stories.

◆ Develop annotated lists of books worth reading.

lection is permanent, many of the borrowed titles change frequently, so there is always something new to encourage browsing.

Books are not in this collection for the sake of quantity. The books are carefully chosen for a variety of reasons, as illustrated by Hickman (1983):

> One teacher of a fourth- and fifth-grade group, for example, often includes many picture books. She chooses some like Mizumura's *If I Were a Cricket* and Foreman's *Panda's Puzzle* for the special purpose of comparing the artists' way with watercolor; others, like Wagner's *The Bunyip of Berkeley's Creek,* are chosen just because they are good stories and the teacher thinks the children will enjoy them. The teacher is sensitive to children's interests and books that will have immediate appeal; thus the presence of *Tales of a Fourth*

Grade Nothing by Blume, *How to Eat Fried Worms* by Rockwell, and *The Mouse and the Motorcycle* by Cleary. The teacher also recognizes that the students need some books that will stretch their imaginations and abilities, stories of sufficient depth to bear rereading and reflection. Some of the titles chosen for this purpose are Babbitt's *Tuck Everlasting,* Cooper's *The Dark Is Rising,* and Steig's *Abel's Island.* Still others, like Konigsburg's *From the Mixed-Up Files of Mrs. Basil E. Frankweiler,* are available in multiple copies so that small groups can read and discuss them. (p. 2)

One notable feature of book selection is that each title bears some relationship to others in the collection. There may be multiple books by an author or an illustrator or several books that represent a genre such as folktales. Other connections may be based on a content theme, such as spooky books, nature books, or survival books.

Choosing Classroom Literature.   To be able to choose literature for classroom collections and to give guidance to students as they choose books to read, a teacher needs to be familiar with children's literature. Because children's literature has expanded extensively in the past 20 years, this is a formidable task.

Several strategies can be used to help choose classroom literature. Here are some tips on how to avoid being overwhelmed as you become familiar with children's literature.

1. *Read and enjoy children's books yourself.* The best way to become familiar with children's books is not to read anthologies or reviews but to read the books themselves. It is a

The extensive expansion of available children's literature makes choosing a classroom literature collection a formidable task.

good idea to keep a card file on the books you have read to jog your memory later. This card file can be used with children to help them in choosing books to read. It can also be used as you share your feelings about particular books with other teachers.

2. *Read children's books with a sense of involvement.* Only by reading books thoroughly can you prepare yourself to share them honestly with children.

3. *Read a variety of book types.* There are various classifications of genres or types of books. By being familiar with specific books in each of the different genres, you can be more helpful when children ask for such things as "a scary mystery" or "something true to life."

4. *Read books for a wide variety of ability levels.* Children at any grade level vary tremendously in their reading abilities and interests. For example, Haywood's *B is for Betsy* is read avidly by some second and third graders. Other children at the same grade level will read somewhat more difficult books such as Sobol's *Encyclopedia Brown Lends a Hand* and Blume's *Tales of a Fourth Grade Nothing.* Still others may benefit from spending time with picture books such as *Where the Wild Things Are* by Sendak or *The Great Thumbprint Drawing Book* by Emberley.

5. *Share how your students respond to particular books with other teachers or other university students.* In the San Antonio, Texas, school district, a book-reporting system was developed. Anyone who read a book and used it with children filled out a review card, which included a brief summary, a rating, comments on the book's unique value, and recommendations for suggested ability levels. No card was turned in unless the book was used with children. Teachers used these cards to help select books for their classrooms. Not unexpectedly, with this teacher-sharing system in place, the children read more along with their teachers.

6. *Start by reading several books of good quality.* Appendix G lists the Newbery and Caldecott award-winning books. As you read these and begin using them with children, you will begin to know books to which children in your class will respond favorably.

Determining Good Literature.   A teacher's first priority is to choose books that children will like and will read. To choose such a collection of books, teachers must be knowledgeable and enthusiastic about children's literature. Through reading children's literature and talking about books with children, teachers learn which books to use in their classrooms. A second consideration is to use accepted ways to judge books according to plot, theme, characterization, and setting. In addition, there are a few criteria to use in building a *balanced* collection of books.

1. *The collection needs to contain modern, realistic literature as well as more traditional literature.* In recent years, some critics have voiced concern about the appropriateness of realism in some children's literature. Other observers feel that realism is justified because it depicts problems children must face while growing up. Each teacher and

school must decide whether to include books that deal with divorce, death, and drug use—issues that touch the lives of many of today's children. Traditional literature, which children have delighted in for many years, should also be a part of the classroom collection of books.

2. *The collection needs to contain books that realistically present different ethnic and minority groups and nontraditional families as well as mainstream Americans.* See Chapter 11 for specific criteria useful in evaluating books for stereotyping.

3. *The collection needs to contain books with different types of themes and books of varying difficulty.* The classroom library needs traditional literature, fantasy, poetry, historical fiction, nonfiction, and picture books. Even upper-grade classroom collections should have some picture books. Picture books often have a good story plot and provide a way to get less enthusiastic students into reading.

Literature with Multicultural Perspectives. In a multicultural society made up of diverse groups who maintain their own cultural traditions and experiences, books help us celebrate our distinctive differences and understand our common humanity. Culturally diverse books in the United States typically tell the stories of people of color—African-Americans, Native Americans, Asian-Americans, and Hispanic Americans. These stories are told through poems, folklore, picture books, realistic and historical fiction, biography, and nonfiction. Junko Yakota (1993) broadens the description of multicultural children's books to include literature that represents *any* distinct cultural group through authentic portrayal and rich detail. Culturally diverse books, therefore, also may represent the literature of regional white and religious groups—for example, Appalachian, Ozark, Jewish, Muslim, or Amish cultures—or the cross-cultural stories of people from other nations. What all culturally diverse books have in common is that they portray what is unique to an individual culture and universal to all cultures.

The power of multicultural literature lies in the human connections that we make. Not only do books about people of color or distinct cultural groups help us understand and appreciate differences among people, but they also show how people are connected to one another through human needs, desires, and emotions (Cullinan & Galda, 1994). At an exhibit of the Cleveland Museum of Art, "Lasting Impressions: Illustrating African-American Children's Books" (featuring original drawings, prints, and collages by 15 illustrators of African-American children's books), we observed a young child standing pensively in front of a drawing from Ann Grifalconi's *Kinda Blue* (1993). The pastel painting that captured her attention depicts the wistful image of Sissy, a young black child living on a farm in Georgia who's "kinda blue" since her father's death. After viewing the illustration for a while, the child began to walk away but then pulled her parents back and said, "I want to be just like her." The emotional connection that she made with Sissy is strong enough to attract her to the book *Kinda Blue*. And the parents do not have to go far to find it. The exhibition includes a reading table with the books for which the illustrations were made. Children, their parents, and other viewers of the exhibition spend as much time browsing through and reading the books as they do viewing the illustrations.

Why Multicultural Literature? There are fundamental social and educational reasons why multicultural literature should be woven into the fabric of children's home and school experiences. Violet Harris, a children's literature scholar and advocate of multicultural books in classrooms, outlines a compelling rationale for making culturally diverse books an integral part of the literacy curriculum. In an interview with Martinez and Nash, Harris (1993) gives five reasons for multicultural literature in the classroom:

1. All children, and especially children of color, need to experience multicultural books. Children receive an affirmation of themselves and their cultures when their life experiences are mirrored in books. The infusion of multicultural literature in the classroom affirms and empowers children and their cultures.

2. Children perceive that members of their cultural group make contributions to the world.

3. Children derive pleasure and pride from hearing and reading stories about children like themselves and seeing illustrations of characters who look as if they stepped out of their homes or communities.

4. Multicultural literature offers hope and encouragement to children who face the types of dilemmas and experiences depicted in some of the books they read.

5. Children who read culturally diverse books encounter authors who use language in inventive and memorable ways, who create multidimensional characters, and who engender aesthetic and literary experiences that can touch the heart, mind, and soul.

Multicultural literature helps readers understand, appreciate, and celebrate the traditions and experiences that make each culture special in its own way. When children read books that depict cultural differences, they not only view the world from another's perspective but also learn more about themselves.

Criteria for Selecting Multicultural Literature. Yakota (1993) notes that the standards for selecting quality literature in general apply to culturally diverse books as well. In addition to these criteria, she suggests that teachers select quality multicultural literature based on these considerations:

1. *Cultural accuracy.* Are issues and problems authentic and do they reflect the values and beliefs of the culture being portrayed?

2. *Richness in cultural details.* Do readers gain a sense of the culture they are reading about?

3. *Authentic dialogue and relationships.* Is the dialogue indicative of how people in the culture really speak, and are relationships portrayed honestly and realistically?

4. *In-depth treatment of cultural issues.* Are issues given a realistic portrayal and explored in depth so that readers may be able to formulate informed thoughts on them?

5. *Inclusion of members of a minority group for a purpose.* Are the lives of the characters rooted in the culture, no matter how minor their role in the story?

We would fly all over the city.
"Mira," Abuela would say, pointing.

And I'd look, as we soared
over parks and streets, dogs and people.

ABUELA, by Arthur Dorros (New York: Dutton, 1991)

MRS. KATZ AND TUSH, by Patricia Polacco
(New York: Bantam, 1992), page 3

THE BOY WHO SWALLOWED SNAKES, by Lawrence Yep (New York: Scholastic, 1993)

"What's that you say?"
Uncle said, comin' closer.

I said it louder:
"I said I'm gonna dig me a hole s-o-o deep,
I can climb right in and hide!"
'Course, it came out real grumpy-like,
'N' Uncle was having none of that!

So he bent his big tall frame
And scooped me right up!
He knowed I loved to be carried
Up on his shoulders, so high.
"How 'bout takin' a ride with me, Sissy?
I'm goin' to visit my corn children!"

KINDA BLUE, by Ann Grifalconi
(Boston: Little, Brown, and
Company, 1993), pages 6-7

The people were always moving from place to place following the herds of buffalo. They had many horses to carry the tipis and all their belongings. They trained their fastest horses to hunt the buffalo.

THE GIRL WHO LOVED WILD HORSES, by Paul Goble (New York: Macmillan, 1978)

EL CHINO, by Allen Say
(Boston: Houghton, Mifflin, 1990), page 25

Now there is a statue of Sadako in Hiroshima Peace Park. She is standing on the Mountain of Paradise, holding a golden crane in out-stretched hands.

Every year, on Peace Day, children hang garlands of paper cranes under the statue. Their wish is engraved at its base:

SADAKO, by Eleanor Coerr and Ed Young (New York: Putnam, 1993), page 44

Then Sarah tried a different hat.
Dark, dark blue, with a red feather.
"This one, Aunt Flossie! This one!"
Aunt Flossie closed her eyes and thought a minute.
"Oh my, yes, my, my. What an exciting day!"

We waited, Sarah and I.
"What happened, Aunt Flossie?" I asked.

AUNT FLOSSIE'S HATS (AND CRAB CAKES LATER),
by Elizabeth Fitzgerald Howard
(New York: Clarion, 1991), page 15

In addition to Yakota's questions, the following checklist is designed by Cullinan and Galda (1994) to help teachers select quality multicultural literature.

◆ Are characters from different cultures portrayed as individuals without stereotyping?

◆ Does the work qualify as good literature in its own right?

◆ Is the culture accurately portrayed from the point of view of someone inside the cultural group?

◆ Are issues presented in their true complexity as an integral part of the story—not just a focus on problems or social concerns?

◆ Does the dialogue maintain the natural melodies of the native language or dialect without making it difficult to read?

◆ Do the books show the diversity within as well as across human cultures?

◆ Do the illustrations contain accurate, authentic representations of people and scenes from different cultural groups?

◆ Do people of color lead as well as follow? Do they solve their own problems, or do they depend on white benefactors?

Appendix H contains a partial listing of children's books representative of African-American, Asian-American, Hispanic American, and Native American cultures. These books, and many others, may easily be incorporated into a literature-based classroom.

Designing the Classroom Library.   As a classroom collection is compiled, the science, art, social studies, and music curricula need to be considered. Include books on topics that will be studied in these subjects areas. Again, make materials on specific topics available in a wide range of reading levels, because of the different reading abilities of students in the same grade level.

As the classroom collection develops, attention must be given to the area of the classroom that houses the library. Specific physical features of classroom libraries can increase children's voluntary use of books (Morrow, 1985; Morrow & Weinstein, 1982; Routman, 1991; Fractor, Woodruff, Martinez, & Teale, 1993). The classroom library should be highly visible; this communicates that it is an important part of the classroom. Clear boundaries should set the library area apart from the rest of the classroom. The library is a quiet place for five or six children to read away from the rest of the classroom. It should afford comfortable seating—perhaps carpet pieces, beanbags, or special chairs. It should hold five or six books per child. Multiple copies of favorites are included. A variety of genres and reading levels should be available, arranged on both open shelves to display attractive covers and shelves to house many books with the spine out. Books in the library are organized and labeled by genre, theme, topic, author, reading level, content area, or some combination of these features. Literature-oriented displays, such as flannel boards, puppets, book jackets, and posters, boost interest and enthusiasm.

Once the classroom library is in place, the literature program itself needs attention. A major part of the program includes reading aloud and telling stories to children.

Listening to Literature

According to Stewig (1980), "most elementary school teachers understand the values that accrue as a result of sharing literature with children" (p. 8). Teachers naturally seem to know that there is no better way for children to become interested in the world of books than through listening to stories and poems. In this way, children learn that literature is a source of pleasure. When they listen to literature, children are exposed to stories and poems they cannot, or will not, read on their own. Often, once children are excited by hearing a selection, they want to read it for themselves. One study found that reading aloud to fifth graders for 20 to 30 minutes a day affected both the quantity and quality of their voluntary reading (Sirota, 1971).

Through hearing stories and poems, children develop a positive disposition toward books. Cumulative experiences with hearing stories and poems are likely to improve reading comprehension and vocabulary development. Cohen (1968) reports that 7-year-olds who were read to for 20 minutes each day gained significantly in vocabulary and reading comprehension. Listening to stories and poems can also provide a basis for group discussion, which often leads to shared meanings and points of reference.

For these reasons, literature listening time can be one of the most productive times in the school day. Sharing literature with children is not a "frill." Most primary teachers include time for reading aloud in their schedules; upper-elementary teachers spend less time reading stories to students. Chow Loy Tom (1969) finds that about 40 percent of third- and fourth-grade teachers read aloud to students, while only 26 percent of sixth-grade teachers read to their students. Among the reasons teachers gave for not reading aloud was lack of time.

A recent national study of read-aloud practices shows that teachers tend to read to children 10 to 20 minutes a day (Hoffman, Roser, & Battle, 1993). However, only 34 percent of the time spent on these read-alouds is related to units of study. Further, the amount of booktalk following read-alouds often lasts fewer than five minutes. Children rarely engage in exploring their response to literature during a read-aloud.

Although teachers may read aloud to students to fill odd moments between a completed activity and the bell or to schedule reading aloud as a calming-down activity, it is important to note that sharing literature is not a time killer. It is too serious and central to the reading program as a whole to be treated in an offhand way. Reading aloud needs to be incorporated into all aspects of the curriculum.

Choosing Literature to Read Aloud.
What kind of thought and planning go into deciding what literature to share? Why not go to the library, pull some books from the shelf, and, when reading-aloud time arrives, pick up a book and read? In classrooms where students become enthusiastic about literature, the teachers have carefully selected which books to read. They have considered the age of the children and what will interest them. They also present different types of literature. Often books read aloud are related to each other in some way. For example, a second-grade teacher read several books by Keats: *The Snowy Day, Dreams,* and *Boggles.* Soon the students could recognize a Keats book by its illustrations.

Hickman (1983) notes the example of a fourth-grade teacher who thought her students would be excited by characters that were transformed magically from one type of being to another. She read to her students tales of magical changes such as "Beauty and the Beast" in Peace's version and Tresselt's retelling of Matsutani's story "The Crane Maiden." Her class also heard Perrault's version of the familiar "Cinderella" and a Native American myth, "The Ring in the Prairie," by Schoolcraft. Last, she read "A Stranger Came Ashore" by Hunter, a fantasy story with magical transformation that is more difficult to understand than the transformations in the preceding stories.

Another teacher might focus on books to demonstrate an assortment of character types.

> In planning experiences with characterization, the teacher chooses books that present a wide variety of characters: male and female, young and old, rich and poor, real and imaginary. The books are read to children and savored. Sometimes the selections are discussed; at other times they are not. Reading occurs each day; the teacher is aware that children may be assimilating unconsciously some of the aspects of successful characterizations exemplified in what they are hearing. (Stewig, 1980, pp. 62–63)

Folktales in which the plot is generally very important can be read to illustrate simple characterization. Other authors give vivid physical descriptions. Consider this description from Judy Blume's *Are You There, God? It's Me, Margaret* (1970):

> When she smiles like that she shows all her top teeth. They aren't her real teeth. It's what Grandmother calls a bridge. She can take out a whole section of four top teeth when she wants to. She used to entertain me by doing that when I was little. . . . When she smiles without her teeth in place she looks like a witch. But with them in her mouth she's very pretty. (pp. 15, 18)

Teachers can also share with children books in which authors show what the characters are like by describing what they do and how they interact with others. Even books for the very young do this. For example, in *Sam* by Ann Herbert Scott, Sam tries to interact with his mother, his brother George, his sister Marcia, and his father, all of whom are too preoccupied with their own concerns. Finally, the family responds. The characters all are developed skillfully by the author and portrayed in subtle monochromatic illustrations by Symeon Shimin. In hearing and discussing such books, children gain an awareness of how authors portray characters.

Preparing to Read Aloud.   Teachers need to prepare for story time. First, before reading a book aloud to the class, they should be familiar with the story's sequence of events, mood, subject, vocabulary, and concepts. Second, teachers must decide how to introduce the story. Should the book be discussed intermittently as it is read, or should there be discussion at the conclusion of the reading? Furthermore, what type of discussion or other type of activity will follow the reading?

Setting the Mood.   Many teachers and librarians set the mood for literature-sharing time with a story hour symbol. One librarian used a small lamp—when the lamp was lit, it was time to listen. Deliberate movement toward the story-sharing corner in the classroom may set the mood for story time. Some teachers create the mood with a record or by playing a piano. As soon as the class hears a specific tune, they know that it is time to come to the story-sharing corner. Norton (1980) describes using a small painted jewelry box from Japan. As she brings out the box, Norton talks with the children about the magical stories contained in it. She opens the box slowly while the children try to catch the magic in their hands. The magic is wonderful, so they hold it carefully while they listen. When the story ends, each child carefully returns the magic to the box until the next story time.

Introducing the Story.   There are numerous ways to introduce stories. The story-sharing corner could have a chalkboard or an easel bearing a question relating to the literature to be shared or a picture of the book to focus the children's attention. Many teachers effectively introduce a story with objects. For example, a stuffed rabbit may be used to introduce *The Velveteen Rabbit* by Williams. A good way to introduce folktales is with artifacts from the appropriate country.

Other ways to introduce a story would be to ask a question, to tell the students why you like a particular story, or to have the students predict what will happen in the story using the title or the pictures. You might tell them something interesting about the background of the story or its author. It is advantageous to display the book, along with other books by the same author or with books on the same subject or theme. Introductions, however, should be brief and should vary from session to session.

Activities After Reading Aloud.   Once the stage is set for literature sharing, the teacher needs to read expressively and clearly. There are many different ways to encourage children to respond after hearing a piece of literature; these will be discussed later in this chapter. After some selections, the teacher can simply allow children to react privately to what they have heard. Davis (1973) calls this the *impressional approach.* The basic idea is that children will take from an experience whatever is relevant to them; therefore, each child will take something from the listening experience. There is no particular reason for the teacher to know precisely what each child gets from each listening experience. Teachers should probably strike a balance between these two approaches. Too many discussions and other follow-up activities may diminish interest; too little will diminish the impact of the literature.

Allowing Others to Present Literature.   Trelease (1989) suggested that in addition to reading literature aloud daily, a good way to promote the importance of reading aloud is to set up guest reader programs in which the principal, parents, the superintendent, and local sports and news personalities read literature favorites to children. Children, too, can present literature to children. In Chapter 6, we described a cross-age tutoring program where older elementary children can be shown how to select and prepare for reading to younger children. Note that selecting the books to be read and preparing the presentation are extremely important. Don't let the reader do this without guidance!

Storytelling

There are three significant reasons for including storytelling in the curriculum.

1. *An understanding of the oral tradition in literature.* Young children in many societies have been initiated into their rich heritage through storytelling; today, few children encounter such experiences.

2. *The opportunity for the teacher to involve the children in the storytelling.* A teacher who has learned the story is free from dependence on the book and can use gestures and action to involve the children in the story.

3. *The stimulus it provides for children's storytelling.* Seeing the teacher engage in storytelling helps children understand that storytelling is a worthy activity and motivates them to tell their own stories (Stewig, 1980).

Each of these reasons is important. Children are sure to be spellbound by a well-told story. Close eye contact, the storyteller's expressions, ingenious props, and the eliciting of the children's participation contribute to the magic. Although we cannot expect everyone to acquire a high level of expertise for a large number of stories, storytelling is a skill one can master with practice, a story at a time.

Selecting the Story to Tell.   Beginning storytellers should choose selections they like and with which they feel comfortable. Simple stories are often the most effective for storytelling. Stories with which many children are familiar and can help with the dialogue are excellent choices for younger children. "The Three Bears," "The Three Little Pigs," and "The Three Billy Goats Gruff" fit in this category. Since ancient and modern fairy tales usually appeal to children aged 6 through 10, consider stories like "The Elves and the Shoemaker," "Rumpelstiltskin," and "The Bremen Town Musicians." Older elementary children frequently prefer adventure; so myths, legends, and epics like "How Thor Found His Hammer," "Robin Hood," "Pecos Bill," and "Paul Bunyan" tend to be popular choices.

You might select several stories about a certain topic. For example, Norton (1980) suggests telling two stories about "forgetting": "Icarus and Daedalus," a Greek legend in which Icarus forgets that his wings are wax, and "Poor Mr. Fingle" (Gruenberg, 1948), who wanders about a hardware store for years because he forgot what he wanted to buy.

One of the purposes of storytelling is to give children an understanding of the oral tradition. Even very young children can understand that today stories are usually passed down in books, whereas many years ago they were handed down orally.

An effective way to help children gain this understanding is to tell stories that are similar in plot, such as "The Pancake" from Norse tales included in Sutherland's *Anthology of Children's Literature* (1984) and *The Bun* by Brown. All of these stories have some kind of personified edible goodie chased by a series of animals and eaten by the most clever animal. Jane, a kindergarten teacher, read these three stories to her class and then guided her students in making a chart showing how the three stories were alike and different. The class then dictated a story titled "The Pizza." In the class's story, the pizza rolled and was chased by the school nurse, some first graders, and the principal. Its fate, of course, was to be gobbled by the kindergartners. Through their experiences, the kindergarten class developed a story using elements from school life, just as storytellers in the oral tradition did from their personal experiences.

Preparing a Story for Telling.   The task of memorizing a story may seem formidable. How can teachers or children prepare for telling a story in front of others? Actually, stories do not need to be memorized. In fact, the telling is often more interesting if the story unfolds in a slightly different way each time. The following steps are helpful in preparing to tell a story.

1. Read the story two or three times to get it clearly in your mind.

2. List the sequence of events in your mind or on paper, giving yourself an outline of the important happenings. Peck (1989) suggested mapping the story by considering the setting, the characters, the beginning event, the problem and attempts at solving it, and the solution. This structure enabled her students to tell stories they had devised without stilted memorization of lines.

3. Reread the story, taking note of the events you didn't remember. Also determine sequences you do need to memorize, such as "Mirror, mirror, on the wall, who's the fairest of them all?" from *Snow White*. Many folk and fairy tales include elements like this, but such passages are not difficult to memorize.

4. Go over the events again, and consider the details you want to include. Think of the meaning of the events and how to express that meaning, rather than trying to memorize the words in the story. Stewig (1980) recommends jotting down the sequence of events on note cards; he reviews the cards whenever he has a few free minutes. He reports that with this technique, it seldom takes longer than a few days to fix the units of action of a story in your memory.

5. When you feel you know the story, tell the story in front of a mirror. After you have practiced it two or three times, the wording will improve, and you can try changing vocal pitch to differentiate among characters. Also try changing your posture or hand gestures to represent different characters.

Once you have prepared the story, decide how to set the mood and introduce it, just as you would before reading a piece of literature. Effective storytelling does not require props, but you may want to add variety and use flannel boards and flannel board figures or puppets. These kinds of props work well with cumulative stories containing a few characters. Jessica, a first grader, told how her teacher had a puppet of "The Old Lady Who Swallowed a Fly" with a plastic see-through window in her stomach. As the story was told, the children delighted in seeing the different animals in the old lady's stomach and helping the teacher tell the repetitive story.

Helping Children Select Books

One trait of independent readers is the ability to select books they can enjoy and from which they can get personally important information. In fact, Anderson, Higgins, and Wurster (1985) finds that good readers know how to select literature relevant to their interest and reading level, while poor readers do not. More often than not, a teacher will hear a child moan, "I can't find a book I want to read." Comments like this usually reveal that students do not feel confident in finding good books by themselves. We have alluded to ways for students to become acquainted with specific books: Teachers can tell exciting anecdotes about authors, provide previews of interesting stories, show films or filmstrips about stories, suggest titles of stories that match students' interests, or compile teacher- and/or student-annotated book lists. To be able to do these things well, teachers need to be well versed in children's literature and know their students.

Beyond this, children need to be shown how to choose books. Hansen (1987) proposes that children be asked to choose and read books of three different difficulty levels. Children should have an "easy book" on hand to encourage fluent reading and the "I can read" feeling. Second, children need a "book I'm working on," in which they can make daily accomplishments by working on the hard spots. Finally, children need a "challenge book," which they can go back to repeatedly over a period of time. This helps them gain a sense of growth over a long period. By letting children know we expect them to read at all levels, children learn to judge varying levels themselves and to give honest appraisals of how well books match their reading ability.

For independent readers, book choice is related to reading purposes and intentions as they read the book. Rick may decide to read *A Wind in the Door* because he liked *A Wrinkle in Time* by the same author, Madeleine L'Engle. When he begins to read, he compares the two books. As he becomes engrossed in the book, he reads to see how the story unfolds. Children need to discuss with each other and their teacher why they chose a specific book and what they are thinking about as they read it.

In addition to their teacher, an even more persuasive source that can help children decide what books to read is their classmates. Peer recommendations make the act of choosing a book more efficient and less risky. Recommendations from friends are the primary way adult readers decide what books to read. For many adults, the next best thing to reading a good book is telling someone else about it.

The use of **dialogue journals** is another effective tool used by teachers to get to know how students feel about their reading and to guide students to "the right book." Jan, a fifth-grade teacher, has her students write daily in a journal. One of her students wrote, "I like it when the whole class reads together. I think it makes me want to read more." Jan responded with, "I'm glad." Another student made the following journal entry: "My favorite book was *Florence Nightingale*. I liked it because of the way she improved the hospitals and made them stay clean. Also she acted differently than any other person I've read about" (Smith, 1982, p. 360). In response to this journal entry, Jan suggested that the student read other biographies of courageous women.

Dialogue journals seem to work well at the beginning of the school year in providing a response to children concerning their thoughts and feelings about the books they are choosing and reading. Later in the year, buddy journals can be instituted as was explained in Chapter 9. Sometimes students will begin recommending books to each other in their buddy journals.

There is another understanding in the world of adult readers that is communicated to students in classrooms where students are into reading: If an adult reader does not like a particular book, he or she doesn't finish it. It is common for an adult to say, "I just couldn't get into that book," or "I never finished that biography." Here is some advice Smith (1982) gave to a classroom of readers concerning what to do about books they have difficulty getting through.

Mark mentioned that he didn't like his version of *Dan Boone*—it didn't pick up his interest, so he stopped reading. That's okay. You should read books you like, because if you spend too long trying to read one you don't like, it may make you doubt reading itself. Jamie asked about this too—she gets discouraged because she reads so slowly. Her mom told her she would get better as she reads more. You do learn to read by reading and by choosing books that interest you. The books should have some new words, but not so many that they discourage you. (p. 359)

Smith also encouraged children to ask for suggestions about which books are interesting. But each child needs to decide if a book is too hard, too easy, or interesting enough to be read cover to cover. Of course, there are times when students need to be nudged to finish a book or to make the next "book I'm working on" a bit more challenging. In the Viewpoint illustrated in Box 10.2, a librarian shares her perspective on how to get books into the hands of children.

BOX 10.2 VIEWPOINT

How One Librarian Gets Children to Read

Classes come to Elizabeth's library for 30 minutes once a week. Elizabeth Gray is a librarian in a K–2 suburban school. She and two mother volunteers work with approximately 20 children. For half the allotted time, Elizabeth either reads them a story or gives a lesson showing them how the library is organized. Then the children find a book. Some take the whole remaining time; others choose their books quickly and began reading, perhaps with an adult to read to. Each child chooses one free-choice book and one reading book. Elizabeth thinks it important for children to find books they want to read. Here are her thoughts on how to do this.

How do you help children find "the right book" for them?
The volunteer mothers and I listen to what the child is looking for. We also help the children to be independent in finding what they want in the library. Since the children are young and are new readers, I have lots of labels, both written and pictures. For example, books about animals are quite popular, so I have a picture of an animal like a zebra in front of where books about that animal are located. Often I display the covers of books, not just the spines. We have an online cataloging system. Even with kindergartners, we model how to use the online cataloging system, and by the second grade, the children are using the keyboard and using the catalog by themselves.

Sometimes children chose books that may be too hard for them. I show them the "five-finger test"—they read a page, and if there are more then five words they don't recognize, they probably need an easier book. I never force a child to change books. If a child is quite interested in a book, he or she will put a lot of effort into it. I consider the taking of books to be a

(Continued)

BOX 10.2 CONTINUED

privilege. The children often chose fairly tales. It surprises me how much they chose nonfiction books, especially books about animals. They often choose books about weather in the news, like tornadoes and hurricanes.

There are so many great children's books being published, plus many classics. How do you keep current?
I constantly read reviews in such journals as the *School Library Journal* and *Horn Book.* Once a month I go to the county library. They arrange new books by the Dewey system—that is, all the science books, math books, biographies, picture books, chapter books, and fiction books are grouped together. At the beginning of the day, someone talks for about an hour on the new books that particular person thinks are extraordinary. The rest of the day, I browse through the books. After this, I decide what books to buy, considering our curriculum needs.

Multicultural literature is much talked about in recent years. How does this trend enter into your work as a school librarian?
I see it as quite important. I think children need to be aware of how many different people there are in the world. I focus on different cultures, and there is so much good material coming out in this area. I go to the Virginia Hamilton Conference of Multicultural Literature, each year, which always spotlights three different authors. One year I heard Eloise Greenfield, an African-American who writes wonderful, elevating poems and stories; Vera B. Williams, who tells stories of Jewish life in New York City; and Ashley Bryant, an African-American illustrator.

How do you work with teachers?
I have a form teachers complete to let me know the topics they are working on. For example, one teacher wants books about the ocean. They also request sets of early readers for their classrooms.

   I bring an author or an illustrator to the school for Right to Read week. The guests generally talk about how they wrote or illustrated their books. Children love this. We are fortunate that the PTA gives us money for this. This year we will have Marilyn Sadler, originally a British author who wrote the Alistar series and the Funny Bunny series.

   We participate in the Buckeye Children's Award. I read the books to the children, and they vote for their favorite books. The children get quite excited to know which books win. During Black History Month, I have African-American parents come to the library and share their favorite books.

ORGANIZING FOR LITERATURE-BASED INSTRUCTION

Organizing patterns for literature-based instruction vary from structured whole class studies of **core books** to independent reading of self-selected books in **literature units, reading workshops,** and **literature circles.** Just as time, response, and choice are important in writing, these factors are also critical to the success of literature-based reading programs.

Core Books

Sometimes teachers will organize literature around the study of core books. In some schools, a set of core books forms the nucleus of the reading program at each grade level (Routman, 1991). A curriculum committee of teachers throughout the district is often assigned to develop a collection of books at each grade that is judged to be age-appropriate and of high quality.

Core books are taught within the framework of whole class study. Students have little or no choice in the selection of core books. As part of a whole class study, teachers assign various activities and use a variety of instructional strategies to support students' interactions with the texts. Many of the comprehension, vocabulary, word identification, and fluency strategies discussed in this book are easily adapted to the study of core books.

Often teachers use core books as springboards for independent reading in which children choose books with related themes and situations or decide to read other works by an author that they have studied. For example, when Brenda Church taught in an inner-city fifth grade in Akron, she introduced a unit on survival by having her students do a whole class study of Jean George's *Julie of the Wolves* (1959). As the unit evolved, the students also read novels in groups. They would select a novel from the choices that Brenda gave them from a book list.

A major problem with the core book approach is the risk of "basalizing" literature. Core books and novels should not be treated like basal textbooks, whose major purpose is to organize instruction around the teaching of reading skills. Basalization could lead to students' completing worksheets, responding to literal comprehension questions, and engaging in round-robin reading (Zarrillo, 1989).

Literature Units

Teachers also organize instruction around literature units. Literature units usually have a unifying element, such as the study of a genre, an author, or a conceptual theme. With literature units, a teacher usually chooses the theme (or negotiates one with the students) and pulls together a collection of books relating to the theme; the children, however, have options as to what books to choose from the collection and what activities they might pursue. Successful literature units strike a balance between whole class, small group, and individually selected activities.

Reading Workshops

Nancy Atwell (1998) originated the reading workshop as a way to integrate the language arts around literature. Reading workshops provide an organizational framework that allows readers to demonstrate their use of reading strategies by responding to books and sharing meaning with others. Reutzel and Cooter (1991) describe how Atwell's reading workshop, with several modifications, can work with elementary school children.

The reading workshop has several key features:

Sparking Interest.   The teacher shares literature. Reutzel and Cooter (1991) provide an example of a teacher reading about vampires and ghouls from Jack Prelutsky's collection of poetry called *Nightmares: Poems to Trouble Your Sleep* (1976) while showing overhead transparencies of some of the book's spooky pen-and-ink sketches. In this way, the teacher sparks interest in various literary genres for free reading.

Minilessons.   The teacher takes several minutes after sharing time to demonstrate a reading strategy through explicit teaching. The focus of a minilesson is often drawn from the observed needs of students, at times discovered during individual reading conferences.

Status-of-the-Class Report.   A status-of-the-class chart helps both teacher and students monitor their responsibilities and progress in a reading workshop. The teacher briefly surveys the class to determine how each student plans to use his or her time during sustained silent reading time and/or group activity. The teacher records students' responses on a chart and, as a result, has a record of each child's commitment for the day. Once children are familiar with the status-of-the-class report, the process takes no more than about five minutes per day to complete.

Sustained Silent Reading.   During sustained silent reading, everyone, including the teacher, reads. This free-reading phase varies from classroom to classroom but accounts for a significant amount of class time as children select and read books of their own choosing. They also keep up-to-date logs recording time spent reading, titles of books read, and when they plan to have individual conferences with the teacher.

Individual Reading Conferences.   Each day, the teacher meets with one or more students for an individual reading conference. Children make appointments on a sign-up board at least one day prior to the conference. Many teachers require that each student have at least three conferences per grading period. During the reading conferences, the teacher and the child discuss the book the child is currently reading. Questions such as the following can be used to guide the conference:

> What part did you find particularly interesting? Funny? Thrilling? Why?

> Did anything in the book bring to mind an experience you have had? What was it? How was it similar to or different from what happened in the story? Why do you think the author wrote this book?

Conferences generally last from five to eight minutes.

Group Sharing Time.   At the end of a reading workshop, the class comes together for ten minutes or so to share details about the books they are engaged in and the activities they have been working on.

Like reading workshops, literature circles involve children in extending personal responses to literature and provide another way of organizing the classroom.

Literature Circles

Historically, teachers grouped children on the basis of measured reading ability. Recently, however, educators have questioned that practice because such grouping limits student choice, interest and motivation. The criticism of grouping children by ability has led practitioners to experiment with heterogeneous groups reading a common text (e.g., Atwell, 1998; Keegan & Shake, 1991) and whole class models such as the previously described use of core books. Further, teachers and researchers have been collaborating on how to work with groups of children leading their own discussions. By studying transcripts of students participating in student-led literature groups (McMahon, 1997), two such teacher-researchers, Deb and Laura, became aware that students they perceived as "average" and "weak" readers were quite articulate when orally expressing their ideas in children-led groups. At the same time, some of the "good" readers responded to their classmates in these groups in ways that were extremely text-based and thus did not connect what they read to other reading or to their own or others' experiences.

Many teachers now seek to move beyond developing reading fluency and comprehension. They want to provide students with time and opportunity to use language to express ideas and explain their thinking to each other and in this way extend their thinking (Villaume, Worden, Williams, Hopkins, & Rosenblatt, 1994). They see literature circles as a way to do this. Teachers who implement literature circles (also known as *literature study groups* and *book clubs*) rely on cooperative learning strategies that show children how to work together and discuss books on the basis of their personal responses to what they have read.

Daniels (1994) defines *literature circles* in this way:

> Literature circles are small, temporary discussion groups [that] have chosen to read the same story, poem, article, or book. While reading each group-determined portion of the text (either in or outside of class), each member prepares to take specific responsibilities in the upcoming discussion, and everyone comes to the group with the notes needed to help preform that job. The circles have regular meetings, with discussion roles rotating each session. When they finish a book, the circle members plan a way to share highlights of their reading with the wider community; then they trade members with other finishing groups, select more reading, and move into a new cycle. Once readers can successfully conduct their own wide-ranging, self-sustaining discussions, formal discussion roles may be dropped. (p. 13)

Gay, a third-grade teacher, organizes literature circles in her classroom. Gay introduces to the class potentially worthwhile books for discussion. If a book is fictional, she builds interest in the story by overviewing its plot, acquainting the student with characters, and reading parts of the story aloud. If the book is informational, she builds anticipation by overviewing the content, reading aloud, and showing the students illustrations from the text. The students then select the books they want to read. Teams are formed not by ability level but by choice of reading material (Vacca & Rasinski, 1992).

Thus in the ideal classroom, the size of the literature circle is determined by the number of children who freely choose a particular book. In real classrooms, some decision making and negotiation may be necessary to achieve groups of productive size. The preferred size for literature circle groups among Chicago-area teachers who worked with Harvey Daniels

(1994) was four or five in the middle grades and three or four in the primary grades. This size allows for a productive mix of perspectives and roles without distractions and inefficiencies. So compromises concerning who reads which books do have to occur. If six children want to read the same book, a decision needs to be made—"Do we want two groups of three or one group of six?" If only two children are interested in a book, the teacher needs to decide if the two will generate enough insightful interactions. If not, the children should be asked to make a second choice to end up in a group of more appropriate size. The teacher may need to say things like, "OK, if you'll read *Hatchet* now and be the fourth member of this group, I'll help you get a group together for *The Phantom Tollbooth* the next cycle" (p. 60).

Jane is a fourth-grade teacher who is enthusiastic about literature circles. When it is time for literature circles, students bring three items to the group: the book their circle is reading, response journals and drawings reflecting their ideas about their reading, and filled-out role sheets for the roles Jane chose for the circles. Jane uses the roles delineated in Daniels' book, *Literature Circles: Voice and Choice in One Student-Centered Classroom* (1994). These roles are defined in the Best Practice illustrated in Box 10.3. On this day, the roles were *discussion director, literary luminary, connector,* and *word wizard.* After a few minutes of settling and joking, the groups began working. For the next 30 minutes, these 10-year-olds conversed with each other using open-ended questions and read passages to prove points or settle disagreements. They kept one eye on the clock to make sure everyone got a fair share of talking. Some of the books discussed in these literature circles were Katherine Paterson's *Bridge to Terabithia,* Daniel Keyes's *Flowers for Algernon,* H. G. Well's *War of the Worlds,* and Beverly Cleary's *Dear Mr. Henshaw.*

Let's explore further how a teacher can give children the opportunity to read and discuss literature in student-led groups by looking at how to share and what to share in literature circles.

Student-Led Literature Circles: How and What to Share.

Teachers whose students lead their own literature circles need to clearly explain that these groups help participants explore different perspectives that each person brings to the discussion. Children are to evaluate, critique, and revise their own individual responses in light of the perspectives their peers express. To clarify how to participate in literature circles, emphasize the differences between "school talk" and "outside-school talk." Through discussion, children will conclude that in most classroom interactions, the teacher asks questions and students answer. "Outside-school talk" is characterized by talking when someone has an idea to share; thus sometimes there is overlapping talk. Further, it is important to note that different members of the group informally assume responsibility for maintaining the conversation. In working with a diverse group of learners, action researcher Virginia Goatley (1997) formulated the following strategies for students participating in literature circles:

HOW TO SHARE

1. Maintain conversations without long pauses.

2. Respond to questions asked by other participants.

3. Elaborate your response to include your reason for the answer.

4. Challenge others' interpretations of the story.

Roles for Literature Circles

The roles rotate every time the group meets. Two students can have the same role in a group meeting.

REQUIRED ROLES

Discussion director	Has the official responsibility to think up some good discussion questions, convene the meeting, and solicit contributions from the other members.
Literary luminary/ passage master	Takes the readers back to memorable, important sections of the text and reads them aloud.
Connector	Takes everyone from the text world out into the real world, where the reader's experiences connect with the literature.
Illustrator	Provides a graphic, nonlinguistic response to the text.

OPTIONAL ROLES

Summarizer	Gives a quick (one- or two-minute) statement of the gist, key points, and highlights of the day's reading when the group convenes.
Vocabulary enricher/ word wizard	Marks down puzzling, interesting, or unfamiliar words encountered while reading, looks them up in a glossary or dictionary if need be, and points them out during literature circle.
Travel tracer	Tracks where the action takes place in the book. (This is useful in books in which the characters move around a lot and the scene changes frequently.)
Investigator/researcher	Digs up background information on any topic related to the book (e.g., geography, history, information about the author).

5. Clarify ideas, questions, answers, and responses.

6. Stay on task.

7. Include all group members in the discussion.

8. Take turns.

WHAT TO SHARE

1. Elaborate written responses to support discussion.

2. Formulate questions for clarification and interest.

3. Share personal responses, prior knowledge, personal experiences.

4. Use comprehension activities to construct meaning and support ideas.

5. Move beyond literal interpretations.

6. Discuss feelings about the text.

7. Relate the text to other books, movies, and shows.

8. Evaluate the text.

These can be modeled and explored in whole class discussions while watching a videotape of a literature circle in action. As children talk to each other in student-led literature circles, the teacher can walk from group to group, facilitating the use of these conversational skills. Sometimes the students' conversations will wander to topics other than the book. Sometimes members will be silent and need to be encouraged to participate. The teacher joins a group just long enough to help members identify the problem and solve it. Laura and Deb found that this modeling and analysis of the literature groups took up significant instructional time at the beginning of the school year; however, as students learned to assume responsibility for their own discussions, the need for modeling, discussion, and intervention diminished.

Another way to guide students to take responsibility for their own literature discussion is through the use of self-assessment (see Figure 10.1). Students complete the form, and then the teacher helps them see how to solve their own dilemmas and what they could do the next time the group meets (McMahon, 1997).

Adapting Literature Circles for the Primary Grades.

Daniels (1994) describes Angie Bynam's 32 second graders in a Chicago housing project who meet regularly in literature circles. Angie has a large number of picture books in multiple-copy sets that she received through a grant from the *Chicago Tribune*. She displays these titles in face-up stacks. When it is literature circle time, the children browse through these books, gradually forming groups of four or five. It takes about ten minutes for the children to look through the books, talk, and negotiate. Some children choose to reread old favorites; others venture into new ones. Each group then checks in at Angie's desk, where she gives role sheets to members of the group.

Within the group, children sit in a circle and take turns reading the book aloud to each other. Then they take a few moments to make some notes on their role sheet. The discussion director begins the conversation. As is true of literature circles with older children, the discussion is natural and spontaneous. The entire process of selecting of books, forming groups, reading, and discussing the books takes about 45 minutes. Daniels (1994) points out that few adults realize that children so young are capable of such child-directed activity.

Here are some guidelines that primary teachers can use to adjust literature circles to their students (Daniels, 1994, pp. 107–109):

◆ Primary literature circles should have a maximum of three or four participants.

◆ The books should be appropriate for emergent readers; that is, they should be picture books, wordless books, big books, or children-made books.

◆ The books are read aloud so that everyone comprehends the story.

◆ Figure 10.1

Self-Assessment in Literature Circle				
Name: _____ Book: _____				
Looking Back and Forward				
	DATE	DATE	DATE	DATE
Did I read the assigned pages?				
If not, I will read the pages during . . .				
Did I write in my log book before starting the literature circle?				
Did I complete my role sheet so that I was prepared for the literature circle?				
Did I share during literature circle?				
Did I listen to others?				
My literature circle was _____ today.				
Important comments:				

◆ The children record their responses in writing with invented spellings or in drawing.

◆ Even with their reading logs or notes, young children may need extra help remembering what they want to share. Some teachers have their students use large Post-it notes to mark their favorite parts of a book.

◆ Some primary teachers organize literature circles in which children read different books and meet in a literature circle to share different books.

◆ Primary literature circles may be organized so that children do not take different roles. In this case, all the children have the same two-part job: (1) to share something of their book using their writing and/or drawing log and bookmarks as cues and (2) to join in an open discussion.

◆ Primary literature circles tend to be one-meeting-per-book events owing to short books and short attention spans.

◆ The teacher is present during the primary literature circle, and just as with older children, the teacher's role is to facilitate the process, not direct it.

ENCOURAGING RESPONSES TO LITERATURE

After reading a book or seeing a movie, we may share the experience by briefly describing the plot. Most often, though, we tell how we felt and why. We point out something in the film or text and/or our personal histories that made us feel the way we did. We give examples from our lives and retell parts of the story. Yet when discussion shifts to the classroom, what usually happens? Often teachers ask questions to elicit a "right answer." Because we have often tried to evaluate what and how much students have understood about the text, teachers spend little time helping students explore, defend, or elaborate on ideas. In this section, we explore the need to lead students in classroom experiences in which they analyze their *personal* reactions to what they have read. Such action supports a **reader-response theory,** a theory that proclaims that *the reader is crucial to the construction of the literary experience.*

Louise Rosenblatt (1982) was one of the earliest proponents of a reader-response theory. She stated:

> Reading is a transaction, a two-way process, involving a reader and a text at a particular time under particular circumstances. . . . The reader, bringing past experiences of language and of the world to the task, sets up tentative notions of a subject, of some framework into which to fit the ideas as the words unfurl. If the subsequent words do not fit into the framework, it may have to be revised, thus opening up new and further possibilities for the text that follows. This implies a constant series of selections from the multiple possibilities offered by the text and their synthesis into an organized meaning. (p. 268)

Rosenblatt took her analysis of reading one step further into implications for classroom literature discussions. In any reading event, the reader adopts one of two stances: the *efferent stance* or the *aesthetic stance.*

When a reader approaches a reading event with an *efferent stance,* attention is focused on accumulating what is to be carried away from the reading. Readers using this stance may be seeking information, as in a textbook; they may want directions for action, as in a driver's manual; or they may be seeking a logical conclusion, as in a political article. In an *aesthetic stance,* however, readers shift their attention inward to center on *what is being cre-*

ated during the reading. Reading is driven by personal feelings, ideas, and attitudes that are stirred up by the text.

In most reading situations, there is both an efferent and an aesthetic response to the text. In reading a newspaper article, for example, a reader may take a predominantly efferent stance, but there may be an accompanying feeling of acceptance or doubt about the evidence cited. Although one stance usually predominates in most reading events, the text itself does not dictate a reader's stance. A text is chosen because it satisfies a reader's intended purpose. Rosenblatt's (1982) description of what happens in predominately aesthetic reading situations holds direct implications for bringing children and literature together.

> In aesthetic reading, we respond to the very story or poem that we are evoking during the transaction with the text. In order to shape the work, we draw on our reservoir of past experience with people and the world, our past inner linkage of words and things, our past encounters with spoken or written texts. We listen to the sound of the words in the inner ear; we lend our sensations, our emotions, our sense of being alive, to the new experience which, we feel, corresponds to the text. We participate in the story, we identify with the characters, we share their conflicts and their feelings. (p. 270)

Teachers create responsive environments in their classrooms by inviting children to react to literature through various symbol systems and modes of expression: art, movement, music, creative drama, talk, writing. Alternative forms of communication, such as art or movement, are especially appealing for students who may have difficulty expressing their feelings and thoughts in words. When children connect drawing with reading, for example, their artwork often helps them discover and shape their response to a story. Various visual arts media—pencil drawings, chalk, markers, crayons, paint, cardboard, paper construction—can be used to encourage responses to literature. In addition, students can design book jackets, mobiles, posters, or comic strips to capture the personal appeal or meaning that texts evoke.

Drawing, creative drama, and role playing often serve as springboards for oral and written responses. Children, especially at the primary level, gravitate naturally to drawing or dramatically performing a story before they talk or write about it.

Sparking Discussion with Book Talks

Whole class study of core books, reading workshops, and literature circles provide numerous opportunities for children to talk about books. Having **book talks** is a great way to evoke children's responses to literature. Here are some suggestions to spark book discussions:

1. Depending on the text, ask questions such as "Did anything especially interest you? Frighten you? Puzzle you? Seem familiar? Seem weird?" Have children tell which parts of the text caused these reactions, and have them compare these experiences to their real-life experiences (Rosenblatt, 1982).

2. Have children tell about the most memorable incident, character, or setting of the book. Then have them share with each other the specific parts of the text they recalled most clearly after hearing or reading a story (Benton, 1984).

3. Ask students to tell about the part of the story or character they remember most vividly. For example, "How did that character feel in this part of the story?" "Have you ever felt like this?" "Describe the situation you were in."

4. Read the opening of a story. Immediately afterward, tell students to jot down what was going on in their heads—pictures, memories, thoughts—during the reading. The jottings should be in a stream-of-consciousness style. Then share the responses and distinguish the common responses from the idiosyncratic ones. This shows students that reading has shared elements as well as highly individual ones and that sharing reactions is a valid way of talking about literature (Benton, 1984).

5. Ask students, "What pictures do you get in your mind of this character, setting, or event?" "If character X were to come through the door now, what would he or she look like?" "If you went to the place where the story occurred (i.e., setting), what would you see?" "Why do you say so?"

6. Ask, "What do you feel about this character? This setting? This event? Why?"

7. Ask, "What opinions do you have of this character? Setting? Incident? The way the story was told? Why?"

Book talks encourage children to go beyond a literal retelling of a story. They can be used in concert with a **free response** heuristic to help students discover and shape their responses to literature. A heuristic, by its nature, is any kind of a prompt that stimulates inquiry and speculation.

Engaging in Free Response

Free response encourages active involvement in reading and an integration of children's background knowledge with the selection's meaning. The technique generates a spirited discussion going far beyond the recall of information. Inferential, evaluative, and analytic thinking are the rule when children's free responses are discussed (Santa, Dailey, & Nelson, 1985).

Free response works well with literature selections that generate diversity of opinion or emotional reactions from readers. The first time a group of children is guided through free response, they hear a portion of a narrative and then stop to respond in writing. Lower-grade students, for example, might be given three minutes to respond in writing, and upper-grade students five minutes. Analyzing the structure of a particular story is useful in determining where to make the breaks for students to respond.

Mrs. Nowak used a free-response heuristic with her second-grade class with *Thomas' Snowsuit* by Robert Munsch and illustrated by Michael Martchenko. This story is a humorous treatment of power struggles between Thomas, who does not want to wear his new snowsuit, and his mother. The power struggle concerning whether he should wear his snowsuit or not continues with his teacher and the principal at school.

Mrs. Nowak introduced the story to her class by asking if the children could recall not wanting to wear some clothing they were supposed to wear. A lively discussion ensued. Then Mrs. Nowak asked what they thought *Thomas' Snowsuit* would be about, and the children had no difficulty predicting that Thomas didn't want to wear his snowsuit. Mrs. Nowak then began reading.

> One day Thomas' mother bought him a nice new brown snowsuit. When Thomas saw that snowsuit, he said, "That is the ugliest thing I have ever seen in my life. If you think I am going to wear that ugly snowsuit, you are crazy!"
>
> Thomas' mother said, "We will see about that."
>
> The next day, when it was time to go to school, the mother said, "Thomas, please put on your snowsuit," and Thomas said, "NNNNNO."

Mrs. Nowak stopped reading and asked her students to write down their reactions to what they had just heard. She emphasized that "any thought related to the story is correct; there are no wrong responses." After several segments of reading and responding, Mrs. Nowak led a discussion in which the children shared their free responses. When she asked their reactions to Thomas's telling his mother, "NNNNNO," Jeremy said, "He's going to get into trouble!" Sue said, "I wouldn't want to wear an old brown snowsuit, either." After each response, Mrs. Nowak probed, "Why do you think so?" Mrs. Nowak remained impartial, and the children's responses became a catalyst for discussion.

When students are freely responding independently, Santa and colleagues (1985) recommend that teachers develop with their students criteria for free response, which are then displayed in the classroom.

Things that I like or dislike about a character or event.

Questions about things I do not understand.

Comments about what I think an unfamiliar word might mean.

Events from my life that come to mind as I read.

Situations or events with which I do not agree.

Can I make predictions? What will happen next? Is the author giving me a clue here?

These heuristic situations prompt students to view reading as a problem-solving activity. As such, free response is easily incorporated into the use of reading journals that help students explore and clarify their responses to text. Various kinds of reading journals, as we explored in Chapter 9, encourage children to solve problems as they respond to meaning during reading. Response journals, in particular, invite children to respond to literature freely and personally. Their responses vary from monitoring understanding to plot and character involvement to literary evaluation.

Exploring Response Options in Literature Journals

Literature journals provide children with the freedom to express their feelings and thoughts about literary texts. The potential for students to do more than summarize the text is omnipresent when they are invited to write freely as they engage in reading. Research on the content of literature journals shows that readers often expand their ways of thinking about a text beyond retelling when they write journal entries or literary letters on a regular basis (Hancock, 1993a, 1993b; Wells, 1993).

Teachers can enhance the variety of reader responses by making children aware of the various options for responding in a literature journal. As Hancock (1993a) explains, "The classroom teacher plays a vital role in the expansion and enrichment of student response to literature. The teacher serves as a catalyst for encouraging exploration [of response options]. . . . Striving to awaken new modes of response within the reader is the responsibility of the teacher in the role of facilitator and response guide" (p. 470).

Hancock (1993b) explores the journal responses of sixth-grade students to several award-winning books: *Hatchet* (Paulsen, 1987), *One-Eyed Cat* (Fox, 1984), *The Great Gilly Hopkins* (Paterson, 1978), and *The Night Swimmers* (Byars, 1980). As a result of her analysis of the content of the students' literature journals, Hancock identified three categories of response: *personal meaning-making, character and plot involvement,* and *literary evaluation.* Table 10.2 outlines response options available to students in these three categories.

Literature journals give children the freedom to express their thoughts and feelings about literary texts.

Options for personal meaning-making encourage students to make sense of the emerging plot and characters. Journal entries might reflect the student's attempts to monitor understanding of the story; make inferences about characters; make, validate, modify, or invalidate predictions about the plot; and express wonder or confusion by asking questions or raising uncertainties.

Options for character and plot responses engage students in character identification, character assessment, and personal involvement in the unfolding events of the story. For example, some students will identify strongly with the goals and problems associated with the main character of the story; they put themselves in the character's shoes. As a result, the reader may express a strong sense of empathy for the character's predicament. Readers will also judge the actions of character within the framework of their own moral standards and value systems. Moreover, students' responses suggest that they become personally involved in the story, expressing satisfaction or dissatisfaction as they become caught up in the plot.

Finally, readers take on the role of literary critic as they evaluate authors or make comparisons with other books that they have read.

A crucial step in becoming a catalyst for student response is to share guidelines, such as those suggested in Chapter 9, for writing in literature journals. In the guidelines, establish an environment for response by encouraging students to react freely and informally without fear of making mechanical writing errors. Also suggest different response options as outlined in Table 10.1.

In addition, one of the most effective ways to extend response options is to state a dialogue with students in their journals. A teacher's comments in response to a journal entry will help students reexamine their responses to the text. When responding to journal entries, it is best to be nonjudgmental, encouraging, and thought-provoking. Once a supportive comment is written, the teacher may decide to direct a child toward an unexplored area of response. Hancock (1993a) describes how Michael wrote many responses (about 40 percent) relating why he did or did not like the book he was reading. He was mainly using his journal as a place to express his *literary evaluations*. Here is one such entry:

> This is getting real boring because the author is writing so much about one thing. The author keeps going back to the same thing "Mistakes" this is getting boring.

His teacher wrote back the following comments:

> I really appreciate your efforts to critique *Hatchet*. It seems that you are a bit disillusioned with some of Brian's actions. You've been attributing that dissatisfaction to the author. Have you thought of sharing your advice with Brian?
> Although he can't really hear you, your suggestions for plot changes may be directed to the main character as well as to the author. You may even find your involvement in the book will increase if you feel you can talk to Brian. Give this a try and see if you feel comfortable with this mode of response. (p. 472)

Interactive comments such as these help students to refocus and redirect their responses to a literary text; they pave the way to personal meaning-making.

TABLE 10.1

Response Options for Literature Journals

Response Option	Example
	PERSONAL MEANING-MAKING
Monitoring understanding	In this story, Brian has divorced parents. *(Hatchet)* Ned's really taking the gun being put away really hard. *(One-Eyed Cat)* Oh, now I get it. The door is too heavy for the animals to open. *(Hatchet)* These past few pages show how one lie can lead to a whole series of lies. *(One-Eyed Cat)*)
Making inferences	I think Gilly is jealous of W.E. because Trotter loves him. *(The Great Gilly Hopkins)* Brian must be very very hungry to eat a raw egg. *(Hatchet)* Ned probably doesn't mean he wants the cat to die. *(One-Eyed Cat)* Retta seems a little like Gilly Hopkins—rebellious and different. *(The Night Swimmers)*
Making predictions	I think the Secret was his mom's dating another man. *(Hatchet)* I was right about the Secret! *(Hatchet)* I bet Gilly's mother won't show up. *(The Great Gilly Hopkins)* I didn't think she'd steal the money. *(The Great Gilly Hopkins)*
Expressing wonder or confusion	I wonder if Gilly is so mean because she wasn't brought up by her own mother. *(The Great Gilly Hopkins)* The author is telling so many things . . . I got lost on p. 28. *(Hatchet)* Is that cat supposed to be playing the role of some sort of sign? *(One-Eyed Cat)* Bowlwater plant? Are these people really cheap or what? TV Ping Pong? *(The Night Swimmers)*

TABLE 10.1 CONTINUED

CHARACTER AND PLOT INVOLVEMENT

Character identification	If I were Ned, I'd want to get the thought out of my head. *(One-Eyed Cat)* Poor Gilly. I guess that's the way it is if you're a foster kid. *(The Great Gilly Hopkins)* Johnny is like my brother. Roy is like my sister. I'm like Retta, not so bossy. *(The Night Swimmers)* He shouldn't waste time waiting for the searchers: he should get food. *(Hatchet)*
Character assessment	Brian is stupid for ripping a $20 bill. *(Hatchet)* It's really mean of Gilly to use W.E. in a plan to run away. *(The Great Gilly Hopkins)* I don't think I like Mrs. Scallop. She is sort of mean and has crazy ideas like that Ned's mother got sick because Ned was born. *(One-Eyed Cat)* Brian is getting better and having less self-pity on himself. *(Hatchet)*
Story involvement	Eyes rolling back in his head until it is white showing. How gross! *(Hatchet)* The scenery sounds so pretty. *(One-Eyed Cat)* I wish Ned hadn't shot that poor cat. He did though. *(One-Eyed Cat)* I can't wait to get on with my reading. I hope Shorty asks Brendelle to marry him. *(The Night Swimmers)*

LITERARY EVALUATION

Literary criticism	These were boring pages because all they talked about were fish. *(Hatchet)* I don't think the author should have Gilly use swear words. *(The Great Gilly Hopkins)* I like this author because she has some suspense like the spy. *(The Night Swimmers)* This is fun reading this part because it's like *My Side of the Mountain*. *(Hatchet)*

Source: Based on "Exploring and Extending Personal Response Through Literature Journals," by Marjorie R. Hancock, *The Reading Teacher, 46*, pp. 466–474. Copyright © 1993 the International Reading Association.

SUMMARY

Capturing children's interest and bringing youngsters together in a literate community, where they can be immersed in books, is a top priority of most reading and language arts teachers. In this chapter, we have offered a variety of ways for teachers to develop students who will choose to read.

As children learn to work together in a community of readers and writers, they talk over their experiences with books and recommend books to each other. Teachers, in turn, facilitate an environment supportive of literature by carefully structuring the classroom, selecting a collection of books, and creating settings and predictable routines. Literature-based reading programs, hooking students on books, storytelling, and classroom libraries all assist children in reading more both in and out of the classroom.

Organizing for literature-based instruction revolves around (1) studies of core books (a collection at each grade level judged to be age-appropriate and of high quality), (2) literature units (around a theme), (3) reading workshops (integrating language arts and literature in responding and sharing), and (4) literature circles (which may be student-led).

We explored strategies for responding to literature, such as book talks, conferences, and response journals, which encourage children to extend their individual thoughts and feelings about books they read through a variety of response options. Finally, we describe how teachers themselves gain confidence and experience as readers and writers through book groups.

TEACHER-ACTION RESEARCHER

1. Think of a child or adolescent whom you would characterize as an avid reader. (Avid readers are enthusiastic about books, empathize with characters, and talk about books with their friends, sharing their reactions and feelings.) Develop a profile of the avid reader you selected. Describe how this child or adolescent exhibits behaviors associated with avid readers. Discuss ways in which you could help this reader further develop these habits and behaviors.

2. Interview several elementary or middle school librarians or media center directors. In what ways do they use technology to support the reading development of children and assist the classroom teacher? Compile their ideas, summarizing them, and report your findings to the class.

3. Work with a group of children and guide them in dramatizing a story after they have read it or heard it read aloud. The selection could be from either a basal reader or a trade book.

4. Collaborate with a fellow student or a classroom teacher to set up a book display to interest children, including those with limited English proficiency, in reading. Decide on a theme and ways to introduce the children to books related to that theme. If possible, observe what happens in the classroom and talk with the teacher about the children's use of the display. Or compile a list of things you would expect to see and questions you would like to have the classroom teacher answer.

5. Prepare a bibliography of children's literature that would be appropriate for a particular grade level's classroom library. Use the school librarian, classroom teachers' recommendations, and bibliographies from journals such as *Language Arts* and *The Reading Teacher* as resources. What books would be the core of the library? What books could be added over time? Include annotations that would explain why each book was chosen. For example, which books would be useful in content area instruction? Which books would help teach letter-sound correspondence?

KEY TERMS

book talks
community of readers
core books
dialogue journals
free response

literature circles
literature journals
literature-based
   reading program
literature units

reader-response
   theory
reading workshops

CHAPTER

11

Basal Readers
and Instructional
Materials

Chapter Overview

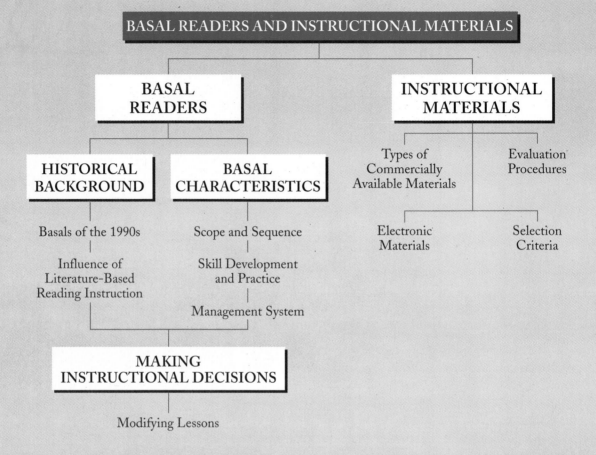

BASAL READERS AND INSTRUCTIONAL MATERIALS

BASAL READERS

HISTORICAL BACKGROUND

Basals of the 1990s

Influence of Literature-Based Reading Instruction

BASAL CHARACTERISTICS

Scope and Sequence

Skill Development and Practice

Management System

MAKING INSTRUCTIONAL DECISIONS

Modifying Lessons

INSTRUCTIONAL MATERIALS

Types of Commercially Available Materials

Electronic Materials

Evaluation Procedures

Selection Criteria

Between the Lines

In this chapter, you will discover:

♦ The history of basal reading programs

♦ What the authors of three major reading programs say about recent trends such as literature-based instruction

♦ An overview of the terminology, components, and characteristics of basal reading programs

♦ How types of instructional decisions and reading materials relate to belief systems

Liz jumped at the chance to be on the selection committee. She wanted to be part of the venture because she was trying to break away from some old practices and implement some of the newer ideas of the whole language, literature approach to reading. Liz was anxious to see what the publishers were offering. "We used an evaluation form that asked questions about the program's philosophy, goals, instructional program, and so on. At first I was overwhelmed by the comprehensiveness, not just of the contents of the materials, but of the descriptions of the components! During one of our meetings we were debating whether the program was child-centered or teacher-centered, literature-based or skills-based. We all stopped and looked at each other and then answered in unison, 'Yes!' As the laughter subsided, I remember feeling that somehow a lot of the pressure was gone. At least for me, I finally realized that I needed to rely on my beliefs as an experienced teacher. I just concentrated on how I thought my first graders and I would like and use this series. The stories were often about animals, a motivating topic for my 6- and 7-year-olds. The stories represented different cultures and refrained from stereotyping. The language sounded whimsical and natural to the ears of first graders. The teacher's guide looked more like a resource book with a variety of activities. It wouldn't meet the needs of all my students; fortunately, I share a planning time with the special education teacher who will help me modify some objectives. If anything, working on the committee made me realize that *I* still have to make choices and decisions about how to use the new materials in my classroom. But the colorful illustrations, bright covers, and authentic literature in our new reading series certainly make my job a lot more pleasant."

Basal reading programs, also known as reading or language arts programs, are the most popular materials used in reading instruction in this country. Elementary students at all grade levels read stories from big books, little books, and anthologies and write in accompanying journals. While the basal of old is disappearing as school systems purchase new materials, the new reading programs are still important to understanding and teaching reading. Many teachers who are becoming increasingly knowledgeable about, comfortable with, and adept at integrating trade books (fact and fiction) into the overall reading program are also using basal reading anthologies on a daily basis. Frequently, selection committees formed by school districts about to adopt a new reading series include teachers representing various grade levels.

In spite of continuing popular support for reading series as the traditional method of teaching reading by teachers and administrators, these "programs have been positioned at the center of the controversy over *best* methods" for the past several decades, according to James Hoffman and his fellow researchers (1998, p. 168). They studied issues relating to basals and teaching practices and reported that the new basals of the 1990s have had an impact that sets them apart from previous basal series. Teachers, much like Liz on the selection committee, viewed the new literature-based programs as more engaging; the quality literature stretched the range of teaching and learning possibilities. While some teachers were more successful than others at taking advantage of new situations, few, if any, of the teachers in the study were blindly following teacher's guides. Teachers faced problems in finding instructional solutions for less skilled readers; they needed support, but there was virtually no professional development offered them.

Knowing and understanding how these sets of materials can support students' literacy development is essential for prospective and veteran teachers, given the "staying power" of basal reading instruction in our schools. Teachers need to assess which educational opportunities are best offered by the reading series and then look for other reading and skill activities without pressure about students' performance on state proficiency and other standardized tests. The chapter overview depicts how the key concepts connected to basal reading and instructional materials relate to each other.

Teachers, according to a recent survey by Baumann and Heubach (1996), are for the most part "discriminating consumers who view basal readers as just one instructional tool available to them as they plan literacy lessons" (p. 522). Teachers in today's classrooms believe that they have flexibility in selecting and using materials and in modifying ideas from the teacher's guides. Nevertheless, in order to do this in an effective, efficient, and professional manner, teachers will continue to benefit from assistance in (1) judging what reading material should be assigned and when supplementary materials are needed; (2) determining which basal teacher's guide suggestions should be omitted, followed, or modified; and (3) evaluating student responses to questions (Barr & Sadow, 1989).

We devote the last section of this chapter to an analysis of instructional materials, beginning with the types of materials available. We will determine how different types of materials correspond to our belief systems. Finally, we'll look into several ways of evaluating and selecting commercial materials for classroom use.

Historical Background

Young newspaper readers in the greater Cleveland area were treated to a historical tour of their basal reading books in a news article written especially for elementary-age students and featuring "McGuffey and His Readers." Pictures of William McGuffey, his birthplace, and his writing desk accompanied an actual page reproduction with a story about Bess and her two goats from Lesson 33 in the *McGuffey Primer*, the very first book in a series used for reading instruction.

Here's how basal readers were described in the news article so that children could understand what they are all about.

There are many different kinds of basal texts.

How and when words are introduced are carefully planned by experts.

The books come in a series.

The words and stories get longer and harder as the child moves from one level to the next.

Moreover, children were informed that McGuffey first published his series in 1836 and that the readers began with the *Primer* and ended with the *Sixth Reader*. As far as the content of the basal readers was concerned, stories were about everyday life and the rewards of good behavior. Does the content sound somewhat familiar? It should. According to a

◆ FIGURE 11.1   *Page from The Appelton Reader (1878)*

28 *SECOND READER.*	*SECOND READER.* **29**

28   *SECOND READER.*

LESSON XV.

drĕss	hĕard	ŭn′-ele	her-sĕlf′
knĭfe	wĭshęd	lăd′-der	stō′-ries
wrŏng	strănge	fĭn′-ġer	lŏŏk′-ing

WILLIE'S STORY.

One day, when Willie had been reading in his new book, his mother wished him to tell her what he had read in it, and Willie said :

"I read about a little girl who wanted to do just as she liked for one whole day.

"Her mother said she could. So the little girl cut her own bread and butter; but she let the knife slip, and cut her finger.

"Then she ate so much candy that she made herself sick. Then she put on her prettiest dress to play in the garden, and tore it.

"And then she went up a ladder, which her mother never would let her climb, and when she was up very high she heard a noise in the garden.

"It was the dog barking at a strange cat, mamma; and while the little girl was looking around to see what it was, she put her foot on the wrong part of the ladder.

"I mean, mamma, she only put her toe on the round; so her foot slipped, and she fell, and was almost killed.

"That was the end of her day of doing just as she liked."

Write a sentence having in it the word knife.
Write a sentence having in it the word ladder.

study by Aaron and Anderson (1981), a remarkable number of values appearing in the readers of the early 1900s appeared in the 1970s as well. Although the stories had changed, apparently "the same virtues are there waiting to be taught" (p. 312).

Just as the young Cleveland readers found insightful differences and similarities between their reading material today and the *McGuffey Readers,* teachers also benefit from such comparisons. A page from an 1878 reader is shown in Figure 11.1.

1683: A Strong Bottom-Up Approach

The New England Primer, published for American colonists in the late 1600s, followed a strong bottom-up model of instruction. The alphabet was taught first; then vowels, consonants, double letters, italics, capitals, syllables, and so on were presented for instruction, in that order. There was, however, no such thing as a controlled vocabulary. Words were not introduced systematically in basal readers until the mid-1800s. Colonial children might meet anywhere from 20 to 100 new words on one page!

By the mid-1800s, the word method, silent reading, and reading to get information from content were introduced in basals. The classics, fairy tales, and literature by American authors became the first supplementary reading materials. Colored pictures, subjects appealing to children's interests, and the teacher's manual had all been introduced by the 1920s. It was then that the work pad was used for seatwork and skills practice in grades 1 through 3.

Basal Readers as We Knew Them

The reading series used in schools at the dawn of the twenty-first century are a far cry, in both appearance and substance, from the first readers. Nevertheless, current reading books retain some of the features that were once innovative. The new basal reading series have grown noticeably in size and price. Though not prescribing the bottom-up teaching approach that was used in the 1600s, today's teacher's manual presents a dilemma that is at the same time intriguing, interesting, and a bit daunting: It often purports to include *everything* that any teacher will ever need to teach reading. As Liz discovered during her stint on the selection committee, the new basal can be downright overwhelming.

Publishing companies began to expand and add new components or features to their basal reading programs around 1925. The preprimer, for example, was added to the basal program to introduce beginning readers to the series and build a beginning reading vocabulary (i.e., words recognized on sight). Inside illustrations and outside covers also became increasingly colorful. Word lists such as Thorndike's became the standard for choosing readers' vocabulary.

As the major author for the Scott, Foresman program, William S. Gray was probably responsible for much of the structure associated with the reading instruction that we experienced as children. Workbooks accompanied our reader. First we worked on skills; then we read for enjoyment. Each book had a different title, and much of the story content was supposed to be "realistic" narrative. Whether the content was or is realistic is an issue both publishers and classroom teachers continue to debate.

As the concept of reading readiness became more popular, teacher's manuals began adding more detail, and readiness books provided opportunities to practice prerequisite skills. One preprimer proliferated into two, three, or even four preprimers.

Instruction in basal reading programs depended in part on a strict adherence to the scope and sequence of reading skills (see Figure 11.2 for a sample from a recent program). The terminology evolved from the 1948 *Ginn Basic Reader,* the objective of which was to provide a *vertical* arrangement of skill development and to ensure continuity in skill development (Smith, 1965, p. 285). Teacher's editions were keyed to the children's books, and diagnostic and achievement tests such as those in the *Sheldon Basic Reading Series* were developed. Basal reading programs had become more sophisticated and, to many teachers, unwieldy. How would they manage the basal reading program?

Sample Page from Program Scope and Sequence

Anthologies: A-F = Student Anthologies, K = Kindergarten Unit
Ancillaries: PR = Practice Book, PJ = Project Book Guide, ILAB = Integrated Language Activity Book, ILTRB = Integrated Language Teacher's Resource Book, BR = Bridge, SPPB = Spelling and Phonics Practice, SPB = Spelling Practice, MH = Multicultural Handbook, IT = Instructional Transparency, GOT = Graphic Organizer Transparency

Use Phonics

	K	1	2
Letter/sound relationships	**Teacher's Guide** **K1•**14, 16, 19, 46–47, 72; **K2•**18–19, 46–47, 72, 73; **K3•**18–19, 44–45, 70–71, 72–73; **K4•**17, 38–39, 40–41, 42–43, 46, 72–73, 76; **K5•**12, 14–15, 38, 42, 44–45, 46–47, 72–73; **K6•**18–19, 44–45, 72–73; **K7•**18–19, 20–21, 22–23, 48–49, 55, 74; **K8•**15, 18–19, 20–21, 24, 47, 49, 70, 72–73, 74	**Teacher's Guide** **A•**T45, T46, T49; **B•**12, 17, 64; **C•**14, 20, 60, 62, 71, 72, 82, 89, 104; **D•**40; **F•**T27, T38, T41, T42, T52–T53, 14, 71, 98 **Ancillaries** **PR•**11–12, 181–182; **PJ•**A5, A6, B3, C3, C4, F5, F8	**Teacher's Guide** **A•**46, 88, 117c–d; **B•**21; **C•**56, 72, 147 **Ancillaries** **PR•**39; **PJ•**F7
Consonants (initial, medial, final)		**Teacher's Guide** **A•**T13, T15, T18–T19, T29, T30, T34–T35, T44, T47, T52–T53, 12, 14, 17h, 19, 21, 26, 29, 37, 43h, 59h; **B•**T60–T61, T62–T63, 22, 44, 48, 61h, 68, 77e–f, 77g–h, 94, 96, 121h; **C•**T57, 12, 35h, 39, 40; **D•**39, 100; **E•**54, 114; **F•**T36, 119g–h, 119i–j **Ancillaries** **PR•**10, 15, 19, 25–26, 27, 41, 45–46, 47, 59, 66, 73, 220–221; **SPPB•**7, 10, 38	**Teacher's Guide** **A•**22, 31e–f, 31g–h, 37, 55h, 103e–f, 103g, 110, 117e–f, 117g; **B•**22, 39h; **C•**63, **D•**88, 106; **E•**59, 67; **F•**59, 105 **Ancillaries** **PR•**6–7, 8, 15, 33–34, 40–41, 58; **SPPB•**4–5, 12–13, 14–15
Consonant blends (initial, medial, final)		**Teacher's Guide** **D•**13, 45e–f, 45g–h, 56, 77h, 119e–f, 119g–h; **E•**T43, T46, T47, 16, 20, 33e–f, 33g–h, 37, 42, 60, 61h, 98, 101e–f, 101g–h, 135e–f, 135g–h; **F•**T44, 119j **Ancillaries** **PR•**112–113, 120, 132–133, 145–146, 161, 170–171, 176–177, 222; **SPPB•**21, 24, 26, 30, 31	**Teacher's Guide** **A•**58, 85h; **B•**10, 39e–f, 39g, 45, 54, 65e–f, 65g, 71, 81h, 86, 97h, 111e–f, 111g, 117e–f, 117g; **C•**22, 29h, 46, 65h, 68, 113; **D•**27h, 58; **E•**11 **Ancillaries** **PR•**27, 56–57, 60–61, 70, 77, 82–83, 89–90, 101, 113, 158; **SPPB•**18–19, 20–21, 26–27, 28–29
Consonant digraphs (initial, medial, final)		**Teacher's Guide** **D•**33e–f, 33g–h, 36, 119h; **E•**86, 95g–h, 95i–j; **F•**23, 53, 81h, 86 **Ancillaries** **PR•**106–107, 134, 164–165, 166, 203; **SPPB•**20, 29	**Teacher's Guide** **A•**17, 92; **B•**31, 78, 81e–f, 81g, 94, 97e–f, 97g, 101, 111e–f, 111g–h, 117h; **C•**53h; **D•**21, 75; **E•**106; **F•**22 **Ancillaries** **PR•**68–69, 75–76, 82–83, 84, 91, 105; **BR•**83; **SPPB•**22–23, 24–25, 26–27

Source: From *Celebrate Reading! Teacher's Guide, Grade 3.* Copyright © 1997. Used by permission of Addison–Wesley Educational Publishers.

Until the 1960s, books in reading series were arranged according to grade placement. Grades evolved into levels (anywhere from 15 to 20) or, as it became known, the management system. By the 1970s, teachers and curriculum committees in general sought clarification about levels in relation to grades. As a result, publishers used the term *level* and cross-referenced this with its traditional grade equivalent. Figure 11.3 shows a listing of the various anthologies and trade books in Level 3A from Scott, Foresman (1997).

Because there were now more than one level (and book) per grade, guidelines for determining the book level for pupils entering the program were suggested. These included pupil placement tests and an informal tryout of a book using a 100-word selection.

Management systems became necessary when publishers significantly overhauled their reading series in the 1970s. The majority of textbook publishers added new components, particularly in the area of assessment, such as pre- and postskill tests, section tests, and end-of-book tests.

The Dick, Jane, Jerry, and Alice characters that some of us grew up with in the 1950s, 1960s, and 1970s are now part of the past. The term *basal* itself may soon follow suit. Today's new basals are known as *integrated reading* or *language programs* and are *literature-based,* a term for a trend that took hold in the mid-1990s.

Basal Programs of the 1990s

The basal reading programs of the 1990s are used in close to 90 percent of elementary classrooms in the United States. The latest trends have now been incorporated into most reading programs sold by various publishers. Goals emphasize the connectedness of the language arts, the importance of meaning-making, and the immersion of children in literature. Thinking, comprehension, and study skills are featured and are often integrated with other subjects, such as music, science, and social studies. Whole language is included as part of the program philosophy, as is skill instruction, which is often done in the form of strategy lessons. More programs are organized thematically and contain stories by well-known children's authors and nonfiction selections. As Johnson (1998) describes it, "Anthologies of predictable literature have replaced preprimers, and the vocabulary control of the past is hardly evident. Word recognition is supported by the illustrations, by patterned repetitive language, by rhythm and rhyme, and by the child's ability to anticipate and quickly memorize the language" (p. 668).

To get an "inside look" at these trends as they influenced the newer literature-based basal reading series of the mid-1990s, see the Viewpoint featured in Box 11.1, in which three authors—Dr. Patricia Edwards, Dr. Jeanne Paratore, and Dr. Lyndon Searfoss—respond to questions about changes, criticisms, and instructional impact of basals used in many schools today.

Most reading series on the market today attempt to satisfy every consumer's appetite when it comes to reading instruction. In order to do that, publishing companies, as the authors quoted in Box 11.1 point out, take great care to include major components. There are certain concepts and terms germane to basal reading instruction; some would say it's like a language of its own. Figure 11.4 presents definitions that should prove helpful in understanding some key concepts.

◆ FIGURE 11.3   Literature in Level 3A (Grade 3)

Literature

A diversity of genres and award-winning selections

A
Pig Tales

Miss Nelson Is Missing!
Mystery by Harry Allard
Illustrations by James Marshall
● Children's Choice
● California Young Reader Medal

Esmeralda and the Pet Parade
Realistic fiction by Cecile Schoberle

Anansi and the Moss-Covered Rock
Animal fantasy retold by Eric A. Kimmel
Illustrations by Janet Stevens

Chicken Little
Animal fantasy by Steven Kellogg
● Children's Choice

Harvey, the Foolish Pig
Folk tale retold by Dick Gackenbach

King Wacky
Fantasy by Dick Gackenbach
● Children's Choice

Featured Poets
Jack Prelutsky, Arnold Lobel

Trade Books
The Cactus Flower Bakery
Animal fantasy by Harry Allard
● Children's Choice Author

Play Ball, Amelia Bedelia
Humorous fiction by Peggy Parish

B
If You Meet a Dragon

Chin Chiang and the Dragon's Dance
Realistic fiction by Ian Wallace
■ Notable Social Studies Trade Book

**The Knight Who Was Afraid
of the Dark**
Humorous fiction by Barbara Shook Hazen
Illustrations by Tony Ross
■ Children's Choice

**A World of Fables from India, China,
America, and Ancient Greece**
Fables retold by Nancy DeRoin, Demi, Anne Terry
White, and John Bierhorst

City Mouse and Country Mouse
Aesop's fable retold as a play by Jane Buxton

Thinking Big
Narrative nonfiction by Susan Kuklin
■ Outstanding Science Trade Book

The Boy and the Ghost
Folk tale by Robert D. San Souci
Illustrations by Brian Pinkney
■ Children's Choice

If You Say So, Claude
Tall tale by Joan Lowery Nixon
Illustrations by Lorinda Bryan Cauley
● Children's Choice

Featured Poets
Alexander Resnikoff, Norma Farber, Frank Asch

Trade Books
Fables
Fables by Arnold Lobel
◀ Caldecott Medal
● ALA Notable Book

What's Cooking, Jenny Archer?
Realistic fiction by Ellen Conford
■ Parents' Choice Author

C
How Many Toes Does
a Fish Have?

Class Clown
Realistic fiction by Johanna Hurwitz
■ Children's Choice
※ School Library Journal Best Book

Louella's Song
Realistic fiction by Eloise Greenfield
Illustrations by Jan Spivey Gilchrist
● Coretta Scott King Award Author
● Coretta Scott King Award Illustrator

Best Enemies
Realistic fiction by Kathleen Leverich
■ Children's Choice

Tacky the Penguin
Animal fantasy by Helen Lester
Illustrations by Lynn Munsinger
■ Children's Choice

Old Henry
Narrative poem by Joan W. Blos
Illustrations by Stephen Gammell
※ Notable Social Studies Trade Book

Chang's Paper Pony
Historical fiction by Eleanor Coerr
● Library of Congress Children's Book of the Year

The Great Flamingo Roundup
Expository nonfiction by Claire Miller

**Kate Shelley and the
Midnight Express**
Historical fiction by Margaret K. Wetterer
※ Notable Social Studies Trade Book

Featured Poet
Joan W. Blos

Trade Books
**She Come Bringing Me That
Little Baby Girl**
Realistic fiction by Eloise Greenfield
■ Children's Choice

The Show-and-Tell War
Realistic fiction by Janice Lee Smith
● Children's Choice

BOX 11.1   VIEWPOINT

A Conversation with Three Authors

Patricia A. Edwards, Jeanne R. Paratore, and Lyndon W. Searfoss, three authors of basal reading series popular in schools in the mid–1990s, shared their viewpoints on basal reading instruction with us. Edwards, a professor at Michigan State University, coauthored the Scott Foresman Reading Series. Paratore, a professor at Boston University, coauthored the Silver Burdett and Ginn Reading Series. Searfoss, a professor at Arizona State University, coauthored the D.C. Heath and Company Reading Series.

ON THE BIGGEST CHANGE IN BASAL MATERIALS IN THE PAST FIVE YEARS

SEARFOSS: The biggest change in basal materials is represented by respect for the teacher as a decision maker. Given an array of choices, how do teachers make decisions? Thematic units, for example, are great, but teachers who have only several hours of built-in inservice a year have very little time to plan them. For example, there is a need to learn how to incorporate reading and writing into instruction across the curriculum. Well-written teacher's manuals have traditionally been the only inservice many teachers receive in a new reading program.

Lyndon Searfoss . . . We have a new day for the basal in classrooms.

PARATORE: There have been several important changes over the past five years: (1) a shift from edited to unedited literature; (2) integration of language arts, particularly writing; (3) an emphasis on teacher and student choices; and (4) numerous changes in assessment, including the inclusion of portfolios and process-based tests. Although it's fair to say that none of these changes has been complete or fully achieved, in each there have been important steps forward.

EDWARDS: Basals have tried to incorporate authentic literature that reflects the multiple student populations. Basal companies have listened to the whole language movement. Entertaining is not teaching. There is a continuing need for balancing. Teachers need control of theory in order to be decision makers. This has been emphasized in the past five years.

Box 11.1 CONTINUED

ON THE CRITICISM THAT PACKAGING AND TERMINOLOGY HAVE CHANGED, ESPECIALLY IN RELATION TO WHOLE LANGUAGE, BUT THE CONTENT OF BASAL MATERIALS HAS NOT

SEARFOSS: This criticism is not valid. If you watch teachers teach and students learn in to-day's classrooms, with a basal based on literature, you do not see or hear the same dialogue you heard ten years ago. There is interaction between and among teachers and students, cooperative learning, and reading and writing for genuine purposes. Coupled with strategy instruction that shows kids how to *use* skills, we have a new day for the basal in classrooms.

EDWARDS: Newly trained teachers are not prepared to make all decisions about instruction. They need structure. Young teachers graduating from college with approximately three courses in reading and language arts need assistance when they are first teaching. They typically have been placed in difficult situations. For example, a new first-grade teacher whom I had worked with was having tremendous difficulty. I went to her school and met with her principal and supervisor, saying, "You need to give Sarah some support." Basal instruction is one way to provide support for teachers who can then make connections.

Patricia Edwards . . . When you're teaching in somebody else's village, what do you need to know?

PARATORE: I don't believe that it is at all valid. There have been some important changes, driven by improved understandings about literacy learning. The shift to unedited text, the availability and integration of trade books with the anthology, emphasis on coreading and rereading of text, and emphasis on teacher and student choices are changes in both materials and in practices that grow out of what some have termed the whole language movement. Other aspects long associated with basal reading programs remain. We have intentionally and deliberately kept a strong instructional component in the basal reading program in both phonics and comprehension because of the belief among the team of authors that at least some children will fail to become successful readers without such instruction.

ON THE MOST IMPORTANT THING A PRESERVICE OR BEGINNING TEACHER NEEDS TO KNOW ABOUT BASAL INSTRUCTION

PARATORE: Perhaps one of the greatest misconceptions about basal readers is that they represent *the* reading program. I don't believe that's the case. Instead, I view the

(Continued)

Box 11.1 CONTINUED

basal as one component of a total program. A beginning teacher should come to the classroom with a basic instructional plan in mind and view the basal reader as one means for operationalizing that plan. As she or he pages through the many suggestions in the teacher's editions, decisions must be made about which parts of the lesson plan fit into the teacher's instructional design and which parts do not; what pieces meet the needs of particular students and which ones do not; which elements link particularly well to the focus in other areas of the curriculum, and so on. The strength of the basal reading program is in its range of options. The weakness is in the suggestion that everything in the teacher's edition is of equal importance for every child.

Jeanne Paratore . . . Children should read the best of children's literature.

EDWARDS: Don't take any one piece of material as the "Bible." Look at the plan, the structure provided, the scope, the sequence. Then think about your region of the country, your students. Draw from literature that would best fit their needs. You can adapt, reconstruct for localized needs. Ask, "What do I—and they—need to know?"

SEARFOSS: New teachers need a good background in children's and adolescent literature. To expect teachers to use literature to drive instruction is realistic; to ask teachers with limited knowledge of literature for children and adolescents to do so is unrealistic.

ON THE MOST IMPORTANT THING AN EXPERIENCED TEACHER NEEDS TO KNOW ABOUT BASAL INSTRUCTION

PARATORE: I'm not sure it's different. It seems that years ago teachers were taught to use the basal reader in a linear fashion, going from lesson to lesson and task to task. The books are no longer planned to be used in that way. Teachers, experienced and new, need to be flexible in their use of a basal reading program, using it when appropriate but choosing from other sources to build a diverse and effective program.

SEARFOSS: Experienced teachers, some of whom are operating on 20 to 25 years of experience, were certified without a course in children's literature. They also may not

BOX 11.1 CONTINUED

have access to libraries in or near their schools. Therefore, they would find it difficult to implement literature-based series.

EDWARDS: A veteran teacher has had numerous experiences; therefore, I would suggest doing a profile of your experiences with basal reading materials. Summarize the positive and negative experiences. Experienced teachers need to update. Keep what you know, and like the beginning teacher, look at who is in your classroom. Keep one foot in the door and one foot in the future.

ON THE EFFECTIVENESS OF BASALS IN PROVIDING A RANGE OF MATERIALS SUITABLE FOR CULTURALLY DIVERSE POPULATIONS IN SCHOOLS

EDWARDS: Basal companies have tried to select good literature and form authoring teams to incorporate a wide range of literature and characters. Yet some materials still miss the mark and don't really appeal to minority children. For too long, multicultural education has focused on artifacts. We need a lens to enable us to learn things about other people's cultures.

SEARFOSS: In current classrooms using basal materials, children are exposed to a broader range of materials than in some classrooms where the reading materials are entirely teacher-selected. Multicultural children's literature is not something most teachers are familiar with. They may even tend to avoid this responsibility if it is placed entirely in their hands. The next wave of basals will need an even better array of resources to provide for better exposure to a broader range of materials.

PARATORE: This can be a strength of a basal reader. It is important that all children, minority and majority, read about people who represent their cultures and their understandings. In a good basal reading program, a systematic and deliberate effort has been made to represent the full range of cultural and linguistic groups represented in our classrooms and in our communities.

The terms in Figure 11.4 may vary from series to series, but it is safe to assume that certain major components will be found in most programs. A brief overview of some of the components that are part of almost every basal series follows.

◆ *Readiness program.* Big books or big storybooks are used to introduce children to shared reading and how reading works. Along with workbooks, they are used to develop basic concepts in language, letter-sound relationships, sense of context, following directions, and listening comprehension. Emergent literacy programs are often organized thematically, include a variety of support materials, and capitalize on children's curiosity about print to get them excited about reading and making predictions. Theme books, picture books, a read-aloud anthology, literature and music cassettes, home and school connection sheets, picture-word cards, an assessment package, and a teacher's edition are all part of the readiness program.

The Language of Basal Instruction

Anthology	A collection of stories and poems bound together in a book for each child.
Classroom libraries	Supplemental children's literature books that are related by theme or genre to the stories in the student anthologies and are offered in addition to anthologies.
Code emphasis	The emphasis of programs from the beginning is on decoding. The content and sequence in teaching sound-symbol correspondence is controlled so that children can learn quickly how to transform unfamiliar printed words into speech.
Computer management systems	Systems that provide teachers with computer disks to check tests automatically, store student progress information, and prepare status reports for reading groups, classes, or grade levels.
Continuous progress	Teachers are encouraged to teach students at their reading levels, not necessarily at their grade levels. The instructional materials in a series are prepared for about 17 to 20 levels ranging from readiness materials in kindergarten and first grade to advanced reading materials in seventh and eighth grades. Instead of using one reader or anthology in each grade, students may be working in different books at different levels in the same classroom.
Controlled vocabulary	Until the mid-1990s, when vocabulary control was being replaced by predictable tests, the number of "new" words that students encounter in each reading lesson was controlled. Publishers control vocabulary in their reading programs in three ways: (1) Many high-interest words are used first, followed by the introduction of more abstract words. (2) High-frequency words appear in the beginning, with low-frequency words gradually inserted in the text. (3) Words that follow regular spelling patterns are used first, and then words with some irregular spelling patterns are used. Words introduced in the lower-level readers are repeated often in subsequent readers.
Criterion-referenced tests	Informal tests devised by either the publishing company or the teacher to measure individual student attainment in skills associated with phonics, vocabulary, and comprehension. The teacher sets the criterion (e.g., 8/10) for adequate performance. The purpose is to assess a reader's performance, regardless of how that performance compares to that of others taking the same test.
Extension (integrating across the curriculum)	After the story is read and the main parts of the suggested lesson framework are completed, teachers continue or extend themes and make cross-curricular connections with fun projects and activities. Art, music, and writing are catalysts to extend ideas and concepts initiated during the lesson. Questioning at the interpretive and applied levels extends comprehension through group discussion.

FIGURE 11.4 Continued

Informal assessment opportunities	Suggestions in the teacher's manual for noticing and observing children's strengths and weaknesses as they read and write to develop a "picture" of their performance. Tips for portfolios, grading suggestions, and student forms are provided, sometimes packaged in a handbook.
Instructional aids	Graphics disks, full-color transparencies, theme logs, write-in booklets, workbooks, blackline activity masters, instructional charts, hands-on manipulatives, audiotapes, videos, and other prepared materials provided at various levels to support classroom instruction.
Kindergarten program	A literature-based basal program's first level for beginning or nonreaders. Ordinarily includes big books, individual big books, and a read-aloud anthology. (Most of these readiness programs are now labeled K.)
Levels	Each level provides a sequential arrangement of student books (readers), teacher's editions, and ancillary materials and builds on those that come before it; each corresponds to a grade level. There may be more than one book for some grade levels, making continuous progress possible. By grade 4, most literature-based series have only one level (book) per grade.
Literature-based reading programs	Anthologies of the newer basal series contain more predictable selections from children's literature and less controlled vocabulary, signaling a shift in focus and philosophy. Traditional components, such as teacher's guide, student texts, practice books, are still offered. Most include activities that reflect current best practice in instruction based on research about cooperative learning, writing process, and modeling comprehension strategies.
Little books	Decodable readers provided for children in early levels that combine predictable elements with phonetically regular words.
Management	The testing program provides teachers with a system to arrange or manage the placement of pupils in different levels of the program. Initial placement tests for "move-ins" are also provided. Tests also help identify skills that students need to acquire or strengthen. In addition, tests may indicate that students have mastered skills at one level and should proceed to the next level. Management combines two major elements: behavioral objectives and criterion-referenced tests.
Meaning emphasis	Newer programs incorporate all the language arts, teaching reading as a communication process rather than as a series of subskills. Meaningfulness of the story content, meaningful ways for children to respond, and integration of language arts activities are some obvious features of this emphasis.

FIGURE 11.4 Continued

Primer	The first book given to children before their first readers. This term is now rarely used.
Readers' and writers' journals	Workbooks for practicing skills to supplement lessons or to provide opportunities for independent, personal response to readings. Writers' journals vary but may include comprehension questions as well as guides for response.
Reading progress cards (running record)	An informal assessment record or individualized record-keeping system to track a student's progress through the entire reading program.
Reinforcement	To ensure that skills have been learned, exercises involving similar and contrasting examples are used to reinforce the learning. This reteaching cycle includes the use of extension activities.
Scope and sequence	The general plan in basal reading programs for the introduction of skills in a sequential or vertical arrangement and with expanding or horizontally conceptualized reinforcement. Students move up through the levels and across within each level (see Figure 11.2).
Skill building	Skills (e.g., basic sight vocabulary, conceptual development, listening facility, comprehension) are not presented only once. They are introduced at one level and then repeated and reinforced at subsequent levels with increasing depth. Instruction begins with simpler subskills and follows this design: introduction of a skill, reinforcement of the skill, and review of the skill.
Skill maintenance	Reviewing recently learned skills as necessary to form the base for new learning to occur.
Strands	Groups of skills that are developed at increasingly higher levels throughout the program. Some popular strands of instruction are word identification, vocabulary development, comprehension, reading study skills, and language arts.
Strategy lessons	Lessons in the teacher's guide; they are not necessarily teaching actual strategies. The lessons are designed to enhance word recognition skills, comprehension, fluency, and vocabulary development. Some target students' achieving English proficiency or children with special needs.
Themes	Topics that tie together the content and materials of totally integrated reading or language arts programs into a meaning-based philosophy.

FIGURE 11.4 Continued

Vocabulary development	Teachers work to increase students' vocabularies. In order to develop a large number of sight words, new words are introduced, these are repeated often in the text selections, and more new words are introduced. Phonics and other word analysis skills and meaning-getting strategies using context are employed to continue vocabulary development.
Whole word method	Words, rather than letters or syllables, are the main instructional unit. Teachers work on the recognition of words, not on sounding out the words.
Workbooks	To supplement lessons in the text, children may independently practice skills in activity books or practice books. Their purpose is to reinforce skills and concepts that teachers have already taught during the lesson framework. Some teachers choose to grade these as daily assignments, using them for assessment.

◆ *Beginning reading.* New basic sight words are introduced; high-frequency sight words accumulate. Children use storybooks and workbooks and eventually construct their own books as they proceed through multiple levels by the end of first grade. Vocabulary and repetition are no longer as controlled; experience charts are used to help word recognition. Predictable features abound in rhyme, rhythm, and repeated patterns. An eclectic phonics approach is built on sight words, phonic analysis, context analysis, and structural analysis. Little books, combining predictable elements with phonetically regular words, are often included.

◆ *Strategy lessons.* A variety of options for strategies are suggested for individual and group lessons and activities to teach sight vocabulary, phonics, structural analysis, and use of context. Teaching vocabulary is usually directly related to the story being read; workbook pages reinforce the words, and teachers are given many alternative choices for activities before and after each story. Students are exposed to new skills, systematically and sequentially; these are often (but not always) logically tied in to the literature selection and taught in a context of making meaning rather than in isolation. Teacher's manuals also offer many ways to build reading fluency, from choral reading to recording stories and poems on tapes.

◆ *Comprehension strand.* Comprehension is stressed strongly, with prereading, during-reading, and postreading strategies and lessons. Quality literature, with considerable attention to multiculturalism, appears in largely unabridged formats.

Ethnically and racially diverse pictures and stories are found in a truly comprehensive variety of literary genres, ranging from animal fantasy, science fiction, autobiography, and poetry to folktale, fable, diary, and legend. The teacher's manual suggests numerous ideas for extending children's understandings; for using a particular story in other subjects like English, art, music, social studies, science, and math; for group and individual activities; and for making the connection to writing. The instructional program follows a set routine, using prompts consistently throughout the book. Questions are fewer in number, inquiring into purpose, motives, and acts of main characters. Emphasis is on critical reading through higher-level questions and encouragement for prediction making.

◆ *Literature.* The majority of stories in each reader are authentic; they are unabridged, excerpted or adapted from award-winning, classic, and contemporary children's literature. Some literature is specially written by popular children's authors for inclusion in these anthologies. Supplemental readings and trade books are suggested and are often available by several titles or entire classroom libraries. Teachers may purchase related reading materials from the company or patronize vendors' book clubs or the school library.

◆ *Language arts.* Creating a literary environment, integrating reading, writing, listening, and speaking at each grade level are promoted; some programs outline, in lesson format, strategies to merge the language arts. Learning centers, workshops, group discussions, cooperative learning projects, library corners, technology, and art and music centers may be set up. Writing activities are frequently mentioned throughout the teacher's manual. Journal entries, posters, charts, letters, thank-you notes, stories, group big books, and thought bubbles, reinforce the focus on the connection between reading and writing. A writing assignment often accompanies a reading comprehension activity. For children with limited English proficiency (LEP) and others with special needs, there are language development exercises and also suggestions for flexible grouping to assist in meeting students' individual needs.

◆ *Management.* Systematic instruction of reading or language arts programs provides teachers with goals and objectives along with teaching plans and assessment tools, all toward the end of documenting individual student and class progress. Their systematic organization is evident and may have special appeal for teachers who view basals "as offering organization, a sequential path for teaching and learning, or as resources . . . useful in doing what . . . is needed to occur for student learning to take place" (Hoffman et al., 1998, p. 183).

◆ *Assessment.* The growing support for portfolio assessment has resulted in the availability of multidimensional ways to assess students as they interact with basal reading series. Teachers are given numerous types of informal and formal assessment options that can be included in each student's portfolio, such as writing center assignments, independent reading logs, and student journals. Although sole reliance on skills mastery tests is not advocated, tests are provided for virtually every story and trade book. The newer, broader approach of ongoing assessment of student performance and attitudes toward the language arts is geared to inform teachers' instructional decision making and students' understanding of their progress toward their own goals.

CHARACTERISTICS OF BASAL READERS

More significant than similarities and differences among reading series are improvements in components over the past decade. Overall physical appearance, literary variety, and efforts to eliminate stereotyping and infuse diversity deserve special recognition. In general, components have become more comprehensive, thorough, or complex, depending on one's viewpoint.

Appearance

Student books, anthologies, trade books, big books, little books, audiotapes, assessment guides, spiral-bound teacher's editions with integrated and strategic lesson ideas, spelling books, practice books, and journals are just some of the physical components now available. Hardcover anthologies are coordinated in cover design, themes, and artwork with corresponding supplemental materials at each level. Appearance is surely a contributing variable when teachers consider the relative merits of a new reading series.

Illustrations

Illustrations reveal an important growth in the quality of basal reading material. One trend is the use of actual illustrations from the original children's literature selection. Many companies intersperse new illustrations with some from original sources. Ginn was one of the first companies to feature real children as characters in the stories with accompanying photographs. First graders could read about Jim and Beth and Ana and Sara and Ken going to visit a book van or taking a trip to Sea World. This is now common practice.

Teachers remain the most important element in terms of critically evaluating and deciding what is appropriate and valuable for their classes to read. When the experience of their culture isn't addressed in the illustrations or text of a basal series, children may not become engaged in meaningful learning. Culturally relevant teaching (Ladson-Billings, 1992) celebrates and builds on the cultural background of students as they move into literacy. Such teaching helps students examine their reading critically asking, "How does this compare to my experiences? My knowledge? My feelings?" The validity and logic of what we read in school can be assessed in terms of how it fits the values not only of our own beliefs and assumptions but also of people with different world views from our own.

Stereotyping

The illustrations and content of basal readers have made strides in guarding against stereotyping, tokenism, and lifestyle oversimplifications. Nevertheless, teachers should continue to be sensitive to these issues as they evaluate and use reading materials, especially basal readers. Some distinctions in terminology are in order.

Stereotyping is an oversimplified generalization about a particular group, race, or sex, with derogatory implications.

Tokenism is a minimal (token) effort to represent minorities, such as nonwhite characters whose faces look like white ones tinted or colored in.

Lifestyle oversimplifications show an unfavorable contrast between minority characters and their setting with an unstated norm of white middle-class suburbia. Typical are inappropriate settings and exaggerations of reality, such as "primitive" living.

Some studies have shown a distinct improvement in the basal reading programs' depiction of gender roles (Hitchcock & Tompkins, 1987), Native Americans, Hispanics, and African Americans (Garcia & Florez-Tighe, 1986; Reyhner, 1986). Yet other studies showed few positive depictions of the elderly (Gutknecht, 1991) and no nonwhite main characters at the third-grade level (Reimer, 1992).

Mem Fox (1993), an educator and children's author, warns that books serve to construct our selves as we read them by presenting us with an image of ourselves. Yet textbooks written to celebrate the 1492 voyage of Christopher Columbus to the Americas called native peoples "savages." Cultural stereotypes, she notes, are easily and unthinkingly reinforced in even our favorite books. Teachers need to be aware of the politically loaded messages in literature and textbooks so that all students can be affirmed by reading books that are not boring yet celebrate diversity.

Students are also changed as they read a good piece of literature. As Bieger (1996) submits, students "see the world in a new way. . . . Literature can be a powerful vehicle for understanding cultures and experiences different from our own" (p. 311). The double benefits that result from exposure to literature that accurately reflects the people of many cultures can be realized when teachers select literature to help students understand their own values and beliefs better and learn about others' contributions. To help both teachers and students choose books with undistorted views and nonracist histories, Slapin (1992) offered these suggestions: (1) Look at how ethnic groups are portrayed in illustrations and in picture books; (2) look for stereotypes; (3) look for loaded words; (4) look for tokenism; (5) look for distortions of history; (6) look at lifestyles; (7) look at dialogue; (8) look for standards of success; (9) look at the role of women; (10) look at the role of elders; (11) look at the authors' or illustrator's background. Reimer (1992) suggested that more literature by, rather than about, people of color needs to be made available in classrooms.

Language Style

The style of written language found in basal readers has been an interest of researchers for decades. Ruth Strickland (1962) was among the first to verify that children's command of oral language surpassed the language appearing in their basal readers. Reading and language researchers of the 1980s and 1990s continued to find out more about *basalese,* a pejorative term for the language style used in basal readers.

With the advent of the newer basal reading series described in this chapter, the style of language found throughout the anthologies reflects probably the greatest change in decades. The shift from controlled vocabulary to predictable stories and authentic literature selections can be observed to some degree in most of the major reading programs. This shift followed extensive criticism and charges that the demands of readability (controlled vocabulary and sentence length) had led to a stilted, unnatural, and bland language, referred to as *basalization* (Goodman, 1988) or *primerese* (Ammon, Simons, & Elster, 1990).

Since controlled vocabulary for beginning readers was always a hallmark of basal programs, there was concern that overreliance on pictures, dialogue, and short sentences would lead young readers to picture dependence, hindering reading acquisition (Simons & Elster, 1990). When basal readers are written to meet readability standards rather than to include authentic and meaningful language, Goodman (1988) and others argued that students are denied the opportunity to rely on what makes sense as a guide to meaningful reading. However, now that most programs have moved away from controlled vocabulary, some questions still remain about how beneficial this will really be for beginning readers.

For example, in the more traditional basal instructional program, children read from their preprimers or primers. Now that we offer children a variety of reading experiences and trade books, "the use of controlled-language texts seems well advised, especially for children who find learning to read difficult," according to Francine Johnston (1998, p. 674). This seems to go hand in hand with previously mentioned concerns that for students who are less skilled readers, the lack of controlled vocabulary may be too challenging and might make success more difficult to achieve in the newer programs. Teachers need to modify their instruction and select stories to serve the needs of their own students, encourage spontaneous conversation, and accept the children's natural language. The idea continues to be to build on children's language strengths.

Workbooks

Many of the workbooks that go along with basal readers are called reader's journals, writer's journals, practice books, or activity books. The contents have expanded somewhat in the 1990s. While still providing practice in spelling, phonics, or decoding skills in the primary grades and comprehension or study skills in the intermediate grades, there are opportunities for open-ended, personal, and creative response too. No longer must teachers merely decide how many workbook pages to assign; today's question is how to choose among and then orchestrate the multiple types of practice books suggested in the manual's

Overreliance on pictures, dialogues, and short sentences to carry meaning can lead young readers to picture dependence, thus hampering reading acquisition.

lesson plan guide! The factor that hasn't changed over the past ten years is the classroom time taken away from actual reading.

In the past, workbooks were criticized because the tasks demanded of the student required little actual reading; many asked students to focus on a single word, rather than supply or compose words in open-ended responses. Mastery of the skill being practiced bore little relation to correct or incorrect responses. Often workbooks were not related to the textbook selections students were reading. The most important consideration for teachers, who have a limited amount of time to devote to reading and the language arts, should be how the workbooks are used.

A fourth-grade teacher we know, comparing his district's decision not to purchase the workbooks or skillbooks that accompanied their new literature anthologies to a nearby district's acquisition of the entire program, commented on the freedom he felt to allow his students time for reading. "There is too much to do in terms of workbook activity to ever get as much reading done as you'd like. And those teachers who have the workbooks feel as if they have to use them." Teachers must take an active role in deciding the appropriate use of workbooks in their classrooms.

If teachers and administrators are trying to decide whether or not to purchase all of the program components that fall into the workbook category (spelling practice book, project book, blackline masters, etc.), they might ask questions to make sure some basic attributes are present:

Do they accurately reflect the concepts being taught?

Do they accurately reflect the content or theme being taught?

Do they use vocabulary tied in to the rest of the program?

Do they contain brief and unambiguous instructions?

Do they contain pictures consistent with the content?

Do they require thoughtful responses connected to writing and reading?

Lesson Framework

Nearly all basal reading programs organize instruction around some variation of the directed reading activity (DRA) first described by Betts in 1946. Although the sequence and suggested activities are relatively standard, enough variation in strategies and emphasis exists to give each publisher's version a unique feel.

The newest basal programs incorporate lessons and activities that are designed to promote strategic reading and to learn strategies for making informed decisions. However, lesson plans in the teacher's manuals can be overwhelming. One publisher devotes 20 pages to a 46-word story; another series has a 42-page lesson plan for a 20-page story.

Nevertheless, teachers who were part of a recent national survey on basal reading instruction said that the manuals "provided them [with] new techniques, reminded them of old favorites, or gave them opportunities to build on or modify the ideas in the teachers' editions" (Baumann & Heubach, 1996, p. 524). While the confusing nature of so many options could be overwhelming to novice teachers, many others have become discriminating consumers who realize that they need not slavishly follow the teacher's manual. The options for teaching strategies in each basal lesson are numerous, but most are organized around three or four phases that correspond to a similar, traditional sequence. As Figure 11.5 illustrates, the new series have lesson planning guides with a sequence laid out but use different terminology ("before," "during," and "after") to label the phases.

Motivation and Background Building. This aspect of the lesson involves getting ready to read. It is sometimes referred to as the prereading phase of instruction. The teacher attempts to build interest in reading, set purposes, and introduce new concepts and vocabulary. Several procedures may include the following:

1. Predicting, based on title, pictures, and background knowledge, what the story might be about

2. Teacher think-alouds to model prediction, set purposes, and share prior knowledge

◆ Figure 11.5   Lesson Planning Guide for a Selection in a Reading Program

Lesson Planning Guide

The Voice of Africa in American Music

	Teaching Strategies	Materials	Integrated Language Arts/ Integrated Curriculum
BEFORE *Reading* pages 42a–f	**Activate Prior Knowledge**		**Speaking/Listening** hear and discuss American music
	Develop Vocabulary	Instructional Transparency 6 Practice Book, p. 15	**Vocabulary** question technique
	Link Spelling and Vocabulary	Spelling Practice Book, pp. 10–11	**Spelling** words with /ü/
DURING *Reading* pages 42–49	**Prereading Strategies**	Student Anthology, pp. 42–49	
	Strategic Reading	Practice Book, pp. 16–17 Orange Tape 2: Side 2	
	Teachable Moments to Develop Skills Sequence: Order of Events ❶ Identify Reading Problem		
	Thinking About It		
AFTER *Reading* pages 49a–h	**Response Activities** Literature Circles Creative Dramatics Writing Prompts Map and Retell Respond Using Vocabulary	Graphic Organizer Transparency 17	**Speaking/Listening** group discussions **Writing** descriptions, music review, song lyrics
	Comprehension Strategies Skill Focus: Identify Reading Problem Supporting Skills: Reread ❶ Use Text Features	Practice Book, p. 18	
	Integrated Language Arts Sequence: Order of Events Definition of a Sentence	Integrated Language Activity Book, p. 39 Integrated Language Teacher's Resource Book, pp. 10, 58	**Writing** informational article **Speaking** sequence events **Grammar** definition of a sentence
	Integrated Curriculum Music: Respond by Playing Art: Culture/Heritage Physical Education: Rhythmic Activities Language Arts: Writing	*Extra Skills Practice Blackline Masters* Vocabulary p. 17 Comprehension pp. 18, 19	**INTEGRATED CURRICULUM** Music: Drumbeats Art: A Drum of Your Own Physical Education: Interpretative Movement Language Arts: Sing Their Praises

Vocabulary
responding
moods
hardship
root
restore

❶ = Holistic Test
🇹 = Skills Test

42c • Anthology A   *The Voice of Africa in American Music*

Source: From *Celebrate Reading! Teacher's Guide, Grade 3.* Copyright © 1997. Used by permission of Addison-Wesley Educational Publishers.

3. Discussion of the pronunciation and meaning of new words; review of words previously taught

4. Location of geographic setting, if important (map and globe skills)

5. Development of time concepts

6. Review of important reading skills needed for doing the lesson

Guided Reading (Silent and Oral).   Depending on the grade level, the story may be read on a section-by-section basis (in the primary grades) or in its entirety. Following silent reading, children may be asked to read the story aloud or orally read specific parts to answer questions. The guided reading phase of the lesson focuses on comprehension development through questioning. Strategic reading, including explicit comprehension and vocabulary skill instruction, are explained in the teacher's guide, along with prompts such as "teachable moments" interspersed throughout the teacher's copy of the story. Teachers, as they have always done during a directed reading activity (DRA), may create their own questions. They may also omit some of the suggestions provided in the teacher's guide, gearing the lesson to the experiences and prior knowledge of their students in relation to a given story. Stopping the students' reading is helpful to articulate predictions, but when they are anxious to find out what happens and totally involved in the piece of literature, teachers should avoid interrupting the reading and let students finish the story.

Skill Development and Practice.   Skill development and practice activities center around direct instruction of reading skills, arranged according to "scope and sequence" and taught systematically. Sometimes this phase of the DRA involves oral rereading, for a specific purpose. Activities and exercises from the various practice books that accompany the basal story are intended to reinforce skills in the broad areas of word analysis and recognition, vocabulary, and study skills. They are interspersed throughout the phases of the lesson in the teacher's guide.

Follow-Up and Enrichment.   There are more possibilities for enrichment and follow-up activities after the actual reading phase of a lesson than teachers will ever be able to incorporate into the curriculum. The options most favored in the 1990s center around integrated curriculum, an effort to connect the language arts with other subject areas, often through themes. Integration is encouraged across all subject areas, including math, previously ignored. Skill development and practice activities are often interspersed with creative enrichment ideas in the teacher's guide. Here is a sample of some follow-up and enrichment activities, which may continue one to three days after reading the literature selection:

- ◆ Writing workshops and portfolios
- ◆ Drama activities, readers' theater
- ◆ Integrated curriculum hands-on projects
- ◆ Response through personal reflection or literature circles
- ◆ Minilessons

◆ Tape recording

◆ Spelling practice books

◆ Additional comprehension strategy lessons and checks

◆ Integrated language activity book

◆ Whole class, community, or family activity

◆ Reading related stories or other genres

MAKING INSTRUCTIONAL DECISIONS

The basal lesson can be a tool at our command, or it can dominate our classroom actions. According to the authors in Box 11.1, teachers who rely solely on their teacher's manual are not following best practice.

Basal programs have certain physical similarities, but a more careful content analysis "reveals that there are significant differences among programs" (Dole & Osborn, 1989, p. 5). Teachers must make informed decisions about using, not using, and/or supplementing basal reading programs. They need to address how whole language and the more traditional use of basal readers can complement each other; how children's literature, electronic texts, and anthologies can each contribute to good instruction.

Let's consider how two experienced fourth-grade teachers handle their teacher's manuals. Barbara has been teaching for seven years. She follows the lessons in her basal assiduously, lesson by lesson and page by page from the teacher's manual. Her compliance, she suggests, is based on a couple of factors. First, the basal program was put together by reading experts "who know far more than I ever will about reading." But do these experts know her students as well as she does? Do they know her children's learning and reading strategies? Their needs? Their fears? Their personal triumphs? Barbara replied, "Perhaps not. But the lessons must be good, or they wouldn't be included in the manual, and besides, they save me hours of planning time."

By contrast, Karen, a fourth-grade teacher with 12 years of experience, follows basal lessons but "reorganizes parts to fit what I think should be taught in my class." Doesn't lesson modification require much planning time? Karen replied, "I guess it does, but it's time well spent. I keep what I think is worthwhile and skip some activities because they don't make sense to me. These decisions take very little time. Planning time is consumed when I decide to do something on my own, like develop my own worksheets or devise a game to reinforce skills."

More and more teachers are taking the same professional stance as Karen. The survey on basal instruction found that rather than passively following the manual, teachers actually find themselves empowered by materials that give them "instructional suggestions to draw from, adapt, or extend as they craft lessons" (Baumann and Heubach, 1996, p. 511).

This image of teachers as informed, thoughtful users of a variety of materials agrees with study results reported by the National Reading Research Center. Hoffman and colleagues (1995) found that 55 percent of teachers supplemented the basals a great deal with additional literature, 10 percent used the basals but didn't use the teacher's manual, 11 percent used only trade books, and 12 percent relied heavily on basals (p. 19).

As teachers become aware of and reflect about why and how they use basals, they will find more opportunities to use their knowledge and skills more fully and effectively. Modifications of basal reading lessons allow teachers to rely on their own strengths as well as those of the students. After all, teachers should not have to face an either/or dilemma in using basals to teach reading. Rather they need to decide where to place instructional emphasis.

It is not unusual to discover very different kinds of reading instruction going on in the same elementary school. Even using just one basal reading program, instructional emphasis often varies from teacher to teacher. It is clearly impossible to teach every activity suggested in a basal reading lesson. There isn't enough time in the day; moreover, we wonder whether a teacher would need to do so to produce proficient readers. From an instructional point of view the question is not "Am I going to do everything as suggested in the teacher's manual?" The more appropriate question was posed this way by an elementary teacher: "If I'm going to skip parts in the teacher's manual or modify the lesson, I have to have the courage to believe that what I am emphasizing is instructionally worthwhile. I ask myself, 'What do I need to change in the lesson to make it work for my students'?"

Modifying Lessons

As teachers of reading become more familiar with instructional strategies in this book and others, they try them out in their classrooms. Many will use alternative strategies in conjunction with their basal anthologies. They may prefer to follow the basic lesson framework, incorporating some alternatives into this structure.

Modifying lessons personalizes reading instruction for teachers and students. The reasons behind this lesson planning are varied, but the most important one is the need to adapt in order to meet the special needs of students. The nature of students as readers, and as individuals within a social situation in which language plays a large role, causes teachers to modify instruction. Debbie Waldron, a teacher of the developmentally handicapped in elementary grades, describes in the Class Works featured in Box 11.2 how she and another primary teacher in her school dealt with the inclusion of a child with special needs.

Children who are reluctant to read, who are just learning English, who are in some way gifted, or who face developmental or other challenges benefit when teachers plan lessons with them in mind. Sometimes lessons may simply be rearranged; at other times parts might be omitted or expanded. If material seems too difficult, teachers may incorporate some content area prereading strategies suggested in Chapter 12. Using the directed reading-thinking activity (DR-TA), in conjunction with suspenseful stories, facilitates prediction making and provides an alternative lesson structure to the DRA. For more ideas and discussion about alternative instruction, see Chapter 13.

Two Choices

I do some teaming in first grade with another teacher. Toward the end of the summer about two years ago, we found out that one of our incoming students, named Simone, was autistic and deaf. Even though I was pleased to be in a first-grade included setting, I remember thinking, "This is going to be a challenge!" We talked, looked through Simone's records, and talked some more. Gradually, we came to a point where we had two choices. We could choose to believe either that Simone would not be able to participate fully in the learning process or that we could use her primary language (signing) to enrich the lives of all our students. If we chose the first option, we could stay with our regular lessons; the routine we'd settled into the year before had worked like a charm. The only problem was that Simone would be excluded from some of our program. If we chose the second option, it would mean more work because we'd need to adapt our lessons.

We chose to use Simone's signing as a means to enrich the lives of everyone in the class. Before the end of the first week of school, we observed that the hearing children seemed to love the intrinsic beauty of sign language; many began trying to sign. During the day there were many times when the hearing children had opportunities to learn sign language. During their daily community meeting, they learned to sign the Pledge of Allegiance and the birthday song. During reading, vocabulary words were frequently taught with the corresponding sign. Many children remembered the written word because they remembered the accompanying sign. They also learned many signs during centers and informal situations.

At midyear, the principal asked us to share some of our experiences in teaching Simone reading and language arts. In response to questions from our colleagues, we cited the following benefits. First and foremost, the children (and their parents) loved learning the new language. Second, the finger positions required to sign strengthen the small muscles needed for printing and other fine motor skills. Third, we often gave directions for classroom transitions using sign language. This added to the repertoire of ways to manage smooth transitions. Finally, it became a way to extend language learning for all the children into all parts of our "normal lesson routine" for reading.

—*Debbie Waldron*

REFLECTIVE INQUIRY

◆ How did these teachers seem to know which parts of a reading lesson would be best to adapt?

◆ Debbie says there is a good sports analogy for their decision to change their instructional plans: "You can't steal second base if your foot is still on first." What does this say about taking risks in teaching?

INSTRUCTIONAL MATERIALS

Due to the proliferation of reading materials and the technological changes induced by computers, we cannot offer teachers a comprehensive listing of current instructional materials in reading. Such a list would be out of date before this book reached your hands. Consequently, it becomes even more essential that teachers be aware of the types of materials available and how to select and evaluate them.

As we already know, over half of elementary teachers use instructional materials in addition to or in place of the basal reading program to teach reading. This willingness to broaden the materials used for instruction is a double-edged sword: There is a lot to choose from and not a lot of guidance on how to go about it. This is especially the case when it comes to electronic materials.

Table 11.1 displays three broad categories of reading materials: basic instructional programs, supplemental materials, and trade books. Basic material such as a comprehensive reading or language arts program will be used by the majority of elementary children. Supplementary programs, in particular technology-based materials, will be used as enrichment for some children and a reinforcement of basic skills for others or will be fully integrated into the lesson. Unlike basic reading programs, supplementary programs are less

TABLE 11.1

Types of Reading Materials

Type	Label	Purpose
Basic instructional literature-based programs and materials	Basal readers and anthologies of literature from a wide range of genres	Intended to provide the majority of reading instruction to the majority of students
Supplementary programs	Skills kits; high-interest, low-vocabulary series; software packages; CD-ROMs, Internet usage, desktop publishing	Intended to meet special needs and enrich classroom instruction; reinforcement of skills; the needs of particular groups such as the gifted, bilingual-bicultural, and learning disabled
Trade books	Library books; popular fiction and nonfiction paperbacks for children and adolescents	Individual titles suited to children's interests; intended for independent reading rather than direct instruction

likely to be scrutinized by selection committees. Trade books, such as library hardcover and paperback books, and sets of trade books related to literature-based programs will be selected by librarians, specialists, and classroom teachers.

Examples of the types of reading materials listed in Table 11.1 can be added as you come into contact with the materials in schools. Take a few minutes now to think of some in each category. Classrooms you visit will differ as to the predominant types of reading material supplied for the children. Some rooms, for example, contain almost exclusively textbooks for reading, science, social studies, mathematics, and so on. Others have hundreds of paperback books and magazines displayed in an assortment of racks. Some classrooms have sturdy cardboard kits and piles of student record books; some have computer workstations along one wall. Few classrooms have the same mix of reading materials.

Many variables could account for a teacher's decision to favor one type of reading material over another for instruction. Grade level, school district policy, influence of colleagues, curriculum objectives, and available resources are some that come to mind. Two others, the impact of technology and the teacher's belief system, are influences that need to be considered.

Electronic Materials

"St. Lucie students to surf the Net." This headline in a local Florida newspaper (*Vero Beach Press Journal*, Aug. 12, 1998) says it all. The article below it announced that by the start of this school year, every class in the county would have access to the Internet, allowing students to "explore horizons more immediate than many of their textbooks." Further, students would be able to research current events, take virtual field trips, and read newspapers from around the world. This was made possible by a yearlong $1.5 million cabling project to enable six computers in each classroom to be connected.

Electronic materials can enrich classroom reading instruction just as trade books and literature-based programs of the 1990s did. Teachers are becoming aware of the possibilities for reading and learning with electronic materials. They are beginning to create multimedia environments in the elementary and middle school by using the Internet and CD-ROM software programs. As they put students in pairs to share a computer to use the Internet or to get information on CD-ROM, teachers are also encouraging social interaction. Students communicate about discoveries they're making and collaborate naturally with other students about the content and process of navigating a multimedia environment. We've come a long way from the computer-aided instruction (CAI) software of the 1980s; electronic materials available today make exciting opportunities for reading and language instruction. Reading and writing on the Internet and communicating through word processing programs are ways to develop students' abilities and create incentives for improvement.

World Wide Web. Access to the Web on the Internet connects students to a vast network of computers around the world that effectively mix text, graphics, sound, and images. This creates a hypermedia system using *hypertext,* a format that is much less linear than printed text because the reader can link through a web of branches to choose different documents.

Students can gather information on every imaginable topic, publish their research reports, and ask questions of experts and other students. Much quicker than a library visit, information access is instantaneous, once students develop some expertise at navigating the hypertext of the Web. Teachers need to provide activities to help their students gain experience with "browsing" or "surfing" the Web. They can take guided tours or be given "bookmarks" to take them directly to sites teachers want them to visit.

E-Mail and Discussion Groups. Students on the Internet can communicate instantaneously via e-mail anywhere in the world. They can connect with students about books they are reading, share information and ask questions about each other's school, hobbies, interests, family, and friends. Students and teachers can join discussion groups by subscribing to a mailing list or listserv.

Word Processors. Computers as word processors in the classroom can help develop students' writing abilities. Students can keep daily journals; write letters and thank-you notes; draft, edit, and revise their writing; and produce attractive stories and reports that others can read. With *desktop publishing* programs, which combine text and graphics in various arrangements, students can contribute their own compositions to the theme or topic under study. For even further extension of the composing process, students can use hypermedia programs called *authoring systems,* which encourage active engagement through the interaction of multiple media. Authoring software facilitates multimedia projects that combine visual images, sounds, graphics, and text. Students fill in computer "cards" with information, pictures, drawings, photographs, music, video, and so on; then "buttons" are created to link the network of completed cards.

Software Programs. In addition to software accompanying comprehensive reading programs, many publishers have inundated the education market with innovative software. Some packages are highly interactive multimedia CD-ROM software, in which students interact with concepts, engaging in investigations using three-dimensional environments. Most major education associations, including the International Reading Association, offer program reviews in their professional journals and newsletters. Teachers who are interested in using commercial CAI for reading and language arts would need to examine it carefully for appropriate use as practice for meeting goals such as skill fluency. Goals for developing higher-level thinking skills are not likely to be met with this type of "drill and practice" software.

Electronic Books. Electronic books, unlike other educational software, have electronic text presented to readers visually and use conventions associated with books, such as a table of contents, pages, and even a bookmark. They have an organizing theme of an existing book or a central focus. Many are available on CD-ROM and are often informational, focusing on in-depth study of subjects. Some are highly interactive storybooks for recreational reading, such as Eastgate Systems' *Afternoon* and Disney's *Animated Storybooks.* Teachers who are looking for ways to increase positive response in children and improve their comprehension would want to consider supplementing their reading or language arts program with these materials.

Educational Games. The instant motivation associated with playing games continues to make them popular in some classrooms. Often used to let students practice or reinforce skills, they have grown in sophistication from cardboard flash cards and spin-the-dial to CD-ROM versions with colorful graphics. Teachers may want to consider using software games to assist students in practicing categorizing, reviewing vocabulary meanings, or sequencing. Students may also benefit from learning how to cooperate with one another because the competitiveness is now redirected toward the computer. Time taken away from other reading activities and the difficulty in making sure everyone gets an opportunity to play are potential problems.

Beliefs About Reading and Instructional Materials

How do teachers' beliefs about reading correspond to their selection and use of instructional materials for reading? There is no definitive answer to this question. There are many complicating factors that prevent teachers from exercising complete freedom of choice and hence prevent us from knowing why certain materials are present in any given classroom. Nevertheless, we believe it is important to consider the relationship between materials used to deliver instruction and the beliefs teachers hold about reading instruction. In other words, it makes sense to assume there is a relationship between what we do and why we do it.

Figure 11.6 illustrates the major types of reading materials across the continuum of beliefs from bottom-up (on the left) to top-down (on the right). Basal reading programs, with their multiple strands, take up the vast middle sections of the continuum. Programmed, prescriptive materials and children's literature books reside in the bottom-up and top-down sections, respectively. Supplementary materials appear in several sections, from flash cards and drill-and-practice software to journals, CD-ROMs, and electronic books.

Differences in beliefs about unit of language to be emphasized are superimposed in the next layer. Letter-sound emphasis corresponds to materials found in prescription programs with a heavy word analysis component. Whole language emphasis corresponds to materials such as library books and paperbacks without arbitrary skill divisions. This unit-of-language emphasis is illustrated further by a dotted boundary line for context. Materials involving minimal use of context are on the left, whereas materials involving maximal use of context are on the right.

A third layer that we might add is instructional strategy corresponding to these materials. We have initiated this with several basic strategies discussed in other chapters. For example, the DRA corresponds to most lessons in reading programs, while the DR-TA corresponds to many stories in anthologies and in supplementary literature. Sustained silent reading (SSR) corresponds to magazines and trade books, that is, personalized rather than prescriptive materials. What other strategies would you place in one spot or move to several points on this continuum?

Unfortunately, often by the time we step back, look at the types of instructional materials we are using, and relate them to our beliefs and priorities, the materials are already in place. How were they selected in the first place?

♦ FIGURE 11.6   Reading Instructional Materials According to Belief Systems

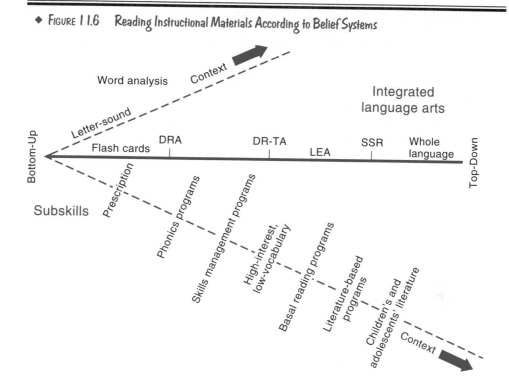

Selecting Reading Materials

Like Liz in the chapter's opening vignette, many teachers have served on textbook selection committees. Some probing would reveal the sophistication of the process: Did the committee seek and obtain information from the various stakeholder groups such as parents, administrators, students, and other teachers? Were there presentations and question-and-answer sessions with company representatives? Was there ample time to pilot one or two of the finalists in classrooms?

Social trends such as treatment of women and minorities, return to basics, and increasing involvement of parents have varying degrees of impact on curriculum development and materials selection. Depending on the community, other issues need to be considered. Censorship is probably the most pervasive issue because it deals with people's values. Examining publications for objectionable matter is not the intended mission of most educational materials selection committees. Yet there is a fine line between examining materials for their contribution to instructional goals and banning materials for their conveyance of implicit or explicit messages to students.

Another issue is the increased media attention to proficiency test scores, especially in reading and writing. Newspapers run feature articles comparing local school districts to each other based on percentages of students passing these tests. Pressure is then put on the school board and administrators of a district to improve their scores. As this filters down to the individual classroom level, teachers devote more instructional time to practicing for the test. How does this affect the use of the various types of instructional strategies and reading materials? Will teachers, for example, feel free to start additional literature circles or take that block of time to drill and practice subskills?

Trends and issues are important as they directly or indirectly influence curriculum materials selection. We need to keep them in perspective. The next time you are asked to assist in selecting materials, here are some questions to use as criteria to guide the process.

1. Have you personally evaluated the content of the materials in terms of accuracy of content, level of presentation, and use of level of language? Have you found the materials acceptable in these areas?

2. Do the data reveal on whom the materials were field-tested? How many students were involved in the use of the materials? In what geographic location were these tests conducted? What were the results?

3. Are authors and publishers readily identifiable within the content of the material?

4. Is there an accompanying instructional guide, and if so, are the curriculum aims, objectives, and instructional strategies presented?

5. Have these materials been used on pupils similar to the pupils in your reading programs? If so, what results were achieved using these materials?

6. Do you feel you will present these materials with honesty and objectivity?

7. Have members of your district formulated specific ways or methods for using these materials?

8. Will these materials complement the other instructional messages of your reading programs?

9. Does the content present information in a fair and nonbiased manner?

10. Are important concepts reinforced so that there is sufficient repetition of major points?

Evaluating Reading Materials

Reading programs, the most prevalent type of instructional material, are also the most likely to be evaluated by teachers and other groups. Publishing companies have become so attuned to this process that they mount high-power, professional presentations to convince school districts to adopt their particular program. School districts have in turn developed extensive evaluation forms to keep track of and compare the programs' elements.

A thorough evaluation of a program currently in use is beneficial for assessing the instructional program in relation to the curriculum goals of the school district. Teachers who participate in answering these questions gain the professional development so often neglected when it comes to reading materials. This process should be done before deciding whether to consider new programs; it's important to have this information as baseline data.

1. What is the overall philosophy of the program? How is reading discussed in the teacher's guide?

2. What kind of learning environment does the program recommend? Is it child-centered? Teacher-centered? Literature-centered? Skills-based?

3. Describe the emergent literacy or readiness program in detail. How does it provide for communication between school and home?

4. Describe the instructional program in detail. How are lessons structured to teach word identification, vocabulary and concepts, reading fluency, comprehension, writing?

5. Describe the literature of the program. What percentage of the selections are in unabridged form? Are different genres included? How culturally diverse is the literature?

6. How well does the program integrate across the curriculum? In what ways is assessment connected to daily instruction? What opportunities are there for connections between the various language arts?

The evaluation sheet in Figure 11.7 illustrates how major components, once examined at some length, can be rated in a kind of "executive summary." Note that the categories under "Additional Information" at the bottom of the form focus on expectations for fair and realistic treatment of people of different races, sexes, ages, cultures, and physical challenges. This form could apply to textbooks in other subject areas and to high school as well as elementary and middle grade levels.

Checklists designed to evaluate reading materials of a supplementary nature may be criticized as rather shallow analysis. Their benefits, however, far outweigh this criticism. Checklists are relatively easy to construct; teachers are more willing to spend the short amount of time it takes to develop a list to help them examine materials. Figure 11.8 presents a sample checklist for examining the potential effectiveness of materials; it is one informal evaluation designed by teachers of elementary reading and language. The form is brief and to the point, deals with teachers' own programmatic goals, and yields useful information. Unlike more elaborate and lengthy commercial evaluation instruments, such checklists can be employed by the people who actually select and use the materials.

With the ongoing proliferation of electronic materials and continuing efforts to develop multicultural, diverse, and authentic materials, teachers need to be more aware than ever about what they are using in instruction. Here are some questions to think about before buying additional materials: Does the material actually contain what its advertisement claims? Are the skill areas that are emphasized really important to literacy? Are the materials likely to hold the interests of the students in your class? Is there sufficient time devoted to reading in relation to other activities? Are thinking and metacognitive strategies included? Is writing integrated in a meaningful way?

◆ Figure 11.7

Textbook Evaluation Profile Sheet TITLE OF TEXTBOOK	Excellent	Good	Acceptable	Poor	Not included	Not applicable
1. Authorship						
2. Learner verification and revision						
3. General characteristics						
4. Physical and mechanical features						
5. Philosophy						
6. Organization of material						
7. Objectives						
8. Subject matter content						
9. Readability						
10. Teaching aids and supplementary material						
11. Teacher's edition or manual						
Total number in each rating classification for all categories						

Additional information

purpose	interest level	sexism
age level	readability	ageism
grade level	racism	diversity

SUMMARY

We examined basal reading programs and other types of instructional materials in this chapter, emphasizing the need for teachers to understand and use materials wisely. Beginning with the predominant vehicle for reading instruction in elementary classrooms, we reminisced about the origins of basals and some instructional concepts that have been associated with their use throughout the years.

After describing the major components of reading and language arts programs, we commented on several basal reading series used in the mid-1990s, pointing out changes, criticisms, and instructional impact.

◆ Figure 11.8

Checklist for Examining the Potential Effectiveness of Materials

Statement	Yes	No	Unsure	Does not apply
1. Reading materials are consistent with philosophy and goals of the program.	_____	_____	_____	_____
2. Materials are adequate for various phases of the program:				
a. Oral language development	_____	_____	_____	_____
b. Listening comprehension	_____	_____	_____	_____
c. Word recognition	_____	_____	_____	_____
d. Reading comprehension	_____	_____	_____	_____
e. Study skills	_____	_____	_____	_____
f. Recreational reading	_____	_____	_____	_____
g. Literature appreciation	_____	_____	_____	_____
3. The materials are				
a. Interesting and stimulating	_____	_____	_____	_____
b. Easy for children to use	_____	_____	_____	_____
c. Readily available	_____	_____	_____	_____
d. Durable	_____	_____	_____	_____
e. Well organized	_____	_____	_____	_____
f. Cost-effective	_____	_____	_____	_____
4. The materials accommodate the range of reading abilities.	_____	_____	_____	_____
5. A variety of cultures is depicted in illustrations and text content.	_____	_____	_____	_____
6. The software integrates with the content and objectives.	_____	_____	_____	_____
7. The software is motivating and thought-provoking.	_____	_____	_____	_____
8. The program is easy to operate.	_____	_____	_____	_____
9. I feel adequately prepared to use all materials available.	_____	_____	_____	_____

Teacher's Name: _____   Grade Level: _____

The new basal programs of the 1990s, best described as comprehensive, have come a long way. Consequently, we investigated their concepts and defined their "language." Rather than assigning pros and cons to basal reading programs, we concentrated on the significant improvements made in several areas. Their appearance, organization, illustrations, and success in publishing authentic literature and reducing stereotyping mark genuine strides made by companies. What teachers choose to do with all the aspects of basal reading instruction is an important issue.

Teachers make decisions daily about instruction best suited to the children in their classrooms. They balance the needs of students with all the materials available, relying on their experience, knowledge, and beliefs about reading and learning to read. They may emphasize whole language activities or prescriptive decoding programs or favor other strategies that may or may not be suggested in the teacher's guide. When teachers modify and adapt lessons, it's often because they need to meet the special needs of their students.

When we considered the wide assortment of instructional materials, we stressed the importance of becoming aware of what is available, especially in light of technological advances. There are current trends and issues teachers should keep in mind as they analyze the materials they are using or considering. They also need to differentiate among the types of commercial reading materials and broaden their view of supplementary materials to incorporate electronic materials. Evaluation criteria are helpful in the selection and use of instructionally worthwhile materials.

In the final analysis, as overwhelming as it might seem to deal sensibly and meaningfully with the array of materials described in this chapter, teachers do exactly that every day.

TEACHER-ACTION RESEARCHER

1. Select a teacher who consistently uses basal reader instruction. Interview the teacher about his or her attitude toward basal instruction. How closely is the teacher's manual followed? How does the teacher use the basal workbooks? In what ways, if any, does the teacher deviate from the suggested steps in the manual? What reasons does the teacher give for making modifications?

2. Plan and teach a basal lesson to a group of your classmates following the guidelines suggested in the teacher's manual. Include *before, during,* and *after* phases. Reflect on the experience; obtain feedback from your "students." How would you amend the lesson to make it better?

3. Create an original lesson for a basal story without consulting the teacher's manual. Then try out the lesson with your fellow students or a group of children. Reflect on the experience. Consult the manual and compare the original lesson you developed with the suggested one. What did you learn from the experience?

4. Compare some selections in a literature-based basal to the actual works of literature. What changes (if any) were made to the authors' original texts? How did that alter your responses to the stories? What instructional decisions might a teacher need to make if the literature selections in her basal series or electronic materials were adapted from children's literature rather than being actual whole texts?

KEY TERMS

anthologies
classroom libraries
code emphasis
computer
    management
    system
continuous progress
controlled vocabulary
criterion-referenced
    tests
extension (integrating
    across the
    curriculum)
informal assessment
    opportunities

instructional aids
kindergarten
    program
levels
literature-based
    reading programs
little books
management
meaning emphasis
primer
readers' and writers'
    journals
reading progress
    cards (running
    record)

reinforcement
scope and sequence
    plan
skill building
skill maintenance
strands
strategy lessons
themes
vocabulary
    development
whole word method
workbooks

CHAPTER

12
Making the Transition to Content Area Texts

Chapter Overview

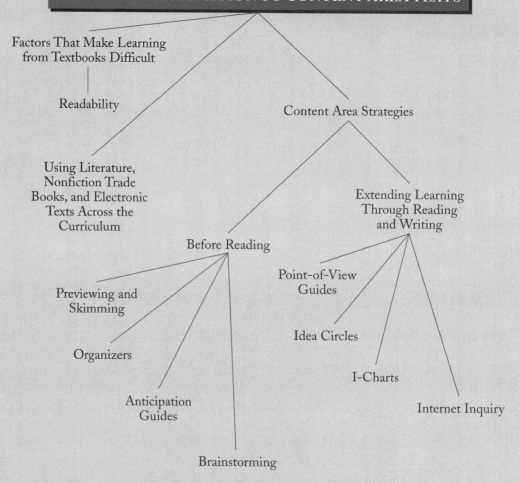

MAKING THE TRANSITION TO CONTENT AREA TEXTS

Factors That Make Learning from Textbooks Difficult

Readability

Using Literature, Nonfiction Trade Books, and Electronic Texts Across the Curriculum

Content Area Strategies

Before Reading

Extending Learning Through Reading and Writing

Previewing and Skimming

Organizers

Anticipation Guides

Brainstorming

Point-of-View Guides

Idea Circles

I-Charts

Internet Inquiry

Between the Lines

In this chapter, you will discover:

◆ Why content area textbooks are difficult for students

◆ Factors that help determine textbook difficulty

◆ How using literature and nonfiction trade books across the curriculum benefits teaching and learning

♦ **How to integrate the use of textbooks, trade books, and electronic texts into units of study and inquiry-centered projects**

♦ **A variety of learning strategies for students to use before and during reading and writing**

Jane and Marie were sitting at the table in the teachers' workroom in mid-September, reviewing their fourth graders' portfolios from last year. "Why is it," Marie asks, "that some kids seem to do so well in reading in third grade and then, when we get them, they seem to go into a slump?" "I'm not certain," replies Jane, "but it may be that it's just too difficult for some students—like Travis—to switch gears from learning to read to reading to learn."

This unnecessary dichotomy between learning to read and reading to learn may actually stand in the way of a child's literacy development. Even before entering school, most children who have had book experiences at home expect print to be meaningful. From as early as age 2, children can be observed engaging in a process of making sense—negotiating meaning—of an author's message (Harste, Woodward, & Burke, 1984). Our contention throughout this book is that children should be learning to read *as* they are reading to learn and to enjoy.

Nonetheless, the problems associated with the transition students make to content area texts, where reading to learn is at a premium, are real. The marked difference in reading ability of good and poor readers known as the "fourth-grade slump" is an indicator that content area texts are inherently difficult. Take, for example, an elementary social studies or a science textbook. It's often devoid of narrative writing; such a textbook doesn't tell stories. Most children, of course, are weaned on narrative writing and come to school with a developing, if not developed, schema for stories. They're on terra firma with the storybook. A textbook, by contrast, relies heavily on an expository style of writing—description, classification, and explanation. By its very nature, a textbook is often dry and uninteresting to the novice reader.

As shown in the chapter overview, you'll explore some of the factors that make content area textbooks difficult, as well as the role of a teacher of reading within the context of content area instruction. Elementary teachers often view their responsibilities in a reading program primarily in terms of skill and strategy development. Their actions are motivated by the question, "How can I help children become more skillful and strategic as readers?" Their main concern, then, is the *process,* or how to guide children's reading development. Yet a concern for the *content* of the reading program should be as important as concern for the process.

The resurgence of children's literature in the 1980s and of children's nonfiction books in the 1990s underscores the importance of meaningful content and authentic texts in elementary classrooms. In addition to reading trade books in content area learning, children

439

can use electronic texts to read extensively and think critically about content. Reading and writing with computers allows children to access and retrieve information, construct their own texts, and interact with others. When a classroom reading program is content-rich, the slump alluded to earlier tends to disappear. In classrooms where literature, nonfiction trade books, and electronic texts are used in abundance, children are more likely to make the transition to content area texts naturally and with ease.

A certain mind-set is often learned as children absorb content from textbooks only: Frequently, they learn at a very early age to focus narrowly on finding the "right" answers to questions that accompany the reading assignment (Vacca & Vacca, 1999, p. 89). This mind-set inhibits children's ability to read literary and informative texts at high levels of literacy. National surveys of reading support claims that the majority of America's children are capable of reading at a basic level of performance—reading for details, identifying main ideas, recognizing relationships among ideas. However, they have difficulty responding to texts at high levels of literacy. At an advanced level, students should be willing to think critically, to extend, elaborate, and examine the meaning of literary and informational texts.

Ennis (1987) defined critical thinking as "reasonable reflective thinking that is focused on deciding what to believe or do" (p. 10) and suggested that the teaching of critical thinking must be integrated into the teaching of all curricular areas. Some of the component abilities of critical thinking that he outlined include identifying or formulating a question, seeing similarities and differences, identifying and handling irrelevancies, summarizing, and asking and answering questions of clarification (p. 12).

The strategies in this chapter focus on how to encourage children to draw from background knowledge and then to be involved in reading and writing using textbooks, trade books, and electronic texts in inquiry learning. In the inquiry learning process, children are guided to identify and formulate questions and find answers to those questions. Moreover, they often enthusiastically use their critical thinking abilities. Now let's focus our attention on factors that make learning from textbooks difficult for many children.

WHY ARE CONTENT AREA TEXTBOOKS DIFFICULT?

Content area textbooks are an integral part of schooling. In most classrooms, textbooks blend into the physical environment, much like desks, bulletin boards, chalkboards, and computers. Even a casual observer expects to see textbooks in use in the elementary classroom. Yet teachers often remark that children find textbooks difficult. When students have trouble reading texts, we are acutely aware of the mismatch between the reading abilities students bring to text material and some of the difficulties of the text.

To compensate for this, some teachers avoid textbook assignments. Instruction revolves around lecture and other activities instead of the textbook. Some teachers abandon difficult materials, sidestepping reading altogether as a vehicle for learning.

In lieu of either abandoning difficult materials or avoiding reading altogether, we need to get answers to some very basic questions. How does the textbook meet the goals of the curriculum? Is the conceptual difficulty of the text beyond students' grasp? Does the author have a clear sense of purpose as conveyed to this audience? How well are the ideas in the text organized? With answers to these and other questions, teachers have some basis on which to make decisions about text-related instruction, exercising their professional judgment.

Factors in Judging the Difficulty of Textbooks

The difficulty of text material is the result of factors residing in both the reader and the text. Therefore, to judge well, you need to take into account several types of information. A primary source of information is the publisher. Consider the publisher-provided descriptions of the design, format, and organizational structure of the textbook along with grade-level readability designations. A second source is your knowledge of students in the class. A third source is your own sense of what makes the textbook useful for learning a particular subject.

The first order of business is to define how the textbook will be used. Will it be used as the sole basis for information or as an extension of information? Will it be used in tandem with informational books and other forms of children's literature? Is it to provide guided activities?

Students in a university reading methods class were curious as to how elementary teachers compensated for difficult or confusing content area textbooks. For a research project, they surveyed over 40 elementary teachers. The college students were surprised that more than 80 percent of the teachers did not think that content textbooks were too difficult. What was even more surprising to the students, however, was the fact that the teachers *did not expect* that the elementary students would learn from the textbooks. One comment summed up most responses: "The students learn the facts and ideas they need when we talk about what is important during class discussions." So while the elementary teachers did not think the textbook was too difficult, they didn't expect students to learn by reading it either! Most elementary teachers, however, continue to use textbooks to teach content subjects, especially those subjects they feel less prepared and confident to teach, like science, even if they believe that the textbooks are often difficult for students to read (Barman, 1992).

How Difficult Is the Text to Understand?   This question might be recast into a set of subsidiary questions: How likely are students to comprehend the text? How difficult are the concepts in the text? Has the author taken into consideration the prior knowledge that students bring to the text? The ability to understand the textbook, to a large extent, will be influenced by the match between what the reader already knows and the text itself. Background knowledge and logical organization of **expository texts** are crucial factors for comprehending new information (Beck & McKeown, 1991).

Irwin and Davis (1980) suggested that teachers analyze a text, using questions such as the following:

Are the assumptions about students' vocabulary knowledge appropriate?

Are the assumptions about students' prior knowledge of this content area appropriate?

Are the assumptions about students' general experiential backgrounds appropriate?

Are new concepts explicitly linked to the students' prior knowledge or to their experiential backgrounds?

Does the text introduce abstract concepts by accompanying them with many concrete examples?

Does the text introduce new concepts one at a time with a sufficient number of examples for each one?

Does the text avoid irrelevant details?

How Usable Is the Text?   To determine how usable a text is, you will need to consider its organizational features and its presentation of material. Your responses to the following questions will help you decide whether you are dealing with a **considerate text** or an *inconsiderate* one. For example, your responses may reveal the extent to which relationships among ideas in the text are clear, the logical organization between ideas, and the use of *signal words* (connectives) to make relationships explicit. To determine if a text is *considerate* and *user-friendly*, ask yourself these questions (Irwin & Davis, 1980).

Does the table of contents provide a clear overview of the content of the textbook?

Do chapter headings clearly define the content of the chapter?

Do chapter subheadings clearly break out the important concepts in the chapter?

Do topic headings provide assistance in breaking the chapter into relevant parts?

Does the glossary contain all the technical terms used in the textbook?

Are graphs and charts clear and supportive of the textual material?

Are illustrations well done and appropriate to the level of the students?

Are the sentence lengths appropriate for the level of students who will be using the text?

Are important terms in italics or boldface type for easy identification by readers?

Are end-of-chapter questions on literal, interpretive, and applied levels of comprehension?

Is an adequate context provided to allow students to determine meanings of technical terms?

How Interesting Is the Text?   Textbooks should appeal to students. The more relevant the text, the more interesting it will be to children. Illustrations and pictures should have appeal, and they will, when they depict persons that students can relate to. Does the cover design and other artwork convey up-to-date, refreshing images? Are type sizes and faces varied? Does the boldface lettering of headings contrast with lightface lettering of the main narrative? Italics and numbering of words and phrases in lists are two other devices that can help make the printed page come alive for elementary students. In addition to the questions just raised, consider these as you analyze a textbook for interest:

Is the writing style of the text appealing to the students?

Are the activities motivating? Will they make the student want to pursue the topic further?

Does the book clearly show how the knowledge being learned might be used by the learner in the future?

Does the text provide positive and motivating models for both sexes as well as for all racial, ethnic, and socioeconomic groups?

Does the text help students generate interest as they relate experiences and develop visual and sensory images?

Perhaps because textbooks need to cover so many subjects to meet state and local curriculum guidelines, nonfiction, expository writing becomes confused in our minds with textbook writing. While it's true that textbooks and nonfiction are different from narratives and fiction, children, even first graders, can be taught to recognize the difference between fantasy or fiction and actual, fact-based explanatory prose.

Once the information accrues about factors contributing to textbook difficulty, you are in a position to use professional judgment. How the more traditional readability formula can be a complement to a teacher's judgment instead of a substitute for it warrants a closer look.

Readability

When elementary teachers judge instructional content area materials, they frequently assess **readability**. Readability formulas can help *estimate* textbook difficulty, but they are not intended to be precise indicators. Of the many readability formulas available, the most popular ones are relatively quick and easy to calculate. They typically involve a measure of sentence length and word difficulty to ascertain a grade-level score for text materials. This score supposedly indicates the reading achievement level students would need to comprehend the material. You do, however, need to be aware of limitations associated with using readability formulas.

Limitations.   Readability formulas yield scores that are simply estimates, not absolute levels, of text difficulty. These estimates are often determined along a single dimension of an author's writing style: vocabulary difficulty and sentence complexity, measured by word and sentence length, respectively. These are two variables most often used to predict the difficulty of a text. Nevertheless, they only *indirectly* assess vocabulary difficulty and sentence complexity. Are long words always harder to understand than short ones? Are long sentences necessarily more difficult than short ones?

Keep in mind that a readability formula doesn't take into account the experience and knowledge that even young readers bring to content material. The reader's emotional, cognitive, and linguistic backgrounds aren't included in readability estimates. Hittleman (1973) maintained that readability is actually a moment in time in which a reader's human makeup interacts with the topic, the purposes for reading, and the semantic and syntactic structures in the material. This makes good sense because formulas are not designed to expose the variables operating within the reader. Thus several factors that contribute to a reader's ability to comprehend text are not dealt with: purpose, interest, motivation, emotional state, and environment. This is an important limitation.

Suggestions. Formulas in and of themselves need not be a liability if you follow Nelson's suggestions (1978, pp. 624–625) for using them:

♦ Learn to use a simple readability formula as an aid in evaluating text material for student use.

♦ Don't assume automatic comprehension will result from matching readability level of material to reading achievement level of students.

♦ Don't assume that automatic reading ease will result from text materials rewritten according to readability criteria. (Leave the rewriting of text material to the linguists, researchers, and editors who have time to analyze and validate their manipulations.)

♦ Do provide materials containing essential facts, concepts, and values of the subject at varying levels of readability within the reading range of your students.

♦ Do recognize that using a readability formula is no substitute for instruction. The elementary teacher still needs to prepare students to read the assignment, guide them in their reading, and reinforce new concepts through rereading and discussion.

Fry Readability Graph. One fairly quick and simple readability formula is the Fry Readability Graph, developed by Edward Fry (1968, 1977). Fry used two variables to predict difficulty and determine grade-level scores for materials from grade 1 through college: sentence length and word length. The total number of sentences in a sample passage determines sentence length, and the total number of syllables in the passage determines word length.

Three 100-word samples from the selected reading material should be used to calculate its readability. Grade-level scores for each passage can then be averaged to obtain an overall readability level. The readability graph in Figure 12.1 is useful in predicting the difficulty of material within one grade level when the accompanying directions for the Fry formula are followed.

In 1990, Fry noted that for short passages of 100 to 300 words in length, a formula for readability should account for difficulty of words and difficulty of sentences, as shown in Figure 12.2. Using the contextual meaning of difficult words and their corresponding grade level gives a more accurate reading level than sentence complexity alone. For example, the word *convention* has three meanings with three levels of difficulty. As a *meeting,* it

Fry Readability Graph

Graph for Estimating Readability—Extended

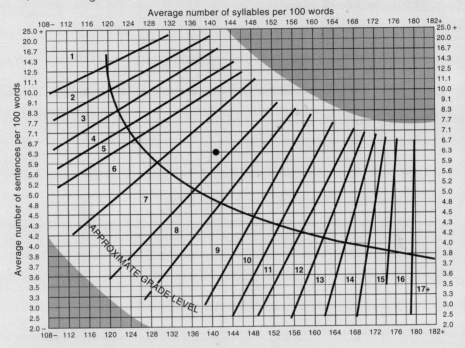

Expanded Directions for Working the Readability Graph

1. Randomly select three sample passages and count out exactly 100 words each, beginning with the beginning of a sentence. Do count proper nouns, initializations, and numerals.

2. Count the number of sentences in the 100 words, estimating length of the fraction of the last sentence to the nearest one-tenth.

3. Count the total number of syllables in the 100-word passage. If you don't have a hand counter available, an easy way is to simply put a mark above every syllable over one in each word, then when you get to the end of the passage, count the number of marks and add 100. Small calculators can also be used as counters by pushing numeral 1, then pushing the + sign for each word or syllable when counting.

4. Enter graph with *average* sentence length and *average* number of syllables; plot dot where the two lines intersect. The area where the dot is plotted will give you the approximate grade level.

5. If a great deal of variability is found in syllable count or sentence count, putting more samples into the average is desirable.

◆ Figure 12.1   Continued

6. A word is defined as a group of symbols with a space on either side; thus, *Joe, IRA, 1945,* and *&* are each one word.

7. A syllable is defined as a phonetic symbol. Generally, there are as many syllables as vowel sounds. For example, *stopped* is one syllable and *wanted* is two syllables. When counting syllables for numerals and initializations, count one syllable for each symbol. For example, *1945* is four syllables, *IRA* is three syllables, and *&* is one syllable.

Source: From *Elementary Reading Instruction,* by E.B. Fry (New York: McGraw-Hill, 1997). Reprinted by permission of McGraw-Hill Companies, Inc.

is a sixth-grade-level word; as a *custom,* it is a tenth-grade-level word; as a *diplomatic agreement,* it is a twelfth-grade-level word. Its use in the particular passage affects the readability of the passage.

Early in their academic lives, students need to develop a healthy respect for textbooks as resources and reference tools. Although they may sometimes find textbooks formidable in size, appearance, or writing style, children shouldn't view them as the sole source of information but rather as one of many sources. Their misperceptions develop when textbooks become the exclusive domain of learning in content areas. As teachers, we can make the transition to textbook study less difficult by creating opportunities for learning that capitalize on a variety of informational sources.

Sue Mathieson, a first-grade teacher in a rural Pennsylvania school district, focuses her reading instruction around content area subject matter. Her students read and write about science. "They want to know about their world and how it works. They study animals with such enthusiasm! But to my amazement, they are equally interested in photosynthesis and how plants grow?" Such natural interest in the working of the world helps Sue design intrinsically motivating reading lessons.

Alternative sources of information—biographies, informational books, picture books, realistic and historical fiction, manuals, magazines, pamphlets, electronic texts, and reference books—help children recognize that learning in content areas requires exposure to many genres in literature. When teachers integrate textbook study with other kinds of prints, they extend and enrich the curriculum.

USING LITERATURE AND NONFICTION TRADE BOOKS ACROSS THE CURRICULUM

The use of children's literature and nonfiction trade books in elementary classrooms extends and enriches information provided in content area textbooks. Often textbooks cannot treat subject matter with the breadth and depth necessary to develop ideas and concepts fully. Literature and nonfiction **trade books** have the potential to capture children's interest and imagination in people, places, events, and ideas. And they have the potential to develop in-depth understanding in ways that textbooks aren't equipped to do.

Fry Short Passage Readability Formula

Rules

1. Use on a passage that is at least three sentences and forty words long.

2. Select at least three key words that are necessary for understanding the passage. You may have more key words.

3. Look up the grade level of each key word in *The Living Word Vocabulary.**

4. Average the three hardest key words. This gives you Word Difficulty.

5. Count the number of words in each sentence and give each sentence a grade level using the sentence length chart.

6. Average the grade level of all sentences. This gives you the Sentence Difficulty.

7. Finally, average the Sentence Difficulty (Step 6) and the Word Difficulty (Step 4). This gives you the Readability estimate of the short passage.

Formula

$$\text{Readability} = \frac{\text{Word Difficulty} + \text{Sentence Difficulty}}{2}$$

Cautions

1. This method should be used only when a long passage is not available. With anything 300 words or longer, use the regular Readability Graph.

2. This method was developed on passages at least three sentences and 40 words long. With anything shorter than that, use the formula at your own risk. It may be better than nothing, but certainly has less reliability.

3. Be careful when looking up the grade level of the key words that you get the grade level for the same meaning as the meaning of that key word as it is used in the passage.

4. The range is grade levels 4–12. In reporting any score 4.0 or below, call it "4th grade or below" and any score above 12.9 call "12th grade or above."

SENTECE LENGTH (DIFFICULTY) CHART

WORDS PER SENTENCE	GRADE LEVEL ESTIMATE	WORDS PER SENTENCE	GRADE LEVEL ESTIMATE
6.6 or below	1	23.2	10
8.6	2	23.8	11
10.8	3	24.3	12
12.5	4	25.0	13
14.2	5	25.6	14
15.8	6	26.3	15
18.2	7	27.0	16
20.4	8	Above 27	17
22.2	9		

*By Edgar Dale & Joseph O'Rourke, Elgin, IL: Dome, 1976.

Source: From "A Readability Formula for Short Passages," by E. B. Fry, in *Journal of Reading, 33*, p. 595. Copyright © 1990. Reprinted with permission of the International Reading Association.

We discussed in Chapter 10 how to choose literature for the classroom. According to Moss (1991), informational book selections should be made on the basis of the "five *A*'s": the *authority* of the *author*, the *appropriateness* of the book for the children in the classroom, the literary *artistry*, and the *appearance* of the book. *Eye Openers II*, by Kobrin (1995), provides brief synopses and teaching ideas for hundreds of high-quality nonfiction trade books.

Nonetheless, having a wide array of literature and nonfiction trade books available for content area learning is necessary but not sufficient to ensure that children make good use of trade books. Teachers must plan for their use by weaving trade books into meaningful and relevant instructional activities within the context of content area study. In this section, the focus is not only on the uses and benefits of literature and nonfiction trade books across the curriculum but also on the preparation of units of study to help you identify concepts, select literature, and develop activities.

Some Uses and Benefits of Literature and Nonfiction Trade Books

There are many benefits to using trade books and **literature across the curriculum,** either in tandem with textbooks or in units of study around a thematic unit. For one, trade books and other literature provide students with intense involvement in a subject; for another, they are powerful schema builders; for a third, they may be used to accommodate a wide range of student abilities and interests. With trade books, children may choose from a variety of topics for intensive study and inquiry. One benefit for the teacher, of course, is that literature may be used instructionally in a variety of ways.

Intense Involvement. A textbook compresses information. Intensive treatment gives way to extensive coverage. As a result, an elementary textbook is more likely to mention and summarize important ideas, events, and concepts rather than develop them fully or richly. Brozo and Tomlinson (1986) underscored this point by illustrating the content treatment of Hitler, the Nazis, and the Jews in a fifth-grade social studies textbook.

> Hitler's followers were called Nazis. Hitler and the Nazis built up Germany's military power and started a campaign against the Jews who lived in that country. Hitler claimed that the Jews were to blame for Germany's problems. He took away their rights and property. Many Jews left Germany and came to live in the United States. The Nazis began to arrest Jews who stayed in Germany and put them in special camps. Then the Nazis started murdering them. Before Hitler's years in power came to an end, six million Jews lost their lives.

A textbook, as you can surmise from this example, often condenses a subject to its barest essentials. The result often is a bland and watered-down treatment of their subjects, which is particularly evident in today's history texts (Sewell, 1987). The paragraph on Hitler's treatment of the Jews is a vivid example of the "principle of minimum essentials" in textbook practice. The passage cited represents the entirety of this particular text's coverage of the Holocaust. Though it may be accurate, it takes one of the most tragic and horrifying events in world history and compresses it into a series of colorless and emotionless summarizing statements.

Greenlaw (1988) noted that most textbooks are written to be "noncontroversial" and have "little style or dramatic flair." What is the alternative to bland and lifeless texts? Greenlaw provides an answer: "Many fine trade books have been published in recent years. . . . We can locate stimulating informational books on almost any topic for almost any level. These books should not become a substitute for the text, but should become an appealing means for students to pursue interests relating to the core topic" (p. 18).

Intense involvement in a subject is one of the major benefits of trade books as a vehicle for content study. What better way to bring to life the realities and horrors of World War II than to have fifth or sixth graders enrich their textbook study by reading (or listening to) trade books.

A favorite story of many middle-grade students involving the German occupation of Europe during World War II is *The Winter When Time Was Frozen* (Pelgrom, 1980). The story is about a young girl, Noortje, and her life as an evacuee on the Everingens' farm in the Netherlands. Brozo and Tomlinson (1986) reported that after hearing her teacher read the story aloud, one fifth grader responded: "This book describes the life of these people so well you'd think the Everingens and the other people were a part of your own family." According to Brozo and Tomlinson, "Were it not for stories like these, most historical events of national and international scope and most notable human achievements and tragedies would remain for many American children distant or even mythical notions with no emotional connections" (p. 290).

Schema Building.

Intense involvement in a subject generates background knowledge and vicarious experience that make textbook concepts easier to grasp and assimilate. As a result, one of the most compelling uses of trade books is as schema builders for subjects under textbook study. Trade books provide background knowledge and vicarious experiences that children are not likely to encounter in textbooks.

The transition to content area reading is smoother when students bring a frame of reference to textbook study. Reading literature strengthens the reading process because reading about a topic can dramatically improve comprehension of related readings on the same topic (Crafton, 1983). The background knowledge acquired in the natural reading of trade books helps students comprehend related discourse. Trade books also create interest and arouse curiosity in areas such as science, health, social studies, and history.

Abilities and Interests.

When teachers use trade books in tandem with textbooks, there's something for everyone. A teacher can provide students with trade books on a variety of topics related to a subject under investigation. Books on related topics are written at various levels of difficulty. Greenlaw (1988) maintained that one of the benefits of trade books is that children can select books on a reading level appropriate to their abilities and interests. Self-selection may range from picture books to books written for adults: "All selections should be valued, and students should be encouraged to share the information they have gleaned in creative ways" (p. 18).

Resources in Instructional Units.

When planning to incorporate trade books in a unit of study, Brozo and Tomlinson (1986) defined several steps in a teaching strategy.

Trade books and informational texts provide students with intense involvement in a subject.

1. Identify salient concepts that become the content objectives for the unit.

   What are the driving human forces behind the events?

   What patterns of behavior need to be studied?

   What phenomena have affected ordinary people or may affect them in the future?

2. Identify appropriate trade books to help teach concepts.

   Read and become familiar with a variety of children's books.

   Use children's literature textbooks and subject guide reference indexes such as *The Best in Children's Books* (Sutherland, 1980).

3. Teach the unit.

   Use textbook and trade books interchangeably.

   Use strategies such as a read-aloud in which a trade book becomes a schema builder before reading the textbook.

   Use trade books to elaborate and extend content and concepts related to the unit.

4. Follow up.

   Engage students in strategies and activities that involve collaboration, inquiry, and various forms of expression and meaning construction.

   Evaluate students' learning by observing how they interpret and personalize new knowledge.

Trade books, electronic texts, and children's book displays can be used as resource materials for units, student projects, and inquiries. Procedures for guiding inquiry-centered projects are outlined in the Best Practice featured in Box 12.1.

BOX 12.1   BEST PRACTICE

Procedures for Guiding Inquiry and Research Projects

I. Raise questions, identify interests, organize information.
  A. Discuss interest areas related to the unit of study.
  B. Engage in goal setting.
    1. Arouse curiosities.
    2. Create awareness of present levels of knowledge.
  C. Pose questions relating to each area and/or subarea.
    1. "What do you want to find out?"
    2. "What do you want to know about _____?"
    3. Record the questions or topics.
    4. "What do you already know about _____?"
  D. Organize information; have students make predictions about likely answers to gaps in knowledge.
    1. Accept all predictions as possible answers.
    2. Encourage thoughtful speculations in a nonthreatening way.

II. Select materials.
  A. Use visual materials.
    1. Trade books and encyclopedias
    2. Magazines, catalogs, directories
    3. Newspapers and comics
    4. Indexes, atlases, almanacs, dictionaries, readers' guides, computer catalogs
    5. Films, filmstrips, slides
    6. Videotapes, television programs
    7. Electronic texts: CD-ROMs, Web site documents, videodisks
  B. Use nonvisual materials.
    1. Audiotapes
    2. Records
    3. Radio programs
    4. Field trips
  C. Use human resources.
    1. Interviews
    2. Letters
    3. On-site visits
    4. Discussion groups
    5. E-mail
    6. Listservs

(Continued)

BOX 12.1 CONTINUED

    D. Encourage self-selection of materials.
        1. "What can I understand?"
        2. "What gives me the best answers?"
III. Guide the information search.
    A. Encourage active research.
        1. Reading
        2. Listening
        3. Observing
        4. Talking
        5. Writing
    B. Facilitate with questions.
        1. "How are you doing?"
        2. "Can I help you?"
        3. "Do you have all the materials you need?"
        4. "Can I help you with ideas you don't understand?"
    C. Have students keep records.
        1. Learning log that includes plans, procedures, notes, and rough drafts
        2. Book record cards
        3. Record of conferences with the teacher

IV. Consider different forms of writing.
    A. Initiate a discussion of sharing techniques.
    B. Encourage a variety of writing forms.
        1. Essay or paper
        2. Lecture to a specific audience
        3. Case study
        4. Story: adventure, science fiction, other genre
        5. Dialogue, conversation, interview
        6. Dramatization through scripts
        7. Commentary or editorial
        8. Thumbnail sketch

V. Guide the writing process.
    A. Help students organize information.
    B. Guide first-draft writing.
    C. Encourage responding, revising, and rewriting.
    D. "Publish" finished products.
        1. Individual presentations
        2. Classroom arrangement
        3. Class interaction

Source: From *Content Area Reading*, 6th ed., by R. T. Vacca and J. L. Vacca (New York: Longman, 1999). Used by permission of Addison Wesley Educational Publishers.

Developing Units of Study

A unit of study organizes instruction around multiple sources of information within the context of meaningful and relevant classroom activity. You can integrate various content areas around reading and writing strategies and the study of different types of narrative and informational books and electronic texts in ways that will give students a real sense of freedom and continuity in what they are learning.

Getting Started.   The title of the unit reflects the topic or theme to be studied. One of the first steps in planning the unit, as was suggested earlier, involves identifying salient concepts to be learned as a result of participation in unit activities. Once the concepts are identified, selecting information sources and developing activities are next in order.

Webbing.   Often constructing a **literature web** for the unit helps you envision the integration of content with activities and/or informational and electronic sources (Huck, Hepler, & Hickman, 1987).

A literature web shows the relationships that exist among the major components of the unit. Study Figures 12.3 and 12.4; each illustrates a web, one developed by a second-grade teacher for a unit on communities and the other developed by a sixth-grade teacher for a unit on the Middle Ages.

In the sixth-grade web, the teacher elects to organize activities and information sources within the various content areas that will be integrated into the unit. In the second-grade web, the teacher organizes trade books around the types of communities that children will be exploring. Either organizational strategy is useful.

Putting a Unit to Work.   "The heart of a unit," according to Coody and Nelson (1982), "is children's day-to-day learning experiences in the classroom" (p. 23). This couldn't be more the case than in Ms. Mark's third-grade class, where students participated in a four-week science unit on birds. Here's how Ms. Mark described the unit, "Birds Are Special Animals":

> "Birds Are Special Animals" is intended for a class of third-grade students. The unit will require approximately four weeks of daily sessions. For the first three weeks, the focus will be on activities planned for the entire class. During the last week of the unit, the focus will be on small group and individual projects. The students will use *The Life of Birds*, edited by Donald Moyle, as their main reading source. Supplemental readings from other sources will be assigned throughout the unit. Audiovisual materials will be used as needed to introduce and reinforce concepts. Students will also have access to a variety of materials with which they can explore areas of individual interest. During this unit, the students will have the opportunity to investigate many aspects of ornithology including the evolution of birds, the adaptation of birds to their habitats, and the interrelation of birds and people.

◆ FIGURE 12.3   A Second-grade Teacher's Literature Web for a Unit on Communities (some sample titles)

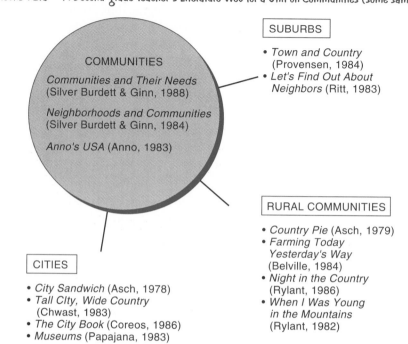

As stated in her description of the unit, *The Life of Birds* was the class's central source of information; it helped form the basis by which students "branched out" into a variety of information sources, both fiction and nonfiction. For example, Ms. Mark used *Mr. Popper's Penguins,* by Atwater, as a read-aloud to introduce children to the study of penguins. *A Chick Hatches,* another read-aloud, was used in conjunction with an experiment on the incubation of an egg. Ms. Mark read different sections of the book during the course of the unit as children observed the egg's hatching and different stages of the chick's development.

The last two weeks of the unit contained equally rich and varied activities but emphasized more writing than the initial assignments. For example, Ms. Mark capitalized on the classroom experiment of hatching a live chick with the following writing activity:

OUR CHICK HAS HATCHED!

After the chick has hatched and the class has decided on its name, each student will write an announcement to his or her family about the new arrival. The announcement will consist of two parts: (1) statistics of the hatching and (2) a personal note.

To help the students write the first part, actual samples of birth announcements were brought in by students and the teacher. These were read aloud and posted on the bulletin

◆ FIGURE 12.4   A Sixth-grade Teacher's Literature Web for a Unit on the Middle Ages

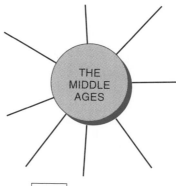

LITERATURE

- *A Door in the Wall*
- *King Arthur and the Knights of the Round Table*
- *Living in a Castle*
- *St. George and the Dragon*
- Poem: "Vision of Piers the Ploughman"
- *The Middle Ages*
- *History of Technology*
- *Medieval People*
- *Sports and Pastimes of England*
- *Looking into the Middle Ages*

RESOURCE PEOPLE

- Calligraphy speaker
- Juggler
- Court jester
- Madrigal singer
- Traveling minstrel

CULMINATING ACTIVITIES

- King Arthur videotape
- Medieval pop-up book
- Manor feast
- Medieval exhibit at art museum

CREATIVE WRITING

- Story starter with the spelling words
- Oath of knighthood
- Dragonfighter diary
- Castle comparison
- Compare life of serf and American slave

THE MIDDLE AGES

ART

- Copies of paintings by Van Eyck, da Vinci, Van der Weyden, Holbein
- Stained glass windows
- Family shield
- Design/build a castle
- Calligraphy
- Manor banners

MUSIC AND DANCE

- *A Tournament of Knights* by Joe Lasker
- *Duet Time Book 2* by Sonya Burakoff
- *A Hole in the Wall:* English dance
- *Road to the Isles* dance: Phylis Weikart
- Introduction to Gregorian chant

SCIENCE AND HEALTH

- The "Black Death"
- Use of metal for armor
- Invention of the longbow
- Discovery of gunpowder
- Roger Bacon's interest in alchemy

ONGOING ACTIVITIES

- Word wall
- Bulletin board timeline
- Mural of village of Camelot

board. The teacher used these samples to walk the students through the process of announcing birth statistics, including name, date, weight, and length.

When the students had some practice with the first part of the assignment, some additional guidelines were given for writing the personal note. The personal note was not to be longer than one page, and it was to focus on the one aspect of the incubation process that most impressed the student.

Developing a unit of study involves deliberate teacher planning to set a tone for students to actively engage in learning around a content theme or topic. It allows a rich opportunity to make reading useful by bridging the gap between children and content area textbooks.

The activities used in a unit of study evolve from your knowledge or reading, writing, discussion, and listening strategies. The reading of electronic texts may be included in these units of study to facilitate learning in content areas.

Learning with Electronic Texts

In Chapters 9 and 11, we discussed the different forms electronic texts may take, such as pages on the World Wide Web, E-mail and discussion groups, word processed documents, and interactive software programs using CD-ROMs. How do electronic texts enhance content area reading and writing? Gates (1988) provides a good explanation of the benefits of using electronic texts in content area study:

> People don't think and learn in a straight line, from one fact to another; they go off on a million tangents, because they're interested in a million things. They don't want to learn only what symphonies Beethoven wrote; they want to hear them, and to know what was going on in Germany—or the world—at the time, who Beethoven's contemporaries were, how literature and art were influenced by his music, and so on. (p. 14)

Blanchard and Rottenberg (1990, pp. 659–660) describe a hypertext application for social studies titled *Presidential Election of 1912*. In this application, students exploring many aspects of information related to American life in 1912 have choices concerning which way to go in their learning. One minute they may read about poverty, race relations, political satire, women's suffrage, unions, trusts, or monopolies; the next minute they can explore the impact of these issues on the presidential election of 1912. Students can also use a detailed simulation of the election to see how results could have been changed.

All this can occur using *Timetable of History*, a hypertext application that integrates graphic representation with speech to permit students to explore links among historical events. With the click of a mouse, students can move from a timeline with a range of dates to a spoken message concerning an important technological invention of that era to a screen giving details of a specific event (Wood, 1989).

It's apparent to students and teachers that electronic media facilitate students' inquiry learning. In a hypertext environment, students can ask questions that have relevance to them, explore answers to these questions, and devise new related questions as they continue to explore electronic texts. The challenge to the teacher then becomes how to guide students in this process. Next we will look at strategies designed to help students learn from texts. They are appropriate with expository texts but in many cases can be adapted to stories.

STRATEGIES BEFORE READING

The strategies in this section augment those found in Chapter 7. For learning to occur, there must be a point of contact between the reader's knowledge of the world and the ideas communicated by the textbook author. As we explained in Chapter 7, what students know, feel, and believe is a major factor in learning; it helps determine the extent to which they will make sense out of any situation. Thus an instructional goal worth pursuing is to help students make contact through a variety of learning strategies that build and activate background knowledge. Such strategies involve prereading preparation.

Teachers can help students learn new ideas by giving them a frame of reference as they get ready to read. A frame of reference is actually an anchor point; it reflects the cognitive structure students need to relate new information to existing knowledge. Helping students organize what they know and showing them where and how new ideas fit is essential for learning to take place.

Previewing and Skimming

A good way to start previewing with a group of children is to model some questions that all readers ask to prepare for reading. **Previewing,** after all, should help students become aware of the purposes for a reading assignment. "What kind of reading are we going to do?" "What is our goal?" "Should we try to remember details or look for the main ideas?" "How much time will this assignment take?" "What things do we already know about _____ (the solar system, for example)?" "What do we still need to find out?" These questions prepare children for what's coming. Raising questions and setting purposes is the beginning of efficient processing of information. It calls for further explicit instruction in previewing.

First, select a subject area in which your textbook contains aids that are obviously visual. The textbook writer has incorporated a number of organizational and typographic aids as guideposts for readers. Point out how the table of contents, preface, chapter introductions or summaries, and chapter questions can give readers valuable clues about the overall structure of a textbook or the important ideas in a unit or chapter. Previewing a table of contents, for example, not only creates a general impression, but also helps readers of all ages distinguish the forest from the trees. The table of contents give students a feel for the overall theme or structure of the course material so that they may get a sense of the scope and sequence of ideas at the very beginning of the unit. You can also use the table of contents to build background and discuss the relatedness of each of the parts of the book. Model for students the kinds of questions that should be raised. "Why do the authors begin with _____ in Part One?" "If you were the author, would you have arranged the major parts in the text differently?" "Why?"

To illustrate how you might use the table of contents, study how a fourth-grade teacher introduced a unit on plants in the environment. Ms. Henderson asked her students to open their books to Part One, titled "Plant Competitors," in the table of contents. "What do you think this part of the book is about?" "Why do you think so?" Key words or terms in the table of contents led to these questions: "What do you think the author means by 'unwanted plants'?" "What does *parasite* mean?" "What do parasites have to do with *nongreen plants*?" Open-ended questions such as these helped Ms. Henderson keep her fourth-graders focused on the material and on the value of predicting and anticipating content.

As these students get into a particular chapter, they will learn how to use additional organizational aids such as the chapter's introduction, summary, or questions at the end. These aids should create a frame of reference for the important ideas in the chapter. Readers can also survey chapter titles, headings, subheadings, words and phrases in special type, pictures, diagrams, charts, and graphs.

Here are some rules or steps to follow when previewing as Ms. Henderson's students did.

◆ Read the title, converting it to a question. ("What are plant competitors in man's environment?")

◆ Read the introduction, summary, and questions, stating the author's main points. ("All living things compete with each other; the competitors of useful plants become the competitors of humans as well; weeds are unwanted plants; nongreen plants living in or on other plants and animals are parasites; people try to control plant competitors.")

◆ Read the heads and subheads; then convert them to questions. (Competition; weeds; nongreen plant competitors; controlling plant competitors. "How are plant competitors controlled?")

◆ Read highlighted print. (Competitors; nongreen plants; parasites; smut. "Chemical sprays are very poisonous.")

◆ Study visual materials; what do pictures, maps, and other displayed elements tell about a chapter's content? (Pictures of mustard plants, destroyed ears of corn, a white pine attacked by tiny nongreen plants, a helicopter spraying a truck farm.)

Until Ms. Henderson's fourth graders were able to do this somewhat independently, she walked them through the steps many times. She also selected one or two pages from the assigned reading and developed transparencies with some questions her students should ask while previewing. Showing the overhead transparencies to the whole class, she explained her reasons for the questions. Then the students opened their books to another section of the chapter, taking turns asking the kinds of questions she had modeled. Soon they raised some of their own questions while previewing.

Skimming.   Learning how to skim content material effectively is a natural part of previewing. *Skimming* involves intensive previewing of the reading assignment to see what it will be about. To help elementary students get a good sense of what is coming, have them read the first sentence of every paragraph (often an important idea). The fourth graders about to study plant competitors read these first sentences.

If you had two pet cats and gave one of them some tuna fish, what would happen?

Plants, of course, don't know they are competing.

Even green plants compete with one another for energy sources.

Plants are often weakened by the parasites growing on them.

Many states passed laws to help with the control of weeds.

An effective motivator for raising students' expectations about their assigned text material is to direct them to skim the entire reading selection rapidly, taking no more than two minutes. You might even get a timer and encourage the children to zip through every page. When time is up, ask the class to recall everything they've read. Both the teacher and the students will be surprised by the quantity and quality of the recalls.

Previewing and skimming are important strategies for helping children develop knowledge of textbook aids and for surveying texts to make predictions. They help get at general understanding as students learn how to size up material, judge its relevance to a topic, or gain a good idea of what a passage is about.

Organizers

To prepare children conceptually for ideas to be encountered in reading, help them link what they know to what they will learn. An **organizer** provides a frame of reference for comprehending text precisely for this reason—to help readers make connections between their prior knowledge and new material. Swaby (1983) defined organizers as involving teacher-directed attempts to clarify and organize students' thinking "in such a way that they know what information they already have that will be important and helpful in comprehending incoming information. . . . Any effort by a teacher to prepare students conceptually for incoming information by hooking the major concepts of the new information to the concepts already possessed by the learners can be interpreted as an advance organizer" (p. 76).

There's no one way to develop or use an organizer. Organizers may also be developed as *written previews* or as *verbal presentations*. Whatever format you decide to use, an organizer should highlight key concepts and ideas to be encountered in print. These should be prominent and easily identifiable in the lesson presentation. Another key feature of an organizer activity should be the explicit links made between the children's background knowledge and experience and the ideas in the reading selection.

An organizer may be developed for narrative or expository text. It can be used for difficult text selections, when the material is unfamiliar to students because of limited schemata. An organizer can be constructed by following these guidelines:

◆ Analyze the content of a reading selection, identifying its main ideas and key concepts.

◆ Link these ideas directly to children's experiences and storehouse of knowledge. Use real-life incidents, examples, illustrations, analogies, or anecdotes to which student readers can relate.

◆ Raise questions in the organizer that will pique interest and engage students in thinking about the text to be read.

Study the advance organizer in Figure 12.5; then read the selection that follows.

UNDERSTANDING THE LANGUAGE OF A DOG

Dogs may not use words to tell how they feel, but they do use parts of their bodies to talk. This is called "body language." When you wave to someone, you are using body language. When a dog wags its tail, it is using body language, too.

Most dogs have a strong sense of *territoriality*. This means they are protective of things that belong to them, including their living space. A dog may feel quite strongly about its bed, a favorite toy, or the backyard. And it is the dog's sense of territoriality that makes it communicate through its body.

A dog may use its body to say many things. By bowing down, wagging its tail, barking, or holding out one front paw, the dog may be saying, "Let's play." When the dog crouches down and rolls over on its back, it means, "Come closer." And if the dog scratches at you with a paw, it may mean, "I want something."

A dog may use body language to warn you away from its territory. To do this, the dog may show its teeth, stick its ears up, growl, or hold its tail out stiffly. This means, "Stay

◆ FIGURE 12.5

Organizer for the Reading Selection "Understanding the Language of a Dog"

Main Idea of Passage to Be Read	Dogs and human beings are alike in an important way. We both use "language" to communicate messages to others. A dog uses a unique language.
Building and Sharing Prior Knowledge and Experiences	When you think of our "language," what comes to mind immediately? *Probably words.* Using words in speaking and writing is one way to communicate a message to someone else. But try to think about how you sit or stand when you're angry or pouting. Can someone get the message you're trying to communicate just by looking at you? How about when you're nervous or excited? How else do we show others what we're feeling or thinking about without using words? (Discuss the other elements of body language.) Can anyone ever tell what your pet is thinking or feeling? How? (Discuss student responses. Compare examples.)
Making the Connection Between Prior Knowledge and the Passage to Be Read	Use what we have just discussed so far to read the passage for today. Look for specific ways in which a dog can communicate with you or with other animals.

away." The dog may growl, crouch, lower its tail, and flatten its ears against its head. This means, "Better stay away. I'm not sure about you."

As we already suggested, the key to a successful organizer lies in the discussion that it initiates. Children must participate actively in making the links between what they know and what they will learn. Much will be lost if they are assigned to read (or listen or view) an organizer without the opportunity to act on it within the context of their own experiences.

Graphic Organizers.   Key concepts or main ideas in the material being studied can also be displayed as a **graphic organizer,** in which key technical terms are arranged to show their relationships to each other.

Ms. Mark designed a graphic organizer to show her third graders vocabulary in relation to more inclusive vocabulary concepts they would meet in their study of birds. Before constructing this activity, Ms. Mark listed the key concepts in her four-week unit, "Birds

Are Special Animals." She then followed the steps suggested by Barron (1968) for developing an organizer and introducing it to her students.

1. *Analyze vocabulary and list important words.* Ms. Mark found these key terms in *The Life of Birds,* edited by Donald Moyle:

   prehistoric birds   protection
   development   language
   behavior   ornithology
   migration   difference

2. *Arrange the concepts to be learned.* Ms. Mark first chose the word *ornithology* as the most inclusive concept, superordinate to all the others. Next she classified the terms immediately *under* the superordinate concept and coordinated them with each other.

3. *Add any other vocabulary terms that you believe students understand.* Ms. Mark added terms like *protect, animals,* and *help.*

4. *Evaluate the organizer.* The interrelationships among the key terms looked like Figure 12.6 and made sense to Ms. Mark and her third graders.

5. *Introduce students to the learning task.* Ms. Mark created as much discussion as possible among her third graders as she presented the vocabulary terms. She drew on their understanding and previous experiences with birds as well as on class activities over the previous few days that introduced the unit (e.g., some preassessment and an anticipation guide).

◆ FIGURE 12.6   A Graphic Organizer

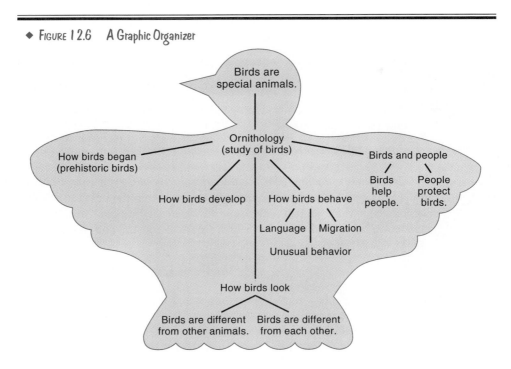

6. *As you complete the learning task, relate new information to the overview.* Using this overview as a study guide throughout the bird unit, Ms. Mark encouraged students to discuss what information was still needed and where it might best be located on the graphic organizer.

Anticipation Guides

By creating anticipation about the meaning of what will be read, teachers facilitate student-centered purposes for reading. An **anticipation guide** is a series of oral or written statements for individual students to respond to before they read the text assignment. The statements serve as a springboard into discussion. Students must rely on what they already know to make educated guesses about the material to be read: They must make predictions.

Let's go back to the fourth-grade class studying about plants in the environment. The teacher, Ms. Henderson, wanted to help students discuss what they knew and believed about the unit in order to raise their expectations about the content matter before reading the text. Above all, she was determined to involve students actively. Here are the guidelines that Ms. Henderson followed in constructing and using anticipation guides.

1. Analyze the material to be read. Determine the major ideas, implicit and explicit, with which students will interact.

2. Write those ideas in short, clear declarative statements. These statements should in some way reflect the world that students live in or know about. Therefore, avoid abstractions whenever possible.

3. Put these statements into a format that will elicit anticipation and prediction making.

4. Discuss readers' predictions and anticipations prior to reading the text selection.

5. Assign the text selection. Have students evaluate the statements in light of the author's intent and purpose.

6. Contrast readers' predictions with the author's intended meaning.

Using these guidelines, Ms. Henderson pinpointed several major concepts, put them in the form of short statements, and wrote each one on the board. After some initial discussion about what students might already know about plants in the environment, Ms. Henderson distributed two 3-by-5-inch pieces of construction paper (one green and one yellow) to each child and explained:

> On the yellow paper, write "unlikely," and on the green paper, write "likely." I will read each of the statements on the board; you will think about it and decide whether it is "likely" or "unlikely." Then, after 15 seconds, I will say, "Go," and you will hold up either your yellow *or* your green card.

The anticipation guide for this activity included several statements.

> A dandelion is always a weed.

> All plants make their own food.

The information in each of the statements was developed in two short chapters in the students' text. After each statement or pair of statements, Ms. Henderson encouraged the children to discuss the reasons for their responses with questions such as "Why?" "Why not?" or "Can you give an example?"

An interesting example of how an anticipation guide may be used in conjunction with a four-day lesson is contained in Figure 12.7. It was designed for use with third graders as an introduction to a unit on primates revolving around *The Story of Nim, the Chimp Who Learned Language*, by Anna Michel.

After the small group discussion, the whole class discusses the trends and ideas that emerged in the groups. These ideas are written on the board in a place where they can re-

---

◆ FIGURE 12.7

Anticipation Guide for THE STORY OF NIM, THE CHIMP WHO LEARNED LANGUAGE

DIRECTIONS: Read the statements below and place a check next to those that you agree with. Discuss your choices in small groups and explain why you agreed with the statements you checked.

_____ 1. Chimpanzees can imitate what humans do but attach no meaning to their actions.

_____ 2. Language can be learned by animals in the same way and sequence in which a child learns language.

_____ 3. Once language is learned, a chimpanzee will forget it and those who taught him, given an absence from one or both.

_____ 4. Scientists undertake projects with animals in order to better understand humans.

_____ 5. Relationships between animals and people aren't as close as those between people and people or animals and animals.

Source: Developed by Elizabeth Martin and reprinted with permission.

main for a day or two. The book is then assigned in its entirety to be read before the next day's class. Next day, students consider each statement on the anticipation guide again and discuss in small groups the ideas that emerged from reading the text. They compare these with the prereading ideas on the board to identify similarities and differences in the two sets of ideas. Students should give reasons for the ideas, and controversial issues arising might then lead to a debate. For example, "What is the real meaning in a chimpanzee's language acquisition compared with a human child's?"

Brainstorming

As a prereading activity, **brainstorming** is especially helpful in getting students to generate ideas they can use to think about the upcoming reading material. The brainstorming procedure involves two basic steps: (1) identifying a broad concept that reflects the main topic to be studied in the assigned reading and (2) having students work in small groups to generate a list of words related to the broad concept within a specified length of time.

Brainstorming sessions are valuable not only from an instructional perspective but from a diagnostic one as well. Observant teachers discover what knowledge their students possess about the topic to be studied. Brainstorming also helps students become aware of how much they know, individually and collectively, about the topic.

Some teachers assign a hypothetical problem to be solved before reading a selection or perhaps a real-life school-related problem. Others simply select a major concept in the reading material and get students actively involved in brainstorming. Mr. Davis, a sixth-grade teacher, used the latter model to develop a brainstorming activity for a story by Robert Zacks, "The Nest."

Mr. Davis began by telling his sixth graders they would soon be reading a story called "The Nest." But first, he said, they would work with one of the major concepts of the story, *restrictions*. He divided the class into small groups, using an alphabetical scheme. (Other times he may choose the groups or let students form their own groups.) Once the groups were formed, Mr. Davis used a three-step brainstorming activity.

1. In your groups, brainstorm as many ideas as possible in three minutes that relate to the concept *restrictions*. Have one member of your group record your ideas.

2. As a group, put the ideas into categories (groups) wherever they seem to be related. Be prepared to explain the reasons behind the grouping of ideas.

3. Following class discussion on how ideas were grouped, examine your own work again and, using these ideas and others gained from the other groups, predict what you believe the story might be about. Be sure to consider the title of the story somewhere in your predictions.

The activity took about 20 minutes and required intermittent teacher direction. Mr. Davis, for example, followed step 1 with a brief oral direction for step 2. Before moving on to step 3, he initiated a class discussion in which groups shared their ideas for grouping ideas into categories and the logic behind the categories. This gave both individuals and groups a chance to react to the various categories. Although a teacher may offer some suggestions to a group that has bogged down in the categorizing process, we caution that this be done sparingly and only to keep the process going.

After step 3 of the brainstorming activity is complete and predictions have been generated, the story is usually assigned. It would, however, also be possible to extend the pre-reading phase. To illustrate, Mr. Davis might have asked students to complete a survey of parents, grandparents, and other adults about restrictions they faced earlier in life and which ones bothered them the most.

Extending Content Learning Through Reading and Writing

Next we examine some teaching strategies that can be used in content areas to increase concept learning: the point-of-view guide, idea circles, I-Charts, and computer-based inquiry using I-Charts. All of these strategies can be used with textbook material, informational books, or narrative stories.

Point-of-View Guide

As noted earlier, at times children may find learning with textbooks challenging or even difficult. The wide range of abilities in most classrooms requires that teachers employ strategies for better comprehension of textbook content. Because comprehension usually occurs when readers *use existing knowledge to reconstruct meaning* from text, teachers need to use strategies that *effect the reconstruction process.* Effecting the reconstruction process involves expanding readers' view, theories, or ideas. A point-of-view guide is designed to activate students' prior knowledge by having them elaborate what is read through the use of alternative perspectives.

Point-of-view guides are questions that are presented in an interview format. Students are instructed to role-play, writing in the *first person* to ensure that different perspectives are being taken, elaborating whenever possible with information from their experiences. In answering the interview questions, students actively contribute their own experiences to the role, which ultimately enhances their recall and comprehension. These questions allow students to elaborate and speculate. The purpose of the point-of-view guide is to develop mental elaboration (students add their own information as they read) and mental recitation (students put new information in their own words, merging text-based and reader-based information). In this way, students learn the content of the reading selection. An example of a point-of-view guide, used in a social studies lesson on the Boston Massacre, appears in Figure 12.8. In the figure, you can see how Billy, a fifth grader, responded to the guide. In this case, the teacher used the guide with the "think, pair, share" strategy: After the children had read the passage, the teacher asked them to *think* about the question, to *pair* with another student and talk about how they would answer the question, and then to *share* by writing down their response.

Point-of-View Guide
Social Studies, Grade 5

The Boston Massacre

Text Passage: On March 5, 1770, Boston did explode. A group of colonists had gathered at Boston Customs House. The group, led by Crispus Attucks and others, began to throw snowballs at the British soldier on duty. Soon eight other British soldiers arrived. "Come on, you rascals," the mob yelled. "You lobster scoundrels. Fire if you dare." For a while, the soldiers did nothing.

The group grew larger and larger. Fearing for their safety, the soldiers began to panic. Suddenly, in the confusion, a soldier fired. Then the other soldiers fired. When the smoke cleared, Attucks and two other men lay dead. Two more would die later from their wounds.

Colonial leaders called the event the Boston Massacre. A **massacre** is the killing of a number of defenseless people. Colonists used the shooting as **propaganda,** information used to win support for a cause. By calling the incident a massacre, the colonists suggested that having British troops in the colonies was dangerous. (*Build Our Nation.* Boston: Houghton Mifflin, 1997, p. 250)

Question 1: Imagine yourself as the British soldier who first fired your gun. Pretend you are talking to your friends after the incident, telling them what happened. What were the reasons for firing your gun? How did you feel when the colonists were yelling at you and throwing snowballs at you? How did you feel and what did you do when the other British soldiers began firing also?

Dear Tom,

I think I started a war with Britain and the colonists. The colonists were calling us names and throwing snowballs at us. There soon was a huge crowd. That was when I was scared and started to fear for my life. It just got to the point where I was so scared that I started to fire. When the smoke cleared I had realized what I had done. That night I thought to myself and said, "I didn't have to take that from them. I had the gun and had to show them who was in control." So I think I was right to show them who was boss. I also think it was wrong for me to fire at them. That is why I had to talk to someone about it.

Sincerly, Billy Kaiser

◆ FIGURE 12.8 Continued

> Question 2: Imagine you were the colonist who followed Crispus Attucks and yelled out to the British soldiers. You admired Attucks, and one of the other colonists was a close friend of yours. Pretend you are talking to your friends after the incident, telling them what happened. What would you say? Why do you think the incident occurred?

Dear Tom,

That incident that happened yesterday was wrong. We were defenseless and they just fired at us. I lost my best friend in that incident. I also lost the person I admired Crispus Attucks. I need to get revenge on them. They invaded my colony, took over my life, and killed my friends. They won't get away with this. If I have to I will fight. They can't invade our territory and kill our friends! It isn't right. Someone has to put a stop to this.

Sincerly, Billy Kaiser

Now let's turn our attention to another strategy that encourages students to integrate learning, idea circles.

Idea Circles

Idea circles are small peer-led group discussions of concepts fueled by multiple text sources. Idea circles are similar to the literature circles discussed in Chapter 10 in that they are composed of three to six students and are peer-led, with interaction rules explicitly discussed and posted. In idea circles, students discuss a concept. Since the students read different informational books, they bring unique information to the idea circle. In the circle, they discuss facts about this concept and relations among the facts and explanations. The teacher provides a chart to guide collaborative discussion, like the one on bats in Figure 12.9. The goal of the idea circle needs to be communicated explicitly. Teachers should tell students what they are expected to accomplish in an allotted time for discussion. The desired product may be individual or collective. Either way, if the desired end product is articulated well at the beginning of the discussion, less time will be spent arguing over what to do, and more time will be invested in actually doing it (Guthrie & McCann, 1996).

See the Class Works featured in Box 12.2 for a description of a third-grade teacher's use of idea circles.

◆ Figure 12.9

Chart to Guide Collaborative Discussion in an Idea Circle

Subject: science in a unit on animals   Topic: bats   Grade 3

Ask your friends and family members what they think about bats. Write their responses here. We will share these responses with the class as a whole.

Find the following information, using your book about bats. It is possible that the book you are using will not include all of these. You may have to get some of this information from others in the idea circle.

Reasons why people are afraid of bats

Myths about bats

Good qualities of bats

Some interesting facts about bats

BOX 12.2 CLASS WORKS

Idea Circles in Third-Grade Science

Michelle McComb's third-grade classroom is filled with students' voices as they work in idea circles. She walks between these student-led groups. The students, each drawing from a different informational text, are involved in debate, often pointing to pictures and captions, taking notes, and composing paragraphs. Michelle engaged her students in these idea circles at about the midpoint in a five-week unit on mammals in which a textbook, literature, and informational trade books were used. At this point, she felt that her students were familiar enough with the topic and one another to be productive in child-led discussion groups. Her lesson plan unfolded in the following way.

TOPIC

Bats

OBJECTIVES

The students will be able to:

◆ Discuss what they have read

◆ Use texts to find specific information

◆ Integrate reading with speaking, listening, viewing, and writing

◆ Explore the importance of various habits of mind in making observations, reports, and decisions

◆ Work collaboratively with peers and learners of different ages and talents to identify characteristics of bats

PROCEDURES

◆ Class members were to ask their friends and family members what they thought about bats. Ideas from a whole class discussion are listed:

  Most people are either frightened a little or very frightened by bats.
  Some people know that bats help us by eating bugs.
  A few thought that bats bite people.

◆ Students are organized into idea circles, first to work on why people are frightened by bats. Once the groups are established, the guidelines for idea circles are reviewed and the expectations for work are outlined.

◆ Students are given time to read their informational books to explore reasons why people are afraid of bats. Groups come together to compile and list their ideas on large chart paper. Some ideas may include:

  Bats carry rabies.
  People can die if they are bitten by a bat.

(Continued)

BOX 12.2   CONTINUED

Bats get tangled in your hair.
Vampire bats eat blood.
They look scary because they show their sharp teeth.

◆ Students are told, "Many people fear bats because they don't know about their good qualities. As members of the B.A.T. (Bats Are Terrific) Club, it is our job to help educate others. In your idea circle, you will use the books about bats to find and chart information about bats. Then you will work together to create a poster. We will hang the posters in our school to help others learn about this gentle creature." Posters may:
Disprove a myth about bats
Tell about their good qualities
Show interesting facts about bats

◆ Students are told what their group is to do:
Read through the bat books for information.
Share what you learned.
Discuss ideas for your poster.
Create a poster using chart paper and markers.
Hang your poster up to share with the whole class.

◆ Students are given time to collaborate in their idea circles. Depending on the ability level of the students, the assignment may take one half-hour session daily for two to four days.

◆ When the posters are completed, the students hang them in the classroom to share with their classmates. Finally, the posters are hung around the school.

ASSESSMENT

During idea circle time, the teacher circulates in the classroom to not only guide the students' work but also informally to assess their progress. She may keep anecdotal records or a checklist that records students' understanding of the concepts and their abilities to work in cooperative groups. The final product, the poster, is used for assessment. In addition to the poster, the students' oral explanation to the class will reveal their understanding of the concepts.

Reflective Inquiry

◆ Why is it helpful to begin idea circles with different ideas about a topic?

◆ How does this teacher view assessment?

◆ What do you think about the importance of a teacher's planning and organizing for inquiry learning?

I-Charts

A common pitfall for elementary students in completing research projects is copying pages of unorganized facts out of encyclopedias using a note card system. **I-Charts,** as explained by Sally Randall (1996), were created to organize note taking, encourage critical thinking that builds on students' prior knowledge, and increase metacognitive awareness. Using I-Charts helps students identify what they want to know, organize the information read, and determine if they have adequately answered their research question.

In using I-Charts, a teacher should introduce the process by guiding the whole class on the same topic with differing subtopics on each I-Chart. The procedures for using I-Charts can be found in the Best Practice featured in Box 12.3.

When examining sources of information, students are encouraged to keep the I-Chart in front of them while they skim each new source to determine if it is helpful. As they read a source, they pull the chart with the subtopic matching the information they were reading

BOX 12.3   BEST PRACTICE

Steps in Using I-Charts for Guiding the Research Project

◆ Each child writes a topic proposal. A proposal explains the topic that interests the student about which he or she wants to learn more. For example, if the unit of study is mammals, that topic might be how a whale, a particular mammal, adapts to its environment, the ocean. In the proposal, students would explain their interest, list what they already know, and detail where they think they will find more information.

◆ The students brainstorm questions that cannot be answered yes or no, to which they would like to find answers. It is helpful for this step to be done in groups of three or four, even when students chose different topics, for example, different mammals. This significantly increases background knowledge and enthusiasm.

◆ Students are given ten copies of blank I-Charts (see Figure 12.10). One copy of the I-Chart is used for each subtopic research question. The I-Charts can be kept in a notebook.

◆ Students find their sources of information in libraries, by conducting interviews with experts, and by requesting letters to agencies. The Internet and CD-ROMs can also be used as sources of information.

◆ In the middle section of the I-Chart, after completing notes on all available information from one such source, students draw a line on the chart after the last recorded fact for that source (see Figure 12.11). On the left, the sources are numbered in the order the student uses them. The references are recorded on a separate sheet.

◆ As the students read sources of information, they will also find and write down interesting related facts and key words near the bottom of the chart. New questions to research often become new subtopics to include in the project.

◆ FIGURE 12.10

I-Chart

Names: Topic:

Subtopic:

What I already know:

Bibliography number:	

Interesting related facts:

Key words:

New questions to research:

◆ Figure 12.11

I-Chart on Whales

Names: Class Example   Topic: Whales

Subtopic: What do whales eat?

What I already know: Whales live in the ocean. They are mammals. They have
blow holes. There are different kinds of whales.

Bibliography number:	
1	Some whales have teeth. They eat mostly fish and squid. Some whales do not have teeth. They have baleen plates in their mouths. They eat mostly krill. Krill are small shrimplike animals.
2	Baleen is a tough material that grows in fringes from the whale's upper jaw. A blue whale may eat 8000 pounds of krill each day. That would be the same as 16,000 servings of spaghetti in a day. Killer whales have teeth and eat warm-blooded animals such as other whales, dolphins, seals, sea lions, and other kinds of fish.
3	Toothed whales use echolocation to navigate and to find their food.

Interesting related facts: Like all mammals, baby whales get milk from their mothers.
They might drink 600 quarts in a day. There are 63 species
of toothed whales and 11 species of baleen whales.

◆ FIGURE 12.11   *Continued*

Key words: baleen, prey, pod, echolocation

New questions to research: How long do toothed whales live?
How long do baleen whales live?

Bibliography for the I-Chart on Whales

1. *Dolphins and Whales,* by Stephen Savage, 1990, Chartwell Books.
2. *Giants of the Deep,* by Q. L. Pearce, 1992, RGA Publishing Group, Inc.
3. *S.O.S. Whale,* by Jill Bailey, 1991, W. H. Smith, Publishers, Inc.

and record the information. As they read new information, they pull out the corresponding I-Chart. This enables children to think critically about the relevance of each piece of information to their subtopics and eliminates random copying of unorganized data. Even with this structure, students occasionally slip up and include under one subtopic information that belongs under another (Randall, 1996).

Completed I-Charts can be used to teach outlining for research reports. Each of eight to ten subtopics on an I-Chart become a Roman numeral. Important facts found on the I-Charts complete the rest of the outline. Sometimes subtopics need to be divided when they are too broad or combined when too closely related. In this way, I-Charts contribute to the outline for the final paper or project. I-Charts can also be used to guide Internet inquiry.

Internet Inquiry

Al Scenna is a fourth-grade teacher who leads his students in inquiry searches using electronic texts, that is, the Internet and CD-ROMs, as well as informational texts and reference books. His students use I-Charts in their classroom inquiry projects and were comfortable "surfing the Net" before he engaged them in an Internet inquiry using electronic texts (see the Class Works featured in Box 12.4).

Al's Electronic Text Inquiry

First, Al Scenna talked with his fourth-grade students about the district's policy on student access to the Internet, gave them copies to take home, and obtained parental permission in writing. The rules for using the Internet are as follows:

◆ Do not go to sites that are not bookmarked or approved in our class address book.

◆ Quickly leave any site that is not appropriate or safe.

◆ Have a teacher preview any site you would like to look up, or have a parent volunteer sit with you while you search.

Al decided to engage his class in an inquiry on dental hygiene within their science curriculum. He introduced the topic with a video clip of short, humorous dental sequences from a number of sources such as *Little Shop of Horrors, Splash,* and *The Return of the Pink Panther.* After viewing these exaggerated dental experiences, Al led a discussion of "going to the dentist" stories in his students' lives. The discussion ranged from losing teeth to toothaches to cavities to braces. Al then told his students they would conduct an inquiry as a review for themselves and to give information to younger students so that they would develop and maintain healthy dental practices. Al shared with his students the following list of dental hygiene topics, drawn from the curriculum:

◆ Anatomy of the tooth

◆ Form and function of different kinds of teeth

◆ Purpose and demonstration of proper toothbrushing

◆ Purpose and demonstration of proper flossing

◆ Protection of mouth and teeth

◆ Role of the dentist

◆ Role of fluoride

◆ Nutrition as it affects teeth and gums

Over the next two days, Al's students signed up for a particular topic until the group reached a maximum of four students. In these groups, the children chose a manager, a scribe, and a liaison to the teacher. Each of the groups brainstormed different sources of information. Then the

(Continued)

Box 12.4 CONTINUED

groups listed what they already knew about their topic and brainstormed questions they would like to answer concerning their topic. The next day, the cooperative groups met to complete the Internet Inquiry Plan form (see Figure 12.12). Once the first part of the form was completed, the liaison arranged a conference time with Al. In conducting the inquiry, students used an I-Chart (see Figure 12.13), which Al reviewed with the groups as they examined their informational resources: the Internet, including Web sites of organizations like the American Dental Association; CD-ROMs; informational books; storybooks; reference books; and pamphlets and brochures. Al encouraged each group to use all of the different kinds of resources. One group had a member whose father was a dentist, and he interviewed his father as an expert resource.

As students worked on their inquiry in the school's computer lab, they each explored at least one approved Internet site for information related to their topic. Al encouraged his students to find at least one text resource on their own. Each material they used was evaluated for its usefulness for primary students. Al recommended that information found on the Internet be reinforced with information found on a CD-ROM or in a book.

Each group organized its answers to the questions concerning its topic in paragraph form and decided how to present its information to the class and to the primary students. The options included a live news show, a live demonstration of a technique, a panel discussion, a video presentation, a dramatization, or a diorama. The student liaison arranged a second meeting with Al once these decisions were made.

In this second meeting, Al helped the students resolve any conflicting information and talked through their presentation. The presentation to the class could be as long as ten minutes, but the presentation to the primary students involved a shortened time of two to three minutes so that the entire class presentation lasted 15 to 20 minutes. The assessment included students assessing their individual and group work, the presentations, and Al's feedback on their conduct of the inquiry and presentations.

Reflective Inquiry

◆ What types of things would you want the students to include in their assessments?

◆ If you were advising the teacher, what suggestions would you make or questions would you like to have answered?

◆ Figure 12.12

Internet Inquiry Plan

Directions: Use this form to help you organize your Internet inquiry. After you have filled out items 1 and 2, send your liaison to me to arrange a conference with your group. After the conference, you may begin conducting your inquiry search.

Names: _____   Date: _____

Title of inquiry: _____

1. The purpose of the inquiry is:

   _____

   _____

   _____

   _____

   _____

2. We will use the following resources:

   _____

   _____

   _____

Once these steps are completed, the liaison will arrange a conference with Mr. Scenna.

3. We will present our information to the class this way:

   _____

   _____

   _____

4. We will present our information to first or second graders this way:

   _____

5. We recommend the following materials to use with the first or second graders:

   _____

   _____

◆ FIGURE 12.13

I-Chart on Dental Hygiene

Names: Cassie A., Amelia Y., Zachary B., Rahiema M. **Topic:** Dental hygiene

Subtopic: Sealant

What I already know: Cassie remembers she had sealant applied the summer after first grade. It didn't hurt.

Bibliography number:	
1	Used on permanent teeth
	Starting around 6 years of age
	Especially good for back teeth—molars
	Fills in little pits in teeth
	Doesn't hurt to have it done
	Plastic coating
	Good for 2–5 years
	Really cuts down on cavities in back teeth
2	Thin plastic coating on back teeth
	Stops bacteria from growing in little pits on the teeth
	For permanent molars starting around 6 years of age and second molars starting around age 12
	Dental solution cleans teeth first and helps sealant stick
	Sealants could last several years but need dentist to check
	Very effective in stopping decay on back teeth
3	Major protection against cavities
	Teeth covered with bacteria film called plaque
	Plaque turns sugars into acid to attack tooth enamel
	Sealant is plastic
	Put on chewing surfaces of back teeth
	Seals the grooves on the back teeth
	Brushes can't get into those grooves
	Easy to apply
	Teeth cleaned, then roughened to help the sealant stick
	Lasts several years
	Dentist will check at regular visits
	Teens and adults can have sealants too

◆ Figure 12.13   Continued

Interesting related facts: Plaque is a film of bacteria on the teeth; plaque uses sugar to make acids that attack the teeth

Key words: molars, permanent teeth

New questions to research: What are first and second molars?

Reference Materials

Primary Resources, Text

Asimov, Isaac. *Why Do We Need to Brush Our Teeth?* Milwaukee: G. Stevens Publishers, 1993

Bunting, Eve. *Trouble on the T Ball Team.* New York: Clarion Books, 1997

Encyclopedia Americana, International Edition. Danbury, CT: Grolier, Inc., 1998

The New Encyclopedia Britannica, 15th ed. Chicago: Encyclopedia Britannica, Inc., 1997

Foster, Malcolm. *Protecting Our Children's Teeth.* New York: Insight Books, 1992

Nardo, Don. *Vitamins and Minerals* (part of the *Encyclopedia of Health* series). New York: Chelsea House Publishers, 1994

① Orth, Ann, "Dental Health." In Jane Fox (Ed.), *Primary Health Care of Children.* St. Louis: Mosby, 1997

Rourke, Arlene. *Teeth and Braces.* Vero Beach, FL: Rourke Publications Inc., 1989

Siegel, Dorothy. *Dental Health* (part of the *Encyclopedia of Health* series). New York: Chelsea House Publishers, 1994

World Book Encyclopedia, Chicago: World Book, Inc., 1997

Primary Resources, CD-ROM

My Amazing Human Body. DK Multipedia

Primary Resources, Internet

③ ADA Online (American Dental Association Web site): www.ada.org/

② The Wisdom Tooth (Dental Hygiene Web site): www.umanitoba.ca/outreach/wisdomtooth/

McNeil (Commercial Manufacturer of Dental Products): www.mrreach.com/

Sources for Primary Grade Readers, Text

Charles, Donald. *Calico Cat's Sunny Smile.* Chicago: Children's Press, 1990

Lutrell, Ida. *Milo's Toothache.* New York: Dial Books for Young Readers, 1992

SUMMARY

Elementary children often experience their first difficulties with reading when they encounter textbooks in content areas. The transition to content area reading should not pose major obstacles, although textbooks are inherently difficult for most students. In classrooms where children are guided to use literature, nonfiction trade books, and electronic texts, children are more likely to make the transition to content area texts naturally and with ease. They learn to approach and appreciate many genres of texts, including the textbook.

To understand what makes a textbook difficult, several factors that contribute to the readability of a text were explained. Also, we explored the uses and benefits of using literature, nonfiction trade books, and electronic texts across the curriculum. Historical and realistic fiction, biographies, and informational books provide children with intense involvement in a subject. Using these different genres of books is a schema builder and can accommodate different reading abilities and interests in the classroom. Moreover, units of study provide teachers with the structure needed to coordinate literature study within the context of meaningful activity.

Various strategies were presented to show how teachers can facilitate textbook study and learning. Some strategies to implement before reading included previewing, organizers, anticipation guides, and brainstorming. Other strategies were explained that can be used to improve the learning of concepts. Point-of-view guides help children reconstruct content learning by using their personal outlook. Students work in idea circles to discuss concepts and how they are related, drawing from different informational sources. I-Charts and Internet inquiry searches are ways teachers can guide students to pursue questions of interest as they learn.

TEACHER-ACTION RESEARCHER

1. Plan a content area lesson using a reading selection from a social studies or science textbook. What prereading strategies will you use? How will you guide reader-text interactions? What follow-up or postreading strategies will you decide on? Teach this lesson to a small group of students. Evaluate the lesson, asking, What concepts did the students acquire through the reading? How well did you establish purpose and activate a schema for reading? Did you sustain motivation throughout the lesson? What was the most effective part of the lesson? What was the least effective part?

2. Construct a graphic organizer using the procedures suggested in this chapter. In a lesson, try out the graphic organizer that you developed. Evaluate your use of this activity.

3. Observe a lesson taught to students in a content area other than reading, such as math, science, health, or social studies. Note all the instructional strategies that the teacher uses to help students learn with texts. How are the students involved in the lesson? Think about the ways that reading to learn did or did not play a role in the lesson. What alternative instructional strategies might have been used?

4. Decide on a content area subject matter and grade level. Surf the Internet to decide where you would place bookmarks for students conducting an inquiry on this topic. Plan how you would guide the inquiry having the students use I-Charts in conducting their search.

KEY TERMS

anticipation guide
brainstorming
considerate text
expository text
graphic organizer
I-Chart

idea circle
Internet inquiry
literature across the
  curriculum
literature web
organizer

point-of-view guide
previewing
readability
trade books

CHAPTER

13

Meeting the Literacy Needs of Diverse Learners*

*This chapter was revised by Patricia R. Schmidt, LeMoyne College, Syracuse, NY.

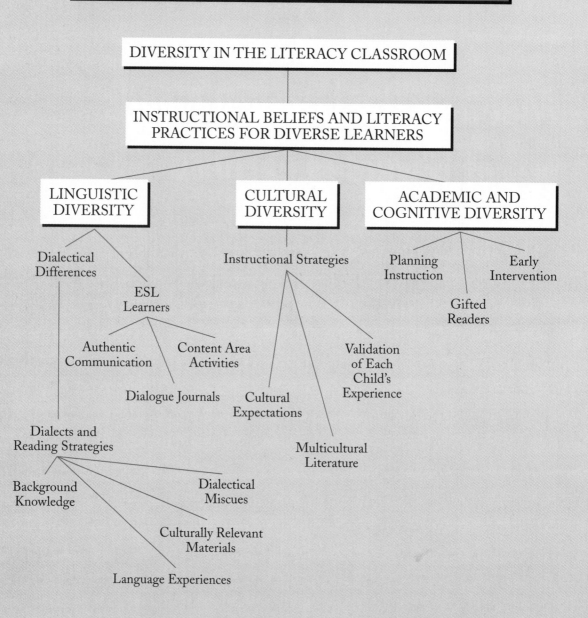

Between the Lines

In this chapter, you will discover:

♦ Linguistic, cultural, cognitive, and academic factors that influence individual diverse learners

♦ Issues about learning to read and write in relation to definitions of literacy and diversity

♦ Illustrations of linguistic, dialectical, cultural, and academic and cognitive diversity in instructional situations

♦ Ways to plan and implement strategies to differentiate instruction, building on students' background knowledge and experiences

*B*eth Arnold's elementary school in a midwestern city school district has been given the task of teaching students whose first languages are Spanish, Arabic, or French, as well as teaching the neighborhood children who speak a dialect of English known as African American Language (AAL), also called Ebonic. On a tour of the school on Community Day, visitors might see classes taught in Spanish, family members in classrooms sharing their language and culture, and the school librarian sharing picture books and children's literature written in the students' first language. They might chat with an African American child who learned to speak and read in Arabic from listening to instruction for students with limited English proficiency (LEP) who are taught some of their content area subjects in his classroom. As the principal of the school, Beth, an energetic African American woman, works hard to keep every student and every parent feeling involved and part of the school community.

"Our job here isn't just to teach students to speak English," Ms. Arnold says. "Part of our job is also to help these students *feel welcome* in school. Feeling welcome is essential for learning, and feeling welcome can't happen if no one understands you or if you can't understand anyone. Our language is totally connected to our sense of who we are. If people don't value our language, they devalue us."

In a rural school, Kelly Stone is proud of the cooperative and collaborative atmosphere in her classroom. Her kindergarten students have had few literacy experiences to prepare them for school. Their families struggle to live at subsistence levels, due to the area's economic difficulties. Consequently, the school has limited resources and materials. Soon after arriving in the district several years ago, Kelly called for help from her children's families. Together they designed and created classroom centers that were relevant to the children's lives and supported their emerging literacy. A family center, animal center, block center, take-apart center, garden center, fishing center, book center, writing and drawing center, and math center were the results of the shared experiences. Families donated items from closets, garages, cellars, fields, and forest. Junk became treasures, and sisters, brothers, aunts, uncles, cousins, mothers, fathers, and neighbors shared their time, materials, and talents. "The children's families seem to understand the culture of the school and literacy development better when the activities for their children relate to their environment. They read stories, tell stories, assist children at the centers, and give what they can to the kindergarten program. They say it takes a whole village to raise our children—well, that's exactly what we are doing."

In an economically, ethnically, and culturally diverse school district, Jennifer Martin, a first-grade teacher, noticed that one of her students was disruptive and inattentive while the rest of the class was eagerly reading the Henry and Mudge series by Cynthia Rylant and writing and sharing in their collaborative reading groups. "Ira was quiet and spoke with a slight impediment," she remembers. "He seemed very ordinary. Yet when I was giving individual reading inventories to the students in October, he read passages at the third-grade level. And even though he seemed to substitute words while reading aloud in the higher-graded passages, he could answer the comprehension questions I asked him with perfect accuracy. I noted that Ira's miscues didn't change meaning. I was chagrined to think I was asking such a gifted reader to sit quietly when the instructional materials I had chosen did not match his needs at all. Now he is reading Cynthia Rylant books with interest too, but he chooses titles that match his reading level more closely."

Jim Brown's third-grade class begins the morning language arts block with a literature read-aloud. After that experience, his room is buzzing with a "healthy hum" as 24 students rotate through centers that develop reading, writing, listening, and speaking. Eight of Jim's students are reading below grade level, and learning disabilities have recently been identified in several of them. At the computer cluster, Jonathan, a student with deficits in written and oral language, is creating silly stories using rhyming words with Julie, his skill buddy, who is reading at a second-grade level. Seven other students of varying literacy levels in the computer cluster are completing programs individually or in pairs.

When the teacher's bell rings for the next rotation, Jonathan moves, with five other students of various talents and differing literacy levels, to the response table, where he will select and complete an activity related to the morning's read-aloud. Materials in this area include Lego blocks, straws, toothpicks, clay, paint, two easels, glitter, scissors, paper, glue, magazines, cloth, yarn, and buttons. A teaching assistant spends an hour during the language arts block to work with students at the response table.

In the last 35 minutes of the block, Jonathan meets with Mr. Brown to prepare for a story with three other students at his reading level. They study story background, analyze vocabulary, make predictions, and ask questions. Then they move to a table with earphones to listen and read along with copies of the story. Tomorrow they will read different parts of the story and discuss them in a group.

Jim Brown is delighted with his classroom this year. He explains, "This is the first time in 20 years of teaching that I think I am actually meeting the diverse needs of my students. Technology and block scheduling have helped me do it."

These stories illustrate some of the factors that influence diverse learners as they approach the task of becoming literate and the challenging decisions that educators, like Beth, Kelly, Jennifer, and Jim must make about content, materials, and teaching in order to meet the needs of all their students. Scores of factors that potentially influence an individual's success in learning to read have been identified and researched, but most fall into three categories:

◆ **Linguistic diversity**—the language the student feels most comfortable communicating in. The first or home language is not the language of instruction in the school.

◆ **Cultural diversity**—the student's home, family, socioeconomic group, culture, and/or society differs from the predominant (middle-class) culture of the school.

◆ **Cognitive and academic diversity**—the child learns at a pace or in a style different from that expected at the school.

These factors influence how, when, and under what circumstances students will best learn to read and write.

Compounding the effects of the three factors is poverty. It has a devastating influence on the social, emotional, and intellectual development of young children. Intellectual deprivation during the preschool years may be profound and long-lasting. In family contexts where parents are illiterate or semiliterate, it is not likely that children will be read to or have reading models, nor will they have easy access to books or writing materials. *Poverty and illiteracy become intergenerational:* Children who are unsuccessful in school are unlikely to become economically successful adults. Thus the cycle of poverty and illiteracy tends to be perpetuated from one generation to another.

What happens when the optimal conditions for certain students' acquisition of literacy do not match what happens in particular classrooms? Such students may be labeled at risk for reading failure. Diverse learners exhibit diverse needs. If they are to learn successfully, their needs must be met. Teachers need to be aware of the nature of diversity and what it means for teaching reading to students who are linguistically, culturally, or academically diverse. These topics are identified in the chapter overview and discussed thoroughly in this chapter.

THE COMPLEXITY OF DIVERSITY IN LITERACY CLASSROOMS

Complicating the choices teachers must make in helping students learn to read and write are the differing definitions both of literacy and of diversity. Kameenui [1993b (Special Issue)] notes that reading research refers to "critical literacy," "occupational literacy," and "pragmatic literacy," as well as "literacy as cultural form." Each definition of literacy implies a different purpose for becoming literate and the appropriate instructional strategy suited for that purpose.

Further complicating the choices teachers must make in the classroom is the complex nature of diversity (Garcia, Pearson, & Jimenez, 1990). The range of needs in learning to read is reflected by the range of children who compose our classrooms. There is no one African American experience, just as there is no one Hispanic American experience or European American experience. Neither are students alike who are identified with learning disabilities. Chall and Curtis (1989) describe such diverse factors contributing to reading disability as neurological irregularities, motor coordination, auditory sequencing and blending, memory, attention, perception, and oral language development. Furthermore, socioeconomic background, geographic location, levels of parental education, cultural heritage, verbal skill, and adequacy of teaching have all been identified as factors influencing student success or lack of it in learning to read.

Beliefs and values about what it means to be literate and who may appropriately become literate lend an emotional and political layer to the diversity issue. Literacy is power, and certain groups have historically been denied access to this power. For example, slaves in the United States were denied access to literacy, and those who struggled to become literate risked punishment by owners or slavebreakers (Harris, 1993). For better or for worse, this appreciation of the power of literacy continues today, with competing views of the appropriateness of both the content and the availability of reading and writing instruction common among educators and theorists. Gadsden (1992) raises the issue of access to literacy by asking, Who controls access? How is it achieved? How do the learners themselves and the classroom situations they are in contribute to learning and developing access to literacy?

Our heightened understanding of the nature of literacy as shaped by cultural and societal influences (see Heath, 1982; Ogbu, 1993) has led to a reexamination among teachers and administrators of the ways in which we describe diversity among learners. Traditionally, school programs were not designed to fit the needs of special learners. Rather, learners were expected to adapt to the needs of the school. Some of the terminology used in describing diversity is explained in Table 13.1.

Although the United States has a long history of non-English-speaking immigrant children attending public school, large-scale bilingual education programs have not experienced wide support. The "melting pot," wherein minority students would become more like the majority, giving up or adjusting whatever linguistic or cultural differences interfered with schooling, served as the metaphor that guided the role of linguistic, cultural, and other minorities in the United States throughout the twentieth century (Mann, 1979; Ogbu, 1993). The underlying basis of the melting pot is the objective to assimilate minorities into the larger society, accompanied by a sacrifice of language and culture for the minority group. However, Cummins (1986) strongly suggests that when children's language and culture are ignored in the classroom, the youngsters feel disempowered and lose the connections necessary for learning in the classroom culture.

In spite of this information, assimilationist objectives still underlie many educational programs. When students were viewed as unable to enter the mainstream, they received remedial or compensatory education. Federal monies that funded programs designed to improve the education of language-minority students or those with low socioeconomic status (Title VII of the Elementary and Secondary Education Act for bilingual students, Title 1 of the same act revised as Chapter 1 of the Education, Consolidation and Improvement Act for reading, Head Start for disadvantaged preschoolers) originated on the assumption that students were deficient and needed to master basic skills before they could be expected to achieve in regular classrooms (Strickland & Ascher, 1992).

Linguistic research has helped us understand that language variation is to be expected and is not good or bad, logical or illogical, in and of itself. Social norms create language options that users of that language choose systematically. Language variations are not random. This view, that language and cultural diversity result from difference rather than deficiency, is paramount to the changed view of how best to teach reading and writing in today's changed and changing classrooms.

In a very real sense, language variations are typical of all readers. No one talks the way books are written. The conventions of oral language differ from the conventions of written language. Very few published materials are simply "talk written down." As readers, we can understand different language forms, even though we might never use them in our own

TABLE 13.1

Terminology Related to Diversity

Term	Definition
LEP	Limited English proficiency
ESL	English as a second language
Chapter 1/Title I	Federally funded program to provide extra reading instruction to children from poor families
Title VII	Federally funded program for children whose first language is not English

CHANGES IN THE WAY WE TALK ABOUT READERS	
Former Term	Current Term
At risk	Of promise
Language-deficient	Language-minority
Culturally deprived	Culturally different
Cultural assimilation	Cultural pluralism

speech. In other words, we don't need to abandon our oral language patterns in order to read. The same is true of our students, of course. When making decisions about reading instruction for linguistically diverse learners, it's wise to remember that one doesn't have to talk like a book in order to read one.

INSTRUCTIONAL BELIEFS AND LITERACY PRACTICES FOR DIVERSE LEARNERS

The emphasis on meeting students' needs as much as possible in the regular classroom means that classroom teachers are now expected to work with students who might once have been sent to a specialist. As the number of languages spoken by immigrants to the United States and Canada rises, teachers may also find (especially in outlying areas or in small districts) that there isn't an available teacher who is fluent in a particular child's home language. Teachers who believe they are unprepared to meet the challenges of **inclusion** (teaching diverse learners in the classroom) may feel frustrated and stressed. Worksheets, isolated exercises, and other skill-related instruction that is not helpful to particular learners may be chosen because it seems easier, even when a specialist is available for

BOX 13.1   VIEWPOINT

Patricia Schmidt on Teaching Diverse Learners

As a reading teacher for 18 years in a suburban middle school in upstate New York, grades 5–8, I worked with students who had been diagnosed with difficulties in reading, writing, listening, and speaking. Each year I was also assigned the one or two new students from places such as Taiwan, Russia, Israel, Detroit, or Appalachia. Similar to other European American teachers in this suburban setting, I believed in the assimilationist perspective. I thought that students from ethnic or cultural minority backgrounds needed to fit into the mainstream to be successful academically and socially. Therefore, my task was to help them learn standard English as quickly as possible. Some students did. They also made friends, followed peer dress codes, and were involved in school activities. They began to look and act exactly like their classmates. However, other students, who maintained their cultural identities, took longer to speak and read standard English. They were often isolated both in and out of the classroom. Their families noticed the difficulties and enlisted my assistance.

Patricia R. Schmidt, LeMoyne College, Syracuse, NY

During the school year, home visits and conferences revealed unfamiliar languages and dialects and diverse cultural perspectives. I began to understand their struggles in making new community connections. I realized that our school was ignoring the rich resources that the new families offered. Reading and study led me to the realization that the additive perspective (Cummins, 1986), which encourages the inclusion of differing languages and cultures in the classroom, could be the approach to guide connections between home and school. Those connections could help the children maintain their own cultural identities as well as see the relevance of the school culture. In addition, students in the mainstream who are unfamiliar with diversity would be gaining from the different people and cultures. So what does this experience mean for our children and schools?

Diversity in our nation's schools is inevitable due to shifting world populations. Also, because the global economy affects all of us, our children will probably work in places very dif-

Box 13.1 CONTINUED

ferent from their home communities. Consequently, our present and future teachers must be prepared to work effectively with linguistic, cultural, and academic diversity. Since most teachers will have grown up in middle-class European American suburbia and have had few opportunities to develop relationships with different groups, they may unconsiously rely on media stereotypes. Differences in the classroom may be viewed as problematic rather than opportunities for children to explore physical, linguistic, cultural, and academic differences and learn to appreciate individual talents and multiple perspectives. Therefore, the classroom as social context can begin to prepare children for an appreciation of differences that gives them social and economic advantages. But how do we do this?

A major means is through effective connections between home and school. Families who are actively involved in the classroom and school community feel comfortable and needed. They see themselves as contributors to their children's education. The task for teachers then is to reach out to families who are culturally and linguistically different from the school and to families who fear and dislike the school because of their own emotional and academic failures. Teachers who realize that families are the children's first teachers and who value the family's knowledge and contributions to the child's literacy development soon begin to communicate in positive ways.

Another key factor relates to the relevance of materials and activities for diverse learners. When children see people like themselves pictured in the resources they are using and can connect an activity with their own life experiences, they tend to stay focused on learning. Drawing on home and community literacy activities and materials as well as children and young adult literature related to diverse groups can be the means for connecting home and school for meaningful literacy development. Furthermore, children from the European American culture are enriched when they learn about diversity through literature and materials introduced and studied in their classrooms.

in-class or pull-out remediation (Bean, Cooley, Eichelberger, Lazar, & Zigmond, 1991). How teachers react to these instructional challenges depends to a large extent on how they believe students become literate and the best ways to meet those needs in the classroom. In the Viewpoint featured in Box 13.1 read how one teacher's perspective changed over time.

The traditional response to remedial reading was to give students with reading difficulty more intense instruction through skill and drill, especially in letter-sound correspondences or phonics (Zucker, 1993). Allington (1977) noted that remedial readers were less likely to read connected text or to work on constructing meaning from print than readers who were considered more able. **Bilingual learners** are often instructed using primary-level worksheets, even when their age or conceptual development means that such work is inappropriate (Freeman & Freeman, 1993).

What is good reading instruction? For all readers, research points to instruction that focuses on reading as a meaning-making activity, with opportunities for practice in connected and meaningful texts and for sufficient and meaningful feedback. Since language activities are based on communicative competence, it is important for all learners to determine how effective their communicative, meaning-making attempts are in the particular contexts in which they find themselves.

For low-achieving, gifted, and linguistically and culturally diverse students, reading remains a process of constructing meaning using both the learner's background knowledge about reading and his or her life experiences with the syntactic, semantic, and graphophonemic cues of the text. When the process breaks down at any point, whether in terms of background knowledge about what it means to read or what a particular word might mean, knowledgeable teachers develop opportunities to expand their students' repertoires of successful strategies for making meaning. Shirley Brice Heath (1991) reminds us that helping students exhibit literate behavior removes the onus associated with focusing on literacy skills, which may not be the true measure of students' understanding if they are nonnative speakers or of their potential if they have culturally different expectations for meaning or literacy. In fact, Allington (1983) attributes the majority of reading failures to poor instruction rather than to any inherent problem in the readers themselves.

A kindergarten study of two bilingual, ethnic minority children by Schmidt (1995) concluded that "schools may actually interfere with children's literacy learning, if educators do not work to understand the diverse cultural backgrounds of the children in classrooms" (p. 408). She recommends instruction based on connections with homes of ethnic minority students to help parents and children understand, for example, the holidays and celebrations in the school. For connections to be made, the school must reach out to the parents, whose difficulties in communicating with the teacher often prevent them from initiating contact, as described in the Class Works featured in Box 13.2.

Linguistic Diversity in Literacy Classrooms

What works in terms of the language and literacy development in first languages is also what works for second-language acquisition (Fitzgerald, 1993). Although the most dramatic examples of linguistic diversity are students whose first language is not English, linguistic diversity is evidenced among native English speakers as well. Geographic location, socioeconomic status, and educational levels, as well as gender, age, and occupation, all affect the way we speak. In the past, these dialectical variations were thought to be confounding factors in certain groups' ability to learn to read.

Dialectical Differences

We all speak a **dialect** of English, although it is much easier for us to see our own speech as natural and the speech of everyone else as the dialect. Depending on how old you are, where you were born or grew up, whether you are male or female, and your economic

BOX 13.2   CLASS WORKS

Home-School Connections

Natoya, an African American girl of 7, attended an urban school where about half the students were white, one-third were black, and the remainder were immigrants from Asia, Ukraine, and Latin America. Natoya was a vivacious second grader with a dramatic flair and an excellent command of oral language. Her colorfully braided and beaded hair always matched her immaculate, stylish outfits. With little encouragement, she sang and danced in perfect tune and rhythm. She loved to expound on the fun activities she enjoyed with her cousins and urged classmates to tell about their social lives. Parties, clothing, songs, friends, and relatives were all favorite topics. Yet despite her talents, Natoya's reading and writing were considered poor for the fall of second grade. She avoided writing activities and complained of a tired hand. She knew the alphabet and could make beginning letter-sound associations but would not concentrate long enough to actually decode or even make sense out of stories. She also recognized sight words quickly but rarely sustained an interest when the teacher read stories aloud. Natoya was assessed for a learning disability by the committee for special education, but the evidence was inconclusive. It was decided that she had a developmental lag in the language area and was suggested that the classroom teacher, Mrs. Knopp, individualize instruction.

Recognizing that home-school connections are key factors in literacy development, Mrs. Knopp realized that she needed to meet with Natoya's family to plan the child's program. During the first weeks of school, Mrs. Knopp had called Natoya's home and introduced herself. Along with telling about the second-grade classroom and Natoya's contributions, Mrs. Knopp shared her own background. She also obtained written permission from Natoya's family to have her reading, writing, listening, and speaking evaluated by the school's reading teacher. So now Mrs. Knopp felt comfortable asking for a meeting to talk about Natoya's literacy development. She and the girl's mother decided on an evening conference at the local community center, where Natoya's three older brothers and baby sister could be entertained and Natoya could pursue other activities until her presence was needed. It would also allow Natoya's father, who worked during the day, to participate in the meeting.

The conference began with Mrs. Knopp asking the parents to contribute any comments, questions, or concerns about Natoya's activities at home or in school. Mrs. Knopp listened as they told about daily and weekend activities. Then Mrs. Knopp asked, "What does Natoya like to do most?" After the parents talked about Natoya, Mrs. Knopp listed Natoya's many positive behaviors. She continued by showing lessons and materials used in the classroom. From their discussion, keeping Natoya focused and motivated emerged as main concerns of both parents and teacher. Together they began to think of ways to engage Natoya. They decided that she would have opportunities to retell and act out stories read aloud in class. She could practice at home with her family. She would then be encouraged to write her own songs and silly stories using rhyming words at home and in school. These could be performed at appropriate times. There

(Continued)

Box 13.2 CONTINUED

were several other students in the class who needed similar experiences, so a teacher aide or parent volunteer could supervise the group.

After conferring for 40 minutes, Natoya was invited into the meeting to hear her parents' and teacher's ideas. Her response was, "So what about clothes so we can be the people in the stories?" Her suggestion for a dress-up center in the classroom was an additional idea and a feature to enhance the second-grade community. Natoya's mother volunteered to gather clothing for the new creative effort.

Reflective Inquiry

◆ Why did everyone involved in the conference leave with the feeling that their contributions would make a difference?

◆ What did Mrs. Knopp gain by getting involved with Natoya's family early in the school year?

◆ How might other students in this classroom community benefit from this home-school connection?

level, your speech will vary. What do you call a sandwich of sliced meats and cheese on a large oblong bun? A "hoagie"? A "grinder"? A "sub"? What would you call something wonderful and out of the ordinary? "Neat"? "Cool"? "Fly"? "Superb"? Would you explain where something "is at" or where it "is"? How would you form the past tense of *dive?* Whether you say *dived, dive, duv,* or *dove* will depend on your geographic region and social class. To a person from the Northeast, a southerner's pronunciation of *drink* sounds more like his own pronunciation of *drank,* while the rest of the country pronounces final *r*'s that the Boston native most likely does not.

These language variations and countless others are examples of the natural evolutions of spoken language, proof of the changing nature of living languages. Latin, a language no longer spoken by people for communicative and social purposes, is considered a dead language. It doesn't change. But change and variation within and among living languages are natural, and linguists know that all languages are equally effective for expressing the needs of their speakers, equally complete, and equally rule-governed, or systematic. Dialects are likewise rule-governed (Labov, 1985).

The difficulties associated with dialectal and linguistic differences in the classroom is the *value* assigned to language, to the perceived goodness or badness of a particular speech variation. Roberts (1985) emphasizes that in and of themselves, language variations are neither good nor bad, and that such judgments are often about the people who speak them rather than about clarity or precision (which are also value-laden judgments!).

Dialects and Reading Strategies

Language variations and associated values affect the instructional job of literacy teachers. For instance, African American Language, or Ebonics, is the dialect of an American community, and to be effective, teachers need to understand it (Locke, 1989). Its rhythm, rate, phonology, syntax, morphology, semantics, lexicon, and stress, along with distinctive nonverbal communication, make it an artistic and verbally agile language (Dillard, 1983). For a time it was thought that beginning readers who spoke a variation of "standard edited English" or "standard American English," the dialect found in textbooks, would read poorly because the language was different from their own. However, this idea is unfounded. When teachers draw on a child's background knowledge, gather culturally relevant materials, effectively monitor oral reading, use language experiences, and bring the study of different language patterns into the classroom, all children can develop reading, writing, listening, and speaking with a similar degree of success.

Background Knowledge.   Connecting the known to the new has long been considered a way to motivate and focus students as well as a means of evaluating the existence of background knowledge. When a teacher draws on a child's prior experiences and helps the child connect those to new vocabulary and story concepts, this provides a basis for making meaning. Children need to see the relevance of a story to their own lives. Classrooms with culturally relevant materials accomplish this task easily.

Culturally Relevant Materials.   When children see books and materials that look and sound like themselves, their lives are validated. The stories they read connect to their own experiences, so new vocabulary and concepts are more easily learned. Furthermore, other children in the classroom gain an understanding of diverse ethnic and cultural backgrounds as they are exposed to multicultural literature. Computer software such as talking books can be helpful for literacy development, but there are few that are relevant to ethnic and cultural minority students.

Dialectical Miscues.   When reading aloud, children often substitute one word for another. Such errors, or miscues, can help teachers understand how—and how successfully—a child is constructing meaning from a text. Language choices are not random; miscues help a teacher decide which cuing system a reader is using to comprehend the text. In oral reading, when a child substitutes words from her or his speaking dialect for the word printed on the page (for example, reading *he don't* for *he doesn't*), the miscue probably shows that the reader is reading the text for meaning. Such a substitution would be impossible if the reader had not comprehended the text.

As more research on reading is done in the classroom, we learn that reading revolves around the experiences that the reader brings to the text to make sense of it. Reading is only partly about the marks on the page. This, in turn, is changing the way we think about dialects and decoding and about how reading teachers should address dialectical differences.

Teachers must of course help their students learn letter-sound correspondences in beginning reading, but they must also help students grow in their understanding that writing is not just speech written down. In fact, writing is like another dialect of English. For example, at the end of a particularly grueling semester of reading and writing, a student complained that friends kept remarking that he was "talking like a book." He had adjusted his speech to match written texts. But vocabulary and syntax that are appropriate for writing may seem stilted and unnatural if we use it in face-to-face conversation. Once we learn "book language," and its rules for conveying meaning, we do not need to see our spoken dialect in print in order to understand a written text.

Using Language Experience.

Helping beginning readers discover the connection between spoken and written language is one of the most important aspects of teaching beginning readers. For beginning readers, and especially students who ordinarily use linguistic variations from school language, the **language-experience approach (LEA)** is a good way to help make the connection between speech and writing concrete. Most important, LEA gives students the kind of reading material that they can most easily read—predictable, meaningful, and contextually complete—because they dictate or write it.

LEA, described in Chapters 2, 3, and 4, begins with ample time for *discussion* of whatever topic interests the students. Rigg (1989) suggests stories that have interest for all students, even students with limited proficiency in English. Discussions leading to stories about pets, recipes, interviews with the class VIP-for-a-day, retellings of a story that has been read aloud, stories patterned after other stories, advice to students in next year's class, and a newcomer's reaction to life in the United States are all popular with children.

The next step, *dictating*, involves the teacher (or a student acting as a peer scribe) writing down the exact words dictated by class members. The scribe rereads each sentence, repeating it to help students remember what they had to say and to help beginning readers read back what is written. While the scribe writes down exactly what the children say, it is important to use conventional spelling and not try to reproduce phonetically what children say. Rigg (1989) points out that the focus is on students' ideas and not on adult grammatical forms. In fact, she notes that copies of LEA dictations help provide running records of student progress in mastering standard forms of English.

Students can revise the LEA text after rereading, either in groups, individually, or as a class with the author's permission. Then the text can be prominently displayed or copies can be made for individuals so that the students can use it for rereading or illustrating or as story starters.

Learning the Language of Books.

Teachers permit students to grow as readers by helping them understand the different patterns of language that give meaning and structure to writing. Reading aloud to children and encouraging wide reading in the classroom and at home can help beginning readers develop an ear for the stylistic conventions of books and written language. Predictable and patterned books, fairy tales, and folklore and books with rich illustration help all students learn the conventions of written language because contextual clues help carry the meaning of the text. These books help all beginning readers, but they offer the extra support that children with limited experience speaking English need.

Special Concerns of ESL Readers

We know that children who receive instruction in their native language learn to read English more easily (Collier, 1989; Cummins, 1989; Hudelson, 1989). Children transfer the knowledge of what it means to read readily from one language to another. What it means to read in Spanish is the same as what it means to read in English, and a native Spanish speaker can use all the cuing systems of language—syntax, semantics, and graphophonemic correspondence—to learn to read in English.

Although the ideal development of second-language literacy would have each nonnative speaker receiving instructional support in the home language while learning to master English, the reality is often quite different. But that does not mean that the regular classroom teacher cannot offer the ESL student rich and meaningful language-based literacy experiences. *The same principles that guide language and literacy learning in a first language should guide literacy learning in a second language.*

The following second-language acquisition principles for classroom practice relate to alphabetic (e.g., Spanish and German) as well as nonalphabetic (e.g., Chinese and Japanese) languages (Vygotsky, 1978; Littlewood, 1984; Moll, 1989).

◆ The social context for learning a second language must be a setting where students feel accepted and comfortable.

◆ Students in small groups and pairs have natural opportunities for meaning-making and authentic communication.

◆ Students need time to listen and process without the pressure of oral and written production. They are often rehearsing and creating systems while silent.

◆ Students must gain confidence in their imperfect second-language learning in order to gain accuracy in performance. They go through a natural sequence of learning a language, so teachers must carefully select one or two specific errors to work on at each stage of development.

Learning a second language should not mean losing a first language (Cummins, 1989). Supporting students' first languages and offering them resources to help them develop proficiency with written language is possible even without special or bilingual language classes. Many activities that teachers may already use in their reading classrooms to teach literacy to native speakers are especially useful for second-language learners. Freeman and Freeman (1993), Barone (1996), and Schmidt (1998a) offer realistic suggestions for support in a first language for ESL learners:

◆ Include environmental print from the child's first language in the classroom. Label objects in the first language and English so that everyone is learning a second language.

The same principles that guide language and literacy learning in a first language should guide literacy learning in a second language.

◆ Make sure that the classroom and school libraries have books in languages other than English as well as books written in English representing the cultures of the children.

◆ Encourage children to bring in artifacts, music, dance, and food from their cultures.

◆ Help children publish and share their writing in their first language.

◆ Enlist the help of bilingual aides—other students, parents, teacher aides, or community volunteers.

◆ Use commercial or student-produced videos and computer software to support language learning and improve self-esteem.

◆ Help ESL students find support on the Internet. There are Web sites, open 24 hours a day, where students can meet others speaking their first language.

They can engage in peer discussions as well as share ideas about learning English.

◆ Connect with the families. Welcome them into the classroom to observe and to share their language and culture. Even though their English may be limited, they often enjoy teaching the numbers, days of the week, greetings, and other common expressions.

Authentic Communication.   It seems logical that a nonnative speaker of English immersed in a literate environment would easily develop competence in reading and writing English. Language learning does not take place, however, without an active, communicative process at work. An example of the primacy of social communication in learning a language is underscored by the case of the hearing child of deaf parents. The child's parents used only American Sign Language, but they exposed the child to the television every day. Although by age 3 he could sign fluently, he did not understand or speak English (Moskowitz, 1985). Television is one-way communication: It asks without answering; it offers no response. Without active communication, language learning suffers.

A similar situation is encountered by the child who speaks little or no English and suddenly finds herself in a classroom where almost none of what she hears makes sense. Without sufficient understanding of English, it is difficult for the nonnative speaker of English to take the active role necessary for constructing meaning. Language learning must involve **authentic communication.**

Freeman and Freeman (1993) note that second-language learners may seem to have shorter attention spans than native speakers, when in actuality they are suffering from the fatigue of struggling to make sense out of a language they barely know. Because they cannot easily express what they do know, nonnative speakers may do poorly on tests. They may remain quiet and uninvolved in the classroom because it takes them longer to process a response or because they are self-conscious about failure. They may lack background knowledge or may not understand which features of the language they hear or see are essential for constructing meaning. Second-language learners need to be involved in activities that require communication. Feedback on whether or not their communication works is indispensable.

Dialogue journals, discussed in Chapter 9, help ESL students understand the conventions of writing while engaged in authentic communication. The student writes in the journal to the teacher; the teacher responds but never corrects errors. Teachers often intentionally include the correct version of a misspelled word or usage in their response, modeling the conventional form for the student.

Dyson's studies of authentic communication through writing activities (1989, 1993) demonstrated the building of classroom communities and the promotion of literacy development for children from different languages and cultures. "What matters about writing in school is not simply the quality of the texts children produce," she noted, "but the quality of life they experience at school and beyond. In a community that values written language, writing can become an important means for individual reflection and social connection" (1989, p. xvii).

Content Area Activities.   Learning with language is easier than learning about language; that is, using language meaningfully to explore, share, decide, react, label, and question helps students develop not only academic concepts but literacy concepts as well. Hudelson (1989, pp. 140–141) suggests five principles for developing activities in content areas that will also help ESL students with English language skills.

◆ Students will learn both content and language more easily when they are active participants in activities that require oral and written language directly related to specific content. Filling out charts individually or in small groups, making notes in a learning log, interviewing family members or peers, conducting experiments and noting results—all these activities can be designed to engage students in both language and content.

◆ Students learn content and language when they are interacting with other students or adults who provide feedback, ideas, and reasons for communication.

◆ Language processes (speaking, reading, writing, listening) are interrelated. Using all of these processes helps students become more adept language users. Activities that give students the opportunity to discuss in whole-class and small-group format, to write, and to act out concepts help them learn English as they come to understand the material being studied.

◆ That literacy is acquired through use, not through the learning of isolated skills, is as true of a second language as of a first. Students need to read and write whole, authentic texts.

◆ Background knowledge facilitates comprehension. Activities involving all the language processes (not just the textbook) can help build background. Semantic webs or maps of what students already know, brainstorming activities, demonstrations, and discussions help students begin reading with a clear focus on the content and the purpose for reading.

Finally, to help students learn the English language, systematic coordination among content area teachers and the ESL teacher is vital. Teachers need to share what they are teaching and how they are teaching. In some ESL programs, students meet with the ESL teacher outside of the classroom several days a week. In other programs, the ESL teacher coteaches with content area teachers in the classroom. In any program, the ESL teacher needs to be actively involved in team planning sessions so that there is congruency in the student's program.

Cultural Diversity in Literacy Classrooms

When the norms for using language, when the learner's and the teacher's expectations about appropriate behavior differ, communication may not be straightforward. Intended cues to meaning may not bring about intended results. Purpose and context also affect our meaning-making, as this story of a young theology student delivering a children's sermon illustrates:

> All of the children were called to the front of the church and the pastor began his sermon:
>
> "Children, I'm thinking of something that is about five or six inches high; that scampers across the ground; that lives in either a nest in the tree or makes its home in the hollowed-out portion of a tree's trunk. The thing I'm thinking about gathers nuts and stores them in winter; it is sometimes brown and sometimes gray; it has a big bushy tail. Who can tell me what I'm thinking of?"
>
> Knowing the proper church behavior, the children remained quiet and reserved. No one ventured an answer. Finally, Robert, age 6, slowly and ever so tentatively raised his hand. The pastor, desperate for a response so he could go on with the sermon, said with some relief, "Yes, Robert, what do you think it was?"
>
> "Well," came the response, "ordinarily I'd think it was a squirrel, but I suppose you want me to say it was Jesus." (Harste, Woodward, & Burke, 1984, p. XV)

Closely related to language and linguistic diversity is cultural diversity. Because native speakers learn language in social settings, they also learn their culture's norms for language use. Native speakers are able to deliberately shift their language to fit their audience, the context, and the purpose of their communication. Different social groups also develop different norms for language use. The subtle cues about meaning in language use become invisible to us, however, and we often take for granted our own knowledge about language as "natural." But language is a shared system; the rules are always culturally defined and culturally specific. Different cultures have different rules.

Because rules for using language are so culturally specific, it is easy for teachers not to recognize that language rules are indeed in effect for speakers of other dialects or speakers with different cultural norms for communicating. Delpit (1988) argues that teachers need to recognize the strengths of the language of minority children but then to move beyond—to help those children acquire the norms or rules for communication in the language of school. Direct teaching of language norms in a meaningful and communicative context, she maintains, can help students who come to school without the background knowledge of the meaning of literacy and school language conventions.

Heath and Mangiola (1991) remind us of the affective dimension of language and schooling. When acceptable means of displaying knowledge clash with cultural means, passivity and disinterest may result. They tell of Alicia, who did not want to be a "schoolgirl." To be a schoolgirl, with her head in a book, not interested in dances or going out, always doing homework, did not interest Alicia. But to be involved in dynamic and collaborative activities that required the knowledge in books—tutoring younger students, writing social studies texts for them, or composing scripts for the school's radio shows— then Alicia was interested. When she saw literacy as useful and compelling, Alicia was eager to be literate.

Instructional Strategies for Culturally Diverse Students

If teachers are aware of the possibilities for cultural incongruence, they can make adjustments in their teaching methods and classroom organization to accommodate difference. For example, among Latin Americans, it is often considered polite to spend a few minutes in small talk about health and home before getting down to actual business. Hawaiian children seemed to learn better when their teachers used the pattern of interaction known as "talk-story" that followed conversational pattern in the students' homes (Au & Mason, 1983).

Determining Cultural Expectations.

How can a teacher decide if cultural misunderstandings are interfering with learning in the classroom? Three things to look for are lessons that continually go awry, an extended lack of student progress, or a lack of student involvement.

Teachers can observe the interactions of students as they work and play together, read about cultural differences as well as cultural similarities, and maintain communication with parents and family in order to determine appropriate classroom changes (Fitzgerald, 1993).

A kindergarten teacher in Patricia Schmidt's 1993 study had not asked the two ethnic minority children in her class about their own families' holiday celebrations. Yet they were totally confused by Christmas, St. Patrick's Day, and Easter—so much so that one child "drew bunnies using red and green as the predominant colors." Finding out about holidays around the world and introducing games and literature to reinforce holiday themes can help teachers turn cultural misunderstandings into student involvement.

Validating Each Child's Experience.

Since we use our previous knowledge of the world to help us construct the meaning of our reading and writing, it is only sensible that students with different experiences will have different readings of books and texts. Our cultural schemata, the beliefs we hold about how the world is organized, influence comprehension. In a study of proficient readers, background knowledge that may be common and familiar for a suburban American child may be unknown and confusing to a child from a center city or a rural farm area and even more confusing to a child who recently arrived in the United States.

Helping students build background knowledge before reading remains an important task for teachers in classrooms with students with culturally diverse experiences. However, cultural groups are difficult to define (Yakota, 1993). Asian students will have varying experiences and languages, depending on their home country and their social class and geographic region within that country. Hispanics in America have vastly divergent backgrounds, ranging from Mexican American and Puerto Rican to Chilean and Peruvian. Students from the former Soviet Union will never say they come "from Russia" if in fact they grew up in one of the other republics, such as Ukraine.

In short, our nation is composed of widely diverse groups of people from around the world, and each group has contributed to the greatness of the nation. Therefore, teaching an appreciation of diversity in rural, urban, and suburban settings is relevant, natural, and appropriate. A model for classrooms is presented in the Best Practice featured in Box 13.3. (A sixth-grade teacher uses this model later in the chapter.)

BOX 13.3   BEST PRACTICE

The ABCs of Cultural Understanding and Communication

The model known as the **ABCs of Cultural Understanding and Communication** was created to help present and future teachers develop culturally responsive pedagogy through literacy activities. When teachers adapt the model in their own classrooms, their students also begin to understand and appreciate differences among classmates. Emphasis is on differences because differences have traditionally been the sources of human conflict. The following is a brief explanation of the model with ideas for classroom practice:

- *Autobiography* is written in detail, including key life events related to education, family, religious tradition, recreation, victories, and defeats.
- *Biography* of a person culturally different is written from in-depth unstructured interviews that include key life events.
- *Cross-cultural analyses* of similarities and differences related to the life stories are listed in chart format.
- *Cultural analyses* of differences are examined with explanations of personal discomfort and admiration.
- *Communication* plans for literacy development and home-school connections are designed with modifications for classroom adaptation.

CLASSROOM PRACTICE

The teacher participates in all of the following activities in order to build classroom community.

Autobiography

- Students bring in family pictures and special family objects to share.
- Students write interview questions and interview family members.
- One student each day brings in a bag of favorite things to share.
- Students draw self-portraits and family portraits using crayons or paints.
- Students write their life stories.
- Students create timelines of their life stories showing significant events.

Biography

- Class learns about interviewing and how to question.
- Students in pairs interview each other and write each other's life stories.
- Students in pairs introduce each other after listening to life stories.
- The whole class interviews the "student of the day" and completes a language experience story.

(Continued)

BOX 13.3 CONTINUED

◆ Each class member draws a picture of the "student of the day" doing his or her favorite activity and writes a sentence or two. The sheets are compiled for a book, and a cover is created. The "student of the day" takes home the special book at the end of the day.

Compare and Contrast Similarities and Differences

◆ Create Venn diagrams showing similarities and differences.

◆ Study physical similarities and differences from self-portraits, photographs, and other artifacts.

◆ Write lists of similarities and differences and discuss them.

Cultural Analysis of Differences

◆ Talk about the differences and why differences are important.

◆ Talk about why we like or don't like some differences.

◆ Talk about why some differences scare us.

Connect Home and School for Communication

◆ Invite family members to come into the class and share food, games, language, customs, and/or home artifacts.

◆ Invite family members to tell a story, sing a song, and/or teach a dance.

◆ Invite family members to talk about their lives and work.

◆ Invite family members to help with all of the ABCs activities

Source: From P. R. Schmidt, *Equity and Excellence in Education,* 31 (2), 28–32, 1988, Greenwood Press.

Choosing Quality Multicultural Literature.   Teachers who use multicultural literature in the classroom help students recognize the unique contributions of each culture and the similarities of the human experience across cultures. At the same time, they help nonmainstream cultures appreciate and value their heritage and give all students the benefits of understanding ways of knowing about the world that are different from their own. Asking several questions can help teachers choose which books will be most useful to them in their classrooms (Yakota, 1993):

◆ *Is this book good literature?* Is the plot strong? Is characterization true to experience? Are setting, theme, and style well developed?

◆ *Is this book culturally accurate?* Will it help readers gain a true sense of the culture?

◆ *Is the book rich in cultural details?* Do details that give readers insight as to the nuances of daily life enhance the story? Or is the culture overgeneralized?

By using multicultural literature in the classroom, teachers help nonmainstream students appreciate and value their heritage.

◆ *Are dialogue and relationships culturally authentic?* For example, *Pacific Crossing* (Soto, 1992), about Mexican American students who go to Japan as exchange students, deals with both cultures authentically.

◆ *Are cultural issues presented comprehensively?* Do they have enough depth and realism for readers to get a true sense of how culture affects the lives of people?

◆ *Are minorities relevant?* Are members of a minority present for a reason, or could the story be told as easily about any cultural group? Token involvement of minority characters gives little sense of their unique, culturally rooted experience.

Choosing books that reflect the insider's perspective not only helps students from non-mainstream cultures read about and validate their own experiences but also helps children understand diverse experiences of groups other than their own. The Class Works featured in Box 13.4 tells how one teacher chooses books for her sixth graders.

ACADEMIC AND COGNITIVE DIVERSITY IN LITERACY CLASSROOMS

As human beings, we make sense of our experiences by putting them into categories and giving the categories labels. Although this ability to categorize and label is essential to help us sort through the amount of information we accumulate, it's of little use as we attempt to describe the diversity of experience and ability we face in our students. Labels can never fully represent the range of experiences that students bring to the task of learning to become literate.

Nonetheless, especially in programs funded by the federal government, such as Chapter 1 remedial math and reading programs, and for special education service in most school districts, labeling becomes necessary for inclusion in the program. Identifying students who may need different or more instruction is a sticky problem. For example, standardized tests do not give teachers useful guidance as to what the instructional needs of their students might be. Occasionally, a district may focus on a curriculum solely designed to raise test scores, leading to instruction focusing on basic skills that do not translate well into reading as a meaning-based activity (Strickland & Ascher, 1992). Legitimate ways of knowing are often not measured by standardized tests; gifted students and linguistically and culturally diverse students often do not test as well as their actual ability would suggest (Tuttle, 1989).

Reading failure is an emotional issue. Among students, parents, and educators alike, the belief that reading is the key to academic as well as personal success is strong. Research indicates that students who experience early reading difficulty maintain or increase below-level performance (Stanovich, 1986). The prestige and power associated with cultural and societal definitions of literacy adds further to the sense of the importance of helping students become literate. However, certain categories can be used to describe learners and their needs that will help us plan the classroom activities that can help all of our students grow as readers and writers, including those with linguistic and cultural differences, those with learning disabilities, young readers having difficulties, and gifted readers.

Planning Instruction for Readers Having Difficulty

The instruction teachers give to students who experience reading difficulty should be much like the instruction they give to other students. No one aspect of the language cuing system should be emphasized over any other. Although phonics-only was at one time touted as the way to help poor readers, we know that especially poor readers need to use their decoding skill in the construction of meaning. Balancing decoding instruction with meaningful reading experiences is the challenge faced by teachers who work with students who struggle with reading. Sacrificing meaningful reading gives students the wrong idea about reading—that it is only about pronouncing words.

Kelly Carpenter's Sixth-Grade Class and Multicultural Literature

Kelly Carpenter, a sixth-grade teacher in a suburban setting, adapted the ABCs of Cultural Understanding and Communication for student research about ancestors (Schmidt, 1998c). Her students interviewed family members about customs and countries of origin. The writing and sharing of family histories in class caught student interest in their own and others' stories and assisted in the building of classroom community and home-school connections. The students also began discovering literature related to their ancestry along with other multicultural literature found in the classroom. They read in interest and ability groups, wrote analyses of books, and shared their ideas in small groups. The following format was used for written and oral discussions.

CULTURAL ANALYSIS OF LITERATURE

Directions: Please answer each question on your own after reading the book in a group.

1. What is the title of the book? Who are its illustrator and author?

2. What is the book about? Give a brief summary.

3. Choose a word that is new or different in the book and define it.

4. What is your most favorite part of the book and why?

5. What is your least favorite part of the book and why?

6. What is your favorite illustration in the book and why?

7. What did you learn from the book?

8. How did the book make you feel when you were reading it?

9. Please complete your cultural analysis on the back:
   a. List the similarities between the book and your culture.
   b. List the differences between the book and your culture.
   c. Analyze the differences, both the ones that you liked and the ones that made you feel uncomfortable. Discuss these in your group.

10. See if people in your group are ready to discuss these questions. If they are, choose a place in the room to meet. If they are not, wait and select a literature response activity from the list of 25. This activity may be shared with the whole class.

(Continued)

BOX 13.4 CONTINUED

Kelly found that this adaptation of the ABCs was a positive way for her class to practice reading, writing, listening, and speaking, as well as a means of developing an appreciation of diversity. "My students and I learned about each other from the beginning of the school year. I learned information not in the files, and they formed a cohesive community as they began to study cooperatively. I am also beginning to integrate reading, writing, listening, and speaking to develop an appreciation of diversity in math and science through ethnomathematics and nonfiction literature."

Reflective Inquiry

◆ What parts of the model would you find most beneficial for use in your classroom? Why?

Activities that require students to be actively involved in constructing meaning, using all the cuing systems of written language, are especially appropriate for struggling readers. Internet projects and activities can offer students with disabilities these opportunities by motivating them to read and write. In addition, strategies discussed in other chapters, such as choral reading, repeated readings, read-alouds, QARs, summary writing, and readers' theater have benefited readers who are having difficulties.

Recently, **inquiry learning,** a classroom approach for teaching math and science, has helped students with special needs in literacy learning. Inquiry learning and teaching is based on the constructivist approach (Piaget, 1970; Confrey, 1990; Fosnot, 1996), which perceives learning as a meaning-making process. Children are seen as little scientists who experiment, solve problems, and discover how the world functions. They are encouraged to become more active classroom participants as they connect with their own environment and the studies at hand and formulate high-level questions. Observations in elementary settings indicate that students exhibited greater focus on content and more positive interactions with classmates during lessons. Finally, their reading, writing, listening, and speaking noticeably improved as they successfully demonstrated oral and written understandings of unit objectives. The Best Practice featured in Box 13.5 describes a framework for helping students form questions in inquiry learning. We see this strategy in use in a second-grade classroom in the Class Works featured in Box 13.6.

Because students with diverse needs often need extra instruction in order to catch up with more able-reading peers, time is always a problem for classroom teachers when dealing with students with special needs. Such teachers need to teach as much as possible with the limited amount of instructional time available. Kameenui (1993b) suggests that teachers keep the following instructional framework in mind as they plan instruction for diverse learners:

◆ Instructional time is limited; teach reading strategies, concepts, or problem-solving analysis in the most efficient manner possible.

KWLQ

At the heart of inquiry learning is questioning, but student ability to ask questions about content is often based on prior knowledge. Furthermore, students with special needs may have difficulty asking questions. To help them with their questioning, a framework was developed using Ogle's (1986) KWL (described in Chapter 7) and an additional Q, as illustrated in Figures 31.1*a* and 13.1*b*. Based on previous personal and school experiences and connected to new experiences, students in kindergarten, second grade, and fifth grade were encouraged to question and discover through the four steps of **KWLQ** (Schmidt, 1999):

1. The students recorded their prior knowledge about a particular subject under *K*. This was completed in pairs with individual charts or on a large class chart (see Figures 13.1*a* and 13.1*b*).

2. The students formulated, recorded, and reported questions, under *W*, in the same manner. The teachers also modeled the different ways to ask questions.

3. The children searched for answers through reading, interviews, field trips, videotapes, the Internet, and firsthand experiences. They recorded and reported their answers under *L*. The teacher anticipated specific answers based on the units of study; the students responded with not only those answers but also with information beyond what the curriculum required.

4. The children noted more questions for further study under *Q*. At the end of the unit, the unanswered questions from *Q* became a focus for those students who continued to be interested in finding answers and reporting them to the class.

In conclusion, KWLQ provided a framework for question formulation and practice for literacy learning as the children naturally connected reading, writing, listening, and speaking for inquiry learning.

Source: From P. R. Schmidt, "KWLQ: Inquiry and Literacy Learning in Science," *The Reading Teacher,* *52,* 789–792, 1999. The International Reading Association.

◆ Intervene and take remedial measures as quickly as possible, and as often as necessary, providing frequent opportunities to read connected texts, activities that require all learners to be active participants in reading (small group or partner reading), and opportunities to develop phonemic awareness and letter recognition as early as possible.

◆ Teach less, but teach well. Select essential objectives and the most important strategies. Spiegel (1992) notes that instruction must be sustained and focused enough for all students to learn strategies and concepts effectively.

◆ FIGURE 13.1a

KWLQ Chart			
K	W	L	Q
What I <u>Know</u>	What I <u>Want</u> to Know	What I <u>Learned</u>	More <u>Questions</u> I Have

◆ Communicate reading strategies clearly and effectively, especially during the beginning phases of instruction. For students who come to school without experiences with or knowledge of the language of school and who have not internalized the rules of that language, direct instruction can be helpful (Delpit, 1988). Since language is learned best in communicative and social situations, direct instruction is most effective when used within the context of connected, meaningful reading and writing.

◆ Reading instruction must be guided strategically by the teacher. Teacher-directed and student-centered activities must all have as their goal not only the improvement of reading but also helping students who have difficulties catch up with their more able-reading peers. The ultimate goal of all reading instruction is for students to direct their own learning.

♦ FIGURE 13.1b

KWLQ Chart	
K What I Know	**W** What I Want to Know
L What I Learned	**Q** More Questions I Have

♦ Effectiveness of instruction and materials should be evaluated during instruction by measuring student performance. Instruction should focus on what students need to learn as well as on how well they are learning it.

Early Intervention for Low-Achieving Readers

Because early reading success is so important for later reading success, and because early reading failure is likely to haunt a student for many years (Stanovich, 1986), **early intervention** *to help lower-than-expected achievers in reading catch up with able-reading peers is essential.* A program designed especially for students in first grade who are experiencing difficulties with reading is Reading Recovery (Clay, 1985; Pinnell, Fried, & Estice, 1990).

BOX 13.6   CLASS WORKS

Kyle and the Insect Unit

Kyle, age 7, was labeled learning-disabled in reading and written language at the beginning of the school year in an urban district. Daily, he and Lonnie, his classmate, received help in the resource room. Kyle often dressed in sweat pants and appeared to be in constant motion. His short, closely cropped blond hair had several cowlicks. A quick, winning smile, articulate language, and agile athletic ability hid his disorganization and lack of focus. Kyle preferred to work alone; his classmates preferred to work away from him. He avoided reading and writing and was unable to complete any reading or writing assignments required of typical second-grade students. He usually preferred to talk about a subject, but during class discussions, he would forget to raise his hand and just shout answers.

In the spring of second grade, Kyle drastically changed his literacy behaviors while participating in an eight-week inquiry unit titled "Insects in My Backyard." This was his teacher's first attempt at inquiry teaching and learning. During this unit, Kyle often showed an initial dislike for working with a buddy but would eventually settle in and produce. For example, when he and his partner, Patrie, were required to write statements about their prior knowledge of insects, they took turns and quickly recorded 20 in five minutes in the *K* section of their KWLQ chart. This was a class record.

After watching a video about backyard insects, the children were asked to record two questions or statements about insects in the *K* or *W* sections of the KWLQ chart. Kyle asked, "A sowbug has how many legs?" and "Are spiders insects?" He also actively participated in a 30-minute discussion about the video, listening to questions and answering numerous questions asked by others, making him the most obviously involved child in the class.

When a container of mealworms was brought into the classroom, Kyle became the expert handler. His observations allowed him to determine whether a worm was alive or dead. He also proudly wrote observations about the life cycle of mealworms and of butterflies. While the class talked about the meanings of the words *larva, pupa,* and *metamorphosis* written on the blackboard, Kyle, equipped with journal and pencil, eagerly moved to a seat near the blackboard and began copying.

Initially, Kyle avoided book exploration for his self-selected research project. While his partner looked up information about bees, Kyle studied a dead bee under a magnifying glass. They both recorded and shared the information discovered in class in the *L* section of the KWLQ chart. A week later, during silent reading time, Kyle asked if he could study a dead wasp along with reading and studying the pictures in a book about bees, wasps, and hornets. He wanted to determine the kind of wasp he was examining and knew he needed a book.

Box 13.6 CONTINUED

For his research, Kyle was required to create a model of his insect. He shaped dough into a model of a queen bee in accurate detail. He surrounded her with eggs and labeled the card that she rested on. He remained focused, needing no repeated directions or guidance throughout the activity.

When Kyle listened to classmates presenting their research, he usually had questions for them, such as "Why does a grasshopper have such a long body and tall legs?" "How are ladybugs born? In a cell? In an egg?" "If a butterfly is flying, could a stick get snagged in its wings?" Unanswered questions were recorded by the teacher in the Q section of the class KWLQ chart.

During class time, Kyle wrote a report on bees and consulted books and classmates for the spelling of certain words he considered important. When he read the report to the class, he spoke clearly and with authority. His classmates clapped as he proudly handed his writing to the teacher.

Do you no keeler bees com form Africa?	*(Do you know killer bees come from Africa?)*
thay do not liv her ths sty.	*(They do not live here in the city.)*
Thay lik hot plais. lik Texas.	*(They like hot places like Texas.)*
One laedi bees work the honey, not boys.	*(Only lady bees work for the honey, not boys.)*
I no wy queen bez re not camoflagd.	*(I know why the queen bees are not camouflaged.)*
thay r terrtorl. thay do nt leve nest.	*(They are territorial. They do not leave the nest.)*
The queen be dont help get hony.	*(The queen bee does not help get the honey.)*
she too buz lyng egs and doing man thngs aernd hive.	*(She is too busy laying eggs and doing many things around the hive.)*
Bees do nt cilct polln in m.	*(Bees do not collect pollen in the rain.)*
th peser poos to grnd.	*(The pressure pushes them to the ground.)*

REFLECTIVE INQUIRY

◆ What do you think were the major benefits for Kyle from this combination of reading, writing, listening, and speaking throughout his science unit?

◆ Do you see any connections between literacy learning behaviors and a sharing classroom community? What are they?

◆ How would you react to Kyle's writing?

Reading Recovery.   A program begun in New Zealand and brought to the United States by Marie Clay, **Reading Recovery** focuses on low-ability readers who work in the program receiving daily, individual instruction for about 15 weeks and catch up to their peers in 70 to 80 percent of cases.

Several of the principles of Reading Recovery are useful for the regular classroom, helping teachers support learners as they acquire word identification strategies:

◆ Use books with illustrations and predictable language to help keep word identification in the context of creating meaning.

◆ Read and reread words and stories to develop fluency.

◆ Keep a running record of children's reading of text. By doing so, the teacher has a way to determine how children are making meaning with text.

◆ Teach words in connection with the whole text. Talk about stories before reading the book; help children understand the big ideas.

◆ Help children develop self-monitoring strategies by helping them problem-solve about what the words are and what they mean.

◆ Use writing activities in connection with reading as writing and reading develop concurrently.

Because Reading Recovery involves intense tutor training, individual tutoring, and pulling students out of the regular classroom, it requires a sincere commitment by schools. However, this commitment to children with reading difficulties is also a commitment to society, since we know that children who do not become literate are on the road to academic failure. Furthermore, the social and emotional suffering that follow often leads to economic failure.

Early Intervention in Reading.   A program that involves supplemental in-class instruction by the regular classroom teacher is known as *Early Intervention in Reading (EIR)* (Taylor, Short, Fry, & Shearer, 1992). EIR involves small group tutoring for the lowest five or so students in a class, with the idea that early supplemental instruction can help prevent the cycle of reading failure and its far-reaching effects on student achievement. Students can be selected for inclusion in the program on the basis of readiness tests, ability to segment words into sounds (phonemic awareness), and sight word and vocabulary knowledge. Materials needed include picture books with strong appeal for first graders, teacher-made summaries of the books on a chart and in booklets for teacher-student reading, and other short, easy-to-read picture books for independent reading. The Best Practice featured in Box 13.7 outlines the procedures for EIR instruction.

Characteristics of Successful Programs.   When considering early intervention for children experiencing reading difficulties, be aware that successful EIR programs have certain characteristics in common, as revealed by Pikulski's 1994 review of five effective programs:

◆ Tutoring takes place with a trained professional.

◆ Tutoring is one to one or in groups of no more than five students.

BOX 13.7 BEST PRACTICE

Early Intervention in Reading Instruction

DAY 1

The teacher begins the session by reading a picture book aloud to the students, modeling fluent reading and appropriate book-reading behaviors. The teacher then reads the summary of the book from a chart. The teacher helps students identify contextual, graphophonemic, and syntactic clues that help identify words. The students practice separating words into their component sounds by writing several words from the story in the back of their booklets. Each word chosen for this kind of practice is written in boxes already duplicated on the page. For example, the student could write the word *that* th/a/t or *cat* c/a/t.

DAYS 2 AND 3

The children, with the teacher's help, reread the summaries. The teacher encourages and instructs the use of reading strategies that help the children identify words. The children also write a sentence in their booklet that is related to the story. The teacher encourages the students to write down the sounds they hear in the words, only supplying letters the children cannot produce by themselves.

Fluency is encouraged throughout the EIR program. Students also reread their summaries, either independently or in pairs with an aide. After the third day, the children take a copy of the booklet home to read to their parents, and another story is begun.

TRANSITION TO INDEPENDENT READING

Four to six months into the program, the children begin to read 50- to 150-word picture books they have not read previously while working with the teacher on 90- to 150-word summaries. As the children read new books, the teacher listens as they read and encourages the use of strategies when they come to difficult words. Eventually, usually about six months into the program, the students begin to read 200-word picture books with teacher assistance. Again, repeated readings and teacher instruction and encouragement with reading strategies help the students gain fluency.

◆ Consistent meetings occur on a daily basis in pull-out or push-in settings.

◆ The reading-writing connection is emphasized along with listening and speaking activities.

◆ Texts are at independent and instructional levels for reading and rereading.

◆ The tutoring complements or is coordinated with classroom literacy instruction.

Gifted Readers

Students who have wide vocabularies, read two or more years above grade level, have excellent memory for story details, understand complex concepts and ideas, and learn quickly and with minimum structure the skills and strategies necessary for reading sophisticated texts may be classified as **gifted readers** (Davis & Johns, 1991). Gifted readers do not automatically learn without instruction, but they learn so quickly that they may not be sufficiently challenged by reading instruction aimed at average readers.

Classroom teachers can differentiate instruction for highly able readers in two ways: by compacting instruction and by modifying curriculum, adapting content and processes (Dooley, 1993).

When *compacting instruction*, identify the needs of readers by pretesting for the strategy or skill that will be taught. Students do not receive instruction for material they have already mastered. For strategies or concepts that need to be taught, the students can join regular instruction, or they can use structured inductive or "discover" learning materials to master the strategy or concepts.

When *modifying curriculum*, you can *adapt content* by having students read longer and more in-depth selections and having them select reading materials that reflect their own needs and interests in studying a particular theme, genre, or author. You can also add an interdisciplinary approach to the topic. To *adapt process*, have students analyze and evaluate their reading. Focus on critical reading strategies through the use of reading guides that include pre-, during-, and after-reading activities. All students should be encouraged to think critically, but highly able readers may need less instruction and less structure to do so.

Identifying Gifted Students in Diverse Settings

Often, the students who are most likely to be identified as gifted come from middle- and upper-middle-class backgrounds. Children of poverty are often just as able, but their creative abilities may go unrecognized. A classroom teacher may need to readjust her ways of seeing her students so that all students can be given the kind of challenging instruction that will help them grow as readers and learners.

Teachers may wish to keep an *observational portfolio* (see also Chapters 14 and 15) based on the following:

◆ Parents' survey: What are your child's strengths? In what areas does your child need guidance or extra practice?

◆ Anecdotal records: What does the child self-select to read? What activities does the child choose independently? Does the child initiate? Explain? Facilitate for others? Show evidence of new and different ways to solve problems?

◆ Observations of lessons

◆ Samples of student work

◆ Peer nomination: Who do other students say knows something special or useful?

SUMMARY

Understanding and accepting children's differences has been a common thread throughout this chapter. Diversity among learners is a fact of life in classrooms. Ignoring this creates unnecessary difficulties and frustrations for both students and teachers. Embracing it leads to effective instructional adaptations in reading.

Adapting instruction to meet the needs of diverse learners was at the core of this chapter. Three types of learner diversity were explored: linguistic, cultural, and academic and cognitive.

Linguistic diversity in the classroom may be the result of a variety of factors. Dialects differ in phonology, syntax, and lexicon. Rather than viewing linguistic diversity as a disadvantage or barrier, teachers and students must understand and value linguistic diversity. Children should have many natural opportunities to use language so that they can experiment with language and discover their options as language users. Teachers must recognize that children may read in their own dialect patterns, but these dialect miscues seldom interfere with the child's quest for meaning. Instruction for linguistically diverse learners should capitalize on children's strengths in comprehension and expression. Our goals for children should center on language growth and flexibility, not change. The same principles that guide language and literacy learning in a first language should guide literacy learning in a second language.

Cultural diversity is closely related to language and linguistic diversity. Teachers need to help children acquire the norms for communication in the language of the school. They need to make adjustments in teaching strategies to accommodate difference, turning cultural misunderstandings into student involvement.

Children with learning disabilities, young readers having difficulties, and gifted readers also benefit from instructional adaptations for their *academic or cognitive diversity*. Teachers often need to provide extra instruction in order to actively involve struggling readers in constructing meaning. Strategies for supplemental in-class instruction are useful for differentiating teaching as well as for pull-out programs such as Reading Recovery.

Teachers who adopt instruction effectively use their understanding of children's needs and their beliefs about reading to make instructional decisions. They reach out to the families of their students in order to connect home and school for literacy instruction. They recognize that whatever adaptations are made for a child's special needs, meaning must be at the heart of reading instruction. They also facilitate meaningful interaction among all students whenever possible, and through carefully attentive observations they convey the uniqueness and value of each individual in the classroom. Finally, they promote an appreciation of similarities and differences across the nation and around the world in their classroom libraries and on the Internet. Their reading to children, discussions with children, and instructional choices for children help their students grow as readers and as understanding human beings.

TEACHER-ACTION RESEARCHER

1. Find out about the language and culture of minority groups that live in your community. Explore the resources available, concentrating on children's books about or from these cultures. Prepare an annotated bibliography of some of the books that could be used during instruction with children from these cultures and their classmates.

2. Experience a modified version of the ABCs of Cultural Understanding and Communication. Sit down with someone who you believe has a different culture than yours. The older person spends four or five minutes sharing earliest memories of family, education, celebrations, food, fun, victories, traumatic events, loves, honors, disappointments, and so on. Next, the younger person does the same. Then, together, make a list of your similarities and differences. Afterward, describe and reflect on this experience in a paragraph or two.

3. Research book lists and annotated bibliographies for books that would be appropriate for readers with special needs, who read English as a second language, or who wish to learn about other cultures. Some journal sources include *Booklist, Language Arts,* and *The Reading Teacher.* Read one (or more) of the recommended books with a student.

    Reflect on the student's response to the books. How does reading these books differ from reading other children's literature?

4. Listen to a child who speaks AAL (African American language) or another dialect of English read aloud. Does the child make miscues that fall into a pattern based on dialectical differences? How can you determine if miscues are dialectically based? Interview classroom teachers about their views on dialectical substitutions in oral reading. Do you agree with the teachers? What evidence about reading and language would you use to support your views?

KEY TERMS

authentic
   communication
bilingual learners
cognitive and
   academic diversity
cultural diversity

dialect
dialogue journals
early intervention
gifted readers
inclusion
inquiry learning

KWLQ
language-experience
   approach (LEA)
linguistic diversity
Reading Recovery

CHAPTER

14

Assessing
Reading Performance

Chapter Overview

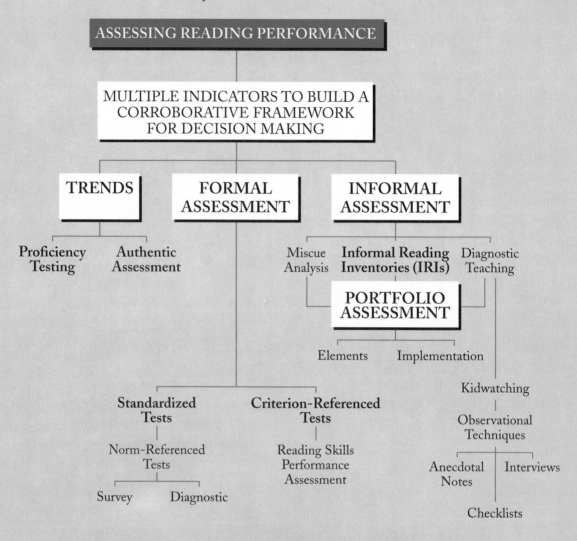

ASSESSING READING PERFORMANCE

MULTIPLE INDICATORS TO BUILD A
CORROBORATIVE FRAMEWORK
FOR DECISION MAKING

TRENDS

FORMAL
ASSESSMENT

INFORMAL
ASSESSMENT

Proficiency
Testing

Authentic
Assessment

Miscue
Analysis

Informal Reading
Inventories (IRIs)

Diagnostic
Teaching

PORTFOLIO
ASSESSMENT

Elements

Implementation

Standardized
Tests

Criterion-Referenced
Tests

Kidwatching

Norm-Referenced
Tests

Reading Skills
Performance
Assessment

Observational
Techniques

Survey

Diagnostic

Anecdotal
Notes

Interviews

Checklists

Between the Lines

In this chapter, you will discover:

♦ **The reasons to use authentic assessments in making decisions about instruction**

♦ **Purposes for formal, standardized assessments**

♦ **Purposes for informal, alternative assessments**

*I*t was springtime, and Sue Latham smiled as she looked through a folder with assessment information on John, a "low" reader in her third-grade classroom. How her assessment of him had changed from early fall to now! She noted that on a *formal,* standardized reading test, given in October, John had scored in the 32nd percentile, which meant that he was below average in comparison to other third graders. Although she did not think this score was particularly useful to her in deciding how to work with John, Mrs. Latham knew that her principal examined these scores. She also noted that on a more *informal* assessment related to his attitude toward reading, John viewed himself positively. He also did well on a section from another informal reading assessment in which he picked questions from a list that he thought would help a person understand the important ideas about a selection. This reminded her of yesterday's social studies lesson on explorers. John and other students had raised some insightful questions as the class previewed the chapter and created a class list of questions that might be answered as they worked on the chapter.

At the start of the school year, Mrs. Latham had decided to work with John in a second-grade basal reader along with four other students. Initially, her decision was based on a conversation with John's second-grade teacher and her review of the *skill mastery tests* administered as part of the basal reader program. One of these tests assessed students' ability to associate the hard and soft sound of the letter *g.* John didn't reach mastery of this particular skill. In other words, he didn't score correctly on 80 percent of the items related to the skill objective; in fact, he answered only six out of ten items correctly. This puzzled Mrs. Latham because just the day before, John had shared a part of a book he was reading about a visit to the zoo, which included seeing *giraffes* and petting *goats.* John didn't experience difficulty reading passages containing words with soft and hard *g* sounds. Later in October, she had a *miscue analysis* compiled from a *running record* of John's oral reading during small group instruction. She had noted no difficulties in his reading of either soft or hard sounds.

Mrs. Latham decided back then to capitalize on John's strength of raising questions about material read both in his reading group and in social studies and science units. She decided *not* to use additional instructional time working on the soft and hard sound of *g,* even though he had not achieved mastery for this objective on the basal reader test. In fact, in November she thought that John was functioning well enough in the second-grade basal reader to reassign him to the third-grade reader. The bottom line is that Mrs. Latham considered information from informal and formal tests *and* her observations of John in actual reading situations. She then made decisions based on *multiple data sources.* Corroborating her instructional decisions was John's *portfolio* of work in progress: some stories and poems he was working on in response to their literature theme unit on tall tales and his personal reading list for sustained silent reading. By using examples of John's actual reading and actual writing, Sue Latham had made an *authentic assessment* of John's *performance in literacy*—a reason to smile.

As depicted in the chapter overview, we support making instructional decisions using multiple ways to assess authentically the *processes* students are engaged in as they read and learn. Diagnostic testing *and* teaching allow you to gather information in order to make inferences about children's reading ability and performance. Tests provide one perspective for becoming knowledgeable about a student's performance; actual teaching situations provide another perspective; and portfolios of student work provide still another.

TOWARD A CORROBORATIVE FRAMEWORK FOR DECISION MAKING

The process that Sue Latham used to develop an authentic assessment of John is another example of how teachers screen and filter information about children's performance through their concepts and beliefs about reading and learning to read. Mrs. Latham holds an interactive view of the reading process. She believes that reading acquisition involves coordinating and integrating many skills during actual reading situations. A child learns to read the way Mrs. Latham first learned to use a stick shift in a car with manual transmission. What needed to be learned was how to coordinate the use of the clutch pedal, gas pedal, brake, and stick in shifting from gear to gear. A beginner may practice pushing the clutch pedal in and out in isolated drill or simulate shifting from gear to gear. However, actually experiencing stick-shifting in traffic makes the difference in learning how to coordinate and integrate the skills.

And so it is with John in his learning to become a fluent reader. When contrasting his performance on the test with his performance in a real reading situation, Mrs. Latham chose to weigh the information from the teaching situation more heavily than the score on the test. Because her students keep portfolios of their work in reading and writing, they too understand their progress in literacy and are learning to evaluate their own strengths and weaknesses in various reading and writing tasks. Portfolios also helped Mrs. Latham plan the kinds of instruction that would move her students toward more mature reading and writing. The student portfolios, works in progress in literacy, are a record of the process of learning in reading and writing for each student. They contain valuable data about growth and progress in literacy performance, and where weaknesses exist, they are useful in planning the instructional next step. Portfolios have become an important aspect of authentic assessment of literacy performance.

Casey Stengel, manager of the New York Yankees in the 1950s and later of the New York Mets, was as renowned for his wonderful use of language as he was for winning baseball games. On one occasion after losing a hard-fought game, Stengel was quoted as saying, "You can know the score of the game and not know the real score." The real score involves understanding and appreciating the dynamics of what happens on the playing field during the game regardless of the outcome.

The real score in reading involves understanding and appreciating *how* children interact with print in authentic reading situations and *why*. "To be authentic, the texts the students read need to relate to things that are interesting and real—that are meaningful for the student" (Farr & Tone, 1998, p. 19).

We advocate using *multiple indicators* of student performance for assessment. Any single indicator—whether it involves commercially prepared or teacher-made tests or observation—provides a perspective, one means of attesting to the accuracy of the score or phenomenon under examination. Multiple indicators, however, build a *corroborative framework* that strengthens decision making. As teachers we must constantly make decisions. Multiple indicators of reading strengthen our decision making as information from one data source builds on or contrasts with information from other data sources. The result is a rich knowledge base for understanding how and why students perform in reading.

Because reading takes place inside the head, the process is not directly observable and therefore not directly measurable. Yet one of the important functions of reading tests, whether formal or informal, should be to help teachers understand a human process that is essentially hidden from direct examination. What are the latest trends in assessment? To what extent do standardized, criteria-referenced, informal, and teacher-made tests play a constructive role in the classroom?

How do teachers keep a running record of performance-based assessments in their classrooms? Finally, how can the process of portfolio assessment involve parents, teachers, students, and administrators in communication about the growth students are making in reading, writing, and language?

Trends in Assessment

Discontent among the public and within the field of education over the state of assessment has reached a fever pitch. On one hand, the public wants assurances that students will leave school well prepared to enter the workforce or embark on postsecondary education. On the other, educators are calling for better, more authentic assessment practices that reunite goals for learning with classroom instruction and assessment. These trends are nearly opposites. As Tierney (1998) explains it, there are two different orientations; one focuses on "something you *do to* students," and the other focuses on "something you *do with* them or help them *do for themselves*" (p. 378).

The trends, proficiency testing and authentic assessment, are analogous to different sides of the same coin. They represent the very different orientations or perspectives held by groups whose needs are not being met in a satisfactory way. Farr and Tone (1998) depict these differences as a "kind of wall" with decision makers on one side, separated by a lack of understanding and acceptance from teachers on the other side (see Figure 14.1).

Proficiency Testing

Throughout the 1990s, state legislators across the country enacted laws requiring students to pass proficiency exams before they can graduate. The premise is that if a student attains

◆ Figure 14.1   *Different Views of Assessment*

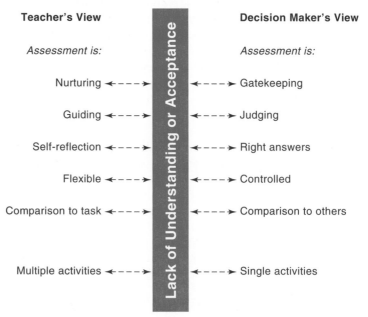

Source: Adapted from *Portfolio and Performance Assessment,* 2nd ed., by R. Farr and B. Tone (Orlando, FL: Harcourt Brace, 1998), p. 19. Reprinted by permission of the publisher.

a certain score on a test that all other students in the state take, the student has demonstrated competence in that body of knowledge (reading, writing, science, math, etc.). **Proficiency testing** is intended to provide the public with a *guarantee* that students can perform at a level necessary to function in society and in the workforce. Of course, there are no guarantees in life itself, let alone on any test, especially based on a one-time performance. Nevertheless, this trend is increasing as "the most recent national efforts to improve education have been on establishing standards that presumably will result in the development of assessments to hold educators accountable" (Farr & Tone, 1998, p. 187). More testing!

Compounding this demand for more standardized testing is the problem that the tests themselves are not adequate, given what we now know about literacy. For example, we know that "any student's performance in reading or writing will vary considerably from task to task and from time to time" (MacGinitie, 1993, p. 557).

What are some of the effects of this trend toward standard setting and proficiency testing? Reliance on high-stakes assessment (in which students, teachers, and school districts are held accountable on the basis of their performance) eliminates the opportunity to track a student's progress in literacy as an individual. Instead, comparisons are made between groups of students, schools, and even school districts based on sets of state and national *standards* for performance in subject areas. In numerous states, newspapers are publishing "report cards" for school districts, then ranking them according to scores attained by their pupils on proficiency tests, with special attention to the overall percentage passing. This in turn spawns "rewarding" districts having higher rates of passing with increased financial subsidies and "punishing" districts having lower rates of passing with decreased subsidies.

Proficiency testing also intrudes into classroom life. The time spent preparing students to take these tests has actually replaced time that would normally be spent on teaching and learning activities. Likewise, the content of the curriculum itself is being examined for its "fit" with the content of the exams. School district personnel are at work trying to align the various subject matter curricula with the areas assessed by the proficiency tests. Is this the best and most efficient way for teachers and administrators to spend their time and use their talent? And is this reallocation of classroom time in the best interests of students and their learning?

Perhaps an even better question to consider is what kinds of assessment are most useful to provide students with the best possible instruction. If, for instance, proficiency test scores were no longer an issue, what kinds of assessments would be effective and efficient? According to Leslie and Jett-Simpson (1997), our "new technology of assessment must be an efficient use of teachers' time. Efficiency means that you get a lot of information from the time invested" (pp. 8–9). For countless teachers, the answers to these and similar questions are not found in their districts' report cards; they are unfolding as teachers become more involved.

Authentic Assessment

The second major trend in assessment is a movement in which teachers are exercising their empowerment as they recapture the vital role they know well—making and sharing decisions about instruction and assessment. Teachers "are being asked to become involved in the design—as well as in the administration—of the assessment procedures . . . to document growth in reading and writing with authentic reading and writing tasks" (Leslie & Jett-Simpson, 1997, p. 9). What do we mean by *authentic?* Several criteria connote **authentic assessment,** as described by Farr and Tone (1998, pp. 18–19): Students are doing reading and writing tasks that look like real-life tasks, and students are primarily in control of the reading or writing task. These two criteria then lead to a third: Students develop ownership, engage thoughtfully, and learn to assess themselves.

Today's teachers want to know more about factors that contribute to their students' literacy achievement (products) and about how the students themselves think about their reading and writing (process). Some teachers strive for more authenticity in *performance-based assessment* by "requiring knowledge and problem-solving abilities" representative of real-world purposes (Leslie & Jett-Simpson, 1997, p. 4). Students respond to a reading task, usually in writing as assigned by the teacher. Other teachers are exploring *portfolio assessment* by involving students themselves in collecting, reflecting on, and assessing their own work. Students develop a sense of ownership as their reading and writing strategies become the focus of attention; teachers benefit from discussions with students about their actual language use.

As shown in Figure 14.1, teachers have many expectations for assessment. Information gathered should be useful in planning classroom instruction, guiding students to become reflective and learn to assess their own strengths and weaknesses. Furthermore, information should permit clear description of a student's literacy growth and achievement

Authentic assessment of literacy—determining what exactly students can and can't do in real-life reading and writing—is one of the major trends in assessment.

for communication with parents and administrators. In the Viewpoint in Box 14.1, third-grade teacher Shawn Jividen tells how she came to take the leadership in changing the way students' literacy development was communicated to parents in her district's report cards.

As teachers learn more about the developmental nature of reading and writing acquisition, they are likely to want more tools with which to do authentic assessment. They will seek ways to collect performance samples (both informally and formally produced), observation techniques, anecdotal records, checklists, interviews, conferences and conversations with students, writing folders, and portfolios. Although teachers will continue to be required to administer standardized tests and assign letter grades, they must also consider their *professional obligation* to meet their students' literacy needs.

Formal Assessment

Pressures for accountability have led many school districts and states to use formal reading tests as a means of assessment. Formal tests may be norm-referenced or criterion-referenced. Many of the recent standardized tests give *both* norm-referenced and criterion-referenced results of students' performance. Norm-referenced test results, in particular, appear to meet decision makers' needs for making comparisons.

Standardized Tests

Standardized reading tests are machine-scorable instruments that sample reading performance during a single administration. Standardized test scores are useful in making com-

Shawn Jividen on Report Cards

Shawn Jividen and the other six third-grade teachers in a suburban and rural district primary school had been unhappy for some time with the requirement that all third-grade children were to receive a reading grade of A through F and a score from a standardized test such as the proficiency test.

Parents wanted to know just what "on grade level" meant for their child. After voicing our displeasure to the principal for over a year, we pursued the idea that there must be something we could do. Finally, she said that if we could all agree on a way to explain to parents exactly how their child is achieving *and developing* in reading, she would be willing to consider replacing the test score. Since I was the "lucky one" taking a graduate course that semester on curriculum evaluation, the principal asked if I would coordinate the effort—an idea immediately seconded by my colleagues!

In no time at all, my steering committee, consisting of all third-grade teachers in the building, met and came up with some basic questions to work from and decided to plunge right into a pilot project. Essentially, we all helped gather information to find out (1) what methods were currently being used by classroom teachers to evaluate children's progress, (2) how teachers collaborated to meet the needs of their students, and (3) which performance areas the teachers felt were appropriate indicators of success in literacy for our third graders. After we finished interviewing teachers and members of the school's curriculum committee, we developed a draft checklist of criteria. These became the focus of a brief survey that we then distributed to teachers, administrators, and some parents. Once the results were analyzed, we agreed on the final checklist, which included "Writes complete sentences," "Exhibits awareness of word meanings and spelling patterns," "Recognizes and self-corrects errors," and nine other items. We assessed each student for each item by marking either a *P*, for *progressing successfully,* or an *E*, for *experiencing difficulty;* comments could be written at the bottom.

When the other teachers heard about our success in developing this checklist, they decided to adopt it (with modifications) as a possible replacement for the standardized test tool for the following year. We know our checklist is far from perfect, but we believe we've improved communication about assessment of our students in a couple of concrete ways. For one, the checklist will accompany each individual child, so the new teacher will have familiar criteria on the child's strengths and weaknesses in reading. For another, parents will receive a copy with their student's report card.

Not only am I relieved that the pilot was successful for personal reasons, but it's been a professionally rewarding experience too. Watching the enthusiasm of my fellow teachers grow, after their initial skepticism, is an unexpected plus after 20 years of teaching—not to mention that our grade level can now use the monies that were to be spent on standardized tests for activities and reading materials for the children!

parisons among individuals or groups at the local, state, or national level. A *norm-referenced test* is constructed by administering it to large numbers of students in order to develop **norms**. It's inefficient and difficult, if not impossible, to test every student in an entire population. Norms therefore represent average scores of a sampling of students selected for testing according to factors such as age, sex, race, grade, or socioeconomic status. Once norm scores are established, they become the basis for comparing the performance of individuals or groups to the performance of those who were in the norming sample. These comparisons allow you to determine whether a child or group is making "normal" progress or performing in "normal" ways.

Normal progress or performance, of course, depends on the *representativeness* of the norming sample. Therefore, the norms of a test should reflect the characteristics of the population. Moreover, it's important to make sure that the norming sample used in devising the tests resembles the group of students tested. Some norm-referenced tests provide separate norms for specific kinds of populations (e.g., urban students). The technical manual for the test should contain information about the norming process, including a description of the norming group.

In developing norm-referenced tests, the scores in the norming sample are distributed along a *normal*, or *bell-shaped, curve*. That is to say, scores cluster symmetrically about the *mean*, the average of all scores. In Figure 14.2, notice that the majority of the scores (about 68 percent) are concentrated within *one standard deviation* above or below the mean. The standard deviation is an important measure because it represents the variability or dispersion of scores from the mean. The standard deviation, roughly speaking, can help you interpret a child's performance. You can judge how well a child performed on a test by examining a score in relation to the standard deviation. A score that falls more than one

◆ FIGURE 14.2   A Bell Curve

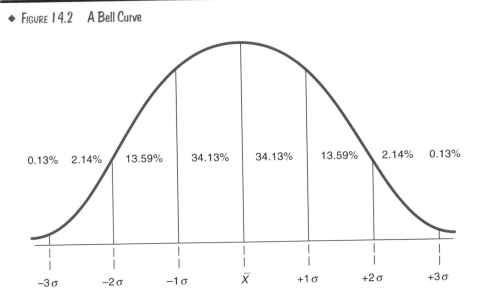

0.13%   2.14%   13.59%   34.13%   34.13%   13.59%   2.14%   0.13%

-3σ -2σ -1σ $\bar{X}$ $+1\sigma$ $+2\sigma$ $+3\sigma$

$\bar{X}$ = Mean σ = Standard deviation

standard deviation below the mean on a reading test would probably be a cause for concern. Recognize, however, that standardized tests aren't error-free: There are measurement problems with any test. Some tests are better than others in helping teachers interpret performance. The more *valid* and *reliable* the reading test, the more likely it is to measure what it says it does.

Reliability refers to the stability of the test. Does the test measure an ability consistently over time or consistently across equivalent forms? The reliability of a test is expressed as a correlation coefficient. Reliability coefficients can be found in examiner's manuals and are expressed in numerical form with a maximum possible value of +1.0. A reliability coefficient of +1.0 means that students' scores were ranked exactly the same on a test given on two different occasions or on two equivalent forms. If students were to take a test on Monday and then take an equivalent form of the same test on Thursday, their scores would be about the same on both tests, if the test were indeed reliable. A test consumer should examine reliability coefficients given in the examiner's manual. A reliability coefficient of +0.85 or better is considered good; a reliability coefficient below +0.70 suggests that the test lacks consistency.

A statistic tied to the idea of reliability is the *standard error of measurement.* The standard error of measurement represents the range within which a subject's *true score* will likely fall. A true score is the score a test taker would have obtained if the test were free of error. Suppose the standard error of measurement was 0.8 for a reading test. If a student achieved a score of 4.0 on the test, his or her true score would fall somewhere between 3.2 and 4.8. Rather than assume that a score received by a student is precisely accurate, the teacher should identify the standard error of measurement in the test manual and interpret each score as falling within a range.

Validity is probably the most important characteristic of a test. It refers to how well a test measures what it is designed to measure. A test developer will validate a test for general use along several fronts. First, the test should have *construct validity*. To establish construct validity, the test developer must show the relationship between a theoretical construct such as *reading* and the test that proposes to measure the construct. Second, the test should have *content validity*. Content validity reflects how well the test represents the domain or content area being examined. Are there sufficient test items? Are the test items appropriate? Third, the test should have *predictive validity*. In other words, it should accurately predict future performance.

Types of Test Scores.   To make interpretations properly, you need to be aware of differences in the types of scores reported on a test. The *raw,* or *obtained, score* reflects the total number of correct items on a test. Raw scores are converted to other kinds of scores so that comparisons among individuals or groups can be made. A raw score, for example, may be converted into a *grade equivalency score.* This type of conversion provides information about reading performance as it relates to students at various grade levels. A grade equivalency score of 4.6 is read as "fourth grade, sixth month in school." Therefore a student whose raw score is transformed into a grade equivalency of 4.6 is supposedly performing at a level that is average for students who have completed six months of the fourth grade.

The idea behind a grade equivalency score is not flawless. When a score is reported in terms of grade level, it is often prone to misinterpretation. For example, don't be swayed by the erroneous assumption that reading growth progresses throughout the school year at a constant rate—that growth in reading is constant from month to month. Based on what is known about human development generally and language growth specifically, such an assumption makes little sense when applied to a human process as complex as learning to read.

One of the most serious misinterpretations of a grade equivalency score involves making placement decisions. Even though a child's performance on a test or subtest is reported as a grade level, this doesn't necessarily suggest placement in materials at that level. Suppose a student received a grade equivalency score of 2.8 on a comprehension subtest. The score may represent information about the student's ability to comprehend, but it doesn't mean that the student should be placed at the second grade, eighth month of basal reading or library materials. First, the standard error of the test indicates that there is a range within which 2.8 falls. Second, the test's norms were in all likelihood not standardized against the content and level of difficulty of the basal reading curriculum in a particular school or library of books. In 1981 the International Reading Association passed a resolution cautioning teachers on the misuse of grade equivalents and advocated the abandonment of grade equivalent scores for reporting students' performance. In place of grade-level scores, the use of *percentile scores* and *standard scores* such as *stanines* provides a more appropriate vehicle for reporting test performance.

Percentiles refer to scores in terms of the percentage of a group the student has scored above. If several second graders scored in the 68th percentile of a test, they scored as well as or better than 68 percent of the second graders in the norming population. Whereas grade equivalency scores are normed by testing children at various grade levels, percentile norms are developed by examining performance only within a single grade level. Therefore, percentile scores provide information that helps teachers interpret relative performance within a grade level only. For this reason, percentiles are easily interpretable.

Stanine is one of several types of standard score. A standard score is a raw score that has been converted to a common standard to permit comparison. Because standard scores have the same mean and standard deviation, they allow teachers to make direct comparisons of student performance across tests and subtests. Specifically, *stanine* refers to a standard *nine*-point scale. When stanines are used to report results, the distribution of scores on a test is divided into nine parts. Therefore, each stanine represents a single digit with a numerical value of 1 to 9. A stanine of 5 is the midpoint of the scale and represents average performance. Stanines 6, 7, 8, and 9 indicate increasingly better performance; stanines 4, 3, 2, and 1 represent decreasing performance.

Types of Tests. Different norm-referenced tests have different purposes. Two broad types of tests are frequently used in schools. An assessment that is based on a **survey test** represents a measure of general performance only. It does not yield precise information about an individual's reading abilities. Survey tests are often used at the beginning of the school year as screening tests to identify children who may be having difficulties in broad areas of instruction. A survey test may be given to groups or individuals.

A standardized **diagnostic test,** by contrast, is a type of formal assessment that is intended to provide more detailed information about individual students' strengths and weaknesses. The results of a diagnostic test are often used to profile a student's strengths and weaknesses of reading performance. Some diagnostic tests are individual; others are designed for group administration.

Most diagnostic tests are founded on a bottom-up, subskills view of reading. Therefore, diagnostic tests are characterized by a battery of subtests that uses large numbers of items to measure specific skills in areas such as phonics, structural analysis, word knowledge, and comprehension.

The concern today is with the type of information provided by the test: What is it for? How useful is it for instructional purposes? In what ways does it apply to culturally diverse populations? Until teachers can readily answer these questions to their own satisfaction, controversy will continue to surround the use of standardized achievement tests in American education. The uses and misuses of standardized tests for reading, writing, and language assessment continue to spur debate.

Uses of Standardized Test Results.

Critics of formal testing tend to argue against the uses to which the standardized test information is put. As noted earlier, scores from formal testing shouldn't be used as the *only* source of information considered in making instructional decisions. Other inappropriate uses of standardized test scores are in the evaluation of teachers, programs, and the distribution of resources.

Some critics call into question whether there is any worth at all to formal testing. For example, Goodman (1975) argued that such tests are mainly measures of intelligence and don't actually assess reading. He contended that the reading measured on reading tests isn't the same as most real-world kinds of reading. Seldom in real life would someone read a short passage and then be required to answer a series of questions about it. Test makers in the 1990s have attempted to make improvements such as increasing the length of passages and using formats other than multiple-choice questions. The state of Illinois even included sections with comprehension questions for which there is more than one "right" answer!

Most test developers assert that their tests can provide accurate and reliable information about groups of 25 or more. From this perspective, scores can show schoolwide trends and differences among groups within a school. Standardized test results can also be used to get an idea of how students in a school compare to other students across the country or indicate if a school as a whole is increasing or decreasing in general reading achievement.

What large-scale single-test batteries cannot do, despite the claims of some test designers, is recommend appropriate instructional or curriculum objectives for schools, classrooms, or students. What they *can* and *should* do, according to Farr and Tone (1998, p. 190), as follows:

FOR READING

Report a global comprehension score.

Omit special subtests on skill areas (such as word recognition and vocabulary).

Make the tests shorter and the passages longer, with more variety (evoking real purposes for reading).

Write items that truly reflect the balance of a passage.

FOR WRITING

Have the students *write* (rather than identify errors in someone else's text).

Rate students by emphasizing content, organization, use of detail, and other writing-relevant factors.

In the meantime, state-by-state comparisons of student achievement in reading and other subject areas, using norm-referenced test scores, are widespread. The National Assessment of Educational Progress (NAEP) periodically makes available to the public data on large-scale reading and writing performance. On what is sometimes called the "nation's report card," NAEP compares several age groups over time and by geographic and other factors. It's important to keep in mind, however, that even though NAEP data make front-page news, it's not appropriate to report large-scale assessment results for individual pupils, classes, or schools (International Reading Association, 1990). Despite their pervasive use, standardized test results are still widely misunderstood.

A phenomenon surrounding the massive use of norm-referenced tests is the "Lake Wobegon effect." Garrison Keillor tells stories about Lake Wobegon, where "the women are strong, the men are good looking, and all the children are above average." Writing about the Lake Wobegon effect, John Pikulski (1989) reported a survey done by a West Virginia physician. He found that 82 percent of 3,503 school districts and 100 percent of the 32 states surveyed with mandated testing programs reported that the average score for students in that district or state was "above average." However, as Pikulski points out, if we are involved in the concept of "average," only 50 percent of the population is above average and the other 50 percent is below average. Consider the Lake Wobegon effect in districts where children come from affluent homes. Teachers and administrators in these districts boast that the average scores for students on their standardized tests are "above average," yet we know that the variable that accounts for the most variance in standardized test scores is socioeconomic status of the test takers. We can only speculate on why the Lake Wobegon effect is so prevalent, but it very clearly demonstrates a misconception concerning norm-referenced testing.

Criterion-referenced testing is another kind of testing conducted in schools, and the assumptions underlying it are different from those of norm-referenced testing. Rather than comparing a student's test performance to that of a norming sample, performance on a criterion-referenced test hinges on mastery of specific reading skills. Let's examine criterion-referenced assessment and how test information is used in classroom decision making.

Criterion-Referenced Tests

Criterion-referenced tests have been used in formal situations for districtwide purposes, in classroom situations, and more recently in statewide testing. The major premise behind criterion-referenced testing is that the mastery of reading skills should be assessed in relation to specific instructional objectives. Test performance is measured against a criterion, or acceptable score, for each of the objectives. Suppose, for example, that there are ten test items for each skill objective. Eight to ten correct items on the test would suggest a level of mastery as specified by the objective. A score of six or seven correct items would signal that additional practice and review of the skill under examination are needed. Fewer than six correct items could mean that a student is deficient in the skill and needs extensive reteaching to achieve mastery.

Performance on a criterion-referenced test, unlike a norm-referenced situation, is judged by what a student can or cannot do with regard to the skill objectives of the test.

The test taker isn't compared to anyone else. The rationale for assessment, then, is that it will indicate strengths and weaknesses in specific skill areas. Whereas norm-referenced test scores are used to screen students and to make general grouping decisions, results from a criterion-referenced assessment are used to make instructional decisions about reading skills development. This same feature is viewed as a restriction by some teachers who want to plan individual instruction on variables other than test-identified weaknesses.

The reliability and validity of criterion-referenced tests have been called into question (Pearson & Johnson, 1978). It has been argued that test makers have tended not to establish statistical reliability and validity for criterion-referenced tests as they do for norm-referenced tests. As a result, users of criterion-referenced tests need to be aware of some of the important issues of reliability and validity surrounding the use of such tests.

Criterion-referenced tests often measure students' performance on a large number of objectives. Because the number of objectives tested is large, the number of items testing each objective may be as low as four or five. Such a practice leads to questions of how *reliable* the measurement of each skill can be with such a small number of items. It's possible that students who perform poorly on a criterion-referenced test won't perform poorly in another situation that assesses the same skill. For example, will a child who cannot count syllables in a word be unable to break down similar words into pronounceable parts when reading orally? Will a child who cannot answer inferential questions as directed on a test be unable to make inferences from a story in an oral retelling?

Test makers assume that mastery of specific skills leads to better reading ability. This is at best a tenuous assumption. A teacher must ask, "Do test items really measure what they are supposed to measure?" Smith and Johnson (1980) pointed out the problem in this respect.

> Test purchasers rightly assume that the tests provided for measuring attainment of objectives are valid indices of the skills at issue. However, if a test uses a paper-and-pencil task, then it ought, at the very least, to validate those measures by administering group and individual tests to a small sample of students. We are not convinced that identifying the initial consonant *f* from the distractor set *f, t, v, r* when given an oral stimulus is the same as saying /f/ when seeing *f*, or reading sentences which contain words starting with *f*. (p. 169)

Smith and Johnson's point is well taken, as is their concern for questions related to the concept of mastery. What does mastery performance mean on a criterion-referenced test? For example, are comprehension skills ever mastered? As Smith and Johnson (1980) asserted, "We hope that no child could 'test out of' main ideas, or sequence . . . for if conceptual difficulty of words or contextual relationships were increased, the same child could fail to show mastery" (p. 170). Comprehension is an ongoing, developing process, as we have maintained throughout this book. To test for mastery of a comprehension skill would provide a teacher with misleading information at best.

Criterion-referenced tests are similar to standardized diagnostic tests in the sense that both attempt to identify strengths and weaknesses in specific skill areas. They share many of the shortcomings of norm-referenced testing and raise new objections among educators (Farr & Tone, 1998). The teacher must recognize that a criterion-referenced test provides only one perspective for understanding children's reading performance. Other indicators of reading should be weighed carefully when planning instruction.

INFORMAL ASSESSMENT

Informal measures of reading such as *reading inventories, miscue analyses,* and *running records* yield useful information about student performance. As the name implies, an **informal assessment** doesn't compare the performance of a tested group or individual to a normative population. Instead, informal tests may be given throughout the school year to individuals or groups for specific instructional purposes.

Informal reading tests gauge performance in relation to the student's success on a particular reading task or a set of reading tasks. In this respect, they are similar to criterion-referenced measures. One of the best uses of informal tests is to evaluate how students interact with print in oral and silent reading situations. We will explore how these measures can be used to inform decision making and strengthen inferences about children's reading behavior and performance.

Informal Reading Inventories

The **informal reading inventory (IRI)** is an individually administered reading test. It usually consists of a series of graded word lists, graded reading passages, and comprehension questions. The passages are used to assess how students interact with print orally and silently. According to the standards set for reading professionals by the International Reading Association (currently under review), classroom teachers across all grade levels and special education teachers should have a basic understanding of multiple forms of assessment, including formal and informal reading inventories.

The information gathered from an IRI should allow you to pair students with appropriate instruction materials with some degree of confidence. Moreover, an analysis of oral reading miscues helps you determine the *cuing systems* that students tend to rely on when reading. In short, IRI information can lead to instructional planning that will increase children's effectiveness with print.

IRIs are commercially available, although teachers can easily construct one. Selections from a basal reading series may be used to make an IRI. If you decide to make and use an IRI, at least three steps are necessary:

1. Duplicate 100- to 200-word passages from basal stories. Select a passage for each grade level from the basal series, preprimer through grade 8. Passages should be chosen from the middle of each basal textbook to ensure representativeness.

2. Develop at least five comprehension questions for each passage. Be certain that different types of questions (based on question-and-answer relationships, discussed in Chapter 7) are created for each graded passage. Avoid the following pitfalls:

   Questions that can be answered without reading the passage (except for on-your-own questions)

   Questions that require yes or no answers

   Questions that are long and complicated

Questions that overload memory by requiring the reader to reconstruct lists (e.g., "Name four things that happened . . .")

3. Create an environment conducive to assessment. Explain to the student before testing why you are giving the assessment. In doing so, attempt to take the mystery out of what can be a worrisome situation for the student.

Administering an IRI. Commercially published IRIs have graded word lists that can be used for several purposes: (1) to help determine a starting point for reading the graded passages, (2) to get an indication of the student's sight word proficiency (e.g., the ability to recognize words rapidly), and (3) to get an indication of the student's knowledge of letter-sound relationships to attack unfamiliar words.

When giving the IRI, the teacher may simply estimate placement in the graded passages instead of using word lists. Select a passage from the inventory that you believe the student can read easily and comprehend fully, for example, a passage two grade levels below the student's present grade. If the passage turns out to be more difficult than anticipated, ask the student to read another one at a lower level. However, if the student reads the passage without difficulty, progress to higher-grade-level passages until the reading task becomes too difficult.

Oral reading is usually followed by silent reading. In both oral and silent reading situations, the student responds to comprehension questions. However, an excellent variation is first to require students to retell everything that they recall from the reading. Note the information given and then follow up with aided-recall questions such as the following:

What else can you tell me about _____ and _____ ?

What happened after _____ and _____ ?

Where did _____ and _____ take place?

How did _____ and _____ happen?

Why do you think _____ and _____ happened?

What do you think the author might have been trying to say in this story?

Do not hurry through a retelling. When asking a question to aid recall, give the student time to think and respond.

Recording Oral Reading Errors. During the oral reading of the passage, the teacher notes reading errors such as mispronunciations, omissions, and substitutions. As the student reads, the teacher also notes how fluent the reading is. Does the student read in a slow, halting, word-by-word fashion? Or does the student read rapidly and smoothly? Errors are recorded by marking deviations from the text on a copy of the passages read by the student. A *deviation* is any discrepancy between what the student says and the words on the page.

The following coding system can be used to mark oral reading errors:

1. *Omissions.* An omission error occurs when the reader omits a unit of written language; that is, a word, several words, parts of words, or one or more sentences. Circle the omitted unit of language.

    Example   Jenny was (still) at school. She never played (after school.)

2. *Substitutions.* A substitution error is noted when a real word (or words) is substituted for the word in the text. Draw a line through the text word and write the substituted word above it.

    Example   The ~~lion~~ looked lonely.
    (monkey written above "lion")

3. *Mispronunciation.* A mispronunciation miscue is one in which the word is pronounced incorrectly. Follow the same procedure as for a substitution error, writing the phonetic spelling above the word in the text.

    Example   Because he was a frog, we called him Hoppy.
    (frag written above "frog")

4. *Insertion.* The insertion miscue results when a word (or words) is inserted in the passage. Use a caret (∧) to show where the word was inserted, and write the word.

    Example   She ∧ ran away.
    (quickly written above the caret)

5. *Repetition.* In repetition, a word or phrase is repeated. Treat the repetition of more than one word as a single unit, counting it as one miscue. Underline the portion of text that is repeated.

    Example   <u>This is a</u> tale about a man who is blind.

6. *Reversal.* The reversal error occurs when the order of a word (or words) in the text is transposed. Use a transposition symbol (a curved mark) over and under the letters or words transposed.

    Examples   He went no his trip

    "See you later," Sue said.

7. *Pronunciation.* A word (or words) is pronounced for the reader. Place the letter *P* over the word pronounced.

    Example   This was a startling development in his life.
    (P written above "startling")

In addition to marking errors, you should also code the reader's attempts to correct any errors made during oral reading. Self-correction attempts result in repetitions, which may have one of three outcomes:

1. *Successful correction.* The reader successfully corrects the error. Correct miscues are coded in the following manner:

   Example   I did not know where I was going. ⓒ why

2. *Unsuccessful correction.* The reader attempts to correct an error but is unsuccessful. Unsuccessful correction attempts are coded in the following manner:

   Example   He felt compelled to leave. ⓊⒸ 1. complied   2. completed

3. *Abandoned correct form.* The student reads the text word (or words) correctly but then decides to abandon the correct form for a different response. Code this behavior in the following manner:

   Example   Mike wondered if the tracks were made by a bear. ⒶⒸ wandered

Familiarity with a coding system is important in marking oral errors. To ensure accurate coding, tape-record the student's reading. You can then replay the student's reading to check whether all errors are recorded accurately. Moreover, tape-recording will help in analyzing the student's responses to comprehension questions or a retelling of the material.

Determining Reading Levels.   The following reading levels can be determined for individual students by administering an IRI.

Independent level: The level at which the student reads fluently with excellent comprehension. The independent level has also been called the *recreational reading level* because not only will students be able to function on their own, but they often have high interest in the material.

Instructional level: The level at which the student can make progress in reading with instructional guidance. This level has been referred to as the *teaching level* because the material to be read must be challenging but not too difficult.

Frustration level: The level at which the student is unable to pronounce many of the words or is unable to comprehend the material satisfactorily. This is the lowest level of reading at which the reader is able to understand. The material is too difficult to provide a basis for growth.

Listening capacity level: The level at which the students can understand material that is read aloud. This level is also known as the *potential level* because if students were able to read fluently, they would not have a problem with comprehension.

The criteria used to determine reading levels have differed slightly among reading experts who have published IRIs. However, the most recommended over the years have been the Betts criteria, named for Emmett Betts (1946), the "father" of the IRI.

In making decisions about a student's reading level, teachers should be cognizant of two powerful correlates that determine whether children will find material difficult or not. First, there is a strong relationship between a student's interest in a topic and reading comprehension. Second, a strong case has been built throughout this book for the relationship that exists between background knowledge and reading comprehension. If children do poorly on a particular passage because they have limited knowledge or schemata for its content, it's easy to err by underestimating reading level.

The point to remember is that reading levels are not chiseled in stone. Levels do fluctuate from material to material depending on a child's schemata and interest in the passage content. The placement information that an IRI yields gives a "ballpark" figure, an indication. Placement decisions should rest on corroborative judgment, with IRI results an important source of information but not the sole determinant.

Analyzing Oral Reading Miscues

Oral reading errors are also called miscues. The terms *error* and *miscue* essentially describe the same phenomenon—a deviation or difference between what a reader says and the word on the page. During the 1970s, the Goodmans and others popularized the term *miscue* to replace

Students need feedback on their efforts to learn how to self-assess their reading progress.

the term *error*. Their impact is still being felt, as teachers have moved away from focusing on what is wrong (an error) to what is a piece of evidence (a miscue). "We cannot let ourselves off the hook by blaming the readers for our lack of success in helping them to learn. The perspective we must adopt is one of building on strength" (Goodman, 1996, p. 15).

A miscue provides a piece of evidence in an elaborate puzzle; it helps reinforce a positive view of error in the reading process for teachers and students alike. Differences between what the reader says and what is printed on the page are not the result of random errors. Instead, these differences are "cued" by the thoughts and language of the reader, who is attempting to construct what the author is saying.

Miscues can be analyzed *quantitatively* or *qualitatively*. A quantitative analysis involves counting the number of errors; it pivots around a search for *deficits* in a student's ability to read accurately. A quantitative analysis is used, for example, to determine the reading levels previously discussed. In addition, a tallying of different types of errors has traditionally been a strategy for evaluating the strengths and weaknesses of a child's ability to analyze words. For example, does the reader consistently mispronounce the beginnings of words? An analysis based on this question helps pinpoint specific difficulties. Does the reader consistently have trouble with single consonants? Consonant clusters?

In a quantitative analysis, each miscue carries equal weight, regardless of the contribution it makes to a child's understanding of the material read. A qualitative miscue analysis, by contrast, offers a radically different perspective for exploring the strengths of students. A qualitative miscue analysis is a tool for assessing what children do when they read. It is not based on deficits related to word identification but rather on the *differences* between the miscues and the words on the page. Therefore, some miscues are more significant than others.

A miscue is significant if it affects meaning—if it doesn't make sense within the context of the sentence or passage in which it occurs. Johns (1985, p. 17) explained that miscues are generally significant in the following instances:

◆ When the meaning of the sentence or passages is significantly changed or altered and the student does not correct the miscue

◆ When a nonword is used in place of the word in the passage

◆ When only a partial word is substituted for the word or phrase in the passage

◆ When a word is pronounced for the student

Miscues are generally *not* significant in these circumstances:

◆ When the meaning of the sentence or passage undergoes no change or only minimal change

◆ When they are self-corrected by the student

◆ When they are acceptable in the student's dialect (e.g., "goed" home for "went" home; "idear" for "idea")

◆ When they are later read correctly in the same passage

We agree with Johns that only significant miscues should be counted in determining reading levels according to the Betts criteria. He recommended subtracting the *total* of all *dialect miscues*, all *corrected miscues*, and all *miscues that do not change meaning* from the total number of recorded miscues.

Miscue analysis can be applied to graded passages from an IRI or to the oral reading of a single passage that presents the student with an extended and intensive reading experience. In the case of the latter, select a story or informational text that is at or just above the student's instructional level. The material must be challenging but not frustrating.

Through miscue analysis, teachers can determine the extent to which the reader uses and coordinates graphic-sound, syntactic, and semantic information from the text. To analyze miscues, you should ask at least four crucial questions (Goodman & Burke, 1972).

1. *Does the miscue change the meaning?* If it doesn't, then it's *semantically acceptable* within the context of the sentence or passage. Here are some examples of semantically acceptable miscues:

   I want to bring him ^back^ home.

   Steve went to the ~~store~~ shop.

   His feet are firmly planted ~~on~~ to the ground.

   ~~Mother~~ Mom works on Wall Street.

   These are examples of semantically unacceptable miscues:

   Bill went to ~~camp~~ court for the first time.

   The mountain ~~loomed~~ leaped in the foreground.

   The summer had been a ~~dry~~ quiet one.

2. *Does the miscue sound like language?* If it does, then it's *syntactically acceptable* within the context of a sentence or passage. Miscues are syntactically acceptable if they sound like language and serve as the same parts of speech as the text words. The examples of semantically acceptable and unacceptable miscues also happen to be syntactically acceptable. Here are two examples of syntactically unacceptable miscues.

   Bill ~~reached~~ carefully for the book.

   I have ~~a~~ to good idea.

   In each example, the miscue doesn't sound like language when the text is read aloud.

3. *Do the miscue and the text word look and sound alike?* Substitution and mispronunciation miscues should be analyzed to determine how similar they are in approximating the graphic and pronunciation features of the text words. High graphic-sound

similarity results when two of the three parts (beginning, middle, and end) of a word are similar, as in this miscue:

He was ~~getting~~ ^{going} old.

Some graphic-sound similarity is present when one of the three word parts is alike.

4. *Was an attempt made to correct the miscue?* Self-corrections are revealing because they demonstrate that the reader is attending to meaning and is aware that the initial miscuing did not make sense.

A profile can be developed for each reader by using the summary sheet in Figure 14.3. Study the following passage, which has been coded, and then examine how each miscue was analyzed on the summary sheet.

Sheep dogs ~~works~~ ^{walk} hard on a farm. They must learn (C) ^{lean} to take the sheep from place to place. They must (C) ^{mostly} see that the sheep do not run away. (C) ^{always} And they ~~must~~ ^{mostly} see that the sheep do not get ~~lost or~~ ^{loose and} killed.

Sometimes these ^{these} dogs are ~~trained~~ ^{trying} to do other kinds of farm work. They earn (UC) ^{learn} the right to be called good ~~helpers~~ ^{helps}, too.

Can you think of ~~one other~~ ^{another} kind of ~~work~~ ^{working} dog? He does not need a coat ^{coat} or strong legs like the sheep dog's. He does not learn to work ~~with~~ ^{doesn't leave} a sled in the deep, cold snow. He ~~doesn't leave~~ ~~does not~~ learn to be a farm worker.

To determine the percentage of semantically acceptable miscues, count the number of yes responses in the column. Then count the number of miscues analyzed. (Do not tally successful self-corrections.) Divide the number of semantically acceptable miscues by the number of miscues analyzed and then multiply by 100.

To determine the percentage of syntactically acceptable miscues, proceed by counting the number of yes responses in the column. Divide that number by the number of miscues analyzed (less self-corrections) and then multiply by 100.

To determine the percentage of successful self-corrections, tally the number of yes responses in the column and divide the number by the number of self-correction attempts and then multiply by 100.

To determine the percentage of higher or some graphic-sound similarity, analyze mispronunciations and substitutions only. Divide the total of high-similarity words by the number of words analyzed and then multiply by 100. Follow the same procedure to determine whether some similarity exists between the miscues and text words.

One final piece of information can be tabulated. Determine the number of miscues that were semantically acceptable or that made sense in the selection *and* the number of successful self-corrections. Divide this number by the total number of miscues. This percentage gives you an estimate of the extent to which the reader reads for meaning.

Inferences can be made about oral reading behavior once the miscues are charted and the information summarized. Although the reader of the passage miscued frequently, his strengths are apparent: He reads for meaning. More than half of the miscues were semantically acceptable. When attempting to self-correct, the reader was successful most of the time. Over 60 percent of his miscues were semantically acceptable or were successfully self-corrected; most of his miscues sounded like language. Moreover, the great majority of his substitution and mispronunciation miscues reflected knowledge of graphic-sound relationships.

Seven significant miscues were made on the passage (which was slightly over 100 words long). This indicates that the material bordered on frustration and is probably not appropriate for instruction. However, the reader has demonstrated strategies that get at meaning.

Miscue analysis is time-consuming. However, when you want to know more about a student's processing of print, miscue analysis is very useful. If you are pressed for time, but you still have a need to know how well a student is processing print, use miscue question 1, "Does the miscue change the meaning?" and look to see if the student self-corrects and how successfully.

Goodman and Marek (1997) recount firsthand examples of how teachers and students grew in their understanding and sense of control over the reading process in *Retrospective Miscue Analysis*. It extends the extensive experience with miscue analysis that led Goodman and Burke, authors of the *Reading Miscue Inventory*, to suggest correlations about reading proficiency (Weaver, 1980).

The following chart gives a quick measure of the percentage of effectiveness in using reading strategies by adding the number of miscues that did not change the meaning of the passage *and* the number of miscues that were successfully self-corrected over the total number of miscues.

Effectiveness in Using Reading Strategies	Miscues That Did Not Change the Meaning of the Passage and Miscues That Were Successfully Self-Corrected
Highly effective	60 to 100 percent
Moderately effective	40 to 79 percent
Somewhat effective	15 to 45 percent
Ineffective	No more than 14 percent

◆ FIGURE 14.3   Qualitative Miscue Analysis Summary Sheet

Text	Miscue	Semantically Acceptable	Syntactically Acceptable	Self-Corrections	Beginning	Middle	Ending	Graphic-Sound Summary
		— Context —			— Graphic-Sound Similarity —			
work	walk	no	yes		X		X	high
learn	lean			yes				
must	mostly			yes				
the	these	yes	yes		X	X		high
away	always			yes				
that		yes	yes					
lost	loose	no	yes		X			some
or	and	no	yes					none
these		yes	yes		X	X	X	XXX
trained	trying	no	yes		X			some
kinds	kind	yes	yes		X	X		high
earn	learn	no	yes	no		X	X	high
helpers	helps	yes	yes		X	X		high
one other	another	yes	yes			X	X	
work	working	yes	yes		X	X		high
dog's	dog	yes	yes		X	X		high
learn	leave			yes				
with	and	no	no					none
sled	sleep	no	yes		X			some
does not	doesn't	yes	yes					

Percentage of semantically acceptable miscues   =   53 percent
Percentage of syntactically acceptable miscues   =   88 percent
Percentage of successful self-corrections   =   80 percent
Percentage of miscues with high graphic-sound similarity   =   58 percent
Percentage of miscues with some graphic-sound similarity   =   25 percent

Throughout this chapter, we have emphasized the point that *multiple indicators* are important; we should not rely on one test score concerning a child's progress in becoming literate. Furthermore, assessments need to show that a student has grown, not just compare the student to other students of similar age. This is particularly important to students who are at risk in reading. Some teachers prefer to keep track of students' progress by using a running record.

Running Records

Keeping track of students' growth in reading, their use of the cuing systems of language—semantics, syntax, and graphophonemics—can help teachers understand the process that goes on in readers' heads. For when readers try to construct meaning as they read aloud, we can begin to see the relationship between the miscues they make and comprehension. We realize that not all deviations from the text are equal in importance, and one miscue is not as informative as a series of miscues.

Rhodes and Shanklin (1993) describe five methods for collecting and analyzing miscues. Each method varies in the time it takes to administer and in the depth and type of knowledge it reveals about the reader. However, one method differs significantly from the others in that it does not require a separate copy of the text in order to keep track of the reading. The **running record**, developed by Marie Clay and explained in her book *The Early Detection of Reading Difficulties* (1985), can be done with only a blank sheet of paper, making it especially good for collecting data about a child's reading during regular classroom activities. To take a running record, the teacher marks a check for each word a child says correctly, matching the number of checks on a line of the paper with the number of words in a line of the text being read. Deviations from print are marked in much the same way as in other miscue analysis procedures; for example:

Correct word	
Insertion	*word spoken*
Omission	—
Substitution	*word spoken*
Self-correction	SC

Detailed explanations of conducting a running record are available in Clay (1985), and Johnston (1992). Teachers of beginning readers (who read aloud more often and read slowly and read shorter, less complicated texts) often prefer to take a running record because it does not require special preparation or disrupt the flow of the classroom lesson. However, as students read faster and read more complicated texts, running records become more difficult to take.

The approximate reading level suggested by an IRI along with information on how a reader uses the cuing systems of language to construct meaning while reading as gathered in a miscue analysis or running record can help teachers understand a child's progress in becoming literate.

It's equally important for *students* to have feedback on their efforts and learn how to assess themselves. By graphically monitoring changes in measures that show that students' efforts have paid off, teachers can help low achievers maintain a keep-trying attitude.

While not a panacea, using graphs is a way to demonstrate graphically to parents and students progress on the factors that contribute to growth in literacy learning.

◆ Figure 14.4   Louisa's Growth in Reading

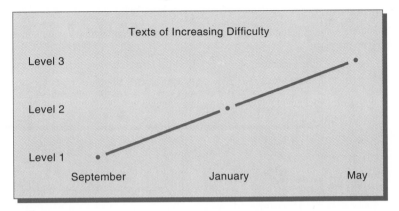

For example, a graph can be made to display Louisa's growth in reading texts of increasing difficulty as in Figure 14.4. The number of books read per month in voluntary reading programs may also be graphed. Figure 14.5 graphically shows both the number of books Susan read each month and the total number of books she read (Flood & Lapp,

◆ Figure 14.5   Susan's Growth in Voluntary Reading

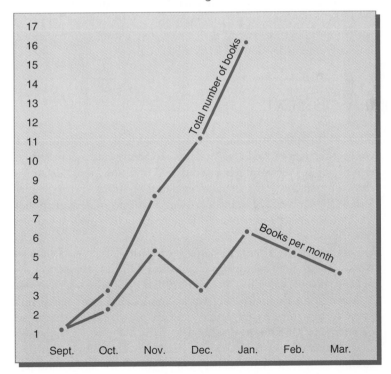

◆ Figure 14.6   Leroy's Responses to an Interview Question

What do you do when you come to a word you don't know?

September: I ask someone.

April: I read the rest of the sentence. Then I try to think of
              a word that has those letters and makes sense in
              the story.

1989). In addition, students like Leroy can be interviewed at different periods, and their responses can be compared to show changes in perception or attitude as in Figure 14.6.

Keeping a running record need not become an overwhelming task. A folder for each child or a notebook with a page for each child that contains a collection of information about his or her literacy learning helps teachers organize the information they collect for assessment. Assessment folders or notebooks could contain information from informal reading tests, miscue analyses, and observational data. Because it is difficult to remember classroom events, we recommend writing down anecdotal records or using a checklist to record important incidents.

The assessment folder that teachers keep for their own use or to share with parents or students is one type of portfolio. As the interest in developing authentic assessment to match our understanding of the constructive nature of the reading process grows, portfolios have emerged as important avenues of assessment.

Portfolio Assessment

Through the process of **portfolio assessment,** teachers seem to have discovered a way to connect instruction and assessment by involving students in reflecting on and making decisions about their work. **Portfolios** are collections that "document the literary development of a student" and include "evidence of student work in various stages" (Noden & Vacca, 1994, p. 292). The evidence that goes into student portfolios is collaboratively chosen by teachers and students and is more likely to represent a process or activity or project than a product.

The items in a portfolio are selected with care. As teachers and students reflect on work samples, they choose those that show merit as examples of significant growth, effort, or achievement. Looking through portfolios, one sees a fairly complete picture of children as learners. Portfolios contain work samples that cross many curriculum areas and take many forms, from essays, letters, stories, poems and anecdotal records to photographs, cassette tapes, and floppy disks.

Portfolios serve many purposes and vary accordingly, but their underlying value is a commitment to students' assessment of their own understanding and personal development. Above all, portfolio assessment is a powerful concept that helps teachers and students alike work toward four important goals: taking risks, taking responsibility for learning, making decisions about how and what to learn, and feeling in control using the language arts to learn (Glazer & Brown, 1993, p. 165).

Essential Elements of Portfolios

Although portfolios differ from each other as literacy profiles of individual learners in different classrooms, they are more authentic than traditional, formal assessment procedures. To varying degrees, they measure the process of the construction of meaning. What makes a portfolio authentic? Michele McCombs, a first-grade teacher, said without hesitation, "It's child-created! The items in the portfolio are unique to each student. Emphasis is placed on making careful choices so that students' learning strengths, styles, and personalities are evident within the collection of items." She then went on to tell the following story to illustrate just what *child-created* means in her class:

> Last January we were studying the Arctic; the children each selected an animal they were interested in learning about. I provided them with a list of ideas to help them explore their topic. Students used books, CD-ROM encyclopedias, and the Internet to find specific information about their animal. Each child planned a presentation for the class in which they included information about the animal's size, enemies, food, and additional interesting information. They could choose a format that would best suit their own learning style and preference; they could write a poem, story, or song, create a model, draw a picture, make a costume, create a fact sheet, or come up with their own idea. The children worked on their projects at school and at home. Parents were encouraged to provide guidance, without taking over the project. The results were wonderful! There were models of papier-mâché, Lego blocks, and watercolored panels. One student, Michael, our resident computer expert, created a Web page! His Web site (see Figure 14.7) not only told information about killer whales but also displayed pictures of the whales he had colored and scanned himself.

Upon completion of their study, Michele took pictures of the children's work for their portfolios, along with any work samples that would fit. She is adamant that the real success of the Arctic unit was not the learning about animals but the exploration of ideas and variety of approaches the children used as they fell in love with learning itself.

Portfolio assessment doesn't mandate or prescribe that portfolios all contain the same elements; that would be contrary to the thoughtful collaboration that is central to this process and makes it so appealing. The following elements are associated with portfolios:

◆ Varied types of work, often completed over time

◆ Written and artistic responses to reading

◆ Writing in several genres

◆ Teacher-assigned and student-generated work

◆ An introduction, summary, or self-reflection by the student about the nature of the piece or what it demonstrates about his or her literacy

Source: Reprinted by permission of Maureen Stauffer.

◆ Collaborative decision making between teacher and student on work assigned and chosen

◆ Work in progress, documenting changes and growth in literacy

◆ Best work, selected for showcasing based on input from teachers and peers conferencing during times set aside to discuss what students are doing and planning, writing and reading and thinking

◆ Notes in a reading log or response journal

◆ List of books read, updated regularly

According to Kieffer and Morrison (1994), portfolios express multiple voices—reflections from students, peers, the community, parents, and other teachers. Moreover, they are multiple stories of what individuals can do, both within the language arts of reading, writing, listening, and speaking and across the curriculum. They document change and help communicate assessment information to parents, school officials, and the public. Ultimately, a portfolio "represents a creation of self . . . ; its contents, like items in a scrapbook, are tangible pieces of the story. Everything is connected" (p. 417).

Implementing Portfolios in the Classroom

Getting started in the implementation of the portfolio assessment process, whether in grade 1 or grade 5, calls for certain decisions and logical steps. Here are a few suggestions:

◆ Introduce the notion of portfolios, the concept itself, and the connection with instructional activities. Show some examples from other occupations and fields; show sample items that might be found in portfolios.

◆ Explain your model for assessment: What is the purpose for the portfolio? Is there more than one purpose? Why are we going to use them? Who are we going to show them to?

◆ Decide what types of items will be included and how they will be selected for inclusion. Who gets to choose? Approximately how large will the portfolio become, and what size will it be? What format will it take? Will different designs be permitted (or even encouraged)? What is the time frame—start date and end date?

◆ Consider in advance appropriate ways to communicate clear explanations of portfolios to your colleagues, your principal, your students' parents, and possibly others in your school district or community.

◆ Develop an array of possible contributions that are most appropriate for your class, the range of students, the language arts, or a reading or writing emphasis: writing samples, videos, conference notes, tests, quizzes, self-evaluations (see Figure 14.8), peer evaluations, daily work samples, personal progress sheets, writing conference logs (see Figure 14.9), semantic maps, inventories (see Figure 14.10), journal entries, interviews, and so on.

◆ FIGURE 14.8

Fifth-Grade Internet Inquiry Project: Rubric for Self-Evaluation

Name: _____

Directions: Evaluate your group's performance in each of the following categories. Be honest. Please also make comments about parts of this project you found successful and parts you found unsuccessful.

Content	Points Possible	Points Earned	Comments
Selection of topic	5		
Evidence of planning	15		
Bibliography of print resources (minimum of 3 per person)	15		
Time on task while doing research in the library computer lab	5		
Web sites (minimum of 5): usefulness, appropriateness	20		
Web site summaries	30		
Evidence of cooperation	10		
Total	100		

When Michele McCombs, who has been doing portfolio assessment for about five years, gets ready to implement the process with a new group of first graders in the fall, she follows the procedures she describes in the Class Works in Box 14.2. Keep in mind that Michele has made numerous adjustments over the years; she suggests talking to teachers who already do this and starting out slowly with one or two new ideas a semester.

As teachers take a more direct, hands-on approach to assessment, they should try to match their beliefs about literacy and instructional practice with the assessment tools they implement. Therefore, teachers who are intent on using portfolio assessment and want to increase the likelihood for succcess may find certain things particularly useful to do with

Writing Conference Log for: __Megan O.__

Date: 1-15-98   Title: Plot Comparison for   Genre: fiction   (nonfiction)
Focus of conference: Story of Three Whales &
    Compare/contrast   Humphrey the Lost Whale
Progress observations:

Strengths	Areas to work on
1) was able to correctly compare/contrast stories	1) more detail for the story endings
2) able to complete the sentences	

Spelling development:

Examples of spelling

thay ✓ ⟩ transitional
traped

banged ⟩ conventional
lived

Developmental stage

* work on double consonants
* able to add "ed" endings

Date: 1-20-98   Title: Double-Entry   Genre: (fiction) nonfiction
Focus of conference: Journal for Whales Song
   reflection/sharing ideas
Progress observations:

Do more double entries! Megan would benefit!!!

Strengths	Areas to work on
1) Megan easily identified passages she liked!	1) identifying more reasons for her choices, connecting to personal life (possibly)
2) She picked meaningful passages	2) risk-taking

Spelling development:

Examples of spelling

deskripting
used, good, words

Developmental stage

transitional
conventional

Date: Jan. 98   Title: Whales   Genre: fiction (nonfiction)
Focus of conference:

Progress observations:

Strengths	Areas to work on
1) many details	commas — for lists
2) topic sentence	
3) lists mammal traits	
4) good closing sentence	

Spelling development:

Examples of spelling

bowhead, whale
fafit (favorite) ⎤
diffrint (different) |
boty (body) |
tempcer (temperature) |
mammel ⎦

Developmental stage

conventional

transitional

◆ FIGURE 14.10

Learning Participation Inventory

Name: _Megan O._

Observations for work
completed Jan. '98

	Often	Occasionally	Seldom
1. Shows enthusiasm for learning	✓		
2. Raises questions		✓	
3. Listens attentively during discussions		✓	
4. Shares ideas		✓	
5. Responds thoughtfully to the ideas of others	✓		
6. Participates in projects enthusiastically	✓		

1. Shows enthusiasm for learning
   Yes!

2. Raises questions
   *This would be a great area
   to work on with her.

3. Listens attentively during discussions
   seems to listen well, but sometimes
   turns away

4. Shares ideas
   Megan is reserved. She sometimes
   hesitates to share her ideas.

5. Responds thoughtfully to the ideas of others
   She enjoys knowing what the teacher
   thinks and responds well.

6. Participates in projects enthusiastically
   She is a hard worker, especially with books
   and topics she enjoys – such as whales.

Observations

All lessons were completed in a one-on-one tutoring session. The student
and teacher know each other very well since they have worked together
twice a week for two school years.

their students. When trying to keep writing projects challenging, even when students can't always choose their own topics, Herrington (1997) recommends that teachers do the following:

◆ Offer guidance

◆ Coach and consult

◆ Be responsive and constructive

◆ Be respectful and instructive

◆ Help focus

BOX 14.2 CLASS WORKS

Michele McCombs on Introducing Portfolios

Modeling is central to everything I teach! When I introduce portfolios to my students, I start by sharing my own portfolio—the one I created when I applied for my teaching position. In it are samples of lessons and units, copies of my transcripts, and photographs of my students engaged in learning. I explain why I put mine together and them let the students look through it.

After I've shared my own portfolio, I tell the kids that they will be creating their own. They excitedly ask questions like "Will mine be in a three-ring binder too? Will mine have pictures? Will I get to keep it?"

In the past, I've used hanging file folders to store work, pictures, and other materials because the children have easy access to them and seem to feel comfortable adding work. I'm constantly saying things like, "WOW—great work; that would be great in your portfolio." I often hear the kids tell each other the very same thing! In fact, we talk all the time about *why* we do *what* we do.

At the end of the year, the children take their portfolios home. I attach a letter to the front stating how proud the children and I are of their work.

Much of what goes into the portfolios is writing samples. I meet with each child in my classroom for an individual or small group conference once every six days (with 24 kids, I meet with four a day). During conference times, we discuss a piece of writing the child is currently working on. I make notes in a writing conference log, which I keep in a three-ring binder and then transfer to the child's portfolio. The four children I'm conferencing with each day and I sit on the rug so that I can easily see what else is happening; after the conference time, the four children share their writing with the whole class. Then the others make comments and suggestions about the writing. These observations are added to the conference log. Finally, I collect the notebooks from the small group I worked with and write personal notes, telling the children my thoughts about their writing. Sometimes I make a recommendation, but I *always* keep the comments encouraging and supportive.

I use the writing conference log and the learning participation inventory for multiple purposes. With the writing log, I'm able to chart the progress of my students all year long. I see their strengths and areas to work on; I see which spelling stage they're at and am able to plan minilessons designed around areas of need—using capitals or punctuation, adding details, or spelling conventions, for example. Mainly, the logs help the children and me see that learning to write is a *process*. Learning participation inventories can be used across the curriculum, with small groups or whole classes. They give me comparative data on student progress in the specific learning behaviors observed and are useful for sharing with parents at conference time. They are also well suited for students in self-evaluation. When we look back through our observations in the logs and inventories, we realize how much they have grown as writers and learners!

REFLECTIVE INQUIRY

◆ Why does Michele McCombs begin by sharing her own portfolio with her first graders?

◆ In what ways does she connect teaching and assessment in her classroom?

◆ How does her attitude toward portfolios help communication with students, parents, and others?

◆ Point to what is well done

◆ Resist taking over the project

For teachers who are trying to enhance involvement of students, the practice of regular conferencing allows students to share their insights (Noden and Vacca, 1994). To help students benefit from reflective, individualized conferences, they recommend that teachers do the following:

◆ Exercise professional judgment on how best to respond

◆ Invite students to share how they think and how they feel

◆ Build on what the student has done

◆ Listen carefully to the student's perception of his or her achievements

◆ Limit the number of goals set mutually by teacher and student

◆ Concentrate on the strategies and process rather than the product

The bottom line is that when a student's work is judged by the standards of growth and positive change and when students play a role in the assessment of their own literacy processes and products, the teacher's role is apt to change. Along with the benefits of portfolio assessment, teachers must deal with drawbacks, most of which center around the amount of time it takes to collect information and analyze outcomes. In fact, one of the most powerful assessment strategies that teachers spend time on is observation, or "kidwatching."

Kidwatching While Teaching

Observing how children interact with print while being taught is what portfolio assessment is all about. The term **kidwatching** has been coined to dramatize the powerful role of observation in helping children grow and develop as language users. Yetta Goodman (1978) maintained that teachers screen their observations of children through their concepts and beliefs about reading and language learning.

In many classrooms, kidwatching is an ongoing, purposeful activity. Because language learning is complex, it's impossible to observe everything that happens in the classroom. The first essential in observing children's reading and language use is therefore to decide what to look for in advance. Clearly, teachers need to watch for signs that signify growth in reading behavior. For example, probably the clearest indicator of word identification difficulties is failure to self-correct. Consequently, this is a behavior that the teacher as an expert process evaluator would take note of as students read orally.

Because it is unobtrusive and does not interfere with ongoing activities, kidwatching enables teachers to catch students in the act, so to speak, of literate behaviors. But knowing what it is that we see and what it means in terms of our students takes practice and good judgment. As Rhodes and Shanklin (1993) note, good anecdotal records and observations depend on teachers who "must understand the developmental nature of reading and writing, the processes of reading and writing, and how both might vary in different literacy contexts" (p. 28).

Dolores Fisette (1993) described the informal reading conference as the ideal place to kidwatch. While her students choose a book and read it to her and then translate the story into their own words, she notes which reading behaviors and strategies each student evidences, as well as how completely a student has comprehended the story as evidenced in the retelling. She can then use this information, recorded on a checklist, to plan instruction. What do students know how to do well? What do they need to learn or to practice?

Anecdotal Notes.   Teachers write short **anecdotal notes** that capture the gist of an incident that reveals something the teacher considers significant to understanding a child's literacy learning. Anecdotal notes are intended to safeguard against the limitations of memory. Record observations in a journal, on charts, or on index cards. These jottings become your "field notes" and will aid you in classifying information, inferring behavior, and making predictions about individual students or instructional strategies and procedures.

Post-it notes and other small pieces of paper that are easily carried about and transferred to a child's folder are perfect for writing on-the-spot anecdotal records.

It isn't necessary or even realistic to record anecdotal information every day for each student, especially in classes with 25 or 30 children. However, over a period of time, focused observations of individual children will accumulate into a revealing and informative record of literacy and language learning.

Charts are particularly useful for keeping anecdotal records. Charts can be devised to record observations in instructional situations that are ongoing: participation in reading and writing activities, small and large group discussions, book sharing, silent and oral reading. For example, the chart in Figure 14.11 was developed to record observations of children's participation in journal-writing sessions.

With improved technology, some data management systems afford teachers the opportunity to use handheld computers, such as the Apple Newton, to record kidwatching as it occurs. In addition, charts can be used to record certain behaviors across instructional activities. Examine the chart in Figure 14.12, devised to monitor and record evidence of risk taking.

A good strategy for developing a permanent record for each child in class is to cut observations apart from the individual charts. Then you can glue each student's notes into a permanent growth record. These can be used during conferences with students or with parents.

Some teachers find that writing anecdotal information can be unwieldy and time-consuming, especially if they are observing students over long stretches of time. An alternative to ongoing anecdotal notes is the use of checklists.

Checklists.   Using a **checklist** is somewhat different from natural, open-ended observation. A checklist consists of categories that have been presented for specific diagnostic purposes.

◆ FIGURE 14.11 Observational Chart for Journal Writing

Mrs. Carter				
Grade __2__				
Time Period: March 27–April 2				

Name	Date	Behavior	Date	Behavior
George	3/27	Frequently asks for assistance with spelling.	4/2	Appears to be writing more independently but still worries about correct spelling of words.
Henry	3/27	Revising draft of April Fool's story; has lots of ideas.	3/29	Writes fluently; ready to publish.
Helen	3/28	Copied a recipe from a cookbook.	4/2	Wrote first original story; was very anxious to have story read; wanted to begin another story.
Maxine	3/29	Draws pictures to rehearse before writing; concentrates on handwriting and neatness.	4/1	Wrote a riddle; wants to share it with class.

Checklists vary in scope and purpose; they can be relatively short and open-ended or longer and more detailed. To be useful, checklists should guide teachers to consider and notice what students can do in terms of their reading and writing strategies. The DR-TA checklist in Figure 14.13 can reveal how a group of students interacts with a text. Collaboratively designed checklists serve the added purpose of helping teachers develop and refine their beliefs about what constitutes important literacy performance.

When Mrs. Cartwright began using an open-ended checklist designed to show evidence of creative thinking and leadership skills on the part of her second graders, she noticed an unanticipated benefit. "It was easy for me to overlook quiet students who were

◆ FIGURE 14.12   Risk-Taking Chart

Mrs. Metzger
Grade __4__
Week: October 11– October 15

Name	Date	Evidence of Risk Taking
Tony	10/11	Showed more willingness to try to spell independently.
Betty	10/12	Volunteered to be the recorder for Radio Reading.
Marie	10/11	Declined to reread portion of story being discussed; reluctant to participate in discussion.
Holly	10/13	Self-corrected miscues during oral reading; wasn't afraid to take guesses at unknown words.

more peer-centered or who kept to themselves but out of trouble. But if I didn't have an annotation for a particular student for a few days, I had to stop and ask myself why. What did I need to do to make sure that all of my students were included in activities? I'm more aware of who I watch and why I watch them."

Interviewing.   Through **interviewing** you can discover what children are thinking and feeling. Periodic student interviews can lead to a better understanding of (1) reading interests and

◆ Figure 14.13   Directed Reading-Thinking Activity Checklist

Teacher: __Mr. Niece__

Grade: __5__

Time Period: __Fourth Period__

Group: __Niece's Nikes__

	Student Name					
	Joe	Fred	JoAnne	Mary	Rich	Emma
Reading Behavior During DRTA						
Reading Title of a Selection						
1. Participates in predicting/is cooperative.	√	√			√	√
2. Makes some predictions with coaxing.	√	√				
3. Initiates own predictions eagerly after prompting with title.	√					
4. Low risk taking/reluctant.		√		√		
5. Predictions are numerous.			√			
After Reading Sections of a Selection						
1. Retelling is accurate.	√		√		√	
2. Retelling is adequate.		√				√
3. Retelling is minimal.				√		
4. Confirms or refutes past predictions.	√		√			√

attitudes, (2) how students perceive their strengths and weaknesses, and (3) how they perceive processes related to language learning.

Cecile Kraus (1983) studied the perceptions of first graders toward reading. She found not only that 6- and 7-year-olds could verbalize their personal constructs of reading but also that their perceptions reflected the way in which they interacted with print. Here are some of the questions that Kraus asked the students in individual interviews:

◆ Suppose someone from another planet happened to land on earth, saw you reading, and said to you, "What are you doing?" You would probably answer, "I'm reading." Then that person might ask, "What is reading?" How would you answer?

◆ What would you do to teach someone to read?

◆ Who is the best reader you know? What makes that person the best reader?

◆ How did you learn to read?

◆ What did your teacher do to help you learn?

◆ If you are reading all by yourself and you come to a word you don't know, what do you do? Why? What do you do if that doesn't help? Why?

◆ What should the teacher do when a person is reading out loud and says a word that is not the same as the word in the story?

◆ Is it important for the teacher to teach you the new words before you read a story? Why or why not? *(If a conditional answer is given:)* When would it be important?

Interviews provide a rich source of information. When coupled with observations made during teaching, interviews strengthen data from formal and informal tests of student performance. Moreover, interviews may reveal information that will not be provided by other means of assessment.

SUMMARY

Reading is a process that takes place inside the head; it isn't directly observable or measurable through any one instrument or procedure. To make an authentic assessment of a human process that's essentially hidden from direct examination, teachers need to base decisions about instruction on multiple indicators of reading performance. Observation and interview, informal reading inventories, miscue analysis, standardized norm-referenced tests, criterion-referenced tests, and running records and portfolio collections all contribute to teachers' understanding.

Trends in reading assessment are almost at cross-purposes with one another. Very different perspectives are held by educators who support standard-setting and proficiency testing and those who promote authentic, performance-based assessment.

The uses to which formal types of assessment can be put were considered, for both norm-referenced and criterion-referenced tests. We examined how to interpret test scores and provided information about validity and reliability of standardized tests. We then explored informal assessment, beginning with informal reading inventories. For example, informal reading inventories can be useful in matching children with appropriate materials and in determining how children interact with print in oral and silent reading situations.

Oral miscue analysis provides insight into the reading strategies children use to make sense out of text. We examined examples of miscue analysis, which can be applied to any oral reading situation and therefore may be used in conjunction with informal reading inventories.

Portfolio assessment has grown in importance; it is influencing the way teachers and students think about and assess the work of students engaged in reading and language arts activities. A way to overcome, or deemphasize, the pressure for comparative scores and grades, portfolio assessment helps demonstrate growth in students' reading performance for parents and students. Numerous illustrations of actual teacher-developed suggestions for implementation, along with samples of assessment procedures that involve both teacher and student input, were offered. With its focus on self-reflection, portfolio assessment often incorporates observation, or kidwatching. This permits teachers to become more aware of students' individual behaviors as they engage in reading and learning activities within the context of the classroom community. Anecdotal notes, checklists, and interviews are some of the techniques that help broaden and deepen our understanding of what children do and why.

TEACHER-ACTION RESEARCHER

1. Plan a reading lesson with an elementary or middle school teacher; then arrange to be the teacher's "eyes" and "ears." Watch what happens during the lesson, taking notes and focusing on how much children are involved in learning. Discuss your notes with the teacher. What instructional decisions would you and the teacher make for the next lesson?

2. Do a miscue analysis with an elementary student to find out more about the student's processing of print. Or ask a classmate to read a passage and purposely make miscues; tape-record the reading. Then follow the procedures in this chapter for conducting miscue analysis to determine the percentage of semantically acceptable miscues, and so forth. Analyze to what extent the reader was able to use and coordinate graphic, sound, and syntactic information from the text.

3. Collaborating with a partner, develop a method of portfolio assessment that you believe would serve to show students' growth in literacy. What would be the essential elements of all of the portfolios? What elements would you leave open to student selection? Design a cover sheet to help organize and explain the portfolio's contents. Determine the criteria for evaluating the contents of the portfolio.

KEY TERMS

anecdotal notes
authentic assessment
checklist
criterion-referenced
    tests
diagnostic test
informal assessment
informal reading
    inventory (IRI)

interviewing
kidwatching
miscue analysis
norms
portfolio
portfolio assessment
proficiency testing
reliability
running record

standardized reading
    test
survey test
validity

CHAPTER

15

Managing and Organizing an Effective Classroom

Chapter Overview

MANAGING AND ORGANIZING AN EFFECTIVE CLASSROOM

IMPROVING
INSTRUCTION

PUTTING IT
ALL TOGETHER

INDIVIDUALIZING
INSTRUCTION

Collaborative and
Cooperative
Learning

Classroom
Teachers of
Reading

Community
of Learners

Groups

Materials

Multiage
Classrooms

Creating a
Physical
Environment

Classroom
of Tomorrow

Learning
Centers

Record
Keeping

Room
Diagrams

Portfolio
Systems

Student
Schedules

Between the Lines

In this chapter, you will discover:

◆ What features make up a cooperative learning-centered classroom
environment

◆ The teacher's roles in facilitating interactive literacy experiences and
explicit instruction

◆ How individualized instruction influences effective reading instruction

- ◆ Characteristics of classroom communities and multiage classrooms
- ◆ Ideas for organizing and managing the classroom through learning centers, record keeping, and portfolio systems
- ◆ Technological features and instructional considerations of the classroom of tomorrow

A teacher in a split third- and fourth-grade classroom in a suburban elementary school decided to broaden her reading program to a more literature-based approach. Colleen VanderSchie had been reading about using collaborative learning and natural texts to teach children to *want to read* as well as how to read. The more she read and the more she talked with her principal about her multiage, multiability students, the more intrigued Colleen became with her idea.

University students visiting Colleen's classroom for their field experience a few months later found the third and fourth graders in the middle of reading and language arts time. They had finished reading a selection and were engaged in a cooperative group assignment.

Children relied on one another, according to the observation field notes submitted by the prospective teachers, for interpreting instruction and for solving problems. Although Colleen circulated among the groups and was available to offer assistance, the children seemed to prefer to collaborate in their groups, resorting to asking the teacher for help only when they continued to be confused or unsure.

QUINCY: I need Mrs. VanderSchie.

SANTOS: No, you don't. I'll show you how to do it.

QUINCY: I don't think she wants you to write them down.

SANTOS: Yeah, that's what these lines are for.

QUINCY: What are details?

SANTOS: Little tiny things. Not the main idea, but little things that make you think of it.

QUINCY: Characteristics of a whale. What are characteristics of a whale?

SANTOS: I'll go get a dictionary. What do we need to look up?

QUINCY: Characteristics of whales.

MAYLEE: C-H, you need C-H-A. Use the guide words.

LaWANDA: Yeah, use the guide words, you guys!

SANTOS: Here it is! I found it!

Most surprising to the students making field observations was the patience and the respect with which children who were not friends and who might avoid one another on the playground or in other settings worked together happily and productively in this setting. Individual friendships, preferences, and gender differences did not appear to affect the collaborative group dynamics. The most able readers were not consistently group leaders. Children of all ability levels were observed participating in the reading activities on an equal basis. The collaborative nature of the project appeared to provide a low-risk setting where children felt comfortable and confident to participate in reading and reading-related activities. In this environment for learning, children's ability levels were not obvious; they did not appear to be a factor in cooperative learning.

When teachers like Colleen take control of the physical arrangement of their classrooms, the grouping of students for instruction, and the way they approach activities and select and use materials, they are managing the classroom. Images of how teachers view their role (technician, expert, learner, etc.) vary, depending on how they view the reading process and, in turn, their instructional beliefs, concerns, and emphases. To manage their classrooms effectively, teachers need to consider a number of important variables shown in the chapter overview. Teachers must conceptualize and organize classroom instruction; select classroom materials, approaches, and activities; and achieve a physical organization in which all the pieces fit together.

Teachers deserve relevant, up-to-date information if they are to be expected to make good decisions about classroom management and organization. Often it is the confluence of newer, researched-based strategies with older, traditional ideas that helps teachers make intelligent decisions about balanced instruction and best practices. We begin this chapter with efforts to improve instruction through collaborative learning and social context, used effectively by Colleen to create the climate for her literature-based, multiage classroom.

Improving Instruction

Teachers, beginning their careers or experienced veterans, want to improve their instructional practice. As we learned in Chapter 2, effective teachers strike a balance between immersing students in integrated reading and writing activities and providing explicit instructional support to show students how to use skills and strategies. To juggle performance-based assessments, authentic texts and contexts, and learners with diverse needs, teachers need a basic knowledge of how to individualize and socialize within their classrooms. They need information about cooperative learning and collaboration in order to develop classroom communities in which their students can be effectively taught, through immersion in integrated language arts and provision of explicit strategy instruction.

Collaborative and Cooperative Learning

The social aspects of reading and learning to read are obvious when one considers the reading process as a communication skill. **Cooperative learning,** described by Slavin (1999) as consisting of programs that "foster the hum of voices in the classroom" and "encourage students to discuss, debate, disagree, and ultimately to teach one another" (p. 193), has been a popular concept since the 1970s. Students work together in small groups to help one another in achieving an academic goal. To this end, classroom management and organization must begin to prepare students to be flexible so that they can recognize and adapt to competitive, cooperative, and individualized interaction situations (Kagan, 1989). Taking both the student and the classroom into account, **collaborative learning** is a cooperative learning environment in which students work effectively together to complete literacy tasks. When cooperative learning programs succeed, the students are engaged in a collaborative learning process. Collaboration and collaborative decision making are also central to portfolio assessment, a classroom-based process discussed in Chapter 14.

We know that the same features that characterize collaborative and cooperative learning are associated with environments that encourage creativity and intrinsic motivation: feelings of safety, acceptance, support, and belonging (Baloche & Platt, 1993). And thanks to Vygotsky's (1978) studies on internalizing language and thinking as we interact with each other socially, we have a variety of ways to look at the importance of the social context of learning.

According to Vygotsky, the best role for the teacher is to mediate between what students are able to do on their own and what they are able to do with support, prompting, and encouragement. Teachers can use this understanding of the role of the social context of thinking and learning to help them organize classroom instruction that will support learners as they construct new meanings through reading and writing.

Teachers are renewing their focus on creating authentic classroom situations that help children become active learners and gain competence in reading and writing. Collaboration and interaction among children during classroom literacy instruction gives them rich opportunities to practice and to refine new literacy learning. Children need to make choices about the type of work they do, to negotiate small groups, to make rules, to delegate tasks to the groups, and to decide on appropriate outcomes. Motivation and enthusiasm for learning come from opportunities for students to make their own choices about tasks and to work together to read, to listen to a book or tape, or to engage in writing activities. They practice strategies the teacher models, often assisting and coaching each other as they work.

Collaborative work is not always smooth and free of conflict, both social and cognitive. How do you decide which group member will be responsible for which task? How can the group decide which source is accurate if research data conflict? Shanahan, Robinson, and Schneider (1993) note that the type of discussion, thinking, reading, and writing that students must do to resolve their disagreements often leads to greater levels of student learning.

Cooperative Learning and the Teacher's Role.   Developing social skills for successful group work is a prerequisite when collaborative learning is a new experience for students. The classroom teacher needs to create activities that encourage and model (1) getting to know and trust group members, (2) communicating accurately and unambiguously, (3) accepting and supporting one another, and (4) constructively resolving conflicts to make mutual achievement of the goals possible (Johnson & Johnson, 1989–1990). The teacher's role becomes one of facilitator and agent for change in a collaborative classroom.

When the teacher is not the sole authority for interpretation in the classroom, when children are assisted in constructing their own reading and writing processes, students learn to connect their life experiences with literacy activities in expanded ways. Pearson (1993) found that even young children can engage in self-directed discussions about books and reading that cover all aspects of comprehension and can evaluate the quality of their writing and their comprehension without direct teacher supervision.

Often readers bring experiences from their own lives to their reading, giving them a logical and valid response that may be different from the teacher's or from other students' responses. If the teacher's experiences and interpretations totally shape school literacy experiences, students with different cultural and academic backgrounds may find they have little or no opportunity to connect their own experiences with their reading and writing.

For example, Cynthia Lewis (1993) describes a student in her class who understood how to do the kind of close reading of texts required in school but used his own "interpretive lens" to build meaning. His view helped him construct a response that did not fit Lewis's cultural expectations, as he sympathized with the klutzy and bumbling guest in a story while showing disdain for the rich but insincere host. Lewis notes that teachers must be aware of how social identity informs our communication and our interpretations. Reading and writing in school should involve helping children learn ways to stretch the boundaries of the familiar and already known, but teachers also need to legitimize the knowledge and experience that students of diverse backgrounds bring to literacy tasks.

Ruth Nathan (1995) sensed that her third-grade students loved projects and capitalized on their curious and social nature "to grab their attention and focus their drive to belong and to communicate with their classmates" (p. 82). Her role is to facilitate the project so that the group efforts are authentic. For example, she says that "big projects *require* that teachers share the burden of parceling out jobs" (p. 84). One of the major benefits of working on a project together is meeting the basic human need to belong. So whether they are working on astronomy, environment, animal habitats, timelines, or food, students begin to exhibit behaviors that we value: "lots of risk-taking with drawing, writing, and talking to others; frequent, independent journeys to the school library . . . ; students begging to work together during lunch break; kids asking to present their projects to other grades" (p. 85). And above all, in meeting the test of truly collaborative and cooperative learning, students bonded with each other in a mutually built, safe environment in which their teacher saw her role as an active agent for change.

Explicit Instruction and the Teacher's Role.

There are times in a collaborative learning environment when the teacher purposefully supports literacy learning by showing students how to use skills and strategies that will lead to independent learning. As discussed in Chapter 2, effective teachers exercise flexibility in their use of approaches and strategies.

They may center instruction around cooperative groups and projects yet provide literacy scaffolds with questions, explanations, demonstrations, practice, and application. The teacher's role shifts to capitalizing on teachable moments, or opportunities to provide **explicit instruction;** this involves explaining and modeling.

When teachers make instruction explicit, they may do so in conjunction with literature-based, integrated language arts approaches. A good illustration of this is Pat Meehan's (1998) description of how her own teaching philosophy had changed from one of "running the class" to one of "teacher-learner in harmony with the other learners in my classroom" (p. 316). She says:

> Today I teach students to use reading strategies purposefully. I no longer teach skills as an "added extra," nor do I ask standard comprehension questions. I grab opportunities within the context of reading literature as a vehicle to teach skills strategically. In this way I also model techniques . . . ; students need a repertoire of comprehension and decoding/encoding strategies in order to respond flexibly in their reading and writing. (p. 319)

Explicit instruction in a meaning-centered classroom, then, is not about isolated phonics drills or extensive practice of discrete skills on worksheets. Rather, teachers focus explicitly on the strategies that proficient readers and writers use to make sense of texts, modeling the strategies themselves, and ways to think about using them flexibly in actual reading and writing situations. A minilesson is an excellent way for teachers to provide explicit instruction. Lasting a few minutes (no more than ten), minilessons follow this pattern: (1) creating an awareness of the strategy, (2) modeling the strategy, (3) providing practice in the use of the strategy, and (4) applying the strategy in authentic reading situations. When teachers take advantage of opportunities to explain and model, students develop understandings about strategy use as they build procedural knowledge of skills and strategies.

Teachers make, verify, and rethink numerous decisions about instruction. Learning more about what teachers know and do to create classroom environments in which best practice can flourish is important.

Classroom Teachers of Reading

To put into practice their knowledge about reading and learning to read, classroom teachers must demonstrate that they are competent professionals who perform multiple roles. As they grow throughout their careers, teachers will acquire more and more expertise; they will have opportunities to reflect on and inquire into their own practice. As introduced in Chapter 1, belief systems help bring into focus what teachers know, believe, and value. What are some guidelines for classroom teachers to follow to look more closely into their roles? What are some instructional practices you are already implementing? Are there certain practices and contexts that most professionals generally agree are facilitating when it comes to instruction in reading?

Standards. According to the International Reading Association (1998), there are three broad categories of standards, or guidelines, that literacy professionals use in developing effective instructional programs: *knowledge and beliefs about reading, instruction and assessment,* and *organizing and enhancing a reading program.* In relation to managing and organizing an effective classroom, teachers need at least a basic understanding of and ability to take action in a large number of important areas:

◆ The impact of physical, perceptual, emotional, social, cultural, environmental, and intellectual factors on learning, language development, and reading acquisition

◆ Students' need for opportunities to integrate their use of literacy through reading, writing, listening, speaking, viewing, and visually representing

◆ How contextual factors in the school can influence student learning and reading (e.g., grouping procedures, school programs, assessment)

◆ The alignment of goals, instruction, and assessment

◆ Cultural, linguistic, and ethnic diversity

◆ Creating programs that address the strengths and needs of individual learners

◆ The instructional implications of research in special education, psychology, and other fields that deal with the treatment of students with learning or reading difficulties

◆ Creating a literate environment that fosters interest and growth in all aspects of literacy

◆ Use of texts and trade books to stimulate interest, promote reading growth, foster appreciation for the written word, and increase the motivation of learners to read widely and independently for information, pleasure, and personal growth

◆ Use of instructional and information technologies to support literacy learning

◆ Conducting assessments that involve multiple indicators of learner progress

◆ Communicating with students about their strengths, areas for improvement, and ways to achieve improvement

◆ Involving parents in cooperative efforts and programs to support students' reading and writing development

◆ Adapting instruction to meet the needs of different learners to accomplish different purposes

◆ Selecting and evaluating instructional materials for literacy, including those that are technology-based

◆ Promoting and facilitating teacher- and classroom-based research

◆ Reflecting on one's practice to improve instruction and other services to students

◆ Interacting with and participating in decision making with teachers, teacher educators, theoreticians, and researchers

Instructional Practices.   As the research base is built about balanced instruction and how teachers manage and organize effective classrooms, there is disagreement over "*how* teaching is conducted and who decides how teachers practice" (Freppon & Dahl, 1998, p. 248). This is often political and connected to curriculum mandates to "fix" school failures. A reality that deals more directly with classrooms and students is how teachers "mediate the research they know according to many factors (e.g., continuous changes in their own learning, students' needs, daily classroom events)" (p. 248).

As teachers, we need to analyze our own attitudes and behaviors, asking whether they are conducive to helping students form positive attitudes. What verbal and nonverbal signals do we send? What is the environment like in our classroom? What expectations are we communicating? It is incumbent on classroom teachers to identify the instructional practices they are using that take students' attitudes, interests, and needs into account. Use the Instructional Practices Inventory in Figure 15.1 to do a quick self-assessment. Check *yes* if you are already implementing a numbered practice; check *perhaps* if you are interested in finding ways to implement the practice; check *no* if you are not implementing or not interested in the practice.

Have you ever wondered what "the experts" in the field of literacy might say are practices worth incorporating into classroom instruction? Rona Flippo (1998) provided a summary of contexts and practices that would facilitate learning to read, as agreed by 11 experts. In relation to contexts, environment, purposes for reading, and materials, these contexts and practices would facilitate learning to read:

◆ Focus on using reading as a tool for learning

◆ Make reading functional

◆ Give your students lots of time and opportunity to read real books as well as time and opportunity to write creatively and for purposeful school assignments (e.g., to do research on a topic, to pursue an interest)

◆ Create environments, contexts in which the children become convinced that reading does further the purposes of their lives

◆ Encourage children to talk about and share the different kinds of reading they do in a variety of ways with many others

◆ FIGURE 15.1

Instructional Practices Inventory

	YES	PERHAPS	NO
1. I am aware of my students' attitudes toward certain aspects of reading.			
2. I plan reading activities that students tend to like.			
3. I use reading materials in which my students can succeed.			
4. I use materials related to the interest and needs of my students' norm group.			
5. I provide situations where the usefulness of reading is apparent, such as reading that is necessary in order to do a certain desired project or activity.			
6. I model reading, either orally or silently, so that my students can see that I value reading.			
7. I provide for recreational reading in my classroom.			
8. I use reading material found in the students' everyday life.			
9. I encourage *parents* to improve attitudes toward reading by reading to their children, providing reading materials, and being examples themselves by reading in front of their children.			
10. I avoid using reading as a punishment.			
11. I use bibliotherapy—I guide my students into books that deal with their problems and relate to their world.			
12. I am enthusiastic when I teach reading.			
13. I am positive in my approach; I emphasize students' abilities instead of constantly referring to their errors and inadequacies.			

◆ Use silent reading whenever possible, if appropriate to the purpose

◆ Include a variety of printed material and literature in your classroom so that students are exposed to the different functions of numerous types of printed materials

Sometimes, despite professional guidelines and preferred practices, teachers find that pressures outside school are overwhelming. Efforts to create responsive, well-organized, effective classrooms don't always work out. Family relationships, nutrition, illness, abuse, addictions, economic hardship, cultural miscommunication, and community pressures can and do override school and classroom-based factors. They are not, however, excuses for inaction. The key for us as teachers is to make certain that our expectations are high and opportunities to succeed are many.

INDIVIDUALIZING INSTRUCTION

The term *individualizing,* more than *individualized,* connotes the process of providing differentiated instruction to students. It reflects the accumulation of previous knowledge and direct experiences in reading classrooms over the years. Many teachers of reading ascribe to this process, which originated as the **individualized instruction** approach. Its relevance today is due in part to the inclusion movement toward meeting the needs and adapting the curriculum for students having special needs. Often misunderstood, the term *individualized instruction* means different things to different people. To some, it means programmed, prescriptive instruction; to others, it means flexible grouping for instruction.

What Is Individualized Instruction in Reading?

This is a key question for anyone interested in classroom organization because it can help clarify the major ways we choose to deliver reading instruction: in small groups, as a whole class, or one to one.

Individualized instruction evolved out of a 150-year-old American goal of providing free schooling for everyone. Its biggest impetus came with the development of reading tests in the early part of the twentieth century. It spawned many experiments in education, such as ability grouping, flexible promotions, and differentiated assignments. Many of the plans followed the ideas outlined in the Dalton and the Winnetka plans, which allowed children to work in reading and content areas at their own pace (Smith, 1965, p. 194).

Gradually, individualized instruction went beyond children's learning rates and reading achievement. The child's interest in reading, attitude toward reading, and personal self-esteem and satisfaction in reading expanded the goal of instruction (Smith, 1965, p. 378). Terms associated with individualization ranged from *individual progression* in the 1920s to *individualized instruction in reading* to *self-selection in reading* to *personalized reading.* Today, we might add *objective-based* and *prescriptive learning.*

An interesting irony is that originally, procedures used in individualized classrooms did not vary widely, whatever it was called. Read the following classic description; does it conjure up a reasonable picture of individualized instruction in your mind?

> Each child selects a book that he wants to read. During the individual conference period the teacher sits in some particular spot in the room as each child comes and reads to her. As he does so, she notes his individual needs and gives him appropriate help. Finally she writes what the child is reading, his needs, and strengths on his record card. Then another individual conference is held, and so on. If several children need help on the same skills, they may be called together in a group for such help. (Smith, 1965, p. 379)

This scenario does, after all, seem like a plausible description of individualized instruction. How it's actually applied in reading classrooms around the country is another matter entirely. In practice, two variations of the original individualized approach to instruction are often found in today's classroom: (1) Individualized procedures are one part of the total program (i.e., one day a week), or (2) parts of individualized reading are integrated into another reading approach (i.e., self-selection during free reading). Individualization can refer to instruction that is appropriate for the student regardless of whether it occurs in a one-to-one, small group, or whole class setting. According to Yanok (1988), individualization is a process of personalizing teaching to provide instruction that recognizes and responds to the unique learning needs of each child.

Although individualized instruction as an approach or a program for reading instruction is not as widespread as others, its influence on reading teachers has been pervasive. For assessment of individual readers' strengths and weaknesses is at the very core of effective reading instruction. This tenet cuts across the delivery of reading instruction, regardless of classroom organization pattern.

Influences of Individualized Instruction

Models of prescriptive and of personalized individualized programs, from skills management systems to literature-thematic units, have been popular off and on over the years. Among the many historical influences of individualized instruction, *groups* and *materials* evolved out of a long tradition yet still help shape the delivery of contemporary reading instruction.

Groups.   The practice of creating and disbanding groups of differing sizes, abilities, and interests of students for the purpose of providing instruction has been part of classroom management and organization since the 1920s. Yet as students were "tracked" and then assessed strictly according to their "ability," one of the effects was to limit opportunities. Children from minority backgrounds and low socioeconomic groups were "placed disproportionately in low-track, remedial programs" (Oakes, 1999, p. 228).

Today, **grouping** is used to organize teaching in content areas and for interdisciplinary instruction across subjects, such as social studies and science, mathematics and language arts. Although small groups are in operation throughout the day in many classrooms, reading instruction is most closely associated with grouping. The reading group or circle is indigenous to reading instruction.

As we think back to our own experiences in elementary school, we may recall reading time with a sense of nostalgia or wince at the memory of being one of the "low" group of readers. There are consequences of placing students in groups. Whether assignment to a group affects students' self-esteem or their chances of being asked or answering higher-level comprehension questions or expectations for success are important considerations.

Grouping serves some instructional purposes especially well; some groups are in existence for a few minutes, others last an entire period; still others are ongoing. Students may split spontaneously into groups of three to five for the purpose of engaging in a discussion strategy; other groups work together through some questions and follow-up writing during their language arts period; a book study group meets every other day for two weeks. Sometimes a large group makes more sense. Silent reading time and free write time are occasions when the whole class participates. And there are times when one-on-one situations are best, such as student-teacher conferences for book sharing or response to writing.

Materials.   Using a wide variety of **materials** for reading instruction is accepted practice across most school districts, as discussed in Chapters 11 and 12. Originally, variety in materials was needed to accomplish the main purpose of matching students with materials on their own reading level. This quickly expanded, with the development and availability of widely diverse materials to meet students' interests and instructional objectives as well. From reference books to videos and CD-ROMs, classroom materials move from shelf to groups of readers or individuals engaged in all types of learning configurations. In balanced instruction, teachers employ a broad range of materials to explicitly demonstrate a strategy or facilitate the reading of personally selected books, short stories, poems, or nonfiction.

Record keeping and the amount of time it requires is a major issue related to materials. Teachers may use computer programs that accompany their basal reading and language arts series, or they might develop a portfolio system of their own, in which students take responsibility for their own completed and in-progress work. Nevertheless, the necessity of keeping classroom records on individual readers' overall and daily performance entails keeping track of the materials used in all facets of the instructional program, including strategy instruction, projects and activities, groups; test scores and other benchmarks of progress; and recommendations for short-term and future placements. Teachers always seek more efficient yet meaningful ways of accumulating, recording, and synthesizing the different components in their teaching and learning environment. How do the parts come together in a classroom community?

PUTTING IT ALL TOGETHER: ORGANIZING A CLASSROOM COMMUNITY

The social nature of reading and writing and the importance of contextual factors in literacy instruction call for teachers to organize their classrooms into nurturing and supportive **communities of learners.** For teachers like Colleen in the chapter's opening, literacy approached collaboratively quickly becomes a useful tool for thinking, learning, *and* enjoyment, just as she had hoped. Reading and writing are the focal activities that students and their teacher use every day to learn about themselves and about the larger world they inhabit.

Community is a quality of an inspirational classroom, according to Merrill Harmin (1994), where students are in "comfortable relationships with other students and with persons of authority" (p. 4). They also listen, respect and solve problems in this environment, which brings out the best in them and their teacher. They do *not* isolate, disconnect, or reject; neither do they become self-centered or resentful.

Teachers and administrators describe classroom community in the Viewpoint in Box 15.1.

BOX 15.1   VIEWPOINT

Defining Classroom Community: What Does It Look Like?

We asked a group of seven experienced teachers and administrators to describe classroom community: How would you know one if you saw it? What would it look like?

◆ I pictured my middle school classroom, but larger and more inclusive. Everyone in the group is a learner; the direction of the class is a united effort. [The students] aid one another and switch roles between expert and resource. They listen to the interruptions of life.

◆ It's the camaraderie the students share, the interactions that take place, the sharing of information and knowledge. This includes formal and informal communication and applies to any age or type of classroom.

◆ Students are talking and interacting in a friendly way.

◆ Teacher and students are working [together or independently] toward an acceptable goal . . . in a structure that allows for the completion of goals. There is sharing of ideas, opinions, techniques, and knowledge at *any* level.

◆ The seating arrangement would permit the sharing of ideas. It would be a cooperative work design in which children and adults respect one another. Whether it's elementary or secondary is insignificant; respect is of the essence.

◆ I see students helping one another with class assignments. There is sharing about situations in which students/parents/teachers helped one another *outside of school*—elementary or middle or high school.

◆ Collaborative work is an essential part of the classroom's learning environment. Members of the class [teacher as well as students] express deep concern for one another's well-being, especially their intellectual well-being.

How do we foster the positive feelings associated with a classroom community of readers and writers? Considering the variety of desirable attributes and depending on the needs of learners, take the following guidelines into account (Clyde & Condon, 1992):

◆ The focus is on authentic reading and writing activities.

◆ Risk taking is encouraged by viewing errors as a natural and normal aspect of learning.

◆ Learners are given options (which books to read, which topics to write on, how long a project might take).

◆ Learners are trusted as teachers give up some control.

◆ Decisions concerning routines, rules, and activities are made collaboratively.

◆ The teacher's role is as facilitator, participant, or guide rather than as transmitter of facts.

◆ Emphasis is on the social nature of learning and knowing.

◆ Reflection and inquiry are essential to learning and to teaching.

◆ Power relationships among students and teachers change as teaching and learning become the valued work of all members of the classroom.

Creating such communities means that teachers must think of classrooms as learning places rather than as workplaces. But moving to such a community takes time. The teacher must help students by planning and setting up routines. Students need to be initiated into the kind of inquiry and collaborative work this definition of learning requires. Teachers need to help students value "thinking, questioning, discussion, learning from mistakes, trying new ideas, responding and challenging ideas, and appreciating diversity" (Clyde & Condon, 1992, p. 92). Multiage classrooms may hasten their initiation.

Multiage Classrooms

School districts are implementing multiage classes at an ever-increasing rate. For our purposes in examining an effective classroom, we need to discover three major things: What is a **multiage classroom,** what are its major features, and what do teachers do that best supports literacy instruction in such a classroom?

Schools might decide to become multiage, but not throughout the entire building. The classrooms that become multiage, however, must meet several requirements: Students are grouped across age levels; they form a single learning community, meeting the academic, social, emotional, physical, and aesthetic needs of its members (Kasten & Lolli, 1998). Clusters of traditional grade levels and ages observed might be K–1 or 3–4, or classes of 6- to 8-year-olds or 9- to 11-year-olds. Teachers might form teams of two, teaching anywhere from 35 to 50 students in one large room. The ages, grades, and teaching combinations are variable.

Some major features have come to be associated with multiage classrooms; Kasten and Lolli (1998) investigated the theories behind nine features, claiming that all but the first cannot be replicated in typically graded classrooms:

1. A stable, nurturing environment is created when children are placed longer with same teacher and group. [This is similar to "looping."]

2. Learners respond to roles as helpers and recipients when interacting with diverse ages.

3. Having multiple encounters with concepts, even those "untaught," prepares the way for future learning.

4. Cross-age tutoring occurs both implicitly and explicitly.

5. Individual paces are accepted and accommodated, making learning suited to developmentally appropriate practice and constructivist theory.

6. Nurturing, altruistic behaviors increase as competitive, aggressive behaviors decrease.

7. When students have opportunities to "be younger and older" in different years, birth-order effect is diminished in classrooms.

8. Social development and self-esteem are enhanced.

9. Decisions about promotion can be flexible with fewer grade-level benchmarks. (pp. 24–25)

A research team reported findings about how ten primary grade teachers created multiage classrooms to meet the needs of a wide variety of readers and writers. These teachers "believed that children benefit from being part of a classroom community for multiple years" (McIntyre et al., 1996, p. 386). Their instruction most supported the children's literacy development in three ways: (1) Teachers created classroom contexts that provided many opportunities for interaction and conversation, a social dimension enabling children to learn concepts, strategies, and skills from each other; (2) teachers differentiated instruction for various groups of children as needed; and (3) teachers provided explicit instruction for specific children for specific purposes, helping all become more metacognitive about what they were learning.

Over time, Colleen's classroom gradually developed into a learning community around collaborative grouping and self-selected reading. She was prepared to take the next step toward a multiage classroom; making the decision to implement it would take a joint commitment of principal and a couple of her teaching colleagues.

Creating a Physical Environment

What actually goes on in any classroom, multiage or traditionally graded, once the door is closed? Colleen and other experienced teachers readily acknowledge that within the walls of their classrooms, there is a certain degree of autonomy impervious to outside pressures. An expression of this autonomy is the physical arrangement or organization of classroom furniture, materials, and space.

Arranging desks, tables, chairs, technology equipment, and materials can contribute greatly to the organization of an entire semester or yearlong reading program. The *physical structure* put into place by the reading teacher can support the goals or underlying structure of the reading program. It can work for the teacher as much as any other component in the total program and total classroom environment.

When you do step back and look carefully at your reading classroom, what do you see? One perspective to take as you look around the room is to examine it for *space usage*, or books, nooks, and crannies. For example, do you see a space suitable for a reading loft? Such a loft might hold four or five readers on top and house a minilibrary underneath. Is there any room for a reading fort made of empty carpet-roll tubes? How about creating student "offices" by using partitions to divide a table into three or four separate areas? If these aren't feasible ways to use space, you might consider establishing several special reading spots, such as a chair, carpet, cupboard, or sofa.

Still another scan of your classroom might be made with *storage techniques* in mind. Boxes, labeled shelves, bulletin boards, and pegboards are multipurpose and inexpensive. Boxes make good filing cabinets; students, too, might like their own filing drawers. Thorough and visible labeling helps students know where to return materials in the room. Interactive and integrative bulletin boards may help students develop positive attitudes toward reading, according to Frager and Valentour (1984). One of the most unusual storage techniques observed was three rows of eight 10-gallon cardboard ice cream containers. They were sturdy and, if nothing else, contributed to positive student attitudes (or memories)!

Storing materials may be overlooked in a classroom equipped with a row of computers, but students at all ages and levels still need designated spots in which to put their belongings and work.

A classroom's physical structure can support the goals or underlying structure of a reading program.

We asked a fifth-grade teacher whose classroom we admired and whose teaching always seemed to be carried out with purpose and reflection to describe how her unusual reading classroom is organized and why. She does so in the Class Works in Box 15.2.

BOX 15.2   CLASS WORKS

Wanda's Deskless Classroom

A fascinating experience in class arrangement took place in my classroom one year—all because a father of one my students worked for a cardboard box factory.

He came to me one day with the free offer of 50 heavy-duty, double-strength cardboard boxes approximately 2 feet square in size. Could I use them? The price was right, so of course I said yes.

Now, how could I use this terrific gift? The answer came to me one day when a student said, "Mrs. Rogers, I haven't sat in my own seat since the first five minutes of today!" I gave this some thought and realized that with the flexible grouping we were constantly using, the children actually did spend very little time at their own desks. So I asked, "Why not do away with desks?" And we did.

Each student was given a box that was to house books, supplies, and so on. We stacked the boxes two tall, and they provided instant dividers to make separate spaces in the room for small groups to meet.

Much of our class instruction was done in small groups with different groupings for each subject. By removing "desk ownership," we eliminated territorial problems. No more did we hear, "Jim wrote all over my desk during reading class." "You can't sit here. I don't want your cooties all over my desk." "Mrs. Rogers, Judy stole my pencil out of my desk when she was sitting there."

Desks were viewed as workbenches and storage areas for learning activities equipment and materials. By removing student-desk associations, the desks themselves became more flexible for rearranging to meet different organizational needs.

An unexpected benefit was that students became more involved. Because they no longer had a desk for retreat where they could while away time unproductively or daydream, they tended to "find something to do" when they finished a task—kibbitz with other students, use the library or resource center, take a book to a corner, or involve themselves in a listening or hands-on activity in special areas set up for that purpose. They learned to move themselves from one task to another, rather than "sit in *their* seats" and wait to be told what to do by the teacher.

One of the best advantages was that it opened new vistas of classroom organization for me as a teacher. I found myself less restricted and more creative and efficient. I could arrange the management of an activity without the confines of "desk ownership."

Reflective Inquiry

♦ Why did Wanda feel more creative when she changed the way desks were used?

♦ How closely connected are classroom organization and management?

Source: Reprinted by permission of Wanda Rogers.

The physical environment teachers of reading create can set the stage for a productive program. As children's or adolescent literature grows in use in classrooms, teachers find ingenious ways to make books accessible to their students. They manipulate physical space, materials, and time to make books, as well as computers, a natural part of their classroom environment. Some of the ideas for organizing classroom communities for whole class, small group, or independent activities are learning centers, room diagrams, student schedules, and portfolio systems.

Learning Centers.   Several advantages to setting up **learning centers** are that they allow more pupil movement, more and diverse opportunities for pupils to work in small groups or independently, and more pupil choice, commitment, and responsibility.

Why teachers choose to use learning centers is important, because their purpose should determine the type of center. Provisions for flexible grouping, individual work, research, and group or committee work are essential for centers in classrooms that foster optimal literacy development for each student (Flood & Lapp, 1993). Such an environment encourages collaborative and social aspects of literacy learning and allows the teacher to plan for various reading and writing activities. Even in the smallest of classrooms, a center for quiet reading and research and a center for groups to meet and talk can usually be arranged, if only by placing desks together to make collaborative work areas.

Supplementing textbooks and basal readers with dictionaries, newspapers and magazines, literature, nonfiction trade books, art supplies, electronic materials, and students' own previously published writing gives students sources to use in developing their ideas for reading and writing. All of these sources can be housed in learning centers organized in creative configurations.

Room Diagrams.   One of the most useful ideas for organizing any classroom, whether you have learning centers or other formats, is a diagram of the classroom. A **room diagram** serves

Classroom learning centers allow more diverse opportunities for students to work alone or in groups, establishing choices, commitment, and responsibility.

three simple yet essential purposes: (1) It helps the teacher keep track of where and how various activities are taking place and with whom; (2) it helps parents and other teachers acclimate to your classroom, whether they are visiting or presiding over another class or study hall (it becomes a handy seating chart); and (3) it gives students an opportunity to see what is available for them to do now and anticipate what other activities are in store for them.

Room diagrams are just as useful to teachers beginning to use activity centers as they are to teachers who long ago stopped using traditional formats. To illustrate, the room in Figure 15.2 is a traditional elementary classroom in which learning centers are separated from regular instructional areas either around the periphery or off to one side. Figure 15.3 outlines a room in which learning or activity areas for collaborative learning are the focal point of the classroom community.

Student Schedules.   The secret to effective implementation of classroom learning centers is teacher organization and the scheduling of students to designated activities. Arranging **student schedules** is time-consuming. In order to develop an *individual schedule* (see Figure 15.4 for a five-week unit), teachers need to consider where and when and in what combinations they want students at the various stations. A student who needs extensive work in a particular area, such as composition or listening, is given more time at that num-

◆ FIGURE 15.2   A Traditional Classroom with Activity Centers

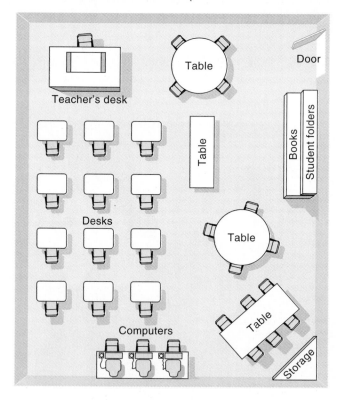

◆ FIGURE 15.3   A Learning-Center Classroom

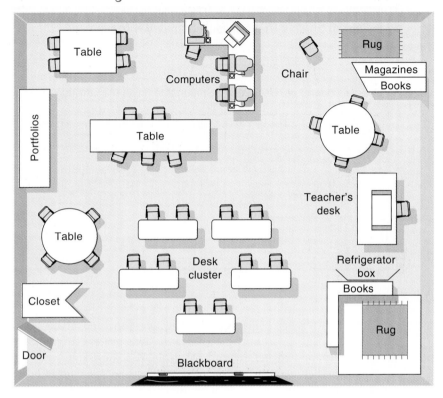

bered station. All students, regardless of their strengths and weaknesses, usually want equal time at certain popular areas, such as games or free-reading stations.

In addition to, or instead of, individual student schedules, teachers may develop *small group schedules* to rotate groups of students to different stations. This type of schedule is often called *rotational*. Figure 15.5 illustrates a schedule designed for second graders to follow during their language arts hour each morning for a week to ten days. The names of stations that the teacher believes are important enough to merit a block of time during language arts are put in the outer, stationary circle. Names of students are listed in the inner circle, which can be rotated daily or more or less frequently. In some cases, teachers let the students decide when to go to the next station or center.

A third way of scheduling students is through *contracting*. Ideally, this is a written agreement between student and teacher in which the student makes a commitment to assume responsibility for a learning experience. Successful contracting is a process that begins during student-teacher conferences. First, the interests of the student are determined through discussion or observation and discussion. Next, the teacher confers with the student about what type of follow-up will benefit this area of interest, and a contract is drawn up and signed. Materials are searched for and organized as the student carries out the plan

◆ FIGURE 15.4

Individual Student Unit Schedule (January 4 to February 1)

Name: _____

Special comments: Use time at Station 2 to finish the introduction to your portfolio.

Week	Monday	Tuesday	Wednesday	Thursday	Friday
A	—	1	2	3	7
B	7	3	9	5	5
C	8	1	4	5	5
D	6	4	4	8	5
E	9	8	1	4	3

of study. The teacher helps by answering questions and giving explicit instruction as needed, when the opportunity presents itself. This process continues until the contract is completed or modified and the student's goals are achieved.

Contracts between teachers and students, then, are the most individual and personal of schedules. Two sample contracts are illustrated in Figure 15.6, the one on the left for use with a primary grader and the one on the right for an intermediate grader.

Record Keeping.   Keeping track of books and stories read by students and materials used by students, or **record keeping,** is a problem for many teachers. It is not feasible for teachers to take on the task of recording who read what, at what level, and what it was all about. Parent volunteers and teacher aides are ideal assistants. However, the most valuable assets to any organized classroom are the students themselves.

Any classroom that has a reading corner or that includes sustained silent reading in its reading program should also have a system to record what students are reading. One system is to have cards or charts attached to the inside back cover of a student folder (or portfolio or reading journal) as shown in Figure 15.7.

Technology can also provide students and teachers with easily accessible ways to chart their self-selected reading, and store information in an uncomplicated and understandable manner. Electronic record-keeping and publishing programs, organizers, and portfolios are also available.

Portfolio Systems.   Collecting students' work and recording their literacy growth for documentation and assessment purposes in a *portfolio system,* described in Chapter 14, also helps in planning and organizing instruction. And when students are evaluated not just on the "correct" answers they give but on their engagement in higher levels of thinking, im-

◆ Figure 15.5   Small Group Student Schedule

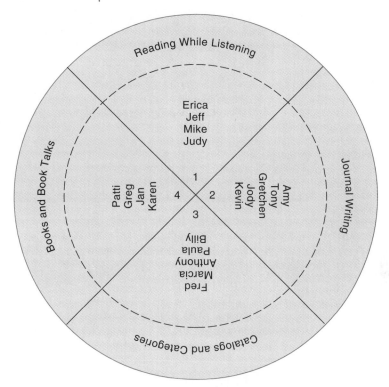

provement in problem solving, and attitudes toward learning, portfolios have the capacity to reinforce curricular and instructional goals. As Hopkin and colleagues (1997) point out, portfolios provide "a tool that clearly communicates information about a student's progress within our specified curricular program. Student portfolios are highly beneficial as transfer documents and, as such, become a practical vehicle to contain our curriculum" (p. 413). They can become catalysts to link parents and the school and to link teachers and other colleagues.

Whereas student work makes up the bulk of a student-generated assessment portfolio, a *teacher's portfolio* needs to include other types of information as well. A loose-leaf binder with a page for each student and room for adding other pertinent data and artifacts should have a place for anecdotal records, observations during lessons, and perhaps surveys from parents, peers, or self about attitudes and aptitudes. Using self-adhesive labels, the teacher can easily write notes about a child as needed and transfer them later to notebook page or an observation form.

A similar idea to the teacher's portfolio is the **teacher's log** organized especially for assessment, with several pages for each student, in which to record observations and narratives (Flood, Lapp, & Nagel, 1993). Teachers can use such logs to record not only reading and writing activities but social behaviors as well. A sample page from a teacher's log that focused on student responses to a unit on multicultural literature and appreciating diversity

◆ FIGURE 15.6   Individual Student Contracts

My name: _____
Today is: _____
1. I will read _____ stories in the library corner.
2. I will write _____ times a week in my journal.
3. I will put _____ key words in my word bank.

    Signed,   (me) _____
               (teacher) _____

Name _____ Date _____
    I'm interested in finding out about _____.
To do this, I will spend _____ hours a week at
the _____ and _____ hours at the _____.
    From my notes, I will prepare a _____
and do a _____, which I will share with
the class on _____.

    Signed,   (me) _____
               (teacher) _____

of cultural heritage shows how students are progressing in ways that go beyond basic facts to critical thinking (see Figure 15.8).

Finally, both student and teacher could fill out a self-evaluation form (see Figure 15.9). They might do this individually and then compare their responses in a conference. The form could be oriented toward the actual classroom activities or serve as a summative statement placed at the end of a student's portfolio.

The Technology Classroom of Tomorrow

It's noon on Tuesday, and the second graders are trooping into the Ameritech Electronic University School Classroom on the campus of Kent State University. The classroom is actually three separate rooms: a lab, an observation room, and a group/distance learning room. Funded by several large corporations and other grant sources, the overall purpose of

◆ FIGURE 15.7   Individual Reading Chart

WHAT HAVE I BEEN READING?				
Date	Title	Author	Rating $\overset{+}{-}$	# pp.
Mar. 13	Lon Po Po: A Red-Riding Hood Story from China	Ed Young	+	87
Apr. 2	Mufaro's Beautiful Daughters	John Steptoe	+	206

this **electronic classroom** is to provide a research laboratory and technology-based classroom for students, college faculty, classroom teachers, and education majors. Due largely to a collaborative effort between local schools and Kent State's College of Education, young students and educators can experience learning in a setting intended to prepare them for the technological challenges of the next century. What are some of the features of this classroom? And what do teachers need to take into consideration in developing the most appropriate instruction in this type of environment?

Hardware and Software.   The classroom is computer-intense; it has 12 desktop computers capable of using CD-ROM software and networking through electronic mail and the Internet. Alphasmart and laptop computers are also available. As shown in Figure 15.10, the teacher station has a computer and the capability to convert anything into a digital picture sent from a student computer to the projection screen. Each computer station consists of two computers with portable eyeball video cameras mounted on top and one desk microphone. At any one of four positions, the combination ceiling camera can activate the mike, if desired by the teacher or researcher-observers. The software, Timbuktu, connects each student's work area to the teacher.

The observation room is located behind a wall of one-way glass on one side of the classroom. Through dome-mounted cameras, observers can view and record student behavior while seated on stools at one of four color video monitors on the counter. Through the use of digital videocassette recorders, data from video and audio sources can be preserved for later analysis. Observers have ample room to discuss their observations and opportunities to ask questions of the instructional specialist. On a typical day, visitors might see the second graders save their work on file servers or using laser pointers during group sharing time in front of the projection screen.

◆ FIGURE 15.8

A Sample Page from a Teacher's Log

Negative Indicators   ### Alternate behaviors

a. Segregated groups   _____

b. Rude remarks   _____

c. Slurs   _____

d. Misconceptions   _____

Positive Skills Observed   ### Examples

a. Caring   _____

b. Teamwork   _____

c. Initiative   _____

d. Effort   _____

e. Problem solving   _____

Community Services Performed   ### Examples

a. Graffiti cleanup   _____

b. Little Brothers and Sisters   _____

c. Publish booklet, "Fighting
   Prejudice at Our School"   _____

Source: From "Assessing Student Action Beyond Reflection and Response," by J. Flood, D. Lapp, and G. Nagel, *Journal of Reading, 36,* p. 422. Copyright © 1993. Used by permission of the International Reading Association.

Ameritech Classroom students also have access to one of four field kits; each has a camcorder, a still digital camera, an audiorecorder, and a laptop computer. These kits permit young students to explore other university and community facilities. The third room is designed to transmit and receive signals from around the country and the world. It has an LCD screen for incoming images and a "smart board" for students and teacher to write on and then project selected parts directly onto the projection screen. There are five computers, more tables grouped for cooperative and collaborative learning, and cameras that automatically turn toward students participating in discussion, activating the microphone on their table. Eventually, distance-learning opportunities with other children should materi-

◆ FIGURE 15.9

Self-Evaluation Form

Name: _____   Date: _____

Directions: Answer *yes* or *no* in each box.

Centers

	1	2	3	4	5	6	7	8	9	10	11

1. Did I improve in this activity?

2. Did I understand and follow directions?

3. Did I write neatly and accurately?

4. Did I do as much as I could?

5. Did I learn anything new?

6. The activities I did my best work on were _____ and _____ .
   It was my best work because _____ .

7. The activities that I had difficulty with were _____ and _____ .
   They were difficult because _____ .

8. The activity I like most is _____ .

9. The activity I dislike most is _____ .

Comments about my portfolio: _____

---

alize as the lessons learned from data gathered here are translated into recommendations for classroom settings in other schools. For a complete listing of the hardware and software available in the Ameritech Classroom, go to this Web site and select from the choices: http://www.educ.kent.edu

Instructional Considerations. As electronic classrooms like this one, or some of its features, become more accessible to teachers, what do teachers need to take into account to make the best possible use of technology and provide quality instruction? Here are some of the things teachers should expect from students:

◆ FIGURE 15.10   The Ameritech Electronic University School Classroom at Kent State University

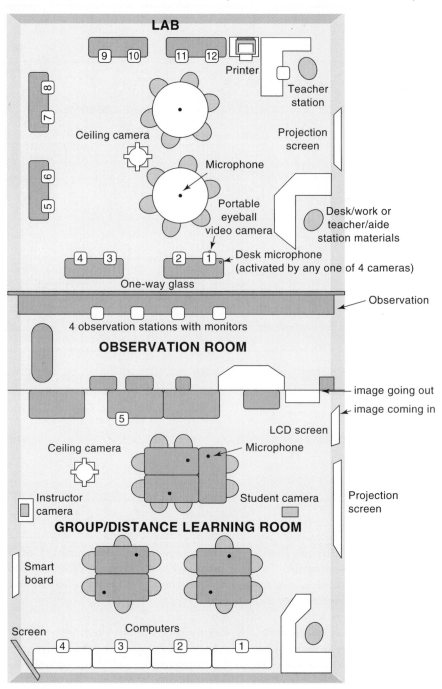

ATTITUDES

◆ Acting comfortable, confident, and capable when using the equipment

◆ Displaying a positive attitude toward using technology; overcoming "phobias" about technology

◆ Realizing the importance of working cooperatively with classmates

◆ Developing flexibility in working relationships with peers

BEHAVIORS

◆ Fluency with specific equipment

◆ A facility for gathering, sorting, analyzing, synthesizing, translating, and presenting information

◆ Sharing knowledge with others

◆ Engaging in cooperative or collaborative learning with classmates

◆ Staying on task and using time productively

As teachers, we need to ask ourselves how to maximize the students' learning and harness their enthusiasm. Moreover, are the children overwhelmed? Do they experience information overload? Are we reasonable in balancing how much of the curriculum should be taught using technologically sophisticated means? Sometimes material that is available doesn't fit naturally into a particular unit of study or project. If that is the case, do not include it. Electronic materials must fit naturally and logically with the curriculum for them to be meaningful—the major consideration for teaching and learning!

SUMMARY

In this chapter, we considered what teachers need to do to manage and organize their classrooms effectively for reading instruction. The guiding principles can be traced back through the evolution of cooperative learning and individualized instruction. Collaborative learning, the social nature of reading and writing, and the teacher's role in creating a classroom community contribute to improved instruction, to meet the overall goal of producing independent readers. We paid close attention to the role of classroom teacher, central to understanding all other factors in an effective classroom. Teachers organize and manage their classroom through daily decision making, guided by professional standards and best practices.

We considered the ways in which teachers put everything together to create an environment and described characteristics of classroom communities and multiage classrooms. Whether facilitating collaborative learning or providing explicit instruction, teachers want to create a classroom environment conducive to learning. How they schedule students, balance activities and materials, and test and keep records differs from teacher to teacher. Just as teachers individualize in various ways, their classroom environments vary from straight-row traditional to flexible-seating open arrangements. Learning centers and their organization were illustrated, along with room diagrams, schedules, record keeping, and portfolio systems. A classroom of tomorrow, replete with the latest in technology, was described from an instructional perspective.

In the end, each individual teacher must decide the best way to manage and organize the classroom in light of students' abilities and needs, priorities, reading program, instructional approach, and technological support. The way we balance all these and other variables in the social and physical context contributes to our reputations as effective teachers.

TEACHER-ACTION RESEARCHER

1. Describe how you would organize your classroom to support the goals of your reading program. Develop a room diagram to illustrate how you would arrange furniture, materials, equipment, student activities, storage, and so on. Label the diagram, and share it with another colleague or student in the class.

2. Visit several elementary schools with different physical facilities and room arrangements. Select an organizational plan that you find effective and efficient, and explain why. Then select one that you believe to be less effective and efficient and explain why.

3. Interview two elementary or middle school teachers, preferably from different schools, asking them how they group children for instruction in reading and language arts. Or interview two of your fellow students and ask how they would group children. Analyze the results, and determine the most prevalent reasons for grouping children for the purposes of reading instruction.

4. Visit a classroom where the teacher uses technology. How does the use of technology affect instruction in this class? What kinds of literacy activities seem to work best with the technology? What doesn't work as well with the technology? Describe or illustrate the placement of technologically advanced equipment in the room.

KEY TERMS

collaborative
  learning
community of
  learners
cooperative learning
electronic classroom

explicit instruction
grouping
individualized
  instruction
learning centers
materials

minilesson
multiage classroom
record keeping
room diagram
student schedules
teacher's log

A

Beliefs About Reading Interview

DETERMINING YOUR BELIEFS ABOUT READING

To determine your beliefs about reading, study the sample responses in this appendix. Then compare each answer you gave to the interview questions in Box 2.1 in Chapter 2 to the samples given here. Using the form in Figure A.1, categorize each response as *bottom-*

◆ FIGURE A.1

Rating Sheet for Beliefs About Reading Interview

	RATING SCALE		
	BU	TD	NI
1. Instructional goals			
2. Response to oral reading when reader makes an error			
3. Response to oral reading when a student does not know a word			
4. Most important instructional activity			
5. Instructional activities reader should be engaged in most of the time			
6. Ordering of steps in a reading lesson			
7. Importance of introducing vocabulary words before students read			
8. Information from testing			
9. How a reader should respond to unfamiliar words during silent reading			
10. Rationale for best reader			

TABLE A.1

Rating Chart

Bottom-up:	Gave zero or 1 top-down response (the rest are bottom-up or not enough information)
Interactive:	Gave 3 to 5 bottom-up responses
Top-down:	Gave 0 or 1 bottom-up responses

up (BU) or *top-down* (TD). If you cannot make that determination, check NI, for *not enough information.*

Ask yourself as you judge your responses, "What unit of language did I stress?" For example, if you said that your major instructional goal is "to increase students' ability to associate sounds with letters," then the unit of language emphasized suggests a bottom-up (BU) response. Bottom-up responses are those that emphasize *letters* and *words* as the predominant units of language.

By contrast, a top-down (TD) response would be appropriate if you had said that your major instructional goal is "to increase students' ability to read library books or other materials on their own." In this response, the unit of language involves the entire selection. Top-down responses emphasize *sentences, paragraphs,* and the *selection itself* as the predominant units of language.

An example of a response that does not give enough information (NI) is one in which you might have said, "I tell the student to figure out the word." Such a response needs to be probed further during the interview by asking, "How should the student figure out the word?"

The following rating sheet will help you determine roughly where you lie on the continuum between bottom-up and top-down belief systems. After you have judged each response to the interview questions, check the appropriate column on the rating sheet for each interview probe.

An overall rating of your conceptual framework of reading is obtained from Table A.1, showing where you fall on the reading beliefs continuum in Figure 2.2 in Chapter 2.

Guidelines for Analyzing Beliefs About Reading Interviews

Directions: Use the following summary statements as guidelines to help analyze your responses to the questions in the interview.

Question 1: Main Instructional Goals

Bottom-Up Responses:

Increase children's ability to blend sounds into words or ability to sound out words.

Increase knowledge of phonetic sounds (letter-sound associations).

Build sight vocabulary.

Increase ability to use word attack skills.

Top-Down Responses:

Increase students' ability to read independently by encouraging them to read library or other books that are easy enough for them on their own.

Increase enjoyment of reading by having a lot of books around, reading aloud to children, and sharing books I thought were special.

Improve comprehension.

Increase ability to find specific information, identify key ideas, determine cause-and-effect relationships, and make inferences. (Although these are discrete skills, they are categorized as top-down because students use higher-order linguistic units—phrases, sentences, and paragraphs—in accomplishing them.)

Question 2: Teacher Responses When Students Make Oral Reading Errors

Bottom-Up Responses:

Help students sound out the word.

Tell students what the word is and have them spell and then repeat the word.

Top-Down Responses:

Ask "Does that make sense?"

Don't interrupt; one word doesn't "goof up" the meaning of a whole passage.

Don't interrupt; if students are worried about each word, they won't be able to remember what is read.

Don't correct if the error doesn't affect the meaning of the passage.

If the error affects the meaning of the passage, ask students to reread the passage, tell students the word, or ask "Does that make sense?"

Question 3: Teacher Responses When Students Do Not Know a Word

Bottom-Up Responses:

Help students sound out the word.

Help them distinguish smaller words within the word.

Help them break the word down phonetically.

Help them sound the word out syllable by syllable.

Tell them to use word attack skills.

Give them word attack clues; for example, "The sound of the beginning consonant rhymes with _____."

Top-Down Responses:

Tell students to skip the word, go on, and come back and see what makes sense.

Ask "What makes sense and starts with _____?"

Questions 4 and 5: Most Important Instructional Activities

Bottom-Up Responses:

Working on skills.

Working on phonics.

Working on sight vocabulary.

Vocabulary drill.

Discussing experience charts, focusing on the words included and any punctuation needed.

Tape-recording students' reading and playing it back, emphasizing accuracy in word recognition.

Top-Down Responses:

Actual reading, silent reading, and independent reading.

Comprehension.

Discussion of what students have read.

Book reports.

Tape-recording students' reading and playing it back, emphasizing enjoyment of reading or comprehension.

Question 6: Ranking Parts of the Directed Reading Procedure

Bottom-Up Responses:

The following are most important:

Introduction of vocabulary.

Activities to develop reading skills.

The following are least important:

Setting purposes for reading.

Reading.

Reaction to silent reading.

Introduction of vocabulary, when the teacher stresses students' using word attack skills to sound out new words.

Top-Down Responses:

The following are most important:

Setting purposes for reading.

Reading.

Reaction to silent reading.

The following are least important:

Introduction of vocabulary.

Activities to develop reading skills.

Question 7: Introducing New Vocabulary Words

Bottom-Up Responses:

Introducing new vocabulary is important because students need to know what words they will encounter in order to be able to read a story.

Previewing new vocabulary isn't necessary; if students have learned word attack skills, they can sound out unknown words.

Introducing new words is useful in helping students learn what words are important in a reading lesson.

Vocabulary words should be introduced if students don't know the meanings of the words; otherwise it isn't necessary.

Top-Down Response:

Vocabulary words need not be introduced before reading because students can often figure out words from context.

Question 8: What a Reading Test Should Do

Bottom-Up Responses:

Test word attack skills.

Test ability to name the letters of the alphabet.

Test sight words.

Test knowledge of meanings of words.

Test ability to analyze letter patterns of words missed during oral reading.

Test visual skills such as reversal.

Top-Down Responses:

Test comprehension: Students should be able to read a passage orally, look at the errors they make, and use context in figuring out words.

Test whether students are able to glean the meanings of words from context.

Answer questions like the following: Do students enjoy reading? Do their parents read to them? Do their parents take them to the library?

Have students read passages and answer questions.

Have students read directions and follow them.

Question 9: What Students Should Do When They Come to an Unknown Word During Silent Reading

Bottom-Up Responses:

Sound it out.

Use their word attack skills.

Top-Down Responses:

Look at the beginning and the end of the sentence and try to think of a word that makes sense.

Try to think of a word that both makes sense and has those letter sounds.

Skip the word; often students can understand the meaning of the sentence without knowing every word.

Use context.

Question 10: Who Is the Best Reader?

READER A	READER B	READER C
Miscue is similar both graphically and in meaning to the text word.	Miscue is a real word that is graphically similar but not meaningful in the text.	Miscue is a nonword that is graphically similar.

Bottom-Up Responses:

Reader C, because *cannel* is graphically similar to *canal.*

Reader B, because *candle* is a real word that is graphically similar to *canal.*

Top-Down Response:

Reader A, because *channel* is similar in meaning to *canal.*

B

The De Ford Theoretical Orientation to Reading Profile (TORP)

Name _____

Directions: Read the following statements, and circle one of the responses that will indicate the relationship of the statement to your feelings about reading and reading instruction. SA = strongly agree; SD = strongly disagree.

Select *one* best answer that reflects the strength of agreement or disagreement.)

	SA	2	3	4	SD

1. A child needs to be able to verbalize the rules of phonics in order to assure proficiency in processing new words.
   1 SA — 2 — 3 — 4 — 5 SD

2. An increase in errors is usually related to a decrease in comprehension.
   1 SA — 2 — 3 — 4 — 5 SD

3. Dividing words into syllables according to rules is a helpful instructional practice for reading new words.
   1 SA — 2 — 3 — 4 — 5 SD

4. Fluency and expression are necessary components of reading that indicate good comprehension.
   1 SA — 2 — 3 — 4 — 5 SD

5. Materials for early reading should be written in natural language without concern for short, simple words and sentences.
   1 SA — 2 — 3 — 4 — 5 SD

6. When children do not know a word, they should be instructed to sound out its parts.
   1 SA — 2 — 3 — 4 — 5 SD

7. It is a good practice to allow children to edit what is written into their own dialect when learning to read.
   1 SA — 2 — 3 — 4 — 5 SD

8. The use of a glossary or dictionary is necessary in determining the meaning and pronunciation of new words.
   1 SA — 2 — 3 — 4 — 5 SD

9. Reversals (e.g., saying "saw" for "was") are significant problems in the teaching of reading.
   1 SA — 2 — 3 — 4 — 5 SD

10. It is good practice to correct a child as soon as an oral reading mistake is made.

$$1 \quad 2 \quad 3 \quad 4 \quad 5$$
SA   SD

11. It is important for a word to be repeated a number of times after it has been introduced to ensure that it will become a part of sight vocabulary.

$$1 \quad 2 \quad 3 \quad 4 \quad 5$$
SA   SD

12. Paying close attention to punctuation marks is necessary to understanding story content.

$$1 \quad 2 \quad 3 \quad 4 \quad 5$$
SA   SD

13. It is a sign of an ineffective reader when words and phrases are repeated.

$$1 \quad 2 \quad 3 \quad 4 \quad 5$$
SA   SD

14. Being able to label words according to grammatical function (e.g., nouns, etc.) is useful in proficient reading.

$$1 \quad 2 \quad 3 \quad 4 \quad 5$$
SA   SD

15. When coming to a word that's unknown, the reader should be encouraged to guess upon meaning and go on.

$$1 \quad 2 \quad 3 \quad 4 \quad 5$$
SA   SD

16. Young readers need to be introduced to the root form of words (e.g., run, long) before they are asked to read inflected forms (e.g., running, longest).

$$1 \quad 2 \quad 3 \quad 4 \quad 5$$
SA   SD

17. It is not necessary for a child to know the letters of the alphabet in order to learn to read.

$$1 \quad 2 \quad 3 \quad 4 \quad 5$$
SA   SD

18. Flash-card drills with sight words is an unnecessary form of practice in reading instruction.

$$1 \quad 2 \quad 3 \quad 4 \quad 5$$
SA   SD

19. Ability to use accent patterns in multisyllable words (pho´ to graph, pho to´ gra phy, and pho to gra´ phic) should be developed as part of reading instruction.

$$1 \quad 2 \quad 3 \quad 4 \quad 5$$
SA   SD

20. Controlling text through consistent spelling patterns (e.g., The fat cat ran back. The fat cat sat on a hat.) is a means by which children can best learn to read.

$$1 \quad 2 \quad 3 \quad 4 \quad 5$$
SA   SD

21. Formal instruction in reading is necessary to ensure the adequate development of all the skills used in reading.

$$1 \quad 2 \quad 3 \quad 4 \quad 5$$
SA   SD

22. Phonic analysis is the most important form of analysis used when meeting new words.

$$1 \quad 2 \quad 3 \quad 4 \quad 5$$
SA   SD

23. Children's initial encounters with print should focus on meaning, not upon exact graphic representation.

$$1 \quad 2 \quad 3 \quad 4 \quad 5$$
SA   SD

24. Word shapes (word configuration) should be taught in reading to aid in word recognition.

$$1 \quad 2 \quad 3 \quad 4 \quad 5$$
SA   SD

25. It is important to teack skills in relation to other skills.

$$1 \quad 2 \quad 3 \quad 4 \quad 5$$
SA   SD

26. If a child says "house" for the written word "home," the response should be left uncorrected.

$$1 \quad 2 \quad 3 \quad 4 \quad 5$$
SA   SD

27. It is not necessary to introduce new words before they appear in the reading text.

1	2	3	4	5
SA				SD

28. Some problems in reading are caused by readers dropping the inflectional ending from words (e.g., jump*s*, jump*ed*).

1	2	3	4	5
SA				SD

Source: From "Validating the Construct of Theoretical Orientation in Reading Instruction," by D. De Ford, *Reading Instruction Quarterly, 20,* Spring 1985. Reprinted by permission of the International Reading Association.

Determining Your Theoretical Orientation

To determine your theoretical orientation, tally your total score on the TORP. Add the point values as indicated on each item, *except for the following items:*

5, 7, 15, 17, 18, 23, 26, 27

For these items, reverse the point values by assigning 5 points for strongly agree (SA) to 1 point for strongly disagree (SD):

5	4	3	2	1
SA				SD

Once your point totals have been added, your overall score on the TORP will fall in one of the following ranges:

THEORETICAL ORIENTATION	OVERALL SCORE RANGE
Phonics	0–65
Skills	65–110
Whole language	110–140

C

Reading and Writing Accomplishments of Young Children by Grade Level

KINDERGARTEN ACCOMPLISHMENTS

◆ Knows the parts of a book and their functions.

◆ Begins to track print when listening to a familiar text being read or when rereading own writing.

◆ "Reads" familiar texts emergently, i.e., not necessarily verbatim from the print alone.

◆ Recognizes and can name all uppercase and lowercase letters.

◆ Understands that the sequence of letters in a written word represents the sequence of sounds (phonemes) in a spoken word (alphabetic principle).

◆ Learns many, though not all, one-to-one letter-sound correspondences.

◆ Recognizes some words by sight, including a few very common ones (a, the, I, my, you, is, are).

◆ Uses new vocabulary and grammatical constructions in own speech.

◆ Makes appropriate switches from oral to written language situations.

◆ Notices when simple sentences fail to make sense.

◆ Connects information and events in texts to life and life to text experiences.

◆ Retells, reenacts, or dramatizes stories or parts of stories.

◆ Listens attentively to books teacher reads to class.

◆ Can name some book titles and authors.

◆ Demonstrates familiarity with a number of types or genres of text (e.g., storybooks, expository texts, poems, newspapers, and everyday print such as signs, notices, labels).

◆ Correctly answers questions about stories read aloud.

◆ Makes predictions based on illustrations or portions of stories.

◆ Demonstrates understanding that spoken words consist of a sequences of phonemes.

◆ Given spoken sets like "dan, dan, den" can identify the first two as being the same and the third as different.

◆ Given spoken sets like "dak, pat, zen" can identify the first two as sharing a same sound.

◆ Given spoken segments can merge them into a meaningful target word.

◆ Given a spoken word can produce another word that rhymes with it.

◆ Independently writes many uppercase and lowercase letters.

◆ Uses phonemic awareness and letter knowledge to spell independently (invented or creative spelling).

◆ Writes (unconventionally) to express own meaning.

◆ Builds a repertoire of some conventionally spelled words.

◆ Shows awareness of distinction between "kid writing" and conventional orthography.

◆ Writes own name (first and last) and the first names of some friends or classmates.

◆ Can write most letters and some words when they are dictated.

First-Grade Accomplishments

◆ Makes a transition from emergent to "real" reading.

◆ Reads aloud with accuracy and comprehension any text that is appropriately designed for the first half of grade 1.

◆ Accurately decodes orthographically regular, one-syllable words and nonsense words (e.g., sit, zot), using print-sound mappings to sound out unknown words.

◆ Uses letter-sound correspondence knowledge to sound out unknown words when reading text.

◆ Recognizes common, irregularly spelled words by sight (have, said, where, two).

◆ Has a reading vocabulary of 300 to 500 words, sight words and easily sounded out words.

◆ Monitors own reading and self-corrects when an incorrectly identified word does not fit with cues provided by the letters in the word or the context surrounding the word.

◆ Reads and comprehends both fiction and nonfiction that is appropriately designed for grade level.

◆ Shows evidence of expanding language repertory, including increasing appropriate use of standard more formal language registers.

◆ Creates own written texts for others to read.

◆ Notices when difficulties are encountered in understanding text.

◆ Reads and understands simple written instructions.

◆ Predicts and justifies what will happen next in stories.

◆ Discusses prior knowledge of topics in expository texts.

◆ Discusses how, why, and what-if questions in sharing nonfiction texts.

◆ Describes new information gained from texts in own words.

◆ Distinguishes whether simple sentences are incomplete or fail to make sense; notices when simple texts fail to make sense.

◆ Can answer simple written comprehension questions based on material read.

◆ Can count the number of syllables in a word.

◆ Can blend or segment the phonemes of most one-syllable words.

◆ Spells correctly three- and four-letter short vowel words.

◆ Composes fairly readable first drafts using appropriate parts of the writing process (some attention to planning, drafting, rereading for meaning, and some self-correction).

◆ Uses invented spelling/phonics-based knowledge to spell independently, when necessary.

◆ Shows spelling consciousness or sensitivity to conventional spelling.

◆ Uses basic punctuation and capitalization.

◆ Produces a variety of types of compositions (e.g., stories, descriptions, journal entries), showing appropriate relationships between printed text, illustrations, and other graphics.

◆ Engages in a variety of literary activities voluntarily (e.g., choosing books and stories to read, writing a note to a friend).

Second-Grade Accomplishments

◆ Reads and comprehends both fiction and nonfiction that is appropriately designed for grade level.

◆ Accurately decodes orthographically regular multisyllable words and nonsense words (e.g., capital, Kalamazoo).

◆ Uses knowledge of print-sound mappings to sound out unknown words.

◆ Accurately reads many irregularly spelled words and such spelling patterns as diphthongs, special vowel spellings, and common word endings.

◆ Reads and comprehends both fiction and nonfiction that is appropriately designed for grade level.

◆ Shows evidence of expanding language repertory, including increasing use of more formal language registers.

◆ Reads voluntarily for interest and own purposes.

◆ Rereads sentences when meaning is not clear.

◆ Interprets information from diagrams, charts, and graphs.

◆ Recalls facts and details of texts.

◆ Reads nonfiction materials for answers to specific questions or for specific purposes.

◆ Takes part in creative responses to texts such as dramatizations, oral presentations, fantasy play, etc.

◆ Discusses similarities in characters and events across stories.

◆ Connects and compares information across nonfiction selections.

◆ Poses possible answers to how, why, and what-if questions.

◆ Correctly spells previously studied words and spelling patterns in own writing.

◆ Represents the complete sound of a word when spelling independently.

◆ Shows sensitivity to using formal language patterns in place of oral language patterns at appropriate spots in own writing (e.g., decontextualizing sentences, conventions for quoted speech, literary language forms, proper verb forms).

◆ Makes reasonable judgments about what to include in written products.

◆ Productively discusses ways to clarify and refine writing of own and others.

◆ With assistance, adds use of conferencing, revision, and editing processes to clarify and refine own writing to the steps of the expected parts of the writing process.

◆ Given organizational help, writes informative well-structured reports.

◆ Attends to spelling, mechanics, and presentation for final products.

◆ Produces a variety of types of compositions (e.g., stories, reports, correspondence).

Third-Grade Accomplishments

◆ Reads aloud with fluency and comprehension any text that is appropriately designed for grade level.

◆ Uses letter-sound correspondence knowledge and structural analysis to decode words.

◆ Reads and comprehends both fiction and nonfiction that is appropriately designed for grade level.

◆ Reads longer fictional selections and chapter books independently.

◆ Takes part in creative responses to texts such as dramatizations, oral presentations, fantasy play, etc.

◆ Can point to or clearly identify specific words or wordings that are causing comprehension difficulties.

◆ Summarizes major points from fiction and nonfiction texts.

◆ In interpreting fiction, discusses underlying theme or message.

◆ Asks how, why, and what-if questions in interpreting nonfiction texts.

◆ In interpreting nonfiction, distinguishes cause and effect, fact and opinion, main idea and supporting details.

◆ Uses information and reasoning to examine bases of hypotheses and opinions.

◆ Infers word meanings from taught roots, prefixes, and suffixes.

◆ Correctly spells previously studied words and spelling patterns in own writing.

◆ Begins to incorporate literacy words and language patterns in own writing (e.g., elaborates descriptions, uses figurative wording).

◆ With some guidance, uses all aspects of the writing process in producing own compositions and reports.

◆ Combines information from multiple sources in writing reports.

◆ With assistance, suggests and implements editing and revision to clarify and refine own writing.

◆ Presents and discusses own writing with other students and responds helpfully to other students' compositions.

◆ Independently reviews work for spelling, mechanics, and presentation.

◆ Produces a variety of written works (e.g., literature responses, reports, "published" books, semantic maps) in a variety of formats, including multimedia forms.

Source: From *Preventing Reading Difficulties in Young Children,* edited by C. E. Snow, S. M. Burns, and P. Griffin. Copyright © 1998, National Academy Press. Reprinted by permission.

D

Trade Books That Repeat Phonic Elements

Short A

Flack, Marjorie. *Angus and the Cat.* Doubleday, 1931.

Griffith, Helen. *Alex and the Cat.* Greenwillow, 1982.

Kent, Jack. *The Fat Cat.* Scholastic, 1971.

Most, Bernard. *There's an Ant in Anthony.* William Morrow, 1980.

Nodset, Joan. *Who Took the Farmer's Hat?* Harper & Row, 1963.

Robins, Joan. *Addie Meets Max.* Harper & Row, 1985.

Schmidt, Karen. *The Gingerbread Man.* Scholastic, 1985.

Seuss, Dr. *The Cat in the Hat.* Random House, 1957.

Long A

Aardema, Verna. *Bringing the Rain to Kapiti Plain.* Dial, 1981.

Bang, Molly. *The Paper Crane.* Greenwillow, 1985.

Blume, Judy. *The Pain and the Great One.* Bradbury, 1974.

Byars, Betsy. *The Lace Snail.* Viking, 1975.

Henkes, Kevin. *Sheila Rae, the Brave.* Greenwillow, 1987.

Hines, Anna G. *Taste the Raindrops.* Greenwillow, 1983.

Short and Long A

Aliki. *Jack and Jake.* Greenwillow, 1986.

Slobodkina, Esphyr. *Caps for Sale.* Addison-Wesley, 1940.

Short E

Ets, Marie Hall. *Elephant in a Well.* Viking, 1972.

Galdone, Paul. *The Little Red Hen.* Scholastic, 1973.

Ness, Evaline. *Yeck Eck.* E.P. Dutton, 1974.

Shecter, Ben. *Hester the Jester.* Harper & Row, 1977.

Thayer, Jane. *I Don't Believe in Elves.* William Morrow, 1975.

Wing, Henry Ritchet. *Ten Pennies for Candy.* Holt, Rinehart & Winston, 1963.

Long E

Galdone, Paul. *Little Bo-Peep.* Clarion/Ticknor & Fields, 1986.

Keller, Holly. *Ten Sleepy Sheep.* Greenwillow, 1983.

Martin, Bill. *Brown Bear, Brown Bear, What Do You See?* Henry Holt, 1967.

Oppenheim, Joanne. *Have You Seen Trees?* Young Scott Books, 1967.

Soule, Jean C. *Never Tease a Weasel.* Parents' Magazine Press, 1964.

Thomas, Patricia. *"Stand Back," said the Elephant, "I'm Going to Sneeze!"* Lothrop, Lee & Shepard, 1971.

Short I

Browne, Anthony, *Willy the Wimp.* Alfred A. Knopf, 1984.

Ets, Marie Hall. *Gilberto and the Wind.* Viking, 1966.

Hutchins, Pat. *Titch.* Macmillan, 1971.

Keats, Ezra Jack. *Whistle for Willie.* Viking, 1964.

Lewis, Thomas P. *Call for Mr. Sniff.* Harper & Row, 1981.

Lobel, Arnold. *Small Pig.* Harper & Row, 1969.

McPhail, David. *Fix-it.* E. P. Dutton, 1984.

Patrick, Gloria. *This Is* . . . Carolrhoda, 1970.

Robins, Joan. *My Brother, Will.* Greenwillow, 1986.

Long I

Berenstain, Stan and Jan. *The Bike Lesson.* Random House, 1964.

Cameron, John. *If Mice Could Fly.* Atheneum, 1979.

Cole, Sheila. *When the Tide Is Low.* Lothrop, Lee & Shepard, 1985.

Gelman, Rita. *Why Can't I Fly?* Scholastic, 1976.

Hazen, Barbara S. *Tight Times.* Viking, 1979.

Short O

Benchley, Nathaniel. *Oscar Otter.* Harper & Row, 1966.

Dunrea, Olivier. *Mogwogs on the March!* Holiday House, 1985.

Emberley, Barbara. *Drummer Hoff.* Prentice-Hall, 1967.

McKissack, Patricia C. *Flossie & the Fox.* Dial, 1986.

Miller, Patricia, and Iran Seligman. *Big Frogs, Little Frogs.* Holt, Rinehart & Winston, 1963.

Rice, Eve. "The Frog and the Ox" from *Once in a Wood.* Greenwillow, 1979.

Seuss, Dr. *Fox in Socks.* Random House, 1965.

Long O

Cole, Brock. *The Giant's Toe.* Farrar, Straus, & Giroux, 1986.

Gerstein, Mordicai. *Roll Over!* Crown, 1984.

Johnston, Tony. *The Adventures of Mole and Troll.* G. P. Putnam's Sons, 1972.

Johnston, Tony. *Night Noises and Other Mole and Troll Stories.* G. P. Putnam's Sons, 1977.

Shulevitz, Uri. *One Monday Morning.* Charles Scribner's Sons, 1967.

Tresselt, Alvin. *White Snow, Bright Snow.* Lothrop, Lee & Shepard, 1947.

Short U

Carroll, Ruth. *Where's the Bunny?* Henry Z. Walck, 1950.

Cooney, Nancy E. *Donald Says Thumbs Down.* G. P. Putnam's Sons, 1987.

Friskey, Margaret. *Seven Little Ducks.* Children's Press, 1940.

Lorenz, Lee. *Big Gus and Little Gus.* Prentice-Hall, 1982.

Marshall, James. *The Cut-Ups.* Viking Kestrel, 1984.

Udry, Janice May. *Thump and Plunk.* Harper & Row, 1981.

Yashima, Taro. *Umbrella.* Viking Penguin, 1958.

Long U

Lobel, Anita. *The Troll Music.* Harper & Row, 1966.

Segal, Lore. *Tell Me a Trudy.* Farrar, Straus, & Giroux, 1977.

Slobodkin, Louis. *"Excuse Me—Certainly!"* Vanguard Press, 1959.

Source: From "Using Children's Literature to Enhance Phonics Instruction," by P. Trachtenburg, *The Reading Teacher, 43,* pp. 648–653. Copyright © 1990. Reprinted by permission of the International Reading Association.

E

Story Frame Example

Story Summary with One Character Included

Our story is about _____

_____. _____ is an

important character in our story. _____

tried to _____ .

The story ends when _____

_____ .

IMPORTANT IDEA OR PLOT

In this story the problem starts when _____

_____ . After that,

_____ .

Next, _____

_____ . Then, _____

_____ . The problem is finally

solved when _____

_____ . The story ends _____

_____ .

SETTING

This story takes place _____

_____ . I know this because the

author uses the words " _____

_____ ." Other clues that

show when the story takes place are _____

_____ .

(Continued)

Story Summary with One Character Included (Continued)

CHARACTER ANALYSIS

_____ is an important character

in our story. _____ is important because

_____ . Once, he/she

_____ . Another time,

_____ . I think that

_____ is _____
(character's name)   (character trait)

because _____ .

Character Comparison

_____ and _____ are two

characters in our story. _____
                                                    (character's name)

is _____ while
                        (trait)

_____ is _____ .
(other character's name)   (trait)

For instance, _____ tries to _____

_____ and _____ tries to _____

_____ . _____ learns a

lesson when _____

_____ .

F

Annotated Bibliography of Read-Aloud Books for Developing Phonemic Awareness

Brown, M. W. (1993). *Four fur feet.* New York: Doubleday.

In this simple book, the reader is drawn to the /f/ sound as the phrase "four fur feet" is repeated in every sentence as a furry animal walks around the world. The same pattern is used throughout the story as we see four fur feet walk along the river, into the country, and so forth. The book must be turned around as the animal makes its way around the world.

Buller, J., & Schade, S. (1988). *I love you, good night.* New York: Simon and Schuster.

A mother and child tell each other how much they love one another. When the child says she loves her mother as much as "blueberry pancakes," the mother responds that she loves her child as much as "milkshakes." The child says she loves the mother as much as "frogs love flies," to which the mother responds she loves her child as much as "pigs love pies." The two go back and forth in this manner until "good night" is said. The rhyme invites the listener to participate and continue the story.

Cameron, P. (1961). *"I can't," said the ant.* New York: Coward-McCann.

Household items discuss the fall of a teapot from the counter in a kitchen and the means by which to put it back. In a series of brief contributions to the conversation, each item says something that rhymes with its own name. "'Don't break her,' said the shaker" and "'I can't bear it,' said the carrot."

Carle, E. (1974). *All about Arthur (an absolutely absurd ape).* New York: Franklin Watts.

Arthur, an accordion-playing ape who lives in Atlanta, feels lonely and travels from Baltimore to Yonkers making friends. In each city he makes a friend whose name matches the initial sound of the city, from a banjo-playing bear in Baltimore to a young yak in Yonkers.

Carter, D. (1990). *More bugs in boxes.* New York: Simon and Schuster.

This pop-up book presents a series of questions and answers about make-believe bugs who are found inside a variety of boxes. Both the questions and answers make use of alliteration: "What kind of bug is in the rosy red rectangle box? A bright blue big-mouth bug." Following a similar pattern is the author's *Jingle* bugs (1992, Simon and Schuster), which has a Christmas theme and makes use of rhyme: "Who's in the chimney, warm and snug? Ho, ho, ho! It's Santa Bug!"

de Regniers, B., Moore, E., White, M., & Carr, J. (1988). *Sing a song of popcorn.* New York: Scholastic.

A number of poems in this book draw attention to rhyme and encourage children to experiment. Also included are poems that play with sounds within words. In "Galoshes" the author describes the slippery slush "as it slooshes and sloshes and splishes and sploshes" around a child's galoshes. In "Eletelephony" sounds are mixed up and substituted for one another: "Once there was an elephant, / Who tried to use the telephant. . . ."

Deming, A. G. (1994). *Who is tapping at my window?* New York: Penguin.

A young girl hears a tapping at her window and asks, "Who is there?" The farm animals each respond, "It's not I," and she discovers that it is the rain. The book is predictable in that each pair of animals rhymes. The loon responds, followed by the raccoon. The dog's response is followed by the frog's.

Ehlert, L. (1989). *Eating the alphabet: Fruits and vegetables from A to Z.* San Diego, CA: Harcourt Brace Jovanovich.

Fruits and vegetables are offered in print and pictures for each letter of the alphabet in this book. The following are displayed for B, for instance: blueberry, brussels sprout, bean, beet, broccoli, banana.

Emberley, B. (1992). *One wide river to cross.* Boston: Little, Brown.

This Caldecott Honor Book is an adaptation of the traditional African-American spiritual about Noah's ark. Through the use of rhyme, the author describes the animals gathering on board one by one (while "Japhelth played the big bass drum"), two by two ("The alligator lost his shoe"), and so on up to ten, when the rains begin.

Fortunata. (1968). *Catch a little fox.* New York: Scholastic.

A group of children talk about going hunting, identifying animals they will catch and where they will keep each one. A frog will be put in a log, a cat will be put in a hat, and so forth. The story concludes with the animals in turn capturing the children, putting them in a ring and listening to them sing. All are then released. The music is included in this book. A different version of this story that includes a brontosaurus (who is put in a chorus) and armadillo (who is put in a pillow) is J. Langstaff's (1974) *Oh, a-hunting we will go,* published by Atheneum, New York.

Galdone, P. (1968). *Henny Penny.* New York: Scholastic.

A hen becomes alarmed when an acorn hits her on the head. She believes the sky is falling, and on her way to inform the king she meets several animals who join her until they are all eaten by Foxy Loxy. This classic story is included here because of the amusing rhyming names of the animals. A recent release of this story is S. Kellogg's *Chicken Little* (1985), published by Mulberry Books, New York.

Geraghty, P. (1992). *Stop that noise!* New York: Crown.

A mouse is annoyed with the many sounds of the forest and implores the cicada to stop its "zee-zee-zee-zee," the frog to stop its "woopoo," until it hears far more disturbing sounds—the "Br-rrm" and "Crrrrr RACKA-DACKA-RACKA-SHOONG" of a bulldozer felling trees. The presentation of animal and machine sounds makes this book useful in drawing attention to the sounds in our language.

Gordon, J. (1991). *Six sleepy sheep.* New York: Puffin Books.

Six sheep try to fall asleep by slurping celery soup, telling spooky stories, singing songs, sipping simmered milk, and so on. The use of the /s/ sound, prevalent throughout, amuses listeners as they anticipate the sheep's antics.

Hague, K. (1984). *Alphabears.* New York: Henry Holt.

In this beautifully illustrated book, 26 teddy bears introduce the alphabet and make use of alliteration. Teddy bear John loves jam and jelly. Quimbly is a quilted bear, and Pam likes popcorn and pink lemonade.

Hawkins, C., & Hawkins, J. (1986). *Tog the dog*. New York: G. P. Putnam's Sons.

This book tells the story of Tog the dog who likes to jog, gets lost in the fog, falls into a bog, and so forth. With the exception of the final page, where the letters *og* appear in large type, the pages in the book are not full width. As the reader turns the narrower pages throughout the text a new letter appears and lines up with the *og* so that when Tog falls into the bog, for example, a large letter *b* lines up with *og* to make the word *bog*. This is a great book for both developing phonemic awareness and pointing out a spelling pattern. Also by the authors are *Jen the hen* (1985), *Mig the pig* (1984), and *Pat the cat* (1993), all published by G. P. Putnam's Sons.

Hymes, L., & Hymes, J. (1964). *Oodles of noodles*. New York: Young Scott Books.

Several of the poems in this collection make use of nonsense words in order to complete a rhyme. In "Oodles of Noodles," the speaker requests oodles of noodles because they are favorite foodles. In "Spinach," the authors list a series of words each beginning with the /sp/ sound until they finally end with the word "spinach." Words include "spin," "span," "spun," and "spoony." Many of the poems point out spelling patterns that will be entertaining with an older audience.

Krauss, R. (1985). *I can fly*. New York: Golden Press.

In this simple book, a child imitates the actions of a variety of animals. "A cow can moo. I can too." "I can squirm like a worm." The rhyming element combined with the charm of the child's imaginative play makes the story engaging. On the final page, nonsense words that rhyme are used, encouraging listeners to experiment with sounds themselves: "Gubble gubble gubble I'm a mubble in a pubble."

Kuskin, K. (1990). *Roar and more*. New York: HarperTrophy.

This book includes many poems and pictures that portray the sounds that animals make. Both the use of rhyme and presentation of animal sounds ("Ssnnaaaarrll" for the tiger, "Hsssssss . . ." for the snake) draw children's attention to sounds. An earlier edition of this book won the 1979 NCTE Award for Excellence in Poetry for Children.

Lewison, W. (1992). *Buzz said the bee*. New York: Scholastic.

A series of animals sit on top of one another in this story. Before each animal climbs on top of the next, it does something that rhymes with the animal it approaches. For instance, the hen dances a jig before sitting on the pig. The pig takes a bow before sitting on the cow.

Martin, B. (1974). *Sounds of a powwow*. New York: Holt, Rinehart & Winston.

Included in this volume is the song "K-K-K-Katy" in which the first consonant of several words is isolated and repeated, as is the song title.

Marzollo, J. (1989). *The teddy bear book*. New York: Dial.

Poems about teddy bears adapted from songs, jump rope rhymes, ball bouncing chants, cheers, and story poems are presented. Use of rhyme is considerable, from the well known, "Teddy bear, teddy bear, turn around, Teddy bear, teddy bear, touch the ground" to the less familiar, "Did you ever, ever, ever in your teddy bear life see a teddy bear dance with his wife?" and the response, "No I never, never, never . . ." Play with sounds is obvious in the poem "Teddy Boo and Teddy Bear" where the author says, "Icabocker, icabocker, icabocker, boo! Icabocker, soda cracker, phooey on you!"

Obligado, L, (1983). *Faint frogs feeling feverish and other terrifically tantalizing tongue twisters*. New York: Viking.

For each letter of the alphabet, one or more tongue twisters using alliteration is presented in print and with humorous illustrations. *S* has smiling snakes sipping strawberry sodas, a shy spider spinning, and a swordfish sawing. *T* presents two toucans tying ties, turtles tasting tea, and tigers trying trousers.

Ochs, C. P. (1991). *Moose on the loose*. Minneapolis, MN: Carolrhoda Books.

A moose escapes from the zoo in the town of Zown and at the same time a chartreuse caboose disappears. The zookeeper runs throughout the town asking citizens if they've seen a "moose on the loose in a chartreuse caboose." No one has seen the moose but each has seen a different animal. Included among the many citizens is Ms. Cook who saw a pig wearing a wig, Mr. Wu who saw a weasel paint at an easel, and Mrs. Case who saw a skunk filling a trunk. Each joins in the search.

Otto, C. (1991). *Dinosaur chase.* New York: HarperTrophy.
A mother dinosaur reads her young one a story about dinosaurs in which "dinosaur crawl, dinosaur creep, tiptoe dinosaur, dinosaur seek." Both alliteration and rhyme are present in this simple, colorful book.

Parry, C. (1991). *Zoomerang-a-boomerang: Poems to make your belly laugh.* New York: Puffin Books.
Nearly all of the poems in this collection play with language, particularly through the use of predictable and humorous rhyme patterns. In "Oh my, no more pie," the meat's too red, so the writer has some bread. When the bread is too brown, the writer goes to town, and so forth. In "What they said," each of 12 animals says something that rhymes with its name. For instance, a pup says, "Let's wake up," and a lark says, "It's still dark."

Patz, N. (1983). *Moses supposes his toeses are roses.* San Diego, CA: Harcourt Brace Jovanovich.
Seven rhymes are presented here, each of which plays on language to engage the listener. Rhyme is predictable in "Sweetie Maguire" when she shouts "Fire! Fire!" and Mrs. O'Hair says, "Where? Where?" Alliteration makes "Betty Botter" a tongue twister: "But a bit of better butter—that will make my batter better!" Assonance adds humor to "The tooter" when the tooter tries to tutor two tooters to toot!

Pomerantz, C. (1993). *If I had a paka.* New York: Mulberry.
Eleven languages are represented among the 12 poems included in this volume. The author manipulates words as in "You take the blueberry, I'll take the dewberry. You don't want the blueberry, OK take the bayberry. . . ." Many berries are mentioned, including a novel one, the "chuckleberry." Attention is drawn to phonemes when languages other than English are introduced. The Vietnamese translation of the following draws attention to rhyme and repetition: I like fish, Toy tik ka; I like chicken, Toy tik ga; I like duck, Toy tik veet; I like meat, Toy tik teet.

Prelutsky, J. (1982). *The baby Uggs are hatching.* New York: Mulberry.
Twelve poems describe unusual creatures such as the sneepies, the smasheroo, and the numpy-numpy-numpity. Although some of the vocabulary is advanced (the Quossible has an irascible temper), most of the poems will be enjoyed by young children who will delight in the humorous use of words and sounds. For instance, "The Sneezysnoozer sneezes in a dozen sneezy sizes, it sneezes little breezes and it sneezes big surprises."

Prelutsky, J. (1989). *Poems of A. Nonny Mouse.* New York: Alfred A. Knopf.
A Nonny Mouse finally gets credit for all her works that were previously attributed to "Anonymous" in this humorous selection of poems that is appropriate for all ages. Of particular interest for developing phonemic awareness are poems such as "How much wood would a woodchuck chuck" and "Betty Botter bought some butter."

Provenson, A., & Provenson, M. (1977). *Old Mother Hubbard.* New York: Random House.
In this traditional rhyme, Old Mother Hubbard runs errand after errand for her dog. When she comes back from buying him a wig, she finds him dancing a jig. When she returns from buying him shoes, she finds him reading the news.

Raffi. (1987). *Down by the bay.* New York: Crown.
Two young children try to outdo one another in making up rhymes with questions like, "Did you ever see a goose kissing a moose?" and "Did you ever see a bear combing his hair?" Music is included.

Raffi. (1989). *Tingalayo.* New York: Crown.
Here the reader meets a man who calls for his donkey, Tingalayo, and describes its antics through the use of rhyme and rhythm. Phrases such as "Me donkey dance, me donkey sing, me

donkey wearin' a diamond ring" will make children laugh, and they will easily contribute additional verses to this song/story.

Sendak, M. (1990). *Alligators all around: An alphabet.* New York: HarperTrophy.

Using alliteration for each letter of the alphabet, Sendak introduces the reader to the alphabet with the help of alligators who have headaches (for *H*) and keep kangaroos (for *K*).

Shaw, N. (1989). *Sheep on a ship.* Boston: Houghton Mifflin.

Sheep sailing on a ship run into trouble when facing a sudden storm. This entertaining story makes use of rhyme (waves lap and sails flap), alliteration (sheep on a ship), and assonance ("It rains and hails and shakes the sails").

Showers, P. (1991). *The listening walk.* New York: HarperTrophy.

A little girl and her father go for a walk with their dog, and the listener is treated to the variety of sounds they hear while walking. These include "thhhhh . . . ," the steady whisper sound of some sprinklers, and "whithh whithh," the sound of other sprinklers that turn around and around. Some phonemes are elongated as in "eeeeeeeyowwwoooo . . . ," the sound of a jet overhead. Some phonemes are substituted as in "bik bok bik bok," the sounds of high heels on the pavement.

Silverstein, S. (1964). *A giraffe and a half.* New York: Harper and Row.

Using cumulative and rhyming patterns, Silverstein builds the story of a giraffe who has a rose on his nose, a bee on his knee, some glue on his shoe, and so on until he undoes the story by reversing the events.

Staines, B. (1989). *All God's critters got a place in the choir.* New York: Penguin.

This lively book makes use of rhyme to tell of the places that numerous animals (an ox and a fox, a grizzly bear, a possum and a porcupine, bullfrogs) have in the world's choir. "Some sing low, some sing higher, some sing out loud on the telephone wire."

Seuss, Dr. (1963). *Dr. Seuss's ABC.* New York: Random House.

Each letter of the alphabet is presented along with an amusing sentence in which nearly all of the words begin with the targeted letter. "Many mumbling mice are making midnight music in the moonlight . . . mighty nice."

Seuss, Dr. (1965). *Fox in socks.* New York: Random House.

Before beginning this book, the reader is warned to take the book slowly because the fox will try to get the reader's tongue in trouble. Language play is the obvious focus of this book. Assonance patterns occur throughout, and the listener is exposed to vowel sound changes when beetles battle, ducks like lakes, and ticks and clocks get mixed up with the chicks and tocks.

Seuss, Dr. (1974). *There's a wocket in my pocket.* New York: Random House.

A child talks about the creatures he has found around the house. These include a "nooth grush on my tooth brush" and a "zamp in the lamp." The initial sounds of common household objects are substituted with other sounds to make the nonsense creatures in this wonderful example of play with language.

Tallon, R. (1979). *Zoophabets.* New York: Scholastic.

Letter by letter the author names a fictional animal and, in list form, tells where it lives and what it eats. All, of course, begin with the targeted letter. "Runk" lives in "rain barrels" and eats "raindrops, rusty rainbows, ripped rubbers, raincoats, rhubarb."

Van Allsburg, C. *The Z was zapped.* Boston: Houghton Mifflin.

A series of mishaps befall the letters of the alphabet. *A* is crushed by an avalanche, *B* is badly bitten, *C* is cut to ribbons, and so forth. Other alphabet books using alliteration include G. Base's *Animalia* (1987), published by Harry N. Abrams, K. Greenaway's (1993) *A apple pie,* published by Derrydale, and J. Patience's (1993) *An amazing alphabet,* published by Random House.

Winthrop, E. (1986). *Shoes*. New York: HarperTrophy.

> This rhyming book surveys familiar and some not-so-familiar types of shoes. The book begins, "There are shoes to buckle, shoes to tie, shoes too low, and shoes too high." Later we discover, "Shoes for fishing, shoes for wishing, rubber shoes for muddy squishing." The rhythm and rhyme invite participation and creative contributions.

Zemach, M. (1976). *Hush, little baby*. New York: E. P. Dutton.

> In this lullaby, parents attempt to console a crying baby by promising a number of outrageous things including a mockingbird, a diamond ring, a billy goat, and a cart and bull. The verse is set to rhyme, e.g., "If that cart and bull turn over, Poppa's gonna buy you a dog named Rover," and children can easily innovate on the rhyme and contribute to the list of items being promised.

From "Read-Aloud Books for Developing Phonemic Awareness," by H. K. Yopp, *The Reading Teacher, 48,* pp. 538–542. Copyright 1995. Reprinted with permission from the International Reading Association and the author.

G
Children's Book Awards

NEWBERY MEDAL

Named in honor of John Newbery (1713–1767), the first English publisher of children's books, this medal has been given annually since 1922 by the American Library Association's Association for Library Service to Children. The recipient is recognized as the author of the most distinguished book in children's literature published in the United States in the preceding year. The award is limited to citizens or residents of the United States.

1922 *The Story of Mankind*, by Hendrik Willem van Loon
Honor Books: *The Great Quest*, by Charles Hawes; *Cedric the Forester*, by Bernard Marshall; *The Old Tobacco Shop*, by William Bowen; *The Golden Fleece and the Heroes Who Lived Before Achilles*, by Padraic Colum; *Windy Hill*, by Cornelia Meigs

1923 *The Voyages of Doctor Dolittle*, by Hugh Lofting
Honor Books: None

1924 *The Dark Frigate*, by Charles Hawes
Honor Books: None

1925 *Tales from Silver Lands*, by Charles Finger
Honor Books: *Nicholas*, by Anne Carroll Moore; *Dream Coach*, by Anne Parrish

1926 *Shen of the Sea*, by Arthur Bowie Christman
Honor Book: *Voyagers*, by Padraic Colum

1927 *Smoky, the Cowhorse*, by Will James
Honor Books: None

1928 *Gayneck, the Story of a Pigeon*, by Dhan Gopal Mukerji
Honor Books: *The Wonder Smith and His Son*, by Ella Young; *Downright Dencey*, by Caroline Snedeker

1929 *The Trumpeter of Krakow*, by Eric P. Kelly
Honor Books: *Pigtail of Ah Lee Ben Loo*, by John Bennett; *Millions of Cats*, by Wanda Gág; *The Boy Who Was*, by Grace Hallock; *Clearing Weather*, by Cornelia Meigs; *Runaway Papoose*, by Grace Moon; *Tod of the Fens*, by Elinor Whitney

1930   *Hitty: Her First Hundred Years,* by Rachel Field
Honor Books: *Daughter of the Seine,* by Jeanette Eaton; *Pran of Albania,* by Elizabeth Miller; *Jumping-Off Place,* by Marian Hurd McNeely; *Tangle-Coated Horse and Other Tales,* by Ella Young; *Vaino,* by Julia Davis Adams; *Little Blacknose,* by Hildegarde Swift

1931   *The Cat Who Went to Heaven,* by Elizabeth Coatsworth
Honor Books: *Floating Island,* by Anne Parrish; *The Dark Star of Itza,* by Alida Malkus; *Queer Person,* by Ralph Hubbard; *Mountains Are Free,* by Julia Davis Adams; *Spice and the Devil's Cave,* by Agnes Hewes; *Meggy Macintosh,* by Elizabeth Janet Gray; *Garram the Hunter,* by Herbert Best; *Ood-Le-Uk the Wanderer,* by Alice Lide and Margaret Johansen

1932   *Waterless Mountain,* by Laura Adams Armer
Honor Books: *The Fairy Circus,* by Dorothy P. Lathrop; *Calico Bush,* by Rachel Field; *Boy of the South Seas,* by Eunice Tietjens; *Out of the Flame,* by Eloise Lownsbery; *Jane's Island,* by Marjorie Allee; *Truce of the Wolf and Other Tales of Old Italy,* by Mary Gould Davis

1933   *Young Fu of the Upper Yangtze,* by Elizabeth Foreman Lewis
Honor Books: *Swift Rivers,* by Cornelia Meigs; *The Railroad to Freedom,* by Hildegarde Swift; *Children of the Soil,* by Nora Burglon

1934   *Invincible Louisa,* by Cornelia Meigs
Honor Books: *The Forgotten Daughter,* by Caroline Snedeker; *Swords of Steel,* by Elsie Singmaster; *ABC Bunny,* by Wanda Gág; *Winged Girl of Knossos,* by Erik Berry; *New Land,* by Sarah Schmidt; *Big Tree of Bunlahy,* by Padraic Colum; *Glory of the Seas,* by Agnes Hewes; *Apprentice of Florence,* by Anne Kyle

1935   *Dobry,* by Monica Shannon
Honor Books: *Pageant of Chinese History,* by Elizabeth Seeger; *Davy Crockett,* by Constance Rourke; *Day on Skates,* by Hilda Van Stockum

1936   *Caddie Woodlawn,* Carol Brink
Honor Books: *Honk, the Moose,* by Phil Stong; *The Good Master,* by Kate Seredy; *Young Walter Scott,* by Elizabeth Janet Gray; *All Sail Set,* by Armstrong Sperry

1937   *Roller Skates,* by Ruth Sawyer
Honor Books: *Phebe Fairchild: Her Book,* by Lois Lenski; *Whistler's Van,* by Idwal Jones; *Golden Basket,* by Ludwig Bemelmans; *Winterbound,* by Margery Bianco; *Audubon,* by Constance Rourke; *The Codfish Musket,* by Agnes Hewes

1938   *The White Stag,* by Kate Seredy
Honor Books: *Pecos Bill,* by James Cloyd Bowman; *Bright Island,* by Mabel Robinson; *On the Banks of Plum Creek,* by Laura Ingalls Wilder

1939   *Thimble Summer,* by Elizabeth Enright
Honor Books: *Nino,* by Valenti Angelo; *Mr. Popper's Penguins,* by Richard and Florence Atwater; *"Hello the Boat!"* by Phillis Crawford; *Leader by Destiny: George Washington, Man and Patriot,* by Jeanette Eaton; *Penn,* by Elizabeth Janet Gray

1940   *Daniel Boone*, by James Daugherty
        Honor Books: *The Singing Tree*, by Kate Seredy; *Runner of the Mountain Tops*, by
        Mabel Robinson; *By the Shores of Silver Lake*, by Laura Ingalls Wilder; *Boy with a
        Pack*, by Stephen W. Meader

1941   *Call It Courage*, by Armstrong Sperry
        Honor Books: *Blue Willow*, by Doris Gates; *Young Mac of Fort Vancouver*, by Mary
        Jane Carr; *The Long Winter*, by Laura Ingalls Wilder; *Nansen*, by Anna Gertrude
        Hall

1942   *The Matchlock Gun*, by Walter D. Edmonds
        Honor Books: *Little Town on the Prairie*, by Laura Ingalls Wilder; *George Washing-
        ton's World*, by Genevieve Foster; *Indian Captive: The Story of Mary Jemison*, by
        Lois Lenski; *Down Ryton Water*, by Eva Roe Gaggin

1943   *Adam of the Road*, by Elizabeth Janet Gray
        Honor Books: *The Middle Moffat*, by Eleanor Estes; *Have You Seen Tom Thumb?*
        by Mabel Leigh Hunt

1944   *Johnny Tremain*, by Esther Forbes
        Honor Books: *These Happy Golden Years*, by Laura Ingalls Wilder; *Fog Magic*, by
        Julia Sauer; *Rufus M.*, by Eleanor Estes; *Mountain Born*, by Elizabeth Yates

1945   *Rabbit Hill*, by Robert Lawson
        Honor Books: *The Hundred Dressed*, by Eleanor Estes; *The Silver Pencil*, by Alice
        Dalgliesh; *Abraham Lincoln's World*, by Genevieve Foster; *Lone Journey: The Life of
        Roger Williams*, by Jeanette Eaton

1946   *Strawberry Girl*, by Lois Lenski
        Honor Books: *Justin Morgan Had a Horse*, by Marguerite Henry; *The Moved-Out-
        ers*, by Florence Crannell Means; *Bhimsa, the Dancing Bear*, by Christine Weston;
        New Found World, by Katherine Shippen

1947   *Miss Hickory*, by Carolyn Sherwin Bailey
        Honor Books: *Wonderful Year*, by Nancy Barnes; *Big Tree*, by Mary and Conrad
        Buff; *The Heavenly Tenants*, by William Maxwell; *The Avion My Uncle Flew*, by
        Cyrus Fisher; *The Hidden Treasure of Glaston*, by Eleanore Jewett

1948   *The Twenty-One Balloons*, by William Pène du Bois
        Honor Books: *Pancakes-Paris*, by Claire Huchet Bishop; *Li Lun, Lad of Courage*,
        by Carolyn Treffinger; *The Quaint and Curious Quest of Johnny Longfoot*, by
        Catherine Besterman; *The Cow-Tail Switch, and Other West African Stories*, by
        Harold Courlander; *Misty of Chincoteague*, by Marguerite Henry

1949   *King of the Wind*, by Marguerite Henry
        Honor Books: *Seabird*, by Holling C. Holling; *Daughter of the Mountains*, by
        Louise Rankin; *My Father's Dragon*, by Ruth S. Gannett; *Story of the Negro*, by
        Arna Bontemps

1950   *The Door in the Wall*, by Marguerite de Angeli
Honor Books: *Tree of Freedom*, by Rebecca Caudill; *The Blue Cat of Castle Town*, by Catherine Coblentz; *Kildee House*, by Rutherford Montgomery; *George Washington*, by Genevieve Foster; *Song of the Pines*, by Walter and Marion Havighurst

1951   *Amos Fortune, Free Man*, by Elizabeth Yates
Honor Books: *Better Known as Johnny Appleseed*, by Mabel Leigh Hunt; *Gandhi, Fighter Without a Sword*, by Jeanette Eaton; *Abraham Lincoln, Friend of the People*, by Clara Ingram Judson; *The Story of Appleby Capple*, by Anne Parrish

1952   *Ginger Pye*, by Eleanor Estes
Honor Books: *Americans Before Columbus*, by Elizabeth Baity; *Minn of the Mississippi*, by Holling C. Holling; *The Defender*, by Nicholas Kalashnikoff; *The Light at Tern Rock*, by Julia Sauer; *The Apple and the Arrow*, by Mary and Conrad Buff

1953   *Secret of the Andes*, by Ann Nolan Clark
Honor Books: *Charlotte's Web*, by E. B. White; *Moccasin Trail*, by Eloise McGraw; *Red Sails to Capri*, by Ann Weil; *The Bears of Hemlock Mountain*, by Alice Dalgliesh; *Birthdays of Freedom*, Vol. 1, by Genevieve Foster

1954   *. . . and Now Miguel*, by Joseph Krumgold
Honor Books: *All Alone*, by Claire Huchet Bishop; *Shadrach*, by Meindert De Jong; *Hurry Home Candy*, by Meindert De Jong; *Theodore Roosevelt, Fighting Patriot*, by Clara Ingram Judson; *Magic Maize*, by Mary and Conrad Buff

1955   *The Wheel on the School*, by Meindert De Jong
Honor Books: *The Courage of Sarah Noble*, by Alice Dalgliesh; *Banner in the Sky*, by James Ullman

1956   *Carry On, Mr. Bowditch*, by Jean Lee Latham
Honor Books: *The Secret River*, by Marjorie Kinnan Rawlings; *The Golden Name Day*, by Jennie Lindquist; *Men, Microscopes, and Living Things*, by Katherine Shippen

1957   *Miracles on Maple Hill*, by Virginia Sorensen
Honor Books; *Old Yeller*, by Fred Gipson; *The House of Sixty Fathers*, by Meindert De Jong; *Mr. Justice Holmes*, by Clara Ingram Judson; *The Corn Grows Ripe*, by Dorothy Rhoads; *Black Fox of Lorne*, by Marguerite de Angeli

1958   *Rifles for Watie*, by Harold Keith
Honor Books: *The Horsecatcher*, by Mari Sandoz; *Gone-Away Lake*, by Elizabeth Enright; *The Great Wheel*, by Robert Lawson; *Tom Paine, Freedom's Apostle*, by Leo Gurko

1959   *The Witch of Blackbird Pond*, by Elizabeth George Speare
Honor Books: *The Family Under the Bridge*, by Natalie S. Carlson; *Along Came a Dog*, by Meindert De Jong; *Chucaro: Wild Pony of the Pampa*, by Francis Kalnay; *The Perilous Road*, by William O. Steele

1960   *Onion John*, by Joseph Krumgold
Honor Books: *My Side of the Mountain*, by Jean George; *America Is Born*, by Gerald W. Johnson; *The Gammage Cup*, by Carol Kendall

1961   *Island of the Blue Dolphins*, by Scott O'Dell
      Honor Books: *America Moves Forward*, by Gerald W. Johnson; *Old Ramon*, by Jack Schaefer; *The Cricket in Times Square*, by George Selden

1962   *The Bronze Bow*, by Elizabeth George Speare
      Honor Books: *Frontier Living*, by Edwin Tunis; *The Golden Goblet*, by Eloise McGraw; *Belling the Tiger*, by Mary Stolz

1963   *A Wrinkle in Time*, by Madeleine L'Engle
      Honor Books: *Thistle and Thyme*, by Sorche Nic Leodhas; *Men of Athens*, by Olivia Coolidge

1964   *It's Like This, Cat*, by Emily Cheney Neville
      Honor Books: *Rascal*, by Sterling North; *The Loner*, by Esther Wier

1965   *Shadow of a Bull*, by Maia Wojciechowska
      Honor Book: *Across Five Aprils*, by Irene Hunt

1966   *I, Juan de Pareja*, by Elizabeth Borten de Trevino
      Honor Books: *The Black Cauldron*, by Lloyd Alexander; *The Animal Family*, by Randall Jarrell; *The Noonday Friends*, by Mary Stolz

1967   *Up a Road Slowly*, by Irene Hunt
      Honor Books: *The King's Fifth*, by Scott O'Dell; *Zlateh the Goat and Other Stories*, by Isaac Bashevis Singer; *The Jazz Man*, by Mary H. Weik

1968   *From the Mixed-Up Files of Mrs. Basil E. Frankweiler*, by E. L. Konigsburg
      Honor Books: *Jennifer, Hecate, Macbeth, William McKinley, and Me, Elizabeth*, by E. L. Konigsburg; *The Black Pearl*, by Scott O'Dell; *The Fearsome Inn*, by Isaac Bashevis Singer; *The Egypt Game*, by Zilpha Keatley Snyder

1969   *The High King*, by Lloyd Alexander
      Honor Books: *To Be a Slave*, by Julius Lester; *When Shlemiel Went to Warsaw and Other Stories*, by Isaac Bashevis Singer

1970   *Sounder*, by William H. Armstrong
      Honor Books: *Our Eddie*, by Sulamith Ish-Kishor; *The Many Ways of Seeing: An Introduction to the Pleasures of Art*, by Janet Gaylord Moore; *Journey Outside*, by Mary Q. Steele

1971   *Summer of the Swans*, by Betsy Byars
      Honor Books: *Kneeknock Rise*, by Natalie Babbitt; *Enchantress from the Stars*, by Sylvia Louise Engdahl; *Sing Down the Moon*, by Scott O'Dell

1972   *Mrs. Frisby and the Rats of NIMH*, by Robert C. O'Brien
      Honor Books: *Incident at Hawk's Hill*, by Allan W. Eckert; *The Planet of Junior Brown*, by Virginia Hamilton; *The Tombs of Atuan*, by Ursula K. Le Guin; *Annie and the Old One*, by Miska Miles; *The Headless Cupid*, by Zilpha Keatley Snyder

1973   *Julie of the Wolves*, by Jean George
      Honor Books: *Frog and Toad Together*, by Arnold Lobel; *The Upstairs Room*, by Johanna Reiss; *The Witches of Worm*, by Zilpha Keatley Snyder

1974 *The Slave Dancer,* by Paula Fox
Honor Book: *The Dark Is Rising,* by Susan Cooper

1975 *M. C. Higgins, the Great,* by Virginia Hamilton
Honor Books: *Figgs and Phantoms,* by Ellen Raskin; *My Brother Sam Is Dead,* by James Lincoln Collier and Christopher Collier; *The Perilous Gard,* by Elizabeth Marie Pope; *Philip Hall Likes Me, I Reckon Maybe,* by Bette Greene

1976 *The Grey King,* by Susan Cooper
Honor Books: *The Hundred Penny Box,* by Sharon Bell Mathis; *Dragonwings,* by Laurence Yep

1977 *Roll of Thunder, Hear My Cry,* by Mildred D. Taylor
Honor Books: *Abel's Island,* by William Steig; *A String in the Harp,* by Nancy Bond

1978 *Bridge to Terabithia,* by Katherine Paterson
Honor Books: *Anpao: An American Indian Odyssey,* by Jamake Highwater; *Ramona and Her Father,* by Beverly Cleary

1979 *The Westing Game,* by Ellen Raskin
Honor Book: *The Great Gilly Hopkins,* by Katherine Paterson

1980 *A Gathering of Days: A New England Girl's Journal, 1830–32,* by Joan Blos
Honor Book: *The Road from Home: The Story of an Armenian Girl,* by David Kherdian

1981 *Jacob Have I Loved,* by Katherine Paterson
Honor Books: *The Fledgling,* by Jane Langton; *A Ring of Endless Light,* by Madeleine L'Engle

1982 *A Visit to William Blake's Inn: Poems for Innocent and Experienced Travelers,* by Nancy Willard
Honor Books: *Ramona Quimby, Age 8,* by Beverly Cleary; *Upon the Head of a Goat,* by Aranka Siegel

1983 *Dicey's Song,* by Cynthia Voigt
Honor Books: *The Blue Sword,* by Robin McKinley; *Dr. De Soto,* by William Steig; *Graven Images,* by Paul Fleischman; *Homesick: My Own Story,* by Jean Fritz; *Sweet Whispers, Brother Rush,* by Virginia Hamilton

1984 *Dear Mr. Henshaw,* by Beverly Cleary
Honor Books: *The Sign of the Beaver,* by Elizabeth George Speare; *A Solitary Blue,* by Cynthia Voigt; *Sugaring Time,* by Kathryn Lasky; *The Wish Giver,* by Bill Brittain

1985 *The Hero and the Crown,* by Robin McKinley
Honor Books: *Like Jake and Me,* by Mavis Jukes; *The Moves Make the Man,* by Bruce Brooks; *One-Eyed Cat,* by Paula Fox

1986 *Sarah, Plain and Tall,* by Patricia MacLachlan
Honor Books: *Commodore Perry in the Land of the Shogun,* by Rhoda Blumberg; *Dogsong,* by Gary Paulsen

1987   *The Whipping Boy*, by Sid Fleischman
Honor Books: *On My Honor*, by Marion Dane Bauer; *Volcano: The Eruption and Healing of Mount St. Helens*, by Patricia Lauber; *A Fine White Dust*, by Cynthia Rylant

1988   *Lincoln: A Photobiography*, by Russell Freedman
Honor Books: *After the Rain*, by Norma Fox Mazer; *Hatchet*, by Gary Paulsen

1989   *Joyful Noise: Poems for Two Voices*, by Paul Fleischman
Honor Books: *In the Beginning: Creation Stories from Around the World*, by Virginia Hamilton; *Scorpions*, by Walter Dean Myers

1990   *Number the Stars*, by Lois Lowry
Honor Books: *Afternoon of the Elves*, by Janet Taylor Lisle; *Shabanu: Daughter of the Wind*, by Suzanne Fisher Staples; *The Winter Room*, by Gary Paulsen

1991   *Maniac Magee*, by Jerry Spinelli
Honor Book: *The True Confessions of Charlotte Doyle*, by Avi

1992   *Shiloh*, by Phyllis Reynolds Naylor
Honor Books: *Nothing but the Truth*, by Avi; *The Wright Brothers: How They Invented the Airplane*, by Russell Freedman

1993   *Missing May*, by Cynthia Rylant
Honor Books: *The Dark Thirty: Southern Tales of the Supernatural*, by Patricia McKissack, ill. by Brian Pinkney; *Somewhere in the Darkness*, by Walter Dean Myers; *What Hearts*, by Bruce Brooks

1994   *The Giver*, by Lois Lowry
Honor Books: *Crazy Lady*, by Jane Leslie Conly; *Dragon's Gate*, by Lawrence Yep; *Eleanor Roosevelt: A Life of Discovery*, by Russell Freedman

1995   *Walk Two Moons*, by Sharon Creech
Honor Books: *Catherine, Called Birdy*, by Karen Cushman; *The Ear, the Eye, and the Arm*, by Nancy Farmer

1996   *The Midwife's Apprentice*, by Karen Cushman
Honor Books: *What Jamie Saw*, by Carolyn Coman; *The Watsons Go to Birmingham, 1963*, by Christopher Paul Curtis; *Yolanda's Genius*, by Carol Fenner; *The Great Fire*, by Jim Murphy

1997   *The View from Saturday*, by E. L. Konigsburg
Honor Books: *A Girl Named Disaster*, by Nancy Farmer; *Moorchild*, by Eloise McGraw; *The Thief*, by Megan Whalen Turner; *Belle Prater's Boy*, by Ruth White

1998   *Out of the Dust*, by Karen Hesse
Honor Books: *Ella Enchanted*, by Gail Carson Levine; *Lily's Crossing*, by Patricia Reilly Giff; *Wringer*, by Jerry Spinelli

CALDECOTT MEDAL

Since 1938, the Association of Library Service to Children of the American Library Association has annually awarded the Caldecott Medal to the illustrator of the most distinguished picture book published in the United States in the preceding year. The recipient must be a citizen or resident of the United States. The medal is named in tribute to the well-loved English illustrator Randolph Caldecott (1846–1886).

1938   *Animals of the Bible,* by Helen Dean Fish, ill. by Dorothy P. Lathrop
Honor Books: *Seven Simeons,* written and ill. by Boris Artzybasheff; *Four and Twenty Blackbirds,* by Helen Dean Fish, ill. by Robert Lawson

1939   *Mei Li,* written and ill. by Thomas Handforth
Honor Books: *The Forest Pool,* written and ill. by Laura Adams Armer; *Wee Gillis,* by Munro Leaf, ill. by Robert Lawson; *Snow White and the Seven Dwarfs,* written and ill. by Wanda Gág; *Barkis,* written and ill. by Clare Newberry; *Andy and the Lion,* written and ill. by James Daugherty

1940   *Abraham Lincoln,* written and ill. by Ingri and Edgar Parin d'Aulaire
Honor Books: *Cock-a-Doodle Doo,* written and ill. by Berta and Elmer Hader; *Madeline,* written and ill. by Ludwig Bemelmans; *The Ageless Story,* ill. by Lauren Ford

1941   *They Were Strong and Good,* written and ill. by Robert Lawson
Honor Book: *April's Kittens,* written and ill. by Clare Newberry

1942   *Make Way for Ducklings,* written and ill. by Robert McCloskey
Honor Books: *An American ABC,* written and ill. by Maud and Miska Petersham; *In My Mother's House,* by Ann Nolan Clark, ill. by Velino Herrera; *Paddle-to-the-Sea,* written and ill. by Holling C. Holling; *Nothing at All,* written and ill. by Wanda Gág

1943   *The Little House,* written and ill. by Virginia Lee Burton
Honor Books: *Dash and Dart,* written and ill. by Mary and Conrad Buff; *Marshmallow,* written and ill. by Clare Newberry

1944   *Many Moons,* by James Thurber, ill. by Louis Slobodkin
Honor Books: *Small Rain: Verses from the Bible,* selected by Jessie Orton Jones, ill. by Elizabeth Orton Jones; *Pierre Pigeon,* by Lee Kingman, ill. by Arnold E. Bare; *The Mighty Hunter,* written and ill. by Berta and Elmer Hader; *A Child's Good Night Book,* by Margaret Wise Brown, ill. by Jean Charlot; *Good Luck Horse,* by Chih-Yi Chan, ill. by Plao Chan

1945   *Prayer for a Child,* by Rachel Field, ill. by Elizabeth Orton Jones
Honor Books: *Mother Goose,* ill. by Tasha Tudor; *In the Forest,* written and ill. by Marie Hall Ets; *Yonie Wondernose,* written and ill. by Marguerite de Angeli; *The Christmas Anna Angel,* by Ruth Sawyer, ill. by Kate Seredy

1946   *The Rooster Crows,* ill. by Maud and Miska Petersham
Honor Books: *Little Lost Lamb,* by Golden MacDonald, ill. by Leonard Weisgard; *Sing Mother Goose,* by Opal Wheeler, ill. by Marjorie Torrey; *My Mother Is the*

Most Beautiful Woman in the World, by Becky Reyher, ill. by Ruth Gannett; *You Can Write Chinese,* written and ill. by Kurt Wiese

1947 *The Little Island,* by Golden MacDonald, ill. by Leonard Weisgard
Honor Books: *Rain Drop Splash,* by Alvin Tresselt, ill. by Leonard Weisgard; *Boats on the River,* by Marjorie Flack, ill. by Jay Hyde Barnum; *Timothy Turtle,* by Al Graham, ill. by Tony Palazzo; *Pedro, the Angel of Olvera Street,* written and ill. by Leo Politi; *Sing in Praise: A Collection of the Best Loved Hymns,* by Opal Wheeler, ill. by Marjorie Torrey

1948 *White Snow, Bright Snow,* by Alvin Tresselt, ill. by Roger Duvoisin
Honor Books: *Stone Soup,* written and ill. by Marcia Brown; *McElligot's Pool,* written and ill. by Dr. Seuss; *Bambino the Clown,* written and ill. by George Schreiber; *Roger and the Fox,* by Lavinia Davis, ill. by Hildegard Woodward; *Son of Robin Hood,* ed. by Anne Malcolmson, ill. by Virginia Lee Burton

1949 *The Big Snow,* written and ill. by Berta and Elmer Hader
Honor Books: *Blueberries for Sal,* written and ill. by Robert McCloskey; *All Around the Town,* by Phyllis McGinley, ill. by Helen Stone; *Juanita,* written and ill. by Leo Politi; *Fish in the Air,* written and ill. by Kurt Wiese

1950 *Song of the Swallows,* written and ill. by Leo Politi
Honor Books: *America's Ethan Allen,* by Stewart Holbrook, ill. by Lynd Ward; *The Wild Birthday Cake,* by Lavinia Davis, ill. by Hildegard Woodward; *The Happy Day,* by Ruth Krauss, ill. by Marc Simont; *Bartholomew and the Oobleck,* written and ill. by Dr. Seuss; *Henry Fisherman,* written and ill. by Marcia Brown

1951 *The Egg Tree,* written and ill. by Katherine Milhous
Honor Books: *Dick Whittington and His Cat,* written and ill. by Marcia Brown; *The Two Reds,* by William Lipkind, ill. by Nicolas Mordvinoff; *If I Ran the Zoo,* written and ill. by Dr. Seuss; *The Most Wonderful Doll in the World,* by Phyllis McGinley, ill. by Helen Stone; *T-Bone, the Baby Sitter,* written and ill. by Clare Newberry

1952 *Finders Keepers,* by William Lipkind, ill. by Nicolas Mordvinoff
Honor Books: *Mr. T. W. Anthony Woo,* written and ill. by Marie Hall Ets; *Skipper John's Cook,* written and ill. by Marcia Brown; *All Falling Down,* by Gene Zion, ill. by Margaret Bloy Graham; *Bear Party,* written and ill. by William Pène du Bois; *Feather Mountain,* written and ill. by Elizabeth Olds

1953 *The Biggest Bear,* written and ill. by Lynd Ward
Honor Books: *Puss in Boots,* by Charles Perrault, translated and ill. by Marcia Brown; *One Morning in Maine,* written and ill. by Robert McCloskey; *Ape in a Cape,* written and ill. by Fritz Eichenberg; *The Storm Book,* by Charlotte Zolotow, ill. by Margaret Bloy Graham; *Five Little Monkeys,* written and ill. by Juliet Kepes

1954 *Madeline's Rescue,* written and ill. by Ludwig Bemelmans
Honor Books: *Journey Cake, Ho!* by Ruth Sawyer, ill. by Robert McCloskey; *When Will the World Be Mine?* by Miriam Schlein, ill. by Jean Charlot; *The Steadfast Tin Soldier,* by Hans Christian Andersen, ill. by Marcia Brown; *A Very Special House,* by Ruth Krauss, ill. by Maurice Sendak; *Green Eyes,* written and ill. by A. Birnbaum

1955   *Cinderella, or the Little Glass Slipper,* by Charles Perrault, tr. and ill. by Marcia Brown
Honor Books: *Book of Nursery and Mother Goose Rhymes,* ill. by Marguerite de Angeli; *Wheel on the Chimney,* by Margaret Wise Brown, ill. by Tibor Gergely; *The Thanksgiving Story,* by Alice Dalgliesh, ill. by Helen Sewell

1956   *Frog Went A-Courtin',* ed. by John Langstaff, ill. by Feodor Rojankovsky
Honor Books: *Play with Me,* written and ill. by Marie Hall Ets; *Crow Boy,* written and ill. by Taro Yashima

1957   *A Tree Is Nice,* by Janice May Udry, ill. by Marc Simont
Honor Books: *Mr. Penny's Race Horse,* written and ill. by Marie Hall Ets; *1 Is One,* written and ill. by Tasha Tudor; *Anatole,* by Eve Titus, ill. by Paul Galdone; *Gillespie and the Guards,* by Benjamin Elkin, ill. by James Daugherty; *Lion,* written and ill. by William Pène du Bois

1958   *Time of Wonder,* written and ill. by Robert McCloskey
Honor Books: *Fly High, Fly Low,* written and ill. by Don Freeman; *Anatole and the Cat,* by Eve Titus, ill. by Paul Galdone

1959   *Chanticleer and the Fox,* adapted from Chaucer and ill. by Barbara Cooney
Honor Books: *The House That Jack Built,* written and ill. by Antonio Frasconi; *What Do You Say, Dear?* by Sesyle Joslin, ill. by Maurice Sendak; *Umbrella,* written and ill. by Taro Yashima

1960   *Nine Days to Christmas,* by Marie Hall Ets and Aurora Labastida, ill. by Marie Hall Ets
Honor Books: *Houses from the Sea,* by Alice E. Goudey, ill. by Adrienne Adams; *The Moon Jumpers,* by Janice May Udry, ill. by Maurice Sendak

1961   *Baboushka and the Three Kings,* by Ruth Robbins, ill. by Nicolas Sidjakov
Honor Book: *Inch by Inch,* written and ill. by Leo Lionni

1962   *Once a Mouse,* written and ill. by Marcia Brown
Honor Books: *The Fox Went Out on a Chilly Night,* written and ill. by Peter Spier; *Little Bear's Visit,* by Else Holmelund Minarik, ill. by Maurice Sendak; *The Day We Saw the Sun Come Up,* by Alice E. Goudey, ill. by Adrienne Adams

1963   *The Snowy Day,* written and ill. by Ezra Jack Keats
Honor Books: *The Sun Is a Golden Earring,* by Natalia M. Belting, ill. by Bernarda Bryson; *Mr. Rabbit and the Lovely Present,* by Charlotte Zolotow, ill. by Maurice Sendak

1964   *Where the Wild Things Are,* written and ill. by Maurice Sendak
Honor Books: *Swimmy,* written and ill. by Leo Lionni; *All in the Morning Early,* by Sorche Nic Leodhas, ill. by Evaline Ness; *Mother Goose and Nursery Rhymes,* ill. by Philip Reed

1965   *May I Bring a Friend?* by Beatrice Schenk de Regniers, ill. by Beni Montresor
Honor Books: *Rain Makes Applesauce,* by Julian Scheer, ill. by Marvin Bileck; *The*

Wave, by Margaret Hodges, ill. by Blair Lent; *A Pocketful of Cricket,* by Rebecca Caudill, ill. by Evaline Ness

1966   *Always Room for One More,* by Sorche Nic Leodhas, ill. by Nonny Hogrogian
Honor Books: *Hide and Seek Fog,* by Alvin Tresselt, ill. by Roger Duvoisin; *Just Me,* written and ill. by Marie Hall Ets; *Tom Tit Tot,* written and ill. by Evaline Ness

1967   *Sam, Bangs and Moonshine,* written and ill. by Evaline Ness
Honor Book: *One Wide River to Cross,* by Barbara Emberley, ill. by Ed Emberley

1968   *Drummer Hoff,* by Barbara Emberley, ill. by Ed Emberley
Honor Books: *Frederick,* written and ill. by Leo Lionni; *Seashore Story,* written and ill. by Taro Yashima; *The Emperor and the Kite,* by Jane Yolen, ill. by Ed Young

1969   *The Fool of the World and the Flying Ship,* by Arthur Ransome, ill. by Uri Shulevitz
Honor Book: *Why the Sun and the Moon Live in the Sky,* by Elphinstone Dayrell, ill. by Blair Lent

1970   *Sylvester and the Magic Pebble,* written and ill. by William Steig
Honor Books: *Goggles!* written and ill. by Ezra Jack Keats; *Alexander and the Wind-Up Mouse,* written and ill. by Leo Lionni; *Pop Corn and Ma Goodness,* by Edna Mitchell Preston, ill. by Robert Andrew Parker; *Thy Friend, Obadiah,* written and ill. by Brinton Turkle; *The Judge,* by Harve Zemach, ill. by Margot Zemach

1971   *A Story: A Story,* written and ill. by Gail E. Haley
Honor Books: *The Angry Moon,* by William Sleator, ill. by Blair Lent; *Frog and Toad Are Friends,* written and ill. by Arnold Lobel; *In the Night Kitchen,* written and ill. by Maurice Sendak

1972   *One Fine Day,* written and ill. by Nonny Hogrogian
Honor Books: *If All the Seas Were One Sea,* written and ill. by Janina Domanska; *Moja Means One: Swahili Counting Book,* by Muriel Feelings, ill. by Tom Feelings; *Hildilid's Night,* by Cheli Duran Ryan, ill. by Arnold Lobel

1973   *The Funny Little Woman,* retold by Arlene Mosel, ill. by Blair Lent
Honor Books: *Anansi the Spider,* adapted and ill. by Gerald McDermott; *Hosie's Alphabet,* by Hosea, Tobias, and Lisa Baskin, ill. by Leonard Baskin; *Snow-White and the Seven Dwarfs,* translated by Randall Jarrell, ill. by Nancy Ekholm Burkert; *When Clay Sings,* by Byrd Baylor, ill. by Tom Bahti

1974   *Duffy and the Devil,* by Harve Zemach, ill. by Margot Zemach
Honor Books: *Three Jovial Huntsmen,* written and ill. by Susan Jeffers; *Cathedral: The Story of Its Construction,* written and ill. by David Macaulay

1975   *Arrow to the Sun,* adapted and ill. by Gerald McDermott
Honor Book: *Jambo Means Hello,* by Muriel Feelings, ill. by Tom Feelings

1976   *Why Mosquitoes Buzz in People's Ears,* retold by Verna Aardema, ill. by Leo and Diane Dillon

Honor Books: *The Desert Is Theirs*, by Byrd Baylor, ill. by Peter Parnall; *Strega Nona*, retold and ill. by Tomie de Paola

1977   *Ashanti to Zulu: African Traditions*, by Margaret Musgrove, ill. by Leo and Diane Dillon
Honor Books: *The Amazing Bone*, written and ill. by William Steig; *The Contest*, retold and ill. by Nonny Hogrogian; *Fish for Supper*, written and ill. by M. B. Goffstein; *The Golem*, written and ill. by Beverly Brodsky McDermott; *Hawk, I'm Your Brother*, by Byrd Baylor, ill. by Peter Parnall

1978   *Noah's Ark*, ill. by Peter Spier
Honor Books: *Castle*, written and ill. by David Macaulay; *It Could Always Be Worse*, retold and ill. by Margot Zemach

1979   *The Girl Who Loved Wild Horses*, written and ill. by Paul Goble
Honor Books: *Freight Train*, written and ill. by Donald Crews; *The Way to Start a Day*, by Byrd Baylor, ill. by Peter Parnall

1980   *Ox-Cart Man*, by Donald Hall, ill. by Barbara Cooney
Honor Books: *Ben's Trumpet*, written and ill. by Rachel Isadora; *The Garden of Abdul Gasazi*, written and ill. by Chris Van Allsburg

1981   *Fables*, written and ill. by Arnold Lobel
Honor Books: *The Grey Lady and the Strawberry Snatcher*, ill. by Molly Bang; *Truck*, ill. by Donald Crews; *Mice Twice*, written and ill. by Joseph Low; *The Bremen-Town Musicians*, ill. by Ilse Plume

1982   *Jumanji*, written and ill. by Chris Van Allsburg
Honor Books: *Where the Buffaloes Begin*, by Olaf Baker, ill. by Stephen Gammell; *On Market Street*, by Arnold Lobel, ill. by Anita Lobel; *Outside over There*, written and ill. by Maurice Sendak; *A Visit to William Blake's Inn*, by Nancy Willard, ill. by Alice and Martin Provensen

1983   *Shadow*, by Blaise Cendrars, translated and ill. by Marcia Brown
Honor Books: *When I Was Young in the Mountains*, by Cynthia Rylant, ill. by Diane Goode; *A Chair for My Mother*, written and ill. by Vera B. Williams

1984   *The Glorious Flight: Across the Channel with Louis Blériot*, written and ill. by Alice and Martin Provensen
Honor Books: *Ten, Nine, Eight*, written and ill. by Molly Bang; *Little Red Riding Hood*, retold and ill. by Trina Schart Hyman

1985   *St. George and the Dragon*, retold by Margaret Hodges, ill. by Trina Schart Hyman
Honor Books: *Hansel and Gretel*, retold by Rika Lesser, ill. by Paul O. Zelinsky; *Have You Seen My Duckling?* written and ill. by Nancy Tafuri; *The Story of Jumping Mouse*, written and ill. by John Steptoe

1986   *The Polar Express*, written and ill. by Chris Van Allsburg
Honor Books: *The Relatives Came*, by Cynthia Rylant, ill. by Stephen Gammell; *King Bidgood's in the Bathtub*, by Audrey Wood, ill. by Don Wood

1987   *Hey, Al!* by Arthur Yorinks, ill. by Richard Egielski
        Honor Books: *The Village of Round and Square Houses,* written and ill. by Ann Gri-
        falconi; *Alphabetics,* written and ill. by Suse MacDonald; *Rumpelstiltskin,* retold
        and ill. by Paul O. Zelinsky

1988   *Owl Moon,* by Jane Yolen, ill. by John Schoenherr
        Honor Book: *Mufaro's Beautiful Daughters,* written and ill. by John Steptoe

1989   *Song and Dance Man,* by Karen Ackerman, ill. by Stephen Gammell
        Honor Books: *The Boy of the Three Year Nap,* written and ill. by Allen Say; *Free
        Fall,* written and ill. by David Wiesner; *Goldilocks and the Three Bears,* adapted and
        ill. by James Marshall; *Mirandy and Brother Wind,* by Patricia McKissack, ill. by
        Jerry Pinkney

1990   *Lon Po Po: A Red Riding Hood Story from China,* adapted and ill. by Ed Young
        Honor Books: *Bill Peet: An Autobiography,* written and ill. by Bill Peet; *Color Zoo,*
        written and ill. by Lois Ehlert; *Hershel and the Hanukkah Goblins,* by Eric A. Kim-
        mel, ill. by Trina Schart Hyman; *The Talking Eggs,* by Robert D. San Souci, ill. by
        Jerry Pinkney

1991   *Black and White,* written and ill. by David Macaulay
        Honor Books: *Puss in Boots,* by Charles Perrault, translated by Malcolm Arthur, ill.
        by Fred Marcellino; *"More, More, More," Said the Baby,* written and ill. by Vera B.
        Williams

1992   *Tuesday,* written and ill. by David Wiesner
        Honor Book: *Tar Beach,* written and ill. by Faith Ringold

1993   *Mirette on the High Wire,* written and ill. by Emily Arnold McCully
        Honor Books: *Seven Blind Mice,* written and ill. by Ed Young; *The Stinky Cheese
        Man and Other Fairly Stupid Tales,* by Jon Scieszka, ill. by Lane Smith; *Working
        Cotton,* by Sherley Anne Williams, ill. by Carole Byard

1994   *Grandfather's Journey,* written and ill. by Allen Say
        Honor Books: *Peppe the Lamplighter,* by Elisa Bartone, ill. by Ted Lewin; *In the
        Small, Small Pond,* written and ill. by Denise Fleming; *Owen,* written and ill. by
        Kevin Henkes; *Raven: A Trickster Tale from the Pacific Northwest,* written and ill. by
        Gerald McDermott; *Yo! Yes?* written and ill. by Chris Raschka

1995   *Smoky Night,* by Eve Bunting, ill. by David Diaz
        Honor Books: *John Henry,* by Julius Lester, ill. by Jerry Pinkney; *Swamp Angel,*
        by Anne Isaacs, ill. by Paul O. Zelinsky; *Time Flies,* written and ill. by Eric
        Rohmann

1996   *Officer Buckle and Gloria,* written and ill. by Peggy Rathman
        Honor Books: *Alphabet City,* written and ill. by Stephen T. Johnson; *Zin! Zin!
        Zin! A Violin,* by Lloyd Moss, ill. by Marjorie Priceman; *Tops and Bottoms,* written
        and ill. by Janet Stevens; *The Faithful Friend,* by Robert D. San Souchi, ill. by
        Brian Pinkney

1997   *Golem,* written and ill. by David Wisniewski
Honor Books: *Hush! A Thai Lullaby,* by Minfong Ho, ill. by Holly Meade; *The Graphic Alphabet,* written and ill. by David Pelletier; *The Paperboy,* written and ill. by Dav Pilkey; *Starry Messenger,* written and ill. by Peter Sis

1998   *Rapunzel,* written and ill. by Paul O. Zelinsky
Honor Books: *The Gardener,* written by Sarah Stewart and by David Small; *Harlem,* written by Walter Dean Myers, ill. by Christopher Myers; *There Was an Old Lady Who Swallowed a Fly,* written and ill. by Simms Taback

H
Recommended Books
for Multicultural Reading Experiences

African and African American Books

Folklore

Aardema, Verna. *Bimwili and the Zimwi.* (P)

————. *Bringing the Rain to Kapiti Plain.* (P)

————. *Oh, Kojo! How Could You!* (I)

————. *Why Mosquitoes Buzz in People's Ears.* (P-I)

Bryan, Ashley. *All Night, All Day: A Child's First Book of African American Spirituals.* (P-I-A)

————. *What a Morning! The Christmas Story in Black Spirituals.* (P-I)

Climo, Shirley. *The Egyptian Cinderella.* (P-I)

Grifalconi, Ann. *The Village of Round and Square Houses.* (P-I)

Hamilton, Virginia. *The All Jahdu Storybook.* Ill. Barry Moser. (P-I)

————. *The People Could Fly.* Ill. Leo and Diane Dillon. (I)

Keats, Ezra Jack. *John Henry.* (I)

Lester, Julius. *How Many Spots Does a Leopard Have?* (I)

————. *John Henry.* (I)

————. *The Tales of Uncle Remus: The Adventures of Brer Rabbit.* (P-I)

McKissack, Patricia. *The Dark.* (I)

Mollel, Tololwa. *The Princess Who Lost Her Hair: An Akamba Legend.* (P-I)

San Souci, Robert. *Sukey and the Mermaid.* Ill. Brian Pinkney. (P-I)

Steptoe, John. *Mufaro's Beautiful Daughters.* (P)

Poetry

Adoff, Arnold. *All the Colors of the Race.* (I)

————. *Black Is Brown Is Tan.* (P)

————. *In for Winter, Out for Spring.* (P-I)

P = primary; I = intermediate; A = adolescent

————. *My Black Me: A Beginning Book of Black Poetry.* (P)

Brooks, Gwendolyn. *Bronzeville Boys and Girls.* (P-I)

Bryan, Ashley. *Ashley Bryan's ABC of African American Poetry.* (P-I)

————. *Sing to the Sun.* (P-I)

Chocolate, Debbi. *Kente Colors.* (P-I)

Clifton, Lucille. *Everett Anderson's Goodbye.* (P)

————. *Everett Anderson's Nine Month Long.* (P)

————. *Some of the Days of Everett Anderson.* (P)

Feelings, Tom. *Soul Looks Back in Wonder.* (I-A)

Giovanni, Nikki. *Spin a Soft Black Song.* (P-I)

Greenfield, Eloise. *"Honey, I Love" and Other Love Poems.* (P-I-A)

Grimes, Nikki. *Come Sunday.* (P-I)

————. *Meet Danitra Brown.* (P-I)

Johnson, James. *Lift Ev'ry Voice and Sing.* (P-I-A)

Myers, Walter. *Harlem.* (I-A)

Price, Leontyne. *Aïda.* Ill. Leo and Diane Dillon. (A)

Steptoe, Javaka. *In Daddy's Arms I Am Tall.* (P)

Winter, Jeanette. *Follow the Drinking Gourd.* (P-I)

Picture Books

Barber, Barbara. *Saturday and the New You.* Ill. Anna Rich. (P-I)

Clifton, Lucille. *Boy Who Didn't Believe in Spring.* (P)

————. *Everett Anderson's Christmas Coming.* (P)

————. *Three Wishes.* Ill. Michael Hays. (P)

Cosby, Bill. *Little Bill Books for Beginning Readers.* Ill. Varnette P. Honeywood. (P-I)

Crews, Donald. *Bigmama's.* (P)

Daly, Nikki. *Something on My Mind.* (P)

Flowers, Art. *Cleveland Lee's Beale Street Band.* Ill. Anna Rich. (P-I)

Greenfield, Eloise. *Grandpa's Face.* (P)

————. *She Come Bringing Me That Little Baby Girl.* (P)

Grifalconi, Ann. *Darkness and the Butterfly.* (P)

————. *Osa's Pride.* (P)

Hamilton, Virginia. *Drylongso.* Ill. Jerry Pinkney. (I)

Hoffman, Mary. *Amazing Grace.* Ill. Caroline Binch. (P)

Hopkinson, Deborah. *Sweet Clara and the Dream Quilt.* Ill. James Ransome. (P-I)

Howard, Elizabeth Fitzgerald. *Aunt Flossie's Hats (and Crab Cakes Later).* Ill. James Ransome. (P)

Johnson, Angela. *One of Three.* Ill. David Soman. (P)

————. *Tell Me a Story, Mama.* Ill. David Soman. (P)

Keats, Ezra Jack. *A Snowy Day.* (P)

————. *Whistle for Willie.* (P)

King, Corretta Scott. *I Have a Dream.* (I-A)

Kurtz, Jane. *Trouble.* Ill. Durga Bernhard. (P-I)

———, and Christopher Kurtz. *Only a Pigeon.* Ill. E. B. Lewis. (P-I)

Lester, Julius. *What a Truly Cool World.* Ill. Joe Cepeda.(P-I-A)

London, Jonathan. *Ali, Child of the Desert.* Ill. Ted Lewin. (P-I)

McKissack, Patricia. *Flossie and the Fox.* (P)

———. *Mirandy and Brother Wind.* Ill. Jerry Pinkney. (P-I)

Mitchell, Margaree. *Uncle Jed's Barbershop.* Ill. James Ransome. (P-I)

Myers, Walter Dean. *Brown Angels.* (P-I)

Pinkney, Brian. *Max Found Two Sticks.* (P)

Pinkney, Gloria Jean. *Back Home.* Ill. Jerry Pinkney. (P)

Polacco, Patricia. *Chicken Sunday.* (P)

———. *Mrs. Katz and Tush.* (P-I)

Ringgold, Faith. *Tar Beach.* (P-I)

Steptoe, John. *Stevie.* (P)

Tarpley, Natasha. *I Love My Hair.* Ill. E. B. Lewis. (P)

Walker, Alice. *To Hell with Dying.* Ill. Catherine Deeter. (I-A)

Williams, Sherley Anne. *Working Cotton.* Ill. Carole Byard. (P)

Wilson, Beth. *Jenny.* Ill. Dolores Johnson. (P)

Fiction

Davis, Ossie. *Just like Martin.* (I)

Greenfield, Eloise. *Koya De Laney and the Good Girl Blues.* (I)

Hamilton, Virginia. *Cousins.* (I)

———. *Drylongso.* Ill. Jerry Pinkney. (I)

———. *M. C. Higgins, the Great.* (I-A)

———. *Planet of Junior Brown.* (I-A)

———. *Zeely.* (I)

Kurtz, Jane. *The Storyteller's Beads.* (I-A)

Myers, Walter Dean. *Fast Sam, Cool Clyde, and Stuff.* (I-A)

———. *Hoops.* (A)

———. *Motown and Didi.* (A)

———. *Somewhere in the Darkness.* (A)

———. *Won't Know till I Get There.* (A)

———. *The Young Landlords.* (A)

Smothers, Ethel Footman. *Down in the Piney Woods.* (I-A)

Taylor, Mildred. *The Road to Memphis.* (A)

———. *Roll of Thunder, Hear My Cry* (A)

Yarbrough, Camille. *Cornrows.* (P)

Nonfiction

Anderson, Laurie. *Ndito Runs.* (P-I)

Bunting, Eve. *Smoky Nights.* (I-A)

Feelings, Muriel. *Jambo Means Hello.* (P-I)

Lester, Julius. *From Slave Ship to Freedom Road.* (I-A)

McKissack, Patricia, and Frederick McKissack. *A Long Hard Journey: The Story of the Pullman Porter.* (I)

Musgrove, Margaret. *Ashanti to Zulu.* (P-I)

Myers, Walter Dean. *Now Is Your Time! The African-American Struggle for Freedom.* (I-A)

Sabuda, Robert. *Tutankhamen's Gift.* (P-I)

Biography

Angelou, Maya. *Kofi and His Magic.* (P-I)

Cooper, Floyd. *Coming Home: From the Life of Langston Hughes.* (I)

Freedman, Florence B. *Two Tickets to Freedom: The True Story of Ellen and William Craft, Fugitive Slaves.* (I-A)

Hamilton, Virginia. *Anthony Burns: The Defeat and Triumph of a Fugitive Slave.* (I-A)

Haskins, James. *Bill Cosby: America's Most Famous Father.* (I)

———. *Diana Ross, Star Supreme.* (I)

Krull, Kathleen. *Wilma Unlimited.* (P-I)

Lester, Julius. *To Be a Slave.* (I-A)

Ringgold, Faith. *My Dream of Martin Luther King.* (P-I)

ASIAN AND ASIAN AMERICAN BOOKS

Folklore

Birdseye, Tom. *A Song of Stars.* Ill. Ju-Hong Chen. (P)

Climo, Shirley. *The Korean Cinderella.* (P-I)

Coerr, Eleanor. *Sadako.* (I-A)

Demi. *The Empty Pot.* (P)

Louie, Ai-Ling. *Yeh-Shen: A Cinderella Story from China.* Ill. Ed Young. (P-I)

San Souci, Robert. *The Samurai's Daughter.* (I)

Tan, Amy. *The Moon Lady.* (I)

Yacowitz, Caryn. *The Jade Stone: A Chinese Folktale.* Ill. Ju-Hong Chen. (I)

Yep, Laurence. *The Butterfly Man.* (I)

———. *The Rainbow People.* (I)

———. *Tongues of Jade.* Ill. David Wiesner. (I)

Poetry

Baron, Virginia Olsen. *Sunset in a Spider Web: Sijo Poetry of Ancient Korea.* (I-A)

Behn, Harry. *Cricket Songs.* (I-A)

Demi. *In the Eyes of the Cat: Japanese Poetry for All Seasons.* Ill. Tze-Si Huang. (P-I-A)

Lee, Jeanne. *The Song of Mu Lan.* (P-I)

Picture Books

Ashley, Bernard. *Cleversticks.* Ill. Derek Brazell. (P)

Baker, Keith. *The Magic Fan.* (P)

Bang, Molly. *The Paper Crane.* (P)

Breckler, Rosemary. *Hoang Breaks the Lucky Teapot.* Ill. Adrian Frankel. (P)

Coutant, Helen, and Vo-Dinh. *First Snow.* (P)

Friedman, Ina. *How My Parents Learned to Eat.* (P)

Garland, Sherry. *The Lotus Seed.* Ill. Tatsuo Kiuchi. (P-I)

Levinson, Riki. *Our Home Is the Sea.* Ill. Dennis Luzak. (P-I)

Say, Allen. *Bicycle Man.* (P)

———. *El Chino.* (P-I)

———. *Grandfather's Journey* (I)

———. *The Lost Lake* (I)

———. *Tree of Cranes.* (P-I)

Tejima. *Ho-limlim: A Rabbit Tale from Japan.* (P-I)

Turner, Ann. *Through Moon and Stars and Night Skies.* Ill. James Graham Hale. (P-I)

Wells, Rosemary. *Yoko.* (P)

Yashima, Taro. *Crow Boy.* (P-I)

———. *Momo's Kitten.* (P)

———. *Umbrella.* (P)

———. *Youngest One.* (P)

Fiction

Merrill, Jean. *The Girl Who Loved Caterpillars.* Ill. Floyd Cooper. (I)

Namioka, Lensey. *Yang the Youngest and His Terrible Ear.* (I)

Uchida, Yoshiko. *The Best Bad Thing.* (I)

———. *The Happiest Ending.* (I)

———. *The Invisible Thread* (I)

———. *A Jar of Dreams.* (I)

Yep, Laurence. *Child of the Owl.* (I-A)

———. *Dragonwings.* (I-A)

———. *Mountain Light.* (I-A)

———. *Sea Glass.* (I-A)

Nonfiction

Banish, Roslyn. *A Forever Family*. (I)

Brown, Tricia. *Lee Ann*. Photos by Ted Thai. (I)

Hoyt-Goldsmith, Diane. *Hoang Anh: A Vietnamese-American Boy*. Photos by Lawrence Migdale. (I)

Maruki, Toshi. *Hiroshima no Pika*. (I-A)

McMahon, Patricia. *Chi-Hoon: A Korean Girl*. (P-I)

Meltzer, Milton. *The Chinese Americans*. (A)

Schlein, Miriam. *The Year of the Panda*. Ill. Kam Mak. (P-I)

Waters, Kate, and Madeline Slovenz-Low. *Lion Dancer: Ernie Wan's Chinese New Year*. (P-I)

Wolf, Bernard. *In the Year of the Tiger*. (I)

Biography

Huynh, Quang Nhuong. *The Land I Lost: Adventures of a Boy in Vietnam*. (I)

Lord, Bette Bao. *In the Year of the Boar and Jackie Robinson*. (I)

Latin American Books

Folklore

Aardema, Verna. *Borreguita and the Coyote*. Ill. Petra Mathers. (Mexico) (P-I)

———. *The Riddle of the Drum: A Tale from Tizapan, Mexico*. (P-I)

Alexander, Ellen. *Llama and the Great Flood*. (Quechua story from Peru) (I)

Belpre, Pura. *Once in Puerto Rico*. (I)

———. *The Rainbow-Colored Horse*. (Puerto Rico) (P-I)

de Paola, Tomie. *The Lady of Guadalupe*. (Mexico) (P-I)

de Sauza, James. *Brother Anansi and the Cattle Ranch*. (Nicaragua) (P)

Hall, Melisande. *Soon Come: A Ptolemy Turtle Adventure*. (P-I)

Hayes, Joe. *A Spoon for Every Bite*. (P-I)

Jaffe, Nina. *The Golden Flower*. (P-I)

Joseph, Lynn. *A Wave in Her Pocket: Stories from Trinidad*. Ill. Brian Pinkney. (I)

Kurtycz, Marcos. *Tigers and Opossums: Animal Legends*. (Mexico) (I)

Schon, Isabel. *Doña Blanca and Other Hispanic Nursery Rhymes and Games*. (P-I)

Vidal, Beatriz. *The Legend of El Dorado*. (I)

Wolkstein, Diane. *Banza: A Haitian Story*. Ill. Marc Tolon Brown. (P)

Poetry

de Gerez, Toni. *My Song Is a Piece of Jade: Poems of Ancient Mexico in English and Spanish*. (I-A)

Delacre, Lulu. *Arroz con Leche: Popular Songs and Rhymes from Latin America*. (P-I)

Joseph, Lynn. *Coconut Kind of Day*. (P-I)

Soto, Gary. *A Fire in My Hands.* Ill. James Cardillo. (I)

―――. *Neighborhood Odes.* Ill. David Diaz. (I)

Picture Books

Belpre, Pura. *Santiago.* Ill. Symeon Shimin. (P)

Bunting, Eve. *How Many Days to America?* Ill. Beth Peck. (I-A)

Cannon, Janell. *Verdi.* (P-I)

Cruz, Martel. *Yagua Days.* (P)

Czernicki, Stefan, and Timothy Rhodes. *The Sleeping Bread.* (P)

Dorros, Arthur. *Abuela.* Ill. Elisa Kleven. (P)

―――. *Isla.* (P-I)

Ets, Marie Hall, and Aurora Latastida. *Nine Days to Christmas: A Story of Mexico.* (P)

Garza, Carmen Lomas. *Family Pictures: Cuadros de Familia.* (P-I)

Gershator, David, and Phillis Gershator. *Bread Is for Eating.* Ill. Emma Shaw Smith. (P-I)

Havill, Juanita. *Treasure Nap.* Ill. Elivia Savadier. (Mexico) (P)

Isadora, Rachel. *Caribbean Dream.* (P)

James, Betsy. *The Dream Stair.* (P)

Jordon, Martin, and Tanis Jordan. *Amazon Alphabet.* (P-I)

Marvin, Isabel. *Saving Joe Louis.* (P)

Politi, Leo. *Pedro, the Angel of Olvera Street.* (P)

Roe, Eileen. *Con Mi Hermano: With My Brother.* (P)

San Souci, Robert. *Cendrillon: A Caribbean Cinderella.* Ill. Brian Pinckney. (P-I)

Tompert, Ann. *The Silver Whistle.* Ill. Beth Peck. (P)

Fiction

Cameron, Ann. *The Most Beautiful Place in the World.* Ill. Thomas B. Allen. (P-I)

Carlson, Lori M., and Cynthia L. Ventura (eds.). *Where Angels Glide at Dawn: New Stories from Latin America.* Ill. José Ortega. (I)

Mohr, Nicholasa. *El Bronx Remembered.* (A)

―――. *Felita.* (I)

―――. *Going Home.* (I-A)

―――. *In Nueva York.* (A)

―――. *Nilda.* (A)

Soto, Gary. *Baseball in April and Other Stories.* (I)

―――. *Taking Sides.* (I-A)

Nonfiction

Ancona, George. *Bananas: From Manolo to Margie.* (P-I)

Anderson, Joan. *Spanish Pioneers of the Southwest.* (P-I)

Brown, Tricia. *Hello, Amigos!* Photos by Fran Ortiz. (P-I)

Brusca, Maria Christina. *On the Pampas.* (I)

Cherry, Lynn. *The Shaman's Apprentice.* (P-I)

Emberley, Rebecca. *My House: A Book in Two Languages/Mi Casa: Un Libro en Dos Lenguas.* (I)

Grossman, Patricia, and Enrique Sanchez. *Saturday's Market.* (P-I)

McDonald's Hispanic Heritage Art Contest. *Our Hispanic Heritage.* (P)

Meltzer, Milton. *The Hispanic Americans.* (A)

Perl, Lila. *Piñatas and Paper Flowers: Holidays of the Americas in English and Spanish.* (I-A)

Shalant, Phyllis. *Look What We've Brought You from Mexico.* (I)

Thomas, Jane. *Lights on the River.* (I)

Zak, Monica. *Save My Rainforest.* Ill. Bengt-Arne Runnerstrom. Trans. Nancy Schimmel. (I)

Biography

Codye, C. *Luis W. Alvarez.* (I-A)

de Treviño, Elizabeth Borten. *El Guero.* (I-A)

———. *I, Juan de Pareja.* (A)

———. *Juarez, Man of Law.* (A)

Gleiter, Jan. *David Farragut.* (A)

———. *Diego Rivera.* (A)

Shorto, R. *David Farragut and the Great Naval Blockade.* (A)

NATIVE AMERICAN BOOKS

Folklore

Bierhorst, John. *Doctor Coyote.* (I)

———. *The Ring in the Prairie: A Shawnee Legend.* (I)

de Paola, Tomie. *The Legend of the Bluebonnet.* (P)

———. *The Legend of the Indian Paintbrush.* (P-I)

Dixon, Ann. *How Raven Brought Light to People.* Ill. James Watts. (P-I)

Goble, Paul. *Beyond the Ridge.* (P-I)

———. *Buffalo Woman.* (P-I)

———. *Crow Chief: A Plains Indian Story.* (I)

———. *Death of the Iron Horse.* (P-I)

———. *Her Seven Brothers.* (P-I)

———. *Iktomi and the Berries: A Plains Indian Story.* (P-I)

———. *Iktomi and the Boulder: A Plains Indian Story.* (P-I)

———. *Iktomi and the Buffalo Skull: A Plains Indian Story.* (P-I)

———. *Iktomi and the Ducks: A Plains Indian Story.* (P-I)

———. *Star Boy.* (P-I)

Goldin, Barbara. *The Girl Who Lived with the Bears.* (P-I)

Harris, Christie. *Once upon a Totem.* (I-A)

Highwater, Jamake. *Anpao: An American Indian Odyssey.* (I-A)

Kusugak, Michael. *Hide and Sneak.* (P-I)

MacGill-Callahan, Sheila. *And Still the Turtle Watched.* Ill. Barry Moser. (P)

Martin, Rafe. *The Rough-Face Girl.* Ill. David Shannon. (P-I)

Monroe, Jean Guard, and Ray Williamson. *They Dance in the Sky.* Ill. Edgar Stewart. (I-A)

Osofsky, Audrey. *Dreamcatcher.* (P)

Oughton, Jerrie. *How the Stars Fell into the Sky.* Ill. Lisa Desimini. (P-I)

Renner, Michelle. *The Girl Who Swam with the Fish: An Athabascan Legend.* (P-I)

Rodanas, Kristina. *Dragonfly's Tale.* (P-I)

Siberell, Anne. *The Whale in the Sky.* (P-I)

Taylor, C. J. *How Two-Feather Was Saved from Loneliness.* (P-I)

Wisniewski, David. *Rain Player.* (P-I)

Poetry

Baylor, Byrd. *The Other Way to Listen.* (P-I)

Bierhorst, John. *A Cry from the Earth: Music of the North American Indians.* (P-I)

Bruchac, Joseph, and Jonathan London. *Thirteen Moons on Turtle's Back: A Native American Year of Moons.* Ill. Thomas Locker. (P-I)

Clark, Ann Nolan. *In My Mother's House.* Ill. Velino Herrera. (P-I)

Jones, Hettie. *The Trees Stand Shining: Poetry of the North American Indians.* Ill. Robert Andrew Parker. (P-I)

Wood, Nancy. *Dancing Moon.* (I-A)

———. *Many Winters.* (I-A)

Picture Books

Baker, Olaf. *Where the Buffaloes Begin.* Ill. Stephen Gammell. (P)

Baylor, Byrd. *Hawk, I'm Your Brother.* (P-I)

Buchanan, Ken. *This House Is Made of Mud.* Ill. Libba Tracy. (P-I)

Joosse, Barbara. *Mama, Do You Love Me?* Ill. Barbara Lavallee. (P-I)

Steptoe, John. *The Story of Jumping Mouse: A Native American Legend.* (P)

Yolen, Jane. *Encounter.* Ill. David Shannon. (I-A)

———. *Sky Dogs.* Ill. Barry Moser. (P)

Fiction

Hobbs, Will. *Bearstone.* (I-A)

O'Dell, Scott, and Elizabeth Hall. *Thunder Rolling in the Mountains.* (A)

Rohmer, Harriet, Octavia Chow, and Morris Vidaure. *The Invisible Hunters.* Ill. Joe Sam. (I-A)

Spinka, Penina Keen. *Mother's Blessing.* (I)

Strete, C. K. *Big Thunder Magic.* (P-I)

———. *When Grandfather Journeys into Winter.* (I)

Wosmek, Frances. *A Brown Bird Singing.* (I)

Nonfiction

Cherry, Lynn. *A River Ran Wild.* (P-I)

Freedman, Russell. *Children of the Wild West.* (I-A)

———. *Indian Chiefs.* (I-A)

Hoyt-Goldsmith, Diane. *Pueblo Storyteller.* Photos by Lawrence Migdale. (I)

Kendall, Russ. *Eskimo Boy: Life in an Inupiaq Eskimo Village.* (I)

Regguinti, Gordon. *The Sacred Harvest: Ojibway Wild Rice Gathering.* Photos by Dale Kakkak. (I-A)

Yolen, Jane. *Encounter.* Ill. David Shannon. (P-I-A)

Biography

Ekoomiak, Normee. *Arctic Memories.* (Inuit in Arctic Quebec) (I)

Freedman, Russell. *Indian Chiefs.* (I-A)

Matthaei, Gay, and Jewel Grutman. *The Ledgerbook of Thomas Blue Eagle.* (I-A)

Books on Other Cultures

Appelt, Kathi. *Bayou Lullaby.* Ill. Neil Waldman.(P)

Archambault, John, and David Plummer. *Grandmother's Garden.* (P)

Bunting, Eve. *Terrible Things.* (P-I-A)

Conrad, Pam. *Animal Lingo.* (P)

Durrell, Ann, and Marilyn Sachs (eds.). *The Big Book for Peace.* (P-I-A)

Goldin, Barbara. *The World's First Birthday: A Rosh Hashanah Story.* (P-I)

Hooks, William. *The Three Little Pigs and the Fox.* Ill. S. D. Schindler. (P-I)

Igus, Toyomi. *Two Mrs. Gibsons.* Ill. Daryl Wells. (P)

Kimmel, Eric. *Baba Yaga: A Russian Folktale.* Ill. Megan Lloyd. (P)

Lacapa, Kathleen, and Michael Lacapa. *Less than Half, More than Whole.* (P-I)

Mayer, Marianna. *Baby Yaga and Vasilisa the Brave.* Ill. K. Y. Craft. (P-I)

Polacco, Patricia. *The Keeping Quilt.* (P-I)

Rosen, Michael. *Elijah's Angel: A Story for Chanukah and Christmas.* Ill. Aminah Robinson. (P-I)

Rosenblum, Richard. *Journey to the Golden Land.* (I-A)

Vagin, Vladimir. *Here Comes the Cat.* (P-I)

Wisniewski, David. *Golem.* (I)

Glossary

active comprehension   Using prior knowledge, schemata, and metacognition to construct textual meaning, fostered by using questioning during reading.

alphabetic principle   Principle that suggests that letters in the alphabet map to phonemes, the minimal sound units represented in written language.

analogy   A comparison of two similar relationships.

analogy-based phonics instruction   Phonics instruction using activities and procedures in which students identify unknown words by comparing and contrasting them to known words.

analytic phonics   An approach to phonics teaching that emphasizes the discovery of letter-sound through the analysis of known words.

anecdotal notes   Brief, written observations of revealing behavior that a teacher considers significant to understanding a child's literacy learning.

anthologies   Bound collections of stories and poems in reading programs.

anticipation guide   A series of written or oral statements for individual students to respond to before reading text assignments.

antonyms   Words opposite in meaning to other words.

aptitude hypothesis   The belief that vocabulary and comprehension reflect general intellectual ability.

assisted reading   A reading strategy that combines all the features of home-centered learning—reading with children, sharing books, repeating favorite stories, memorizing text, and providing needed assistance.

authentic assessment   Asking students actually to perform tasks that demonstrate sufficient knowledge and understanding of a subject.

authentic communication   An essential component of language learning requiring active communication and participation.

automated reading   A reading approach in which students listen individually to tape-recorded stories while reading along with the written text.

automaticity   The automatic, almost subconscious recognition and understanding of written text.

basal reading approach   A major approach to reading that occupies the central and broadest position on the instructional continuum. Built on scope and sequence foundations and traditionally associated with bottom-up theory, basal programs have been modified in recent years with the inclusion of language experience and literature activities.

belief systems   Theoretical orientations and philosophical approaches to the teaching of reading.

best practice   Thoughtful, informed, state-of-the art teaching in which literacy-related practices are theoretically sound and supported by research.

big books   Enlarged versions of children's storybooks, distinguished by large print and illustrations, designed to offer numerous opportunities for interaction.

bilingual learners   Students whose first language is different from the language of instruction in the school and who may or may not be fluent in the language of instruction.

book talks   Discussion opportunities for children to engage in conversations about their responses to reading books from class core study, reading workshops, or literature circles.

bottom-up model   A type of reading model that assumes that the process of translating print to meaning begins with the printed word and is initiated by decoding graphic symbols into sound.

brainstorming   Prereading activity that identifies a broad concept reflecting the main topic to be studied in an assigned reading and organizes students in small groups to generate a list of words related to the topic.

buddy journal   Written conversations between children in a journal format; promotes student interaction, cooperation, and collaboration.

categorization   Critical manipulation of words in relation to other words through the labeling of ideas, events, or objects.

checklist   A list of categories presented for specific diagnostic purposes.

choral reading   Oral reading, often of poetry, that makes use of various voice combinations and contrasts to create meaning or highlight the tonal qualities of a passage.

class relationships   Conceptual hierarchies organized according to the superordinate and subordinate nature of the concepts.

classroom libraries   Collection of children's literature and trade books selected to supplement textbooks; may be teacher-created or part of a basal reading series.

cloze passages   Quotations with one or more word deletions within each sentence; used to elicit responses from students.

code emphasis   Emphasis on decoding, the translation of unfamiliar printed words into speech.

cognitive and academic diversity   The situation that results when children learn faster than, slower than, or differently from what is expected at school.

collaborative learning   Learning in an environment where students work effectively together to complete literacy-related tasks.

community of learners   The classroom conceptualized as a nurturing and supportive environment.

community of readers   The conceptualization of children, in alliance with their friends and teacher, work together in classrooms in which school reading imitates adult reading; an effect created by literature-based reading programs.

computer management system   Any system that allows teachers to use computers to score tests, record skill progress information, and prepare status reports.

concept   A mental image of anything; can be used as the basis for grouping by common features or similar criteria.

concept circles   A vocabulary activity in which students identify conceptual relationships among words and phases that are partitioned within a circle.

considerate text   A textbook distinguished by its user-friendliness, particularly in regard to organizational features and presentation of material.

consolidated alphabetic phase   The final phase in children's ability to identify words in which they rely less on individual letter-sound relationships and use their knowledge of predictable letter patterns to speed up the process of reading words.

consonant-based phonics instruction   Phonics instruction activities and procedures that make use of reader's knowledge of consonants to identify words.

consonants   The sounds represented by all the letters of the alphabet except *a, e, i, o,* and *u.*

constructivism   Learning theory associated with Jean Piaget that describes meaning-making as cognitively constructing knowledge by using prior knowledge and experience in interaction with the environment.

continuous progress   Teaching reading at students' individual reading levels, not grade levels.

controlled vocabulary   Vocabulary taught progressively by controlling the number of new words students will encounter in each reading lesson.

cooperative learning   Learning that occurs as students work together in small groups to help each other achieve an academic goal.

core books   Collection of books that form the nucleus of a school reading program at each grade level; usually selected by a curriculum committee.

criterion-referenced tests   Informal tests devised to measure individual student achievement according to a specific criterion for performance (e.g., eight words out of ten spelled correctly).

cross-checking   Using letter-sound information and meaning to identify words.

cultural diversity   Situation that results when a student's home, family, socioeconomic group, culture, and society differ from the predominant culture of the school.

decoding   The conscious or automatic processing and translating of the printed word into speech.

definitional knowledge   The ability to relate new words to known words; can be built through synonyms, antonyms, and multiple-meaning words.

desktop publishing   Using software programs that combine word processing with layout and other graphic design features that allow children and teachers to integrate print and graphics on a page.

developmentally appropriate practice   The matching or gearing of the reading curriculum to children's developing abilities.

developmental stages of spelling   Stages in the gradual recognition and understanding of spelling rules, from letter-sound associations to vowels, transitional spelling, and conventional spelling.

diagnostic test   Formal assessment intended to provide detailed information about individual students' strengths and weaknesses.

dialect   A set of rule-governed variations of a language.

dialog journal   A journal written as a conversation between child and teacher that emphasizes meaning while providing natural, functional experiences in both writing and reading.

directed reading-thinking activity (DR-TA)   An activity that builds critical awareness of the reader's role and responsibility in interacting with the text through the process of predicting, verifying, judging, and extending thinking about text material.

discussion web   A strategy used in cooperative learning that requires students to explore both sides of issues during postreading discussions before drawing conclusions.

double-entry journal   A two-column journal format that gives students an opportunity to identify passages from texts and explore in writing why those passages are interesting or meaningful.

dramatic play   Unstructured, spontaneous, and expressive classroom activities requiring little planning.

early intervention   Intervening to help lower-than-expected achievers catch up with able reading peers.

eclectic instruction   The teacher's use of a combination of approaches and strategies to teach reading.

electronic classroom   A computer-intense classroom in which students can experience learning in a technology-rich instructional environment.

electronic texts   Texts that are created and read on a computer screen.

emergent literacy   Children's literacy learning conceptualized as developmental, with no clear beginning or end, rather than as proceeding in distinct sequence. Thus children begin to develop literacy through everyday experiences with print long before they enter school.

explicit   Based on stated information.

explicit instruction   Teacher-centered or teacher-facilitated instruction.

explicit strategy instruction   Instruction that makes clear the *what, why, when,* and *how* of skill and strategy use.

expository texts   Books (particularly textbooks) that rely heavily on discourse distinguished by description, classification, and explanation.

extension (integrating across the curriculum)   Using activities such as art, music, and writing as catalysts to extend ideas and concepts initiated during a formal lesson.

family literacy   How family interactions influence the language development of young children and provide the context in which they learn to read and write.

fluency   The ability to read easily and well.

fluency development lesson (FDL)   An instructional framework designed to develop oral reading fluency. It incorporates the use of various repeated reading techniques such as choral reading and paired reading routines.

free response   Active involvement or participation in reading through discussion or writing that includes inferential, evaluative, and analytic thinking about a book based on the reader's response.

full alphabetic phase   One of four stages in children's ability to identify words. This stage is evident when children have developed enough knowledge about letter-sound relationships to unlock the pronunciations of unknown words.

function words   Grammatically necessary words, such as articles, conjunctions, pronouns, verbs of being, and prepositions, that bind information-bearing words.

gifted readers   Students who have wide vocabularies, read two or more years above grade level, have excellent memory for story details, understand complex concepts and ideas, and learn skills and strategies quickly and with minimum structure.

graphic organizer   Any diagram of key concepts or main ideas that shows their relationships to each other.

graphophonemic cues   Letter-sound information that readers process during reading.

grouping   The creation and disbanding of groups of differing sizes, abilities, and interests for the purpose of providing specific instruction.

group share session   Discussion period intended to help students reflect on the day's work. As part of a writing workshop plan, the session focuses on specific writing concerns.

high-frequency words   Words that appear often in printed material.

I-Chart   A chart that helps students research, organize, and integrate information from multiple text sources.

idea circle   A *literature circle* in which readers engage in discussions of concepts that they have been exploring in trade books and other types of texts.

immediate word identification   The rapid recognition of words, a process often triggered by a reader's well-developed schemata for different words.

implicit   Based on unstated assumptions in conjunction with given information.

inclusion   Incorporating the diverse needs and abilities of all students into classroom instruction.

individualized instruction   Any strategy or instructional plan that allows students to work at their own pace and level.

inferential strategy   Elementary student strategy built around prereading questions and postreading discussion.

informal assessment   Informal measures of reading that yield useful information about student performance without comparisons to the performance of a normative population.

informal assessment opportunities   Occasions identified in basal program teacher's manuals for noticing children's strengths and weaknesses as they write.

informal reading inventory (IRI)   An individually administered informal test, usually consisting of graded word lists, graded reading passages, and comprehension questions that assess how students orally and silently interact with print.

inquiry learning   A process in which students engage in experimentation and problem solving as they research issues and interests, gathering information from a variety of sources.

instructional aids   Charts, workbooks, skill packs, cards, game boxes, and other devices that accompany a basal reading program.

instructional scaffolding   Providing enough instructional guidance and support for students so that they will be successful in their use of reading strategies.

instrumental hypothesis   Belief in a causal chain between vocabulary knowledge and comprehension; that is, if comprehension depends in part on the knowledge of word meanings, vocabulary instruction should influence comprehension.

interactive model   A type of reading model that assumes that translating print to meaning involves using both prior knowledge and print and that the process is initiated by the reader making predictions about meaning and/or decoding graphic symbols.

interactive reading   Teachers and children reading books together, collaborating to construct meaning and enjoy stories.

interactive writing   Shared writing activity in which children are invited to volunteer to write parts of a story.

Internet inquiry   An instructional strategy designed to help students engage in research on the Internet based on the questions they raise or their interests in various topics of study.

interviewing   Periodic communication with individual students to assess reading interests and attitudes, self-perceptions, and understanding of the language-learning process.

invented spellings   Spellings children use early in their reading and writing development as they begin to associate letters to sounds.

key words   Words charged with personal meaning and feeling selected for use in helping beginning readers identify words quickly and easily.

kidwatching   See *observation.*

kindergarten program   The literature-based basal program's first level for beginning or nonreaders.

knowledge hypothesis   The suggestion that vocabulary and comprehension reflect general knowledge rather than intellectual ability.

KWL   (What do you *know?* What do you *want* to find out? What did you *learn?*) Three-step teaching model designed to guide and motivate children as they read to acquire information from expository texts.

language experience   See *language-experience approach (LEA).*

language-experience activities   Activities using the natural language of children and their background experiences to share and discuss events, listen to and tell stories, dictate words, sentences, and stories, and write independently.

language-experience approach (LEA)   A major approach to reading, located on the holistic side of the instructional continuum, tied closely to interactive or top-down theory. Often considered a beginning reading approach, connections between reading and writing are becoming more prevalent in classrooms.

learning centers   Classroom areas set aside to offer students more and diverse opportunities to work in small groups or independently and more student choice, commitment, and responsibility.

levels   Sequential arrangements of readers, teacher's editions, and ancillary materials for each grade level in basal reading programs.

linguistic awareness   Understanding the technical terms and labels needed to talk and think about reading.

linguistic diversity   The diversity that results when a student's first language, or language of communication at home, is not the language of instruction in the school.

linguistic instruction   A traditional approach to teaching phonics popular in the 1960s.

literacy club   The group of written language users with whom a child interacts.

literacy development   The stages of language experience.

literacy event   Any powerful, authentic instance of the use of language to convey meaning and understanding between a writer and reader.

literacy play center   Designated classroom area designed around familiar contexts or places and furnished with props to provide an environment where children may play with print on their own terms.

literary letters   Correspondence about literary texts between children or between children and teachers; popularized by Nancy Atwell (1988).

literate environment   An environment that fosters and nurtures interest in and curiosity about written language and supports children's efforts to become readers and writers.

literature across the curriculum   Weaving an array of literature into meaningful and relevant instructional activities within the context of content area study.

literature-based instruction   A major approach to reading that encourages students to select their own trade books, with the sessions followed by teacher-student conferences at which students may be asked to read aloud from their selections; used by teachers who want to provide for individual student differences in reading abilities while focusing on meaning, interest, and enjoyment.

literature-based reading program   Reading program based on instructional practices and student activities using literature, books, novels, short stories, magazines, plays, and poems that have not been rewritten for instructional purposes.

literature circle   Discussion or study group based on a collaborative strategy involving self-selection of books for reading; each group consists of students who independently selected the same book.

literature journal   Journal that invites readers to respond to literary texts; less structured than reading logs and other journals.

literature unit   A lesson organized around book collections featuring unifying elements such as genre, author, or conceptual theme.

literature web   Any graphic device that illustrates the relationships among the major components in a unit of study.

macrocloze stories   Stories given to students with passages deleted from the text; students read the stories and discuss the missing text either orally or in writing.

management   Testing program that provides a system for arranging or managing the placement of pupils in different levels of basal reading programs.

materials   Reference books, catalogs, paperback books, magazines, and ancillaries provided in the classroom to meet students' interests and to offer instructional variety.

meaning emphasis   A focus on reading as a communication process rather than as a series of subskills.

metacognition   Awareness of one's own cognitive processes, including task knowledge and self-monitoring of activity.

minilesson   A brief, direct instructional exchange between teacher and students to address specific, observed learning needs of students.

miscue analysis   Informal assessment of oral reading errors to determine the extent to which readers use and coordinate graphic-sound, syntactic, and semantic information.

multiage classroom   A single learning community meeting the numerous needs of its student members, grouped across age levels.

multimedia authoring   Using software programs that allow students to produce text, color pictures, sound, and video in combination.

norms   Average scores of a sampling of students selected for testing according to factors such as age, sex, race, grade, or socioeconomic status; basis for comparing the performance of individuals or groups.

observation   Informal assessment by classroom teachers to document growth in learning by watching and recording students' literate behaviors.

onset   The initial part of a word (a consonant, consonant blend, or digraph) that precedes the vowel.

oral recitation lesson (ORL)   Lesson that makes use of direct instruction and student practice, including reading in chorus, as a means of incorporating fluency into daily reading instruction.

organizer   A frame of reference established to prepare children conceptually for ideas to be encountered in reading.

orthographic knowledge   Knowledge of common letter patterns that skilled readers use rapidly and accurately to associate with sounds.

paired reading   Structured collaborative work involving pairs of children of the same or different reading ability to foster reading fluency.

paired-word sentence generation   Teaching strategy that asks students to take two related words and create one sentence that correctly demonstrates an understanding of the words and their relationship to one another.

partial alphabetic phase   One of four developmental phases in children's ability to identify words. This phase is evident when children develop some knowledge about letters and begin to detect letter-sound relationships.

phonemic awareness   An understanding that speech is composed of a series of written sounds; a powerful predictor of children's later reading achievement.

phonics   The relationships between letters and sounds, taught so as to provide readers with a tool to analyze or "attack" the pronunciation of words that are not recognized immediately.

phonograms   Letter clusters that help form word families or rhyming words; see also *rime*.

point-of-view guide   An instructional activity for supporting comprehension in which readers approach a text selection from various perspectives or points of view.

portfolio   A compilation of an individual student's work in reading and writing, devised to reveal literacy progress as well as strengths and weaknesses.

portfolio assessment   Informal evaluation of a portfolio to determine a student's literacy development; a process in which teachers and students make decisions and reflect on collaboratively chosen work samples.

possible sentences   Sentences generated using vocabulary words and contrast words as a part of class discussion.

prealphabetic phase   A stage of word learning that occurs in early childhood when young children can recognize some words on sight because of distinctive visual and contextual cues in and around the recognized words; also known as the *logographic* or *visual cue phase*.

predictable texts   Literature that is distinguished by familiar or predictable characteristics of setting, story line, language patterns, or rhyme and consequently can promote fluency.

prereading activities   Activities designed to help students activate prior knowledge, set purpose, and/or engage their curiosity before reading.

pretend play   The spontaneous creation of stories—including setting, characters, goal, plot, and resolution—during children's play.

previewing   Establishing purposes and priorities before reading to help students become aware of the goals of a reading assignment.

primer   A first-grade-level reading book given to children before their first readers.

professional knowledge   Knowledge acquired from an ongoing study of the practice of teaching.

proficiency testing   Standardized testing designed to determine competence ratings for students nationwide.

psycholinguistics   The study of the mental faculties involved in acting on and interact with written language in an effort to make sense of a text.

question-answer relationships (QARs)   A comprehension strategy that enhances children's ability to answer comprehension questions by teaching them how to find the information they need to respond.

questioning the author (QtA)   A comprehension-centered instructional strategy designed to show readers how to question the author's intent while reading.

readability   The relative accessibility or difficulty of a text. Sentence length and word difficulty are among the elements used in formulas that assign grade-level readability scores for text materials.

reader-response theory   The belief that responsibility for constructing textual meaning resides primarily with the reader and depends to a great extent on the reader's prior knowledge and experience.

reader's theater   The oral presentation of drama, prose, or poetry by two or more readers.

reading journal   A journal used in conjunction with literary texts. After a period of sustained reading, teachers use prompts to guide students' written responses to the text.

reading progress cards (running records)   Informal assessment records and individualized record-keeping systems that track student progress in basal reading programs.

reading readiness   The level of physical, mental, and emotional maturity that children need to reach to benefit from reading instruction.

Reading Recovery   An early intervention program begun in New Zealand that focuses on low-ability readers who receive intense, individual instruction daily over a 15-week period.

reading workshop   Method, introduced by Nancy Atwell (1988), for integrating the language arts around literature through an organizational framework that allows readers to demonstrate reading strategies by responding to books and sharing meaning with their peers.

reading-writing connections   The natural links between reading and writing. Evidence suggests that writing and reading develop together and should therefore be nurtured together.

reciprocal teaching   An instructional strategy that builds readers' awareness of and expertise in the use of various comprehension skills and strategies.

record keeping   Tracking the books and stories read by students; records can be maintained by teachers or students.

reinforcement   Exercises involving similar and contrasting examples that are used to reinforce learning in basal programs.

reliability   Consistency of test results over time and administrations.

repeated readings   Reading short passages of text more than once, with different levels of support, to develop rapid, fluent oral reading.

ReQuest   Reciprocal questioning encourages students to ask their own questions about material they have read.

response journal   See *literate journal.*

rime   The part of the letter pattern in a word that includes the vowel and any consonants that follow; also called a *phonogram or word family.*

running records   Method for marking miscues of beginning readers while they read. Also see *reading progress cards.*

schemata   Mental frameworks that humans use to organize and construct meaning.

scope and sequence plan   General plan in basal reading programs for the introduction of skills in sequential or vertical arrangement.

scrambled stories   Stories separated into parts and jumbled; students read the stories and put them back in order.

scribbling   One of the primary forms of written expression; the fountainhead for writing that occurs from the moment a child grasps and uses a writing tool.

self-monitoring   Being aware of miscues, the pronunciation of unknown words, and comprehension processes during reading to develop the ability to correct oneself.

semantic cues   The prior knowledge and experience that readers bring to a reading situation.

semantic mapping   A strategy that shows readers and writers how to organize important information.

shared book experience   Strategy allowing all children in a classroom or small group to participate in the reading of a story, usually through the use of a big book with large print and illustrations.

skill building   The introduction, repetition, and reinforcement of skills at all levels of basal reading programs.

skill maintenance   Review of recently acquired skills to form the foundation for new learning in basal reading programs.

skills-based curriculum   A curriculum based on the assumption that learning to read successfully presumes the acquisition of a finite but sizable number of skills and specific abilities.

sociolinguisitics   The study of the everyday functions of language and how interactions with others and with the environment aid language comprehension and learning.

spelling-based phonics instruction   Using activities and procedures in which students use orthographic knowledge to study words.

stages in the writing process   Sequential activities involved in the production of written texts, include rehearsing, drafting, revising and editing, and publishing.

standardized reading test   A formal test of reading ability administered according to specific, unvarying directions; usually norm-referenced and machine-scored.

storybook experiences   Read-alouds, readalongs, interactive reading, interactive writing, rereadings of favorite texts, and independent reading and writing.

story frames   Skeletal paragraphs represented by a sequence of spaces tied together with transition words and connectors signaling lines of thought; frames can emphasize plot summary, setting, character analysis, character comparison, and problem.

story grammar   The basic elements that make up a well-developed story, such as plot and setting.

story impressions   Prereading strategy that helps students anticipate what stories could be about, using content fragments to make predictions.

story map   An analysis of a story's organizational elements; used to strengthen instructional decisions.

story schema   The underlying structure and relationships in a story that act as catalysts for constructing meaning and distinguishing important ideas and events.

strands   Areas of skills developed at increasingly higher levels throughout basal reading programs.

student schedule   Organization of an individual student's activities in different learning-center areas based on the student's strengths, weaknesses, and interests.

subordinate   Inferior in rank, class, or status.

superordinate   Superior in rank, class, or status.

survey test   Broad type of test that measures general performance only.

sustained silent reading (SSR)   Structured activity in which children are given fixed time periods for reading self-selected materials silently.

syllable   A vowel or a cluster of letters containing a vowel and pronounced as a unit.

synonyms   Words similar in meaning to other words.

syntactic cues   Grammatical information in a text that readers process, along with graphophonemic and semantic information, to construct meaning.

synthetic phonics   A building-block approach to phonics intended to foster the understanding of letter-sound relationships and develop phonic knowledge and skill.

teacher's log   Observational record of student reading and writing activities and social behaviors organized especially for assessment.

Theoretical Orientation to Reading Profile (TORP)   A survey instrument designed by Diane De Ford (1985) that uses three belief systems—phonics, skills, and whole language—to determine teacher beliefs about practices in reading instruction.

think sheet   List of questions used to elicit responses about texts for discussion purposes.

top-down model   A type of reading model that assumes that the construction of textual meaning depends on the reader's prior knowledge and experience.

trade books   Literature and informational books widely available in bookstores; used by teachers to supplement or replace sole dependence on textbooks in reading or content area instruction.

units of language   Categories of written language, ranging from the smallest units, letters, to the largest unit, the whole text selection, that are emphasized for instructional purposes.

uses of oral language   Language functions that can and should be adapted to print at the beginning of instruction.

validity   The accuracy with which a test measures what it is designed to measure—the most important characteristic of a test.

vocabulary   The panoply of words we use, recognize, and respond to in meaningful acts of communication.

vocabulary-building skills   Linguistic skills that allow children to construct word meanings independently on the basis of context clues.

vocabulary development   Introduction and repetition of words for reinforcement in basal reading programs.

vowels   All sounds represented by the letters *a, e, i, o,* and *u.*

whole language curriculum   A curriculum that integrates all the language arts—reading, writing, speaking, and listening—to create child-responsive environments for learning that are supported by literature-based instruction.

whole word method   Technique in which word recognition, rather than letters or syllables, is the main instructional unit.

word analysis   Translating print to speech through an analysis of letter-sound relationships.

word attack   The reader's ability to use letter-sound relationships to analyze unknown words; used interchangeably with the terms *phonics, word analysis,* and *decoding.*

word banks   Boxes of word cards that individual students are studying as it relates to phonics, spelling, or vocabulary learning.

word identification   The use of phonemic and meaning cues to identify unfamiliar words.

word processing   Using computers to create and publish texts.

word recognition   Rapid identification of words from memory.

word sorting activities   Vocabulary development through categorization activities with groups of words.

word walls   Words compiled on sheets of shelf paper hung on the wall of a classroom. Word wall are used by teachers to engage students in word study for a variety of instructional purposes.

workbooks   See *readers' and writers' journals.*

writing workshop   Classroom writing time during which students are given the structure and direction they need to understand, develop, or use specific writing strategies in planning and revising drafts.

Bibliography

Aaron, R. L., & Anderson, M. K. (1981). A comparison of values expressed in juvenile magazines and basal reader series. *The Reading Teacher, 35,* 305–313.

Adams, M. J. (1990). *Beginning to read: Thinking and learning about print: A summary.* Urbana: University of Illinois, Center for the Study of Reading.

Agnew, A. T. (1982). Using children's dictated stories to assess code consciousness. *The Reading Teacher, 34,* 448–452.

Allen, R. V. (1976). *Language experiences in communication.* Boston: Houghton Mifflin.

Allington, R. L. (1977). If they don't read, how they gonna get good? *Journal of Reading, 21,* 57–61.

Allington, R. L. (1983). Fluency: The neglected reading goal. *The Reading Teacher, 36,* 556–561.

Alvermann, D. E. (1991). The discussion web: A graphic aid for learning across the curriculum. *The Reading Teacher, 45,* 92–99.

Ammon, P., Simons, H., & Elster, C. (1990). Effects of controlled, primerese language on the reading process. Technical Report No. 45. Center for the Study of Writing, Berkeley and Pittsburgh. ERIC Document Reproduction Service, No. ED 334542.

Anderson, R. C., & Freebody, P. (1981). Vocabulary knowledge. In J. T. Guthrie (Ed.), *Comprehension and teaching: Research perspectives.* Newark, DE: International Reading Association.

Anderson, R. C., Hiebert, E. H., Scott, J., & Wilkinson, I. A. G. (1985). *Becoming a nation of readers.* Washington, DC: National Institute of Education.

Anderson, R. C., Higgins, G. D., & Wurster, S. R. (1985). Differences in the free reading books selected by high, average, and low achievers. *The Reading Teacher, 39,* 326–330.

Armbruster, B. B., Echols, C., & Brown, A. L. (1982). The role of metacognition in reading to learn: A developmental perspective. *Volta Review, 84,* 45–56.

Armbruster, B. B., & Nagy, W. E. (1992). Vocabulary in content area lessons. *The Reading Teacher, 45,* 550–551.

Ashton-Warner, S. (1959). *Spinster.* New York: Simon & Schuster.

Ashton-Warner, S. (1963). *Teacher.* New York: Simon & Schuster.

Ashton-Warner, S. (1972). *Spearpoint: Teachers in America.* New York: Knopf.

Atwell, N. (1998). *In the middle: New understandings about writing, reading, and learning* (2nd ed.). Portsmouth, NH: Heinemann.

Atwell, N. (1993). Forward to *Teachers are researchers.* In L. Patterson, C. Santa, K. Short, & K. Smith (Eds.), *Teachers are researchers.* Newark, DE: International Reading Association.

Au, K., & Mason, J. (1983). Cultural congruence in classroom participation: Achieving a balance of rights. *Discourse Processes, 6,* 145–167.

Avery, C. (1990). Learning to research/researching to learn. In M. Olson (Ed.), *Opening the door to classroom research.* Newark, DE: International Reading Association.

Baloche, L., & Platt, T. J. (1993). Sprouting magic beans: exploring literature through creative questioning and cooperative learning. *Language Arts, 70,* 264–271.

Barman, C. R. (1992). An evaluation of the use of a technique designed to assist prospective elementary teachers using the learning cycle with science textbooks. *School Science and Mathematics, 92*(2), 59–63.

Barone, D. (1996). Whose language? Learning from bilingual learners in a developmental first-grade classroom. In D. J. Leu, C. K. Kinzer, & K. Hinchman (Eds.), *Literacies for the 21st century: Research and practice.* Chicago: National Reading Conference.

Barr, R., & Johnson, B. (1997). *Teaching reading and writing in elementary classrooms* (2nd ed.). New York: Longman.

Barr, R., & Sadow, M. W. (1989). Influence of basal programs on fourth-grade reading instruction. *Reading Research Quarterly, 24,* 44–71.

Barrentine, S. J. (1996). Engaging with reading through interactive read-alouds. *The Reading Teacher, 50,* 36–43.

Barron, R. (1968). The use of vocabulary as an advance organizer. In H. L. Herber & P. Sanders (Eds.), *Research in reading in the content areas: First report.* Syracuse, NY: Syracuse University Reading and Language Arts Center.

Baumann, J. F., & Heubach, K. M. (1996). Do basal readers deskill teachers? A national survey of educators' use and opinions of basals. *Elementary School Journal, 96,* (5), 511–526.

Baumann, J. F., Hoffman, J. V., Moon, J., & Duffy, A. M. (1997). *It's not whole language versus phonics but a matter of balance, eclecticism, and common sense: Results from a survey of U.S. elementary school teachers.* Athens, GA: National Reading Research Center.

Baumann, J. F., Hoffman, J. V., Moon, J., & Duffy-Hester, A. M. (1998). Where are teachers' voices in the phonics/whole language debate? Results from a survey of U.S. elementary classroom teachers. *The Reading Teacher, 51,* 636–650.

Bean, R., Cooley, W., Eichelberger, R., Lazar, M. & Zigmond, N. (1991). Inclass or pullout: Effects of setting on the remedial reading program. *Journal of Reading Behavior, 23,* 445–463.

Bear, D. R., Invernizzi, M., Templeton, S., & Johnston, F. (1996). *Words their way: Word study for phonics, vocabulary, and spelling instruction.* Upper Saddle River, NJ: Merrill.

Bear, D. R., & Templeton, S. (1998). Explorations in developmental spelling: Foundations for learning and teaching phonics, spelling, and vocabulary. *The Reading Teacher, 52,* 222–242.

Beck, I. L., & Juel, C. (1995). The role of decoding in learning to read. *American Educator, 19*(2), 8, 21–25, 39–42.

Beck, I. L., & McKeown, M. G. (1983). Learning words well: A program to enhance vocabulary and comprehension. *The Reading Teacher, 36,* 622–625.

Beck, I. L., & McKeown, M. G. (1991). Research directions social studies texts are hard to understand: Mediating some of the difficulties, *Language Arts, 68,* 482–490.

Beck, I. L., McKeown, M. G., Hamilton, R. L., & Kucan, L. (1997). *Questioning the author: An approach for enhancing student engagement with text.* Newark, DE: International Reading Association.

Beck, I. L., McKeown, M. G., & McCaslin, E. (1983). All contexts are not created equal. *Elementary School Journal, 83,* 177–181.

Beck, I. L., McKeown, M. G., McCaslin, E., & Burket, A. (1979). *Instructional dimensions that may affect reading comprehension: Examples of two commercial reading programs.* Pittsburgh: University of Pittsburgh Language Research and Development Center.

Beck, I. L., McKeown, M. G., & Omanson, R. (1987). The effects and uses of diverse vocabulary instructional techniques. In M. McKeown & M. Cartis (Eds.), *The nature of vocabulary acquisition.* Mahwah, NJ: Erlbaum.

Beck, I. L., Perfetti, C. A., & McKeown, M. G. (1982). Effects of long-term vocabulary instruction on lexical access and reading comprehension. *Journal of Educational Psychology, 74,* 506–521.

Benjamin, L. A., & Lord, J. (1996). *Family literacy.* Washington, DC: Office of Educational Research and Improvement.

Benton, M. (1984). The methodology vacuum in teaching literature. *Language Arts, 61,* 265–275.

Betts, E. A. (1946). *Foundations of reading instruction.* New York: American Book Company.

Beyersdorfer, J. M., & Schauer, D. K. (1989). Semantic analysis to writing: Connecting words, books, and writing. *Journal of Reading, 32,* 500–508.

Bieger, M. (1996). Promoting multicultural education through a literature-based approach. *The Reading Teacher, 49*, 308–312.

Bissex, G. (1980). *GNYS AT WRK: A child learns to write and read.* Cambridge, MA: Harvard University Press.

Blachowicz, C. L. (1986). Making connections: Alternatives to the vocabulary notebook. *Journal of Reading, 29*, 643–649.

Blanchard, J. S., & Rottenberg, C. J. (1990). Hypertext and hypermedia: Discovering and creating meaningful learning environments. *The Reading Teacher, 43*, 656–661.

Bloomfield, L., & Barnhart, C. (1961). *Let's read: A linguistic approach.* Austin, TX: Holt, Rinehart and Winston.

Blume, J. (1970). *Are you there, God? It's me, Margaret.* New York: Dell.

Bond, G., & Dykstra, R. (1967). The cooperative research programs in first-grade reading. *Reading Research Quarterly, 2*, 135–142.

Bradley, J. M., & Talgott, M. R. (1987). Reducing reading anxiety. *Academic Therapy, 22*, 349–358.

Bransford, J. D., & Johnson, M. K. (1973). Considerations of some problems of comprehension. In W. C. Chase (Ed.), *Visual information processing.* Orlando, FL: Academic Press.

Braunger, J., & Lewis, J. P. (1997). *Building a knowledge base in reading.* Newark, DE: International Reading Association.

Bredekamp, S. (1987). *Developmentally appropriate practice.* Washington, DC: National Association for the Education of Young Children.

Bromley, K. (1989). Buddy journals make the reading-writing connection. *The Reading Teacher, 43*, 122–129.

Brown, A. L. (1985). Metacognition: The development of selective attention strategies for learning from texts. In H. S. Singer & R. B. Ruddell (Eds.), *Theoretical models and processes of reading* (3rd ed.). Newark, DE: International Reading Association.

Brozo, W. G., & Tomlinson, C. M. (1986). Literature: The key to lively content courses. *The Reading Teacher, 40*, 288–293.

Bunting, E. (1989). *The Wednesday surprise.* New York: Clarion Books.

Bus, A., Van Ijzendoorn, M., & Pellegrini, A (1995). Joint book reading makes for success in learning to read: A meta-analysis on intergeneration transmission of literacy. *Review of Educational Research, 65*, 1–21.

Butler, A. (1988). *Shared book experience.* Crystal Lake, IL: Rigby.

Calkins, L. M. (1983). *Lessons from a child.* Portsmouth, NH: Heinemann.

Calkins, L. M. (1994). *The art of teaching writing.* Portsmouth, NH: Heinemann.

Cambourne, B. (1984). Language, learning, and literacy. In A. Butler & J. Turbill (Eds.). *Towards a reading-writing classroom.* Portsmouth, NH: Heinemann.

Carnine, D., Silbert, J., & Kameenui, E. T. (1990). *Direct instruction reading* (2nd ed.). Columbus, OH: Merrill.

Celebrate reading! (1997). Glenview, IL: Scott, Foresman.

Chall, J., & Curtis, M. (1989). Responding to individual differences among language learners: Children at risk. In J. Flood, J. M. Jensen, D. Lapp, & J. Squire (Eds.), *Handbook of research on teaching the English language arts.* Old Tappan, NJ: Macmillan.

Chenfield, M. (1978). *Teaching language arts creatively.* Orlando, FL: Harcourt Brace.

Chomsky, C. (1970). Reading, writing, and phonology. *Harvard Educational Review, 40*, 287–309.

Chomsky, C. (1976). After decoding, what? *Language Arts, 53*, 288–296, 314.

Chomsky, C. (1979). Approaching reading through invented spelling. In L. B. Resnick & P. A. Weaver (Eds.), *Theory and practice of early reading*, Vol. 2. Mahwah, NJ: Erlbaum.

Clay, M. M. (1966). *Emergent reading behavior.* Unpublished doctoral dissertation, University of Auckland, New Zealand.

Clay, M. M. (1979a). *Concepts about print test.* Portsmouth, NH: Heinemann.

Clay, M. M. (1979b). *Reading: The patterning of complex behavior* (2nd ed.). Auckland, New Zealand: Heinemann.

Clay, M. M. (1979c). *Stones.* Portsmouth, NH: Heinemann.

Clay, M. M. (1985). *The early detection of reading difficulties: A diagnostic survey with recovery procedures.* Portsmouth, NH: Heinemann.

Clay, M. M. (1988). Exploring with a pencil. *Reading Today.*

Clay, M. M. (1991). *Becoming literate: The construction of inner control.* Portsmouth, NH: Heinemann.

Clyde, J. A., & Condon, M. W. F. (1992). Collaborating in coursework and classrooms: An alternative for strengthening whole language teacher preparation cultures. In C. Weaver & L. Henke (Eds.), *Supporting whole language: Stories of teacher and instructional change.* Portsmouth, NH: Heinemann.

Clymer, T. (1963). The utility of phonic generalizations in the primary grades. *The Reading Teacher, 16,* 252–258.

Cohen, D. (1968). The effect of literature on vocabulary and reading achievement. *Elementary English, 45,* 209–213, 217.

Collier, V. (1989). How long? A synthesis of research on academic achievement in a second language. *TESOL Quarterly, 23,* 509–532.

Confrey, J. (1990). What constructivism implies for teaching. In R. B. Davis, C. A. Maher, & N. Noddings (Eds.), *Constructivist views on the teaching and learning of mathematics.* Reston, VA: National Council of Teachers of Mathematics.

Connelly, F. M., & Clandinin, D. J. (1988). *Teachers as curriculum planners: Narrative of experience.* New York: Teachers College Press.

Coody, B., & Nelson, D. (1982). *Teaching elementary language arts.* Belmont, CA: Wadsworth.

Cooper, P., & Gray, P. (1984). *Teaching listening as an interactive process.* Paper presented at the annual convention of the International Reading Association, Atlanta.

Cowley, J. (October, 1991). Joy of big books. *Instructor, 19.*

Crafton, L. (1983). Learning from reading: What happens when students generate their own background knowledge. *Journal of Reading, 26,* 586–593.

Cramer, R. L. (1975). Reading to children: Why and how. *The Reading Teacher, 28,* 460–463.

Cramer, R. L. (1978). *Children's writing and language growth.* Columbus, OH: Merrill.

Cullinan, B., & Galda, L. (1994). *Literature and the child* (3rd ed.). New York: Harcourt Brace.

Cullinan, B., Jaggar, A., & Strickland, D. S. (1974). Language expansion for black children in primary grades: A research report. *Young Children, 29,* 98–112.

Cummins, J. (1986). Empowering minority students: A framework for intervention. *Harvard Educational Review, 56,* 18–36.

Cummins, J. (1989). *Empowering minority students.* Sacramento, CA: Association of Bilingual Education.

Cunningham, J. W., Cunningham, P. M., Hoffman, J. V., & Yopp, H. R. (1998). *Phonemic awareness and the teaching of reading: A position statement from the board of directors of the International Reading Association.* Newark, DE: International Reading Association.

Cunningham, P. M. (1995). *Phonics they use: Words for reading and writing* (2nd ed.). New York: HarperCollins.

Cunningham, P. M., & Allington, R. L. (1999). *Classrooms that work: They can all read and write* (2nd ed.). New York: Longman.

Dale, E. (1965). Vocabulary measurement: Techniques and major findings. *Elementary English, 42,* 895–901.

D'Alessandro, M. (1990). Accommodating emotionally handicapped children through a literature-based reading program. *The Reading Teacher, 44,* 288–293.

Daniels, H. (1994). *Literature circles: Voice and choice in one student-centered classroom.* York, ME: Stenhouse.

Davis, D. C. (1973). *Playway: Education for reality.* Minneapolis: Winston.

Davis, F. B. (1944). Fundamental factors of comprehension in reading. *Psychometrika, 9,* 185–197.

Davis, S., & Johns, L. (1991). Identifying and challenging gifted readers. *Illinois Reading Council Journal, 19,* 34a–34d.

De Ford, D. E. (1985). Validating the construct of theoretical orientation in reading instruction. *Reading Research Quarterly, 20,* 366–367.

Deighton, L. (1970). *Vocabulary development in the classroom.* New York: Teachers College Press.

Delpit, L. (1988). The silenced dialogue: Power and pedagogy and educating other people's children. *Harvard Educational Review, 58,* 280–298.

Dillard, J. M. (1983). *Multicultural counseling: Toward ethnic and cultural relevance in human encounters.* Chicago: Nelson-Hall.

Dole, J. A., & Osborn, J. (1989). *Reading materials: Their selection and use.* Technical Report No. 457. Urbana: University of Illinois, Center for the Study of Reading. ERIC Document Reproduction Service No. ED 305592.

Dooley, C. (1993). The challenge: Meeting the needs of gifted readers. *The Reading Teacher, 46,* 546–551.

Dowhower, S. L. (1987). Effects of repeated reading in second-grade transitional readers' fluency and comprehension. *Reading Research Quarterly, 22,* 389–406.

Dowhower, S. L. (1989). Repeated reading: Research into practice. *The Reading Teacher, 43,* 502–507.

Downing, J. (1979). *Reading and reasoning.* New York: Springer-Verlag.

Downing, J. (1982). Reading: Skill or skills? *The Reading Teacher, 35,* 534–537.

Duin, A., & Graves, M. (1987). Intensive vocabulary instruction as a prewriting technique. *Reading Research Quarterly, 22,* 311–330.

Dupuis, M. M., & Snyder, S. L. (1983). Develop concepts through vocabulary: A strategy for reading specialists to use with content teachers. *Journal of Reading, 26,* 297–305.

Durkin, D. (1966). *Children who read early.* New York: Teachers College Press.

Durkin, D. (1980). *Teaching young children to read* (3rd ed.). Needham Heights, MA: Allyn & Bacon.

Durkin, D. (1988). *A classroom observation study of reading instruction in kindergarten.* Technical Report No. 422. Champaign: University of Illinois, Center for the Study of Reading.

Durrell, D. D. (1958). Success in first-grade reading. *Journal of Education, 148,* 1–8.

Durrell, D. D. (1963). *Phonograms in primary grade words.* Boston: Boston University Press.

Dyson, A. H. (1989). *Multiple worlds of child writers: Friends learning to write.* New York: Teachers College Press.

Dyson, A. H. (1993). Whistle for Willie, lost puppies, and cartoon dogs: The sociocultural dimensions of young children's composing. *Journal of Reading Behavior, 24,* 433–462.

Earle, A. (1995). *Zipping, zapping, zooming bats.* New York: HarperCollins.

Ehri, L. C. (1991). Development of the ability to read words. In R. Barr, M. L. Kamil, P. Mosenthal, & P. D. Pearson (Eds.), *Handbook of reading research* (2nd ed.). New York: Longman.

Ehri, L. C. (1992). Reconceptualizing the development of sight word reading and its relationship to reading. In P. Grough, L. C. Ehri, & R. Trelman (Eds.), *Reading acquisition.* Mahwah, NJ: Erlbaum.

Ehri, L. C. (1994). Development of the ability to read words: Update. In R. Ruddell & H. Singer (Eds.), *Theoretical models and processes of reading* (4th ed.). Newark, DE: International Reading Association.

Ehri, L. C. (1995). Teachers need to know how word reading processes develop to teach reading effectively to beginners. In C. N. Hedley, P. Antonacci, & M. Rabinowitz (Eds.), *Thinking and literacy: The mind at work.* Mahwah, NJ: Erlbaum.

Elkind, D. (1989). Developmentally appropriate practice: Philosophical and practical implications. *Phi Delta Kappan, 71,* 113–117.

Ennis, R. H. (1987). A taxonomy of critical thinking dispositions and abilities. In J. Baron & R. Steinberg (Eds.), *Teaching thinking skills: Theory and practice.* New York: Freeman.

Farr, R., & Tone, B. (1998). *Assessment portfolio and performance* (2nd ed.). Orlando, FL: Harcourt Brace.

Fawcett, G. (1990). Literacy vignette: The gift. *The Reading Teacher, 43,* 504.

Fielding, L. G., Wilson, P. T., & Anderson, R. C. (1986). A new focus on free reading: The role of trade books in reading instruction. In T. Raphael (Ed.), *The contexts of school-based literacy.* New York: Random House.

Fisette, D. (1993). Practical authentic assessment: Good kid watchers know what to teach next! *The California Reader, 26*(4), 4–9.

Fitzgerald, J. (1993). Literacy and students who are learning English as a second language. *The Reading Teacher, 46,* 638–647.

Flippo, R. (1998). Points of agreement: A display of professional unity in our field. *The Reading Teacher, 52,* 30–40.

Flood, J., & Lapp, D. (1989). Reporting reading progress: A comparison portfolio for parents. *The Reading Teacher, 42,* 508–514.

Flood, J., Lapp, D., & Nagel, G. (1993). Assessing student action beyond reflection and response. *Journal of Reading, 36,* 420–423.

Fosnot, C. (1996). *Constructivism: Theory, perspectives, and practice.* New York: Teachers College Press.

Fowler, G. L. (1982). Developing comprehension skills in primary students through the use of story frames. *The Reading Teacher, 36,* 176–179.

Fox, B. J. (1996). *Strategies for word identification: Phonics from a new perspective.* Columbus, OH: Merrill.

Fox, B. J., & Wright, M. (1997). Connecting school and home literacy experiences through cross-age reading. *The Reading Teacher, 50,* 396–403.

Fox, M. (1993). Politics and literature: Chasing the "isms" from children's books. *The Reading Teacher, 46,* 654–658.

Fractor, J. S., Woodruff, M. C., Martinez, M. G, & Teale, W. H. (1993). Let's not miss opportunities to promote voluntary reading: Classroom libraries in the elementary school. *The Reading Teacher, 46,* 476–484.

Frager, A., & Valentour, J. (1984). Beyond book jackets: Creative bulletin boards to encourage reading. *Reading Horizons, 24,* 259–262.

Freeman, D., & Freeman, Y. (1993). Strategies for promoting the primary languages. *The Reading Teacher, 46,* 551–558.

Freppon, P. A., & Dahl, K. L. (1998). Balanced instruction: Insights and considerations. *Reading Research Quarterly, 33,* 240–251.

Fry, E. B. (1968). A readability formula that saves time. *Journal of Reading, 11,* 513–516, 575–578.

Fry, E. B. (1977). Fry's readability graph: Clarifications, validity, and extension to level 17. *Journal of Reading, 21,* 242–252.

Fry, E. B. (1980). The new instant word list. *The Reading Teacher, 34,* 284–290.

Gadsden, V. (1992). Literacy and the African-American learner: The struggle between access and denial. *Theory into Practice, 31,* 274–275.

Gambrell, L. B. (1985). Dialogue journals: Reading-writing interactions. *The Reading Teacher, 38,* 512–515.

Garcia, G., Pearson, P. D., & Jimenez, R. (1990). *The at-risk dilemma: A synthesis of reading research.* Champaign: University of Illinois, Reading Research and Education Center.

Garcia, J., & Florez-Tighe, V. (1986). The portrayal of Blacks, Hispanics, and Native Americans in recent basal series. *Equity and Excellence, 22*(4), 72–76.

Gaskins, I. W., Ehri, L. C., Cress, C., O'Hara, C., & Donnelly, K. (1997). Procedures for word learning: Making discoveries about words. *The Reading Teacher, 50,* 312–327.

Gates, B. (1988). Computers in schools, today and tomorrow. *T.H.E. Journal, 16,* 14–15.

Gentry, J. R., & Henderson, E. H. (1980). Three steps to teaching beginning readers to spell. In E. H. Henderson & J. W. Beers (Eds.), *Developmental aspects of learning to spell: A reflection of word knowledge.* Newark, DE: International Reading Association.

Giff, P. R. (1980). *Today was a terrible day.* New York: Viking.

Glazer, S. M., & Brown, C. S. (1993). *Portfolios and beyond.* Norwood, MA: Christopher- Gordon.

Goatley, V. (1997). Talk about text among special education students. In S. I. McMahon & E. Raphael (Eds.), *The book club connection.* New York: Teachers College Press.

Goff, P. (1998). Where's the phonics? Making a case for its direct and systematic instruction. *The Reading Teacher, 52,* 138–141.

Goodman, K. S. (1973). Psycholinguistic universals in the reading process. In F. Smith (Ed.), *Psycholinguistics and reading.* Austin, TX: Holt, Rinehart and Winston.

Goodman, K. S. (1975). Do you have to be smart to read? Do you have to read to be smart? *The Reading Teacher, 28,* 625–632.

Goodman, K. S. (1986). *What's whole in whole language?* Portsmouth, NH: Heinemann.

Goodman, K. S. (1988). Look what they've done to Judy Blume! The basalization of children's literature. *New Advocate, 1,* 18–28.

Goodman, K. S. (1997). Principles of revaluing. In Y. M. Goodman & A. M. Marek (Eds.), *Retrospective miscue analysis.* Katonah, NY: Owen.

Goodman, Y. M. (1978). Kid-watching: An alternative to testing. *National Elementary Principal, 10,* 41–45.

Goodman, Y. M., & Burke, C. L. (1972). *Reading miscue inventory manual: Procedure for diagnosis and evaluation.* Old Tappan, NJ: Macmillan.

Goodman, Y. M., & Marek, A. M. (1997). *Retrospective miscue analysis,* Katonah, NY: Owen.

Gordon, C. J., & Braun, C. (1983). Using story schemata as an aid to reading and writing. *The Reading Teacher, 37,* 116–121.

Goswami, U. (1998). The role of analogies in the development of word recognition. In J. Metsalan & L. Ehri (Eds.), *Word recognition in beginning literacy.* Mahwah, NJ: Erlbaum.

Goswami, U., & Bryant, P. (1990). *Phonological skills learning to read.* Mahwah, NJ: Erlbaum.

Gough, P. (1985). One second of reading. In H. Singer & R. Ruddell (Eds.), *Theoretical models and processes of reading* (3rd ed.). Newark, DE: International Reading Association.

Graves, D. H. (1983). *Writing: Teachers and children at work.* Portsmouth, NH: Heinemann.

Graves, D. H. (1994). *A fresh look at writing.* Portsmouth, NH: Heinemann.

Graves, D. H., & Sunstein, B. S. (1992). *Portfolio portraits.* Portsmouth, NH: Heinemann.

Gray-Schlegel, M. A., & King, Y. (1998). Introducing concepts about print to the preservice teacher: A hands-on experience. *The California Reader, 32*(1), 17–21.

Greenlaw, M. J. (1988). Using informational books to extend the curriculum. *The Reading Teacher, 42,* 18.

Griffith, P. L., & Olson, M. (1992). Phonemic awareness helps beginning readers break the code. *The Reading Teacher, 45,* 516–523.

Gruenberg, R. (1948). Poor Mr. Fingle. In *More favorite stories.* New York: Doubleday.

Gunning, T. G. (1995). Word building: A strategic approach to the teaching of phonics. *The Reading Teacher, 48,* 484–489.

Guthrie, J. T., & McCann, A. D. (1996). Idea circles: Peer collaborations for conceptual learning. In L. B. Gambrell & J. F. Almasi (Eds.), *Lively discussions! Fostering engaged reading.* Newark, DE: International Reading Association.

Gutknecht, B. (1991). Mitigating the effects of negative stereotyping of aging and the elderly in primary grade reading instruction. *Reading Improvement, 28,* 44–51.

Haggard, M. R. (1986). The vocabulary self-collection strategy: Using student interest and world knowledge to enhance vocabulary growth. *Journal of Reading, 29,* 634–642.

Hall, D. (1979). *Ox-Cart Man,* ill. by Barbara Cooney. Viking, 1979.

Halliday, M. A. K. (1975). Learning how to mean: Exploration in the development of language. London: Arnold.

Hancock, M. R. (1993a). Exploring and extending personal response through literature journals. *The Reading Teacher, 46,* 466–474.

Hancock, M. R. (1993b). Exploring the meaning-making process through the content of literature response journals: A case study investigation. *Research in the Teaching of English, 27,* 335–369.

Hansen, J. (1981). An inferential comprehension strategy for use with primary children. *The Reading Teacher, 34,* 665–669.

Hansen, J. (1987). *When writers read.* Portsmouth, NH: Heinemann.

Harmin, M. (1994) *Inspiring active learning: A handbook for teachers.* Alexandria, VA: Association for Supervisor and Curriculum Development.

Harris, T. H., & Hodges, R. E. (1995). *The literacy dictionary: The vocabulary of reading and writing.* Newark, DE: International Reading Association.

Harris, V. (1993). Bookalogues: Multicultural literature. *Language Arts, 70,* 215–217.

Harste, J. C., & Burke, C. L. (1977). A new hypothesis for reading teacher research. In P. D. Pearson & J. Hansen (Eds.), *Reading: Theory, research, and practice.* Clemson, SC: National Reading Conference.

Harste, J. C., Short, K. G., & Burke, C. (1988). *Creating classrooms for authors: The reading-writing connection.* Portsmouth, NH: Heinemann.

Harste, J. C., Woodward, V. A., & Burke, C. L. (1984). *Language stories and literacy lessons.* Portsmouth, NH: Heinemann.

Heath, S. B. (1982). What no bedtime story means: Narrative skills at home and at school. *Language and Society, 11,* 49–77.

Heath, S. B. (1991). The sense of being literate: Historical and cross-cultural features. In R. Barr, M. L. Kamil, P. Mosenthal, & P. D. Pearson (Eds.), *Handbook of reading research* (2nd ed.). New York: Longman.

Heath, S. B., & Mangiola, L. (1991). *Children of promise: Literate activity in linguistically and culturally diverse classrooms.* Washington, DC: National Education Association.

Heilman, A. W., Blair, T. R., & Rupley, W. H. (1986). *Principles and practices of teaching reading* (6th ed.). Columbus, OH: Merrill.

Henderson, E. H., & Beers, J. W. (Eds.). (1980). *Developmental and cognitive aspects of learning to spell: A reflection of word knowledge.* Newark, DE: International Reading Association.

Henderson, E. (1990). *Teaching spelling* (2nd ed.). Boston: Houghton Mifflin.

Henderson, J. G., & Hawthorne, R. D. (1995). *Transformative curriculum leadership.* Columbus, OH: Merrill.

Henry, G. (1974). *Teaching reading as concept development.* Newark, DE: International Reading Association.

Hepler, S. I. (1982). *Patterns of response to literature: A one-year study of a fifth- and sixth-grade classroom.* Unpublished doctoral dissertation, Ohio State University, Columbus.

Hepler, S. I., & Hickman, J. (1982). "The book was okay. I love you": Social aspects of response to literature. *Theory into Practice, 21,* 278–283.

Herman, P. A. (1985). The effect of repeated readings on reading rate, speech, and word recognition. *Reading Research Quarterly, 20,* 553–565.

Herring, R. D. (1997). *Counseling diverse ethnic youth.* Orlando, FL: Harcourt Brace.

Herrington, A. J. (1997). Developing and responding to major writing projects. In M. D. Sorcinelli & P. Elbow (Eds.), *Writing to learn: Strategies for assigning and responding to writing across the disciplines.* San Francisco: Jossey-Bass.

Herrmann, B. A. (1988). Two approaches for helping poor readers become more strategic. *The Reading Teacher, 42,* 24–28.

Hickman, J. (1983). Classrooms that help children like books. In N. Roser & M. Frith (Eds.), *Children's choices.* Newark, DE: International Reading Association.

Hilbert, S. B. (1993). Sustained silent reading revisited. *The Reading Teacher, 46,* 354–356.

Hitchcock, M. E., & Tompkins, G. E. (1987). Basal readers: Are they still sexist? *The Reading Teacher, 41,* 288–292.

Hittleman, D. (1973). Seeking a psycholinguistic definition of readability. *The Reading Teacher, 26,* 783–789.

Hoffman, J. V. (1985). *The oral recitation lesson: A teacher's guide.* Austin, TX: Academic Resource Consultants.

Hoffman, J. V., McCarthy, S. J., Bayles, D. L., Price, D. P., Elliot, B., Dressman, M., & Abbott, J. A. (1995). *Reading instruction in first-grade classrooms: Do basals control teachers?* Report No. 43. Athens: University of Georgia, National Reading Research Center.

Hoffman, J. V., McCarthy, S. J., Elliot, B., Bayles, D. L., Price, D. P., Ferree, A., & Abbott, J. A. (1998). The literature-based basals in first-grade classrooms: Savior, Satan or same-old? *Reading Research Quarterly, 33,* 168–197.

Hoffman, J. V., Roser, N. L., & Battle, J. (1993). Reading aloud in classrooms: From the modal to a "model." *The Reading Teacher, 46,* 496–503.

Holdaway, D. (1979). *The foundations of literacy.* Portsmouth, NH: Heinemann.

Holdaway, D. (1980). *Independence in reading* (2nd ed.). Sydney: Ashton-Scholastic.

Holdaway, D. (1982). Shared book experience: Teaching reading using favorite books. *Theory into Practice, 23,* 293–300.

Hong, L. K. (1981). Modifying SSR for beginning readers. *The Reading Teacher, 34,* 888–891.

Hopkin, M., Hopkin, M., Gunyuz, P., Fowler, A., Edmison, R., Rivera, H., & Ruberto, L. (1997), Designing a user-friendly curriculum guide for practical application in an integrated language arts classroom. *The Reading Teacher, 50,* 410–416.

Hornsby, D., Sukarna, D., & Parry, J. (1988). *Read on: A conference approach to reading.* Portsmouth, NH: Heinmann.

Hoskisson, K. (1975). The many facets of assisted reading. *Elementary English, 52,* 312–315.

Huck, C. S., Hepler, S. & Hickman, J. (1987). *Children's Literature in the Elementary School* (4th ed.). Fort Worth, TX: Holt, Rinehart & Winston.

Hudelson, S. (1989). Teaching English through content area activities. In J. Flood, J. M. Jensen, D. Lapp, & J. Squire (Eds.), *Handbook of research on teaching the English language arts.* Old Tappan, NJ: Macmillan.

Hunt, L. C. (1970). Effect of self-selection, interest, and motivation upon independent, instructional, and frustrational levels. *The Reading Teacher, 24,* 146–151.

Hymes, D. (1974). *Foundations in sociolinguistics: An ethnographic approach.* Philadelphia: University of Pennsylvania Press.

Hymes, J. L. (1958). *Before the child reads.* Evanston, IL: Row & Peterson.

Ignoffo, M. (1980). The thread of thought: Analogies as a vocabulary building method. *Journal of Reading, 23,* 519–521.

International Reading Association. (1998). *Standards for reading professionals.* Newark, DE: International Reading Association.

International Reading Association and National Association for the Education of Young Children. (1998). *Learning to read and write: Developmentally appropriate practices for young children: A joint position statement of the International Reading Association and the National Association for the Education of Young Children.* Newark, DE: International Reading Association.

International Reading Association and National Council of Teachers of English. (1996). *Standards for English language arts.* Newark, DE: International Reading Association.

Irwin, J. W., & Davis, C. A. (1980). Assessing readability: The checklist approach. *Journal of Reading, 24,* 124–130.

Isakson, M. B., & Boaty, R. M. (1993). Hard questions about teaching research. In L. Patterson, C. M. Santa, K. Short, & K. Smith (Eds.), *Teachers are researchers.* Newark, DE: International Reading Association.

Johns, J. L. (1985). *Basic reading inventory* (3rd ed.). Dubuque, IA: Kendall-Hunt.

Johns, J. L., & Ellish-Piper, L. (1997). *Balanced reading instructions: Teachers' visions and voices.* Dubuque, IA: Kendall-Hunt.

Johnson, D. W., & Johnson, R. T. (1989–1990). Social skills for successful group work. *Educational Leadership, 47*(4), 29–33.

Johnston, F. R. (1998). The reader, the text, and the task: Learning words in first grade. *The Reading Teacher, 51,* 666–675.

Juel, C. (1988). Learning to read and write: A longitudinal study of fifty-four children from first through fourth grade. *Journal of Educational Psychology, 80,* 437–447.

Kagan, S. (1989). *Cooperative learning: Resources for teachers.* San Juan Capistrano, CA: Resources for Teachers.

Kameenui, E. T. (1993a). Diverse learners and the tyranny of time: Don't fix blame; fix the leaky roof. *The Reading Teacher, 46,* 376–383.

Kameenui, E. T. (1993b). A special issue on innovations in literacy for a diverse society. *The Reading Teacher, 46,* 539.

Kameenui, E. T., Simmons, D. C., Clark, D., & Dickson, S. (1997). Direct instruction reading. In S. A. Stahl & D. A. Hayes (Eds.), *Instructional models in reading.* Mahwah, NJ: Erlbaum.

Kamii, C. (1991). What is constructivism? In C. Kamii, M. Manning, & G. Manning (Eds.), *Early literacy: A constructivist foundation for whole language.* Washington, DC: National Education Association.

Kamil, M. L., & Pearson, P. D. (1979). Theory and practice in teaching reading. *New York University Education Quarterly,* 10–16.

Kasten, W. C., & Lolli, E. M. (1998). *Implementing multiage education: A practical guide.* Norwood, MA: Christopher-Gordon.

Keegan, B., & Shake, K. (1991). Literature study groups: An alternative to ability grouping. *The Reading Teacher, 44,* 542–547.

Kieffer, R. D., & Morrison, L. S. (1994). Changing portfolio process: One journey toward authentic assessment. *Language Arts, 71,* 411–418.

Kirby, D., Latta, D., & Vinz, R. (1988). Beyond interior decorating: Using writing to make meaning in the elementary school. *Phi Delta Kappan, 69,* 718–724.

Klein, M. L. (1985). *The development of writing in children: Pre-K through grade 8.* Upper Saddle River, NJ: Prentice Hall.

Klesius, J. P., & Griffith, P. H. (1998). Interactive storybook reading for at-risk learners. *The Reading Teacher, 49,* 552–560.

Kobrin, B. (1995). *Eye openers II: How to choose and use children's books about real people and things.* New York: Penguin.

Koskinen, P., & Blum, I. (1986). Paired repeated reading: A classroom strategy for developing fluent reading. *The Reading Teacher, 40,* 70–75.

Kraus, R. (1971). *Leo the late bloomer.* New York: Windmill Books.

Labbo, L., & Teale, W. (1990). Cross-age reading: A strategy for helping poor readers. *The Reading Teacher, 43,* 362–369.

Laberge, D., & Samuels, S. J. (1976). Toward a theory of automatic information processing in reading. In H. Singer & R. Ruddell (Eds.), *Theoretical models and processes of reading* (2nd ed.). Newark, DE: International Reading Association.

Labov, W. (1985). The study of nonstandard English. In V. Clark, P. Escholz, & A. Rosa (Eds.), *Language* (4th ed.). New York: St. Martin's Press.

Ladson-Billings, G. (1992). Reading between the lines and beyond the pages: A culturally relevant approach to literacy teaching. *Theory into Practice, 28,* 312–320.

Lamme, L. L. (1984). *Growing up writing.* Washington, DC: Acropolis.

Larrick, N. (1987). Illiteracy starts too soon. *Phi Delta Kappan, 69,* 184–189.

Lauritzen, C. (1982). A modification of repeated readings for group instruction. *The Reading Teacher, 35,* 456–458.

Leland, C., & Fitzpatrick, R. (1994). Cross-age interaction builds enthusiasm for reading and writing. *The Reading Teacher, 47,* 292–301.

Leslie, L., & Jett-Simpson, M. (1997). *Authentic literacy assessment.* New York: Longman.

Leu, D. J., Jr., & Leu, D. D. (1999). *Teaching with the Internet: Lessons from the classroom* (2nd ed.). Norwood, MA: Christopher-Gordon.

Levine, S. G. (1984). USSR: A necessary component in teaching reading. *Journal of Reading, 27,* 394–400.

Lewis, C. (1993). "Give people a chance": Acknowledging social differences in reading. *Language Arts, 10,* 454–461.

Liberman, I. Y., Shankweiler, D., Fisher, F. W., & Carter, B. (1974). Explicit syllable and phoneme segmentation in the young child. *The Journal of Experimental Child Psychology, 18,* 201–212.

Liberman, I. Y., Shankweiler, D., Liberman, A., Fowler, C., & Fischer, F. (1977). Phonetic segmentation and recoding in the beginning reader. In A. Reber & D. Scarborough (Eds.), *Toward a psychology of reading.* Mahwah, NJ: Erlbaum.

Littlewood, W. (1984). *Foreign and second language learning.* New York: Cambridge University Press.

Locke, D. C. (1989). Fostering the self-esteem of African-American children. *Elementary School Guidance and Counseling, 23,* 254–259.

MacGinitie, W. H. (1993). Some limits of assessment. *Journal of Reading, 26,* 556–560.

Mandler, J., & Johnson, N. (1977). Remembrance of things parsed: Story structure and recall. *Cognitive Psychology, 9,* 111–151.

Mann, A. (1979). *The one and the many: Reflections on American identity.* Chicago: University of Chicago Press.

Manzo, A. V. (1969). The request procedure. *Journal of Reading, 11,* 123–126.

Marchbanks, G., & Levin, H. (1965). Cues by which children recognize words. *Journal of Educational Psychology, 56,* 57–61.

Marzolo, J. (1993). *Happy birthday, Martin Luther King.* New York: Scholastic.

McCaslin, N. (1990). *Creative drama in the classroom* (5th ed.). New York: Longman.

McCracken, R. A. (1971). Initiating sustained silent reading. *Journal of Reading, 14,* 521–524, 582–583.

McCracken, R. A., & McCracken, M. J. (1978). Modeling is the key to sustained reading. *The Reading Teacher, 31,* 406–408.

McDonald, F. J. (1965). *Educational psychology.* Belmont, CA: Wadsworth.

McDonnell, G. M., & Osburn, E. B. (1978). New thoughts about reading readiness. *Language Arts, 55,* 26–29.

McGinley, W. J., & Denner, P. R. (1987). Story impressions: A pre-reading/writing activity. *Journal of Reading, 31,* 248–253.

McIntyre, E., Kyle, D. W., Gregory, K. M., Moore, G. H., Wheatley, V. A., Clyde J. A., & Houda, R. A. (1996). Teaching young readers and writers in multi-age classrooms. *Language Arts, 73,* 384–394.

McMahon, S. I. (1997). Book clubs: Contexts for students to lead their own discussions. In S. I. McMahon & T. E. Raphael (Eds.), *The book club connection.* New York: Teachers College Press.

McTighe, J., & Lyman, F. T. (1988). Cueing thinking in the classroom: The promise of theory-embedded tools. *Educational Leadership, 45*(7), 18–24.

Meehan, P. (1998). Beyond a chocolate crunch bar: A teacher examines her philosophy of teaching reading. *The Reading Teacher, 51,* 314–324.

Mezynski, K. (1983). Issues concerning the acquisition of knowledge: Effects of vocabulary training on reading comprehension. *Review of Educational Research, 53,* 258–279.

Mike, D. G. (1996). Internet in the schools: A literacy perspective. *Journal of Adolescent and Adult Literacy, 40,* 4–13.

Moffett, J. (1975). An interview with James Moffett. *Media and Methods, 15,* 20–24.

Moll, L. C. (1989). Teaching second language students: A Vygotskian perspective. In D. M. Johnson & D. H. Roen (Eds.), *Richness in writing: Empowering ESL students.* New York: Longman.

Moorehead, M. (1990). Leslie Anne learns to read. *The Reading Teacher, 44,* 332.

Morphett, M. V., & Washburne, C. (1931). When should children begin to read? *Elementary School Journal, 31,* 496–503.

Morris, D., & Nelson, L. (1992). Supported oral reading with low-achieving second graders. *Reading Research and Instruction, 31,* 49–63.

Morrow, L. M. (1985). *Promoting voluntary reading in school and home.* Bloomington, IN: Phi Delta Kappa Educational Foundation.

Morrow, L. M. (1990). Preparing the classroom environment to promote literacy during play. *Early Childhood Research Quarterly, 5,* 537–554.

Morrow, L. M., & Weinstein, C. S. (1982). Increasing children's use of literature through program and physical design changes. *Elementary School Journal, 83,* 131–137.

Moskowitz, B. (1985). The acquisition of language. In V. Clark, P. Escholz, & A. Rosa (Eds.), *Language* (4th ed.). New York: St. Martin's Press.

Moss, B. (1991). Children's nonfiction trade books: A complement to content area texts. *The Reading Teacher, 45,* 26–31.

Munsch, R. N. (1980). *The paperbag princess.* Toronto: Annick Press.

Munsch, R. N. (1985). *Thomas' snowsuit.* Toronto: Annick Press.

Munsch, R. N. (1989). *Love you forever.* Toronto: Firefly Books.

Murphy, H. A. (1957). The spontaneous speaking vocabulary of children in primary grades. *Journal of Education, 146,* 1–105.

Nagy, W. (1988). *Teaching vocabulary to improve reading comprehension.* Urbana, IL: National Council of Teachers of English.

Nathan, R. (1995). Parents, projects, and portfolios: 'Round and about community building in Room 14. *Language Arts, 72,* 82–87.

National Institute of Education, Commission on Reading. (1985). *Becoming a nation of readers: The report of the commission on reading.* Washington, DC: National Institute of Education.

Neisser, U. (1976). *Cognition and reality: Principles and implications of cognitive psychology.* New York: Freeman.

Nelson, J. (1978). Readability: Some cautions for the content area teacher. *Journal of Reading, 21,* 620–625.

Neuman, S. B., Caperelli, B. J., & Kee, C. (1998). Literacy learning: A family matter. *The Reading Teacher, 52,* 244–252.

Neuman, S. B., & Roskos, K. A. (1990). Play, print, and purpose: Enriching play environments for literacy development. *The Reading Teacher, 44,* 214–221.

Neuman, S. B., & Roskos, K. A. (1993). Access to print for children of poverty: Differential effects of adult mediation and literacy-enriched play settings in environmental and functional print tasks. *American Educational Research Journal, 30,* 95–122.

Neuman, S. B., & Roskos, K. A. (1997). Literacy knowledge in practice: Contexts of participation for young writers and readers. *Reading Research Quarterly, 32,* 10–32.

Noden, H., & Vacca, R. T. (1994). *Whole language in middle and secondary classrooms.* New York: HarperCollins.

Nolte, R. Y., & Singer, H. (1985). Active comprehension: Teaching a process of reading comprehension and its effects on reading achievement. *The Reading Teacher, 39,* 24–28.

Norton, D. E. (1980). *The effective teaching of language arts.* Columbus, OH: Merrill.

Oakes, J. S. (1999). Limiting students' school success and life chances: The impact of tracking. In A. C. Ornstein & L. S. Behar-Horenstein, *Contemporary issues in curriculum* (2nd ed.). Needham Heights, MA: Allyn & Bacon.

Ogbu, J. (1993). Adaptation to minority status and impact on school success. *Theory into Practice, 31,* 287–295.

Ogle, D. M. (1986). K-W-L: A teaching model that develops active reading of expository text. *The Reading Teacher, 39,* 564–571.

Ohnmacht, D. C. (1969). *The effects of letter knowledge on achievement in reading in the first grade.* Paper presented at the annual meeting of the American Education Research Association, Los Angeles.

Owens, R. E. (1988). *Language development* (2nd ed.). Columbus, OH: Merrill.

Palincsar, A., & Brown, A. L. (1984). Reciprocal teaching of comprehension-fostering and comprehension-monitoring activities. *Cognition and Instruction, 1,* 117–175.

Pearson, P. D. (1982). *Asking questions about stories.* New York: Ginn.

Pearson, P. D. (1984). Guided reading: A response to Isabel Beck. In R. C. Anderson, J. Osborn, & R. Tierney (Eds.), *Learning to read in American schools: Basal readers and content texts.* Mahwah, NJ: Erlbaum.

Pearson, P. D. (1993). Teaching and learning reading: A research perspective. *Language Arts, 70,* 502–511.

Pearson, P. D. (1996). Reclaiming the center. In M. Graves, P. Vanden Broek, & B. Taylor (Eds.), *The first R: Every child's right to read.* New York: Teachers College Press.

Pearson, P. D., & Gallagher, M. (1983). The instruction of reading comprehension. *Contemporary Educational Psychology, 8,* 317–344.

Pearson, P. D., & Johnson, D. W. (1978). *Teaching reading comprehension.* Austin, TX: Holt, Rinehart and Winston.

Peck, J. (1989). Using storytelling to promote language and literacy development. *The Reading Teacher, 43,* 138–141.

Pelgrom, E. (1980). *The winter when time was frozen.* New York: Morrow.

Perfetti, C. A. (1985). *Reading ability.* New York: Oxford University Press.

Piaget, J. (1970). *The science of education and the psychology of the child.* New York: Orion Press.

Piaget, J. (1973). *The language and thought of the child.* New York: World.

Pikulski, J. J. (1989). Questions and answers. *The Reading Teacher, 42,* 533.

Pikulski, J. J. (1994). Preventing reading failure: A review of five effective programs. *The Reading Teacher, 48,* 30–38.

Pils, L. (1993). I love you, Miss Piss. *The Reading Teacher, 46,* 648–653.

Pinnell, G., Fried, M., & Estice, R. (1990). Reading recovery: Learning how to make a difference. *The Reading Teacher, 43,* 282–295.

Pressley, M. (1996). Concluding reflections. In E. McIntyre & M. Pressley (Eds.), *Balanced instruction: Strategies and skills in whole language.* Norwood, MA: Christopher-Gordon.

Pressley, M., Rankin, J., & Yokoi, L. (1996). A survey of instructional practices of primary grade teachers nominated as effective in promoting literacy. *Elementary School Journal, 96,* 363–384.

Pressley, M., Wharton-McDonald, R., Rankin, J., Yokoi, L., & Ettenberger, S. (1996). The nature of outstanding primary grade literacy instruction. In E. McIntyre & M. Pressley (Eds.), *Balanced instruction: Strategies and skills in whole language.* Norwood, MA: Christopher-Gordon.

Randall, S. N. (1996). Information charts: A strategy for organizing student research. *Journal of Adolescent and Adult Literacy, 39,* 536–542.

Raphael, T. E. (1982). Question-answering strategies for children. *The Reading Teacher, 36,* 186–191.

Raphael, T. E. (1986). Teaching question-answer relationships, revisited. *The Reading Teacher, 39,* 516–622.

Rasinski, T. V., & DeFord, D. (1986). Students and their writing: perceptions and motivations. In J. Niles & R. Lalik (eds.), *Solving Problems in Literacy: Learners, Teachers, and Researchers* (pp. 294–295). Thirty-fifth yearbook of National Reading Conference. Rochester, NY: National Reading Conference.

Rasinski, T. V., & Fredericks, A. D. (1991). The Akron paired reading project. *The Reading Teacher, 44,* 514–515.

Rasinski, T. V., & Padak, N. D. (1996). *Holistic reading strategies: Teaching children who find reading difficult.* Columbus, OH: Merrill.

Rasinski, T.V., Padak, N. D., Linek, W. L., & Sturtevant, E. (1994). Effects of fluency development on urban second-grade readers. *Journal of Educational Research, 87,* 158–165.

Read, C. (1971). Preschool children's knowledge of English phonology. *Harvard Educational Review, 41,* 1–34.

Reid, J. F. (1966). Learning to think about reading. *Educational Research, 9,* 56–62.

Reimer, K. M. (1992). *Multiethnic literature: Holding fast to dreams.* Technical Report No. 551. Champaign, IL: Reading Research and Educational Center. ERIC Document Reproduction Service, No. ED 343128.

Reinking, D. (1995). Reading and writing with computers: Literacy research in a post-typographical world. In K. A. Hinderman, D. J. Leu Jr., & C. K. Kinzer (Eds.), *Perspectives on literacy research and practice.* Chicago: National Reading Conference.

Reutzel, D. R., & Cooter, R. B. (1991). Organizing for effective instruction: The reading workshop. *The Reading Teacher, 44,* 548–554.

Reyhner, J. (1986). Native Americans in basal reading textbooks: Are there enough? *Journal of American Indian Education, 26,* 14–22.

Rhodes, L. K. (1981). I can read! Predictable books as resources for reading and writing instruction. *The Reading Teacher, 34,* 314–318.

Rhodes, L. K., & Shanklin, N. (1993). *Windows into literacy: Assessing learners K–8.* Portsmouth, NH: Heinemann.

Rigg, P. (1989). Language experience approach: Reading naturally. In P. Rigg & V. Allen (Eds.), *When they don't all speak English: Integrating the ESL student into the regular classroom.* Urbana, IL: National Council of Teachers of English.

Roberts, P. (1985). Speech communities. In V. Clark, P. Escholz, & A. Rosa (Eds.), *Language* (4th ed.). New York: St. Martin's Press.

Rose, K. (1982). *Teaching language arts to children.* Orlando, FL: Harcourt Brace.

Rosenblatt, L. (1982). The literary transaction: Evocation and response. *Theory into Practice, 21,* 268–277.

Roser, N. L., Hoffman, J. V., & Farest, C. (1990). Language, literacy, and at-risk children. *The Reading Teacher, 43,* 554–559.

Roskos, K. A. (1986). *The nature of literate behavior in the pretend play episodes of four- and five-year-old children.* Unpublished doctoral dissertation, Kent State University, Kent, OH.

Roskos, K. A. (1988). Literacy at work in play. *The Reading Teacher, 41,* 562–566.

Rosow, L. (1992). The story of Irma. *The Reading Teacher, 45,* 525.

Routman, R. (1988). *Transitions: From literature to literacy.* Portsmouth, NH: Heinemann.

Routman, R. (1991). *Invitations.* Portsmouth, NH: Heinemann.

Ruddell, R., Ruddell, M., & Singer, H. (1994). Theoretical models and processes of reading (4th ed.). Newark, DE: International Reading Association.

Rumelhart, D. E. (1982). Schemata: The building blocks of cognition. In J. Guthrie (Ed.), *Comprehension and teaching: Research reviews.* Newark, DE: International Reading Association.

Rupley, W. H., Logan, J. W., & Nichols, W. D. (1999). Vocabulary instruction in balanced reading programs. *The Reading Teacher, 52,* 336–346.

St. Lucie students surf the net. (1998, August 12). *Vero Beach Press Journal,* p. A3.

Samuels, S. J. (1972). The effect of letter-name knowledge on learning to read. *American Educational Research Journal, 1,* 65–74.

Samuels, S. J. (1976). Hierarchical subskills in the reading acquisition process. In J. T. Guthrie (Ed.), *Aspects of reading acquisition.* Baltimore, MD: Johns Hopkins University Press.

Samuels, S. J. (1979). Method of repeated readings. *The Reading Teacher, 32,* 403–408.

Samuels, S. J. (1988). Decoding and automaticity. *The Reading Teacher, 41,* 756–760.

Samuels, S. J. (1994). Toward a theory of automatic information processing in reading, revisited. In R. Ruddell, M. Ruddell, & H. Singer (Eds.), *Theoretical models and processes of reading* (4th ed.). Newark, DE: International Reading Association.

Samuels, S. J. (1996). Howling in the wind: Academics try to change classroom reading instruction. In M. Graves, P. Vanden Broek, & B. Taylor (Eds.), *The first R: Every child's right to read.* New York: Teachers College Press.

Santa, C. M., Dailey, S. C., & Nelson, M. (1985). Free response and opinion proof: A reading and writing strategy for middle grade and secondary teachers. *Journal of Reading, 28,* 346–352.

Schickedanz, J. A. (1986). *More than the ABCs.* Washington, DC: National Association for the Education of Young Children.

Schickedanz, J. A. (1998). What is developmentally appropriate practice in early literacy? Considering the alphabet. In S. B. Neuman & K. A. Roskos (Eds.), *Children achieving: Best practices in early literacy.* Newark, DE: International Reading Association.

Schmidt, P. R. (1995). Working and playing with others: Cultural conflict in a kindergarten literacy program. *The Reading Teacher, 48,* 404–412.

Schmidt, P. R. (1998a). *Cultural conflict and struggle: Literacy learning in a kindergarten program.* New York: Lang.

Schmidt, P. R. (1998b). The ABCs of cultural understanding and communication. *Equity and Excellence in Education, 31*(2), 28–38.

Schmidt, P. R. (1998c). The ABCs model: Teachers connect home and school. In T. Shanahan & F. Rodriguez-Brown (Eds.), *Forty-seventh yearbook of the National Reading Conference.* Chicago: National Reading Conference.

Schmidt, P. R. (1999). KWLQ: Inquiry and literacy learning in science. *The Reading Teacher, 52,* 789–792.

Schreiber, P. (1980). On the acquisition of reading fluency. *Journal of Reading Behavior, 12,* 177–186.

Searcy, B. (1988). Getting children into the literacy club—and keeping them there. *Childhood Education, 65,* 74–77.

Sewell, G. T. (1987). *American history textbooks: An assessment of quality.* New York: Educational Excellence Network, Teachers College, Columbia University.

Shanahan, T. (1988). The reading-writing relationship: Seven instructional principles. *The Reading Teacher, 41,* 636–647.

Shanahan, T. (1990). *Reading and writing together. New perspectives for the classroom.* Norwood, MA: Christopher-Gordon.

Shanahan, T., & Neuman, S. B. (1997). Literacy research that makes a difference. *Reading Research Quarterly, 32,* 202–210.

Shanahan, T., Robinson, B., & Schneider, M. (1993). Integration of curriculum or interaction of people? *The Reading Teacher, 47,* 158–160.

Shanklin, N. L., & Rhodes, L. K. (1989). Comprehensive instruction as sharing and extending. *The Reading Teacher, 42,* 496–501.

Sharpley, A. M., & Sharpley, C. F. (1981). Peer tutoring: A review of the literature. *Collected Original Resources in Education 5*(3), 7–11.

Shatz, E. K., & Baldwin, R. S. (1986). Context clues are unreliable predictors of word meanings. *Reading Research Quarterly, 21,* 429–453.

Simons, H., & Elster, C. (1990). Picture dependence in first-grade basal texts. *Journal of Educational Research, 84,* 86–92.

Simpson, M. (1987). Alternative formats for evaluating content area vocabulary understanding. *Journal of Reading, 31,* 20–27.

Singer, H. (1978). Active comprehension: From answering to asking questions. *The Reading Teacher, 31,* 901–908.

Singer, H., & Ruddell, R. (Eds.). (1985). *Theoretical models and processes of reading* (3rd ed.). Newark, DE: International Reading Association.

Sirota, B. S. (1971). *The effect of a planned literature program of daily oral reading by the teacher on the voluntary reading of fifth-grade children.* Unpublished doctoral dissertation, New York University.

Slapin, B. (1992). *How to tell the difference: A checklist for evaluating children's books for anti-Indian bias.* Philadelphia: New Society.

Slavin, R. E. (1999). Synthesis of research on cooperative learning. In A. C. Ornstein & L. S. Behar-Horenstein (Eds.), *Contemporary issues in curriculum* (2nd ed.). Needham Heights, MA: Allyn & Bacon.

Smith, F. (1976). Learning to read by reading. *Language Arts, 53,* 297–299, 322.

Smith, F. (1977). The uses of language. *Language Arts, 54,* 638–644.

Smith, F. (1985). *Reading without nonsense* (2nd ed.). New York: Teachers College Press.

Smith, F. (1988). *Joining the literacy club: Further essays into education.* Portsmouth, NH: Heinemann.

Smith, F. (1989). Demonstrations, engagement, and sensitivity. The choice between people and programs. In G. Manning & M. Manning (Eds.), *Whole language: Beliefs and practices, K–8.* Washington, DC: National Education Association.

Smith, L. B. (1982). Sixth graders write about reading literature. *Language Arts, 59,* 357–366.

Smith, N. B. (1965). *American reading instruction.* Newark, DE: International Reading Association.

Smith, R. J., & Johnson, D. D. (1980). *Teaching children to read.* Reading, MA: Addison-Wesley.

Snow, C. E., Burns, M. S., & Griffin, P. (1998). *Preventing reading difficulties in young children.* Washington, DC: National Academy Press.

Soto, G. (1992). *Pacific crossing.* Orlando, FL: Harcourt Brace.

Sowers, S. (1982). Six questions teachers ask about invented spelling. In T. Newkirk & N. Atwell (Eds.), *Understanding writing: Ways of observing, learning, and teaching.* Chelmsford, MA: Northeast Regional Exchange.

Spearitt, D. (1972). Identification of subskills in reading comprehension by maximum likelihood factor analysis. *Reading Research Quarterly, 8,* 92–111.

Spiegel, D. L. (1981). *Reading for pleasure: Guidelines.* Newark, DE: International Reading Association.

Squire, J. R. (1984). Composing and comprehending: Two sides of the same basic process. In J. M. Jensen (Ed.), *Composing and comprehending.* Urbana, IL: National Conference on Research in English.

Stahl, S. A. (1983). *Vocabulary instruction and the nature of word meanings.* Paper presented at a meeting of the College Reading Association, Atlanta.

Stahl, S. A. (1986). Three principles of effective vocabulary instruction. *Journal of Reading, 29,* 662–668.

Stahl, S. A. (1992). Saying the "p" word: Nine guidelines for exemplary phonic instruction. *The Reading Teacher, 45,* 618–625.

Stahl, S. A., Duffy-Hester, A. M., & Stahl, K. A. (1998). Everything you wanted to know about phonics (but were afraid to ask). *Reading Research Quarterly, 33,* 338–355.

Stahl, S. A., & Fairbanks, M. (1986). The effects of vocabulary instruction: A model-based meta-analysis. *Review of Educational Research, 56,* 72–110.

Stanovich, K. E. (1986). Matthew effects in reading: Some consequences of individual differences in the acquisition of literacy. *Reading Research Quarterly, 21,* 360–407.

Stanovich, K. E. (1994). Romance and reality. *The Reading Teacher, 47,* 280–291.

Stauffer, R. G. (1970). *The language experience approach to the teaching of reading.* New York: Harper-Collins.

Stein, J. (1990). *The Random House rhyming dictionary.* New York: Random House.

Stein, N., & Glenn, C. (1979). An analysis of story comprehension in elementary school children. In R. Freedle (Ed.), *New directions in discourse processing.* Norwood, NJ: Ablex.

Stewart, O., & Tei, E. (1983). Some implications of metacognition for reading instruction. *Journal of Reading, 27,* 36–43.

Stewig, J. W. (1980). *Read to write* (2nd ed.). Austin, TX: Holt, Rinehart and Winston.

Stoll, D. R. (1997). *Magazines for kids and teens.* Newark, DE: International Reading Association.

Strickland, D. S. (1996). In search of balance: Restructuring our literacy programs. *Reading Today, 14*( ), 32.

Strickland, D. S., & Ascher, C. (1992). Low-income African-American children and public schooling. In P. Jackson (Ed.), *Handbook of research on curriculum.* Old Tappan, NJ: Macmillan.

Strickland, D. S., & Morrow, L. M. (1990). Family literacy: Sharing good books. *The Reading Teacher, 43,* 518–519.

Strickland, R. (1962). *The language of elementary school children: Its relationship to the language of reading textbooks and the quality of reading of selected children.* Bloomington: Indiana University School of Education.

Sutherland, Z. (Ed.). (1980). *The best in children's books: The University of Chicago guide to children's literature, 1973–1978.* Chicago: University of Chicago Press.

Sutherland, Z. (Ed.). (1984). *The Scott, Foresman anthology of children's literature.* Glenview, IL: Scott, Foresman.

Swaby, B. (1983). *Teaching and learning reading.* New York: Little, Brown.

Taylor, B., Short, R., Frye, B., & Shearer, B. (1992). Classroom teachers prevent reading failure in low-achieving first-grade students. *The Reading Teacher, 45,* 592–597.

Taylor, D. (1983). *Family literacy: Young children learning to read and write.* Portsmouth, NH: Heinemann.

Taylor, D., & Dorsey-Gaines, C. (1989). *Growing up literate: Learning from inner-city families.* Portsmouth, NH: Heinemann.

Taylor, N. E., & Vawter, J. (1978). Helping children discover the functions of written language. *Language Arts, 55,* 941–945.

Teale, W. H. (1978). Positive environments for learning to read: What studies of early readers tell us. *Language Arts, 55,* 922–932.

Teale, W. H., & Sulzby, E. (1986). *Emergent literacy: Writing and reading.* Norwood, NJ: Ablex.

Thelen, J. (1986). Vocabulary instruction and meaningful learning. *Journal of Reading, 29,* 603–609.

Thorndyke, P. (1977). Cognitive structures in comprehension and memory of narrative discourse. *Cognitive Psychology, 9,* 77–110.

Thurstone, L. L. (1946). A note on a reanalysis of Davis' reading tests. *Psychometrika, 11,* 185–188.

Tierney, R. J. (1998). Literacy assessment reform: Shifting beliefs, principled possibilities, and emerging practices. *The Reading Teacher, 51,* 374–390.

Tierney, R. J., & Shanahan, T. (1991). *Research on reading-writing relationships: Interactions, transactions, and outcomes.* In R. Barr, M. L. Kamil, P. Mosenthal, & P. D. Pearson (Eds.), *Handbook of reading research* (2nd ed.). New York: Longman.

Tom, C. L. (1969). *What teachers read to pupils in the middle grades.* Unpublished doctoral dissertation, Ohio State University, Columbus.

Topping, K. (1989). Peer tutoring and paired reading: Combining two powerful techniques. *The Reading Teacher, 42,* 488–494.

Trachtenburg, P. (1990). Using children's literature to enhance phonic instruction. *The Reading Teacher, 43,* 648–654.

Trelease, J. (1989). *The new read-aloud handbook.* New York: Penguin.

Tunnell, M., Calder, J., Justen, J., & Waldrop, P. (1988). An affective approach to reading: Effectively teaching reading to mainstreamed handicapped children. *The Pointer, 32,* 38–40.

Tuttle, F. (1989). Responding to individual differences: Teaching the gifted. In J. Flood, J. M. Jensen, D. Lapp, & J. Squire (Eds.), *Handbook of research on teaching the English language arts.* Old Tappan, NJ: Macmillan.

Tyler, R. W. (1949). *Basic principles of curriculum and instruction.* Chicago: University of Chicago Press.

Vacca, R. T., & Newton, E. (1995). Responding to literary texts. In C. N. Hedley, P. Antonacci, & M. Rabinowitz (Eds.), *Thinking and literacy: Mind at work in the classroom.* Mahwah, NJ: Erlbaum.

Vacca, R. T. & Rasinski, T. V. (1992). *Case studies in whole language.* Orlando, FL: Harcourt Brace.

Vacca, R.T., & Vacca, J. L. (1999). *Content area reading: Literacy and learning across the curriculum* (6th ed.). New York: Longman.

Veatch, J., & Acinapuro, P. (1966). *Reading in the elementary school.* Katonah, NY: Owen.

Veatch, J., Sawicki, F., Elliot, G., Flake, E., & Blakey, J. (1979). *Key words to reading* (2nd ed.). Columbus, OH: Merrill.

Venezky, R. L. (1978). Reading acquisition: The occult and the obscure. In F. B. Murray & J. J. Pikulski (Eds.), *The acquisition of reading.* Baltimore: University Park Press.

Venezky, R. L., & Massaro, D. W. (1979). The role of orthographic regularity in work recognition. In L. Resnick & R. Weaver (Eds.), *Theory and practice of early reading.* Mahwah, NJ: Erlbaum.

Villaume, S. K., Worden, T., Williams, S., Hopkins, L., & Rosenblatt, C. (1994). Five teachers in search of a discussion. *Language Arts, 47,* 480–489.

Viorst, J. (1972). *Alexander and the terrible, horrible, no good, very bad day.* New York: Atheneum.

Vygotsky, L. S. (1962). *Thought and language.* Cambridge, MA: MIT Press.

Vygotsky, L. S. (1978). *Mind in society.* Cambridge, MA: Harvard University Press.

Walley, C. (1993). An invitation to reading fluency. *The Reading Teacher, 46,* 526–527.

Watson, D. (1978). Reader selected miscues: Getting more from sustained silent reading. *English Education, 10,* 75–85.

Watson, D. (1989). Defining and describing whole language. *Elementary School Journal, 90,* 129–141.

Weaver, C. (1980). *Psycholinguistics and reading: From process to practice.* New York: Little, Brown.

Webster's compact rhyming dictionary. (1987). Springfield, MA: Merriam-Webster.

Wells, G. (1986). *The meaning-makers: Children learning language and using language.* Portsmouth, NH: Heinemann.

Wells, M. C. (1993). At the juncture of reading and writing: How dialogue journals contribute to students' reading development. *Journal of Reading, 36,* 294–303.

Whaley, J. F. (1981). Story grammar and reading instruction. *The Reading Teacher, 34,* 762–771.

Wharton-McDonald, R., Pressley, M., Rankin, J., Mistretta, J., Yokoi, L., & Ettenberger, S. (1997). Effective primary-grades literacy instruction equals balanced literacy instruction. *The Reading Teacher, 5,* 518–521.

Winn, M. (ed.). (1974). *The fireside book of fun and game songs.* New York: Simon & Schuster.

Wolf, J. (1985). Teaching young writers to revise. *The Ohio Reading Teacher, 19,* 28–30.

Wood, R. (1989, January-February). Hypercard and CD-ROM. *Hyperlink,* 52–54.

Wylie, R. E., & Durrell, D. D. (1970). Teaching vowels through phonograms. *Elementary English, 47*, 787–791.

Yakota, J. (1993). Issues in selecting multicultural literature for children and adolescents. *Language Arts, 70*, 156–167.

Yanok, J. (1988). Individualized instruction: A good approach. *Academic Therapy, 24*, 163–167.

Yopp, H. K. (1992). Developing phonemic awareness in young children. *The Reading Teacher, 45*, 696–703.

Yopp, H. K. (1995). A test for assessing phonemic awareness in young children. *The Reading Teacher, 49*, 20–29.

Yopp, R. H., & Yopp, H. K. (1993). *Literature-based reading activities.* Needham Heights, MA: Allyn & Bacon.

Zarrillo, J. (1989). Teachers' interpretations of literature-based reading. *The Reading Teacher, 43*, 22–28.

Zucker, C. (1993). Using whole language with students who have learning disabilities. *The Reading Teacher, 46*, 660–670.

Credits

Name Index

Subject Index